THE JURISPRUDENCE OF LORD HOFFMANN

Lord Leonard Hoffmann remains one of the most important and influential English jurists. Born in South Africa, he came to England as a Rhodes Scholar to study law at the University of Oxford. After graduating from the Bachelor of Civil Law as Vinerian Scholar, he was elected Stowell Civil Law Fellow of University College. There followed an extremely distinguished judicial career, including 14 years as a member of the Judicial Committee of the House of Lords (from 1995 to 2009).

In 2009, Lord Hoffmann returned to the Oxford Law Faculty as a Visiting Professor. In this volume, current and past colleagues of Lord Hoffmann from the University of Oxford examine different aspects of his jurisprudence in diverse areas of private and public law. The contributions are testament to the clarity and creativity of his judicial and extra-judicial writings, to his enduring influence and extraordinary intellectual breadth, and to the respect and affection in which he is held.

The Jurisprudence of Lord Hoffmann

Edited by
Paul S Davies
and
Justine Pila

·HART·
PUBLISHING
OXFORD AND PORTLAND, OREGON
2015

Published in the United Kingdom by Hart Publishing Ltd
16C Worcester Place, Oxford, OX1 2JW
Telephone: +44 (0)1865 517530
Fax: +44 (0)1865 510710
E-mail: mail@hartpub.co.uk
Website: http://www.hartpub.co.uk

Published in North America (US and Canada) by
Hart Publishing
c/o International Specialized Book Services
920 NE 58th Avenue, Suite 300
Portland, OR 97213-3786
USA
Tel: +1 503 287 3093 or toll-free: (1) 800 944 6190
Fax: +1 503 280 8832
E-mail: orders@isbs.com
Website: http://www.isbs.com

Hart Publishing is an imprint of Bloomsbury Publishing plc.

British Library Cataloguing in Publication Data
Data Available

ISBN: 978-1-84946-591-5

Typeset by Compuscript Ltd, Shannon
Printed and bound in Great Britain by
CPI Group (UK) Ltd, Croydon CR0 4YY

Foreword

LORD SUMPTION*

It is not easy to write objectively about a friend. Forewords and prefaces, as Proust observes at the end of *Le Temps retrouvé*, are an inherently insincere genre. But judges are different. They leave behind when they retire a corpus of judgments which, as Lord Hoffmann himself once observed, cease to be their author's property as soon as they are published and become instead sources of disembodied law. Their work therefore lends itself to objective clinical examination in a way that would hardly be possible for actors, artists, politicians or even chartered surveyors.

Lennie Hoffmann was probably the most creative legal mind to sit on the Judicial Committee of the House of Lords in the last half-century of its existence. His prose style, with its combination of informality, precision and humour, its arresting turns of phrase and its absence of pomposity or clichés, has always made his the first speech that one turns to. The range of subjects on which he spoke with authority, including some with which he had had no previous acquaintance, was remarkable. His ability to turn his colleagues round to his own way of thinking was legendary. The common law, with its narrative and highly personalised style of judgments and its acceptance of idiosyncrasy and dissent, offers unique opportunities for one man's power of intellect and fluency of expression to influence the development of the law. In a less collaborative system, it could have been a weakness. But no one who thinks of Mansfield, Brougham (on a good day), Esher, Atkin, Reid, Denning, Goff or Bingham would say that it has been. It is to this class that Lord Hoffmann belongs.

The chapters in this volume examine Lord Hoffmann's contribution to the law from many specialised points of view. But it is also worth looking at his approach to resolving legal problems at a more general level. Of course, any generalisations about such a prolific thinker who sat on the English bench for 24 years will be found to fray a bit at the edges, and some may not be recognised by Lord Hoffmann himself. But it is I think possible to point to a number of persistent themes in his judicial work which explain at least in part what made him such an outstanding judge.

Lord Hoffmann had a marked ability to surmount the partitions between different specialised areas of law. This reflects the exceptional range of his

---

* Justice of the Supreme Court of the United Kingdom.

legal interests. Specialisation is the natural result of the growing complexity of law and its increasing penetration into the interstices of human affairs. But most specialisations are bogus, and all of them are enemies of coherence. How many lawyers approach legal problems by reaching for their familiar kit of special rules without asking themselves how these rules relate to broader legal principles common to many other areas of law? The common law has grown up organically around a number of basic techniques and instincts that apply across the board. When one finds that a body of rules has grown up in a particular specialised area which appears to be at variance with principles applied everywhere else, the chances are that they are either wrong or misunderstood. An appellate judge must therefore be able to survey the common law as a whole and to perceive connections that its division into different subject areas tends to obscure. Lord Hoffmann had this ability to a supreme degree.

Allied to Lord Hoffmann's facility for jumping over the law's party walls was a striking propensity to approach old problems as if they were new, which accounts for the refreshing absence of off-the-shelf opinion in his judgments. One of the problems about an ancient, precedent-based system is that there are a lot of ready-made answers to choose from. It is only too easy to reach for the packaged product, the received view, the maxims which on closer inspection turn out to be devoid of analytical content. In a famous lecture in 1999, Lord Hoffmann berated judges for resorting to 'common sense' as a substitute for thought.[1] The observation was characteristic of a judge who never took anything for granted. Much of his own judicial work has been characterised by a willingness to reclassify familiar problems in order to identify a unifying principle in an apparently disparate and inconsistent body of law. Yet this has been combined with a genuine respect for authority and a disposition to find the answer there even if old cases need to be reinterpreted and outliers discarded. He proceeds like the explorer of a distant landscape, familiar in outline but uncharted in detail, pausing only to give a respectable burial to the desiccated skeletons of earlier authorities who expired by the roadside because they did not know where they were going. Lord Hoffmann always knew where he was going.

A good example of the technique is the series of lectures and judgments on causation and its relationship to duty, which began with his speech in the *SAAMCO* case[2] and produced a coherent test to replace the unprincipled body of special rules which had previously populated the field. Another is his reordering of the difficult body of law relating to the imputation of a mental state to a corporation. It is now impossible to approach this question

---

[1] Lord Hoffmann, 'Common Sense and Causing Loss' (Lecture to the Chancery Bar Association in London on 15 June 1999).

[2] *South Australia Asset Management Corp v York Montague Ltd* [1996] UKHL 10, [1997] AC 191 (hereinafter *SAAMCO*).

without reference to his judgments in *El Ajou v Dollar Land Holdings plc*[3] and *Meridian Global Funds Management Asia Ltd v Securities Commission*.[4] Other illustrations will be found in his treatment of the construction of contracts, the sources of duty in the law of tort, the statutory duties of public bodies, the barring of claims based on illegal acts, the problems of international corporate insolvency and the meaning of novelty in patent law. Some of his judgments, for example, those which deal with the construction of commercial contracts, remain controversial. Others, such as his views on the power of the English courts to impose universal solutions on international insolvencies, have been partially abandoned by his successors. But all of them have been influential and most will leave a legacy that will endure for as long as the problems to which they are addressed.

Perhaps the principal hallmark of Lord Hoffmann's judicial work is the avoidance of redundant moralising. Not all moralising is redundant, but some judges are unduly partial to it. There is a tendency to view legal problems in moral terms, even in areas such as commercial or public law which rarely lend themselves to it. Let me take a minor but revealing illustration. *Co-operative Insurance Society Ltd v Argyll Stores (Holdings) Ltd*[5] reaffirmed the longstanding practice by which the courts do not specifically enforce covenants to carry on a business. Argyle Stores had closed down a supermarket in a shopping centre in deliberate disregard of an express covenant in its contract with the developer to keep it open. It did this because the supermarket lost money and it was cheaper to pay damages. The Court of Appeal thought that this was a very poor show and granted the injunction, but Lord Hoffmann thought that it was just a question of money, and depended simply on the contractual apportionment of risk; honour did not come into it. The appropriate standard of business conduct was derived from the contract and from legal principles governing remedies, which were based on social efficiency and not moral principle. 'On the scale of broken promises, I can think of worse cases, but the language of the Court of Appeal left them with few adjectives to spare.' Lord Hoffmann spoke for a unanimous committee, but it is rumoured that he had a lot of difficulty with his colleagues on that one.

There are striking analogies between the pragmatic realism which Lord Hoffmann brought to the resolution of business disputes and his approach to public law. In *R (Bancoult) v Secretary of State for Foreign and Commonwealth Affairs (No 2)*,[6] the House of Lords held by a majority that colonial

---

[3] *El Ajou v Dollar Land Holdings plc* [1993] EWCA Civ 4, [1993] 3 All ER 717.

[4] *Meridian Global Funds Management Asia Ltd v Securities Commission* [1995] UKPC 5, [1995] 2 AC 500.

[5] *Co-operative Insurance Society Ltd v Argyll Stores (Holdings) Ltd* [1997] UKHL 17, [1998] AC 1.

[6] *R (Bancoult) v Secretary of State for Foreign and Commonwealth Affairs (No 2)* [2008] UKHL 61, [2009] 1 AC 453.

legislation providing for the deportation of the whole settled population of the Chagos Islands in the Indian Ocean and preventing them from returning was not void as being inconsistent with fundamental principles of the common law. Lord Hoffmann, delivering the leading speech for the majority, accepted that the legislation had been passed with a 'callous disregard of their interests', but he declined to decide the case on a point of constitutional principle which could have no practical application. The islanders had been deported half a century before. There was no realistic possibility of their returning. Their real object was to bring pressure on the government to compensate them for the loss of their right of abode. 'The law gives it and the law may take it away', he observed, 'in this context I do not think that it assists the argument to call it a constitutional right.' The grant of an injunction against Argyll Stores to uphold the sanctity of contracts would not have resulted in the contract being performed; it would just have upped the price of a financial settlement. Just so, the relief sought in the Chagos Islands case would not have restored the Chagossians to their ancestral abode; it would only have altered the terms of a financial negotiation. Many people would be indignant at the analogy. What has a crude bargain for financial advantage between a supermarket operator and a property developer got in common with the noble constitutional principles which the House of Lords put to one side in *Bancoult*? The answer, I suspect, that Lord Hoffmann would give is that they are both cases in which moral principle was redundant because it had no bearing on the realities of the situation. Its assertion served a purely rhetorical function, which is a commonplace of litigants, but rarely the proper role of a judge.

None of this means that Lord Hoffmann was indifferent to principle or that he was naturally subservient to the demands of the state. He is a liberal individualist. His formulation of the principle of legality in *R v Secretary of State for the Home Department ex p Simms*[7] has set narrow limits on the state's ability to use powers conferred in general terms to interfere with fundamental rights. He has been a staunch defender of individual rights against oppression by the state. At the same time, he has always been sceptical of collective claims against the state whose acceptance would transpose abstract principle without qualification into law and transfer decision-making powers from democratically accountable institutions to the courts. He recognises the practical limits of judicial intervention. He approached moral and constitutional principle as tools for conferring practical benefits, and not simply as sources of declaratory rhetoric. The distinction is important, for the demands of idealism are absolute, whereas their practical application gives rise to difficult dilemmas which judges are often poorly

---

[7] *R v Secretary of State for the Home Department ex p Simms* [1999] UKHL 33, [2000] 2 AC 115.

placed to resolve. Lord Hoffmann was always conscious of the realities of government and legislation. Public affairs involve difficult compromises that are not always consistent with moral or intellectual purity. The law's interventions, however admirable in conception and intention, have a cost in terms of money, efficiency and democratic principle, and therefore in terms of public utility. These instincts are coupled with a profound understanding of his adoptive country, its history, its collective values and instincts, and its traditionally equivocal attitude to the state.

Thus, the Lord Hoffmann who declared in *Secretary of State for the Home Department v Rehman*[8] in the aftermath of the attack on the Twin Towers in New York that in matters of national security the cost of error was too high for judges to challenge the executive's assessment of risk was the same Lord Hoffmann who rejected the right of the state to authorise the indefinite detention of non-nationals without trial in *A v Secretary of State for the Home Department*[9] on grounds altogether more fundamental than any of his colleagues. Alone of the nine members sitting, he decided the case on the ground that nothing had happened to 'threaten the life of the nation', which was capable of justifying a departure from a fundamental principle of the constitution. His speech is worth quoting, for it was perhaps his finest moment and its language is an excellent example of his clarity of thought and vigorous prose style:

> The 'nation' is a social organism, living in its territory (in this case, the United Kingdom) under its own form of government and subject to a system of laws which expresses its own political and moral values. When one speaks of a threat to the 'life' of the nation, the word life is being used in a metaphorical sense. The life of the nation is not coterminous with the lives of its people. The nation, its institutions and values, endure through generations. In many important respects, England is the same nation as it was at the time of the first Elizabeth or the Glorious Revolution. The Armada threatened to destroy the life of the nation, not by loss of life in battle, but by subjecting English institutions to the rule of Spain and the Inquisition. The same was true of the threat posed to the United Kingdom by Nazi Germany in the Second World War. This country, more than any other in the world, has an unbroken history of living for centuries under institutions and in accordance with values which show a recognisable continuity...

> Of course the government has a duty to protect the lives and property of its citizens. But that is a duty which it owes all the time and which it must discharge without destroying our constitutional freedoms. There may be some nations too fragile or fissiparous to withstand a serious act of violence. But that is not the case in the United Kingdom. When Milton urged the government of his day not to censor the press even in time of civil war, he said: 'Lords and Commons of England, consider what nation it is whereof ye are, and whereof ye are the governours'.

---

[8] *Secretary of State for the Home Department v Rehman* [2001] UKHL 47, [2003] 1 AC 153.
[9] *A v Secretary of State for the Home Department* [2004] UKHL 56, [2005] 2 AC 68.

This is a nation which has been tested in adversity, which has survived physical destruction and catastrophic loss of life. I do not underestimate the ability of fanatical groups of terrorists to kill and destroy, but they do not threaten the life of the nation. Whether we would survive Hitler hung in the balance, but there is no doubt that we shall survive Al-Qaeda.[10]

Lord Hoffmann famously concluded that: 'The real threat to the life of the nation, in the sense of a people living in accordance with its traditional laws and political values, comes not from terrorism but from laws such as these.'[11] The then Prime Minister made no secret of his indignation and suggested after the terrorist incidents in London in July 2005 that Lord Hoffmann must now be privately eating his words. But he fundamentally mistook both the man and the point that he had been making.

The chapters in this volume are a tribute to a remarkable legal mind and to the respect in which Lord Hoffmann is held even by those who profoundly disagree with him. But we are not just lawyers, and a portrait which was confined to his legal mind would be sadly incomplete. There are some judges whose voice and personality sing out from the written page. Sometimes this can be a rather depressing experience. It is, however, difficult to read a judgment or a lecture by Lennie Hoffmann without being struck by the energy and zest, the unlimited intellectual curiosity, the cultivated values and the wit that make their author such excellent company.

---

[10] ibid [91], [95]–[96].
[11] ibid [97].

Preface

This volume contains edited versions of papers presented at a conference that was held in honour of Lord Hoffmann on the occasion of his eightieth birthday at St Catherine's College, Oxford, on 25 and 26 April 2014. Their order of presentation largely follows the order of their presentation at the conference itself, beginning with introductory remarks by Professor Colin Tapper, including a discussion of Lord Hoffmann's contribution to the law of evidence, followed by 18 chapters focused on different aspects of his jurisprudence in the areas of tort law, human rights law, administrative law, media law, intellectual property law, employment law, contract and commercial law, the law of unjust enrichment, tax law, property law and corporate law.

Lord Hoffmann has been a central figure in the life of the Oxford Law Faculty, including a friend and close colleague of many current and past Faculty members. Most recently, since his appointment to a Visiting Professorship in September 2009, he has taught seminars in causation with his former tutor, Professor Tony Honoré, led the patent law seminars on the Final Honours School (undergraduate) intellectual property law courses and participated in many Faculty seminars and conferences across a broad range of areas. His teaching reflects the very qualities that have been recognised as having distinguished him as a judge—qualities valued enormously by his current students. They include the ability to 'suffuse even the most technical subject with intellectual excitement' remarked upon by Lord Walker in *Generics (UK) Ltd v H Lundbeck A/S*[12] and the ability to perceive the deep connections that exist between different areas of law noted by Lord Sumption in his Foreword to this volume.

These activities are only the most recent in an academic life that has spanned more than half a century since his arrival from South Africa in 1954 as a Rhodes Scholar to read for the BA in Jurisprudence and Bachelor of Civil Law at Queen's College. In 1961, four years after completing those degrees and being elected to the Vinerian Scholarship, Lord Hoffmann was appointed Stowell Civil Law Fellow of University College. In 1964, he was called to the English Bar by Gray's Inn, marking the beginning of a nine-year period in which he combined legal practice with a career as an Oxford tutorial fellow. That period continued until his decision to focus on his practice at the Chancery Bar in 1973. Four years later, in 1977, he was appointed Queen's Counsel.

---

[12] *Generics (UK) Ltd v H Lundbeck A/S* [2009] UKHL 12, [2009] 2 All ER 955 [31].

Many Oxford Dons combine academic life with legal practice, but in the 150-year history of the Oxford Law Faculty, it is difficult to imagine a more distinguished legal career than that of Lord Hoffmann. In England alone, that career has included 24 years as a judge and 14 years (from 1995 to 2009) as a Lord of Appeal in Ordinary. (He has also served as a part-time member of the Courts of Appeal in Jersey and Guernsey from 1980 to 1985, and since 1998 has been a non-permanent member judge of the Court of Final Appeal of Hong Kong.) Some indication of the breadth and depth of his contributions to English jurisprudence during those years is given by his extra-judicial writings, which span a wide range of areas of private and public law, including those covered by the contributions to this volume.

As a study of Lord Hoffmann's jurisprudence, this volume is not intended to be exhaustive, nor is it intended to represent all (academic and non-academic) legal perspectives. Rather, the volume shares the aim of the conference that preceded it, namely, to use the occasion of Lord Hoffmann's birthday to engage with his work and, in doing so, to acknowledge the contribution he has made to both English law and the legal academy, including the Oxford Law Faculty specifically. We would like to thank St Catherine's College, the Oxford Law Faculty and Hart Publishing for their support in bringing this project to fruition. We are also grateful to the conference participants, including Lord Hoffmann himself, for their lively engagement with the papers presented, and to Binesh Hass for research assistance.

Lord Hoffmann is a towering figure in the English legal community. The contributions to this volume reflect the depth and breadth of his judicial and non-judicial writings over the years, which continue to exercise the minds of academics, students and practitioners in England and beyond. At the same time, they are a mark of the deep affection and respect in which he is held by his past and present academic colleagues at Oxford. It is a privilege and a pleasure to present this Festschrift in his honour.

Justine Pila
Paul S Davies
Oxford, 26 November 2014

Contents

List of Contributors

Roderick Bagshaw is Associate Professor of Law, University of Oxford, and Fellow of Magdalen College.

Alan Bogg is Professor of Labour Law, University of Oxford, and Fellow of Hertford College.

Andrew Burrows QC, FBA is Professor of the Law of England, University of Oxford, and Fellow of All Souls College.

Hugh Collins, FBA is Vinerian Professor of English Law, University of Oxford, and Fellow of All Souls College.

Paul S Davies is Associate Professor of Law, University of Oxford, and Fellow of St Catherine's College.

Sandra Fredman QC, FBA is Rhodes Professor of the Laws of the British Commonwealth and the USA, University of Oxford, and Fellow of Pembroke College.

Judith Freedman CBE is Pinsent Masons Professor of Taxation Law, University of Oxford, and Fellow of Worcester College.

James Goudkamp is Associate Professor of Law, University of Oxford, and Fellow of Keble College.

Sarah Green is Associate Professor of Law, University of Oxford, and Fellow of St Hilda's College.

Tony Honoré QC, FBA is Emeritus Regius Professor of Civil Law at All Souls College, Oxford.

Ben McFarlane is Professor of Law at University College, London.

Jennifer Payne is Professor of Corporate Finance Law, University of Oxford, and Fellow of Merton College.

Justine Pila is University Lecturer in Intellectual Property Law, University of Oxford, and Fellow of St Catherine's College.

Francis Reynolds QC, FBA is Emeritus Professor of Law, University of Oxford, and Emeritus Fellow of Worcester College.

Jacob Rowbottom is Associate Professor of Law, University of Oxford, and Fellow of University College.

Roger Smith is Associate Professor of Law, University of Oxford, and Fellow of Magdalen College.

Robert Stevens is Herbert Smith Freehills Professor of Private Law, University of Oxford, and Fellow of Lady Margaret Hall.

Colin Tapper is Emeritus Professor of Law, University of Oxford, All Souls Reader in Law, and Fellow of Magdalen College.

Frederick Wilmot-Smith is Fellow of All Souls College, Oxford.

Alison L Young is Associate Professor of Law, University of Oxford, and Fellow of Hertford College.

Table of Cases

Bold page references indicate where cases are discussed at length.

Tables of Legislation

Statutes

Statutory Instruments

Other National Jurisdictions

Australia

Hong Kong

India

US

International Treaties and Conventions

European Legislation

1

Introductory Remarks and the Law of Evidence

COLIN TAPPER*

LENNIE (aka Lord Hoffmann) was good enough to provide a foreword for my own Festschrift[1] and it is pleasing to be allowed the opportunity of helping to introduce this Festschrift for him. I did not come to know Lennie until some time after we had both been students here in Oxford. We were however born in the same year, and studied law in Oxford at much the same time. I propose in these remarks, first, to describe the state of legal education in Oxford at that period and, second, to say something of Lennie's work in Evidence, which was the subject of his one academic monograph[2] and is not otherwise represented in this book.

I shall start in the year of our birth, 1934. At about that time legal education in Oxford was at an extremely low ebb.[3] The subject was widely regarded as lacking academic respectability. Corpus Christi College surrendered the Chair of Jurisprudence to University College for that reason, many Colleges had no Law Fellow and none more than one. Not that having such a Fellow represented any certain guarantee of academic quality since many such Fellows were either unqualified or incompetent. Nor were these categories identical since some of the qualified were incompetent and a very few of the unqualified were competent. My own college, Magdalen, provides an example. The Law Fellow hoped to become Bursar and avoided teaching law to the extent of actually hiding away from students. In Christ Church the relevant Student was regarded as so incompetent by a particularly forceful undergraduate, one JHC Morris, as to provoke a demand to be transferred for tuition to Balliol, where the Fellow, Theo Tyler, was both

---

* This is a written version of an oral address and differs from what was said in minor respects.

[1] P Mirfield and R Smith (eds), *Essays for Colin Tapper* (Oxford, Oxford University Press, 2003).

[2] LH Hoffmann, *South African Law of Evidence* (1st edn, Durban, Butterworths, 1962).

[3] For a fuller account upon which I have drawn, see AW Brian Simpson, *Reflections on the Concept of Law* (Oxford, Oxford University Press, 2011).

qualified and competent, despite being blind. These two examples became linked when Magdalen cast off its incompetent and unenthusiastic Fellow, appointing John Morris in his place. Things began to change. Morris was extremely efficient; for example, he is reputed to have been the first tutor to use typed reading lists. He was also a very good judge of academic talent, as proved by his first two appointments to Fellowships in Law at Magdalen, Rupert Cross and Guenter Treitel, each in turn later elected Vinerian Professor.[4] Academic respectability in the faculty more generally was further enhanced by the appointment of a number of first-rate teachers after the war, including Tony Honoré.

There remained problems with consistency in the quality of students. In most colleges there were avenues to admission for what have recently been dubbed the 'thick and rich'. Heads of House had places in their gift irrespective of admissions tutors, and some Law Fellows were not themselves averse to such admissions. Simpson recounts the practice of one Law Fellow who encouraged oarsmen to apply and then regularly invited the members of the Eton first eight to a lavish party in June to which examiners in Law Moderations were invited in the hope that they would be lenient to some of the budding oarsmen.[5] This side of the problem of respectability was tackled by increasing the rigour of University examinations. One of the newly appointed Law Fellows, Peter Carter at Wadham College, was particularly fierce. In his second year as an examiner in the Final Honours School of Jurisprudence, only four candidates of a field of about 200 were awarded first class honours, and three of those already had other degrees. Yet in his first year, despite a huge increase in failures, 11 firsts were awarded. That was Lennie's year, and that same cadre of students secured seven firsts in the examination for the degree of Bachelor of Civil Law in the following year. It was an annus mirabilis, six of those seven became Law Fellows of Oxford Colleges and the other became Head of a Law School elsewhere, Vice-Chancellor of that University and an Honorary Bencher of Gray's Inn. In both of these years Lennie was pre-eminent. There was then no formal recognition of the best candidate in the undergraduate examination, but it seems clear from informal sources that it was Lennie, and in the BCL where the best candidate was, and still is, awarded the Vinerian Scholarship, Lennie secured it. It is also worth mentioning that in those days when options were strictly limited, meaning that all the candidates took very nearly the same set of papers, such a ranking order was much more reliable than it is now, given the current proliferation of options. In my opinion, Lennie's year marked the final advent of complete academic respectability of law as a subject in this University.

---

[4] John Morris was also himself offered the Chair, but declined it.
[5] Above n 3, 66.

I now offer a few remarks about Lennie's scholarship in the law of evidence. Evidence was then a compulsory subject in the BCL and at the time was taught by Rupert Cross, who in Lennie's BCL year published the first edition of his textbook on evidence. Lennie, after his subsequent return to South Africa, was sufficiently impressed by it as to use it as a model for his own book on the South African law of evidence. When he came back to Oxford as a Fellow of University College, he joined Rupert Cross in the seminar in the law of evidence for the BCL. I became a third member of that seminar a year later and found the experience of working with two such marvellous colleagues as daunting as it was rewarding. Lennie had a great gift of clarity of thought and expression, and was sufficiently self-confident to reject the conventional wisdom in the subject without compunction or regret.

I can illustrate this by reference not to Lennie's work on the South African law, of which I know too little, but by reference to an article of his commenting on a decision of the House of Lords some years later.[6] This was a decision on the admissibility of evidence of the accused's bad character, then invariably described as 'similar fact' evidence, and traced back to a decision of the Privy Council in *Makin v Attorney-General for New South Wales*.[7] This case arose from the widespread incidence of the murder of infants, usually illegitimate, whose mothers, usually very poor, were desperate to find someone to care for a child. Advertisements to take in such infants for payments of a very small premium were common. For the advertisers it was much more profitable to murder the infants than to rear them. In most common law jurisdictions there were prosecutions in respect of such murders.[8] The Makin family advertised for children in Sydney and became suspected of wrongdoing by their evasive surreptitious movements between houses, and eventually 13 bodies of children were found buried in four different houses which they had occupied. They were charged with the murder of one of the children they had taken in, although the paucity of evidence can be discerned from the fact that there were two counts in the indictment, one for the murder of a named child and the other for the murder of an unnamed child. In other words, it was impossible even to identify the child from its remains, still less to ascertain the cause of death. The evidential issue related to the admissibility of evidence of finding the other 12 bodies. At every stage the evidence was admitted, and in the Privy Council Lord Herschell, LC, delivered a Delphic judgment attempting to justify this result. This judgment came to be regarded as the epicentre of the rule relating to

---

[6] LH Hoffmann, 'Similar Facts after Boardman' (1975) 91 *LQR* 193, commenting on *R v Boardman* [1975] AC 421 (HL).
[7] *Makin v Attorney-General for New South Wales* [1894] AC 57 (PC).
[8] In England one such case related to the most murders ever laid to the responsibility of a single defendant, exceeding the numbers in the relatively recent case of Dr Shipman.

the admissibility of 'similar fact' evidence. It failed to quell dispute about the application of the law, which Lord Hailsham described in *Boardman* as having become 'a pitted battlefield'.[9] It remained the case that in the most serious cases the evidence was always admitted.[10] The classic illustration of the operation of the 'similar fact' rule occurred in *R v Straffen*,[11] where the accused had been confined to Broadmoor Hospital, having pleaded insanity in relation to the murder of two young girls whose dead, but not sexually molested, bodies had been left unconcealed at the side of the road. Straffen subsequently escaped from Broadmoor and, within a few hours, a dead, but sexually unmolested, body of a young child was found unconcealed by the roadside nearby. The evidence of the previous events was, obviously rightly, admitted.

Then came the case of *Boardman*. Boardman was a schoolmaster accused of homosexual relations with three[12] boys at his school. There were several incidents in relation to each boy and the issue related to the admissibility of other incidents as evidence to prove any one of them. Here, as in *Makin*, the evidence of each of them was extremely weak, but, as in *Makin*, the lower courts admitted the evidence. Lord Hailsham was anxious to clarify the law and to provide an authoritative gloss on Lord Herchell's speech in *Makin*. To his consternation, he discovered on the day that the speeches were to be delivered that Lords Cross and Wilberforce had come with dissenting speeches. He told them that to dissent would send quite the wrong message and would cause the House of Lords to be deluged by similar appeals in unwholesome criminal cases. He further pointed out that, unlike the other members of the House, Lords Cross and Wilberforce had always practised in Chancery and ought to defer to the opinions of their brethren who were thoroughly experienced in the operation of the law of evidence in criminal cases. This failed to persuade Lords Cross and Wilberforce to abstain from delivering the speeches they had prepared, but did induce them to add a few grudging words at the end concurring in the result, if only as a matter of fact or of deference to the courts below, rather than as a matter of legal principle. There was an interesting sub-plot. Although Lord Hailsham was right in his assessment of the dissenters' experience of criminal law, he also knew, or would have guessed, that Lord Cross' speech would have been heavily influenced by the views of his brother Sir Rupert Cross, who was an acknowledged master of the law of criminal evidence. However, he also

---

[9] *R v Boardman* (n 6) 445.
[10] There seems to be no reported English case of murder where the evidence was ever excluded.
[11] *R v Straffen* [1952] 2 QB 911 (CCA).
[12] Reduced to two before the case reached the House of Lords.

knew that Lord Cross could not, with dignity or amour propre, admit as much. The outcome, from Lord Hailsham's point of view, then and thus became completely counter-productive. Once Lords Cross and Wilberforce were party to the decision but still delivered their contrasting reasons, and given that Lord Morris' speech was sufficiently equivocal to be claimed to support all possible views, commentators could claim to find the ratio decidendi not in the speeches of Lord Hailsham and Lord Salmond, but in those of Lords Cross and Wilberforce.

Lennie was one such commentator. The significance of his commentary lay not so much in its espousal of the reasoning of Lords Cross and Wilberforce as in the boldness of his demolition of the hitherto sacrosanct reasoning of Lord Herschell in *Makin*. He even went so far as to deny that *Makin* was a 'similar fact' case at all. His argument was that ever since that case, two quite different situations had been confused: first, there were cases like *Straffen* where there was clear evidence that the accused had acted in the past in a particular, and particularly unusual, way and was now accused of having repeated his conduct; and, second, there were cases like both *Makin* and *Boardman* where there was some rather weaker evidence to show that the accused may have done something rather similar on a number of occasions and by statistical arguments might be found to be guilty of the commission of all. This distinction later became orthodox, but when first articulated by Lennie was completely contrary to all of the accepted 'wisdom'. The penetration, clarity and originality of analysis so displayed continued to characterise his contributions to jurisprudence and legal scholarship, as the remainder of these chapters will show.

2

Responsibility for Harm to Others: A Brief Survey

TONY HONORÉ QC, FBA

I AM HAPPY to help introduce and contribute to this Festschrift in honour of Lord Hoffmann. He came up to Queen's in the 1950s when I was the law tutor there. A fellow South African and Rhodes Scholar from Cape Town, I looked forward to his arrival and was not disappointed. He did outstandingly well in law at Oxford, as he has done since. But I remember a comment he made to the effect that to be a good lawyer, unlike a leading physical scientist, you need not be outstandingly clever. That is just as well and Rhodes would have agreed. But you do need a modest talent, common sense and stamina. The latter Lennie has kept through regular cycling.

I will not go into the details of his notable career, which others have outlined. So what may an ex-tutor properly say of an ex-pupil who has reached a decently advanced age? Thales of Miletus is supposed to have introduced into teaching the principle that a pupil need not agree with his teacher. Indeed, reasoned dissent is the basis of progress in learning. Nor need a teacher agree with his pupil. I think Lennie may disagree, at least in part, with what I shall shortly argue. That does not debar me from saying a word in appreciation of his career, in particular of his contribution to judicial office. For while law is made in our system on the basis of arguments between counsel and judges, judges in the higher courts have to decide which arguments to accept, and this often brings out disagreements between them. It is important in a higher court that there should be a judge or judges capable of giving a lead when it comes to settling these differences of opinion. We have been fortunate to have in our House of Lords and Supreme Court such figures as Richard Wilberforce and Tom Bingham. They were not always right, but they had a clear view of the potentialities and limits of the judicial office, and were prepared to say where they thought that pointed in the particular case. To my mind, Lord Hoffmann has been one of those cardinal figures who have helped to guide our law to the high reputation it still enjoys. That is reason enough for this volume that will examine some of his wide-ranging contributions in detail.

Now for a short piece on one of his concerns: responsibility for harm to others.

Start from the principle that human beings, like other living creatures, are responsible for the misfortunes that befall them. We all have to cope with what happens to us and hence to bear the risk of events that befall us. These include such misfortunes as ill-health, loss of property or employment, the death of friends or relatives and similar mishaps. Our need to adapt to risk is a natural form of responsibility, since life rests on the pursuit of continuity by survival or reproduction. This 'having to cope' burden is pre-legal. On the other hand, we are not normally responsible for the misfortunes that befall others. So our responsibility to others for misfortunes that befall them, when it exists, involves a transfer of this pre-legal burden from the person who suffers the misfortune to another.

The transfer comes about, in my view, in two main ways. The person held responsible for another's misfortune has either: (i) brought about or helped to bring about the event for which he is held responsible; or (ii) bears the risk of having to cope with or answer for that event. These two ways of becoming responsible may seem disconnected, but they relate to the same enterprise. This is the enterprise of explaining and coping with events in a way that attaches the explanation and means of coping, so far as possible, to human action. It fits a society that seeks to answer and draw conclusions from two questions about what happens to people. Does the explanation of an event point to human agency? What human action does the event call for? The posing and, up to a point, the answering of these questions is also pre-legal. But the processes of law combine these two forms of inquiry and may formalise them as a ground for recognising rights and duties. Has something come about through wrongful human agency? If so, what official action, if any, should be taken?

To begin with the explanation of how a misfortune has come about. To have brought about an event is to be responsible for that event. There will normally be a reason to attach credit or discredit to the person responsible. The most straightforward ground is responsibility for conduct. We are responsible because we have chosen to do something. If the person whose conduct is in question lacked freedom to choose, his or her responsibility may be reduced or non-existent. But a person who possesses the capacity to choose and decide is responsible for what he or she has done and, within certain limits, for its outcome.

However, positive voluntary action is not the only ground of responsibility for conduct. We may be passively responsible for our conduct in failing to do in our duty. Sometimes this duty is self-imposed. We have undertaken but failed to do something. Other duties are imposed on us through our relations to others, for instance, through family ties, friendship or membership of a community. In that case, too, we are within limits responsible for the outcome of a failure to do our duty. And the only explanation may involve showing that someone's conduct has *helped* to bring about a given event or state of affairs, without causing it in the strict sense. In that case the person helping has a lesser degree or responsibility for what has happened than the person causing the outcome and a lesser degree of credit or discredit is appropriate.

Something needs to be said about the notion of 'cause' that is used here. Though it has given rise to a complex philosophical literature, the importance of causation in ordinary life rests on a quite simple idea. Since we live in a world in which many events occur in regular sequence, it is helpful to discover under what conditions we can rely on these sequences to be sure of achieving a given outcome. We find by observation, coupled with trial and error, that when A, B and C are present, X can be relied upon to follow, but that the presence of D is not necessary. We thereby build up recipes, based on conditions that are individually necessary and together sufficient to ensure what we want. We call these causal principles. We project them to explain past or predict future events and they form the bedrock of science, history and other disciplines. But this procedure is subject to certain caveats. Causal principles incorporate not merely the cause and outcome but also the process by which that outcome is reached. To cause death by poisoning does not involve the same causal principle as to cause death by dehydration or shooting. Moreover, since there is usually an interval of time between cause and outcome, the application of a causal principle to explain a given event is not appropriate if the regular causal process has been frustrated in the interval by an intervening event. In the case of a frustrating event, the question may arise whether the initial wrongdoer has by wrongdoing attracted a normative change that imposes on him or her a responsibility for risk that covers the frustrating event.

Indeed a person who is not responsible on the basis of his or her conduct may be responsible in another way. He or she may have a duty independent of conduct to deal with or make reparation for the event in question. The two forms of responsibility, though often connected, are in principle distinct. The first assigns or fails to assign authorship to one who intervenes or fails to intervene in the world. The second assigns a duty in a way that resembles certain other social duties independent of conduct which resemble guarantees. Responsibility in this second sense must of course be based on a good reason. In both cases conventions determine how the situation should be dealt with and what form the reparation, if any, should take.

Apart from responsibility for conduct, responsibility on the ground that as individuals we bear certain risks of harm to others also seems basic. Indeed, responsibility for conduct is sometimes based on the risk to others that the conduct is likely to create, as in the case of strict legal liability for engaging in dangerous operations. But there are also areas in which a person is responsible because he or she bears a risk, though his or her conduct has not brought about the event for which he or she is responsible. We bear the burden of ill fortune to ourselves unless that risk of having to cope with it is displaced by being transferred to another. But to transfer the risk of responsibility for misfortune to another is also a feature of human society and can found responsibility outside the law.

A second ground of responsibility is therefore present when a person bears the risk of another person's misfortune which he or she has not brought about. We guarantee or insure, as it were, another person against misfortune. This form of responsibility may, again, be active or passive. It is active when we take on responsibility for another by agreement, such as an insurance contract. Although this responsibility is based on our conduct in making the agreement, the resulting responsibility, if any, is not responsibility *for one's conduct*. We may also be responsible for risks imposed on us apart from agreement. For instance, we may be responsible (at least outside the law) for harm done by our young children, not only if we have failed in our duty to supervise them properly, but simply by virtue of the relationship that exists between us. Parenthood, marriage ('for better, for worse'), partnership and many other relations involve the assumption or imposition of risks as well as benefits. Indeed, the imposition of risk is often seen as the counterpart of the benefit. *Ubi emolumentum ibi onus.*

A good example of the second form of responsibility is *Baker v Willoughby*,[1] where the plaintiff was injured by the defendant's negligence, so that he was disabled from earning in the future. In a later unrelated incident he was shot by robbers, so that he would in any case have been disabled from then on. The plaintiff's loss of earnings after the second incident was not caused by the first injury, since the second wrongdoer injured a person who was already disabled. It was nevertheless held, I think rightly, that the first wrongdoer was liable for the plaintiff's loss of earnings after the second injury. To injure someone wrongfully may alter the normative position between the injurer and the victim. It may impose on the injurer, by transferring a risk, a liability which would not otherwise fall on him. Of course, there must be a good reason for a court to do this, but, if there is, the outcome is morally in order from the point of view of the injurer (who is as a consequence of his wrongdoing made to insure the victim against the effect of later wrongful injury), the court (which does justice in the circumstances by imposing compensation for successive unlawful injuries) and the victim (who receives what is rightly due to him or her).

This example concerns a frustrating event, which is overridden by the court's duty to do justice. Another example concerns the balance between benefit and liability. Why is the employer responsible in tort for his or her employee's wrong? The employee has in most cases caused harm to a third party, for instance, by driving a van belonging to his or her employer without due care. But the employer has in general done nothing to cause harm

---

[1] *Baker v Willoughby* [1969] UKHL 8, [1969] 3 All ER 1528.

to the third party. It is true that he or she has taken the employee into his or her employment, but, unless the employer knew at the time that the employee was incompetent in the relevant respect (for example, that he or she was a poor driver), he or she has not caused or contributed to harming the third party. The employer is held liable for a different reason. He or she benefits from the employee's services and, in return, it is thought fair that he or she should take the risk that the employee may harm a third party in the course of his employment. He or she is legally responsible in that event. The legal liability results from the combination of faulty conduct on the part of the employee and the transfer of the risk of injury from the third party to the employer. Both responsibility for conduct and responsibility based on the transfer of risk are in play. There must of course be a good reason to transfer the risk from the person injured to another. In this instance the transfer to the person who in general benefits from the employment is morally in order and commended itself to the courts that created this branch of the law.

These, then, are the two main grounds of human responsibility to others in ordinary life and in the law. We are responsible either because we have brought or helped to bring about harm to another by our conduct, or because the duty of dealing or risk of having to deal with harm to another rests on us.

In thinking about responsibility in ordinary life and the law, we need to bear in mind both conduct and risk. As regards risk, the correlation of benefit and risk is not the only ground for transferring risk as a supplement to responsibility for wrongful conduct. Another good reason is to be found in the duty of courts to do justice to those injured by wrongs. This involves, among other things, ensuring that a plaintiff who has suffered unlawful injuries is, if possible, compensated. The House of Lords, rightly in my opinion, took a similar view in the case of *Fairchild v Glenhaven*.[2] Mesothelioma, an incurable cancer, is caused by exposure to asbestos fibres. When two or more employers in turn negligently exposed an employee to asbestos fibres and the employee later suffered from the disease, it was decided that each employer who, by a similar process of exposure, materially increased the danger could be made liable, though it could not be shown which of the exposures actually caused the disease. The decision can be justified on the basis that an employer who commits a wrong by negligently exposing another to asbestos has to bear the risk that, in view of a similar exposure by others, the victim will contract the disease, but that it will be impossible to prove which employer's exposure to the danger caused it. The moral justification for so deciding lies, again, in the law's duty to ensure that a victim who is injured through two or more wrongful acts is, if possible, not denied compensation. It can be argued that it is for legislators, rather than judges,

---

[2] *Fairchild v Glenhaven* [2002] UKHL 22, [2002] 3 WLR 89.

to extend causal liability in this way.[3] But judges have a duty to do justice, which includes seeing that a victim of wrongful conduct or his or her estate receives compensation when the matter is litigated in appropriate (in this case civil) proceedings.

It should be noted that the suggested explanation of liability for causing harm in this case depends on the fact that the basis of liability is civil, not criminal. Civil liability leads to the payment of money, not to punishment. The allocation of legal responsibility on the basis of risk consists of transferring it from one person to another, and this transfer of responsibility is not a feature of criminal law, which in principle penalises people for their own conduct and not that of others. The criminal wrongdoer does indeed take the risk that what he or she does will bring about unexpected consequences, for example, that his or her careless driving will result in the death of the victim rather than mere injury, but not that the conduct of another will do so. Participation in crime forms only an apparent exception, marked by the use of a different terminology, such as aiding, abetting, counselling or procuring a crime. The language of participation brings out that the offender is held responsible for his or her conduct in facilitating a wrongful act, which is a type of conduct, not for assuming a risk.

There may be other types of case in which the transfer of risk from the person who suffers harm to another is defensible and morally appropriate. The examples mentioned are merely intended to draw attention to its place, easily overlooked, in moral and legal judgments of responsibility.

---

[3] Eg, L Hoffmann, 'Fairchild and after' in A Burrows, D Johnston and R Zimmermann (eds), *Judge and Jurist: Essays in Memory of Lord Rodger of Earlsferry* (Oxford, Oxford University Press, 2013) 3–70.

3

But for Lord Hoffmann, How Would the Causal Inquiry in Negligence Look?

SARAH GREEN

I. INTRODUCTION

THERE IS LITTLE doubt that the answer to the question posed in the chapter title above is 'significantly different'. In the spirit of a proper counterfactual assessment, this question will be answered by considering what the causal inquiry in negligence would look like if, instead of Lord Hoffmann's judgments, the common law had been (in)formed by opposing views.

There are three principal areas in which the causal inquiry would look different from the way it currently does were it not for the influence of Lord Hoffmann:

— the tort of negligence would have recovery for 'lost chances' where no such thing has been lost;
— the tort of negligence would have a less constrained *Fairchild* principle;
— there would be no sensible foil to the result in *Chester v Afshar*[1] and it might therefore have had more of a practical impact on the tort of negligence.

II. 'LOST CHANCES'

Lord Hoffmann was in the majority of three who decided against the imposition of liability in *Gregg v Scott*,[2] a case in which the claimant argued that he had lost a chance of recovery from illness as a result of the defendant's negligence. But For his Lordship's contribution to this decision, therefore, the outcome would have been different. And it would have been wrong.

[1] *Chester v Afshar* [2004] UKHL 41, [2005] 1 AC 134.
[2] *Gregg v Scott* [2005] UKHL 2, [2005] 2 AC 176.

In *Gregg*, the claimant visited the defendant GP, complaining of a lump under his left arm, which the defendant diagnosed as a benign lipoma. In failing to refer the claimant to a specialist at that point, the defendant was held to have been in breach of his duty of care. It was not until a biopsy was carried out by a specialist, following a referral by another GP nine months later, that the claimant discovered that he had cancer in the form of non-Hodgkin's lymphoma. The trial judge found that the claimant's chance of being 'cured' (defined in this context as a period of 10 years' remission) was 42 per cent when he made his visit to the defendant, but that the nine-month delay, consequent upon the defendant's negligent failure to diagnose his illness correctly, reduced his chance of being cured to 25 per cent. As the claimant had only a 42 per cent chance of a cure in the first place, however, he was unable to prove on the balance of probabilities that the defendant's negligence caused him to be in a worse state than he would have been in had his treatment not been delayed by nine months. In the light of this fact, the claimant argued that the defendant's negligence had caused him to lose the chance of being cured.[3] In so doing, he invited the Court to address a similar question to the one first considered by the House in *Hotson v East Berkshire Health Authority*[4] as to whether or not such a 'loss' should be recoverable.

By a majority of three to two,[5] the House of Lords dismissed Gregg's appeal and held that it was (still) not prepared to extend loss of a chance claims to such cases. Whilst on the facts as found by the trial judge, it had been established that the defendant's breach of duty had reduced the epidemiological likelihood of survival by 17 per cent, the House of Lords correctly declined to recognise this as actionable damage. It was Lord Hoffmann who succinctly identified the significance of the issue: 'A wholesale adoption of possible rather than probable causation as the criterion of liability would be so radical a change in our law as to amount to a legislative act.'[6] Had Lord Hoffmann decided in favour of imposing liability on Dr Scott, the tort of negligence would have taken a turn for the worse. A move towards liability based on 'possible rather than probable' causation or, in other words, not requiring claimants to prove their cases on the balance of probabilities, but instead awarding them damages according to the probability that they deserve compensation (often referred to as 'proportional liability') would not have been a positive development. There are a number of reasons why this is so, all of which demonstrate why Lord Hoffmann's approach is to be preferred.

---

[3] That is, the 17 per cent difference between his 'chances' (42 per cent) when he first saw the defendant and his 'chances' (25 per cent) by the time he was correctly diagnosed.

[4] *Hotson v East Berkshire Health Authority* [1988] UKHL 1, [1987] AC 750.

[5] Lords Hoffmann, Nicholls, and Hope in the majority and Lord Walker and Lady Hale dissenting.

[6] *Gregg* (n 2) [90].

In refusing to depart from the orthodox approach to causation, the Court recognised that it is epistemic limitations which pose the most consistent problem for the causal inquiry and, to use Lord Hoffmann's words once more: 'What we lack is knowledge and the law deals with that lack of knowledge by the concept of the burden of proof.'[7] In other words, although the law cannot expect to deal in certainties, the least it can do is expect its probabilities to be more likely than not. The formulation of the claim in *Gregg*, misleadingly couched in terms of a 'lost chance', was an attempt to sidestep the orthodox standard of proof on the basis that the claimant had lost something of value to him in having his 'already likely to suffer an adverse outcome' position made, by the defendant's breach, into 'even more likely to suffer an adverse outcome'. In legal terms, however, such a 'chance' is less a prediction of what would have happened to a particular claimant than an approximation of the forensic margin of error:

> If it is proved statistically that 25 per cent of the population have a chance of recovery from a certain injury and 75 per cent do not, it does not mean that someone who suffers that injury and who does not recover from it has lost a 25 per cent chance. He may have lost nothing at all. What he has to do is prove that he was one of the 25 per cent and that his loss was caused by the defendant's negligence. To be a figure in a statistic does not by itself give him a cause of action. *If the plaintiff succeeds in proving that he was one of the 25 per cent and the defendant took away that chance*, the logical result would be to award him 100 per cent of his damages.[8]

As the emphasis shows, what is uncertain in these cases is whether the claimant ever had a greater than evens chance of recovery and whether the defendant's breach affected the substance of that possibility, making it into a less than evens chance. On facts such as these, a claimant is deemed to have had a chance of avoiding a detriment only where she *starts off* in a position in which it is more likely than not that she will avoid the adverse outcome. If a breach of duty reduces this chance to a level at which it is still greater than evens, the defendant in question is not liable in negligence, despite having affected the likelihood of that outcome occurring. If a breach of duty brings the claimant's chances below the evens threshold, however, that defendant will be liable in negligence for having made the claimant worse off in the eyes of the law. Since the assessment of the claimant's chances in such cases is intrinsic to the question of whether she deserves compensation from the defendant, the degree to which her chances have been reduced is not as important as the comparative

---

[7] ibid [79].
[8] *Hotson v East Berkshire Health Authority* [1987] 1 All ER 210 (CA) 223 (Croom-Johnson LJ) (emphasis added).

effect of the defendant's breach on her position. In *McGhee v National Coal Board*,[9] Lord Salmon gave the following well-known illustration:

> Suppose ... it could be proved that men engaged in a particular industrial process would be exposed to a 52% risk of contracting dermatitis even when proper washing facilities were provided. Suppose it could also be proved that that risk would be increased to, say, 90% when such facilities were not provided. It would follow that ... an employer who negligently failed to provide the proper facilities would escape from any liability to an employee who contracted dermatitis notwithstanding that the employers had increased the risk from 52% to 90%. The negligence would not be a cause of the dermatitis because even with proper washing facilities, ie without the negligence, it would still have been more likely than not that the employee would have contracted the disease—the risk of injury then being 52%. If, however, you substitute 48% for 52% the employer could not escape liability, not even if he had increased the risk to, say, only 60%. Clearly such results would not make sense; nor would they, in my view, accord with the common law.[10]

Fortunately, in *Sienkiewicz v Grief*,[11] Lord Phillips made direct reference to this argument and said of it:

> I can understand why Lord Salmon considered that to base a finding of causation on such evidence would be capricious, but not why he considered that to do so would be contrary to common law. The balance of probabilities test is one that is inherently capable of producing capricious results.[12]

Although this comment has the obvious merit of aligning the result in Lord Salmon's example with the orthodox common law position, it also has the unfortunate effect of fortifying the view that such a position is capricious. It is not. Whilst the balance of probabilities approach might sometimes produce results which seem harsh either to a particular claimant or defendant considered discretely, those results will at least be consistent across the spectrum of *causal relationships between parties*. That is, a defendant found liable in negligence for having caused a four per cent reduction in a claimant's statistical 'chances' (say, from 52 per cent to 48 per cent) might look hard done by, as compared to another who was found not liable, despite having caused a 42 per cent reduction (say, from 48 per cent to six per cent) in another claimant's statistical 'chances'. Comparing the positions of defendants alone, however,[13] is not an authentic means of evaluating a mechanism

---

[9] *McGhee v National Coal Board* [1973] 1 WLR 1 (HL).
[10] ibid 12.
[11] *Sienkiewicz v Grief* [2011] UKSC 10, [2011] 2 AC 229.
[12] ibid [25]–[26].
[13] Or, indeed, claimants, to whom the argument applies with equal force.

intended to allocate the risk of error as between defendants and claimants as distinct, but related, classes. If the positions of claimants are considered alongside those of the defendants with whom they are correlative,[14] results will be consistent, and this is the comparison which really matters. For every losing defendant whose breach reduces a claimant's chances from 51 per cent to 49 per cent, for instance, there will be a losing claimant whose chances have been reduced by, say, 45 per cent, but who only ever had a chance amounting to 46 per cent. In other words, the potential for harsh results cuts both ways. But it *always* cuts both ways, so it cannot accurately be described as 'capricious'. Indeed, since we are all potentially claimants in negligence as much as we are potential defendants, splitting the risk of error in this way is the least capricious way of dealing with the inherent imperfections of the forensic process.[15] Consequently, it is not open to claimants to re-characterise a claim which does not reach this evidentiary standard as being a claim for a lesser *degree* of loss,[16] because the legal result of falling short of this standard is that no loss has been suffered. Therefore, claimants in such cases are not those who have lost a less than evens chance, but those for whom there is a less than evens chance that they have lost anything at all. In *Gregg*, Lord Hoffmann made the significance of this point very clear:

> [T]he law regards the world as in principle bound by laws of causality. Everything has a determinate cause, even if we do not know what it is ... There is no inherent uncertainty about what caused something to happen in the past or about whether something which happened in the past will cause something to happen in the future.[17]

The fact that the claimants in both *Hotson* and *Gregg* attempted to repackage facts otherwise bound for forensic failure suggests that there is some dissatisfaction with the polarity of outcomes generated by the balance of probabilities standard. It is perhaps the fiction inherent in a system which purports to give certain answers on the basis of uncertain evidence which generates such disquiet, and makes a proportional approach to liability (of the sort rejected by Lord Hoffmann in *Gregg*)[18] appear on its face to be more appealing. Currently, a defendant can part-cause an injury or cause part of an injury, but what he cannot do is *possibly* cause an injury. As Lord Hoffmann has made clear in an extra-judicial context:

> The law operates a binary system in which the only values are 0 and 1. If the evidence that something happened satisfies the burden of proof ... then it is

---

[14] See E Weinrib, *Corrective Justice* (Oxford, Oxford University Press, 2012) 20.
[15] See *Sienkiewicz* (n 11) [187] (Lord Brown).
[16] As the claimants in both *Hotson* (n 4) and *Gregg* (n 2) did; they claimed not for the full extent of their final injury, but for a proportion of it, calculated according to the 'chance' of avoiding the injury they claimed to have lost.
[17] *Gregg* (n 2) [79].
[18] ibid.

assigned a value of 1 and treated as definitely having happened. If the evidence does not discharge the burden of proof, the event is assigned a value of 0 and treated as definitely not having happened. There is no forensic space for the conclusion that something which has to be proved may have happened.[19]

This might seem strange, given that:

> Evidence is never perfect; uncertainty always exists. Why not recognise the uncertainty entailed in any attempt to reconstruct history, particularly with the difficulties of the necessarily counterfactual inquiry required by causation? Shouldn't law frankly acknowledge the probabilistic nature of factual assessments such as causation and adjust the extent of liability accordingly?[20]

However, even if proportional liability were a fairer or more effective approach to take,[21] it is simply not compatible with a system which has the balance of probabilities standard at its core. An adversarial system is better served by the balance of probabilities standard, and the production of all-or-nothing results. That way, not only do the winners know they are winners and the losers know they are losers, but, more often than not, both will have their deserts. By contrast, a system of proportional liability is highly unlikely ever fully to compensate or to correct.[22] The law cannot indulge in the luxury of indecision. Whilst it might be argued that granting an award on the basis of proportional liability *is* a decision because it effects some form of transfer, that decision is one defined by its own uncertainty and therefore amounts to a form of forensic capitulation. Were any form of proportional approach to be the norm, this argument would lack force, but whilst the default standard remains that of all or nothing, the making of an exception based on proportionality undermines its whole conceptual basis. To equate the probability of causation with the quantity of damages awarded to the claimant is to misunderstand both the nature of the causal inquiry in negligence and the role of probability within it:

> Probability theory is intended as a mathematical description of the world. Its goal is to bring the uncertainty in our world view as closely as possible into congruence with the uncertainty in the world. Our mathematicians have done a great job of constructing and elaborating mathematical systems and theorems towards that end. Our scientists have made considerable progress in discovering which physical systems obey which models. But no adequate philosophical explication of probability theory exists as yet, nor can one do so until we learn a good deal more logic

---

[19] L Hoffmann, 'Causation' in R Goldberg (ed), *Perspectives on Causation* (Oxford, Hart Publishing, 2011) 8.

[20] M Green, 'The Future of Proportional Responsibility' in M Madden (ed), *Exploring Tort Law* (Cambridge, Cambridge University Press, 2005) 354.

[21] And this is by no means a universally accepted truth: ibid 385.

[22] J Gardner, 'What is Tort Law for? Part 1: The Place of Corrective Justice' (2011) 30 *Law and Philosophy* 1, 21; Weinrib (n 14) 87–96.

and a good deal more physics than we presently know. We may never be sure we have it right, perhaps, until we possess a general theory of rationality and know for certain whether or not God play dice with the Universe.[23]

Probability is a tool and not a conclusion. Eliding the two is the same as attributing greatness to Ashkenazy's piano, Tendulkar's bat or Shakespeare's quill; unfortunately, a tool itself generates no outcome. Probability should not therefore be used to quantify what it has not been able to justify. But for Lord Hoffmann, this point might have been lost on the tort of negligence.

III. A LESS CONSTRAINED *FAIRCHILD* PRINCIPLE

Despite the fact that Lord Hoffmann's contribution to the unanimous decision in *Fairchild v Glenhaven Funeral Services Ltd*[24] was a significant one, its absence would not have prevented the development therein of the exceptional causal principle now generally associated with that case.[25] However, the way in which his Lordship subsequently dealt with that principle has helped to ensure that it is more constrained in its application than it would otherwise have been. The importance of this constraint can hardly be over-estimated, since the *Fairchild* principle is an exception which validates the rule.

The defendants in *Fairchild* were former employers of mesothelioma victims, who had exposed their employees to asbestos in breach of their duties of care. It was accepted that, for the purposes of the case, any exposure to asbestos other than that for which the defendants were responsible (such as general environmental exposure) could be discounted. The major complications, however, were, first, that each individual had been exposed to asbestos by more than one employer and, second, that medical knowledge about mesothelioma was incomplete and was therefore unable to associate the development of the disease with any particular source of asbestos (in other words, with any particular employer). Lord Hoffmann succinctly identified the significant features of the case thus:

> First, we are dealing with a duty specifically intended to protect employees against being unnecessarily exposed to the risk of (among other things) a particular disease. Secondly, the duty is one intended to create a civil right to compensation for injury relevantly connected with its breach. Thirdly, it is established that the greater the exposure to asbestos, the greater the risk of contracting that disease. Fourthly, except in the case in which there has been only one significant exposure to asbestos, medical science cannot prove whose asbestos is more likely than not

---

[23] R Weatherford, *Philosophical Foundations of Probability Theory* (London, Routledge & Kegan Paul, 1982) 252.

[24] *Fairchild v Glenhaven Funeral Services Ltd* [2002] UKHL 22, [2003] 1 AC 32.

[25] Despite having started life in *McGhee* (n 9).

to have produced the cell mutation which caused the disease. Fifthly, the employee has contracted the disease against which he should have been protected.[26]

The House of Lords held the defendants in *Fairchild* liable on the basis that they had *materially increased the risk* of the claimants developing mesothelioma, despite the fact that no claimant could (ever) prove on the balance of probabilities that any one of multiple defendants had caused his illness. In the process, the Court emphasised the exceptional nature of what it was doing and limited it by reference to, inter alia, the intractable epistemic problems associated with mesothelioma:

> In these circumstances, a rule requiring proof of a link between the defendant's asbestos and the claimant's disease would, with the arbitrary exception of single-employer cases, empty the duty of content. If liability depends upon proof that the conduct of the defendant was a necessary condition of the injury, it cannot effectively exist. It is however open to your Lordships to formulate a different causal requirement in this class of case. The Court of Appeal was in my opinion wrong to say that in the absence of a proven link between the defendant's asbestos and the disease, there was no 'causative relationship' whatever between the defendant's conduct and the disease. It depends entirely upon the level at which the causal relationship is described. To say, for example, that the cause of Mr Matthews's cancer was his significant exposure to asbestos during two employments over a period of eight years, without being able to identify the day upon which he inhaled the fatal fibre, is a meaningful causal statement. The medical evidence shows that it is the only kind of causal statement about the disease which, in the present state of knowledge, a scientist would regard as possible. There is no a priori reason, no rule of logic, which prevents the law from treating it as sufficient to satisfy the causal requirements of the law of negligence. The question is whether your Lordships think such a rule would be just and reasonable and whether the class of cases to which it applies can be sufficiently clearly defined.[27]

The crux of the issue in *Fairchild*, characterised by Lord Bingham as the 'rock of uncertainty',[28] is that the nature of mesothelioma makes it (currently) impossible to discern in principle which exposures contributed to the disease and which did not. Therefore, in these 'rock of uncertainty' cases, the issue is not that factual evidence is *unavailable* in any given instance, but that, on the basis of current knowledge, factual evidence is *not capable* of answering the causal question.[29] It is essential that this specific type of

---

[26] *Fairchild* (n 24) [61].

[27] ibid [62].

[28] ibid [7].

[29] It is entirely possible, according to our current state of knowledge, that all but one defendant on the facts of *Fairchild* (or, indeed, every defendant, if Stapleton's point that environmental exposure cannot defensibly be discounted, despite what their Lordships decided in *Fairchild*; see J Stapleton, 'Lords A'Leaping Evidentiary Gaps' (2002) 10 *Torts Law Journal* 293–96) could have had no effect whatsoever on the claimant. This is what makes the issue so difficult—a point which is missed by the example of the multiple stabbing given in C Miller,

impossibility is distinguished from the impossibility which can arise on the facts of any given case, when the available evidence is unable to provide the court with a scientifically conclusive answer, despite the fact that it is in principle possible to provide such an answer on such facts. In the absence of this critical distinction, the material contribution to risk analysis loses one of its principle justificatory bases and becomes potentially applicable to any case in which proof of causation is physically (as opposed to theoretically) impossible. One of the most important means of maintaining this distinction, and keeping the exceptional *Fairchild* principle within acceptable limits, is an adherence to the 'single agent' criterion. Unfortunately, this has not been universally acknowledged:

> Since *Fairchild* and *Barker* there has been much academic focus on a supposedly critical distinction between so-called 'single agent' and 'multiple agent' cases, the suggestion being that the former more readily lend themselves to special rules of causation than the latter. For my part I have difficulty even in recognising the distinction between these categories, at any rate in some cases.[30]

With respect, this distinction is indeed critical. For a start, 'the claimant must prove that his injury was caused by the eventuation of the kind of risk created by the defendant's wrongdoing'.[31] Despite not having recognised its importance in *Fairchild* itself,[32] Lord Hoffmann explicitly emphasised the relevance of this distinction in *Barker v Corus*.[33] His Lordship made it clear that, for the exceptional principle to apply, 'the mechanism by which it caused the damage, whatever it was, must have been the same'[34] and that he was 'wrong' to think otherwise.[35] Lord Rodger explained the significance

---

'Causation in Personal Injury after (and before) *Sienkiewicz*' (2012) 32 *Legal Studies* 396, 400. His example is one of material contribution to injury, since all of those stabbing Caesar caused him some injury, regardless of whether they triggered his death by dealing the fatal blow. This is an orthodox causal situation and is not subject to the evidentiary gap which is such an intractable problem in the mesothelioma cases.

[30] *Sienkiewicz* (n 11) [187] (Lord Brown).

[31] *Fairchild* (n 24) [170] (Lord Rodger).

[32] ibid [73].

[33] *Barker v Corus* [2006] UKHL 20, [2006] 2 AC 572.

[34] ibid [24]. However, see the wording used by Lord Mance in *Durham v BAI (Run-off Ltd)* [2012] UKSC 14, [2012] 2 AC 273 [65]: 'In the present state of scientific knowledge and understanding, there is nothing here that enables one to know or suggest that the risk to which the defendant exposed the victim actually materialised. What materialised was at most a risk of the same kind to which someone, who may or may not have been the defendant, or something or some event had exposed the victim.' With respect, this wording is a little misleading because all sources of asbestos create the same risk: that of causing an individual to develop mesothelioma. What scientific knowledge cannot yet establish is whether a particular defendant's *contribution* to that single risk was necessary for a particular claimant to develop mesothelioma.

[35] *Barker* (n 33) [23]. However, see also L Hoffmann, '*Fairchild* and After' in A Burrows, D Johnston and R Zimmermann (eds), *Judge and Jurist: Essays in Memory of Lord Rodger of Earlsferry* (Oxford, Oxford University Press, 2013) 66.

of single as opposed to multiple sources of risk at the time that the *Fairchild* principle was formulated:

> [T]he principle does not apply where the claimant has merely proved that his injury could have been caused by a number of different events, only one of which is the eventuation of the risk created by the defendant's wrongful act or omission. *Wilsher* is an example.[36]

Wilsher remains good law, and long may this be true. The issue in that case, in which the defendant's breach was one of five different potential causes of the claimant's injury,[37] was that the *agent* of cause was indeterminate. This is not true of the mesothelioma cases, in which it is accepted that the causal agent is asbestos, and so it is the *source* of the causal agent which is indeterminate. In the mesothelioma cases, therefore, we know more than we did in *Wilsher*. We know, for instance, that the defendant's behaviour contributed to *the* specific risk which came to fruition in the form of the claimant's ultimate injury. In *Wilsher*, this was not known; all that was established therein was that the defendant had created *a* risk which might have resulted in the claimant's injury. For a distinction that calls for such a minor textual alteration, it has major implications. Deciding in favour of liability in *Wilsher*-type situations would effectively mean imposing liability for risk creation, regardless of whether or not that risk actually resulted in injury. Not only would this rail against the law of torts' (correct) refusal to award damages for risk creation *simpliciter*,[38] but, in practical terms, it would mean potentially crushing liability for defendants, and particularly those likely by dint of their nature to create such risks on a regular basis, such as the NHS. Adherence to this criterion thereby ensures that defendants will not be held liable when it cannot be established that the claimant's injury fell within *the* risk created by their negligent behaviour. Such a limitation, in making the exception more exceptional, also makes it more acceptable: first, only rarely will it apply; and, second, it is far easier to defend the aggregation of defendants where they have all contributed to the creation of the same risk, which has then eventuated in harm to the claimant, than it is where they have all created different and independent risks.

It is a crucial limitation of the *Fairchild* principle that it does not lead to liability for the creation of risk *simpliciter*. Although in *Barker*, Lord Hoffmann presented the basis of the principle as one which recognises risk creation, it is clear that this was a means by which the imposition of proportionate liability for an indivisible injury could both be carried out and

---

[36] *Fairchild* (n 24) [170] (Lord Rodger).
[37] The other four of which were not breaches of duties of care.
[38] See *Rothwell v Chemical & Insulating Co Ltd* [2007] UKHL 39, [2008] 1 AC 281; and S Green, 'Risk Exposure and Negligence' (2006) 122 *LQR* 386.

justified, and would only occur where that risk has eventuated in damage to the claimant:

> Although the *Fairchild* exception treats the risk of contracting mesothelioma as the damage, it applies only when the disease has actually been contracted. Mr Stuart-Smith, who appeared for Corus, was reluctant to characterise the claim as being for causing a risk of the disease because he did not want to suggest that someone could sue for being exposed to a risk which had not materialised. But in cases which fall within the *Fairchild* exception, that possibility is precluded by the terms of the exception. It applies only when the claimant has contracted the disease against which he should have been protected. And in cases outside the exception, as in *Gregg v Scott* [2005] 2 AC 176, a risk of damage or loss of a chance is not damage upon which an action can be founded.[39]

In *Durham v BAI (Run-off) Ltd*,[40] Lord Mance confirmed this interpretation of the exceptional principle:

> In reality, it is impossible, or at least inaccurate, to speak of the cause of action recognised in *Fairchild* and *Barker* as being simply 'for the risk created by exposing' someone to asbestos. If it were simply for that risk, then the risk would be the injury; damages would be recoverable for every exposure, without proof by the claimant of any (other) injury at all. That is emphatically not the law ... The cause of action exists because the defendant has previously exposed the victim to asbestos, because that exposure *may* have led to the mesothelioma, not because it did, and because mesothelioma has been suffered by the victim ... The actual development of mesothelioma is an essential element of the cause of action. In ordinary language, the cause of action is 'for' or 'in respect of' the mesothelioma, and in ordinary language a defendant who exposes a victim of mesothelioma to asbestos is, under the rule in *Fairchild* and *Barker*, held responsible 'for' and 'in respect of' both that exposure and the mesothelioma.[41]

The *Fairchild* principle constitutes an undoubtedly exceptional approach to the causal inquiry. It does not, however, allow claimants to recover for having been exposed to a risk which has not eventuated in harm,[42] nor

---

[39] *Barker* (n 33) [48]. See also Hoffmann (n 35) 67.

[40] *Durham* (n 34).

[41] ibid [65]; see also [68], [72], [73], [77], [85], [87] and [90].

[42] For an explanation of why this interpretation of the principle is so crucial in practice, see R Merkin and J Steele, *Insurance and the Law of Obligations* (Oxford, Oxford University Press, 2013) 373–81. Essentially, if liability is based on the reformulated gist of increased risk, it cannot therefore be associated with a particular policy year, because there is no 'single indivisible loss' in each year of cover (which is the accepted artifice by which claims in asbestos-mesothelioma cases are made post-*Trigger*) and, consequently, coverage can be hard to establish. This is a dire outcome for claimants and amounts to the same 'remarkable' outcome which the Supreme Court in *Trigger* aimed to avoid (see [89]). Conversely, on the interpretation approved in *Trigger*, which retains mesothelioma as the gist of the damage caused, albeit by modified causal connections, each and every insurer on risk is liable. See also *Phillips v Syndicate 992 Gunner* [2003] EWHC 1706 (Comm), [2004] Lloyd's Rep IR 418. It has also been established that the application of the *Fairchild* principle does not modify the formulation of the duty of care: see *Williams v University of Birmingham* [2011] EWCA Civ 1242, [2012] ELR 47.

does it apply to each and every situation in which a claimant faces difficulty in establishing causation. But for Lord Hoffmann, the exception may well have started to erode the rule.

IV. NO SENSIBLE FOIL TO THE RESULT IN *CHESTER*

In his dissent in *Chester*, which was as convincing as it was concise, Lord Hoffmann was the only panel member who recognised (at least explicitly) the true implications of deciding in favour of liability on the facts of that case. Whilst, therefore, the law would be no different but for Lord Hoffmann's contribution, the impact of that decision might well have been greater without it. This would be no good thing.

In *Chester*, the defendant performed elective surgery on the claimant in order to alleviate her severe back pain. Although he did so without negligence, she suffered significant nerve damage and was consequently left partially paralysed. The defendant breached his duty of care by failing to warn his patient of the one to two per cent risk of such paralysis occurring as a result of the operation. The causal problem arose in this case because the claimant did not argue that, had she been warned of the risk, she would *never* have had the operation or even that, duly warned, she would have sought out another surgeon to perform the operation.[43] Her argument was simply that, had she been properly warned of the risks inherent in the procedure, she would not have consented to having the surgery within three days of her appointment and would have sought further advice on alternatives. A majority of the House of Lords held Mr Afshar liable on the basis that,[44] since the ultimate injury suffered by the claimant was a product of the very risk of which she should have been warned, it could therefore *be regarded* as having been caused by that failure to warn.

In the course of his dissent, Lord Hoffmann made the following point:

> Even though the failure to warn did not cause the patient any damage, it was an affront to her personality and leaves her feeling aggrieved. I can see that there might be a case for a modest solatium in such cases.[45]

The very fact that the majority decision in *Chester* was one in favour of liability suggests that what the claimant was *really* being compensated for was the denial of her right to make a free choice, since that denial led in

---

[43] *Cf Chappell v Hart* (1998) 195 CLR 232, in which Kirby and Gaudron JJ found that the claimant's hypothetical actions in that case, in seeking out a more experienced surgeon, would have decreased her risk of injury as a result of the procedure. There was no agreement on this point.

[44] Lord Bingham also dissented.

[45] *Chester* (n 1) [34].

her case to no consequential loss.[46] It is not, however, a straightforward exercise to justify *Chester* in this way. First, although in *Rees v Darlington Memorial NHS Trust*,[47] there is an explicit recognition at the highest level that an infringement of autonomy can amount to actionable damage in negligence, none of the judgments in *Chester* made reference to that decision.[48] Second, the House of Lords in *Chester* departed substantively from the *Rees* approach in any event by awarding substantial damages for the infringement, far in excess of the £15,000 conventional award granted in the earlier case. Finally, these contextual issues aside, the outcome in *Chester* is simply not presented as one based on the idea of autonomy as a freestanding right; rather, it is presented as a conclusion reached on causal grounds.

The majority in *Chester* decided that[49] although Miss Chester could not recover on the basis of conventional principles of causation,[50] her claim should nevertheless be successful. This decision was supported by two principal arguments: that her injury lay within the scope of the surgeon's duty of care and that, were she to be denied recovery, such a duty to warn would be drained of meaningful content. With respect, neither of these claims adequately supports the radical departure from established principles of causation demanded by that conclusion. First, the fact that the injury fell within the scope of the surgeon's duty of care is not a *substitute* for causal involvement; rather, it is a *limiting* device which applies once causally relevant factors have been identified. So, a causally relevant factor can be deemed legally irrelevant because it causes a result which falls outside of a defendant's duty of care. It does not follow, however, that a factor which has no causal relevance to an outcome can be made legally relevant because that outcome (which was not caused by the factor in question) just happens to be the mischief against which the defendant's duty of care was intended to guard. This is a clear non sequitur and is not, unsurprisingly, an argument that has been repeated elsewhere in the tort of negligence.[51] In *Chester*, the defendant's breach had not been established, on the balance of probabilities, to have played any historical role in the claimant's injury because, but for

---

[46] Because the chance available to her as a result of the breach was identical to the one that would have been available to her but for the breach: see R Stevens, *Torts and Rights* (New York, Oxford University Press, 2007) 76–78; and *Chappell* (n 43) [40]–[43] (McHugh J).

[47] *Rees v Darlington Memorial NHS Trust* [2003] UHKL 52, [2004] 1 AC 309.

[48] Despite the fact that both counsel in *Chester* (n 1) referred directly to *Rees* in their respective submissions. For an assessment of the implications of *Rees*, see D Nolan, 'New Forms of Damage in Negligence' (2007) 70 *MLR* 59, 70–80.

[49] Lord Hope, Lord Steyn and Lord Walker.

[50] Because she did not argue that, but for the failure to warn, she would not have had the procedure at any point. Had she done so successfully, she would have established causation on orthodox grounds: see *McWilliams v Sir William Arroll Co Ltd* [1962] UKHL 3, [1962] 1 WLR 295 (HL).

[51] Although Lord Walker and Lord Steyn attempted to make an analogy with the causal exception in *Fairchild* (n 24), the two situations are, as we have seen, far from analogous.

the failure to warn, she would have run exactly the same risk (the one to two per cent risk of cauda equine syndrome inherent in the procedure itself, however carefully performed) on a different day. The fact, therefore, that the failure to warn did not make Miss Chester any worse off renders the *scope* of the defendant's duty irrelevant—in negligence, individuals do not have a duty to compensate for damage that they do not cause.

Second, a finding of no liability which follows a failure to establish a factual causal link between a breach of a duty of care and a claimant's damage has no effect whatsoever on the *content* of that duty of care. The form of the negligence inquiry is such that a breach of a duty of care is a necessary but not sufficient element of a successful negligence claim. This inevitably means that duties will be breached with impunity from negligence liability, so long as no damage has thereby been caused (or at least so long as no damage can be established on the balance of probabilities to have thereby been caused).[52] This does not detract from the point or the worth of the duty of care concerned. A patient's dignity and right to decide is protected by the law of tort's recognition that a medical professional has a duty to warn, not by a readiness to override causal considerations in the claimant's favour. If a breach of that duty to warn causes the claimant no loss, then a finding of no liability does not violate that right; it merely serves as an acknowledgement that the patient's inability to exercise that right did not, on this occasion, cause any loss. This point was emphasised by Lord Hoffmann in the opening paragraph of his judgment:

> My Lords, the purpose of a duty to warn someone against the risk involved in what he proposes to do, or allow to be done to him, is to give him the opportunity to avoid or reduce that risk. If he would have been unable or unwilling to take that opportunity and the risk eventuates, the failure to warn has not caused the damage. It would have happened anyway.[53]

It is, of course, trite that damage is the gist of a claim in negligence and, whilst Mr Afshar was negligent and Miss Chester damaged, the two were not connected in the way in which this axiom anticipates. The fact that both the negligence and the damage occurred within the same factual matrix was no more than coincidental. In this context, an outcome is described as coincidental if the breach of duty is not one which increases the general risk of that outcome materialising. An oft-cited example is that of the claimant who, having had his leg broken by the defendant, is being taken to hospital when the ambulance in which he is travelling is struck by lightning. The fact that the claimant is killed by the lightning strike is coincidental in terms of the defendant's actions, since breaking someone's leg does not generally increase the risk of their being killed by lightning. In *Chester*, the risk which

---

[52] Stevens (n 46) 44.
[53] *Chester* (n 1) [28].

eventuated in the injury to Miss Chester (paralysis brought about by cauda equine syndrome) was integral to the surgical procedure she underwent and was not a risk which was, or could be, increased by a surgeon's failure to warn a patient of its existence. Once more, this crucial point is one that has since been emphasised by Lord Hoffmann:

> The doctor's failure to warn neither affected the patient's choice to have the operation nor increased the risk of the complication occurring. It was simply a coincidence that the risk happened to eventuate in a case in which the patient had not been warned about it.[54]

Jane Stapleton disagrees with this and argues that an increase in failures to warn patients of such risks will lead to a greater number of surgical procedures being undertaken, which will then in turn lead to a greater number of cases of paralysis occurring.[55] Since the net result will be a greater *incidence* of such injuries, the relationship between the failure to warn and cauda equina syndrome is not coincidental. In so doing, Stapleton makes it very clear that it is the incidence of such injuries and not the degree of risk of the injury occurring on any given occasion which will thereby be increased. Unfortunately, this is precisely the point which undermines her argument. If the tort of negligence were concerned chiefly with the incidence of injuries and had as one of its avowed aims the optimisation of risks, this would be a persuasive argument. It is what Law and Economics scholars would argue for, but it is not the premise on which the English law of negligence rests—a tort which, in its current form, serves corrective ends at the expense of distributive values.[56] The question, therefore, of whether *this* defendant increased the risk of injury to *this* claimant trumps any macro-level considerations about damage across a population. In these terms, the eventuation of the risk of cauda equine syndrome in Miss Chester's unfortunate case was coincidental upon Mr Afshar's failure to warn her. This was a fact acknowledged by all of those in the majority,[57] who nevertheless decided that there existed sufficient 'policy' concerns to impose liability in spite of it.[58]

The fact that the occurrence of the claimant's damage in *Chester* was coincidental upon the defendant's breach says something important about the correct way to analyse the case. One of the many remarkable features

---

[54] Hoffmann (n 19) 7.

[55] See J Stapleton, 'Occam's Razor Reveals an Orthodox Basis for *Chester v Afshar*' (2006) LQR 426, 441.

[56] Fortunately, the task of arguing this point has been tackled by those far better suited to the task than I: see Gardner (n 22); E Weinrib, *The Idea of Private Law* (revised edn, Oxford, Oxford University Press, 2012); J Coleman, *The Practice of Principle* (New York, Oxford University Press, 2011); A Beever, *Rediscovering the Law of Negligence* (Oxford, Hart Publishing, 2009).

[57] *Chester* (n 1) [22], [81] and [101]. See also Stevens (n 46) 165.

[58] *Chester* (n 1) [22] (Lord Steyn), [87] (Lord Hope) and [101] (Lord Walker).

of this decision is that it is not generally thought to fit within any of the recognised analytical categories into which negligence cases divide. As such, it has been characterised as a 'failure to warn' case and is often analysed as if it were *sui generis*.[59] In actual fact, however, *Chester* is hard to see as anything other than a loss of autonomy case, as suggested by Lord Hoffmann. Classifying *Chester* in this way not only achieves the most consistency in terms of the broader tort of negligence, but it also facilitates the clearest analysis of the issues outlined above. The 'chance' in *Chester* was the one to two per cent risk of developing cauda equine syndrome, and this risk was *inherent in the surgical procedure*.[60] The same risk could of course be represented as a 98–99 per cent chance of the procedure *not* having this adverse outcome. As Stuart-Smith LJ makes clear in *Allied Maples*, it matters not how such an uncertainty is perceived: 'I can see no difference in principle between the chance of gaining a benefit and the chance of avoiding a liability.'[61] The magnitude of this chance was not affected by anything that occurred between the parties to the dispute in *Chester*; rather, their relationship determined only whether the claimant could avail herself of the chance in question. Mr Afshar's failure to warn his patient meant that he performed her operation on Monday 21 November 1994 as opposed to a date sometime later. Consequently, Miss Chester ran the one to two per cent risk of developing cauda equine syndrome. (She also, and simultaneously, availed herself of the 98–99 per cent chance of avoiding that eventuality.) But for Mr Afshar's negligence, Miss Chester would probably, according to her own evidence, have run an identical risk, and taken an identical chance, on a different day. To conclude from this that the defendant's failure to warn made any material difference to the claimant is, according to Lord Hoffmann:

> [A]bout as logical as saying that if one had been told, on entering a casino, that the odds on the number 7 coming up at roulette were only 1 in 37, one would have gone away and come back next week or gone to a different casino. The question is whether one would have taken the opportunity to avoid or reduce the risk, not whether one would have changed the scenario in some irrelevant detail. The judge found as a fact that the risk would have been precisely the same whether it was done then or later or by that competent surgeon or by another.[62]

---

[59] It is categorised in J Steele, *Tort Law: Text, Cases and Materials* (2nd edn, Oxford, Oxford University Press, 2009) as a 'Particular Causation Problem', in Stevens (n 46) as 'Coincidental Loss' and in WVH Rogers (ed), *Winfield & Jolowicz on Tort* (18th edn, London, Sweet & Maxwell, 2010) under the heading 'What Would Have Happened'. In A Dugdale, *Clerk & Lindsell on Torts* (20th edn, London, Sweet & Maxwell, 2013) 2–14, the case is said to stand in a 'third category' of its own (the first one being made up of situations in which properly advised claimants would have followed the same path regardless, and the second covering those who would have acted differently).

[60] And not therefore affected in its magnitude by the way in which the surgery was conducted.

[61] *Allied Maples Group Ltd v Simmons & Simmons* [1995] EWCA Civ 17, [1995] 1 WLR 1602, 1611.

[62] *Chester* (n 1) [31].

Of course, it is true that, on 21 November 1994, Miss Chester was unfortunate enough to succumb to this relatively small risk of injury and that the consequences for her were dire. This is, however, irrelevant in negligence terms. The tort is not one which seeks to compensate those who suffer loss as a result of misfortune; ideological considerations aside, it is staggeringly ill-equipped to do so.[63] The causal element of the negligence inquiry is what binds it to corrective, as opposed to distributive, ends and for courts to choose to override this on an ad hoc basis is to do the common law a disservice:

> To be acceptable the law must be coherent. It must be principled. The basis on which one case, or one type of case, is distinguished from another should be transparent and capable of identification. When a decision departs from principles normally applied, the basis for doing so must be rational and justifiable if the decision is to avoid the reproach that hard cases make bad law.[64]

With the greatest of respect to those in the majority in *Chester*, it is neither 'rational' nor 'justifiable' to take account of what *actually happened* as a result of a risk run by the claimant, where that risk is identical to the one which would have been run but for the breach of duty. To compare, as judges and commentators have done,[65] the one to two per cent ex ante risk of injury with the 100 per cent ex post knowledge that the injury occurred is an inauthentic exercise. To state the truism that had the operation been performed some days later, the injury would probably not have occurred (since it was 98–99 per cent likely not to have done so), but then to conclude from this that the defendant's breach thereby caused the injury because it exposed the claimant to an identical risk *which is now known to have eventuated* is not to compare like with like. It would have been unlikely that injury would have resulted on 28 November, but *no more* unlikely than it was on 21 November. The only difference between the two events is that we (now) know what happened as a result of one of them, but it is an eventuality which is both independent of, and coincidental to, the defendant's actions. Put simply, the defendant made no difference to the claimant's normal course of events and should therefore not have been subject to negligence liability.

Lord Hoffmann has described the fact that Afshar was nevertheless found liable as 'startling',[66] and it is clear from both his judicial and extra-judicial analyses that it is not a result which fits with his Lordship's understanding

---

[63] See Gardner (n 22) 26: "'[C]orrective justice" tells us ... what it is that the law of torts is supposed to be efficient *at*. It is supposed to be efficient at securing that people conform to a certain (partly legally constituted) moral norm of corrective justice. If it is not efficient at this job then, from the point of view of corrective justice itself, the law of torts should be abolished forthwith'.

[64] *Fairchild* (n 24) [36] (Lord Nicholls).

[65] See, eg, Stapleton (n 55) and *Chester* (n 1) [21] (Lord Steyn).

[66] Hoffmann (n 19) 7.

of what it means *in law* to be the cause of something else. It may well be this understanding which has ensured that Lord Hoffmann's legacy in terms of the causal inquiry in negligence is an overwhelmingly positive one. Perhaps the most distinctive feature of his approach to the causal inquiry is that it is self-consciously crafted to serve forensic, as opposed to philosophical, concerns. In response to the academic tendency to search for a comprehensive and universal explanation for causal outcomes, he has written:

> In my view, all this wringing of hands is quite unnecessary. It might be easier if, instead of speaking of 'proof' of causation, which makes it look as if we are dealing with one monolithic concept ... we spoke of 'causal requirements' of a legal rule. That would make it clear that causal requirements are creatures of the law and nothing more. The causal requirements of one rule may be different from those of another ... But different casual requirements are nevertheless causal requirements.[67]

But For Lord Hoffmann, several of those causal requirements would be different. And the tort of negligence would thereby have suffered a loss.

---

[67] ibid 9.

4

A Long, Hard Look at Gray v Thames Trains Ltd

JAMES GOUDKAMP*

I. INTRODUCTION

THIS CHAPTER ADDRESSES the landmark decision in *Gray v Thames Trains Ltd.*[1] Although it was decided in the twilight years of the House of Lords, it was the first occasion on which the House considered at any length the doctrine of illegality in the tort setting.[2] The goal of this chapter is to explore *Gray*, focusing on Lord Hoffmann's speech, which is the principal opinion. It will be argued that *Gray*, owing to Lord Hoffmann's speech, significantly improved the law (for which there was much scope). However, it will also be contended that the reasons given by Lord Hoffmann for embracing the rules that he laid down are suspect in certain respects and that those rules can be improved upon. Finally, it will be shown that *Gray* has been marginalised somewhat by two subsequent decisions at the highest level, namely, *Stone & Rolls Ltd v Moore Stephens*[3] and *Hounga v Allen,*[4] and that its status is therefore open to some doubt.

* Paul Davies and Lorenz Mayr provided me with insightful thoughts on a draft of this chapter. I am grateful to them and also to Jodi Gardner for her research assistance.

[1] *Gray v Thames Trains Ltd* [2009] UKHL 33, [2009] 1 AC 1339. The decision is noted in P Davies, 'The Illegality Defence and Public Policy' (2009) 125 *LQR* 556 and J Goudkamp, 'The Defence of Illegality: *Gray v Thames Trains Ltd*' (2009) 17 *Torts Law Journal* 205.
[2] The House of Lords touched upon the defence in the tort context in *National Coal Board v England* [1954] AC 403 (HL) and *Gardner v Moore* [1984] 1 AC 548 (HL).
[3] *Stone & Rolls Ltd v Moore Stephens* [2009] UKHL 39, [2009] 1 AC 1391.
[4] *Hounga v Allen* [2014] UKSC 47, [2014] ICR 847, noted in J Goudkamp and M Zou, 'The Defence of Illegality in Tort: Beyond Judicial Redemption?' (2015) 74 *CLJ* 13.

II. THE DECISION IN *GRAY*

A. The Facts

On 5 October 1999, Mr Kerrie Gray was injured in a train accident.[5] The accident was caused by the negligence of the company that operated the train in which he was travelling, and by the negligence of a company that was responsible for the rail infrastructure. Mr Gray suffered only minor physical injuries in the accident, but the experience caused him to develop post-traumatic stress disorder and depression. His work suffered because of his mental injuries. Nearly two years later, Mr Gray was involved in an altercation with an intoxicated pedestrian, whom he stabbed and killed. Mr Gray surrendered himself to the police shortly thereafter. He was charged with murder and the Crown accepted a plea of guilty to manslaughter on the ground of diminished responsibility. He was ordered to be detained in hospital pursuant to section 37 of the Mental Health Act 1983. This detention was subject to a restriction order under section 41 of the same Act.

B. Proceedings are Commenced

In 2005, Mr Gray commenced proceedings in negligence against the defendants. A critical contention in his claim was that he only committed the manslaughter because of the mental injuries that he suffered in the train accident. He sought the following relief:

(1) damages for the personal injuries (both mental and physical) that he suffered in the accident;
(2) damages for the loss of earnings that he suffered between the date of the accident and the date of the manslaughter;
(3) damages for the loss of earnings that he suffered from the date of the manslaughter;
(4) an indemnity in respect of any liability that he might incur to the dependants of the pedestrian whom he killed;
(5) damages for feelings of guilt and remorse from which he suffered as a result of killing the pedestrian; and
(6) damages for the harm done to his reputation as a result of the conviction.

No claim for damages was made by Mr Gray in respect of his loss of freedom as a result of his detention. The defendants made various concessions. They accepted that they were negligent and that, but for their negligence,

---

[5] The accident was the Ladbroke Grove train disaster. For the official report into the accident, see Lord Cullen, *The Ladbroke Grove Rail Inquiry* (London, Health and Safety Executive Books, 2001).

Mr Gray would not have committed the manslaughter. They also conceded that they were liable for the relief sought in items (1) and (2) above. However, they denied that they were liable to provide the relief enumerated in items (3)–(6) on the ground of illegality.

C. The Decisions of the Courts Below

Standing in the way of Mr Gray's claim was the decision of the Court of Appeal in *Clunis v Camden and Islington Health Authority*,[6] from which the House of Lords had refused leave to appeal.[7] In *Clunis*, it had been held that one could not recover damages in tort in respect of losses suffered as a consequence of a criminal law sanction. *Clunis* had been applied by the Court of Appeal in *Worrall v British Railways Board*,[8] *Cooper v Reed*[9] and *DN v Greenwich LBC*,[10] all of which added to the height of the precedential hurdle that confronted Mr Gray.[11] The trial judge in *Gray*, Flaux J, correctly held that *Clunis* was binding on him and that it was indistinguishable.[12] His Lordship concluded that 'in so far as the claimant's claim relates to losses suffered after the commission of the act of manslaughter ... that claim will not be entertained'.[13] Consequently, the relief sought in items (3)–(6) was denied.

Mr Gray appealed to the Court of Appeal. Sir Anthony Clarke MR, who delivered the reasons of the Court, concluded that the question of whether the claimant was entitled to the relief that he sought depended on whether the claim for relief was 'so closely connected or inextricably bound up with his criminal or illegal conduct that the court could not permit him to recover without appearing to condone that conduct'.[14] Sir Anthony concluded that this test prevented items of relief (4)–(6) from being granted, but that damages for loss of earnings after the date of the manslaughter (item (3)) were recoverable. His Lordship asserted that items (4)–(6) were inextricably linked with the illegal conduct, while item (3) was not.[15] No reasons were given for this differential treatment of items (4)–(6) on the one hand and item (3) on the other. The Master of the Rolls simply said 'it does

---

[6] *Clunis v Camden and Islington Health Authority* [1998] QB 978 (CA).
[7] [1998] 1 WLR 1093.
[8] *Worrall v British Railways Board* [1999] CLY 1413 (CA).
[9] *Cooper v Reed* [2001] EWCA Civ 224.
[10] *DN v Greenwich LBC* [2004] EWCA Civ 1659, [2005] 1 FCR 112 [79].
[11] *Cf KR v Bryn Alyn Community (Holdings) Ltd* [2003] EWCA Civ 85, [2003] QB 1441 [131]: 'Notwithstanding anything said by this court in Clunis's case, an argument may survive that damages are recoverable in respect of tortious acts that have resulted in a law-abiding citizen becoming a criminal.'
[12] *Gray v Thames Trains Ltd* [2007] EWHC 1558 (QB) [49].
[13] ibid [60].
[14] [2008] EWCA Civ 713, [2009] 2 WLR 351 [20].
[15] ibid [24].

not seem to us that it can fairly be said that the loss of earnings [after the manslaughter] was inextricably linked with the claimant's illegal act'.[16]

D. The Decision of the House of Lords

The defendants appealed to the House of Lords against the decision of the Court of Appeal that Mr Gray was entitled to damages in respect of the earnings that he lost from the date of the manslaughter (item of relief (3)). Mr Gray cross-appealed against the decision to withhold items of relief (4)–(6). The House of Lords unanimously allowed the appeal and held that the orders of the trial judge should be restored. The result was that items of relief (3)–(6) were denied. Lord Hoffmann delivered what has come to be regarded as the principal speech in the House. Lord Phillips, Lord Rodger and Lord Brown delivered opinions in which they substantially agreed with Lord Hoffmann. Lord Scott concurred with Lord Hoffmann and Lord Rodger without offering reasons of his own.

Lord Hoffmann described what he took to be the main issue in this case as follows: 'The question in this case is in my opinion whether the intervention of Mr Gray's criminal act in the causal relationship between the defendants' breaches of duty and the damage of which he complains prevents him from recovering that part of his loss caused by the criminal act.'[17] The answer to this question depended upon the applicability of the doctrine of illegality. Lord Hoffmann held that the doctrine came in a wider and narrower form. In its narrower form, it prevents recovery 'for damage which flows from loss of liberty, a fine or other punishment lawfully imposed on [the defendant] in consequence of [his] own unlawful act'.[18] 'In its wider form', the rule, Lord Hoffmann said, 'is that [the defendant] cannot recover compensation for loss which [he has] suffered in consequence of [his] own criminal act.'[19] Lord Hoffmann invoked *Jobling v Associated Dairies Ltd*[20] and concluded that the Court would not shut its eyes to what had happened since the date of the tort and treat Mr Gray's earning capacity as having been destroyed from the date of the train accident.[21] Accordingly, he applied the narrow rule to deny recovery for income that Mr Gray would have derived from the date of the manslaughter had he not been injured in the train accident

---

[16] ibid.
[17] *Gray* (n 1) [27].
[18] ibid [29].
[19] ibid.
[20] *Jobling v Associated Dairies Ltd* [1982] AC 794 (HL).
[21] *Gray* (n 1) [49].

(item of relief (3)).[22] The inability to earn a living while imprisoned was a consequence of the act that resulted in the sentence of imprisonment. The narrow rule, Lord Hoffmann said, also meant that item of relief (6) would be denied.[23] The harm done to Mr Gray's reputation was 'caused by the lawful sentence imposed upon him for manslaughter'.[24] It was, in other words, also part of the punishment. The wide rule was held to preclude Mr Gray from obtaining relief in respect of items (4) and (5). In Lord Hoffmann's words, 'Mr Gray's liability to compensate the dependants of the dead pedestrian was an immediate "inextricable" consequence of his having intentionally killed him. The same is true of his feelings of guilt and remorse'.[25]

An important move that Lord Hoffmann made near the beginning of his speech was to put to one side the issue of whether Mr Gray relied (or needed to rely) on his unlawful conduct to establish his entitlement to the relief that he sought.[26] His Lordship noted that this was a decisive consideration in 'cases about rights of property'[27] and cited the famous decision in *Tinsley v Milligan* as an illustration.[28] But Lord Hoffmann held that the issue of reliance on unlawful conduct did not matter in a case such as *Gray*. The significance of this is discussed later.[29] Lord Hoffmann also distanced himself from the 'inextricable link' test,[30] although he occasionally used language reminiscent of that test.[31] He preferred to see the entire matter as one of causation. Some words will also be said about Lord Hoffmann's attempt to marginalise the inextricable link test later.[32]

III. THE IMPACT OF *GRAY*

The decision in *Gray* has been influential in at least four ways. First, *Gray* largely swept away the pre-existing law on the defence of illegality in the context of actions in negligence.[33] The wide and narrow rules enunciated by

---

[22] ibid [50].
[23] ibid.
[24] ibid.
[25] ibid [55].
[26] ibid [30].
[27] Regarding the doctrine of illegality in relation to cases involving interference with chattels, see J Goudkamp and L Mayr, 'The Doctrine of Illegality and Interference with Chattels' in A Dyson, J Goudkamp and F Wilmot-Smith (eds), *Defences in Tort* (Oxford, Hart Publishing, 2015) ch 12.
[28] *Tinsley v Milligan* [1994] 1 AC 340 (HL).
[29] See section IV below.
[30] *Gray* (n 1) [47]–[48].
[31] See the quotation accompanying n 25.
[32] See section V below.
[33] See also the discussion in section VIII below.

Lord Hoffmann were installed in place of the prior rules.[34] It is interesting to note that *Gray* has been applied in cases where it is not strictly binding. A good example of this concerns joint illegal enterprise cases. These cases had previously been decided in accordance with the principles established in *Pitts v Hunt*.[35] In that case, the Court of Appeal, adopting rules laid down by the High Court of Australia,[36] held that a duty of care would not arise as between participants in a joint illegal enterprise where the nature of the enterprise was such that it was not possible or not feasible to ask how much care the reasonable person would have taken.[37] *Gray* was obviously not a joint illegal enterprise case. The defendants in *Gray* were not implicated in any way in Mr Gray's offending. However, in *Delaney v Pickett*,[38] which was the first joint illegal enterprise case that the Court of Appeal considered after *Gray*, the Court applied *Gray*, and ignored *Pitts* (even though *Pitts* was binding on it and *Gray* was distinguishable). Precisely the same thing occurred in *Joyce v O'Brien*, which was the second joint illegal enterprise case since *Gray* to come before the Court of Appeal.[39] The covert burial of the approach espoused in *Pitts* is complete. Second, Lord Hoffmann's speech in *Gray* caught the attention of the courts in several other jurisdictions. It has been cited (although not adopted) by the highest courts in Australia[40] and New Zealand.[41] Third, Lord Hoffmann's opinion triggered an avalanche of academic writing.[42] By and large, this writing has heaped praise on his speech.[43] Fourth, Lord Hoffmann's reasons in *Gray* seem to

---

[34] It might be queried whether this proposition is valid in view of *Moore Stephens* (n 3). That case is discussed below in section VIII. Although an alternative action in negligence was pleaded in that case, it was not really argued as a negligence case and was certainly not treated as such by the House of Lords. Accordingly, this case does not really threaten the accuracy of the proposition that has been advanced.

[35] *Pitts v Hunt* (1991) 1 QB 24 (CA).

[36] *Smith v Jenkins* (1970) 119 CLR 397; *Jackson v Harrison* (1978) 138 CLR 438. The High Court of Australia subsequently abandoned these rules: see *Miller v Miller* [2011] HCA 9, (2011) 242 CLR 446.

[37] For criticism of this test, see J Goudkamp, 'The Defence of Joint Illegal Enterprise' (2010) 34 *Melbourne University Law Review* 425.

[38] *Delaney v Pickett* [2011] EWCA Civ 1532, [2012] 1 WLR 2149, noted in J Goudkamp, 'The Defence of Illegality in Tort Law: Whither the Rule in *Pitts v Hunt?*' (2012) 71 *CLJ* 481.

[39] [2013] EWCA Civ 546, [2014] 1 WLR 70.

[40] *Miller* (n 36) [56].

[41] *Leason v Attorney-General* [2013] NZCA 509, (2014) 2 NZLR 224 [97]–[101], [106], [115].

[42] Among countless examples, see Davies (n 1); Goudkamp (n 1); J Morgan, 'Manslaughter as a "Vicissitude of Life"' (2009) 68 *CLJ* 503; M Fordham, 'Not So Different after All? A Causation-Based Approach to Joint Illegal Enterprises' [2013] *Singapore Journal of Legal Studies* 202; PJ Yap, 'Rethinking the Illegality Defence in Tort Law' (2010) 18 *Tort Law Review* 52; JR Spencer, 'Civil Liability for Crimes' in M Dyson (ed), *Unravelling Tort and Crime* (Cambridge, Cambridge University Press, 2014) 310–18; G Virgo, 'Illegality's Role in the Law of Torts' in M Dyson (ed), *Unravelling Tort and Crime* (Cambridge, Cambridge University Press, 2014).

[43] For example, Margaret Fordham writes that Lord Hoffmann's speech brought 'welcome consistency to the concept of illegality': Fordham (n 42) 210.

lie, at least in part, behind the decision of the Law Commission, at the end of its marathon investigation into the illegality defence in private law generally,[44] to recommend that statutory reform of the illegality defence was not needed in the tort context. The Law Commission had suggested in one of its consultation papers that that the application of the illegality defence in tort law should be determined according to a 'structured discretion'.[45] In its final Report, the Commission concluded that *Gray* had signalled a greater willingness on the part of judges to discuss more transparently the policy considerations that support the illegality defence, which was what the Commission was hoping its postulated 'structured discretion' would achieve.[46]

IV. THE RELIANCE TEST

As mentioned earlier,[47] Lord Hoffmann dismissed as irrelevant the issue of whether Mr Gray had relied or needed to rely on his illegal conduct in order to substantiate his claim for relief. The reliance test is best associated with the decision of the House of Lords in *Tinsley v Milligan*,[48] a case in the law of trusts, although it has not infrequently been invoked in negligence cases.[49] In *Tinsley*, two women (X and Y) who cohabitated with each other had put the legal title of their house in the name of Y only despite the fact that both had contributed to the purchase price of the house. They did this so that X could misrepresent her assets with a view to claiming fraudulently welfare benefits to their mutual advantage. The relationship broke down and Y sought to evict X. X argued that she had a share of the beneficial title to the house. Y, in reply, invoked the doctrine of illegality. It was held that X had a beneficial interest in the house and that the doctrine was inapplicable. The doctrine did not apply, the House of Lords said, because X did not need to rely on her illegality in order to obtain the relief that she sought. This was because she benefited from the presumption of a resulting trust. All that X needed to do in order to enliven that presumption was to prove

---

[44] Law Commission, *Illegal Transactions: The Effect of Illegality on Contracts and Trusts* (Law Com CP No 154, 1999); Law Commission, *The Illegality Defence in Tort* (Law Com CP No 160, 2001); Law Commission, *The Illegality Defence: A Consultative Report* (Law Com CP No 189, 2009); Law Commission, *The Illegality Defence* (Law Com No 320, 2010).

[45] 'We suggest that the current rules applied by the courts when considering the effect of illegality on a tortious claim should be replaced by a structured discretion, under which the court would be directed to consider whether, in the light of the underlying rationales and taking into account a number of guiding factors, the claim should be allowed or disallowed': Law Commission (2001) (n 44) para 1.18.

[46] ibid paras 3.37–3.41.

[47] See text accompanying n 26.

[48] *Tinsley* (n 28).

[49] See, eg, *Clunis* (n 6) 987; *Vellino v Chief Constable of the Greater Manchester Police* [2001] EWCA Civ 1249, [2002] 1 WLR 218 [71]; *Hewison v Meridian Shipping Services Pte Ltd* [2002] EWCA Civ 1821, [2003] ICR 766 [29], [45], [62], [64]–[65], [78].

that she had contributed to the purchase price. She did not need to disclose her unlawful conduct to do that and, hence, her illegality was irrelevant. The position would have been otherwise but for the presumption of a resulting trust.

The reliance test should have no role in the law of torts or, indeed, in private law generally. No convincing reason has ever been given as to why it should matter whether the claimant relied or needed to rely on his illegal conduct. Why should the fact of reliance be important? Merely stating that a claimant cannot succeed in his action if he relies on or is required to rely on his illegal conduct (which is all that the House of Lords did in *Tinsley* in articulating the reliance test) is no justification at all for such a rule; it is simply a description of the rule. It is also worth remembering that the issue of whether or not a claimant needs to rely on his illegal conduct turns on how matters that are relevant to liability happen to be allocated according to the divide between the elements of the material cause of action and defences. If an element of the cause of action cannot be established without the claimant pointing to some fact that reveals illegal conduct on his part, the claimant will need to rely on his illegality to make good his claim for relief, since he bears the onus of proof in relation to the elements of his action. Conversely, if the fact in question is material only to a defence, because defences must be established by defendants,[50] the claimant will not need to rely on his unlawful behaviour. However, the courts have never articulated a coherent theory for allocating issues that are relevant to liability as between causes of action, on the one hand, and defences, on the other.[51] Issues tend to get allocated to one category rather than to the other at random, when the courts even bother to make it clear to which category a particular issue is allocated (which they frequently do not).[52] Accordingly, it will often be a matter of luck whether a given claimant needs to rely on his illegal conduct in order to establish his cause of action. It is patently unsatisfactory for the applicability of the doctrine of illegality to be determined on this basis.

It should be noted that Lord Hoffmann rejected the reliance test for reasons that differ from those that have just been given. His Lordship seems to have focused on the issue of whether the authorities supported the proposition that claimants who cause themselves loss as a result of their own illegal act cannot recover damages in respect of that loss. Lord Hoffmann appears to have reasoned that if the outcome in *Gray* was to turn on the existence of such a rule, the issue of reliance was a distraction.[53] Lord Hoffmann is of

---

[50] J Goudkamp, *Tort Law Defences* (Oxford, Hart Publishing, 2013) 12, 138–39.
[51] ibid ch 2.
[52] For a depressing illustration of the lack of care that the courts have taken in relation to specifying whether a rule is part of the cause of action or a defence, see ibid 65–68 (discussing consent).
[53] *Gray* (n 1) [49].

course correct in this connection. But there are more fundamental reasons—
reasons that have just been set out—why the reliance test should have no
role in the law of torts (or in private law generally). No argument (let alone
a *persuasive* argument) has ever been made to show why the fact of reliance
is something to which attention ought to be paid.

V. THE INEXTRICABLE LINK TEST

The inextricable link test for determining the application of the doctrine of
illegality was developed, it seems, in *Cross v Kirkby*.[54] The claimant had
assaulted the defendant with a baseball bat. The defendant wrested the bat
from the claimant and used it to inflict significant injury upon the claimant.
The claimant brought proceedings in battery. The Court of Appeal held that
the claim failed on the ground of self-defence.[55] But it also rejected it on the
basis of the doctrine of illegality.[56] Beldam LJ and Judge LJ both thought
that the issue of illegality should be resolved according to the 'inextricable link' test.[57] Beldam LJ wrote that in his view, the doctrine of illegality
'applies when the claimant's claim is so closely connected or inextricably
bound up with his own criminal or illegal conduct that the court could not
permit him to recover without appearing to condone that conduct'.[58] Judge
LJ contended that the question of illegality should be resolved as follows:

> [W]here the claimant is behaving unlawfully, or criminally, on the occasion when
> his cause of action in tort arises, his claim is not liability to be defeated *ex turpi
> causa* unless it is ... established that the facts which give rise to it are inextricably
> link with his criminal conduct. I have deliberately expressed myself in language
> which goes well beyond causation in the general sense.[59]

Judge LJ's comments clearly indicate that he regarded the inextricable link
test as posing a different enquiry from causation. He seemed to think that it
presented a broader question than that of whether the claimant caused his
loss by his own illegal act.

The shortcomings of the inextricable link test are both significant and
obvious. First, why should it matter whether the claimant's illegal conduct
was inextricably linked with his damage? No answer to this question was
given by the Court of Appeal. The metaphor of the 'inextricable link' may
sound intuitively attractive. It is, in this regard, like tests that turn on issues

---

[54] *Cross v Kirkby* (2000) *The Times*, 5 April (CA).
[55] ibid [35], [92].
[56] Regarding the interplay between the doctrines of self-defence and illegality, see J Goudkamp, 'Self-defence and Illegality under the Civil Liability Act 2002 (NSW)' (2010) 18 *Torts
Law Journal* 61.
[57] Otton LJ agreed with Beldam LJ's reasons.
[58] *Cross* (n 54).
[59] ibid [103].

such as reasonableness and proportionality. These concepts all have an instinctive appeal. But the cold, hard fact is that no matter how seductive a test may sound, the issue of whether it is justified remains to be determined. Second, assuming that the doctrine of illegality should sometimes apply when the claimant's illegal conduct is linked with his damage, why should the matter turn upon whether the link is inextricable? Why should not a stronger link be required or a weaker link be sufficient? Again, the Court of Appeal did not give any reasons in this connection. Third, when is a link 'inextricable'? Seeing as the matter is not, to Judge LJ's mind at least, the same as asking whether the claimant's illegal act caused his own damage, the normal rules of causation cannot be used to answer this question. What, therefore, does the phrase 'inextricable link' mean? No direct guidance was offered by Judge LJ. This third objection might be stated as follows: assuming that the closeness of the connection between the claimant's illegal act and his damage should even be important, the inextricable link test tells us what we are searching for, but does not tell us how to find it.

Lord Hoffmann eschewed the inextricable link test.[60] For the foregoing reasons, his Lordship, it is submitted, was right to do so. However, these were not, apparently, the reasons that Lord Hoffmann had in mind. His Lordship appears to have shunned the inextricable link test because, in his view, it merely re-stated the fact that the applicability of the doctrine of illegality turned on whether the claimant caused his own damage by his unlawful act.[61] In short, Lord Hoffmann seemed to avoid the inextricable link test because he preferred to call a spade a spade. Whether or not the inextricable link test is really just an application of established causal rules is unclear. Judge LJ clearly thought, as has been noted, that the test was different from the general principles of causation, although it is debatable whether this is the case. Certainly, Judge LJ did not explain what the suggested difference was.

VI. THE WIDE RULE

A. A New Rule?

The wide rule, it will be recalled, is that 'you cannot recover compensation for loss which you have suffered in consequence of your own criminal act'.[62] Was the wide rule created in *Gray* or did Lord Hoffmann merely uncover a pre-existing principle? The latter view is preferable. In 1969, in *Boyle v*

---

[60] See text accompanying n 30.
[61] *Gray* (n 1) [49], where Lord Hoffmann wrote: 'Stripped of the metaphor of the inextricable link, the question is whether [Mr Gray's] act of manslaughter caused his inability to earn.'
[62] ibid [29].

Kodak, Lord Diplock said: 'To say "you are liable to me for my own wrong-doing" is neither good morals nor good law.'[63] This statement is effectively equivalent to the wide rule. Furthermore, in many cases that preceded *Gray*, it had been held that the claimant, because he had caused his own damage by his illegal conduct, had no right to compensation good against the defendant. The well-known decision in *Vellino v Chief Constable of the Greater Manchester Police* is such a case.[64] In this matter, the claimant suffered horrific injuries when, in an attempt to avoid being arrested by police, he threw himself out of a window of an apartment that was situated on the second storey of a building. He sued the Chief Constable for what he asserted was an unreasonable failure on the part of the arresting constables to prevent him from leaping from the window. One of the routes via which the majority of the Court of Appeal reached the conclusion that the claimant could not recover damages was that of causation.[65] Accordingly, Lord Hoffmann in *Gray*, in articulating the wide rule, can fairly be said to have been invoking existing law rather than laying down a new principle.

B. What Sort of Rule is the Wide Rule?

The wide rule is obviously a causal rule.[66] It turns on whether the claimant suffered loss as a consequence of his own criminal act. But there are other causal rules that feature in negligence actions. Two such rules need to be mentioned here. First, causation is one of the elements of the action in negligence.[67] Second, a claimant who establishes liability and who seeks damages in respect of a given loss must prove that the loss was caused by the defendant's tort if he is to be awarded compensation in respect of it. Causation, therefore, is also relevant in relation to the quantum of damages to which a claimant who has managed to establish liability is entitled. It follows that an issue arises as to the nature of the relationship between the wide rule on the hand and these two other causal principles on the other hand.

It is clear from *Gray* that the wide rule can leave a finding of liability intact and operate only at the stage at which the claimant's damages are

---

[63] *Boyle v Kodak* [1969] 1 WLR 661 (HL) 673.

[64] See also *Sacco v Chief Constable of the South Wales Constabulary* (CA, 15 May 1998).

[65] *Vellino* (n 49) [25] (Schiemann LJ suggesting that a person who injures himself while attempting to escape from police custody is 'the author of his own misfortune'). *cf* [28], where Schiemann LJ placed his decision on the lack of a duty of care.

[66] It is 'simply a question of causation': *Les Laboratoires Servier v Apotex Inc* [2014] UKSC 55, [2014] 3 WLR 1257 [19] (Lord Sumption).

[67] Judges have enumerated the elements of negligence in an astonishing diversity of ways: see DG Owen, 'The Five Elements of Negligence' (2007) 35 *Hofstra Law Review* 1671. This renders it difficult to know what the elements of the action actually are. But there is, despite this instability in the law, widespread agreement that causation is one of the elements of the action.

quantified. Because Mr Gray was found to have caused certain losses about which he complained as a result of his criminal act, those losses were irrecoverable. But the wide rule did not cause his action to fail completely. He was, for instance, entitled to damages for the physical and mental injuries that he suffered in the train accident and also for the loss of earnings that he suffered as a result of the accident between the date of the accident and the date of the manslaughter. How, exactly, does the wide rule function to eliminate recovery in respect of particular items of loss? There can be little doubt that when the wide rule operates at the damages stage, as it did in *Gray*, it prevents the claimant from establishing the causal link between the tort and a particular item of loss that must be demonstrated in order to recover damages in respect of that loss. Put differently, the wide rule, insofar as it is relevant to the quantification of damages, is just another way of expressing the principle that a claimant who establishes liability can only recover damages in respect of a given loss if he shows that the loss in question was caused by the tort.

The wide rule can also prevent liability from arising where *all* of the damage about which the claimant complains was caused by his own criminal act. This occurred in *Joyce v O'Brien*.[68] In this case, the parties stole a ladder from a residential property. The claimant was injured when he fell from a van that was being driven by the defendant onto which he had loaded the ladder. The Court of Appeal held that the wide rule prevented liability from arising altogether. How, precisely, did the wide rule yield that result? According to a popular view, all liability rules are either part of the claimant's cause of action or are defences.[69] Which type of rule is the wide rule when it operates in relation to liability? The stronger view is that it is a mere re-statement of the causation element of the action in negligence. The wide rule prevents liability from arising where all of the claimant's damage was caused by his criminal act. However, if the claimant caused all of his own damage, it is impossible for the causation element of the action in negligence to be satisfied. This means that the claimant's action should fail at that stage and the issue of defences, which properly falls for consideration only once all the elements of the action are present,[70] is never reached.[71] It seems, therefore, that the wide rule, insofar as it can prevent liability from arising completely, is nothing more than a manifestation of the fundamental principle that the

---

[68] *Joyce v O'Brien* [2013] EWCA Civ 546, [2014] 1 WLR 70.
[69] This view is addressed in Goudkamp (n 50) ch 2.
[70] ibid 13–14.
[71] Virgo contends that the wide rule is a defence since it arises for consideration only once the elements of the tort of negligence have been established: Virgo (n 42) 179. Virgo's overlooks the basic fact that the tort of negligence is not committed unless the claimant's damage was caused by the defendant's breach of duty. Where the claimant causes all of his damage by his own criminal act (and thereby triggers the wide rule), the causation element of the action in negligence cannot possibly be satisfied. If the elements of the action are not satisfied, the issue of defences cannot arise. Therefore, when the wide rule prevents liability from arising, it is impossible for it to do so as a defence.

tort of negligence permits recovery only if the claimant's damage was caused by the defendant's breach of duty. A defendant who relies on the wide rule in an effort to show that he should not be liable at all is actually *denying* part of the claimant's action and is not, strictly speaking, invoking a defence.[72]

The analysis in this section has various implications for how we should understand the wide rule. Most obviously, it bears upon the allocation of the onus of proof in relation to that rule. When the wide rule prevents liability from arising, it is a mere re-statement of the causation element of the action in negligence. When it prevents a claimant who has established liability from recovering damages in respect of a given item of loss, it is a re-statement of the principle that such a claimant must show that losses for which he seeks compensation were caused by the defendant's tort. It is trite law that the claimant bears the onus of proving both that the elements of his action are satisfied and that the items of loss in respect of which he claims damages are compensable. It follows that the onus of proof should rest on the claimant to show that the wide rule does not apply.

C. The Unexplained Focus on the Criminal Nature of the Claimant's Act

One puzzling feature of Lord Hoffmann's description of the wide rule is the emphasis that it places on the fact that the claimant injured himself as a result of his own '*criminal* act'. It has been argued that the wide rule merely re-states the rules: (1) that causation is an element of the action in negligence; and (2) that a claimant who has established liability must, in order to recover compensation in respect of a particular item of loss, prove that the loss was caused by the defendant's tort. If this is right, it is very hard to explain the stress that the wide rule places on the fact that the claimant was injured while acting illegally. *Any* conduct of the claimant, *criminal or not*, that is an intervening cause will be sufficient to prevent causation from being established, whether for the purposes of the causation element of the action in negligence or causation insofar as it is relevant to the quantification of damages. Why, then, is the wide rule couched in terms of intervening causation attributable to the claimant's criminal act? Perhaps Lord Hoffmann used this language simply because Mr Gray's act in question, which Lord Hoffmann found to be an intervening cause, was a criminal act. Another possibility is that these words were chosen because Lord Hoffmann saw the wide rule as doing something other than re-stating the other two principles that have just been mentioned. If this is how he understood the wide rule, it is respectfully submitted that he fell into error. As has been contended, the wide rule is not an independent rule; it merely re-states other rules.

---

[72] See further Goudkamp (n 50) 61–62.

D. Lord Hoffmann's Attempt to Justify the Wide Rule

For the reasons that have been given, the wide rule is nothing more than a re-statement of other rules. It is not clear that this was understood by Lord Hoffmann. It has already been noted that the fact that he spoke of the wide rule as being triggered by a *criminal* act on the part of the claimant suggests that he failed to grasp how the wide rule operates. Adding to these doubts is the fact that he endeavoured to justify the wide rule. He said the following (and only the following) in support of the wide rule: '[It] has to be justified on the ground that it is offensive to public notions of fair distribution of resources that a claimant should be compensated (usually out of public funds) for the consequences of his own criminal conduct.'[73] However, the wide rule is not an independent rule and therefore does not require justification in its own right.

However, let us put to one side the issue of how the wide rule should be classified and consider the adequacy of Lord Hoffmann's rationalisation of it, which has just been noted. There are several points to observe in this connection. First, it is not clear what Lord Hoffmann meant when he said that the rule '*has to be* justified' on the ground that he gave. Does that mean that he thinks that all other possible rationalisations are inadequate? If this is what he believed, why did he not set out his reasons for thinking that other arguments that might be made in support of the wide rule were unsatisfactory? A further oddity in Lord Hoffmann's language here is that it seems to presuppose that the wide rule *is* justifiable.

Second, it is mystifying what Lord Hoffmann had in mind when he suggested that claimants who are injured by their own criminal conduct would, if they succeed in their tort action, 'usually [be compensated] out of public funds'. Very few of the cases in which the doctrine of illegality is in issue are brought against the state. Lord Hoffmann seems to be conflating here the distinction between taxpayer-funded compensation and compensation that is paid by liability insurers (and hence by the premium-paying population). Admittedly, there might not be a great difference between the persons who comprise these groups, but it is strange that Lord Hoffmann appeared to treat these groups as synonymous when clearly they are not. It should also be noted that it is in fact *more likely* if actions by claimants 'who are injured by their own criminal conduct' are refused that such claimants will have recourse to public funds. This is because if tort damages are unavailable, many such claimants will turn to social security for support. In short, Lord Hoffmann's concern about claimants who suffer damage as a result of their own criminal conduct tapping public funds, far from supporting the rejection of their claims is, if anything, something that points in favour of allowing them. Finally, and most fundamentally, Lord Hoffmann did not explain

---

[73] *Gray* (n 1) [51].

why he thought that it should matter that claimants in wide rule cases would, if their actions succeed, be compensated out of public funds. The suggestion that the source of the compensation should matter to entitlements to damages in tort law is heretical. According to conventional wisdom, liability in tort should be determined without reference to whether the claimant would be paid by an insurer, the tortfeasor, the state, etc.

Third, it is not terribly clear what Lord Hoffmann's justification for the wide rule actually is. His Lordship spoke of the need to ensure 'the fair distribution of resources'. There are several ambiguities in this brief passage. Lord Hoffmann did not indicate what he meant by 'resources'. Presumably he intended to refer to money. The class of persons among whom the resources are distributed is also not identified. Is the relevant class the claimant and the defendant in the particular lawsuit? Or is the group society generally? The last interpretation seems to be the most plausible given Lord Hoffmann's earlier reference, discussed in the previous paragraph, to 'public funds'. Finally, Lord Hoffmann did not propound the criterion or criteria by which he thought that the fairness of a given distribution of resources should be measured.

Fourth, if, as has been suggested, the resource that Lord Hoffmann had in mind is money and the class of persons to which he was referring was society as a whole, his rationale for the wide rule is unsatisfactory. It presupposes that tort law should strive to promote a just distribution in financial wealth among persons generally. Tort law is, however, not particularly well positioned to do that. Some of tort law's most basic rules mean that it is prone to perpetuate or aggravate already gross distributive inequalities in financial wealth. One such rule is the principle that the victim of a tort is entitled to full compensation (which commits tort law to providing income replacement). Because of this rule, if a destitute man negligently runs over with a car a wealthy banker and renders him unable to work, tort law holds the former liable to compensate fully the latter for his loss of income. It is irrelevant that imposing liability will worsen the pre-existing distributive inequality. Adopting the wide rule in the hope of promoting a just distribution of resources throughout society seems rather futile given the full compensation principle and the many other rules (which cannot be discussed here due to limitations of space) that render tort law largely insensitive to whether its impact on the distribution of wealth in society is just.

John Spencer contends that I am reading Lord Hoffmann's speech too literally. Spencer interprets Lord Hoffmann as saying, in essence, that the wide rule is justified on the ground that it produces outcomes of which public opinion would approve and that it thereby promotes public confidence in the law. Spencer writes:

> [I]f (as I suspect) the phrase 'public notions of the fair distribution of resources' really means no more than 'the man on the Clapham omnibus's instinctive sense

of right and wrong', I believe Lord Hoffmann's justification is a sound one. There can be no question, surely, but that good legal rules are ones which avoid results offensive to this sense. And although no one (so far as I am aware) has carried out an opinion poll on this precise issue, it is not difficult to guess what the result would be if they did.[74]

Let us assume that Spencer is correct in saying that this is what Lord Hoffmann had in mind. Suppose also that the wide rule promotes public confidence in the law because it prevents the law from producing results that would cause the public to think less of the law. Would this mean that the wide rule is justified? This leads us into very difficult territory. I have argued elsewhere that the wide rule almost certainly does nothing to deter offending[75] or to prevent wrongful profiting (which are two reasons which have often been advanced by judges and commentators for denying a remedy to claimants who were injured while acting illegally).[76] I have also argued that the wide rule is unfair to claimants since it is liable to impose on them punishment that is grossly disproportionate to the gravity of their wrongdoing.[77] I will not repeat these arguments here. I incorporate them by reference. I believe that, disregarding for the moment the effect of awarding damages to claimants who were injured while acting illegally on public confidence in the law, there is an overwhelming case for doing away with the wide rule. It hits out indiscriminately at claimants without accomplishing anything worthwhile in the process. The relevant question to my mind, therefore, is should a defective rule be retained simply because members of the public, who have not thought deeply about it, would be in favour of the outcomes that it produces? In other words, should a rule that inspires public confidence in the law be adopted for that reason alone, even if is quite damaging? There is no doubt that it is of great importance that the law inspires public confidence. If the law does not enjoy the confidence of the public, there is an increased risk that the public will cease to have recourse to the law in order to resolve their disputes. It is therefore arguable that even if, as I believe, the wide rule is in reality a defective rule, it should be embraced.

There is not enough space available to me here to get anywhere near the bottom of this thorny issue, so I will instead note that there is an interesting parallel problem that exists elsewhere in the law from which tort law might be able to glean some guidance. It is a basic principle of the law governing judicial bias that a decision that appears to the ordinary, fairminded observer to be infected with bias should be set aside even if the

---

[74] Spencer (n 42) 316.
[75] *Cf* NJ McBride and R Bagshaw, *Tort Law* (4th edn, Harlow, Pearson Education, 2012) 732, who support the wide rule on the grounds of deterrence (without giving any reasons for thinking that it deters offending).
[76] Goudkamp (n 1) 212–13.
[77] ibid.

judge who reached it was actually impartial.[78] This rule—the rule against apparent bias—is rooted in the need to maintain public confidence in the law.[79] The logic is that public confidence is just as likely to be destroyed by decisions that appear to the public to have been made by a biased judge as by decisions that are reached by a judge who is in fact biased, and therefore decisions that are contaminated with either apparent or actual bias must be set aside. The law consequently sometimes sets aside decisions as a result of, say, something that the judge said or did, or some association between the judge and someone else involved in the case, which was innocuous from a lawyer's perspective (such that lawyers would not think that the judge is actually biased), but which might cause the lay observer to suspect that something was wrong.[80] In one sense, the rule against apparent bias is a defective principle, since it leads to resources being consumed retrying cases where the original judge was actually impartial. Undoubtedly conscious of this, judges have often imputed detailed knowledge of the legal system to the hypothetical observer to make him less likely than the ordinary member of the public to suspect impropriety,[81] with the result that decisions are set aside less frequently for apparent bias than would otherwise be the case. In another sense, however, the rule against apparent bias is an essential one given the overriding concern that the public have confidence in the law. From this perspective, increasing the knowledge of the hypothetical observer of the legal system to make him more like a lawyer is highly objectionable.[82] This puzzle in the law on apparent bias resembles, to a degree, that which I have canvassed in relation to the wide rule in *Gray*. Both the rule against apparent bias and the wide rule, it might be said, aspire to uphold public confidence in the law by producing results which might otherwise be absurd. Whether or not it is sensible for the law deliberately to produce bad outcomes because doing so inspires public confidence in the law is a debate for another day.

There is one small addition to the foregoing discussion that needs to be added to prevent it from being misunderstood. The analysis that has been offered should not be taken as endorsing the 'public conscience' test for illegality. That test, which was developed in *Thackwell v Barclays Bank Ltd*[83]

---

[78] *Porter v Magill* [2002] 2 AC 357 (HL).

[79] For discussion, see J Goudkamp, 'The Rule against Bias and the Doctrine of Waiver' (2007) 26 *Civil Justice Quarterly* 310.

[80] See, eg, *Smith v Kvaerner Cementation Foundations Ltd* [2006] EWCA Civ 242, [2007] 1 WLR 370 (apparent bias found to exist on the ground that a company appearing in proceedings before a recorder was a client of the recorder).

[81] 'The fictitious postulate [ie, the hypothetical observer] has been stretched virtually to snapping point. Courts throughout the common law world have built up a profile of the hypothetical observer, identifying features which this paragon will manifest and features that will be absent': *Smith v Roach* [2006] HCA 36, (2006) 80 ALJR 1309 [96] (Kirby J).

[82] Consider *R v Secretary of State for the Environment ex p Kirkstall Valley Campaign Ltd* [1996] 3 All ER 304 (QBD) 316, where Sedley J complains about the fact that judges, in determining apparent bias cases, are essentially holding up a mirror to themselves.

[83] *Thackwell v Barclays Bank Ltd* [1986] 1 All ER 676 (QBD).

and abandoned in *Tinsley v Milligan*,[84] determined the effect of illegal conduct by the claimant according to whether allowing recovery would shock or cause affront to the public. The argument above has simply suggested that maintaining public confidence in the legal system may form part of a rationale for the wide rule. Moreover, the discussion in this regard has been directed at the rationales for withholding relief on the ground of illegality rather than at the test that should be used to determine when actions that are contaminated with unlawful conduct on the part of the claimant will succeed and fail. Accordingly, the discussion does not imply that any stance has been taken in relation to the public conscience test. Because the public conscience test was not discussed by the House of Lords in *Gray*, nothing more will be said about it here.

VII. THE NARROW RULE

A. The Provenance of the Narrow Rule

According to the narrow rule, tort law will not award compensation in respect of loss 'which flows from loss of liberty, a fine or other punishment lawfully imposed upon you in consequence of your own unlawful act'.[85] This rule has a long history. It can be traced at least to the decision of the Court of Common Pleas in *Colburn v Patmore*.[86] The claimant publisher in that case had been held liable for a criminal libel on account of material printed in his newspaper. He sought an indemnity from the editor in respect of the loss that he suffered as a result of the conviction. Although the Court found in the defendant's favour due to a defect in the claimant's pleadings, the Court made it clear that, had it not been for this defect, it would have dismissed the claimant's action on the grounds of illegality. The narrow rule has been applied on countless subsequent occasions (in the UK and in many other jurisdictions), as Lord Hoffmann noted in his speech.[87]

---

[84] *Tinsley* (n 28).
[85] *Gray* (n 1) [29].
[86] *Colburn v Patmore* (1834) 1 CM & R 73, 149 ER 999.
[87] Some additional cases are collected in J Goudkamp, 'Can Tort Law Be Used to Deflect the Impact of Criminal Sanctions? The Role of the Illegality Defence' (2006) 14 *Torts Law Journal* 20.

B. What Sort of Rule is the Narrow Rule?

It was noted earlier[88] that the wide rule can both prevent liability from arising and, when the finding of liability remains intact, stop damages from being recovered in respect of certain losses. The same goes for the narrow rule. In *Gray*, the narrow rule stopped Mr Gray from obtaining damages for particular losses, such as damage to his reputation done by the conviction. However, it can also, in the right type of case, completely prevent liability from arising. Consider the decision in *Clunis*. The claimant in this case stabbed a man to death in an unprovoked attack. He pleaded guilty to manslaughter on the basis of diminished responsibility and was sentenced to detention in hospital. The claimant then sued the defendant health authority for failing to detain and treat him. He contended that had the defendant done these things, he would not have committed the manslaughter and would not have suffered as great a loss of freedom. The claimant's action failed entirely. This outcome, as Lord Hoffmann noted in *Gray*,[89] was the result of the application of the narrow rule.

It was explained earlier that the wide rule is merely a re-statement of two causal principles, namely, the causation element of the action in negligence, and the rule that a claimant who has established liability and who wishes to recover damages in respect of certain losses must prove that the losses in question were caused by the defendant's tort. The narrow rule is also a re-statement of these rules. When it precludes liability from arising, it does so by stopping the causation element of the tort of negligence from being satisfied. When it leaves a finding of liability undisturbed but stands in the way of damages for certain losses from being obtained, it does so on the ground that the claimant failed to establish that the losses concerned were causally related to the defendant's tort. One upshot of the foregoing is that the claimant must bear the onus of proving that the narrow rule does not apply,[90] as is the case in relation to the wide rule. This is by virtue of the well-established principle that claimants carry the onus of proving both the elements of the tort in which they sue and that items of loss in respect of which they seek damages were caused by the defendant's tort.

C. The Scope of the Narrow Rule

The scope of the narrow rule is unclear in certain respects. Two doubts regarding its ambit will briefly be noted. First, it is not entirely unclear

---

[88] See section VI above.

[89] *Gray* (n 1) [37].

[90] It was held in *West v Ministry of Defence* [2006] EWHC 19 (QB) [9]–[11] that the claimant has the burden of showing that the narrow rule is inapplicable, roughly for these reasons.

whether the narrow rule precludes damages from being recovered in respect of criminal law penalties imposed for all types of offences or just for certain types of offences. The offence committed by Mr Gray—manslaughter—cannot be committed faultlessly. The narrow rule as articulated by Lord Hoffmann in *Gray* certainly dictates, therefore, that one cannot recover damages in respect of criminal law penalties imposed for fault-based offences. But what about criminal law penalties imposed for strict liability offences? Does the narrow rule prevent damages from being recovered in respect of such penalties? This issue did not arise in *Gray*. But Lord Hoffmann's description of the narrow rule is unqualified.[91] It is thus arguable that the rule applies irrespective of the type of crime—fault-based or involving strict liability—that the claimant committed. However, this argument is very difficult (if not impossible) to maintain in view of remarks made in *Les Laboratoires Servier v Apotex Inc*. In this case, Lord Sumption, with whom Lord Neuberger and Lord Clarke agreed, remarked, without referring to Lord Hoffmann's speech in *Gray* on this point, that the commission of 'strict liability [offences] where the claimant was not privy to the facts making his act unlawful'[92] will not engage the doctrine of illegality. Many older cases support this view.[93] It is true that *Les Laboratoires Servier* was not a narrow rule case and so the weight that this remark is capable of bearing is debatable. However, this comment by Lord Sumption targets the issue precisely and has been endorsed by a majority of the Supreme Court. It would require a heroic effort to show that it does not represent the law.

Second, there is some uncertainty as to whether the purpose of the sentence imposed on the claimant is relevant to the applicability of the narrow rule. Lord Hoffmann was firmly of the view that the civil courts should not enquire as to the purpose of the criminal law court in sentencing the claimant. His Lordship thought that tort law should not award damages in respect of criminal law penalties regardless of the criminal court's purpose in imposing a particular penalty. Lord Hoffmann was of this opinion because he felt that criminal courts invariably try to accomplish several things in sentencing offenders.[94] However, Lord Phillips,[95] Lord Rodger[96] and Lord Brown[97] left open the possibility that, where the criminal court's decision to order the detention of the claimant was not based on the need to punish him, compensation might be granted in respect of loss caused to the claimant by that order. The situation that they envisaged was a purely rehabilitative sentence. Lord Scott agreed with both Lord Hoffmann and

---

[91] See text accompanying n 18.
[92] *Les Laboratoires Servier* (n 66) [29].
[93] See, eg, *Osmand v J Ralph Moss Ltd* [1970] 1 Lloyd's Rep 313 (CA).
[94] *Gray* (n 1) [41].
[95] ibid [14]–[15].
[96] ibid [83].
[97] ibid [103].

Lord Rodger and did not mention this difference of opinion between them. Accordingly, it seems that it is open for a person who breaches the criminal law as a result of a tort being committed against him to argue that he should be compensated for the consequences of the sentence imposed on him, provided that it was clear from the sentence that he had no significant personal responsibility for the offending.

D. Lord Hoffmann's Attempt to Justify the Narrow Rule

Lord Hoffmann sought to justify the narrow rule on the ground that it prevents tort law and the criminal law from coming into conflict with each other.[98] His Lordship's thinking was that the law would be inconsistent if it imposed a criminal law penalty on a person and then permitted that person to use tort law to 'shift' that penalty onto someone else (insofar as it is possible for a criminal penalty to be deflected by an award of compensation). This justification for the narrow rule has been endorsed by the courts in several other jurisdictions, most clearly in Canada.[99] My view is that there remains much thinking to be done about what, precisely, the notion of 'inconsistency' means here. Narrow rule cases present the threat of inconsistency in two ways: (1) in relation to the law's goals ('goal inconsistency'); and (2) in respect of the formal pronouncements of responsibility made by the law ('pronouncement inconsistency'). If tort law grants relief in respect of a criminal law sanction, it takes some of the sting out of it and thereby undermines whatever goal the criminal law court was trying to serve in imposing the sanction. This is goal inconsistency. However, the spectre of pronouncement inconsistency is also present here. This is because if tort law awards compensation in respect of the loss caused by the penalty, it would be casting doubt on the criminal law's determination regarding responsibility for the offence. A finding of liability in narrow rule cases sends a message that the defendant (and not the claimant) in the tort suit is the person who is really responsible for the criminal law offence in question. This is at odds with the criminal law's pronouncement that the claimant is criminally responsible. It appears, therefore, that there are two consistency rationales that might be capable of supporting the narrow rule. They are as follows: (1) the narrow rule is justified because it prevents tort law from undermining efforts to realise the criminal law's goals; and (2) the narrow rule is justified because it prevents the law from making inconsistent pronouncements regarding the claimant's responsibility for the act that led to his being convicted and sanctioned. Obviously, both rationales have a lot going for them.

---

[98] ibid [37].
[99] *Hall v Hebert* [1993] 2 SCR 159; *HL v Canada (AG)* [2005] SCC 25, [2005] 1 SCR 401; *British Columbia v Zastowny* [2008] SCC 4, [2008] 1 SCR 27.

No one can seriously doubt that consistency in the law (in both senses) is in principle a good thing. But are either of these rationales sufficient (whether taken alone or in combination) to justify the narrow rule?

Let me take the goal consistency rationale first. One reason for doubting whether this rationale fully supports the narrow rule is that it assumes that tort law's goals are never worth pursuing when promoting them would detract from the realisation of the criminal law's goals. However, it is far from obvious that the criminal law's goals should always take priority over those of tort law. Certainly, the suggestion that they should invariably take priority ought to be rejected by, for example, someone who believes that the function of the law generally is or should be to deter inefficient behaviour. According to this philosophy, there is no reason to suppose that the criminal law is somehow inherently superior to tort law, such that its goals are more important, let alone qualitatively more important.[100] Indeed, according to this philosophy, both tort law and the criminal law have precisely the same goal (that is, the maximisation of societal wealth), and it is entirely possible that tort law might actually deter unwanted behaviour more efficiently than the criminal law in a given case, in which case it ought to be given priority. Proponents of this utilitarian view of the law contend that when tort law deters unwanted behaviour more efficiently than the criminal law, the law should opt to regulate the behaviour in question by way of tort law instead of the criminal law.

A second reason for thinking that the goal consistency rationale may not fully support the narrow rule is that the objectives of the criminal law might paradoxically sometimes be *promoted* if tort law 'shifts' a criminal law penalty from the person on whom it was initially imposed to another person. The idea here is that the criminal law occasionally makes targeting mistakes. By 'mistakes', I do not mean to refer to the possibility of a person who is guilty being acquitted and a person who is innocent being convicted; rather, by mistakes, I am talking about errors in the *design* of the criminal law. I mean, to be specific, that the criminal law might, as a result of a badly formulated rule, result in liability being imposed on the wrong person in the sense that (depending on one's philosophy of what the criminal law is for) he is not the person who is most to blame for the breach of the criminal law or is not the most efficient loss avoider. Were it not for the narrow rule, tort law might be able to step in here and correct such targeting errors and thereby advance the goals of the criminal law. Consider the Singaporean case of *United Project Consultants Pte Ltd v Leong Kwok Onn*.[101] In this decision, the claimant had faultlessly committed a tax offence as a result of the negligence of his auditor. The Court of Appeal allowed the claimant to

---

[100] Consider WM Landes and RA Posner, *The Economic Structure of Tort Law* (Cambridge, MA, Harvard University Press, 1987) 154–55.

[101] *United Project Consultants Pte Ltd v Leong Kwok Onn* [2005] 4 SLR (R) 214 (CA).

recover damages from the auditor in respect of the penalty. Obviously, the result would be different in the UK under the narrow rule, assuming that the offence in question would be thought sufficiently serious to attract the rule in the first place.[102] The crucial point to note for present purposes is that allowing the claimant to use tort law to deflect the impact of the criminal law penalty from the claimant to the auditor actually promoted the goals of the criminal law (at least insofar as those goals are understood in terms of punishment or deterrence). The penalty was in effect transferred from the claimant to the auditor. The auditor was the blameworthy party and was also in a better position than the claimant to ensure that the tax offence was not committed. To summarise, the second objection is that the goal consistency rationale, far from justifying fully the narrow rule, might actually support suspending the narrow rule on occasion.

What about the pronouncement consistency rationale? According to this rationale for the narrow rule, the narrow rule is justified because it prevents tort law from granting relief where awarding compensation would cast or tend to cast doubt on the criminal law's determination that the claimant is criminally responsible. The danger here is that the legal system might send mixed messages. The first objection that was voiced in relation to the goal consistency rationale applies here too. That objection, in relation to the goal consistency rationale, was that it is not clear that the criminal law's goals should take absolute priority over those of tort law. The same objection can be made mutatis mutandis to the pronouncement consistency rationale. Why should tort law always defer to the criminal law's pronouncements? Depending on one's legal philosophy, one might be committed to rejecting the proposition that the criminal law should always take precedence over tort law. Reasons why this is so have been discussed above. The second objection that was raised in relation to the goal consistency rationale was that tort law might paradoxically promote the criminal law's goals if it deflects a particular criminal law sanction. The idea was that where the criminal law has made a targeting error as a result of a rule the design of which is sub-optimal, tort law might usefully step in to diminish the impact of that error by holding the defendant in the tort claim liable to the claimant. The same objection does not really apply to the pronouncement consistency rationale. If tort law sends a message that is inconsistent with that promulgated by the criminal law, there is a danger that neither message will be understood.

Neither version of the consistency rationale is without difficulty, for the reasons that have been given. It is doubtful whether they (even if taken together) support the narrow rule. More generally, I very much doubt that

---

[102] It is clear that the offending by the claimant must reach a threshold of seriousness to engage either the wide rule or the narrow rule. What is unclear, however, is what that threshold is. In *Moore Stephens* (n 3) [179], Lord Walker opined that a mere regulatory offence not involving dishonesty would be insufficient.

the puzzle of what rule should be embraced in narrow rule cases can be dissolved by considering only the issue of consistency. Ultimately, the goal should be to produce a just rule for the resolution of narrow rule cases, and consistency is only one of several considerations that will be in play in this regard. This point is captured by Lord Atkin's dictum in *Ras Behari Lal v The King Emperor* that 'consistency is a good thing, but justice is better'.[103] For example, one argument in support of the narrow rule that has nothing to do with either consistency rationale has to do with efficiency. Arguably, tort law should not be in the business of cleaning up messes created by the criminal law.[104] That requires extra litigation (and therefore cost and delay) and it is not clear that this is worth the candle. Perhaps the most efficient thing for tort law to do when the criminal law has produced a sub-optimal outcome is nothing, given the cost of intervening.

In conclusion, it is doubtful whether the twin arguments from consistency justify the narrow rule. The narrow rule might be justified, but the justification must be sought in a consideration of all of the pros and cons of that rule. It is a mistake to concentrate exclusively on consistency, since that is surely not the only factor to bear in mind in determining whether a particular rule is just.

VIII. THE RETREAT FROM *GRAY*

In many respects, the decision in *Gray* improved the pre-existing law significantly. Prior to *Gray*, it was unclear even what the core rules in this area were. The Court of Appeal had developed a dizzying number of formulae,[105] including the reliance test,[106] the inextricable link test,[107] the proportionality test[108] and a test that asked whether it was possible or feasible to determine the standard of care that the reasonable person would have taken for the claimant's interests.[109] This mess was swept away by Lord Hoffmann in *Gray* (explicitly in the case of the reliance test[110] and the inextricable link test[111]) for the purposes of proceedings in negligence. The solution that he

---

[103] *Ras Behari Lal v The King Emperor* (1933) 50 TLR 1 (PC) 2.

[104] Lord Hoffmann hinted at this rationale in *Gray* (n 1) [41].

[105] In *Hewison v Meridian Shipping Services Pte Ltd* [2002] EWCA Civ 1821, [2003] ICR 766 [56], Ward LJ complained that 'the search for principle' had been 'elusive'.

[106] See section IV above.

[107] See section V above.

[108] In *Saunders v Edwards* [1987] 1 WLR 1116 (CA) 1133, Bingham LJ seemed to suggest that it was relevant, in applying the doctrine of illegality, to consider the unlawfulness of the claimant's act on the one hand and the quantum of the claimant's loss on the other. Many other judges have often thought this to be a significant consideration too: see, eg, *Cross* (n 54) [53]; *Clarke v Clarke* [2012] EWHC 2118 (QB) [30].

[109] *Pitts v Hunt* (1991) 1 QB 24 (CA).

[110] See section IV above.

[111] See section V above.

installed in its place—the wide rule and the narrow rule—brought welcome clarity to the law. In the process of laying down these rules, Lord Hoffmann also demonstrated convincingly that the arguments for denying the claimant's action on the ground of illegality (in whole or in part) differed depending on whether one was dealing with a wide rule case or a narrow rule case. 'The questions of fairness and policy are different.'[112] The fundamental differences between these types of cases had not really been appreciated prior to *Gray*. Judges had often made the error of thinking that narrow rule cases supported denying recovery in wide rule cases.[113] However, as Lord Hoffmann made clear, these cases are materially different from each other, and the difference is such that the consistency rationale only operates in favour of the narrow rule.[114] (The argument (or arguments) from consistency plainly do not support the wide rule, as Lord Hoffmann made clear, because in wide rule cases, the claimant's tort action does not threaten to stultify the criminal law.) The inappropriateness of drawing on narrow rule cases to resolve wide rule cases is now much more visible.

What has happened since *Gray*, and what is the current status of *Gray*? There have been two major developments. First, the House of Lords handed down its mammoth decision in *Moore Stephens*,[115] in which it also considered the doctrine of illegality. Skating over most of the detail, the facts in *Moore Stephens* were as follows. A fraudster incorporated a company in order to defraud several banks. He engaged an auditor, the defendant, to give his purported business an air of respectability, which helped him to dupe the victim banks. The banks eventually uncovered the fraud and obtained judgments against the company.[116] The company's liquidators commenced proceedings in negligence and contract against the auditor, seeking an indemnity in respect of the company's liability to the banks. The auditor maintained that the proceedings should be struck out on the basis that they were founded on the company's illegal conduct. The House of Lords, by a majority, upheld the orders of the judge at first instance striking out the action on this ground. In doing so, the House effectively treated the proceedings as a contractual claim,[117] and the most significant issue in the case[118] was said to be whether the fraudster's acts should be attributed to the company (it was held that they should be). Consequently, *Moore*

---

[112] *Gray* (n 1) [31].

[113] See, eg, *Wilson v Coulson* [2002] PIQR P22 (QBD) [70] and text accompanying n 120.

[114] *Gray* (n 1) [32].

[115] The decision runs to 277 paragraphs, not including the annex.

[116] *Komercni Banka AS v Stone and Rolls Ltd* [2002] EWHC 2263 (Comm), [2003] 1 Lloyd's Rep 383.

[117] See, eg, *Moore Stephens* (n 3) [26] (Lord Phillips focusing on the maxim *ex turpi causa non oritur actio* in its application to contractual claims), [98] (Lord Scott stating expressly that it was appropriate to concentrate on the claim in 'contractual negligence' rather than 'tortious negligence').

[118] 'The central bone of contention between the parties': *Moore Stephens* (n 3) [38].

Stephens is of relatively little interest to tort lawyers. However, two striking features of it are worth noting for present purposes. First, *Gray* hardly featured in it at all. It was mentioned only once and then only in passing,[119] despite the fact that the reasons given by the House in *Moore Stephens* were exceptionally prolix. The neglect of *Gray* is surprising considering that it was decided just five weeks before judgment was given in *Moore Stephens* and in view of the fact that two of the judges in *Moore Stephens* (Lord Phillips and Lord Scott) also heard the appeal in *Gray*. The House's lack of engagement with *Gray* might have been a reflection of the fact that it treated *Moore Stephens* as a contractual case only. Second, their Lordships lost sight of the distinction between wide rule cases and narrow rule cases. *Moore Stephens* was a wide rule case. The company was obviously not seeking a remedy in respect of any criminal law sanction that had been imposed on it. However, several members of the House of Lords cited narrow rule cases or postulated hypothetical narrow rule cases in support of their conclusion that the doctrine of illegality applied.[120] As noted in the preceding paragraph, Lord Hoffmann had explained convincingly in *Gray* that this was inappropriate given the basic difference between wide rule cases and narrow rule cases. As Lord Hoffmann put it: 'One cannot simply extrapolate rules applicable to a different kind of situation.'[121]

The second major development was the delivery by the Supreme Court of its decision in *Hounga*.[122] The defendants, Mr and Mrs Allen, arranged for the claimant, a Nigerian national, to enter the UK under false pretenses. The claimant knowingly participated in these arrangements. The claimant then went to live with the Allens and worked illegally for them. Approximately 18 months later, Mrs Allen evicted the claimant from the Allens' home and dismissed her from her employment. The Employment Tribunal held that the Allens had unlawfully discriminated against the claimant on the ground of nationality in dismissing her contrary to what is now section 39(2)(C) of the Equality Act 2010. The Tribunal ordered Mrs Allen to pay compensation.

---

[119] ibid [25].

[120] Perhaps the best illustration of this tendency is found in the opening paragraph of Lord Brown's speech. Lord Brown postulated a hypothetical narrow rule case, apparently believing that it encapsulated the issue at stake in *Moore Stephens*: see (n 3) [195].

[121] *Gray* (n 1) [31].

[122] The Supreme Court very recently also delivered its decision in *Les Laboratoires Servier* (n 66). This case is of limited relevance for present purposes. The claimant pharmaceutical company obtained an interim injunction restraining the importation and sale in the UK by the defendant company, which was based in Canada, of medicine which it said had been manufactured in breach of a UK patent. The usual undertaking regarding damages was given. The UK patent was subsequently found to have been invalid and the defendant sought compensation. One issue for the Supreme Court was whether compensation could be recovered in view of the fact that the defendant in manufacturing the medicine was in breach of a Canadian patent. The Supreme Court held that the doctrine of illegality was not engaged because the conduct was not sufficiently turpitudinous. This was obviously quite a different point from that in issue in *Gray*, and it is not surprising that *Gray* barely featured in the reasons of the Supreme Court.

The case reached the Supreme Court on the issue of whether the defence of illegality prevented this liability from arising. The Court unanimously held that it did not. *Gray* was, again, mentioned only once, by Lord Wilson, who delivered the principal opinion.[123] Lord Wilson doubted the usefulness of the causal approach[124] to the doctrine of illegality promoted by Lord Hoffmann. He also disagreed with Lord Hoffmann's criticism of the inextricable link test[125] and said that the test was unsatisfied in the instant case.[126] However, Lord Wilson then said that the 'bigger question'[127] than that of whether the inextricable link test was satisfied was whether it applied. He did not give an answer to that question, an omission that seems to have been accidental. Lord Hughes, who delivered the only other opinion in the case, did not notice this omission and mistakenly concluded that Lord Wilson had held that the inextricabe linked test was the relevant rule to apply.[128]

Given the foregoing, the status of *Gray* must be open to some doubt. It was certainly not endorsed in either *Moore Stephens* or in *Hounga*, and in those cases the House of Lords and the Supreme Court might be read as trying to distance themselves from it. However, it is true that *Moore Stephens* was treated as a contractual case and *Hounga* was a case involving a statutory tort. So perhaps those cases merely demonstrate limits to the applicability of the analysis adopted in *Gray* and should not be read as suggesting that *Gray* ought not to be applied in the context of the tort of negligence. *Gray* has so far been regarded by the Court of Appeal as laying down the approach that is to be taken in the negligence setting,[129] although it will be interesting to see whether *Gray* will be treated differently in that context in the light of *Hounga*.[130] It is strongly arguable that *Gray* remains binding on the Court of Appeal in the negligence setting.

IX. CONCLUSION

Lord Hoffmann's speech in *Gray* was a triumph in more ways than one. It extracted from the jurisprudential debris created by a series of decisions

---

[123] *Gray* (n 1) [35].
[124] ibid [36]–[38].
[125] Lord Hoffmann's criticism of that test is discussed above: see section V.
[126] *Gray* (n 1) [39].
[127] ibid [40].
[128] ibid [58].
[129] *Delaney v Pickett* [2011] EWCA Civ 1532, [2012] 1 WLR 2149; *Joyce* (n 68). See the discussion of these cases in section III above and in the text accompanying n 68.
[130] *Flint v Tittensor* [2015] EWHC 466 (QB) was decided just before this chapter was published. It came too late to make substantive engagement with it possible. However, very briefly, that decision, which was a wide rule case, followed the approach adumbrated in *Gray*. No mention is made of *Hounga*. *Flint*, therefore, suggests that the rules expounded in *Gray* will continue to be applied in at least the negligence context.

of the Court of Appeal two rules (the wide rule and the narrow rule) for determining the applicability of the doctrine of illegality in context of proceedings in negligence. His Lordship was able to express those rules in beautifully clear terms, both of which, fortunately, do not actually add to the corpus of law in this area since they are mere re-statements of fundamental principles in the law of torts. Finally, Lord Hoffmann demonstrated the necessity of distinguishing between wide rule and narrow rule cases. Even though there are certain difficulties with Lord Hoffmann's speech, it is nevertheless, if I may respectfully say so, a wonderfully rich yet succinct exploration of one of the most challenging corners of the law of torts.

5

Lord Hoffmann and the Economic Torts

RODERICK BAGSHAW

I. INTRODUCTION

IN *OBG LTD v Allan*,[1] the House of Lords re-organised the general economic torts.[2] One of the two leading speeches was delivered by Lord
Hoffmann, the other being given by Lord Nicholls. The new scheme
for the general economic torts adopted by the Court, which I will refer to
as 'Lord Hoffmann's scheme', separated the tort of procuring or inducing
breach of contract from the tort of intentionally causing loss by unlawful means and exterminated the misbegotten chimera of direct interference
with contractual relations. In explaining this scheme, the Court clarified
that intentionally causing loss by unlawful means (hereinafter 'the unlawful
means tort') imposes a special form of primary liability, while the procuring
breach tort imposes accessorial liability. Thus, the latter tort was said to be
simply an emanation of general secondary civil liability that had acquired a
distinct label.[3] Where the Court divided, Lord Hoffmann spoke for a majority that favoured restricting the scope of the former tort so that it only
imposes liability, at least in a three-party case,[4] where the means used by

---

[1] *OBG Ltd v Allan* [2007] UKHL 21, [2008] 1 AC 1.

[2] *OBG* also determined whether the tort of conversion ought to be extended to the conversion of contractual rights, with a majority rejecting this innovation, and whether a claimant
could properly claim that *all* photographic images of a wedding were confidential information.
But in this chapter I consider only the decision's effect on the general economic torts. I follow
Hazel Carty in using the phrase 'general economic torts' as an organising category which can be
separated conveniently from the 'misrepresentation economic torts': see H Carty, *An Analysis of
the Economic Torts* (2nd edn, Oxford, Oxford University Press, 2010) especially chs 8 and 13.

[3] *OBG* (n 1) [8] and [36]. In the subsequent case of *Total Network SL v Revenue and Customs
Commissioners* [2008] UKHL 19, [2008] 1 AC 1174, a differently constituted House of Lords
refused to accept that 'unlawful means conspiracy' was a superfluous but nominate mirror of
general civil secondary liability: see, eg, [225]–[226] (per Lord Neuberger).

[4] A 'three-party case' is where the defendant uses unlawful means against a third party with
the intention of causing loss to the claimant. Typical examples include where the defendant
uses unlawful means against the claimant's potential customers, suppliers or employees. In
this chapter I will often refer to the participants in three-party scenarios as D (defendant), C
(claimant) and T (third party).

the defendant amount to a civil wrong against the person to which they are applied,[5] or would have amounted to an actionable civil wrong if that person had suffered damage,[6] an alternative that he treated as also including situations where the defendant *threatened* to commit acts that would have amounted to an actionable civil wrong to the person concerned, but never had to go through with this threat because the person had 'caved in'.[7] He also insisted that the unlawful means had to restrict that person's freedom or liberty to deal with the claimant.[8]

The scope of the general economic torts is significant for a broad range of people, not just law students and textbook writers, because they impose liability where various techniques are resorted to by competitors seeking a larger share of the market, employees or suppliers seeking better terms or conditions, and protestors seeking influence, and consequently they restrict the liberty of competitors, employees, suppliers and protesters. Such restrictions can be beneficial in that they can provide welcome protection for the valuable expectations of individuals, businesses and other enterprises against disruption by unfair and egregious methods, such as the use of lies, threats, theft and violence against customers, suppliers or employees. But, equally, extensive restrictions might go too far in preventing interference with existing distributions of wealth and power, and restrictions of uncertain scope might discourage the cautious and responsible from competing or protesting. Lord Hoffmann has informally described the motivation behind his speech in *OBG* as being to confine the liabilities recognised in the leading cases within clear boundaries, so as to ensure that the general economic torts were not a 'hazard to navigation'.[9] And this description of his project resonates with recurring themes found elsewhere in his tort law jurisprudence: for instance, commitment to establishing predictability without showing disrespect for precedent, and a preference for a minimalist general common law, which can be supplemented by precise, specialised statutes.[10] The primary purpose of this chapter is not to take issue with these underlying goals, still less to encourage either the Supreme Court or the legislature to strike out in a new direction, overturning *Allen v Flood*[11] and establishing general tortious liability for economic harm intentionally caused without a sufficient justification. Instead, this chapter has the more modest goal of illuminating some

---

[5] *OBG* (n 1) [49] and [59].

[6] ibid [50].

[7] ibid [49].

[8] ibid [51]. The significance of the different phrases used to describe the same limit in other paragraphs (eg, at [47]) will be discussed below.

[9] Statement by Lord Hoffmann (in discussion of the prototype of this chapter presented at the conference 'The Jurisprudence of Lord Hoffmann' held at St Catherine's College, University of Oxford, 25 April 2014).

[10] *OBG* (n 1) [59]–[60].

[11] *Allen v Flood* [1898] AC 1 (HL).

of the pressures that exist at the edge of the concepts that Lord Hoffmann's scheme uses to confine liability, and the additional tension resulting from the House of Lords' pronouncements on the conspiracy torts in the *Total Network* case.[12] Such exegesis may be useful because there is no doubt that Lord Hoffmann's speech immediately became the foundational document for modern understanding of the general economic torts. But my discussion of points of detail is also necessary groundwork in preparation for addressing the more general question whether Lord Hoffmann's attractively simple and clear scheme has oversimplified the economic torts.

II. THE RELATIONSHIP BETWEEN THE UNLAWFUL MEANS TORT AND PROCURING A BREACH OF CONTRACT

Lord Hoffmann's scheme reduces the general economic torts to protection of two economic[13] interests of a potential claimant: an interest in receiving due performance of a valid contract and an interest in third parties being free to deal with him or her without interference. Clearly these interests are not exclusive, in that the second, broader interest includes cases where the interference with a third party's freedom has prevented a claimant from receiving due performance of a contractual obligation.[14] Indeed, the tort of procuring breach provides nothing close to full protection for a claimant's interest in receiving due performance of contracts; it only covers a fraction of those cases where a person other than the non-performing party can be said to have *caused* the non-performance. The precise scope of that fraction is contentious and will be discussed below; at this stage, it is sufficient to say that situations where a defendant *encourages* or *persuades* the non-performing party to break the contract are undoubtedly within

---

[12] *Total Network* (n 3).

[13] It is doubtful whether either interest ought to be treated as *exclusively* economic. For example, due performance of a valid contract may prevent physical damage to a claimant's property or personal injury (such as where the contract is for veterinary or medical treatment) and, similarly, the significance of a third party's liberty vis-a-vis the claimant *may* sometimes be a result of the third party's ability to protect the claimant against personal injury or property damage. Perhaps a defendant who procured a breach of a contract between a medical professional and the claimant, or used unlawful means to prevent treatment being provided with the intention of causing loss to the claimant, could be held liable for *negligence* (since this tort surely covers intentionally causing personal injury by indirect means). But it is not easy to imagine why anyone would want to insist that these claims could not be described as being for procuring breach of contract and the unlawful means tort respectively.

[14] The economic interest protected by the tort of inducing a breach of contract is *probably* not merely a sub-category of the broader interest protected by the unlawful means tort, because cases of simple *encouragement* or *persuasion* to break a contract with the claimant do not *interfere with* the encouraged or persuaded party's *liberty* to deal with the claimant, which is *probably* the interest protected by the unlawful means tort. (The word 'probably' appears in the previous sentence in order to allow for the issue debated below: see section III.A.)

the fraction, and situations where a defendant *prevents* the party from performing are undoubtedly outside it, whilst controversy surrounds situations where a defendant *tricks* or *coerces* the party into breaking the contract, *enables* the party to do so or *facilitates* a breach. Where a defendant has *caused* a claimant not to receive due performance of a valid contract otherwise than by behaviour within the procuring breach fraction, then the claimant's interest will only be protected in tort law if he or she can establish that the defendant committed the unlawful means tort or some adjacent tort.[15] And in such cases the claimant will have to demonstrate that the use of unlawful means caused the non-performance by affecting the promisor's actions in a way that falls within the scope of that tort.[16]

III. THE UNLAWFUL MEANS TORT

A. The Effect of the Unlawful Means

Simon Deakin and John Randall have argued that the unlawful means tort should only protect interests that can be described as involving 'trade, business or employment'.[17] However, it is not easy to understand what advantages might flow from having to debate whether particular interests fall inside or outside this bracket. Why should intimidating an elderly gentleman into changing his butcher or sacking his butler be actionable at the instance of the butcher or butler, but intimidating him into halving the allowance he pays to his daughter, disinheriting his son or recalling the loan of his Rubens to the National Gallery not be?[18]

Lord Hoffmann's scheme gives no special advantage to 'trade, business or employment', though one paragraph refers to the 'essence of the tort' as 'interference with the actions of a third party in which the claimant has an *economic* interest'.[19] Whilst he does not elaborate, the adjective 'economic'

---

[15] The reference to 'adjacent torts' is intended to accommodate uncertainties about what other wrongs have been absorbed into the unlawful means tort. For example, where a defendant deceives a promisor into ceasing to deal with the claimant, there is some uncertainty as to whether this can only be actionable if it is an instance of the unlawful means tort or whether an adjacent tort called 'three-party deceit' (committed where D *deceives* T in order to get T to harm C) exists.

[16] Below I discuss the important question whether what is necessary is a restriction on liberty or a mere interference with actions.

[17] S Deakin and J Randall, 'Rethinking the Economic Torts' (2009) 72 *MLR* 519, 533.

[18] See also R Stevens, *Tort and Rights* (Oxford, Oxford University Press, 2007) 189.

[19] *OBG* (n 1) [47] (emphasis added). This is echoed by Lord Walker in *Total Network* (n 3) [100]; indeed, he goes so far as to suggest that one feature that distinguishes the tort of unlawful means conspiracy from the unlawful means tort is that in the former, 'the claimant need not be a trader who is injured in his trade, though that is the most common case'. He offers no explanation, however, as to why it should not be a tort for D to intimidate T into not making donations to C's charity or for D to use unlawful means to make it impossible for T to pay a tax to C.

may have been intended to prevent the tort being used to pursue actions for interference in family and social relationships, though it may be insufficient to prevent this when these have an economic dimension.[20] The reference to 'interference *with the actions* of a third party' was more obviously intended to be significant: a critical feature of Lord Hoffmann's scheme is that it confines the unlawful means tort, at least in three-party cases, to situations where the means cause harm to the claimant through restricting or interfering with a third party's liberty,[21] for example, by *preventing* a potential customer from trading with the claimant. The primary effect of this limit is to preclude liability where the unlawful means make a claimant's relationship with a third party less profitable without having any effect on the third party's behaviour. And this effect was clearly intended: Lord Hoffmann wanted to prevent the tort from covering a class of cases exemplified by a defendant bootlegger's production and sale of unlicensed recordings reducing the value of a claimant recording company's exclusive licence with a recording artist.[22]

The attraction of protecting the bootlegger from liability to the record company through a limit on *how* the means led to the claimant's loss stems from the fact that it would have proved difficult to achieve the same result through a narrow definition of 'unlawful means': bootlegging might qualify as 'unlawful means' even within a regime that insists that only civil wrongs will suffice, since it might support a civil claim by the copyright holder.[23] Moreover, a no-liability result could not be reached by relying on a lack of intention to harm the record company on the part of the defendant. For Lord Hoffmann, where a bootlegger knows that some proportion of his sales will be to people who would have otherwise bought a licensed recording, the bootlegger cannot maintain that he or she only intends to gain sales and does not intend the record company to lose them. One of the most attractive features of Lord Hoffmann's scheme is that it does not rely on an artificial and morally dubious curtailment of 'intention' in order to restrict liability.

---

[20] Clearly, the statutes that abolished the actions for enticement (Law Reform (Miscellaneous Provisions) Act 1970, s 5) and loss of family services (Administration of Justice Act 1982, s 2) would *obstruct* an attempt to impose tort liability on D for use of *unlawful means* to prevent a spouse or child of C from continuing a relationship with C. But common law authority also leans against such claims: *F v Wirral Metropolitan Borough Council* [1991] Fam 69 (CA). *cf* claims for deceit where a lie *induced* a claimant to continue a relationship: *P v B (Paternity: Damages for Deceit)* [2001] 1 FLR 1041; *A v B* [2007] EWHC 1246 (QB), [2007] 2 FLR 1051.

[21] *OBG* (n 1) [6]: 'The defendant's liability is primary, for intentionally causing the plaintiff loss by unlawfully *interfering with the liberty of others*' (emphasis added).

[22] ibid [52]–[53], analysing *RCA Corp v Pollard* [1983] 1 Ch 135 (CA).

[23] ibid [52]: 'This was an infringement of section 1 of the Dramatic and Musical Performers Protection Act 1958, which made bootlegging a criminal offence and, being enacted for the protection of performers, would have given Elvis Presley a cause of action: see Lord Diplock in *Lonrho Ltd v Shell Petroleum Co Ltd (No 2)* [1982] AC 173, 187.'

Lord Hoffmann clearly intended this new device (a limit defined in terms of the *effect* of the unlawful means on the third party) not to cause difficulties in standard cases where D's unlawful means *physically prevent* T from dealing with C, and D's *threat* of unlawful means convinces T not to deal with C. But his speech did not explore whether the device would be easy to apply in less frequently encountered situations or whether the pattern of outcomes it might be expected to produce in these cases would be defensible. Investigation of these issues is impeded, however, by uncertainty surrounding the precise formulation of the new limit. I have already quoted Lord Hoffmann's description of the essence of the tort as 'a wrongful interference *with the actions* of a third party'. But in the next paragraph he refers to a defendant 'interfering *with the liberty of action* of a third party' and subsequently to 'interfering *with the freedom* of a third party' to deal with the claimant.[24] Plainly, these formulations are not identical—a defendant can act in a way which changes ('interferes with'?) a third party's *actions* without restricting that person's *liberty*. For example, D might commit a tort against T in order to obtain an opportunity to *advise*, or *encourage*, him to act in some way that will harm C.[25] Similarly, D's unlawful means might cause T to act to C's detriment by *facilitating some alternative mode of behaviour* that T is likely to select as an alternative to dealing with C.[26] A further situation where it seems easier to describe D as 'interfering' with T's *actions*, as opposed to restricting T's *liberty*, is where D misleads T.[27] In *Lonrho v Fayed*,[28] one of the claims pursued alleged that three defendants had made false statements to the Secretary of State, which led him not to refer a takeover bid to the Monopolies and Mergers Commission, which in turn caused the claimants to lose the opportunity to make a rival bid. If these events potentially amounted to the unlawful means tort, as Lord Hoffmann's reference to the case in *OBG* suggests,[29] then we must conclude

---

[24] *OBG* (n 1) [47], [48] and [51] respectively (emphasis added). See also [129], [306] ('inhibiting his freedom to trade', per Baroness Hale) and [320] ('interfering with a third party's freedom to deal with [the claimant]', per Lord Brown).

[25] The 'unlawful means' (civil wrong) used might be breaking into T's house in order to talk to him or breaking a contractual promise to T not to communicate with him again.

[26] For example, D might wrongfully grant T access to a substantial quantity of cocaine, knowing that if that drug becomes easily available, then T is likely to choose to spend the weekend consuming it rather than dealing with C. (Of course, in accordance with Lord Hoffmann's definition of 'unlawful means', to have committed the tort, D's act would also have to be a private law wrong to T. But this might be the case if, for instance, D had promised T that he would use his best endeavours to prevent him from gaining access to cocaine.)

[27] Yet another example might be where the defendant uses unlawful means to facilitate a third party's actions to the claimant's detriment, for example, by kidnapping the third party and taking him against his will to a place where he will have an easy opportunity of acting in a way which will cause loss to the claimant.

[28] *Lonrho v Fayed* [1990] 2 QB 479 (CA), discussed by Lord Hoffmann in *OBG* (n 1) [50].

[29] *OBG* (n 1) [50].

that deception can affect a third party's actions in a way which falls within the scope of the tort. It should be noted, though, that if this is the case, then an exclusive licensee may be able to use the unlawful means tort to sue a bootlegger, provided that the 'pirate' recordings are so good that customers are deceived, but not if they knew that they were buying fakes.

The question whether the unlawful means must *restrict* the third party's liberty, or need only influence his or her actions, might also be significant in determining whether the tort will cover situations where a defendant uses *bribery* to persuade a third party not to deal with the claimant. Is there any reason for thinking that deceiving the Secretary of State to prevent him or her from exercising his or her powers should be a tort, whilst bribing him or her to similar effect should not be?[30] In *Constantin Medien AG v Ecclestone*,[31] a recent case involving an allegation of causing loss by unlawful means through bribery, the Court formulated the tort in accordance with the passage in Lord Hoffmann's speech which only refers to the need for 'a wrongful interference with the actions of a third party in which the claimant has an economic interest'.[32]

Regardless of the precise formulation of the new device, how can one defend a pattern of outcomes that distinguishes cases of physical prevention and intimidation from those where the unlawful means merely reduce the profitability of C's relationship with T? Suppose, for example, that a famous soprano, T, contracts to sing exclusively for C during January, and D, a rival opera promoter, seeks to cause economic harm to C by publishing private information about T, for instance, that she has expressed outrageously illiberal views in private settings. Even if this scheme involves committing a civil law wrong in relation to T,[33] it does not appear to restrict her liberty to perform her contract with C and need not alter her actions with regard to C. What reasons might there be for distinguishing D's scheme from one where he intentionally causes similar harm to C by physically injuring T, or imprisoning her, so that she cannot sing?

---

[30] Where it is a public official who is bribed by a defendant, then a claimant *may* be able to establish that the defendant is liable for participating in the tort of misfeasance in public office. But whilst this possibility may provide a satisfactory solution in *some* cases, it clearly cannot cover all cases where a defendant gains an unfair advantage over the claimant through bribery of third parties. In *Crofter Hand Woven Harris Tweed Co v Veitch* [1941] UKHL 2, [1942] AC 435, one of the hypothetical cases that seems to have caused some concern amongst members of the House of Lords involved a defendant who offered a payment to a trade union if its members would obstruct a claimant's business.

[31] *Constantin Medien AG v Ecclestone* [2014] EWHC 387 (Ch).

[32] *OBG* (n 1) [47], quoted by Newey J at [2014] EWHC 387 (Ch) [322]. A further problem in bribery cases is that under Lord Hoffmann's formulation, the unlawful means must be unlawful vis-a-vis the person whose actions are affected by them: the tensions caused by this additional restriction on the scope of the tort will be discussed below.

[33] Perhaps a breach of confidence, a breach of contract or a wrongful publication of private information.

One suspicion that should be openly confronted is that there is no good reason for the new limit and it is simply an unjustifiable residue of the 'interference with contract' era. During this period, a tort of 'interference with contract' was thought to exist and to be related to the tort of procuring breach of contract. In these circumstances, analysis of the bootlegger situation focused on the effect of the defendant's unlawful behaviour on the exclusive licence between the artist and the record company—this was the only *contract* that might possibly have been *interfered* with. And in the circumstances, someone inclined not to impose liability could hang that conclusion on the argument that the type of interference was not 'close enough' to the procuring of a breach.[34] As noted above, however, in Lord Hoffmann's scheme, the unlawful means tort is not a relative of procuring breach of contract and liability under it does not depend on interference with performance of any contract; many of the paradigm cases involve unlawful means that prevent new contracts being made, for example, by scaring off potential customers.[35] Is there some *other* reason for attaching importance to the *effect* of the unlawful means on the third party?

One justification that might be suggested is that where D's use of unlawful means interferes with T's ability to make his or her own decision as to whether to deal with C and to act in accordance with those decisions, then the effect of D's behaviour is worse from some significant perspective than if D simply reduces the benefit that C will receive from his or her relationship with T. But it is not self-evident in what way it is *worse*. For instance, suppose that D threatens T with a civil wrong which, had the threat been carried out, would *not* have restricted T's liberty, in order to get T to act to C's detriment. (This general description would cover D *threatening* T, the soprano, that he will publish the discreditable private information unless she exercises her right to terminate her engagement to sing for C.) It is hard to identify any way in which using a threat to coerce T into terminating the engagement would be 'worse' for C than the consequence of D immediately publishing the information so as to render his expectation valueless.

A second possible candidate as a justification for the limit might be that in many of the cases where it is *not* satisfied, the harm to C will have been caused by a free choice made either by T or some further party, such as those of C's potential customers who will elect to purchase bootlegged recordings or refuse to buy tickets to hear illiberal sopranos. Perhaps it can be contended that where C has been injured by another person's *sufficiently free* choice, C has less of a basis for complaint, even if D has used 'unlawful means' in order to influence that choice. But three problems face this candidate.

---

[34] Clearly, the production of unauthorised recordings by a bootlegger did not interfere with the artist's ability to perform any of the obligations he or she owed to the record company under the contract.

[35] *Garret v Taylor* (1620) Cro Jac 567, 79 ER 485 (KB); *Tarleton v M'Gawley* (1794) Peake 270, 170 ER 153 (NP).

First, within the law of torts generally, another person's *free* choice will *not* preclude a defendant from being held responsible for the consequence of that choice if he or she *intended* to bring about such a choice.[36] Second, in some situations the civil law will have established that the means used by D are 'unlawful means' partly in order to limit opportunities for such *free* choices. For example, one of the reasons why it is unlawful to publish private information is to restrict the freedom of others to choose (freely) to discriminate against the person who the information is about. Third, the argument cannot provide a *complete* justification because *not* all of the situations where the new limit precludes liability involve free choices. For example, where D has contracted with T that he will supply a tool to X, X needs the tool in order to benefit C, and D breaks his contract with T in order to harm C, then the harm to C will not have been a result of any *free* choice by either T or X.

This third problem reveals that the new limit will leave a lacuna: when the civil law is securing a person's capacity to achieve his or her goals, it goes beyond securing merely his or her *freedom of action*, so the new limit will mean that there is no liability in some cases where a defendant has caused loss to a claimant by using unlawful means to diminish a third person's legally protected capacity to achieve his or her goal of benefiting the claimant. Ironically, one of the cases Lord Hoffmann discussed in *OBG* probably falls within this lacuna. In *GWK Ltd v Dunlop Rubber Co Ltd*,[37] which Lord Hoffmann described as 'a good example of intentionally causing loss by unlawful means',[38] GWK Ltd, a car manufacturer, agreed that its cars should be fitted and sold with tyres manufactured by Associated Rubber Manufacturers Ltd unless the customer requested otherwise and impliedly agreed that they should be displayed with such tyres at motor shows.[39] The claims against Dunlop arose from that company's employees substituting the tyres on two GWK Ltd cars at the Scottish Motor Show in November 1924. The cars, which belonged to GWK Ltd, had been sent to Scotland to appear on the stand of an Edinburgh motor dealer, and there was evidence that this dealer had agreed to the substitution in exchange for a credit rebate note from Dunlop.[40] From these facts, we can see that GWK Ltd's *capacity* to confer the intended benefit on ARM Ltd depended on more than its own

---

[36] This is the position in, for example, the tort of procuring a breach of contract.

[37] *GWK Ltd v Dunlop Rubber Co Ltd* (1926) 42 TLR 376 (KB).

[38] *OBG* (n 1) [24].

[39] The two companies do not seem to have been unconnected, in that the Managing Director and Chairman of ARM Ltd was also the Chairman of GWK Ltd, and there was mention during the trial of ARM Ltd having lent money to GWK Ltd.

[40] Lord Hewart LCJ was not impressed by the defendants; before giving judgment, he described them as having employed a 'system of contemptible dishonesty, aided and abetted by corruption': 'The Action Against Dunlop's: Judges Comments' *The Times* (London, 28 January 1926) 5, column 4. His reported questioning of the defendant's sub-manager for Edinburgh appears to have focused on the idea that the scheme misled *the public* into believing that GWK Ltd had deliberately selected Dunlop tyres: 'Action Against Dunlops: Alleged Substitution of Tyres' *The Times* (London, 20 January 1926) 5, column 4.

freedom of action; it also depended on its capacity to prevent anyone else interfering with the cars and the tyres even when they were several hundred miles away from anyone whose *actions* would be attributed to GWK Ltd. In 1926, Dunlop was held liable for committing trespass to the goods of GWK Ltd and for maliciously interfering with the contractual rights of ARM Ltd, with the jury awarding £500 for the first tort and £2,000 for the second.[41] But the new limit in Lord Hoffmann's scheme seems capable of embarrassing any attempt to treat ARM Ltd's claim as for the unlawful means tort: GWK's *actions* were not altered by Dunlop's employees, though its property, and hence its legally protected capacity to achieve its goals, was undoubtedly interfered with.

Alongside the difficulties with formulating and justifying the 'interference with liberty' limit, we should note an additional problem arising from the decision of the House of Lords in *Total Network*: how should we deal with a case of conspiracy to cause harm to a claimant by using unlawful means vis-a-vis a third party to whom the claimant is economically linked, but without interfering with that third party's liberty? An example of such a case might be a conspiracy of rival opera promoters to cause harm to C by publishing discreditable private information about T.[42] The *Total Network* case does not expressly address this conundrum. Moreover, portions of the reasoning in it can be deployed to support opposite conclusions; the argument that special limits on tortious liability are required whenever a defendant harms a claimant through the behaviour of an intermediary might be thought to pull against liability for the opera conspirators, since C is not the immediate target of the wrongful publications, whilst the argument that a conspiratorial dimension can compensate for a shortfall with regard to the 'unlawfulness' of the means might be thought to pull the other way.

Given the difficulties surrounding the 'interference with liberty' concept, we should consider whether some alternative device might have fared better. Although Lord Nicholls supported a broader definition of 'unlawful means' in *OBG*, he also sought to limit the scope of the tort in terms of how the means brought about the claimant's harm. Thus, he discussed a case similar to the bootlegging example, where D, a manufacturer, managed to gain an advantage over a rival by using a patented innovation in its manufacturing process without paying any licence fee to T, the owner of the

---

[41] Using a simple RPI calculator, £2,000 in 1926 can be treated as equivalent to just over £100,000 in 2014. See LH Officer and SH Williamson, 'Five Ways to Compute the Relative Value of a UK Pound Amount, 1270 to Present' www.measuringworth.com/ukcompare. The 1923 GWK models cost £295 for a four-seater and £285 for a two-seater.

[42] The claimant in *Lonrho v Fayed* (n 28) also alleged a conspiracy to use unlawful means, but the dispute as to whether this should be struck out, which eventually reached the House of Lords, turned on whether the conspirators had to be shown to have the predominant purpose of injuring the claimant: see [1992] 1 AC 448 (HL).

patent,[43] and stated that one reason why D would avoid liability here was because C, the disadvantaged rival, would not have been 'harmed through the instrumentality of a third party'.[44] He also discussed a hypothetical case involving a courier company that gained an advantage over its rivals by committing road traffic offences, such as by speeding and running red lights, which Lord Walker suggested was another case where the 'instrumentality' concept could prevent liability.[45] It is not immediately clear, however, why anyone should concede that the manufacturer's and the courier company's wrongdoing do not cause harm to their rivals through the *instrumentality* of the customers who they succeed in diverting from the claimants.[46] So far as the unlawful acts *changed the expected behaviour* of the claimants' potential customers, and the defendants committed those acts with the intention of harming their rivals, it is not easy to see why the potential customers are less of an *instrument* than they would have been if the defendants were threatening them with violence or property damage for proposing to trade with the claimants. Why is a person who is threatened unless he or she ceases dealing with the claimant more of an 'instrument' than a person who is enticed away by an attractive offer?

This is not to deny that there are cases where it can be argued that there should be no liability because the *unlawfulness* of the means is *irrelevant* to their *effectiveness* as a means of damaging the claimant. This description might cover cases such as that mentioned earlier where D trespasses on T's land in order to get him to listen to persuasive advice about avoiding future dealing with C: the trespass may provide D with the opportunity to cause damage to C through advising T, but it is not the trespass which makes the advice effective qua advice. However, neither the patent nor the courier case involves similarly *irrelevant* unlawfulness; in each it is the unlawful behaviour that allows D to make an offer to T that is more attractive than C's. That said, we might predict that in the real world it would frequently be very difficult to determine whether a manufacturer's product was purchased because of its price being lower than what it would have been in the absence of patent infringement, or whether a courier's business would have fallen away if its delivery drivers had kept to the speed limit. Thus, in such cases, it seems plausible that the practical cost of investigating the relevant questions would be unattractively high when compared to the potential advantages

---

[43] *OBG* (n 1) [157].

[44] ibid [159].

[45] ibid [160]. Lord Walker discussed a pizza delivery company in place of a courier, but attributed the no-liability result to the 'instrumentality' device: [266] and [268]. Lord Nicholls, however, did not expressly state that it would be the 'instrumentality' device that prevented liability in the courier case; instead, he explained that: 'The couriers' criminal conduct is not an offence committed against the rival company in any realistic sense of that expression.'

[46] Perhaps the 'instrumentality' also has to be the victim of the wrong?

of defining the civil law wrong in such a nuanced way. Similarly, we might want to be more cautious when designing rules that could 'chill' innovations by defendants eager to reduce their manufacturing costs or improve their communication with the public than rules focused on defendants inclined to resort to intimidation, deceit or physical interference with persons or property. If such arguments are valid, then they could lend support to using a device that excludes from the scope of the tort methods of harming the claimant that work in particular ways, such as by allowing the defendant to reduce its product price or to increase the attractiveness of its offer, rather than a device that attempts to identify *directly* whether the unlawfulness was *irrelevant* to the effectiveness of the means.

Do the difficulties with clarifying and explaining the new 'interference with liberty' concept mean that the device should not have been adopted so as to save the bootlegger from liability? One reason why the bootlegger ought not to be held liable to the claimant record company is because Parliament, when it devised a scheme to protect copyright, consciously chose not to grant new civil rights to those with only a licence to exploit; thus, it might be thought to subvert the intentions of Parliament to allow a general economic tort to provide such a civil right.[47] This reason, however, could have been addressed without a general limit on how the unlawful means causes the harm; the bootlegger could have been saved from liability by a special exception to the general tort focused on this specific reason.

In summary, I have identified some concerns arising from the inclusion of the 'interference with liberty' limit within Lord Hoffmann's scheme: it appears to exclude some unlawful methods without a good justification for doing so, lacks clarity and is non-transparent (in the sense that it does not openly explain its own existence). But I have not recommended either removal of the limit without replacement or the adoption of the rival 'instrumentality' device. Instead, I have formulated a cautious case in favour of narrower exclusions from liability, focused on identifying: (i) situations where the illegality is irrelevant to the effectiveness of the means; (ii) situations where it would be too costly, or otherwise contrary to good public policy, to investigate how far, if at all, the illegality was significant to the effectiveness of the means; and (iii) situations where the creation of tort liability would be inconsistent with Parliament's intentions.

B. Means that are Unlawful vis-a-vis Someone Other than the Third Party

I noted above that a further problem in bribery cases is that under Lord Hoffmann's formulation, the unlawful means must be unlawful vis-a-vis the

---

[47] Lord Nicholls invoked this explanation in *OBG* (n 1) [157].

person whose actions are affected by them.[48] This requirement also has the potential to restrict liability for the tort of three-party intimidation in a way that demands explanation; thus, D will commit the tort if he threatens to injure T if he fails to act in a way that will cause loss to C, but if he instead threatens to injure T's spouse, G, then his scheme will fall outside the tort; carrying out the latter threat would be a civil wrong to G, but it is not G's actions that are interfered with.[49] Can arguments to justify this limit be identified?

A strong argument against the limit is that it imports into the three-party unlawful means tort an artificial insistence on the insularity of individuals that civil law uses to serve purposes that are relevant primarily in a different context. Thus, tort law insists that deliberately breaking G's leg is a tort to G and not to G's spouse or children or employer, and consequently ignores most of the ways in which G's welfare is linked to that of other people, because this self-imposed myopia avoids the complexities that would flow from a multiplicity of actions, channels claims efficiently and reduces the risks of over-deterrence. But none of these reasons provides a good justification for continuing to treat individuals as insular when considering what means a defendant should be prohibited from using in order to persuade one individual to act to the detriment of another.

Someone inclined to impose liability on D for loss he intentionally coerces T into inflicting on C by threatening to injure T's spouse, or indeed on D for loss he persuades T to inflict on C by bribing him with the promise of battering his worst enemy, might be tempted to achieve these ends by the simple expedient of stipulating that unlawful means do not have to be unlawful vis-a-vis the person whose actions are affected. Doing this, however, might be thought to jeopardise the goal of avoiding liability in the bootlegger situation; in that situation, the *actions* of the potential purchasers of the claimant's official recordings may be affected (they choose to buy the bootlegged recordings instead) by the defendant's use of means which are unlawful vis-a-vis the copyright holder. But at the end of the previous section, I noted that the law could use other methods to protect the bootlegger from liability. With respect, I would contend that given the availability of those other methods, it was an unnecessary and unjustifiable oversimplification to insist that the unlawful means must be unlawful vis-a-vis the person whose freedom of action is interfered with. This limit unnecessarily restricts the capacity of the tort to address forms of outrageous behaviour

---

[48] In *some* bribery cases, it may be possible to circumvent the limit by switching focus onto the fact that paying a bribe to T may have involved the 'unlawful means' of procuring a breach of contract between T and his or her employer; thus, liability will turn on whether *this* wrong interfered with *the employer's* liberty of action vis-a-vis C.

[49] The problem is not confined to threats: suppose that D deliberately injures T's spouse, with the intention of bringing about a situation where T ceases to perform tasks that benefit C, but provides care for his spouse instead.

(eg, threatening to harm the spouses of a rival's potential customers) that can be defined relatively clearly and should obviously be prohibited.

C. Unlawful Means

I noted above that the majority in *OBG* accepted Lord Hoffmann's opinion that liability under the unlawful means tort should only be imposed where D used means which amounted to a civil wrong[50] against T, or would have amounted to an actionable civil wrong if T had suffered damage, with that alternative treated as extending to situations where D had threatened to commit acts that would have amounted to a civil wrong to T, but had not had to go through with the threat because T had 'caved in'. This stipulation as to what can count as 'unlawful means' excited immediate dissent from Lord Nicholls, an expression of uncertainty from Lord Walker and has been jeopardised through being unconvincingly distinguished by the House of Lords in the course of elucidating the tort of conspiracy to cause loss by unlawful means in the *Total Network* case.[51] In the aftermath of the latter, Hazel Carty complained that 'the *Total* decision has arguably undermined the prospect for clarity that *OBG* represented, and thrown the economic torts back into the mess in which they were before *OBG*'.[52]

Was Lord Hoffmann's definition of 'unlawful means' justifiable? Or is the best that can be said in its favour that it confines the scope of the tort *more narrowly* than the minority's definition would have done, and hence preserves more freedom for economic actors to compete and tussle without fear of civil liability? A first step towards answers is to survey briefly the types of case which might be decided differently using a broader interpretation of 'unlawful means'. In dissent, Lord Nicholls expressly mentioned that his broader definition would sometimes impose liability for the commission of crimes and threats to commit them. A broader definition could also hold *public* defendants liable more frequently, where their acts were unlawful (ultra vires) as a matter of public law. Relatedly, it might impose liability after a breach of a statutory duty that Parliament created without any sanction (either criminal or civil).

Against the background of this survey, it may be helpful to consider why the general economic tort is limited by a requirement of 'unlawful means' at all. I suggest that liability depends on the use of 'unlawful means' because a majority of the House of Lords in *Allen v Flood*[53] decided against regulating

---

[50] For discussion of whether equitable wrongs should be treated as 'civil wrongs' for these purposes, see Carty (n 2) 87–88.
[51] *Total Network* (n 3).
[52] H Carty, 'The Economic Torts in the 21st Century' (2008) 124 *LQR* 641, 642.
[53] *Allen v Flood* (n 11).

behaviour that was intended to cause economic harm to others through evaluation of the potential defendant's reasons for pursuing such a course; instead, they decided to base liability around a catalogue of 'methods' that defendants are prohibited from deploying in order to cause loss to claimants on pain of civil liability. Ideally, such a catalogue would include all 'methods that a defendant should be prohibited from using in order to cause (economic) harm to the claimant, on pain of incurring civil liability' and nothing else. But to leave judges free to compile such a catalogue and to decide whether every contentious innovation in the techniques of competition or protest should be added to it might create a dangerous degree of uncertainty and give judges an undesirable responsibility for developing controversial law that will have a direct effect on the distribution of wealth and power. Hence the attraction of incorporating some pre-existing catalogue of 'unlawful means' into the general economic tort; transplanting a pre-existing catalogue will enhance certainty and reduce the political exposure of the judiciary. From this perspective, the 'unlawful means' requirement serves as a certainty-enhancing surrogate for a bespoke catalogue of 'methods that a defendant should not be permitted to use in order to cause (economic) harm to the claimant on pain of civil liability'.

From this perspective, tension will principally arise where a particular form of behaviour is classified as 'unlawful' in the selected pre-existing catalogue, but for reasons that have nothing to do with how the defendant should have been behaving with regard to the claimant's interests. For instance, it is an offence under section 1 of the Wildlife and Countryside Act 1981 to damage or destroy the nest of any wild bird while that nest is in use or being built. Suppose that in a particular tourist destination, two cafés, belonging to C and D respectively, face each other across the main street. Suppose also that one spring, C's café obtains an unexpected advantage over its rival through the fact that a rare bird builds its nest on the wall of D's building, and this nest can best be observed from the upstairs windows in C's café. If D destroys the nest in order to re-level the 'playing field', then he will, of course, have committed a crime and will have done so in order to reduce C's takings and boost his own. But clearly the reason that it is a crime to destroy the nest of a wild bird is not because anyone thinks that nest destruction should be defined as an unfair method of competition between café proprietors. If D discovered that tourists were selecting C's café because it provided such a good vantage point from which to watch the amusing antics of his (D's) pet cockatoo, no one would suggest it was unfair competition for him to get rid of the bird. So it might be thought to be an arbitrary windfall for C if he could establish that it is a private law wrong to his business interests for a rival to destroy the nest of a bird simply because, fortuitously, it had been protected in order to advance environmental interests. A parallel point can be made about preventing private liability in tort being based on behaviour that has only been classified as unlawful by Parliament for the purposes of public law, for instance, to enhance democratic accountability or transparency rather than the business interests of a claimant,[54] or behaviour that has only been classified as unlawful by Parliament as a gesture.

A related argument in favour of Lord Hoffmann's definition is that it prevents statutory provisions that were not intended by Parliament to create new civil entitlements from being used as an element in establishing a new civil entitlement. For example, section 224(3) of the Town and Country Planning Act 1990 makes it a criminal offence to display many types of advertisement without the consent of the local planning authority. However, it is far from clear that Parliament intended this provision to create an opportunity for one business to sue another that intentionally lured potential customers away from it by means of criminal fly-posting. Parliament may often draft criminal offences in a particular way because it expects there to be a prosecutorial discretion as to whether and when they are enforced and because it has a power to specify the appropriate sanction. If such offences are transplanted into tort law as potential gateways to liability, then these safeguards will be circumvented. And this argument based on parliamentary intentions can be reinforced by highlighting that Lord Hoffmann's position avoids the oddity of statutory wrongs becoming elements in the three-party unlawful means tort even when they cannot be used *directly* as the basis for a civil claim for breach of statutory duty.

There are passages in *Total Network* which suggest that these objections can be neutralised by only allowing *some* criminal offences to constitute 'unlawful means'. For example, Lord Mance emphasised that the particular criminal offence in *Total Network*—cheating the public revenue—was 'integrally related' to the claimant, Her Majesty's Revenue and Customs, 'and recognised specifically to protect it from such injury'. And he treated these elements as delimiting the liability for conspiracy to use unlawful means which the House was recognising.[55] Clearly, a similar limit on when crimes can constitute unlawful means for the purposes of the unlawful means tort would ensure that liability could rarely be based on such reasoning; the café owner could not demonstrate that nest protection legislation was 'recognised specifically' to protect business interests such as his, and the rival of the patent-infringing manufacturer would also probably fail. It is unclear, however, whether a majority of the House of Lords supported Lord Mance's narrow approach. In an opaque passage, Lord Walker stated that he accepted that 'the sort of considerations relevant to determining whether a breach of statutory duty is actionable in a civil suit ... may well overlap,

---

[54] Clearly, other tort judgments of Lord Hoffmann have also addressed the importance of distinguishing between public law unlawfulness and tort liability: see, eg, *Stovin v Wise* [1996] UKHL 15, [1996] AC 923; *O'Rourke v Camden* [1997] UKHL 24, [1998] AC 188 (HL).

[55] *Total Network* (n 3) [124]. See also Lord Nicholls in *OBG* (n 1) [161].

or even occasionally coincide with, the issue of unlawful means in the tort of conspiracy',[56] but he did not explain how this reasoning related to his more general holding that 'criminal conduct (at common law or by statute) can constitute unlawful means, provided that it is indeed the means'.[57] In *OBG* itself, Lord Nicholls stated that a claimant would not be permitted to treat a statutory crime as 'unlawful means' for the purposes of the tort if the resultant tort liability would be 'inconsistent with the statutory scheme' and also suggested that the tort might only be available where the crime was committed against the claimant.[58] However, he did not explain why a *criminal offence* must be committed against *the claimant* in order to establish the tort, whilst Lord Hoffmann's scheme insisted that a civil wrong must be committed against *the third party* whose actions were influenced.[59] Yet, if the objections are neutralised in some such way, then there will be a price to be paid by way of a reduction in certainty—only *some* criminal offences will constitute 'unlawful means', but there will be scope to argue about which.[60] Moreover, if the dividing line is not to be between 'those statutory provisions that Parliament intended to create new private rights' and others, then it is likely to be a boundary that depends on judicial assessment of which statutory provisions it would be good public policy to utilise as components in civil liability, and there must be scope to doubt whether the necessary decisions will be predictable or transparent. These costs must be assessed against the background of the primary reasons for incorporating a pre-existing list of 'unlawful means' rather than compiling a bespoke catalogue of 'prohibited methods': to enhance predictability and reduce the political exposure of the judiciary.

If a broader definition of 'unlawful means' had been adopted in the *OBG* case, then uncertainty would not have been confined to three-party cases; a difficult issue would also have arisen with regard to two-party cases. If it became a tort for D to commit a crime in order to prevent C's potential customers from dealing with C, then should it also be a crime for D to commit crimes against C directly, with the intention of interfering with his business? For example,

---

[56] *Total Network* (n 3) [96] (citation of *Cutler v Wandsworth Stadium Ltd* [1949] AC 398 (HL) omitted). The passage is obscure since the 'considerations relevant to determining whether a breach of statutory duty is actionable in a civil suit' are those factors which help a court to determine whether Parliament intended the statutory provision to create new *civil law* rights, whilst the general thrust of the judgment is that a conspiracy to use unlawful means can be actionable even when the unlawful means on their own did not involve any violation of civil law rights.

[57] *Total Network* (n 3) [95].

[58] ibid [157] and [160].

[59] The fact that Lord Nicholls did not draw attention to this distinction means that there is scope to doubt whether he *intended* to propose that the crime must be against *the claimant*.

[60] No doubt, it will remain the case that the offence of *perjury* cannot be relied on as the 'unlawful means' in an action for conspiracy to use unlawful means: *Marrian v Vibart* [1963] 1 QB 528 (CA).

should it be considered a tort for D to display an abusive message (likely to cause distress to C) whilst C is working in public, with the intention of interfering with her business?[61] If it is an actionable wrong for D to abuse T in public so as to persuade T to stop trading with C, it might seem 'passing strange' if it was not also an actionable wrong for D to do the same thing to C directly as a way of interfering with the same business. Lord Nicholls' response to a similar argument in *OBG* was to suggest that the relevant two-party wrong should exist, at least where the claimant's 'economic interests had been deliberately injured by a crime committed against him by the defendant'.[62] But this view is in tension with some of the reasoning subsequently relied on in *Total Network*: if intention to cause harm to a claimant is enough to make the use of unlawful means civilly actionable even without that additional element of 'conspiracy', then the tort of conspiracy to use unlawful means becomes tautologous; the conspirators can be held liable as joint participants in the newly recognised two-party civil wrong.[63] Moreover, if D committing a crime against C in order to interfere with C's business is an actionable civil wrong against C, then this will undermine the way in which the *OBG* case was distinguished in *Total Network*:[64] that distinction depended on a narrower sense of unlawful means being appropriate in three-party cases, but recognition of an extended two-party civil wrong will indirectly create a situation where the difference evaporates: the extended two-party *civil wrong* will become available to *satisfy* the three-party wrong's narrow limit.[65]

Some theorists insist that there is a further, stronger reason for accepting that for the purposes of the unlawful means tort, 'unlawful means' must be confined to means that are civilly actionable. They maintain that it is essential to the nature of the tort that the means should be such as might support a civil action by the third party because the unlawful means tort operates as a 'privity extension': the third party has a civil right that the defendant should not behave in a particular way, but in circumstances where the defendant acts in that way in order to inflict harm on the claimant, intentionally, it is

---

[61] This behaviour is intended to amount to a criminal offence under the Public Order Act 1986, s 5 (as amended).

[62] *OBG* (n 1) [161].

[63] A fundamental element in the reasoning in *Total Network* (n 3) was that the tort of conspiracy to use unlawful means is not simply a sub-category of general secondary liability for a civil wrong that has acquired a separate label.

[64] *Total Network* (n 3) [43] (per Lord Hope), [99] (per Lord Walker) and [124] (per Lord Mance).

[65] An illustration may help. Suppose that D abuses T in public (a crime) to prevent her from dealing with C. In *Total Network* (n 3), it was said that limiting 'unlawful means' to civil wrongs (and not crimes) in *OBG* was explained by the special need for narrow limits in three-party cases. But if D abusing T in public (a crime) with the intention of interfering with *her* business is a two-party *civil wrong* to T, then this *civil* wrong will *satisfy* the special narrow limit and complete a three-party tort to C where D is seeking to interfere with T's business *as a means* of harming C.

justifiable to permit the claimant to sue for the violation of the third party's right.[66] This theory seems particularly attractive where the defendant commits the wrong without inflicting any damage on the third party, since in such a case it appears as if the private law claim is transferred from the third party to the claimant, the true victim in the circumstances. But the unlawful means wrong is not, of course, only available in situations where there seems to have been such a 'transfer'; in many cases where a defendant commits a wrong to the third party as a means of preventing his or her trade with the claimant, there will be damage to both the third party and the claimant. Thus, in such cases the unlawful means tort is additional to the third party's potential claims. For example, where D shoots a hole in T's canoe to prevent him from trading with C, C's claim for his economic losses will be supplementary to T's claim for the repair costs. Further, in cases of three-party intimidation, where the defendant has only had to threaten to commit the wrong to the third party, the notion of a claim being 'transferred' seems attenuated; the right that the defendant threatened will not have actually been violated. For example, if D threatens to burn T's house down unless T ceases to trade with C, it is artificial to assert that C's claim for the profits he would have made through such trade is somehow the 'transfer' of a claim based on violation of a right to the integrity of real property. In summary, the description of the unlawful means tort as a 'privity extension' seems more like a rhetorical device to disguise the inconsistency between the tort and a popular grand theory, as opposed to a justification for the tort.[67]

What arguments can be raised against Lord Hoffmann's definition? In discussing crimes as potential 'unlawful means', Lord Nicholls primarily invokes a comparison:

> In seeking to distinguish between acceptable and unacceptable conduct it would be passing strange that a breach of contract should be proscribed but not a crime.[68]

This draws its strength from the premise that behaviour which is classified as criminal is *more seriously wrongful* than behaviour which is primarily dealt with in private law. But, with respect, this exaggerates the significance that Parliament attaches to criminalisation when seeking to exert influence through legislation in a wide range of spheres[69] and downplays the wrongfulness of *intentionally* violating private law rights in order to achieve an

---

[66] See Stevens (n 18) 188–89.

[67] Adoption of the 'privity extension' theory would also make it much harder for the law to deal in a satisfactory way with cases where the means used were not unlawful vis-a-vis the person whose actions were interfered with, for example, D threatening T that if he did not harm C, then his spouse would be battered.

[68] *OBG* (n 1) [152].

[69] The number of criminal offences created in the previous 15 years became a matter of political comment in the lead-up to the 2010 general election; in September 2008, the claim that over 3600 offences had been created since May 1997 was widely reported. See, eg, N Morris, 'More than 3,600 New Offences under Labour' *The Independent* (4 September 2008) 6.

ulterior goal.[70] Moreover, the pivotal question is not simply whether the defendant's behaviour can be castigated as *unacceptable* from a general social perspective, but whether the claimant can plausibly describe it as such an unacceptable method of interfering with his or her expectations that he or she ought to be entitled to make a private claim.

  I have identified two arguments in favour of the definition of 'unlawful means' used in Lord Hoffmann's scheme: (1) it avoids the problem of statutory provisions being put to uses that Parliament did not intend; (2) it is more certain and less politically exposed than a device that must distinguish between different crimes. But neither of these arguments points decisively and positively in favour of defining 'unlawful means' solely in terms of 'civil wrongs'.

  Someone seeking to develop a positive argument in support of Lord Hoffmann's definition might begin by sketching out what a legislator making a fresh start ought to include in a catalogue of 'methods that a defendant should be prohibited from using on a claimant's potential customers, employees and suppliers in order to cause (economic) harm to the claimant, on pain of incurring civil liability to the claimant'. In a legal system that is based around private entitlements and individual autonomy, I suggest that such a catalogue might be built around two lists: (1) methods that wrongfully deprive a potential customer, employee or supplier of the resources that the law secures *to them* as those available for use in pursuing their goals; and (2) methods that are incompatible with the freedom of potential customers, employees and suppliers to select their own goals. Building on this, list (1) might include actionable civil wrongs, particularly those that protect person, property and contractual entitlements. However, it might also extend to methods that wrongly deprive potential customers, employees or suppliers of *common goods* that are secured to all, such as access to public highways. List (2) would include prohibited methods of coercion and misleading, and perhaps more exotic methods such as hypnotism. Whilst an elaboration of this sketch might coincide with Lord Hoffmann's definition to a considerable extent, there is scope to doubt whether either respect for parliamentary intentions or a desire for certainty demanded *such* simplicity. For example, it is arguable that the forms of coercion on list (2) could be extended beyond threats to commit civil wrongs without jeopardising certainty. Just as the crime of blackmail extends to cover threats to do things that it would not be unlawful to do, the civil law of wrongs might have good reason to prohibit use of a broader range of threats than simply those which threaten to destroy secure private resources.[71]

---

[70] Such 'calculated' civil wrongdoing has frequently been identified as more serious than quotidian negligence and hence as potentially justifying *punitive* damages.

[71] The breadth of the doctrine of economic duress may also support this proposition.

D. Summary

Lord Hoffmann's formulation of the unlawful means tort in *OBG* has been praised as narrow, relatively clear and capable of defending the appropriate conclusions reached in leading cases.[72] But while I agree with each of those plaudits, I have argued that there is a lack of clarity in the 'interference with liberty' concept and that the device may be unduly limiting. Moreover, I have suggested that the tort was oversimplified, and hence prevented from dealing with some forms of excessive behaviour, through the insistence that the unlawful means must be unlawful vis-a-vis the party whose actions are affected and the stipulation that only a threat of an actionable civil wrong can constitute prohibited coercion.

IV. PROCURING A BREACH OF CONTRACT

A. Secondary Liability

I reported above that Lord Hoffmann's scheme preserved the tort of procuring breach of contract and explained its scope on the basis that it imposes secondary, or accessory, liability for the contract-breaker's breach of contract. This vision of the tort's function contradicts an alternative account,[73] which urged that contracts should be treated as valuable devices that persons should avoid knowingly 'damaging' in defined ways unless they have a justification for doing so, and impliedly rejects the contention that the tort ought never to have been recognised at all. How convincing is the case for the secondary liability model?

A starting point here might be that the most obvious justification for imposing secondary liability for civil wrongs—that without it, people might be able to avoid liability by arranging for others (who might be difficult to trace or without resources) to commit wrongs on their behalf—cannot be extended to explain the existence of secondary liability for *breaches of contract*. Only a party to the contract can break it, and consequently someone who procures a breach will usually not have been capable of breaking the

---

[72] Most academic responses praised the decision, whilst identifying residual concerns. According to H Carty, '*OBG v Allan*: The House of Lords Shapes the Economic Torts and Explores Commercial Confidences and Image Rights' (2007) 15 *Torts Law Journal* 283, 293, the decision deserved 'two cheers'. See also G Chan, 'Of Unities and Disunities in Economic Torts: *OBG, Douglas and Mainstream*' (2008) 19 *King's Law Journal* 158; B Ong, 'Two Tripartite Economic Torts' (2008) 8 *Journal of Business Law* 723; J Thomson, 'Redrawing the Landscape of the Economic Wrongs' (2008) 12 *Edinburgh Law Review* 267.

[73] For a defence of this account, see R Bagshaw, 'Inducing Breach of Contract' in J Horder (ed), *Oxford Essays in Jurisprudence, Fourth Series* (Oxford, Oxford University Press, 2000) 131.

contract himself or herself. Of course, it can be argued that people should be liable for persuading others to commit wrongs even if they could not have committed those wrongs themselves. But the force of this argument is likely to depend on the significance, within the rationale for the wrong, of the element that makes it impossible for the procuring defendant to have committed the tort. An analogy may assist here: if a private citizen persuades a public official to abuse his or her powers so as to harm the claimant, then it is a difficult question whether the citizen should be held secondarily liable for misfeasance in public office because the citizen is not a public official. On one view, the misfeasance tort recognises a special responsibility of those who have accepted public office, and thus its existence does not necessarily support the imposition of accessory liability on private citizens, who have not accepted any special office. An alternative view, however, is that because it is so important that public officials do not abuse their powers, it is appropriate to recognise a duty of private citizens not to encourage officials to behave corruptly. Do the reasons why *only* a party to a contract commits a primary wrong by breaking it and disappointing the other party's expectations weigh against the proposal that there should be secondary liability on those who encourage such behaviour?

Lord Hoffmann states that: '[T]he real question which has to be asked in [a procuring breach case is] did the defendant's acts of encouragement, threat, persuasion and so forth have a *sufficient causal connection* with the breach by the contracting party to attract accessory liability?'[74] But the word 'sufficient' needs careful attention. It is clear that the degree to which the defendant can be said to have *caused* the breach cannot be the key to accessory liability. There are many circumstances in which a defendant can act so as to make a breach inevitable which will not trigger liability, even if the defendant acts in this way with the intention of bringing about a breach, and similarly liability *may well* be imposed even when a defendant's act has not increased the likelihood of a breach occurring.[75] For example, if X intends to give a painting to T and, in anticipation, T has contracted to sell it to C, then D will not be liable to C for procuring a breach of this contract if he acquires the painting from X by offering him an outrageous price and then refuses to supply it to T, even if his goal throughout is to ensure that T breaks his contract.

Andrew Simester and Winnie Chan suggest that for D to procure T to break a contract with C is a wrong to C because 'D subverts the peremptory nature of [T]'s contractual promise, something to which [C] has a beneficial

---

[74] *OBG* (n 1) [36] (emphasis added).
[75] This last proposition reflects the fact that D's *persuasion* may well *cause* T's breach of contract even if T was already aware of other strong reasons for breaking the contract and even if D simply pre-empted someone else's identical persuasion. (Throughout this section, I assume that T has breached a contract with C, and C is claiming that D is liable in tort for having procured this breach.)

right'.[76] By this they mean that D persuades T to treat his or her promise as less than a promise and to give it less than 'pre-emptive status in [his or her] reasoning'.[77] But at first glance this is an unusual justification for a private law wrong, since, from the disappointed claimant's perspective, it probably makes little difference what rational processes the contract-breaker went through before breaking the contract. Moreover, the liability described by Lord Hoffmann in *OBG* did not depend on showing that the contract-breaker had a different *attitude* to contractual promises before the defendant's intervention. But the argument finds a reason for secondary liability in the harm done to the public interest, through damage to the 'institution of promising', when a defendant encourages or *reinforces* a promisor's inappropriate thinking about promises.

If Simester and Chan's suggestion is correct,[78] however, then there is no obvious reason for thinking that the scope of accessory liability for breach of contract should match the scope of accessory liability for other civil wrongs. Why would the appropriate scope of accessory liability for, say, false imprisonment consist of all those forms of behaviour that might potentially do sufficient damage to the 'institution of promising' if deployed against a promisor with the intention of causing a breach of contract? This can be illustrated by considering how Simester and Chan's rationale might be used to clarify the appropriate scope of the procuring breach tort. For instance, their rationale suggests that a defendant should not be held liable for the procuring tort if he engineers a breach by tricking a party, perhaps by telling the soprano that her engagement at Her Majesty's Theatre will not start for another month.[79] Similarly, it ought not to be actionable for a defendant to take advantage of a promisor's momentary forgetfulness or ignorance about the terms of a contract in order to persuade her to act in some way that will make it impossible (or extremely difficult) for her to perform at a later date.[80] And instances of making possible, or facilitating,

---

[76] AP Simester and WMF Chan, 'Inducing Breach of Contract: One Tort or Two?' (2004) 63 *Cambridge Law Journal* 132, 152–53.

[77] ibid 151.

[78] Their rationale is more clearly expressed, but probably similar in scope, to that supported by Carty (n 2) ch 3, who requires 'corruption of the claimant's contract partner' (at 61) and quotes (at 56), with apparent approval, the opinion of Robert Stevens that 'The essence of the tort is that by inducing a voluntary breach the claimant undermines the bond of trust between persons': see Stevens (n 18) 280. Two sentences further on, Stevens cites Simester and Chan (n 76) as consistent with his account.

[79] Liability for the unlawful means tort in these circumstances would depend on both the trickery amounting to 'unlawful means' and the defendant having an intention to injure the claimant. (There may be a significant distinction between intending T to break a contract with C and intending C to suffer harm; sometimes a defendant may honestly believe that C will suffer no harm as a result of a breach.)

[80] Suppose that D knows that T has promised to sell seven Picasso prints to C for a price well below their market value if he ever has to leave his home and go into sheltered accommodation. Suppose also that D discovers that T has forgotten this and in order to prevent C obtaining the prints, he immediately buys them from T.

a breach of contract by a party who has already determined that she wants to do this would perhaps also fall outside the tort.[81] But are we sure that we would want D to avoid joint liability for false imprisonment if he tricked T into imprisoning C, or took advantage of T's forgetfulness to persuade him to perform an act that would make it impossible for him to release C when C wanted to be let out, or made it possible for T to imprison C, in each case with the intention that C should be imprisoned?

Lord Hoffmann does not discuss in any detail the scope of the general civil accessory liability with which he aligns the procuring breach tort.[82] Clearly there is an advantage by way of simplicity in using uniform principles to determine the reach of accessory liability across the full breadth of the civil law. But there are also disadvantages in doing so—preoccupation with uniformity may mean that differences with regard to the costs and practical consequences of extending the principles into each specific context are overlooked. David Howarth has argued that the common law took a wrong turning when it established the procuring breach tort and that, even if it would now be impolitic to abolish it, a defence should be made available whenever it would not be 'fair, just and reasonable' for a defendant to be held liable.[83] His foundational position appears to be that there is insufficient evidence that the benefits of providing protection for contractual expectations beyond the remedies that can be obtained against the party in breach outweigh the costs of doing so,[84] particularly since in some circumstances, it will not be immoral to break contracts or will be efficient to do so.[85] Clearly, such arguments cannot be assessed on their merits if we are committed to recognising uniform principles of accessory liability across the civil law.

---

[81] This might apply in the situation where T asks D to tie her to a chair in order to help her to go through with her plan of not performing her contract to sing at C's theatre.

[82] In *OBG* (n 1) [8] and [36], he invokes 'general principles' to be found in *CBS Songs Ltd v Amstrad Consumer Electronics plc* [1988] UKHL 15, [1988] AC 1013 and *Unilever plc v Chefaro Proprietaries Ltd* [1994] FSR 135 (CA).

[83] D Howarth, 'Against *Lumley* v *Gye*' (2005) 68 MLR 195.

[84] ibid 209–17. At 217, he states: 'Certainty is costly and we might already have enough of it. *Lumley*'s effects seem more to be on the distribution of income and wealth between employers and employees than on the efficiency of the allocation of resources.' The underlying suggestion is that the tort facilitates exploitation and injustice by reducing the power of employees vis-a-vis their employers through impeding the freedom of trade unions to organise strikes.

[85] ibid 217–21. However, he accepts (at 221) that the existence of the tort does not prevent efficient re-negotiation of contracts, but instead influences the way in which the parties will have to settle such new arrangements. To summarise, where T has contracted to do x for C and there are now grounds for thinking that this might be inefficient and that T ought to do x for D instead, with C being paid an amount equal to his or her expectation loss, the existence of the tort may require D to make a proposal to C as well as T. Including C in the re-negotiation may help to ensure that any new arrangements really do produce a surplus, since C will be well-placed to quantify his or her expectation loss accurately. But doing so may also increase transaction costs, principally through allowing C to negotiate for a share of any surplus.

If we seek to determine the *ideal* scope of liability for procuring a breach of contract, what questions ought to be pivotal? One must be whether there is something special about intentionally persuading someone to break a contract *voluntarily* which sufficiently distinguishes it from other forms of behaviour which might intentionally be used to *cause* a breach, such as tricking the promisor, coercing them or providing them with the necessary assistance to break the promise.[86] To address this question, I would propose assessing each potentially actionable form of behaviour against two benchmarks: how far it is appropriate to attach responsibility to a defendant who has used this form of behaviour relative to pre-existing problems with the promisor's capacity to perform and relative to any choices made by the promisor; and whether attaching liability to such behaviour might lead to heavy costs investigating the relevant facts and undue caution on the part of potential tortfeasors. For example, whilst D's refusal to deal with T, or refusal to deal on particular terms or at a particular price might be sufficient to *cause* T to breach a contract with C, the popular view that these forms of behaviour should be outside the scope of the tort[87] might be explained by the fact that where D's refusal is sufficient to cause T's breach, it seems likely that there was a *pre-existing* problem with T's capacity to perform the contract, and an obligation to assist people like T to perform their contracts might be thought to be an undesirable intrusion on autonomy and efficiency, or at least to invite costly inquiries into the justifications for such a refusal. Clearly, analysis of, say, making threats to T to discourage him from performing or taking advantage of his forgetfulness in order to persuade him to do something that will later prevent him from performing a contract would look very different from the perspective of these benchmarks.

B. Summary

I have contended that Lord Hoffmann did not present an irresistible case for treating the tort of procuring breach of contract as an example of accessory liability, with the principles governing that liability identical to those that will be used to determine whether a secondary party is liable for having procured a battery or a libel. Moreover, even if there is some attractive simplicity in the notion that uniform principles of secondary liability apply across

---

[86] Lord Hoffmann expresses the opinion that intentionally causing a party to break a contract by means of a threat can amount to the procuring breach tort: see *OBG* (n 1) [21] and [36]. Although he does not say so expressly, there seems no reason why in this context the threat should have to be to commit a civil wrong. It seems, however, that persuading a party to break a contract by means of a threat to do something that could have been done lawfully *and* would have brought about a breach will establish a defence of justification: *Edwin Hill and Partners v First National Finance Corp* [1989] 1 WLR 225 (CA).

[87] See, eg, Simester and Chan (n 76) 149.

the civil law, difficult decisions must still be made about difficult cases, such as where D intentionally facilitates T's commission of a wrong against C or tricks T into committing such a wrong.

V. CONCLUSION

Any scheme which is designed to enhance certainty across a broad range of factual contexts is likely to require a controversial trade-off between bright-lines and normative defensibility. I have argued, however, that some elements in Lord Hoffmann's scheme unnecessarily oversimplify the general economic torts, and minor modifications would allow them to regulate a broader range of excessive behaviours in a defensible way without a significant reduction in certainty. Of course, an even more flexible and responsive version of the economic torts could also be designed; indeed, this prospect may have appealed to the members of the House of Lords who decided the *Total Network* case. But I share Lord Hoffmann's conviction that predictability is important, particularly in contexts where its absence might diminish innovation, chill protest and expose judges to having regularly to make decisions with immediate consequences for the distribution of wealth and power. *OBG* provides the best foundations on which to build the future of the general economic torts.

6

Salvaging of the Law of Torts

ROBERT STEVENS

I. INTRODUCTION

I SHALL NOT waste the reader's time with flattery. No doubt this work
contains plenty of that. However, when I wrote my first book[1] and
thought whether I would want someone to write a foreword, and if so
who, the only person I asked (or would have asked) was Lord Hoffmann,
a man I only knew through his judicial decisions. The only other plausible
candidates had, rather selfishly, long since died.

Lord Hoffmann made many important contributions to the law of torts.
Severely edited highlights include *Hunter v Canary Wharf Ltd*[2] on nuisance,
Tomlinson v Congleton Borough Council[3] on occupiers' liability, *Transco
plc v Stockport Metropolitan Borough Council*[4] on the rule in *Rylands v
Fletcher*,[5] *White v Chief Constable of South Yorkshire*[6] on nervous shock,
Williams v Natural Life Health Foods Ltd[7] on economic loss and many contributions to the meaning of causation. He managed in *OBG Ltd v Allan*[8]
what had seemed to me to be the impossible task of sorting out the dog's
dinner that the Court of Appeal had made of the economic torts, although
this triumph was subsequently partially undone by the mess that a differently constituted House made of unlawful means conspiracy in *Total Network SL v HMRC*,[9] to which I shall return at the end of this chapter.

Despite carrying the grand title of Professor of Law, I do not hobnob with
members of our ultimate appellate court very often, but I once suggested to
Lord Rodger that Lord Hoffmann's greatest contribution was his achieve-
ment in correcting the terrible mess that the liability of public bodies in

---

[1] R Stevens, *Torts and Rights* (Oxford, Oxford University Press, 2007).
[2] *Hunter v Canary Wharf Ltd* [1997] AC 655 (HL).
[3] *Tomlinson v Congleton Borough Council* [2003] UKHL 47, [2004] 1 AC 46.
[4] *Transco plc v Stockport Metropolitan Borough Council* [2003] UKHL 61, [2004] 2 AC 1.
[5] *Rylands v Fletcher* [1868] LR 3 HL 330.
[6] *White v Chief Constable of South Yorkshire* [1999] AC 455 (HL).
[7] *Williams v Natural Life Health Foods Ltd* [1998] 1 WLR 830 (HL).
[8] *OBG Ltd v Allan* [2007] UKHL 21, [2008] 1 AC 1.
[9] *Total Network SL v HMRC* [2008] UKHL 19, [2008] 1 AC 1174.

tort, particularly for negligence, had become. Lord Rodger enthusiastically agreed. Of particular importance are the judgments in *Stovin v Wise*[10] and *Gorringe v Calderdale Metropolitan Borough Council*.[11]

Now, in the light of what I am going to say, the correctness of those decisions may seem obvious, but that is not how they were perceived at the time. Indeed, *Stovin v Wise*, the pivotal case, was decided by a bare majority, Lords Goff and Jauncey simply agreeing with Lord Hoffmann.

II. PUBLIC BODIES

Dicey's principle of equality of treatment of public bodies and private citizens has two limbs.[12] First—and much the more important of the two—it is basic to the rule of law that real persons who are the agents of public bodies do not acquire any blanket privileges or immunities in carrying out their public duties, something which has been accepted in the common law in relation to local authorities for centuries.[13] At one time, the Crown, unlike local authorities, did have a special immunity from suit, but this has been removed by legislation everywhere in the common law world.[14]

Some special privileges are necessary if state agents are to carry out their functions. So, highway authorities may have a privilege to dig up the road for purposes of repair, thereby creating what would otherwise be a public nuisance, which persons generally do not have.[15] Police officers may be conferred a special privilege, sometimes mistakenly called a power, to stop and search suspects.[16] If there are to be any special privileges or immunities of this kind, then they should in principle be authorised by legislation, as the above examples are, and not by judicial decision.

The second limb of the equality principle is that we do not have greater rights against the state or its agents than we do against persons generally. Again, the legislature may depart from this default position. The largest and most significant departure from the second limb concern those rights we have against the state that it secures for each of us a range of 'human' goods.[17] These rights restrict the state's sovereignty to behave as it pleases. In some jurisdictions they are embodied in a constitution and so may be termed constitutional rights. Sometimes they go under the name of civil or civic rights, labels reflecting the party against whom they are exigible. Over

---

[10] *Stovin v Wise* [1996] AC 923 (HL).

[11] *Gorringe v Calderdale Metropolitan Borough Council* [2004] UKHL 15, [2004] 1 WLR 1057.

[12] AV Dicey, *The Law of the Constitution* (London, Macmillian, 1885) 178.

[13] *Entick v Carrington* (1765) 2 Wils KB 275, 95 ER 807.

[14] In England, Crown Proceedings Act 1947, s 2.

[15] Highways Act 1980.

[16] Police and Criminal Evidence Act 1984, ss 1–23.

[17] Human Rights Act 1998.

recent decades, the more common label has been that of human rights, in order to reflect their supposed universal applicability in all times and places. (Although as they are conditional upon the existence of a state against which they are exigible, this cannot be true. Cavemen had no right to education exigible against anyone.)[18] In the UK, as we are signatories to the European Convention on Human Rights now given force as a matter of domestic law by the Human Rights Act, the list includes a right to privacy, a right to marriage and a right to join a trade union.

III. FAILURES TO CONFER BENEFITS

The cases that have occasioned most difficulty are where the state attempts to confer a benefit upon its citizens and, through the fault of an individual or a system, negligently fails to do so. Should there be a claim available to the person left worse off than they otherwise would be? If our starting point is that all those left worse off than they otherwise would be by the negligence of another should have a claim, unless we can come up with a good reason why not, we might think the answer should be yes.[19] This is not the correct starting point.

I have a right that you do not punch me on the nose, or that you do not negligently damage my lorry, or that you do not call me an axe murderer in print. I do not have a right that you cure my illness, mend my broken bicycle or speak well of me.

The claim here is not that it is impossible to conceive, as a matter of analytic truth, of positive legal duties of rescue or benevolence, easy or otherwise, owed to other people. We can imagine a system of positive law which imposes such duties and we have a name for it: France.[20] Rather, the claim is that our common law is not such a system.

Lord Hoffmann in *Stovin v Wise* gave three reasons seeking to justify this rule:

> One can put the matter in political, moral or economic terms. In political terms it is less of an invasion of an individual's freedom for the law to require him to consider the safety of others in his actions than to impose upon him a duty to rescue or protect. A moral version of this point may be called the 'why pick on me?' argument. A duty to prevent harm to others or to render assistance to a person in danger or distress may apply to a large and indeterminate class of people who happen to be able to do something. Why should one be held liable rather than

---

[18] See generally J Raz, '*Human Rights without Foundations*' in J Tasioulas and S Besson (eds), The Philosophy of International Law (Oxford, Oxford University Press, 2010) 321.

[19] See for an example of this approach *Michael v CC of South Wales Police* [2015] UKSC 2, [189] *per* Lady Hale.

[20] See J Kortmann, *Altruism in Private Law* (Oxford, Oxford University Press, 2005).

another? In economic terms, the efficient allocation of resources usually requires an activity should bear its own costs. If it benefits from being able to impose some of its costs on other people (what economists call 'externalities') the market is distorted because the activity appears cheaper than it really is. So liability to pay compensation for loss caused by negligent conduct acts as a deterrent against increasing the cost of the activity to the community and reduces externalities.[21]

Unfortunately, none of these three reasons is convincing and none has any weight when applied to a public body.

First, all duties imposed by law are an invasion of our freedom of action. Some duties to take care when we choose to act are very burdensome indeed, such as the duty on a driver to take care in driving. Some duties of benevolence would by contrast be of negligible onerousness, such as to call the emergency services when you see your neighbour's house on fire or to pick up a baby drowning in an inch of water.

Further, the onerousness of steps necessary to comply is a factor that can be taken into account in determining whether a defendant has been negligent, falling below the standard of reasonable care. Why should it rule out the existence of the duty altogether?

When applied, as in *Stovin v Wise*, to public bodies, this argument seems to lose whatever force it may have. Why are we ever concerned with the liberty of public bodies as opposed to individuals? This is especially so where the public body is already, as in *Gorringe v Calderdale Metropolitan Borough Council*, under a public law duty of action. The public body has no freedom of action in such a case, and so there is no further invasion of its liberty (even if we were concerned with such) by holding it liable in tort.

Lord Hoffmann's second 'Why Pick on Me?' argument has little appeal, especially to those who have been responsible for the education of the young. If one student seeks to exculpate himself for failure to deliver an essay by pointing out that another student has done the same or has behaved far worse by repeated failures, a tutor will give him short shrift. It is one of the very first lessons we learn as children (or should be) that trying to evade sanction by pointing to the equivalent or worse wrongdoing of our sibling does not avail us. In law, one tortfeasor may be more culpable than a co-tortfeasor, but if we 'pick' on him, this is solved by allowing a contribution claim, not by ruling out any claim at all.

Again, when applied to public authority defendants who have failed to exercise their statutory powers (as in *Stovin v Wise*) or to comply with their public duties (as in *Gorringe*), the argument has even less force. We are picking on the public body because the law has pinpointed it as the relevant party with the power or duty to do something about this adverse state of affairs.

---

[21] [1996] AC 923 (HL), 943–44.

The third economic argument is predicated on the idea that externalities that are the result of inaction do not need to be internalised. But what is the justification for this? If the answer is that an enterprise is not responsible for failing to benefit others, which includes failures to prevent harm coming to them, we are back where we started. Why are we not responsible for failing to benefit others? Why not internalise the external costs of failing to benefit others? Again, whatever power this argument may have, it seems to have little force when applied to public bodies already under a statutory duty to act.

IV. EQUAL FREEDOM

Despite the failure of these arguments, Lord Hoffmann was clearly right in his conclusion. The lack of any general duty to confer benefits on other people is the starkest illustration there is that private law is based upon the rights we have one against another. It also allows us to understand the basis of those rights. The law's starting point is not that we should virtuously behave or arrive at the economically optimal result.

If, as some beginners think, the law was concerned with our virtue, then there would be no justification for drawing the sharp line that the law does. However, the maxim of Jesus Christ that we should 'do unto others as you would have them do unto you'[22] or the maxim in Leviticus to 'love your neighbour as yourself' is a maxim of personal morality or virtue, not of interpersonal moral right. The man who fails to pick up a baby drowning in an inch of water when he could, if he chose, easily rescue it behaves in a way which is, as a matter of personal morality, deeply wrong and reprehensible. However, he does not, by his failure to rescue, violate any right of the child.

Similarly, if we reason in wholly consequentialist terms, as economists do, there is simply no viable distinction between drowning babies and failing to rescue them. The end result—one dead baby—is precisely the same. If the law were solely concerned with preventing adverse outcomes, then there is no merit in the sharp divide between acts that injure and failures to rescue.

How then do we ascertain the rights we have, one against another?

In a world of absolute liberties, each of us would be free to stab one another in the neck, to steal a farmer's crops and to shout 'fire!' in crowded theatres. Freedom for the pike is death for the minnow,[23] but we are all of us both pikes and minnows. In order for each of us to be able to choose how to live our lives, it is necessary that we have rights against others that they refrain from interfering with our freedom. We each have a right to be secure

---

[22] Matthew 7:12; Luke 6:31.
[23] I Berlin, *Two Concepts of Liberty* (Oxford, Clarendon Press, 1958).

from interference by others in order that we may be free. The correlative general duties are ones to refrain from behaving in certain ways. This results in a system of equal freedom.

If we see rights as justified by seeking to ensure that each of us has equal freedom to live our lives, the absence of general rights that others take positive steps to confer benefits upon us follows as a matter of course. The point here is *not* that positive duties limit the freedom of the person subject to the duty, when a duty to refrain from acting in a certain way does not. All rights limit the freedom of others. Rather, your damaging my lorry interferes with my freedom to choose how to live my life, whereas your not repairing my bicycle does not. Further, we are not concerned with whether I would or would not have made use of the undamaged lorry. Whether, as a matter of fact, the consequence of your wrong removes from me options that I would in fact have exercised is irrelevant. It is for me to choose how to use my body and my things, not you. We are unconcerned here with whether the claimant is, as a matter of how things turn out, worse off as things turn out than he otherwise would be.

Now, a system of positive law could, and some systems do, go further than this. It could be that it is thought that the world would be better if we enforced duties of altruism, so that more babies are rescued (although the evidence that these good ends are in fact achieved by such laws is scanty to non-existent). We may be persuaded, rightly or wrongly, that it is worth the price of using people as a means to an end by imposing such positive law duties. The creation of such duties, which go beyond the basic duties required by the principle of equal freedom, is beyond the legitimate power of judges. Whether we should have rights that others act benevolently towards us, whether public bodies or otherwise, is a matter for the legislature. Judge-made private law retains its legitimacy from its basic and minimalist nature.

It might be objected that the common law imposes many positive duties to act, the duty of the driver of a car to hit the brakes when he sees a child running in front of his car, for example. One source of confusion is the usage of non-feasance and misfeasance as if they were opposites, which they are not. Feasance, although it is not much used in English anymore, means 'doing'. Feasance has the same root as the French *faisance*, with the stem *faire*, 'to do'. The opposite of non-feasance ('not doing') is feasance ('doing'). Misfeasance, wrongdoing, is a species of feasance. The opposite of misfeasance is non-misfeasance (not-wrongdoing). There are many examples of wrongs which involve failure to act (mis-nonfeasance). If in driving my car I hit a pedestrian because I failed to hit the brakes in time, this can be described, as a matter of language, as either misfeasance (negligent driving) or wrongful nonfeasance (negligent failure to use the brakes). It is consequently tempting to dismiss the distinction between non-feasance and misfeasance as illusory.

Clarity is aided not by a false contrast between non-feasance and misfeasance, but instead by employing the language of rights. The common law does not recognise general rights against others that they confer benefits upon us. This reflects a basic difference of interpersonal justice between damaging someone's bicycle and not repairing it.

Of course, we can also impose upon ourselves positive duties to confer benefits upon others, most obviously by way of contract. However, these assumed duties are wider than the narrow province of contract, a point frequently overlooked. A public hospital assumes a duty to take positive steps to place an emergency patient in the better position that reasonable care would ensure. You owe me a duty not to damage my trousers, but no duty to ensure that care is taken of them. If, however, you borrow my trousers, you come under a positive duty to take steps to ensure that care is taken of my trousers. This non-contractual bailment is one example of a common phenomenon within our law. These positive custodial duties are only owed to those to whom responsibility has been assumed, not the whole world. Public bodies can assume these positive custodial duties by accepting a patient into hospital, a child into foster care, or inviting an individual on to government premises, just as much as a private actor can.

V. PUBLIC AND PRIVATE LAW

Private law may be distinguished from public law in different ways. One method is to focus on the person or body that is subject to a duty or upon which a power is conferred. Is it an agent or part of the state? By this method of demarcating public law, the criminal law is not part of its subject matter as private individuals are subject to its duties (indeed, it is difficult to imagine situations where the state itself as such could be subject to criminal law sanctions).

A different method of distinguishing private from public is to focus on the nature of a duty owed.[24] Some duties are public in the sense that they are not owed to any particular individual; they are duties 'in the air'. Duties not to commit insider trading or not to be in possession of heroin are of this kind. Other duties are private because they are owed to other individuals who have control over their performance. On this definition, the criminal law falls within the public sphere as the duties are public, although these do not exhaust all the public duties that there are.

Confusion is caused by the fact that the same action may be simultaneously a public wrong and a private wrong (such as punching someone on the nose, which is both a crime and a tort). If, however, individuals are left worse off as a result of a wholly public wrong, they have no claim to damages as they have not themselves been wronged.

---

[24] I explore this more fully in R Stevens, 'Private Rights and Public Wrongs' in M Dyson (ed), *Unravelling Tort and Crime* (Cambridge, Cambridge University Press, 2014).

So, private individuals may owe both private duties (eg, not to trespass on another's land) and public ones (eg, not to commit blasphemy). Public bodies (and their agents) may also owe private duties (eg, not to trespass on another's land) and public ones (eg, to house the homeless).

The law commonly imposes upon public bodies the power, and sometimes the duty, to confer benefits upon members of the public in a way that it does not with private individuals. So, public bodies may be required to treat the sick, or regulate finance, or repair the roads, or educate the young, or protect us from crime, or prevent fires, or inspect building works for defects in a way that private individuals are under no obligation to do. The reason why the law is more willing to impose such positive obligations upon public bodies is that we are unconcerned with their liberty. Indeed, obliging state agencies to pick up babies drowning in inches of water may be thought to be one of the central purposes of having a state.

That said, if legislation confers upon a public body a power of action, or a *public* duty for the benefit of the public or a particular class, this does not tell us that a *private* right is intended to be created for the benefit of those affected. We cannot assume the latter from the existence of the former. It is not the case that the mere fact that I have been left worse off as a result of the breach of a public duty gives me a claim, whether that duty is a criminal law duty generally imposed upon private individuals generally or a public duty imposed upon public bodies in particular.

Absent one of the rights that exist against persons generally, if a claimant wishes to sue a public body for damages for conduct that is not normally wrongful, such as the failure to protect the claimant from injury by a third party such as a criminal,[25] the only possible source of such a right is the legislation under which the public body acts. Sometimes the legislature is explicit in its intention to confer rights upon individuals, as the Highways Act is in relation to the duty to repair the roads. If the legislation is silent as to whether any personal right is created, the most natural interpretation is that none is. In some cases, a right may be implied although not express and a claim for 'breach of statutory duty' allowed, but outside of the realm of employment safety, this has rarely proven successful. After the amendments to the Health and Safety at Work Act 1974 by the Enterprise and Regulatory Reform Act 2013, which states that a breach of health and safety regulations shall be presumed not to be actionable,[26] such claims will now rarely succeed.

In England, the greatest twentieth-century judicial disaster in the law of torts, which departed from the principles stated above, was the decision of the House of Lords in *Anns v Merton London Borough Council*.[27]

---

[25] Eg *Michael v CC of South Wales Police* [2015] UKSC 2.
[26] Health and Safety at Work Act 1974, s 47, as amended by the Enterprise and Regulatory Reform Act 2013, s 69.
[27] *Anns v Merton London Borough Council* [1978] AC 728 (HL).

Anns concerned the liability of a local authority for negligently failing to inspect the foundations of building work. The claimants were lessees who subsequently acquired their interest in the premises. Cracks began to appear in the plaster on their walls, and the claimants successfully argued that the local authority owed them a duty of care and was consequently potentially liable for expenditure necessary to restore the dwelling to a condition in which it was no longer a danger to health and safety. In allowing the claim, the House of Lords made a number of errors, of which the easiest to spot was the view that the claim was one for property damage.[28] The House corrected this mistake, first in *D & F Estates v Church Commissioners for England*,[29] where the defendant was the builder, and then in *Murphy v Brentwood District Council* by overruling *Anns* itself where the defendant was a local authority.[30]

If, however, in exercising a statutory power or carrying out a statutory *public* duty, a public body fails to confer a benefit upon someone, it cannot without more be liable. It does not matter that the failure of the public body was grossly below the standard of conduct which could have been expected. That this is the law was established by the House of Lords in *East Suffolk Rivers Catchment Board v Kent*.[31] The claimant's land flooded as a result of a breach in a sea wall. The defendant public body in the exercise of its statutory powers took on the job of repairing the wall. Because of the inefficient way in which the work was carried out, the repair work took much longer than was necessary. The claimant, a farmer, sought compensation for the loss consequent upon the land being flooded for longer than it would have been if all reasonable care had been taken. The majority of the House of Lords dismissed the claim. It was not shown that the claimant, or anyone else, would have repaired the wall if the authority had not intervened. No right to the claimant's land was therefore infringed. There was no implicit assumption of responsibility as the efforts of the defendant did not exclude anyone else from effecting repairs. The legislation under which the public body had the power to act did not create a right good against it for the careful completion of the work.

Lord Atkin dissented in *East Suffolk* and, much like his dissent in *Liversidge v Anderson*,[32] this undermined the weight subsequently attached to the majority's decision. The dissent in *East Suffolk* was given particular weight, coming as it did from the founding father of the neighbour principle

---

[28] For the other errors, see R Stevens, 'Torts' in L Bloom-Cooper, B Dickson and G Drewry (eds), *The Judicial History of the House of Lords 1876–2009* (Oxford, Oxford University Press, 2009) 637–43.

[29] *D & F Estates v Church Commissioners for England* [1989] AC 177 (HL).

[30] *Murphy v Brentwood District Council* [1991] 1 AC 398 (HL).

[31] *East Suffolk Rivers Catchment Board v Kent* [1941] AC 74 (HL).

[32] *Liversidge v Anderson* [1942] AC 206 (HL).

in *Donoghue v Stevenson*.[33] Unfortunately, whilst in *Liversidge v Anderson* Lord Atkin was arguably right, in *East Suffolk* he was plainly wrong. In *Anns*, the House of Lords followed the approach of Lord Atkin, whilst not formally overruling *East Suffolk* itself. Although purchasers or lessees of property do not have a right against persons generally that they provide them with the benefit of a careful house inspection, and the legislation under which the local authority acted did not on its true construction confer such a right, the House in *Anns* gave the lessee a claim for damages where the local authority had failed to confer upon the lessee this benefit.

Although *Anns* itself was overturned in *Murphy*, this was not on the basis that the court could not take the step of imposing a positive duty to confer a benefit where this was not discoverable in the wording of the legislation under which the public body acted. Where the injury which the public body had reasonably foreseeably failed to prevent was property damage or personal injury, it remained arguable even after *Murphy* that liability should be imposed. The attempt to retreat from this misstep has led to a continuing stream of cases coming before the House of Lords and Privy Council on the liability of public bodies for failure to confer benefits,[34] such as against the police for failing to catch criminals.

Eventually, orthodoxy was re-established by Lord Hoffmann, first in respect of the exercise of statutory powers by the House of Lords in *Stovin v Wise*,[35] where a public body failed to exercise a statutory power to remove a raised bank that restricted visibility on the highway and, subsequently and more decisively, in respect of the carrying out of statutory duties by a unanimous decision in *Gorringe*. So, the negligent failure of a public body to paint a 'STOP' sign on the highway was not actionable by someone injured as a result any more than the failure by anyone else to paint such a sign would be actionable. A road without such a sign does not want of repair, so that the claimant cannot rely upon his statutory private right. The public body may be under a *public* duty to act in a particular way, a duty which an individual may have standing to enforce by judicial review, but the essential question in a claim for damages for a civil wrong is whether this was intended to confer upon the claimant a personal right. Although not alone responsible for the

---

[33] *Donoghue v Stevenson* [1932] AC 562 (HL).

[34] Eg, *Yuen Kun-Yeu v Attorney-General of Hong Kong* [1988] AC 175 (PC, HK); *Rowling v Takaro Properties Ltd* [1988] AC 473 (PC, NZ); *Hill v Chief Constable of West Yorkshire* [1989] AC 53 (HL); *Murphy v Brentwood District Council* (n 28); *X v Bedfordshire County Council* [1995] 2 AC 633 (HL); *Stovin v Wise* (n 10); *Barrett v Enfield London Borough Council* [2001] 2 AC 550 (HL); *Phelps v Hillingdon London Borough Council* [2001] 2 AC 619 (HL); *Gorringe* (n 11); *D v East Berkshire Community NHS Trust* [2005] UKHL 23, [2005] 2 AC 373; *Brooks v Commissioner of Police for the Metropolis* [2005] UKHL 24, [2005] 1 WLR 1495; *Chief Constable of the Hertfordshire Police v Van Colle* [2008] UKHL 50, [2009] 1 AC 225.

[35] Lord Goff, Lord Jauncey of Tullichettle and Lord Hoffmann; Lord Nicholls and Lord Slynn dissenting.

reassertion of orthodoxy, Lord Hoffmann's speeches were by far the most significant. However, 26 years of confusion cannot be eradicated overnight, and the law is still not generally understood, at least not apparently by the Court of Appeal[36] or the English Law Commission.[37] In principle, the law today has returned to the position established in the 1940s.

If, by contrast, one starts from the position that a claimant who now finds himself in a worse position than he would be if the defendant was careful is entitled to compensation, it seems natural to assume that the claim in *Anns* should succeed. Why should the public body have an 'immunity' from having to pay for the loss which, but for its negligence, would not have occurred?

If in *East Suffolk Rivers Catchment Board v Kent* the public body's intervention had caused either the landowner or a third party to change their behaviour, so that they themselves did not attempt to repair the wall, a claim could potentially have succeeded. If it could be shown that repairs would have been successful but for the public body's intervention, the public body has wronged the claimant by causing his land to be flooded. Precisely the same would be true of a well-meaning officious neighbour. Specific reliance of this kind is simply one way in which our actions can result in another being wronged.

When a public body negligently fails to confer a benefit upon us, as in *Gorringe*, this is not actionable without more. This does not involve the public body asserting any 'immunity' or invoking an 'exclusionary rule'.

VI. CONCLUSION

Public law and private law are not oil and water, but we must be extremely careful before slipping between the two. That I have a private right against you that you behave in a certain way does not necessitate the recognition of a public duty that you do so. Conversely, public duties the performance of which will benefit particular individuals do not necessitate the existence of private rights. My job description as Professor of *Private* Law is not a lie. Individuals may have standing to enforce a public duty, but they do not do so on the basis that the duty is owed to them. Public law's standing requirements reflect the fact that proceedings are not conducted on the basis of (private) right.

---

[36] *Smith v Chief Constable of Sussex* [2008] EWCA Civ 39, overturned by *Chief Constable of the Hertfordshire Police v Van Colle* (n 32).

[37] Law Commission, *Administrative Redress Public Bodies and the Citizen* (Law Com CP No 187, 2008) 45–46. These curious proposals, criticised by Lord Hoffmann extra-judicially, have been abandoned.

This takes me back to *Total Network Solutions v HMRC*, a case apparently far removed from my topic. Where two or more persons conspire to cause another loss, when can they be liable? If the actions of one of them constitute a tort, a violation of a right of the claimant, it is possible to say that because of their conspiracy, their actions are attributed to one another so as to constitute a tort by both. Similarly, if the actions of one conspirator constitute a crime, it is possible for the law to say that both are liable for this crime because of the effect of their conspiring together. Where the actions do not constitute a crime, the agreement cannot as a matter of principle transform it into one. Where the actions do not constitute the violation of any private right, so as to be a tort, the agreement alone cannot create one. For conspirators to be criminals, what they must conspire to do must be a crime, and for conspirators to be tortfeasors, what they must conspire to do must be a tort. A conspiracy to commit a tort is not necessarily a crime, and a conspiracy to commit a crime is not necessarily a tort. By holding that the conspiracy to commit a crime can potentially constitute a tort, the House of Lords confused together public duties and private rights—precisely the same mistake as had been made decades before in *Anns* and corrected by Lord Hoffmann.

Sadly, Lord Hoffmann was not part of the panel in *Total Network Solution v HMRC*. Good judges matter.

7

Are Human Rights Culturally Determined? A Riposte to Lord Hoffmann

SANDRA FREDMAN QC, FBA

I. INTRODUCTION

[O]f course we share a common humanity ... Nevertheless ... the specific answers, the degree to which weight is given to one desirable objective rather than another, will be culturally determined. Different communities will, through their legislature and judges, adopt the answers which they think suit them.[1]

THE RELATIONSHIP BETWEEN issues which go to our 'common humanity' and those which are 'culturally determined' is a vexed one. Between a commitment to a thoroughgoing relativity and pure universalism lie many stopping points. Lord Hoffmann's primary target is the European Court of Human Rights (ECtHR). The aim of this chapter, however, is to examine his arguments in the light of the increasingly lively transnational judicial conversation about the resolution of similar human rights questions in different jurisdictions. I argue that it is a mistake to address the question as if there were only two options: a universal right answer to human rights disputes or an answer which is culturally determined, precluding any further common ground. Instead, the interpretation of both the substance and limitations of human rights should be a deliberative process. There can be no aspiration to achieve absolute answers which apply in all contexts over all time, but to engage in constant reasoned attempts to develop the understanding of human rights. It is through the process of deliberation, consensus building and accountability that human rights take on a dynamic role in society.[2]

---

[1] L Hoffmann, 'Human Rights and the House of Lords' (1999) 62 *MLR* 159, 165.

[2] See further S Fredman, 'From Dialogue to Deliberation: Human Rights Adjudication and Prisoners' Rights to Vote' (2013) *Public Law* 292; S Fredman, 'Adjudication as Accountability: A Deliberative Approach' in N Bamforth and P Leyland (eds), *Accountability in the Contemporary Constitution* (New York, Oxford University Press, 2013).

It will be argued here that the particular form of legal discourse permits a deliberative approach, which can use legal reasoning and deliberative techniques to navigate between the general and specific. Judges making decisions on complex issues of human rights law need to adopt a reasoning process which is thorough and persuasive. Even if the outcome is contested and may even change over time, its authority lies in its deliberative content, that is, in its use of reasons which are rigorous, convincing, and well-supported by evidence, be it factual or legal. While there are clearly appropriate variations based on institutional, historical or social differences, these should not be taken for granted, but openly defended by means of reasons which are identifiable, understandable and persuasive. This necessitates a consideration of how other decision-makers, faced with similarly worded human rights instruments, have come to their conclusions. Comparative materials, on this approach, constitute an important contribution to the rigour of the deliberative process. In Waldron's terms, this is equivalent to consulting the laboratory of the world;[3] in Barak's terms, this is the judge's 'experienced friend'.[4]

The chapter begins by assessing Lord Hoffmann's critique of the universality of human rights. Lord Hoffmann's primary argument is that the weight to be given to different and possibly conflicting 'desirable objectives' is culturally determined and therefore a local matter, for different communities, through their legislature and judges. Behind this is the much stronger claim that, ultimately, different human rights values and public policy objectives are incommensurable. Otherwise, there could be open discussion about what weight should be given to different objectives and why such weight is given. Cultural pluralism cannot be a stopping point: either it slides into purely subjective decision-making or it must be open to transnational scrutiny. I therefore contest the view that the weighing of different objectives is entirely a local matter. Local variation, while possible, must be defended on the basis of explicitly articulated local differences, whether in the form of the balance of power between executive, legislature and judiciary, or the text of the bill of rights, or the legal tradition. In the second section, I develop this argument by considering two issues which have been confronted by courts in several different jurisdictions in recent years: equality on grounds of sexual orientation and the ever-contentious question of prisoners' right to vote.

II. CULTURALLY DETERMINED OR A COOPERATIVE ENTERPRISE?

Lord Hoffmann's main argument is that only domestic courts and legislatures can make decisions as to the meaning and application of human rights

---

[3] J Waldron, *Partly Laws Common to Mankind: Foreign Law in American Courts* (New Haven, CT, Yale University Press, 2012) 89, 199.

[4] A Barak, 'Response to the Judge as Comparatist: Comparison in Public Law' (2005) 80 *Tulane Law Review* 195.

in their jurisdiction. For him, human rights decisions, particularly those which are disputed enough to come before courts or tribunals, necessarily involve the weighing of several 'desirable objectives'.[5] The hierarchy of values or priorities is, in his view, 'culturally determined'. Lord Hoffmann's main target is the ECtHR, which he contrasts with domestic courts such as the US Supreme Court, citing decisions from the latter which he regards as demonstrating the superiority of a court which is culturally in tune with its subjects. Although he accepts that 'Jefferson would have regarded at least some of the provisions of the Bill of Rights amendments as universals in the sense of being founded upon moral imperatives which were applicable to all human beings', he argues that:

> [T]he concrete application of these provisions by the Supreme Court ... were not at all universal. They were founded on the day-to-day realities of American life, federalism, the American doctrine of the separation of powers, American political culture and legal tradition.[6]

This has meant, he concludes, that the American Bill of Rights is often interpreted differently from very similar formulations in other legal systems. He gives some selected examples, such as the total inadmissibility in the US of any evidence obtained by an unlawful search, and the extent to which the balance drawn between freedom of speech and the right to a fair trial is tilted towards the former in the US.

The conclusion he draws is that while, at the level of abstraction, human rights may be universal, at the level of application, 'the human rights which these abstractions have generated are national. Their application requires trade-offs and compromises, exercises of judgment which can be made only in the context of a given society and its legal system'.[7] It is for this reason, he argues, that the role and jurisdiction of the ECtHR are fundamentally misconceived. He gives three examples from the ECtHR jurisprudence to support his point. The first is the ECtHR decision on the right to silence in the *Saunders* case.[8] Lord Hoffmann criticises the judgment on the basis that it failed to draw on the rich domestic jurisprudence that had developed around the right to silence. Thus, it ignored Lord Mustill's rigorous discussion of the right to silence and the 200-year-old history of similar provisions in English bankruptcy and company law. Most of all, it failed to mention Lord Templeman's insightful comment that, given the risk that the right to silence could protect the guilty and may be unnecessary to safeguard the innocent, it could only be justified on the basis that it discouraged ill-treatment of a

---

[5] Hoffmann (n 1) 165.
[6] Lord Hoffmann, 'The Universality of Human Rights: Judicial Studies Board Annual Lecture' (19 March 2009) [15] www.brandeis.edu/ethics/pdfs/internationaljustice/biij/BIIJ2013/hoffmann.pdf.
[7] ibid.
[8] *Saunders v UK* (1997) 23 EHRR 313.

suspect and the production of dubious confessions.[9] Where none of these dangers exist, English law has introduced important statutory protections. Instead, the ECtHR simply stated that the privilege applied to all types of criminal offences without distinction.

The criticism of the *Saunders* case is well made. However, the question is whether Lord Hoffmann is correct to conclude that the defects of the judgment are due to the fact that the application of the right to silence in any domestic context is culturally determined. Instead, I would argue that the defects in the Court's reasoning were due to flaws in its deliberation rather than being an inevitable result of its status as an international court. One could easily think of similar criticisms of the decisions of national courts. This can partly be tested by asking the question in the reverse direction. Is Lord Templeman's insightful comment applicable only in the UK? Or is it a relevant set of arguments which a court embarking on a judgment should take account of? It is not obvious why this line of reasoning should be considered to be culturally specific to the UK and therefore entirely alien to the 'culture' of Canada, the US, India or South Africa. Indeed, the implication of Lord Hoffmann's position is that the ECtHR should have considered it. There are certainly potentially relevant differences: the constitutional text might differ in material respects; the institutional competence of the Court might be broader or more restricted; and there might be legal categories which are misunderstood in the translation to other jurisdictions. On the other hand, none of these factors might be materially different. This suggests that human rights decision-makers at a local level should have valid reasons for differentiating their own jurisdiction from others rather than simply hiding behind a claim of cultural pluralism.

As further support for this diagnosis, we could look to the later case of *O'Halloran v UK*,[10] in which the Grand Chamber rejected a challenge to the duty of car owners to reveal the identity of the driver in cases in which the car was caught speeding by speed cameras. Lord Hoffmann regards this case as evidence of his own position, arguing that the ECtHR's decision in *Saunders* prompted the challenge in *O'Halloran*, which he regards as a *reductio ad absurdum* of the *Saunders* principle.[11] However, I would argue that it is evidence of the dynamism of the deliberative approach. In *O'Halloran*, many of the defects in the *Saunders* reasoning were addressed. The Court made it clear that the right to silence was not absolute, but that it needed to be considered in the context of the nature and degree of compulsion used to obtain the evidence, the existence of any relevant safeguards in the procedure and the use to which any material so obtained was put.[12] Although the decision

---

[9] See *AT&T Istel Ltd v Tully* [1993] AC 45 (HL) 53.
[10] *O'Halloran v UK* (2008) 46 EHRR 21.
[11] See Hoffmann (n 6) [30].
[12] See *O'Halloran* (n 10) [55].

in relation to Saunders himself still stands, the ability of legal reasoning to continually develop and self-reflect is nothing new; it is the basis after all of the common law. Lord Hoffmann rather disarmingly continues his critique of the Court not by affirming its more nuanced approach in *O'Halloran*, but by quoting in detail from one of the two dissenting opinions, which he cites 'in order that you may appreciate the type of reasoning employed in Strasbourg'.[13] His third example is similar: having criticised the Chamber decision in *Hatton v UK*,[14] in which the Court held that a relaxation in the restrictions of night flights at Heathrow was a breach of the applicants' Article 8 rights, he acknowledges that the decision on Article 8 was overturned by the Grand Chamber.[15] This again demonstrates that the defects in the reasoning were deliberative ones, which could be corrected by more careful argument before the Court rather than being necessarily attributable to cultural difference. Yet again, Lord Hoffmann focuses his criticism on the dissenting opinion in *Hatton*'s case. We could very easily find dissenting opinions in domestic courts to criticise, if we disagreed with their conclusions. But it is difficult to see these as good enough evidence that the application of human rights is necessarily culturally determined. This does not mean to say that there are not potential situations in which local variation is required. But a deliberative stance does not allow this to be taken as a fiat, simply under the label of cultural difference. Instead, variation on grounds of local difference should itself be vigorously and openly defended.

It is not proposed here to discuss Lord Hoffmann's critique of the appointment process or constitution of the Court. Instead, I would like to develop the critique of his claim that the application of what he calls abstractions is necessarily culturally determined by considering the ways in which courts in different jurisdictions have dealt with similar questions. I suggest that the claim of cultural pluralism creates boundaries between nations which are unnecessarily watertight. While there may not be absolute truths, the common resource of judicial deliberation should be drawn on by all courts in applying similarly worded human rights principles. Local variations should be fully defended on the basis of justifiable differences rather than simply being attributed to cultural determinism.

III. PRISONERS' RIGHT TO VOTE

I begin by stepping straight into the hotly contested question of whether prisoners should have the right to vote, a question that has appeared before courts in many jurisdictions, including the US, South Africa, Canada,

---

[13] Hoffmann (n 6) [15].
[14] *Hatton v UK* (2002) 34 EHRR 1.
[15] See *Hatton v UK* (2003) 37 EHRR 28 (Grand Chamber).

Australia, the UK and the ECtHR. Lord Hoffmann would presumably regard this as one of the prime examples where the application of an abstract principle is 'culturally determined'. In this section, I consider what reasons could be brought forward to support this position and why they are difficult to sustain. The alternative, deliberative approach is far more compelling.

The fundamental nature of the right to vote in a democracy is hard to gainsay. There are those who have argued that this right is not contained in the ECHR, which provides more obliquely for a duty on states to 'hold free elections at reasonable intervals by secret ballot, under conditions which will ensure the free expression of the opinion of the people in the choice of the legislature'.[16] However, the Court has emphatically endorsed the clear implication that this includes a subjective individual right to vote,[17] and it is difficult to see how free elections ensuring the free expression of the opinion of the people can be achieved without the right to vote. The struggle for women's suffrage, for the vote for African Americans and for the vote for the black majority in South Africa should make us pause long and hard before we accept that the right to vote should be culturally determined. In Saudi Arabia, women have only just been granted some form of right to vote, in a move that does not come into effect until 2015. Does Lord Hoffmann's cultural pluralism endorse a position according to which it would be entirely up to the domestic authorities to determine whether the right to vote should be restricted on grounds of race or sex? If the application of the right to vote is entirely culturally determined, then even a restriction on the right to vote on the grounds of race or sex would be beyond scrutiny. Conversely, if such a restriction could be condemned as breaching the right to vote, it is difficult to see how its restriction in relation to prisoners could be regarded as culturally determined. This is not to say that no restrictions are permissible, but rather to argue that restrictions can and should be subject to transnational scrutiny.

If, as I hope is the case, Lord Hoffmann would not accept that the right to vote is culturally determined to the extent of permitting restrictions based on race or sex, then we need to ask further what his cultural pluralism entails. It has been acknowledged that the right to vote is not absolute, but can be limited. This has been accepted by courts in Canada, Australia and South Africa, as well as by the ECtHR.[18] It is generally uncontroversial to limit the right to vote to those who are over 18 years old. The question therefore is how we determine whether those limits are justified. What sorts of reasons should be legitimate and who should evaluate them? It is this

---

[16] ECHR Protocol 1, art 3.

[17] *Mathieu-Mohin v Belgium* (1988) 10 EHRR 1.

[18] See *August v Electoral Commission* (CCT8/99) [1999] ZACC 3 (South African Constitutional Court); *Minister of Home Affairs v National Institute for Crime Prevention and the Re-integration of Offenders* (CCT 03/04) [2004] ZACC 10 (South African Constitutional Court) (hereinafter *NICRO*); *Hirst v UK (No 2)* (2006) 42 EHRR 41; *Sauvé v Canada (Chief Electoral Officer)* [2002] 3 SCR 519; *Roach v Electoral Commissioner* [2007] HCA 43; *Scoppola v Italy (No 3)* [2013] 56 EHRR 19.

latter question that Lord Hoffmann puts into the sphere of cultural pluralism: it is national courts which should make these decisions in the light of
local conditions. This suggests that the reasoning process used by a national
court cannot be subject to scrutiny outside its national borders and is of
no relevance to a national court in a different country faced with the same
question. Yet courts in jurisdictions all over the English-speaking world are
referring to each other's judgments in addressing this question. Are they
wrong to do so? To determine this, it is worth looking more closely at the
way in which this transnational conversation has taken place.

Lord Hoffmann's central concern is with the difficulty in weighing desirable objectives, the assumption being that there is no real way of assessing
the process of evaluation cross-nationally. It is here that the deliberative
approach departs from Lord Hoffmann's cultural pluralism. It is argued
here that courts can and do provide a deliberative framework within which
evaluation can take place. For example, under the European Convention
on Human Rights (ECHR), the Court must satisfy itself that the conditions
placed on the right to vote:

> [D]o not curtail the rights in question to such an extent as to impair their very
> essence and deprive them of their effectiveness; that they are imposed in pursuit
> of a legitimate aim; and that the means employed are not disproportionate ... In
> particular, such conditions must not thwart 'the free expression of the opinion of
> the people in the choice of the legislature'.[19]

The South African Court in *NICRO* was even more specific. While accepting that the right to vote could be subject to limitations, it insisted that
proper justification be put in evidence before it to justify deprivation of so
fundamental a right. As Chaskalson CJ put it:

> In a case such as this where the government seeks to disenfranchise a group of its
> citizens and the purpose is not self-evident, there is a need for it to place sufficient
> information before the Court to enable it to know exactly what purpose the dis-
> enfranchisement was intended to serve. In so far as the government relies upon
> policy considerations, there should be sufficient information to enable the Court
> to assess and evaluate the policy that is being pursued.[20]

Nor was this a framework for evaluation which Chaskalson CJ reached in
isolation. He made it clear that he agreed with the comments of the Canadian
Supreme Court Chief Justice McLachlan in the major Canadian prisoners'
right to vote case, *Sauvé*. Indeed, he quoted at length from the part of the
judgment when McLachlan J stated:

> At the end of the day, people should not be left guessing about why their *Charter*
> rights have been infringed. Demonstrable justification requires that the objective

---

[19] *Mathieu-Mohin* (n 17) [52].
[20] *NICRO* (n 18) [65].

clearly reveals the harm that the government hopes to remedy, and that this objective remains constant throughout the justification process. As this Court has stated, the objective 'must be accurately and precisely defined so as to provide a clear framework for evaluating its importance, and to assess the precision with which the means have been crafted to fulfil that objective'.[21]

Chaskalson CJ's stance is paradigmatically deliberative. Since the Court did not have sufficient information to enable it to assess and evaluate the policy being pursued and since this was a blanket ban on all prisoners, the restriction on the fundamental right had not been justified and should be struck down. Prisoners now have the right to vote in South Africa, with no discernible ill effects.

The ECtHR's decision in *Hirst* to strike down the blanket ban in the UK has been widely vilified in the UK and is usually the chief reason why those with similar views to Lord Hoffmann argue for withdrawal from the European Convention. However, *Hirst* is far from an outlier. On the basis of evaluative frameworks along the above lines, courts in Canada, South Africa and Australia have held that a blanket ban is incompatible with the right to vote.[22] In coming to this conclusion, they have liberally cited from each other. Similarly, when it came to *Scoppola*, the ECtHR had the benefit of a string of decisions, including the South African decision striking out a blanket ban and the Australian decision doing the same. The Court also canvassed similar practice in European countries who were members of the Council of Europe. Thus, it was far from alone in reaffirming its position in *Hirst* that a blanket ban on prisoner voting is a breach of Article 3 of Protocol 1.[23]

Apart from the ECtHR, these are national courts coming to national decisions. None of these took the view that conditions in their own country in relation to prisoners were sufficiently unique that they could not regard other courts as providing helpful contributions to their own reasoning process. Importantly, this was not to say that other jurisdictions were binding on the domestic court, but rather that their reasoning process was valid and therefore relevant to their own decision-making.

The powerful outlier in this picture is the US, which continues to countenance large-scale disenfranchisement of prisoners in many states, a bar which continues after the end of the sentence. Figures suggest that this disenfranchises 5.85 million citizens, nearly 4.4 million of whom have been released from prison and are living and working in the community. The impact is highly racialised. As many as 13 per cent of African-American men have lost their right to vote, seven times the average. According to the American

---

[21] *Sauvé* (n 18) [23].
[22] See *NICRO* (n 18); *Sauvé* (n 18); *Sauvé v Canada (Attorney-General) (No 1)* [1993] 2 SCR 438; *Hirst* (n 18); *Roach* (n 18); *Scoppola* (n 18).
[23] *Scoppola* (n 18) [96].

Civil Liberties Union (ACLU): 'Over the last few decades, the number of disfranchised citizens has been increasing because of an incarceration boom fueled by mandatory minimum sentences and the "war on drugs".'[24] Until 2010, these included mandatory five-year minimum sentences for simple possession of five grams of crack cocaine, while possession of 10 grams led to a mandatory 10-year sentence. A much more lenient regime applied to offences for possession of powder cocaine. Because crack cocaine was the drug of choice for black users, about 80 per cent of those convicted on crack charges were black. Users and sellers of powder cocaine, who were more often white, were subject to a more lenient sentencing regime. The Fair Sentencing Act 2010 raised the threshold for a five-year mandatory sentence to 28 grams and to 280 grams for a 10-year sentence. However, this was not retrospective and many of those convicted under the previous regime remain in prison and, depending on what state they live in, might be additionally subject to disenfranchisement.[25]

Nevertheless, the US Supreme Court has steadfastly maintained that a blanket ban on prisoners' right to vote is not constitutionally invalid. This is not to say, however, that this approach can simply be regarded as an appropriate exercise of cultural pluralism. It is argued here that, at the very least, it needs to be opened to deliberative scrutiny. One reason which could be put forward is the very real textual difference. In *Richardson v Ramirez* in 1974, the Supreme Court upheld prisoner voter disqualification on the grounds that this was set out expressly in section 2 of the Fourteenth Amendment, which provides for the denial by states of the right to vote to persons 'for participation in rebellion, or other crime'.[26] However, even this could be open to further deliberative scrutiny. Should 'other crime' mean any crime whatsoever or just crimes on the same level as rebellion as the dissent in *Richardson* suggested? Equally important, should the US Court not be openly faulted for failing to consider the kind of arguments that have moved other courts, in particular, a resistance to an indiscriminate and blanket ban? Some glimmerings of such an approach can be seen in the form of cases challenging the ban on equal protection grounds. There are now several conflicting decisions from lower courts in the US as to whether the Voting Rights Act (VRA), which prohibits discrimination on grounds of

[24] American Civil Liberties Union, 'The Democracy Restoration Act' www.aclu.org/files/images/asset_upload_file494_39408.pdf.
[25] See E Eckholm, 'Congress Moves to Narrow Cocaine Sentencing Disparities' *New York Times* (28 July 2010) www.nytimes.com/2010/07/29/us/politics/29crack.html?_r=1&; L Greenhouse, 'Crack Cocaine Limbo' *New York Times* (5 January 2014) www.nytimes.com/2014/01/06/opinion/greenhouse-crack-cocaine-limbo.html; L Greenhouse, 'Voting Behind Bars' *New York Times* (29 July 2010) http://opinionator.blogs.nytimes.com/2010/07/29/voting-behind-bars.
[26] *Richardson v Ramirez* 418 US 24, 55 (1974). See further *Romer v Evans* 517 US 620, 634 (1996) (describing the principle that states may disenfranchise a convicted felon as 'unexceptionable').

race, is applicable to prisoner voter disqualification. In a strongly worded case in 2009, the Ninth Circuit Court of Appeals held that the discriminatory impact of Washington's felon disenfranchisement was attributable to racial discrimination in Washington's criminal justice system and therefore that its felon disenfranchisement law violated section 2 of the VRA.[27] However, the First Circuit Court of Appeals, also in 2009, held that Congress never intended section 2 of the VRA to apply to currently incarcerated felons.[28] The Supreme Court in 2010 ordered the Solicitor General to 'express the views of the United States' on whether laws that take away the right to vote from people in prison or on parole could be challenged under the VRA as racially discriminatory,[29] but it is not clear what has happened subsequently. In any event, it is maintained here that to put a stop to any kind of debate about the validity of these arguments under the cloak of cultural determinism is a serious mistake. Both courts and legislature need to be held to account for the quality of their reasoning.

The question of whether a disqualification which only applies to more severe sentences has received a more mixed response from different courts. Whereas the Supreme Court of Canada was unwilling to countenance any ban,[30] the Australian High Court accepted a ban for prisoners serving sentences above three years[31] and the ECtHR in *Scoppola* accepted the Italian regime, which applied to prisoners serving sentences above five years.[32] Such divergences need not, however, be attributed to cultural determinism. Instead, courts continue to refer to each other and to weigh up the arguments. The rigour with which they do so should remain open to ongoing critique and analysis.

IV. SEXUAL ORIENTATION

A second major issue which has confronted courts in many jurisdictions is the question of equality on grounds of sexual orientation. Since many bills of rights are silent as to whether the equality guarantee applies to this issue, this is a clear example of the need to apply what Lord Hoffmann would call an abstraction in particular situations. We can again ask the question of whether this is an issue which is purely culturally determined, one which only national courts can address in a national context and which by definition cannot be generalised in any sense. The question has analogies with the

---

[27] See *Farrakhan v Gregoire* 590 F 3d 989 (US Court of Appeals (9th Cir), 2010). See also the earlier decision in *Farrakhan v Washington* 338 F 3d 1009 (US Court of Appeals (9th Cir), 2003), cert denied, 543 US 984 (2004).

[28] See *Simmons v Galvin* 575 F 3d 24 (US Court of Appeals (1st Cir) (2009)).

[29] See *Simmons v Galvin* 130 S Ct 2428 (2010).

[30] See *Sauvé* (n 18).

[31] See *Roach* (n 18).

[32] See *Scoppola* (n 18).

prisoners' right to vote issue because both concern a fundamental right—the right to equality and the right to vote. In both cases, we can highlight the implications of cultural pluralism by asking if it is wholly a matter for domestic determination whether the right could be withdrawn or restricted.

It is of course optimal for the move to be taken by the legislature, as it was indeed in Britain after the Wolfenden Report, which eventually led to the repeal of laws punishing homosexual conduct in the Sexual Offences Act 1967. Judicial intervention to enforce human rights would not be necessary if legislative action were always forthcoming. It is when a group systematically lacks political power that such intervention becomes democratically legitimate. Such was the case in Northern Ireland, which retained its criminalisation of sodomy laws well into the 1980s. In such a situation, is it entirely a matter for local determination whether such a prohibition remains in effect? In its groundbreaking decision in *Dudgeon v UK*,[33] the ECtHR held that this amounted to a breach of the right to privacy under the Convention. The Court was clear that the law interfered with the applicant's right to respect for his private life, which included his sexual life, in breach of Article 8:

> Either he respects the law and refrains from engaging—even in private with consenting male partners—in prohibited sexual acts to which he is disposed by reason of his homosexual tendencies, or he commits such acts and thereby becomes liable to criminal prosecution.[34]

As in the right to vote cases, much of the decision was therefore concerned with whether the restrictions could be justified as necessary in a democratic society for the pursuance of a legitimate aim. Lord Hoffmann would regard the weighing of objectives as a matter for local decision. Indeed, the government in its defence made much of the cultural differences between Northern Ireland and Great Britain, drawing attention to:

> [W]hat they described as profound differences of attitude and public opinion between Northern Ireland and Great Britain in relation to questions of morality. Northern Irish society was said to be more conservative and to place greater emphasis on religious factors, as was illustrated by more restrictive laws even in the field of heterosexual conduct.[35]

As the Court acknowledged, this was a relevant factor, but did not shut down the question: 'Where there are disparate cultural communities residing within the same State, it may well be that different requirements, both moral and social, will face the governing authorities.'[36] Similarly, some degree of regulation of sexual conduct could be justified where necessary to preserve public order and decency. The Court drew heavily on the Wolfenden Report

---

[33] *Dudgeon v UK* [1982] 4 EHRR 149.
[34] ibid [41].
[35] ibid [56].
[36] ibid [56]–[57].

for its view that some degree of control could even extend to consensual acts committed in private, notably to provide sufficient safeguards against the exploitation of vulnerable people.[37]

The question therefore was whether it was 'necessary' in a democratic society to achieve these legitimate aims. Clearly, the task of weighing these different objectives is not an easy one. However, human rights frameworks are not agnostic as to how the process should be conducted. By their nature, human rights are very weighty. Only considerations which are particularly urgent or pressing can counteract the necessity to respect them. Unless one regards the values as totally incommensurate and therefore the process of weighing them as purely subjective, there is no reason why it should be considered impervious to cross cultural discussion, scrutiny and influence. Thus, in *Dudgeon*, the Court concluded that 'the moral attitudes towards male homosexuality in Northern Ireland and the concern that any relaxation in the law would tend to erode existing moral standards cannot, without more, warrant interfering with the applicant's private life to such an extent'.[38] Therefore, 'the restriction imposed on Mr Dudgeon under Northern Ireland law, by reason of its breadth and absolute character, is, quite apart from the severity of the possible penalties provided for, disproportionate to the aims sought to be achieved'. Notably, too, the Court made sure that it was not an isolated decision. It noted that:

> [I]n the great majority of the member States of the Council of Europe it is no longer considered to be necessary or appropriate to treat homosexual practices of the kind now in question as in themselves a matter to which the sanctions of the criminal law should be applied.[39]

Thus, while it did not itself set the norm, it took upon itself the responsibility to bring the outliers into the mainstream.

The possibility and value of cross-cultural discussion and influence is further demonstrated by the fact that the *Dudgeon* case became influential in the decision by the US Supreme Court in the landmark case of *Lawrence v Texas*,[40] in which the Court reversed its previous judgment in *Bowers*,[41] which had upheld the criminalisation of sodomy. Kennedy J was able to draw on this resource to refute 'the sweeping references by Chief Justice Burger to the history of Western civilization and to Judeo-Christian moral and ethical standards'. As well as citing the Wolfenden Report and the UK Sexual Offences Act 1967, Kennedy J referred to *Dudgeon* as follows:

> Of even more importance, almost five years before *Bowers* was decided, the European Court of Human Rights considered a case with parallels to *Bowers*

---

[37] ibid [49].
[38] ibid [61].
[39] ibid [60].
[40] *Lawrence v Texas* 539 US 558 (2003).
[41] *Bowers v Hardwick* 478 US 186 (1986).

and to today's case. An adult male resident in Northern Ireland alleged he was a practicing homosexual who desired to engage in consensual homosexual conduct. The laws of Northern Ireland forbade him that right. He alleged that he had been questioned, his home had been searched, and he feared criminal prosecution. The court held that the laws proscribing the conduct were invalid under the European Convention on Human Rights ... Authoritative in all countries that are members of the Council of Europe (21 nations then, 45 nations now), the [*Dudgeon*] decision is at odds with the premise in *Bowers* that the claim put forward was insubstantial in our Western civilization.[42]

The Court also rejected the attempt to rely entirely on a culturally determinist position. Thus, it endorsed Justice Stevens' dissenting opinion in *Bowers*:

> The fact that the governing majority in a State has traditionally viewed a particular practice as immoral is not a sufficient reason for upholding a law prohibiting the practice; neither history nor tradition could save a law prohibiting miscegenation from constitutional attack.[43]

The ECtHR's later judgment in *Norris v Ireland*,[44] which replicated the *Dudgeon* decision for Ireland, was also influential in the groundbreaking decision of the South African Constitutional Court when it, too, decided to overturn the longstanding criminalisation of sodomy under South African law. Thus, Ackerman J, citing *Norris*, stated in *NCGLE* that 'the European Court of Human Rights has correctly, in my view, recognised the often serious psychological harm for gays which results from such discriminatory provisions'.[45] Nor is the ECtHR the only source for such transnational interaction. Ackerman J also cited the Supreme Court of Canada in *Vriend v Alberta*, both for the psychological harm of sexual orientation discrimination, and:

> [T]he implicit message conveyed by the exclusion, that gays and lesbians, unlike other individuals, are not worthy of protection. This is clearly an example of a distinction which demeans the individual and strengthens and perpetrates [sic] the view that gays and lesbians are less worthy of protection as individuals in Canada's society. The potential harm to the dignity and perceived worth of gay and lesbian individuals constitutes a particularly cruel form of discrimination.[46]

Far from rendering it inapplicable, the contextual difference—*Vriend* was a case about sexual orientation discrimination in employment—strengthened its applicability. As Ackerman J stated: 'These observations ... would apply

---

[42] *Lawrence v Texas* (n 40) 573.
[43] ibid 578.
[44] *Norris v Ireland* (1991) 13 EHRR 389.
[45] *National Coalition for Gay and Lesbian Equality v Minister of Justice* (CCT11/90) [1988] ZACC 15 (South African Constitutional Court) (hereinafter *NCGLE*) [23], citing *Norris* (ibid [21]).
[46] *Vriend v Alberta* [1998] 1 SCR 493 [102] (per Cory J).

with even greater force to the criminalisation of consensual sodomy in private between adult males.'[47]

The trend towards decriminalisation of homosexuality has, however, been abruptly interrupted by the Indian Supreme Court's decision to overturn a strongly argued decision of the Delhi High Court which had struck down section 377 of the Indian Penal Code criminalising sodomy.[48] In the *Naz Foundation* case,[49] the Delhi High Court drew on the growing common resource of comparative materials to support its finding that section 377 violated the right to full personhood, which it held was implicit in the notion of the right to life under Article 21 of the Indian Constitution. In an impressive demonstration of the ways in which cultures can and should interact with each other, it cited extensively from the ECtHR cases of *Dudgeon, Norris v Ireland*, the South African *NCGLE* case, the US Supreme Court decisions in *Romer v Evans* and *Lawrence v Texas*, and the Canadian case of *Vriend v Alberta*, as well as from Indian judicial and non-judicial sources. This is summed up in the following dictum from Justice Muralhidur:

> This vast majority (borrowing the language of the South African Constitutional Court) is denied 'moral full citizenship'. Section 377 IPC grossly violates their right to privacy and liberty embodied in Article 21 insofar as it criminalises consensual sexual acts between adults in private. These fundamental rights had their roots deep in the struggle for independence and, as pointed out by Granville Austin in 'The Indian Constitution—Cornerstone of a Nation', 'they were included in the Constitution in the hope and expectation that one day the tree of true liberty would bloom in India'. In the words of Justice V.R. Krishna Iyer these rights are cardinal to a decent human order and protected by constitutional armour. The spirit of Man is at the root of Article 21, absent liberty, other freedoms are frozen.[50]

However, the Supreme Court of India gave short shrift to all these arguments, holding that the presumption of constitutionality of a statute, even one which had been agreed prior to the Constitution, had not been displaced.[51] It was also unimpressed with the High Court's use of comparative law:

> In its anxiety to protect the so-called rights of LGBT persons and to declare that Section 377 IPC violates the right to privacy, autonomy and dignity, the High Court has extensively relied upon the judgments of other jurisdictions. Though

---

[47] *NCGLE* (n 49) [23].

[48] 'Unnatural offences—Whoever voluntarily has carnal intercourse against the order of nature with any man, woman or animal, shall be punished with imprisonment for life, or with imprisonment of either description for a term which may extend to ten years, and shall also be liable to fine. Explanation—Penetration is sufficient to constitute the carnal intercourse necessary to the offence described in this section.'

[49] *Naz Foundation v Government of Delhi* (Delhi High Court, 2 July 2009) www.nazindia. org/judgement_377.pdf.

[50] ibid [52].

[51] *Koushal v Naz Foundation* (Supreme Court of India, 11 December 2013) http://judis.nic. in/supremecourt/imgs1.aspx?filename=41070.

these judgments shed considerable light on various aspects of this right and are informative in relation to the plight of sexual minorities, we feel that they cannot be applied blindfolded for deciding the constitutionality of the law enacted by the Indian legislature.[52]

It cited its own 1973 death penalty decision of *Singh v State of UP*,[53] in which the Court emphatically rejected the relevance of US materials cited before it. In that case, the Constitutional Bench had 'grave doubts about the expediency of transplanting Western experience in our country. Social conditions are different and so also the general intellectual level'.[54] The Supreme Court similarly cited a 1974 case, *Pal v Arora*,[55] in which counsel who appeared for the appellant had relied upon a passage from *Halsbury's Laws of England* on the issue of presumption of undue influence in the case of parties engaged to be married. In that case, the Court had spent some time explaining that the context in which marriage took place in India and, in particular, the continued prevalence of arranged marriages made *Halsbury's Laws of England* irrelevant to the Indian context. Without more ado, the Supreme Court in *Naz* concluded that the comparative law relied on by the Delhi High Court was irrelevant and that its conclusion should be overturned.

This raises in stark terms the dilemma facing Lord Hoffmann's position. Is it correct to say that the right to privacy for gay people should be protected in South Africa, the UK, Northern Ireland, Ireland and the USA, but not in India? That there is nothing in the reasoning used in these other jurisdictions that has relevance to India? Lord Hoffmann would argue that the balance between conflicting objectives of equality for LGBT people and some version of public morality are entirely a matter for the domestic court. While this is clearly descriptively true in this case, it is hard to see why it should be normatively the case too. At the very least, the Indian Supreme Court should provide public justification for its finding that these reasons do not apply in India. It might well be that the specific laws in some areas, such as those relating to marriage, might differ to reflect different understandings of what constitutes undue influence in marriage. But even this requires justification. By ignoring the reasoning in other courts and retreating behind the screen of cultural pluralism, the Indian Supreme Court should be regarded as failing in its function of providing determinations on difficult questions which, while not necessarily right or wrong, are nevertheless capable of being convincing, plausible and rigorously argued.

The assumption of cultural determinism also assumes that legal systems are far more insulated from each other than they are. Section 377 of the

---

[52] ibid [52].
[53] *Singh v State of UP* (1973) 1 SCC 20.
[54] *Koushal* (n 51) [14].
[55] *Pal v Arora* (1974) SC 1999.

Indian Penal Code, which criminalises sodomy as an 'unnatural offence', was never explicitly enacted by the Indian legislature, but was instead imported from British law through the colonial code drawn up in the nineteenth century. The Court's strong presumption of the constitutionality of statutes was therefore based on a further, much weaker, presumption that, by failing to repeal it, the legislature must be taken to have approved it. The result was that in practice, a British colonial relic was upheld—some steps away from a culturally determined result. This raises the further question of whose culture counts.[56] The appeal against the Delhi High Court decision was not brought by the original respondents in the case, namely, the Union of India, the government of Delhi and the police. Instead, as permitted by the wide laws of standing in India, it was brought by Suresh Kumar Koushal and others who are described as 'citizens of India who believe they have the moral responsibility and duty in protecting cultural values of Indian society'. To what extent should these petitioners be regarded as expressing Indian cultural values any more than the minority of LGBT people whose rights they were denying? It is arguably exactly in these situations that a broader, transnational value system should be part of the Court's deliberative approach.

The steps beyond decriminalising homosexuality towards establishing full equality for same-sex partnerships have attracted less consensus, but, as in the case of minimum qualification periods for prisoners' voting rights, this does not make them any less open to transcultural conversation and interaction. It is again preferable to achieve this through legislative action, as has finally happened in Britain. The South African Constitutional Court has systematically addressed barriers to equality, culminating in the *Fourie*[57] decision requiring equality in marriage. The ECtHR has progressed more slowly. In its 2010 decision of *Schalk v Austria*,[58] it rejected an argument by a same-sex couple that the refusal to allow them to marry breached their Convention rights. The applicants had initially to confront the explicit wording of Article 12 ECtHR, which states that: 'Men and women of marriageable age have the right to marry and to found a family, according to the national laws governing the exercise of this right.' This contrasts with the more recent EU Charter of Fundamental Rights, which entered into force on 1 December 2009. Article 9 of the Charter reads as follows: 'The right to marry and to found a family shall be guaranteed in accordance with the

---

[56] M Kirby, 'Sodomy Revived: The Supreme Court of India Reverses Naz' (*Oxford Human Rights Hub*, 22 April 2014) http://ohrh.law.ox.ac.uk/the-hon-michael-kirby-sodomy-revived-the-supreme-court-of-india-reverses-naz.

[57] *Minister of Home Affairs v Fourie* (CCT 60/04) [2005] ZACC 19 (South African Constitutional Court).

[58] *Schalk v Austria* (2011) 53 EHRR 20.

national laws governing the exercise of these rights.' The Commentary on the Charter makes it clear that:

> [S]ince there is no explicit reference to 'men and women' as the case is in other human rights instruments, it may be argued that there is no obstacle to recognize same-sex relationships in the context of marriage. There is, however, no explicit requirement that domestic laws should facilitate such marriages.[59]

Notably, the Court held that the text was no longer an insuperable obstacle. Indeed, having regard to Article 9 of the Charter, it held that it:

> [W]ould no longer consider that the right to marry enshrined in Article 12 must in all circumstances be limited to marriage between two persons of the opposite sex. Consequently, it cannot be said that Article 12 is inapplicable to the applicants' complaint.[60]

However, given the lack of European consensus, the question of whether to recognise same-sex marriages was one for the national law of Contracting States and not for the ECtHR:

> In that connection the Court observes that marriage has deep-rooted social and cultural connotations which may differ largely from one society to another. The Court reiterates that it must not rush to substitute its own judgment in place of that of the national authorities, who are best placed to assess and respond to the needs of society.[61]

It therefore found that Article 12 did not impose an obligation to grant same-sex couples access to marriage. The Court did take a small step forward and hold that the relationship of a cohabiting same-sex couple living in a stable de facto partnership fell within the conception of 'family life' in Article 8, which gives everyone a right to respect for private and family life.[62] However, given that the applicants, by the time of the case, had an equivalent alternative in the form of a Registered Partnerships Act, there was no breach of Articles 8 and 14. Strikingly, the Court held that it could not 'but note that there is an emerging European consensus towards legal recognition of same-sex couples. Moreover, this tendency has developed rapidly over the past decade. Nevertheless, there is not yet a majority of States providing for legal recognition of same-sex marriage'.[63] It therefore held that as long as the institutions were roughly equivalent, there was no need to determine that each and every aspect of the partnership was identical to marriage. Therefore, the state had not exceeded its margin of appreciation in relation to marriage.

However, this devolving of decision-making to the states does not signify a resort to cultural pluralism. Instead, the Court had to air its reasoning process and show openly why it has come to this decision. Moreover, its

---

[59] ibid [25].
[60] ibid [61].
[61] ibid [62].
[62] ibid [94].
[63] ibid [105].

adherence to a living instrument doctrine (itself a source of criticism from Lord Hoffmann) leaves it open to the Court to change its conclusion when there is sufficient consensus among states. Both of these strongly support the argument that restrictions on human rights need to be openly defended. When the context changes, such restrictions can then be modified or lifted.

V. CONCLUSION

In this chapter, I have argued against a conception of human rights which regards their application as culturally determined. Judges making decisions on complex issues of human rights law need to adopt a reasoning process which is thorough and persuasive. Even if the outcome is contested and may even change over time, its authority lies in its deliberative content, that is, in its use of reasons which are rigorous, convincing and well supported by evidence, be it factual or legal. While there are clearly appropriate variations based on institutional, historical or social differences, these should not be taken for granted, but openly defended by means of reasons which are identifiable, understandable and persuasive. This necessitates a consideration of how other decision-makers, faced with similarly worded human rights instruments, have come to their conclusions.

8

Lord Hoffmann and Public Law: TV Dinner or Dining at the Savoy?

ALISON L YOUNG

I. INTRODUCTION

WHEN YOU ARE asked to evaluate the contribution of an extremely eminent member of the judiciary to a particular area of the law, it is hard to know where to start. Alas, the first thing that sprang to mind was something that probably appeared to Lord Hoffmann as a throwaway remark. In *Moyna v Secretary of State for Work and Pensions*,[1] one of the issues that arose before the court was whether an individual was unable to cook for herself and so was entitled to an extra disability living allowance. In addition, the court had to determine whether any mistake made by the administrative bodies called upon to determine this issue was an error of law or an error of fact. The Court of Appeal and the House of Lords were only able to overturn any determination by an administrative body or tribunal if an error of law had been made. When contemplating how an individual might solve the problem of not being able to cook for herself, Lord Hoffmann remarked that:

> A person who cannot cook for himself is entitled to the allowance, now £14.90 a week, whether he solves the eating problem by obtaining help, having a wife, buying television dinners or dining at the Savoy.[2]

One of the issues that has always intrigued me about this quotation is how it is possible to dine at the Savoy for £14.90.[3]

As well as furnishing an attention-grabbing title, *Moyna* is one of the cases that will form the focus of my assessment of Lord Hoffmann's contribution to public law. This chapter will begin by comparing and contrasting the fortunes of two of Lord Hoffmann's contributions to public law,

---

[1] *Moyna v Secretary of State for Work and Pensions* [2003] UKHL 44, [2003] 1 WLR 1929.
[2] ibid [17].
[3] An issue on which, alas, Lord Hoffmann remains silent.

both of which were discussed in recent decisions of the Supreme Court. In addition to *Moyna*, I will investigate Lord Hoffmann's account of the principle of legality in *R v Secretary of State for the Home Department ex p Simms*.[4] These two cases appear to have experienced contrasting fortunes. Whilst *Moyna* originally appeared to have little influence, Lord Hoffmann's approach to the distinction between law and fact would now appear to be on the verge of playing a predominant role. The principle of legality, however, which enjoyed a prominent role in public law, appears to have had its importance side-stepped, if not eroded. These contrasting fortunes serve to illustrate Lord Hoffmann's more important and potentially more permanent contribution to public law; an approach to public law that focuses more on principles and their specific application to the particular circumstances of the case as opposed to one based upon the application of axiomatic rules and broad taxonomies. However, it is also important to realise that this approach is not suited to all areas of public law and that, when misapplied, it can do more harm than good.

II. CONTRASTING FORTUNES OVER MISCARRIAGES OF JUSTICE

It is probably fair to say that Lord Hoffmann would not describe himself as a public law specialist. Nevertheless, his time as a judge in the Court of Appeal and the House of Lords occurred during an explosion of public law cases in the run-up to and following the enactment of the Human Rights Act 1998. As such, it was hard for any member of the senior judiciary at that time not to have had an influence upon the development of public law. Perhaps Lord Hoffmann's most important contribution was one that is indirectly as opposed to directly concerned with public law—his important judgments on the liability of public authorities in tort law, particularly *Gorringe v Calderdale Metropolitan Borough Council*.[5] Lord Hoffmann has also been involved in high-priority public law cases, particularly those concerning the balance to be made between the protection of national security and human rights and civil liberties, most notably *A v Secretary of State for the Home Department (Belmarsh Prisoners)*,[6] concerning whether the indefinite detention of prisoners without trial found in section 23 of the Anti-terrorism Crime and Security Act 2001 was compatible with Convention rights and *Secretary of State for the Home Department v AF*,[7] which

---

[4] *R v Secretary of State for the Home Department ex p Simms* [1999] UKHL 33, [2000] 2 AC 115.

[5] *Gorringe v Calderdale Metropolitan Borough Council* [2004] UKHL 15, [2004] 1 WLR 1057.

[6] *A v Secretary of State for the Home Department (Belmarsh Prisoners)* [2004] UKHL 56, [2005] 2 AC 68.

[7] *Secretary of State for the Home Department v AF* [2009] UKHL 28, [2010] 2 AC 269.

assessed the Convention-compatibility of closed material proceedings. It may seem odd, therefore, to choose to focus on two aspects of public law that may not appear to have as high a profile: the distinction between errors of law and errors of fact and the principle of legality. However, these elements of public law not only provide an illustration of the mixed reaction to Lord Hoffmann's contributions to public law, but also help to illustrate how his main contribution to public law is one of approach as opposed to substance.

A. The Law–Fact Distinction

The distinction between errors of law and errors of fact plays an important role in English administrative law. It plays a foundational role in judicial review, determining the extent to which courts are able to review the decisions of administrative bodies and administrative tribunals. English administrative law traditionally delineates between jurisdictional and non-jurisdictional errors. Jurisdictional errors are errors that may be made by an administrative body when determining whether it has the power to act. Non-jurisdictional errors are errors that can be made when an administrative body is acting within its powers. Courts can correct jurisdictional errors, but cannot correct non-jurisdictional errors. For example, a statute may provide that 'a college may give scholarships to students who obtained a First in their first-year examinations'. This empowers the college to act—to distribute scholarships—when certain conditions are met: students have obtained a First in their first-year examinations. 'Obtaining a First' determines the jurisdiction of the college. It can only give scholarships to students who obtained a First in their first-year examinations. If a scholarship were given to a student without a First, then the college would have made an error as to its jurisdiction; it would have given a scholarship to someone when it did not have the power to do so. The court would therefore correct this error. If a college were to give scholarships to those who had obtained a First, but only to students who went to state schools who obtained a First, then the court could not replace the college's assessment that only state school-educated students with a First deserved scholarships with its own assessment favouring a different sub-section of students who obtained a First. The court would be able to strike down a decision were the college to act irrationally—eg, giving scholarships on the basis of hair colour[8]—but would not be able to replace the college's assessment of who should get a scholarship with its own.

---

[8] See *Associated Provincial Picture Houses v Wednesbury Corporation* [1948] 1 KB 223 (CA).

The seminal cases of *Anisminic v Foreign Compensation Commission*[9] and *R (Visitor of the University of Hull) ex p Page*[10] are regarded as authority for the principle that all errors of law are jurisdictional errors. Consequently, courts can correct any error of law made by an administrative body. However, not all errors of fact are jurisdictional errors. Instead, courts can only control factual errors in certain specific situations. This delineation between error of law and error of fact is reiterated in the Tribunals, Courts and Enforcement Act 2007, where appeals from the First-Tier Tribunal to the Upper Tribunal and from the Upper Tribunal to the Court of Appeal are available for points of law only.[11] The way in which courts distinguish between 'points of law' and 'points of fact' or 'errors of law' and 'errors of fact' plays an important role in English administrative law as it determines whether, and to what extent, a court can review decisions of administrative bodies and tribunals.

The distinction between 'law' and 'fact' may appear to be straightforward. The definition of a legal term is a question of law. The determination of the facts is clearly a question of fact. However, difficulties arise when dealing with legal definitions that are open to a range of interpretations, particularly when the best interpretation of the legal term depends predominantly on the circumstances in which it is applied. This is best explained by an example. Imagine that legislation had empowered a college to give scholarships not to those who had obtained a First in their first-year examinations, but to those who were 'poor'. We can define 'poor' in the abstract as those who have fewer assets than others. We can assess the facts as they apply to students, determining the income and outgoings of their parents, for example. But difficulties arise when deciding how few assets are required to determine that a student is 'poor'. A student whose family earns an average income may be 'poor' when compared with a cohort of students whose parents earn above-average incomes as partners in law firms. The same student would, however, be 'rich' if all the other students in her cohort come from families earning the minimum wage.

Our example is regarded by some as an illustration of the problems that arise when refining a legal definition in order to provide a precise definition of the term.[12] Others argue that difficulties arise when applying legal definitions to the facts.[13] Lord Hoffmann's contribution to this issue, in these grey areas of refinements of legal definitions or applications of law to the facts, seemed at first to have had only marginal impact. However, it has been

---

[9] *Anisminic v Foreign Compensation Commission* [1968] UKHL 6, [1969] 2 AC 147.
[10] *R (Visitor of the University of Hull) ex p Page* [1992] UKHL 12, [1993] AC 682.
[11] Tribunals, Courts and Enforcement Act 2007, ss 11–14.
[12] PP Craig, *Administrative Law* (7th edn, London, Sweet & Maxwell, 2012).
[13] TAO Endicott, 'Questions of Law' (1998) 114 *LQR* 292; and R Williams 'When is an Error Not an Error? Reform of Jurisdictional Review of Error of Law and Fact' [2007] *Public Law* 793.

recently used to signal a sea-change in the approach of the court away from focusing on the distinguishing characteristics of 'law' and 'fact' and towards an assessment of whether it is expedient for the court to correct decisions of administrative bodies or tribunals.

As mentioned above, the issue in *Moyna* was whether Mrs Moyna was entitled to an additional disability living allowance. Section 72(1)(a)(ii) of the Social Security Contributions and Benefits Act 1992 established that Mrs Moyna was entitled to this allowance if she was so severely disabled that she 'cannot prepare a main meal for herself if she has the ingredients'.[14] Mrs Moyna had indicated that she was unable to lift heavy pans, had difficulties chopping some vegetables and that she sometimes had to rest when preparing meals. She believed that she would require help for one to three days a week to help her to cook. The original assessment by the doctors of the local authority and the Disability Appeal Tribunal had been that she was sufficiently able to cook for herself and so was not entitled to the extra allowance. An appeal was then made to the Social Securities Commissioner, who was able to overturn decisions where there had been a legal error. The Commissioner determined that no legal error had been made. The Court of Appeal, however, disagreed. It concluded that a legal error had been made. There was evidence of a wide range of divergent conclusions when applying section 72(1)(a)(ii) to different individuals who would appear to be in similar situations. As such, it concluded that legal errors must have been made—there must be an incorrect legal definition if the definition appears to give divergent results when applied to similar facts.

On appeal to the House of Lords, Lord Hoffmann, giving the leading judgment, concluded that, had any error been made in *Moyna*, it was best classified as an error of fact and not an error of law. The importance of Lord Hoffmann's contribution lies not in the outcome, but in the way in which he approached the distinction between law and fact. First, he rejected the argument of the Court of Appeal that an error of law must have occurred if the same legal test has produced divergent results in similar situations. He recognised that some legal terms were issues of judgment as opposed to a purely empirical determination. This was the case with a determination of whether an individual was so disabled that she could not cook for herself. The legal interpretation of the term could still be correct even if apparently divergent conclusions were reached on similar facts as the term included an element of evaluative judgment. Second, Lord Hoffmann rejected the approach of *Brutus v Cozens*,[15] where a distinction was drawn between legal terms that had their own normal meaning and those that carried more technical meanings. A term such as 'insulting' should be interpreted according to its ordinary meaning and is best understood as a question of fact as

---

[14] Social Security Contributions and Benefits Act 1992, s 72(1)(a)(ii).
[15] *Brutus v Cozens* [1973] AC 854 (HL).

opposed to a question of law. Lord Hoffmann concluded that this was a misreading of the case. The approach in *Brutus v Cozens* was best understood as recognising that context, background and syntax should be taken into account when interpreting statutory terms.

Lord Hoffmann, instead, proposed taking an approach to the distinction between law and fact based on expediency, stating that:

> [T]here are two kinds of question of fact: there are questions of fact; and there are questions of law as to which lawyers have decided that it would be inexpedient for an appellate tribunal to have to form an independent judgment.[16]

The issue as to whether Mrs Moyna was able to cook for herself fell into the grey area of application of law to the facts or where legal definitions are refined in a manner that is highly dependent on the circumstances in which the definition is applied. It was best understood as a question of law on which it was not expedient for the appellate tribunal to form an independent judgment. As such, it is best dealt with by the court as a question of fact; one where the court has no ability to substitute its assessment for that of the administrative body or tribunal.

Lord Hoffmann's approach to the definition of law and fact in this complicated area—despite it amounting to a potential 'revolution' in approach[17]—initially appeared to have had little impact on the law. Lord Hoffmann repeated his approach in *Lawson v Serco*,[18] which concerned the interpretation of 'employee', particularly relating to whether British legislation regulating employees had territorial restrictions and, if so, how these were to be determined. Here, the court had to determine whether, inter alia, individuals employed by British firms to work abroad or peripatetic employees based in Great Britain were 'employees'. Lord Hoffmann concluded that this issue did not concern an assessment of primary facts—eg, how and when the individual was employed—or the legal meaning of 'employee'. Instead, it concerned an evaluation of primary facts according to the legal definition. As such, its classification as 'law' or 'fact' depends 'upon whether as a matter of policy one thinks that it is a decision which an appellate body with a jurisdiction limited to errors of law should be able to review'.[19] Lord Hoffmann was reluctant to classify the issue as to whether peripatetic employees were 'employees' for the purposes of the legislation as an issue of fact as opposed to law, thus excluding a right of appeal. Nevertheless, he argued that the issue was one where the original finding of the primary fact-finder was 'entitled to considerable respect'.[20]

[16] *Moyna* (n 1) [27].
[17] See R Carnwath, 'Tribunal Justice: A New Start' [2009] *Public Law* 48, 63.
[18] *Lawson v Serco* [2006] UKHL 3, [2006] 1 All ER 823.
[19] ibid [34].
[20] ibid.

Lord Hoffmann's flexible approach to the distinction between errors of law and errors of fact was recently endorsed in the Supreme Court decision of *Jones v First Tier Tribunal*.[21] In *Jones* the issue arose as to whether the Criminal Injuries Compensation Authority should grant an award to Mr Jones, who had been severely injured in a road traffic incident. A collision occurred between Mr Jones's gritter lorry and a truck. The truck had stopped in order to try to avoid an individual who had walked out into the middle of a busy road to commit suicide. In order to receive an award, Jones had to demonstrate that his injuries had been caused by a 'crime of violence' under section 20 of the Offences Against the Person Act 1861. An issue arose as to whether the individual committing suicide had the relevant mens rea—the intention to cause harm or recklessness as to whether harm is caused. The Criminal Injuries Compensation Authority refused to make an award, concluding that no crime of violence had been committed. The First Tier Tribunal and the Upper Tribunal agreed, concluding that no error of law had been made in this assessment. The Court of Appeal disagreed, arguing that the Criminal Injuries Compensation Authority had made an error of law. The Supreme Court agreed with the First Tier and the Upper Tier Tribunal, concluding that no error of law had been made.

In his judgment, Lord Carnwath referred to Lord Hoffmann's judgments in *Moyna* and *Lawson*, as well as citing his own academic writing on the tribunal system. He endorsed the adoption of the emerging new approach to the distinction between law and fact, proposed by Lord Hoffmann. First, as regards the distinction between tribunals and appellate courts, Lord Carnwath stated that the distinction between law and fact should be determined according to factors based on expediency and policy. In particular, the appellate court should determine whether there is any utility in hearing an appeal from the decision of the specialist tribunal, making its assessment according to the need for the development of the law in this area and an assessment of the relative competences of the tribunal and the appellate court. Even if the court determines that the issue is one of law, and therefore an appeal should be permitted, the appellate court should give weight to the conclusion of the tribunal.[22] Second, when determining whether a specialist appellate tribunal should hear an appeal from a first-tier tribunal, similar criteria apply, but do so in a different manner due to the specialist nature of the appellate tribunal. The appellate tribunal should have greater flexibility to venture into the facts, in particular ensuring that the errors of law that it can hear on appeal include issues of principle affecting that specialist jurisdiction.[23] Although Lord Carnwath's statements are technically obiter

---

[21] *Jones v First Tier Tribunal* [2013] UKSC 19, [2013] 2 AC 48.
[22] ibid [46].
[23] ibid.

dicta, nevertheless they are widely regarded as endorsing a sea-change in the approach to the distinction between law and fact, completing the move to greater flexibility proposed by Lord Hoffmann.

B. The Principle of Legality

The principle of legality was not created by Lord Hoffmann. However, his reference to this principle in *Simms* is frequently referred to as a definitive authority for the principle of legality. The principle of legality is a principle of statutory interpretation. It recognises that Parliament does not legislate in a vacuum; rather, it legislates against a backdrop of principles of the common law. As such, broad legislative terms are to be interpreted so as to comply with this backdrop of common law principles. Parliament would have understood, when legislating, the context of these principles and so is not to have been taken to have intended to legislate in a manner that contradicts these principles unless it clearly and specifically expresses its intention to do so. This principle of interpretation is found in the third edition of *Cross: Statutory Interpretation*.[24] Although originally used to ensure that broad legislative principles were not interpreted so as to remove the rights of natural justice and procedural fairness,[25] the principle was later interpreted to extend to include a presumption that Parliament would not intend to legislate contrary to substantive principles of the common law. For example, in *Leech*, the principle was used to conclude that a statutory provision that empowered the creation of general prison rules would not empower the restriction of communications between prisoners and their solicitors due to this being in conflict with common law principles.[26] In *Witham*, a general provision empowering the Lord Chancellor to set legal fees did not empower the Lord Chancellor to set fees that would preclude individuals from pursuing legal cases, thus restricting the common law principle of access to justice.[27]

The principle of legality was also discussed extensively by Lord Browne-Wilkinson and Lord Steyn in *Pierson* before the discussion of this principle by Lord Steyn and Lord Hoffmann in *Simms*.[28] The analysis in *Pierson* explains why Lord Hoffmann's account of the principle of legality is cited so frequently. In *Pierson*, both Lord Browne-Wilkinson and Lord Steyn

---

[24] R Cross, G Engle and J Bell, *Cross: Statutory Interpretation* (3rd edn, Oxford, Oxford University Press, 1995).

[25] See, eg, *R v Home Secretary ex p Doody* [1993] UKHL 8, [1994] AC 531.

[26] *R v Secretary of State for the Home Department ex p Leech (No 2)* [1993] EWCA Civ 12, [1994] QB 198.

[27] *R v Lord Chancellor ex p Witham* [1997] EWHC Admin 237, [1998] QB 575.

[28] *R v Secretary of State for the Home Department ex p Pierson* [1998] AC 539 (HL).

discussed the principle of legality. Lord Steyn regarded the principle of legality as a general principle of statutory interpretation:

> Parliament does not legislate in a vacuum. Parliament legislates for a European liberal democracy founded on the principles and traditions of the common law. And the courts may approach legislation on this initial assumption. But this assumption only has prima facie force. It can be displaced by a clear and specific provision to the contrary. These propositions require some explanation.[29]

Although the statute provided the Home Secretary with a large discretionary power to determine the mandatory component of a life sentence, he did not have the power to exercise this discretion in a manner that would undermine the common law principle preventing the imposition of retrospective criminal sentences. However, Lord Browne-Wilkinson's judgment appeared to have a narrower focus. He recognised the same earlier authorities as Lord Steyn in support of the principle of legality. Nevertheless, his interpretation focused more specifically on the way in which statutory provisions *empowering administrative bodies* were to be interpreted. He therefore articulated the following principle:

> A power conferred by Parliament in general terms is not to be taken to authorise the doing of acts by the donee of the power which adversely affect the legal rights of the citizen or the basic principles on which the law of the United Kingdom is based unless the statute conferring the power makes it clear that such was the intention of Parliament.[30]

As well as a difference in the breadth of the application of the principle of legality, a further possible distinction emerges as to the justification for the principle of legality. Lord Steyn regards the principle of legality as a key constitutional principle: a means of reconciling common law principles designed to protect the values of a European liberal democracy in a constitutional setting which upholds the sovereignty of Parliament as a legal principle such that the courts cannot overturn legislation or directly contradict the will of Parliament when interpreting legislative provisions. Lord Browne-Wilkinson's defence of the principle of legality arguably derives from principles of administrative law, focusing on an analysis in line with conceptions of the ultra vires principle, where courts are empowered to strike down actions of the administration that are beyond the scope of their powers. The principle of legality illustrates more specifically how common law principles are used to restrict the scope of general powers granted to administrative bodies. Parliament is aware of these principles operating in the background and therefore, by applying the principle of legality, courts are striving to enforce the will of Parliament, interpreted in line with common law principles.

---

[29] ibid 587 [C].
[30] ibid 575 [C]–[D].

Lord Hoffmann's account of the principle of legality in *Simms* supports Lord Steyn's interpretation of the principle and merits reciting in full:

> Parliamentary sovereignty means that Parliament can, if it chooses, legislate contrary to fundamental principles of human rights. The Human Rights Act 1998 will not detract from this power. The constraints upon its exercise by Parliament are ultimately political, not legal. But the principle of legality means that Parliament must squarely confront what it is doing and accept the political cost. Fundamental rights cannot be overridden by general or ambiguous words. This is because there is too great a risk that the full implications of their unqualified meaning may have passed unnoticed in the democratic process. In the absence of express language or necessary implication to the contrary, the courts therefore presume that even the most general words were intended to be subject to the basic rights of the individual. In this way the courts of the United Kingdom, though acknowledging the sovereignty of Parliament, apply principles of constitutionality little different from those which exist in countries where the power of the legislature is expressly limited by a constitutional document.[31]

Following his justification of the principle of legality, Lord Hoffmann explains how the principle of legality relates to the Human Rights Act 1998, as well as explaining how the principle applies to the interpretation of secondary as well as primary legislation so as to justify its application in *Simms*.

Despite the strong support for the principle of legality, particularly as expressed by Lord Hoffmann in *Simms*, the principle was arguably 'sidestepped' in the recent Supreme Court decision of *Bank Mellat v Her Majesty's Treasury (1)*.[32] The case concerned a challenge to the Financial Restrictions (Iran) Order 2009, made under Schedule 7 to the Counter-Terrorism Act 2008, which directed institutions in the financial sector not to enter into, or to continue to pursue, financial transactions or other business with, inter alia, Bank Mellat. Bank Mellat issued proceedings under section 68 of the 2008 Act to set aside the Order. Due to the sensitive nature of the material relied on, the government applied for and was granted permission for the hearing to be conducted as a closed material proceeding. As such, sensitive information would not be given to Bank Mellat, being given instead to a Special Advocate who was required to give the gist of the information to Bank Mellat in order to enable it to challenge the order. The Bank was unsuccessful in overturning the order and appealed to the Court of Appeal and then to the Supreme Court. As the appeal would concern an examination of aspects of the judgment reached in closed proceedings, the issue arose as to whether the Supreme Court would be able to conduct a closed material proceeding.

---

[31] [2000] 2 AC 115, 131 [E]–[G].
[32] *Bank Mellat v Her Majesty's Treasury (1)* [2013] UKSC 38, [2013] 3 WLR 179.

Al Rawi v Security Service[33] had established that closed material proceedings were contrary to the principle of open justice—a fundamental principle of the common law—that could not be eroded unless there were compelling reasons to do so and, preferably, by statute. As such, only Parliament should have the power to introduce closed material proceedings through detailed legislative provisions. The Counter-Terrorism Act empowered courts to develop 'rules of court' to hear closed material proceedings. However, section 68 of the Act defined 'rules of court' as 'rules for regulating the practice and procedure to be followed in the High Court or the Court of Appeal or in the Court of Session'. No express mention was made of the power to develop rules of the court for the Supreme Court—which was unsurprising given that although the Constitutional Reform Act 2005 empowered the creation of the Supreme Court, at the time of the enactment of the Counter-Terrorism Act, the Supreme Court did not exist. The Constitutional Reform Act empowers the Supreme Court to 'determine any question necessary to be determined for the purposes of doing justice to an appeal to it under any enactment'.[34] Section 45(1) of the Act empowers the President of the Supreme Court to enact the 'Supreme Court Rules' which govern 'the practice and procedure to be followed by the Court'. The Supreme Court Rules enacted under this section state that the Supreme Court has all the powers of the court below,[35] as well as having the ability to conduct hearings in private, provided there is a prior public announcement of its reasons for doing so.[36]

The Supreme Court concluded that it did have the power to hear closed material proceedings. Lords Hope, Kerr and Reed disagreed. All three relied on *Al Rawi* as authority for the need for parliamentary authority for closed material proceedings. The establishment of closed material proceedings was contrary to the fundamental right of open justice. As such, legislation would only empower the holding of closed material proceedings in specific and express terms or by necessary implication.[37] All three concluded that this authority could not be found in the Counter-Terrorism Act, which did not refer to the Supreme Court, or in the broad provisions of section 40 of the Constitutional Reform Act. Lord Kerr argued that the power to carry out closed material proceedings could only be granted 'in the most unambiguous and forthright terms or by unmistakeably necessary implication'.[38] Both Lord Reed and Lord Hope referred to Lord Hoffmann's judgment in *Simms* to argue that the Constitutional Reform Act would only have been able to

---

[33] *Al Rawi v Security Service* [2011] UKSC 34, [2012] 1 AC 531.
[34] Constitutional Reform Act 2005, s 40(5).
[35] RSC, r 29(1).
[36] ibid r 27(3).
[37] *Bank Mellat* (n 32) [85] (Lord Hope), [105] (Lord Kerr), [135] (Lord Reed).
[38] ibid [105] (Lord Kerr).

empower the Supreme Court to create closed material proceedings if it did so by express words, the broad words in the Act being insufficient.[39] Lord Neuberger, giving the majority judgment, concluded that there was a strong case for enabling the Supreme Court to hold closed material proceedings, focusing in particular upon the practical consequences that would arise were the Supreme Court to hear an appeal from the Court of Appeal where closed material proceedings had been used. If the Supreme Court were not able to hear closed material proceedings it could either: not hear the appeal; hear the appeal with the materials that were previously subjected to a closed material proceeding being heard in open court; hear the appeal with the Supreme Court being unable to consider the materials subject to the closed material proceedings; be bound to allow the appeal; or be bound to refuse the appeal.[40] In essence, the Supreme Court would not be able to do justice to the appeal if it were not able to hear a closed material proceeding.[41] Lord Neuberger did recognise the importance of the principle of legality, but he concluded that this principle had to be interpreted according to the context and the purpose of the statute before the court.[42] As regards section 40(2) of the Constitutional Reform Act 2005, the provision was best understood as 'broad' as opposed to 'general'. It provided that all decisions of the Court of Appeal could be appealed to the Supreme Court unless this was precluded by another statute. Given that the Court of Appeal can hold closed material proceedings, this purpose could only be achieved by the broad provision of the Constitutional Reform Act if the Supreme Court were empowered to hold closed material proceedings.[43]

Critics of the decision might well regard this as a weakening of the principle of legality in favour of expediency, adding to this the concerns that are raised against closed material proceedings as a whole. However, Lord Neuberger's contribution could be seen as being more in line with Lord Hoffmann's account of the principle of legality than that of the minority, who relied on the principle to reject the ability of the Supreme Court to entertain closed material proceedings. This will become evident in the next section.

III. PURPOSES, CONTEXT AND PUBLIC LAW REASONING

This section will argue that Lord Hoffmann's principal contribution to public law is not his contribution to the substantive principles of public law, but the way in which he decides public law cases. In particular, I will argue that Lord Hoffmann prefers a contextual to an abstract approach, looking at

---

[39] ibid [85] (Lord Hope), [135] (Lord Reed).
[40] ibid [39]–[42] (Lord Neuberger).
[41] ibid [43] (Lord Neuberger).
[42] ibid [55] (Lord Neuberger).
[43] ibid [56] (Lord Neuberger).

the purpose of a rule, legal principle or distinction as opposed to applying these in an axiomatic manner. Understanding Lord Hoffmann's contribution in this manner explains how Lord Neuberger's account of the principle of legality in *Bank Mellat* is more in line with Lord Hoffmann's approach than that of the dissenting judges.

Rules, doctrines and definitions can be applied in diverse ways. The first difference—between a contextual and an abstract analysis—is best understood as a spectrum. All rules involve an element of generalisation. When a rule is applied in an abstract manner, the focus is on the application of the rule in general with less attention paid to specific circumstances. When applied in a contextual manner, there is detailed analysis of the specific circumstances in which the rule is to be applied. This can be illustrated by thinking about the different ways in which the court could have determined whether an individual was so disabled that she was unable to cook for herself. A more abstract approach would focus on broad categorisations, looking either at a general series of tasks that an individual was or was not able to complete, or by determining categories of disability. Applied in this manner, an assessment of whether Mrs Moyna was so disabled that she was not able to cook for herself would focus on determining whether she could or could not perform these tasks, or on the classification of her disability and whether it fell within those listed as meaning an individual was unable to cook for herself. A more contextual approach would examine more specifically the precise range of tasks that Mrs Moyna was able to perform, looking in more detail at her disability.

The second difference concerns whether one takes a purposive or axiomatic approach. Purposive approaches apply legal terms and rules according to the purpose of the legal term or rule. An axiomatic approach does not examine the purpose of the legal rule; it focuses on an assessment of the criteria of a particular legal rule or legal term. This can be illustrated by the different approaches taken to the distinction between law and fact. An axiomatic approach would apply the distinction by determining the criteria of 'law' and 'fact', and assessing the extent to which the matter to be assessed by the court possessed the criteria of 'law' and 'fact'. A purposive approach focuses on why a distinction is made between 'law' and 'fact'. If, for example, the distinction were made to delineate between issues where courts were more likely to have greater expertise and so should be able to overturn an earlier assessment of an administrative body, one would look to whether the matter was one where the court or the administrative body had greater expertise. As with the delineation between an abstract and a contextual approach, this is best understood as a spectrum. Approaches can be more or less purposive or axiomatic.

This approach to public law reasoning can clearly be seen in Lord Hoffmann's account of the application of the law/fact distinction in *Lawson*. He recognises that disputes can arise as to the evaluation of facts to determine whether they meet the requirements of a particular legal definition. His approach focuses on the purposes of the distinction between law and fact. In the context of these cases, appeals are allowed for issues of law, but not for issues of fact. Therefore, whether an issue as to the evaluation of the facts to meet a legal definition is treated as a matter of fact or law depends 'upon whether as a matter of policy one thinks that it is a decision which an appellate body with jurisdiction limited to errors of law should be able to review'.[44] In *Lawson*, Lord Hoffmann was of the opinion that there should be a right of appeal, so the issue was classified as a matter of law. Lord Hoffmann then adds further flexibility into this distinction by recognising that when the evaluations of facts is a 'question of degree', the 'decision of the primary fact-finder is entitled to considerable respect'.[45] Lord Hoffmann's analysis was purposive and focused on the particular application of the legal statute in question in the case before him: the problem of whether peripatetic workers should be classified as workers for the purposes of employment protection in UK statutes.

Lord Hoffmann's approach is also evident in his account of the principle of legality. What distinguishes his contribution in *Simms* is his account not just of the legal principle, but also of the purpose of the principle. He explains the constitutional importance of the principle of legality. The principle ensures that, were Parliament to legislate contrary to human rights, it would do so taking account of the full political cost. Clear and specific words in legislation are required to ensure that Parliament is aware that it is legislating in a way that will restrict fundamental rights. This general principle applies to all legislation. When applied to legislative provisions that empower administrative bodies, the legislative provision will not be interpreted as granting the power to act contrary to fundamental rights unless this is clearly and specifically articulated. The justification of the principle also requires that secondary legislation be interpreted in a manner so as not to restrict fundamental rights unless the secondary legislation clearly and specifically requires this restriction. Lord Hoffmann's concern is not to develop a rule that is applied axiomatically, but to focus on the reason behind the principle of legality, ensuring that it is applied according to its purpose. The purpose of the principle is to ensure as strong a protection of human rights as possible in a system with a legal principle of parliamentary sovereignty. Although Parliament can legislate contrary to human rights, it should only do so clearly and openly, where there has been a full democratic debate over these issues to ensure that there is clear parliamentary will to legislate contrary to human rights.

When we re-examine the impact of Lord Hoffmann's approach to the distinction between law and fact and the principle of legality, we see that

---

[44] *Lawson* (n 18) [34].
[45] ibid.

both of the two recent Supreme Court cases are positively influenced by the approach of Lord Hoffmann, even though *Bank Mellat* appears, at first glance, to side-step the principle of legality. It is easy to see how *Jones* follows Lord Hoffmann's approach to public law reasoning. Lord Carnwath explicitly adopts Lord Hoffmann's approach. His aim in *Jones* was to change the focus of the courts: away from an assessment of whether an issue is one of 'law' or 'fact' towards an assessment of whether the issue is one where a further appeal to the court would be beneficial. Again, in line with Lord Hoffmann's approach in *Lawson*, he added in further flexibility by ensuring that, even when faced with an issue of law, the court could defer to the assessment of the tribunal. Deference entails a modification of stringency. This implies that courts will not automatically correct legal definitions of lower tribunals whenever they disagree. Rather, courts may correct if they think that the legal definition of the tribunal is irrational or where there are strong reasons for disagreeing with the assessment of the tribunal.

To understand why the decision in *Bank Mellat* also illustrates an adoption of Lord Hoffmann's approach to reasoning in public law, we need to look more closely at Lord Neuberger's judgment, contrasting that with the approach of the dissenting judgments. Lord Neuberger recognises the principle of legality in his judgment and refers expressly to Lord Hoffmann's account of this principle in *Simms*.[46] However, he also recognises that this principle 'should not be applied without regard to the purpose and context of the statutory provision in issue'.[47] Section 40 of the Constitutional Reform Act 2005 is plainly intended to ensure that the Supreme Court can hear all appeals and decide them justly. This would not be possible unless they were enabled to hear closed material proceedings. Lord Neuberger's contextual and purposive approach is also illustrated in his argument in favour of allowing the Supreme Court to hear closed material proceedings. Lord Neuberger focuses on the specific problems that would arise were the Supreme Court to be unable to hear closed material proceedings. In doing so, he does not examine issues of expediency in the abstract, focusing instead on the range of specific options with which the Supreme Court would be faced were it not to hear closed material proceedings.[48] Lord Neuberger also focuses on the legal and constitutional principles operating in the background, specifically the need to ensure the protection of national security and the maintenance of the rule of law, and the role of the European Court of Human Rights.[49]

For the minority, the principle of legality applies more as a bright-line rule whose provisions cannot be crossed. Once it is established that closed

---

[46] *Simms* (n 4) [55].
[47] ibid [56].
[48] ibid [37]–[42].
[49] ibid [52].

material proceedings transgress fundamental principles of natural justice, there is a need for clear and specific statutory language to empower the Supreme Court to hold closed material proceedings hearings. Yet the 2008 Act does not provide this authorisation and the 2005 Act provides no specific authorisation providing a broad power to hear appeals. As fundamental rights cannot be overridden by implication or by anything other than manifestly necessary implication, the Constitutional Reform Act cannot empower the Supreme Court to hold closed material proceedings, even if this may cause logistical difficulties.

When analysed in a purposive and contextual manner, we can understand how *Bank Mellat* is not an illustration of the principle of legality being sidestepped by the courts, but of where the purposes of the principle are fulfilled even if, at first sight, its application is ignored in favour of expediency. The broad purpose of the principle of legality is to ensure that any restriction of fundamental rights has been carefully considered and is a true reflection of the will of Parliament. Fundamental principles are to be protected from inadvertent or accidental erosion. Although the Counter-Terrorism Act did not expressly include the Supreme Court, the Act does provide evidence of a clear intention of Parliament to introduce a proceeding that would normally transgress the fundamental principles of natural justice in order to protect national security. Parliament established clear rules to apply in this situation that can apply by analogy in the Supreme Court, who can adopt its own procedural rules in line with the legislative requirements. Although the legislature had not specifically debated granting the power to hold closed material proceedings to the Supreme Court, there had been legislative debate surrounding closed material proceedings during the enactment of the Counter-Terrorism Act. In addition, the European Court of Human Rights had scrutinised this provision,[50] requiring the adoption of 'gisting', which was subsequently followed by the House of Lords.[51] If the purpose of the principle of legality is to draw attention to a restriction on human rights, one could argue that this objective had already been achieved prior to *Bank Mellat*.

IV. SHOULD PUBLIC LAW BE PURPOSIVE?

This chapter has argued that Lord Hoffmann's most important contribution to public law has not been in terms of substantive outcomes or the development of important principles of public law, but instead in his approach to legal reasoning in public law cases. We have argued that his approach

---

[50] *A v UK* (2009) 49 EHRR 625.
[51] *Secretary of State for the Home Department v AF (No 3)* [2009] UKHL 28, [2010] 2 AC 269.

has two distinctive features. First, he takes a contextual as opposed to a general approach, ensuring that he focuses on the specific details and context of public law cases as opposed to employing broad generalisations. Second, his approach is purposive as opposed to axiomatic. He focuses on an assessment of the purpose of the rule as opposed to applying the rule in a vacuum, paying little if any attention to the purpose of a rule. The distinction between a general, axiomatic approach and a specific, purposive approach is similar to Frederick Schauer's distinction between a particularistic and a rule-based approach to decision-making.[52] Those adopting a particularistic approach to decision-making apply rules as 'rules of thumb' that have little weight in the decision-making process. The decision-maker focuses instead on the particular circumstances before her and the purposes behind the rule that she is applying. However, those adopting a rule-based approach to decision-making focus predominantly on the terms of the rule itself, applying the rule in a general manner. There are costs and benefits to each of these approaches. An analysis of these costs and benefits in the field of public law can help us to assess the merits of Lord Hoffmann's approach to public law reasoning.

When assessed in terms of outcome, an easy case can be made for adopting a particularistic approach. All rules contain generalisations. Consequently, rules are over and under inclusive. When applying the rule, there will be some situations where matters that should have been included in the rule, if the rule is to achieve its purpose, are not included. And, in a similar way, examples can be given of situations that fall within the rule that are not required to be covered by the rule if the rule is to achieve its purpose. To take the classic example of 'no dogs in the café', an application of this rule would exclude guide dogs, whose access to the café would not thwart the purposes of the rule—to maintain hygiene and to prevent disruption to the customers in the café. An application of the rule would also allow animals into the café that may be just as disruptive and unhygienic—eg, enabling people with pet crocodiles to take them to the café. A particularistic approach to rule applying avoids these instances of over- and under-inclusiveness. By treating the rule of 'no dogs in the café' as a rule of thumb, the café-owner can determine whether, nevertheless, the purposes of the rule would not be thwarted were guide dogs allowed and crocodiles prohibited from the café.

There are, however, advantages to adopting a rule-based approach to decision-making. A rule-based approach would appear to achieve fairness and consistency in decision-making. If all dogs are excluded from the café, there can be no potential issues of favouritism or discrimination that may arise were the café-owner to take a specific decision as to the admission

---

[52] F Schauer, *Playing by the Rules: A Philosophical Examination of Rule-Based Decision-Making in Law and in Life* (New York, Oxford University Press, 1993) 77–78.

of each dog appearing at the café door.[53] Rule-based approaches may also promote reliance, predictability and certainty in a similar manner. Dog-owners know in advance that they cannot take their dog into the café and will plan their lives accordingly.[54] In addition, rule-based approaches may further efficiency. The café-owner can spend less time determining whether a dog should be admitted to the café and more time preparing and serving food to his customers.[55] It may also be a desirable solution for decision-makers who are risk-averse. Rather than facing the risks involved in annoy-ing customers by refusing access to the café for their dogs, the café-owner can point to the rule as a justification for his decision. The rule-maker as opposed to the decision-maker takes responsibility for the risks of drawing up the rule.[56] Stability may also be achieved. The status quo is maintained and dogs are excluded from the café.[57]

However, a rule-based decision-making approach may not always have these advantages. Whilst a rule-based approach may promote fairness, it may also miss genuine distinctions that require differential treatment. Guide dogs should be allowed in cafés as there is a genuine distinction between a guide dog and other dogs. To treat them in the same manner would be to transgress fairness in the opposite manner: treating as alike two situa-tions that merit differential treatment. Predictability and certainty are only promoted if those making, applying and being governed by the rules have a shared common understanding of the terms used in the rule. Certainty is promoted where there is a common understanding of the term 'dog'. This would not be promoted were a more contestable term used in the rule—eg, if the rule excluded 'badly behaved domestic pets' as opposed to 'dogs'. In addition, the advantages of a rule-based approach need to be balanced against the costs of over- and under-inclusiveness. Are certainty, stability, efficiency and the potential removal of risk from decision-makers more or less important than ensuring that the rule fulfils its purpose and reaches the right outcome?

It is impossible to perform this assessment for public law as a whole. However, an argument can be made for the advantages of adopting a par-ticularistic as opposed to a rule-based approach to the law/fact distinction. The distinction between law and fact has proved to be particularly elusive. Academics point to the way in which the distinction is problematic given that issues of fact may involve the same degree of evaluation as issues of law.[58] To determine whether someone is tall, for example, requires one not

---

[53] ibid 135–37.
[54] ibid 137–43.
[55] ibid 143–49.
[56] ibid 149–55.
[57] ibid 155–58.
[58] J Beatson, 'The Scope of Judicial Review for Error of Law' (1984) 4 *OJLS* 22.

only taking accurate measurements of height, but in addition requires an evaluation of whether this measurement satisfies the requirement of being 'tall'. Should this be assessed according to the average height of those in your community, or the world, taking into account age and gender or being age and gender-neutral? How far above average height does an individual need to be in order to be assessed as 'tall'? Legal definitions may also be more or less dependent on their factual basis. The difficulties faced when determining whether Mrs Moyna was sufficiently disabled so as to be unable to cook for herself illustrates the relative factual dependency of this legal definition. It also illustrates the evaluative nature of applying some legal definitions.[59] Even if we argue that these alleged grey areas can be made clearer by assessing whether an administrative decision-maker got the legal definition or the facts wrong,[60] further confusion can still arise as there is a lack of agreement as to whether the distinction between law and fact refers to issues or errors. Given this lack of consensus, a rule-based approach to this distinction is unlikely to bring the advantages of fairness, consistency, stability and efficiency. Moreover, there is a high likelihood that a rule-based approach will give rise to too many instances of over- and under-inclusiveness.

Two further differences between adopting a rule-based and a particularistic approach to public law reasoning may be particularly relevant to ascertaining whether Lord Hoffmann's approach is suited to public law decision-making. First, a rule-based approach vests decision-making authority in the rule-maker as opposed to the authority applying the rule. A particularistic approach to rule-making places more authority in the hands of the authority applying the rules as opposed to the author of the rules. For example, a rule-based approach to the division between law and fact places more decision-making power in the legislature which enacted the Tribunals, Courts and Enforcement Act 2007. The decision-applying authority—here the Upper Tribunal and the Court of Appeal—has less decision-making power. The Upper Tribunal and the Court of Appeal merely examine an issue to determine whether it is one of law or of fact. By taking a particularistic approach, greater authority is given to the Upper Tribunal and the Court of Appeal. They examine the purpose of distinguishing between law and fact, determining whether, in the particular circumstances, these purposes would be served by determining that an appeal should be allowed and so the issue should be classified as law as opposed to fact. Second, a rule-based approach maintains the status quo, whereas a particularistic approach is more dynamic, adapting to the particular situations before the court. A rule-based approach would classify a particular issue as one of law. This would then establish a clear precedent, where all issues in future that shared these characteristics would be matters of law. A particularistic

---

[59] See Williams (n 13) and Endicott (n 13).
[60] See Craig (n 12).

approach examines each issue specifically, allowing for greater flexibility over time.

These considerations may appear to provide a prima facie argument in favour of adopting a particularistic approach to public law reasoning. Public law decisions increasingly involve an assessment of human rights. Arguably, courts are better at protecting human rights than the legislature. In particular, courts may be best placed to identify situations in which the application of a general rule may harm individual rights in a specific situation. Adopting a particularistic approach may also ensure that human rights protections adapt as society evolves, recognising new human rights. It is also easy to argue that, when protecting human rights, it is more important that the right decision be reached than that consistency, efficiency and stability are achieved. However, problems may also arise when adapting a particularistic approach to public law. First, whether courts or legislatures—the archetypal law-makers and law-appliers—are better placed to determine human rights depends upon the extent to which human rights are contestable. There may be as great a risk that the judiciary will take decisions that reinforce old stereotypes and prejudices as the legislature. And the relative risk may well depend upon the particular right in question as well as the specific composition of the legislature and the judiciary.

Second, whether a particularistic approach is preferable may well depend upon the nature of the rule being applied. In public law in particular, some rules, principles and distinctions are important because they establish the relative powers of constitutional actors. The principle of legality is one such principle. The principle does provide a means of protecting human rights, but it also rests on a constitutional settlement as to the relative powers of the legislature and the courts. Courts may read statutory provisions so as to ensure that legislation does not inadvertently transgress fundamental rights, but, to date, do not have the power to override legislation that contravenes fundamental rights. To adopt a particularistic approach to the principle of legality may mean that there are fewer instances of over- and under-inclusiveness. As explained above, adopting a particularistic approach to the principle of legality in *Bank Mellat* arguably ensured that the purpose of the principle of legality was better achieved than if the court had adopted a rule-based approach. However, when applying a particularistic approach, the court is also given more authority to determine the scope of the principle of legality. Moreover, if a rule-based approach is taken towards the principle of legality, then this entrenches this principle, providing a greater safeguard of the principle of legality from a piecemeal application in the face of ever-changing events. Adopting a particularistic approach to the principle of legality may jeopardise a constitutional principle designed to divide power between the legislature and the judiciary as regards the protection of human rights. As such, this may be a principle where stability and the need to avoid the risk of an accidental erosion of the protection of human rights is more important than ensuring that the right outcome is reached on the circumstances. This suggests that it is better to take a rule-based as opposed to a particularistic approach to the principle of legality.

V. CONCLUSION

Lord Hoffmann was a senior member of the judiciary at an important time in the history of the development of public law. The enactment of the Human Rights Act 1998, the growing influence of EU law and the European Convention of Human Rights, and the need to respond to the 'war on terror' whilst continuing to protect human rights gave rise to a greater proportion of decisions of the House of Lords and the Supreme Court dedicated to public law issues. This chapter has recognised that Lord Hoffmann has played an important role in the development of public law, his most important contribution being in the way in which he approaches public law cases. Lord Hoffmann prefers to take a particularistic as opposed to a rule-based approach, focusing on ensuring that public law achieves its purposes in the particular situation before the court. This approach is attractive and is generally advantageous for public law. However, it also has the danger of undermining constitutional safeguards, particularly those concerning the distribution of power between different institutions of the constitution. Perhaps this suggests that we should take a particularistic approach to assessing whether a particularistic or rule-based approach is best suited to public law.

9

A Trump Card Which Sometimes Wins: Lord Hoffmann, Free Speech and the Media

JACOB ROWBOTTOM

WHEN I WAS asked to write about Lord Hoffmann's contribution to free speech and media freedom, it was difficult to know where to start. Throughout his legal career, Lord Hoffmann has been involved in many of the key cases concerning freedom of expression. For example, in 1975, he was junior counsel in the landmark case of *Attorney-General v Jonathan Cape Ltd*,[1] led by Brian Neill QC in successfully representing the publishers of Richard Crossman's diaries. In that case—which is still found on constitutional law reading lists—Lord Widgery famously decided that publishing the former minister's account of events in the Cabinet from 10 years earlier did not amount to a breach of confidence. This ruling provided a step towards more open government. Over a decade later, as a judge in the High Court, Hoffmann J gave the first instance decision in *X Ltd v Morgan Grampian (Publishers) Ltd*,[2] in which he ordered a journalist and his publisher to disclose notes of a conversation with an anonymous source.[3] While the Court of Appeal and the House of Lords upheld the orders, the case went to the European Court of Human Rights (ECtHR) in *Goodwin v UK*,[4] which found the UK to be in breach of Article 10 of the European Convention on Human Rights (ECHR). The Strasbourg Court used the case to underline the importance of protecting journalists' sources and found the disclosure orders to be a disproportionate interference with freedom of expression. The ECtHR's decision received a mixed response in the UK. To many, the case highlighted the limited protection for journalists' sources in the domestic law at the time, but to the Major government, it was

---

[1] *Attorney-General v Jonathan Cape Ltd* [1976] QB 752 (QB).
[2] *X Ltd v Morgan Grampian (Publishers) Ltd* (1990) *The Times*, 11 April (Ch).
[3] For background, see *X Ltd v Morgan Grampian (Publishers) Ltd* [1991] 1 AC 1 (HL).
[4] *Goodwin v UK* (1996) 22 EHRR 123.

further evidence of the ECtHR over-reaching itself. Government figures at the time called for the Strasbourg Court to be reformed[5]—a familiar refrain in contemporary debates about the ECtHR.

Prior to his time in the House of Lords, Lord Hoffmann's best-known contribution to the law on freedom of expression was as a Court of Appeal judge in *R v Central Independent Television plc*[6] (again, alongside Sir Brian Neill). In this case, the claimant argued that a television report on a criminal investigation should not include images of a man convicted of child sex offences years earlier, on the grounds that it would lead to the identification of (and cause distress to) the man's former wife and child. The Court of Appeal rejected this argument, finding that the publicity was not directed at the child and that the court had no power to restrain the publication. Hoffmann LJ began his judgment with some powerful remarks that are worth quoting in full:

> There are in the law reports many impressive and emphatic statements about the importance of the freedom of speech and the press. But they are often followed by a paragraph which begins with the word 'nevertheless'. The Judge then goes on to explain that there are other interests which have to be balanced against press freedom. And in deciding upon the importance of press freedom in the particular case, he is likely to distinguish between what he thinks deserves publication in the public interest and things in which the public are merely interested. He may even advert to the commercial motives of the newspaper or television company compared with the damage to the public or individual interest which would be caused by publication.
>
> The motives which impel Judges to assume a power to balance freedom of speech against other interests are almost always understandable and humane on the facts of the particular case before them. Newspapers are sometimes irresponsible and their motives in a market economy cannot be expected to be unalloyed by considerations of commercial advantage. And publication may cause needless pain, distress and damage to individuals or harm to other aspects of the public interest. But a freedom which is restricted to what Judges think to be responsible or in the public interest is no freedom. Freedom means the right to publish things which government and Judges, however well motivated, think should not be published. It means the right to say things which 'right-thinking people' regard as dangerous or irresponsible. This freedom is subject only to clearly defined exceptions laid down by common law or statute.[7]

He then went on to say:

> It cannot be too strongly emphasised that outside the established exceptions, or any new ones which Parliament may enact in accordance with its obligations

---

[5] M White, 'Ministers Seek Curb on Rights' *The Guardian* (London, 2 April 1996).
[6] *R v Central Independent Television plc* [1994] Fam 192.
[7] ibid 202.

under the Convention, there is no question of balancing freedom of speech against other interests. It is a trump card which always wins.[8]

Those final words proved to be highly quotable and were often used by those seeking stronger protection for the press. For example, counsel for *The Sun* once relied upon those words to argue that the Protection from Harassment Act 1997 should not apply to published newspaper articles—though that argument was rejected by the first instance judge.[9] Hoffmann LJ's words could easily be mistaken for suggesting absolute protection for the press, but on closer inspection his position is more qualified. He clearly accepts that freedom of expression can be qualified, but only where there are 'clearly defined exceptions laid down by common law or statute'. According to this view, the trump card operates only outside of 'the established exceptions'.[10] Really, Hoffmann LJ was warning of the danger of judges developing 'ad hoc exceptions' to freedom of expression as a result of their sympathy for the plight of claimants in a case. It is also worth noting that at the time of this decision, domestic law did not recognise a right to privacy or to protect private information, while freedom of expression had been recognised as a common law right.[11] As a result, Lord Hoffmann's statement can be read as prioritising expression rights over privacy insofar as the latter was not yet a clearly defined exception in domestic law.[12] We will see how this position changed during Lord Hoffmann's time in the House of Lords.

Once in the House of Lords, Lord Hoffmann heard a number of important free speech and media law cases. In *Simms*, he concurred with Lord Steyn's judgment that underlined the importance of freedom of expression and upheld a prisoner's speech rights. Lord Hoffmann did not discuss the importance of free speech in that case, but referred to the principle of legality, which allows Parliament to abrogate a right only through express words or necessary implication. Just as his principle in *Central Independent Television* permitted exceptions to expression only where clearly established in law, the principle of legality also requires clarity from the legislature when it introduces a new restriction. The two cases fit together, as both allow for

---

[8] ibid 203.

[9] For an account of *Thomas v News Group Newspapers Ltd* in the Lambeth County Court, see C Dyer, 'But the Sun Can Say Anything it Likes. Can't it?' *The Guardian*, (London, 13 March 2001) 10 (Judge Cox, finding that the Protection from Harassment Act 1997 was one of the statutory exceptions provided for by Lord Hoffmann). The decision was later upheld in the Court of Appeal: see *Thomas v News Group Newspapers Ltd* [2001] EWCA Civ 1233, [2002] EMLR 4.

[10] The point was also confirmed by Lord Hoffmann in 'Mind Your Own Business' (Goodman Lecture, 22 May 1996), quoted in *Venables v News Group Newspapers Ltd* [2001] EWHC QB 32, [2001] Fam 430 [18].

[11] *Derbyshire County Council v Times Newspapers Ltd* [1992] UKHL 6, [1993] AC 534; *R v Secretary of State for the Home Department ex p Simms* [1999] UKHL 33, [2000] 2 AC 115.

[12] Although he accepted that privacy could be an exception to expression rights under the Convention, this step had not yet been taken in the domestic law.

the legal restriction of expression rights, but require any interference to be authorised in an open and public process. That way, if expression rights are to be curtailed, 'Parliament must squarely confront what it is doing and accept the political cost'.[13]

While Lord Hoffmann's career touched on a wide range of free speech issues, the main focus of this chapter is his contribution in the House of Lords once the Human Rights Act 1998 (HRA) was in force. In particular, I will look at three of Lord Hoffmann's major decisions in this area: *Jameel v Wall Street Journal Europe Sprl*,[14] *Campbell v MGN Ltd*[15] and *R v British Broadcasting Corporation ex p ProLife Alliance*.[16] At first sight—and judging by the response from a number of commentators—these cases might appear to point to a mixed record on free speech. *Jameel* got an emphatic thumbs-up as a step forward for the protection of press freedom. Lord Hoffmann's contribution to *Campbell* got a more mixed reception—while he helped to establish the new approach to breach of confidence/misuse of private information, he also dissented on the facts and would have found in favour of the newspaper. Finally, *ProLife Alliance* attracted considerable criticism from a number of commentators, who argued that it provided insufficient protection to expression rights. Yet such an evaluation of Lord Hoffmann's contribution in the three cases is too simplistic. Decisions are not to be categorised as 'pro-speech' or 'anti-speech' simply based on whether an outcome favours a speaker or not. Most cases are more complex and we have to look at the reasoning underlying the decision. Here it will be argued that while the three decisions of Lord Hoffmann provoked very different reactions, his concern for editorial autonomy provides a common thread running through each.

I. LIBEL AND *JAMEEL*

I will begin by looking at Lord Hoffmann's contribution to the law of libel, focusing on *Jameel* and his intervention in the debate over libel reform prior to the Defamation Act 2013. In *Jameel*, the *Wall Street Journal* published a story in 2002 identifying the claimant as one of several businessmen whose bank accounts were being monitored, at the request of the US, by the authorities in Saudi Arabia as part of an effort to prevent funds being channelled to terrorist organisations. In the subsequent defamation action, the newspaper did not advance a defence of justification, but relied on

---

[13] *Simms* (n 11) 131.
[14] *Jameel v Wall Street Journal Europe Sprl* [2006] UKHL 44, [2007] 1 AC 359.
[15] *Campbell v MGN Ltd* [2004] UKHL 22, [2004] 2 AC 406; see also *Campbell v MGN Ltd* [2005] UKHL 61, [2005] 1 WLR 3394 (hereinafter *Campbell (No 2)*).
[16] *R v British Broadcasting Corporation ex p ProLife Alliance* [2003] UKHL 23, [2004] 1 AC 185.

qualified privilege under *Reynolds v Times Newspapers Ltd.*[17] In *Reynolds*, the House of Lords had established a defence for those publishing stories in the public interest, as long as the publisher met the requirements of responsible journalism. Lord Nicholls set out 10 non-exhaustive factors to indicate when a journalist had acted responsibly. At first instance in *Jameel*,[18] Eady J rejected the *Wall Street Journal*'s defence on the grounds that the newspaper had not fulfilled the requirements of the *Reynolds* defence.

The House of Lords found for the newspaper on appeal and Lord Hoffmann used the opportunity to set out the principles underlying the defence. He noted that while *Reynolds* had attempted to secure 'greater freedom for the press to publish stories of genuine public interest', it had made little difference in the lower courts.[19] He therefore sought to revive the liberalising spirit of *Reynolds*. He found that *Reynolds* was quite different from traditional qualified privilege as there was 'no question of the privilege being defeated by proof of malice' once the requirements of responsible journalism were satisfied.[20] Instead, *Reynolds* was better named a 'public interest defence' rather than privilege.[21] In his re-statement of the *Reynolds* principles, Lord Hoffmann stated that three questions must be addressed when applying the defence. The first was whether the story itself is in the public interest, a test which he found the *Wall Street Journal* article 'easily passes'.[22]

The second question was whether the inclusion of the defamatory statement was justifiable.[23] So, while it might have been in the public interest to publish a story about the monitoring of bank accounts, the question at this stage was whether it was justifiable to identify Jameel in the story. In addressing this second stage, it was particularly important to show respect for the judgment of newspaper editors:

> [W]hereas the question of whether the story as a whole was a matter of public interest must be decided by the judge without regard to what the editor's view may have been, the question of whether the defamatory statement should have been included is often a matter of how the story should have been presented. And on that question, allowance must be made for editorial judgement. If the article as a whole is in the public interest, opinions may reasonably differ over which details are needed to convey the general message. The fact that the judge, with the advantage of leisure and hindsight, might have made a different editorial decision should not destroy the defence. That would make the publication of articles which are, *ex hypothesi*, in the public interest, too risky and would discourage investigative reporting.[24]

---

[17] *Reynolds v Times Newspapers Ltd* [2001] 2 AC 127 (HL).
[18] *Jameel v Wall Street Journal Europe Sprl* [2004] EWHC 37 (QB), [2004] EMLR 196.
[19] *Jameel* (n 14) [38].
[20] ibid [46].
[21] ibid.
[22] ibid [49].
[23] ibid [51].
[24] ibid.

The point is particularly important in stressing editorial autonomy and the dangers of excessive judicial interference with the journalist's discretion. On the facts, the inclusion of the names was justified to show that people at the centre of Saudi society, such as prominent businessmen, were being monitored.

The third question was whether the publisher had acted as a 'responsible journalist'.[25] In *Jameel*, Lord Hoffmann took issue with Eady J's conclusion that the requirements for this part of the defence had not been fulfilled. First, Lord Hoffmann found that the jury's findings of fact—that the reporter's story had not been confirmed by independent sources—were 'vitiated' by Eady J's direction to them.[26] No weight should have been placed on those findings. Furthermore, Lord Hoffmann stated that a failure to include the claimant's comment did not defeat the defence in this case. The journalist had sought a comment from the claimant the night before publication. The claimant was unavailable until the following day and the newspaper decided not to delay publication to wait for Jameel's comment. Both Eady J and the Court of Appeal had found that the newspaper had not acted responsibly under the *Reynolds* test as a result of the failure to delay publication. Lord Hoffmann disagreed and found that Jameel, having no knowledge of the covert operations in Saudi Arabia, would have only been able to comment 'that he knew of no reason why anyone should want to monitor his accounts'.[27] As a result, while it 'might have been better if the newspaper had delayed publication', failure to do so was not fatal to the *Reynolds* defence.[28]

More generally, Lord Hoffmann was particularly critical of the decision of Eady J at first instance for applying a high threshold for the *Reynolds* defence:

> In *Reynolds*, Lord Nicholls gave his well-known non-exhaustive list of ten matters which should in suitable cases be taken into account. They are not tests which the publication has to pass. In the hands of a judge hostile to the spirit of *Reynolds*, they can become ten hurdles at any of which the defence may fail. That is how Eady J treated them. The defence, he said, can be sustained only after 'the closest and most rigorous scrutiny' by the application of what he called 'Lord Nicholls'

---

[25] ibid [53].
[26] ibid [60]. The reporter argued that information from his principal source had been confirmed by four other sources from Saudi Arabia. While the jury found that the sources had not provided such confirmation, Lord Hoffmann stated that no weight should be placed on that finding, as it had been affected by Eady J's direction that the jury should assume that the allegations were untrue. If the jurors were to make that assumption, Hoffmann reasoned, 'it is not surprising that they were unconvinced' that the four sources had confirmed the story ([61]). Putting that point to one side, Lord Hoffmann also found that there was evidence from sources in the US to confirm the story, which had not been given much attention in the trial or in the Court of Appeal.
[27] ibid [84].
[28] ibid [85].

ten tests'. But that, in my opinion, is not what Lord Nicholls meant. As he said in *Bonnick* (at p 309) the standard of conduct required of the newspaper must be applied in a practical and flexible manner. It must have regard to practical realities.[29]

According to Lord Hoffmann, Eady J applied the law as if '*Reynolds* had changed nothing' and had relied on the traditional duty/interest test for qualified privilege.[30] This, Lord Hoffmann argued, was 'quite unrealistic'.[31] From this, we can see Lord Hoffmann's awareness of the realities of the newsroom and pressures faced by journalists. If such demanding standards are applied, then much journalistic activity would not withstand judicial scrutiny. Both in granting respect to editorial judgment and in applying the responsible journalism criteria flexibly, Lord Hoffmann sought to give the press considerable leeway and showed respect for professional judgment.

Unsurprisingly, the decision gained positive coverage in the media. In an editorial, *The Times* described it as 'an important victory not only for the British press but for the vital democratic principle of free expression'.[32] The emphasis on flexibility was also welcomed by the House of Commons, Culture Media and Sport Select Committee in 2010, though it noted the scope for further liberalisation.[33] The decision received praise from several legal academics (including the current author)[34]—although it also received criticism from other commentators, who argued that it gave too much freedom for the press to get things wrong.[35] The decision also proved to be influential on later case law. In *Flood v Times Newspapers Ltd*, Lord Mance noted how the flexibility of the test ensures respect for editorial discretion by 'giving weight to the judgement of journalists and editors' in relation to both the news-gathering process and the content of the material.[36] While the *Reynolds* defence has since been replaced by a statutory public interest defence, Lord Hoffmann's flexible approach lives on in the new test, which provides that 'the court must make such allowance for editorial judgement' and 'must have regard to all the circumstances of the case'.[37] Given that the basic question in *Jameel* was whether the *Reynolds* defence should be construed narrowly or broadly, Lord Hoffmann's position came down unambiguously in favour of press freedom and freedom of expression.

---

[29] ibid [56].
[30] ibid [57].
[31] ibid.
[32] Editorial, 'The Public Interest' *The Times* (London, 12 October 2006) 19.
[33] Culture, Media and Sport Select Committee, *Second Report of 2009–10, Press Standards, Privacy and Libel* (HC 2009–10, 362–I) para 161.
[34] J Rowbottom, 'Libel and the Public Interest' (2007) 66 *CLJ* 8.
[35] See D Price and A Melville-Brown, 'Another, More Subjective, Side of the Argument' *The Times* (London, 24 October 2006) Law Section, 1; and J Coad, 'Reynolds and Public Interest' [2007] *Entertainment Law Review* 75.
[36] *Flood v Times Newspapers Ltd* [2012] UKSC 11, [2012] 2 AC 273 [122]–[132], [137].
[37] Defamation Act 2013, s 4.

Lord Hoffmann's judgment in *Jameel* also addressed another important issue in libel law, namely whether a libel against a company should be actionable per se or whether proof of special damage must be shown. The majority of the House of Lords found that there is no reason to treat a company differently from anyone else and that special damage is not required. Lord Hoffmann, along with Baroness Hale, took a different view. He argued that in the case of an individual, reputation forms part of his or her personality. By contrast, he argued, a commercial entity 'has no soul and its reputation is no more than a commercial asset'.[38] Such a view echoed the sentiments expressed by Tony Weir, over 30 years earlier, that companies have 'no feelings which might have been hurt and no social relations which might have been impaired'.[39] According to the minority view, the reputation of a company does not warrant the same protection as that of an individual, and a different balance should be struck with freedom of speech. While Lord Hoffmann was in a minority on that point, his view was later taken up in section 1(2) of the Defamation Act 2013, which provides that a statement referring to 'a body that trades for profit' is not defamatory 'unless it has caused or is likely to cause the body serious financial loss'.

Having seen Lord Hoffmann's role in incrementally liberalising the law of defamation, one might have expected him to be a strong ally of the campaign for libel reform that led to the enactment of the Defamation Act 2013. He was certainly supportive of several of the reforms being advocated (such as the requirement for companies to show damage), but had 'misgivings' about some of the reform proposals.[40] For example, he was sceptical of claims that *Reynolds* privilege needed to be replaced with a new statutory public interest defence. If a 'stronger' defence meant something modelled on the US approach in *New York Times Co v Sullivan*,[41] then Lord Hoffmann thought that this would offer too little protection to reputation. In the House of Lords debate on the Defamation Bill, he noted that the US is the exception in its robust protection for expression, and warned that the comparison with the US was being pushed by parts of the media in hope of tilting the law in their own favour.[42] However, not all libel reformers took inspiration from the US, and the proposals that were eventually included in the Defamation Act provided a variation on the *Reynolds/Jameel* approach. While Lord Hoffmann expressed no strong objection to codifying the approach in *Reynolds*, he did wonder what it would add.[43] In short, he did not feel that there was a strong case for reform in this area: 'As the *Jameel*

---

[38] *Jameel* (n 14) [38].
[39] JA Weir 'Local Authority v. Critical Ratepayer—A Suit in Defamation' (1972) 30 *CLJ* 238, 240.
[40] HL Deb 9 July 2010, vol 720, cols 430–31.
[41] *New York Times Co v Sullivan* 376 US 254 (1964).
[42] HL Deb 9 July 2010, vol 720, col 432.
[43] ibid.

case appeared to be generally welcomed by the press and has been followed by the Canadians, I should have thought that there was a case for leaving well alone.'[44]

Lord Hoffmann's strongest criticism of the libel reform campaign aimed at the arguments concerning 'libel tourism', the classic case being where a person residing overseas brings an action in the English courts against a publication that is also based outside of jurisdiction. In the Dame Anne Ebsworth Memorial Lecture in 2010, he argued that the reform campaign had been initiated 'entirely from the Americans' and was 'based upon a belief that the whole world should share their view about how to strike the balance between freedom of expression and the defence of reputation'.[45] Parts of the British media had then, he argued, seized on the issue and subjected Sir David Eady to 'disgraceful personal abuse'.[46] The problem of libel tourism, he argued, had been exaggerated and he thought that more evidence was required before action became necessary. The intervention attracted criticism from some within the libel reform campaign, with one journalist suggesting that he had overlooked several examples and was more concerned with protecting the legal establishment, in particular Sir David Eady.[47] Rachel Ehrenfeld, the American referred to by Lord Hoffmann, described his speech as 'an effort to silence demands by British free speech proponents to change British libel laws'.[48] John Kampfner described Lord Hoffmann's speech as defensive and full of 'Little Englander appeals', and claimed that the intervention (along with those of others) showed how the 'forces of reaction, those who are hostile to the very idea of a First Amendment defending free speech, have entered the fray'.[49]

There was clearly a debate to be had about libel tourism[50] and, in my view, a change in the law was desirable.[51] However, many of the criticisms made of Lord Hoffmann were unfair. Far from seeking to shield other judges from criticism, we should remember that Lord Hoffmann was strongly critical of Eady J's decision in *Jameel*. Lord Hoffmann's objection was to abuse

---

[44] ibid.

[45] Edited version of L Hoffmann, 'Fifth Ebsworth Memorial Lecture "Libel Tourism"' (London, 2 February 2010) www.indexoncensorship.org/2010/02/the-libel-tourism-myth.

[46] ibid.

[47] See, eg, N Cohen, 'Libel Tourists Will Love the Tales of Lord Hoffmann' *The Observer* (London, 7 February 2010) 37 (caricaturing Lord Hoffmann's stance on the American campaigners): 'Damn them to hell for impugning the fine work of Mr Justice Eady and dear old Carter-Ruck.'

[48] R Ehrenfeld, 'America Must Defend its Writers' *The Guardian* (London, 1 March 2010) www.theguardian.com/commentisfree/libertycentral/2010/mar/01/congress-bill-protect-libel.

[49] J Kampfner, 'Let Battle Commence over Privacy' *The Independent* (London, 6 February 2010) 36.

[50] *Cf* Lord Steyn, 'Defamation and Privacy: Momentum for Substantive and Procedural Change?' (The 3rd Annual Boydell Lecture, London, 26 May 2010) https://inforrm.files.wordpress.com/2010/05/lord-steyn-boydell-lecture.pdf.

[51] For example, even if relatively few examples of genuine libel tourism were litigated, there could still be examples of a chilling effect.

and ill-informed criticism. Far from being a force of reaction and trying to silence opponents of change, he himself had taken steps to liberalise defamation law. Finally, he did not ignore libel tourism, but was on to the problem in *Berezovsky v Forbes*[52]—over a decade before the Defamation Act 2013 was passed. In *Berezovsky*, a Russian multi-millionaire brought an action against an American magazine in the English courts. The first instance judge found that the English courts were not an appropriate forum to hear the case. The Court of Appeal and a majority of the House of Lords disagreed, allowing the case to go ahead in London on account of Berezovsky's reputation within the jurisdiction. In his dissent, Lord Hoffmann thought that Berezovsky was not really concerned with his UK reputation, but sought a 'verdict of an English court that he has been acquitted of the allegations in the article, for use wherever in the world his business may take him'.[53] Berezovsky was, Lord Hoffmann said, a 'forum shopper' who thought he was unlikely to win in the US and had decided that a victory in the Russian courts would lack credibility. The claimants had therefore 'weighed up the advantages to them of the various jurisdictions that might be available and decided that England is the best place in which to vindicate their international reputations'.[54] Lord Hoffmann shared the first instance judge's concern that 'the English court should not be an international libel tribunal for a dispute between foreigners which had no connection with this country'.[55]

Despite the difference of opinion, libel reform campaigners later echoed Lord Hoffmann's words when arguing that 'London has become an international libel tribunal'.[56] The points of disagreement between Lord Hoffmann and the reformers seemed to be in relation to the extent to which libel tourism was a pressing problem, and whether the existing safeguards at the time (such as the forum non conveniens doctrine and the power to strike out trivial libel claims as an abuse of process) were sufficient. Ultimately, the arguments of the libel reformers were carried into law and the 2013 Act provides that a 'court does not have jurisdiction to hear and determine' a defamation action unless it is 'is satisfied that, of all the places in which the statement complained of has been published, England and Wales is clearly the most appropriate place in which to bring an action in respect of the statement'.[57] While I regard this change as welcome (although I will wait to see how it is applied), my point is that Lord Hoffmann was not a foe to libel reform and in several areas anticipated the arguments made for change. He

---

[52] *Berezovsky v Forbes* [2000] UKHL 25, [2000] 2 All ER 986.
[53] ibid 1004.
[54] ibid 1005.
[55] ibid 1006.
[56] J Glanville and J Heawood, *Free Speech is Not for Sale. The Impact of English Libel Law on Freedom of Expression. A Report by English PEN & Index on Censorship* (London, English PEN & Index on Censorship, 2009).
[57] See Defamation Act 2013, s 9.

was, however, wary of legislation being made in haste, emphasised the need for full evidence and thought it necessary to locate exactly which defects in the law were causing problems and needed correction.

Finally, in the debates on libel reform, Lord Hoffmann noted that some of the practical difficulties with defamation law lay not in the substance of the law, but in the cost of litigation.[58] These issues had already been discussed in *Campbell*, in which the defendant argued that an order to pay the claimant's costs, including success fees under a conditional fee agreement, was a disproportionate infringement of Article 10 ECHR. The House of Lords dismissed the *Daily Mirror*'s appeal in *Campbell (No 2)*, with Lord Hoffmann stating that the Conditional Fee Agreements (CFA) regime was a 'choice open to the legislature' to fund litigation.[59] The ECtHR, however, found the costs regime to violate Article 10.[60] Funnily enough, in making this finding against the UK government, the Strasbourg Court relied on the government's own reviews of the costs regime, which identified flaws in the system.[61]

The Court also relied on judicial dicta from the domestic courts on the effects of CFAs, including those of Lord Hoffmann in *Campbell (No 2)*. CFAs, Lord Hoffmann had said, could have a 'blackmailing effect' on a newspaper.[62] Where a CFA was taken out by an impecunious claimant without insurance to cover legal costs, the defendant would have little chance of recovering its own legal costs if successful, but would have to pay the claimant's success fees if unsuccessful. A further problem, Lord Hoffmann pointed out, was that claimants could conduct the case in a way that 'runs up substantial costs' for both claimant and defendant.[63] While it was therefore desirable to moderate the costs of defamation actions, Lord Hoffmann thought that a 'legislative solution' was the answer. This criticism of CFAs was cited by and influenced the reasoning of the Strasbourg Court. So, while Lord Hoffmann may have found the scheme to be consistent with Article 10 in domestic law, parts of his reasoning persuaded the Strasbourg Court to come to the opposite conclusion in the same case.

The discussion of Lord Hoffmann's contribution to libel law shows his role in liberalising the law and giving greater weight to expression rights. There were important ways in which the laws needed to be developed to better protect the press, but this was not a journey in one direction towards an

---

[58] HL Deb 9 July 2010, vol 720, col 432, when discussing the problems of *Reynolds* privilege.

[59] *Campbell (No 2)* (n 15) [28].

[60] *MGN Ltd v UK* [2011] ECHR 66, (2011) 53 EHRR 5.

[61] Some of the reviews relied on by the court were published after the House of Lords' decision: ibid [203].

[62] *Campbell (No 2)* (n 15) [31].

[63] See discussion of the development in R Wacks, *Privacy and Media Freedom* (Oxford, Oxford University Press, 2013) chs 3 and 4.

ever-stronger shield for media freedom. His was not an absolutist approach to expression rights; he was also committed to the traditional approach that protected other legal interests. For this reason, he resisted arguments to tilt the law in favour of the media and other speakers along the lines of the US *Sullivan* model. Decisions such as *Jameel* were, instead, about striking a better balance between speech and reputation. This balanced and to some degree conditional approach to press freedom can be seen more clearly in the next area for discussion, the law of privacy.

II. PRIVACY

It is often noted that while the law of defamation has (to some degree) been reined in, the law of privacy is in the ascendency. While the common law famously recognised no right to privacy in *Kaye v Robertson*,[64] the action for breach of confidence was gradually been widened to give greater protection to personal information. The HRA gave momentum to this development by incorporating the ECHR into domestic law, including the protection of private and family life under Article 8. Soon after the enactment of the HRA, the lower courts found themselves to be under an obligation to develop the doctrine of breach of confidence in a way that protects Article 8 rights. This led to a type of 'indirect horizontal effect' in which Article 8 obligations could be asserted, parasitically on the back of breach of confidence, against privately owned news organisations. In an early ruling in *Douglas v Hello! Ltd*,[65] Sedley LJ said that 'we have reached a point at which it can be said with confidence that the law recognises and will appropriately protect a right of personal privacy'.[66] He found that the claimants had a 'powerfully arguable case' for 'a right of privacy which English law will today recognise and, where appropriate, protect'.[67] The decision rang alarm bells in some parts of the press, which had lobbied the government to prevent the HRA creating a 'backdoor privacy law'. A feature in the *Sunday Times* warned that the ruling 'opens up fertile new territory for lawyers and for rich folk with the means and incentive to avoid unwanted personal publicity'.[68] Yet the case law did not move solely in one direction and early decisions such as *A v B plc*[69] emphasised the rights of the press. Given these various changes and mixed messages, Naomi Campbell's appeal to the House of Lords in her case against the *Daily Mirror* gave an important opportunity for the top court to clarify the law.

---

[64] *Kaye v Robertson* [1991] FSR 62 (CA).
[65] *Douglas v Hello! Ltd* [2001] QB 967 (CA).
[66] ibid [110].
[67] ibid [125].
[68] Opinion, 'Our New Legal Tyranny' *Sunday Times* (London, 24 December 2000).
[69] *A v B plc* [2002] EWCA Civ 337, [2002] 3 WLR 542.

Just months before the *Campbell* ruling, Lord Hoffmann had given the lead judgment in *Wainwright v Home Office*,[70] in which he held that there was no right to privacy in the UK. A general tort of privacy, he thought, was something to be left to the legislature and not to be established by the judiciary. Article 8 required only that remedies be provided for infringements of private and family life, which could be achieved through a piecemeal range of laws. He read Sedley LJ's comments in *Douglas* to mean merely that the law of confidence had reached a point where a confidential relationship is not necessary. According to Lord Hoffmann, privacy was not an organising principle, but a background value. While such a ruling might have been seen to reassert the status quo, any reassurance for the press was to be short-lived following *Campbell*.

The decision in *Campbell* is a landmark, and it is possibly the most important media law case in recent years. The facts are well known. The *Daily Mirror*, then edited by Piers Morgan, ran a story detailing how the model Naomi Campbell was being treated for drug addiction and included photographs of her leaving Narcotics Anonymous. A majority of the House of Lords held that the newspaper was entitled to publish the fact that Campbell had taken drugs and was seeking treatment, as it was legitimate to correct her earlier denials of drug abuse. However, the majority held that to include details of the treatment from Narcotics Anonymous and publish photographs of her outside the treatment venue went beyond what was necessary to make their point. Unsurprisingly, the decision proved to be unpopular with some parts of the press. Dominic Mohan, writing in *The Sun*, warned of politicians abusing the law to cover up embarrassing details and stated that our own freedoms are being 'gradually chipped away'.[71] A *Daily Mail* editorial described the decision as a 'red-letter day for crooks, con artists and sleazy politicians'.[72] The *Daily Mirror* described its loss in the courts as creating a 'charter for deceit'.[73]

While the issue could have been decided under the existing law of breach of confidence, the Lords took the opportunity to re-state the law in the light of the gradual changes and the influence of Article 8. This re-statement of the law included a two-stage test for courts to apply when asked to protect private information. The first stage asks whether the information itself is private, namely whether the claimant had a reasonable expectation of privacy. If the answer to the first question is yes, then the court goes on to balance the privacy right with the right to freedom of expression under Article 10. Many of the same issues considered in traditional breach of confidence remained relevant in this new test, and the extent to which it

[70] *Wainwright v Home Office* [2003] UKHL 53, [2004] 2 AC 406.
[71] D Mohan, 'Farewell Freedom' *The Sun* (London, 8 May 2004).
[72] Editorial, 'Freedom in Peril' *Daily Mail* (London, 7 May 2004) 12.
[73] Editorial, 'Liars Licence' *Daily Mirror* (London, 7 May 2004) 8.

changed the old law is a matter for debate. However, I would argue that the House of Lords set the law off on a new course, the consequences of which are still being played out.

Lord Hoffmann's judgment played a key part in that reformulation. Following the view expressed in *Wainwright*, he said that privacy was one of the values underlying breach of confidence.[74] He noted that in the recent applications of the law, there had been a 'shift in the centre of gravity of the action for breach of confidence'.[75] Breach of confidence 'was an equitable remedy' which 'traditionally fastens on the conscience of one party to enforce equitable duties which arise out of his relationship with the other'.[76] By contrast, when protecting personal information, the focus is not upon good faith, but rather on 'the protection of human autonomy and dignity—the right to control the dissemination of information about one's private life and the right to the esteem and respect of other people'.[77] The courts are still grappling with this shift. For example, in *Weller v Associated Newspapers Ltd*,[78] Dingemans J noted that the emphasis on the defendant's state of mind in some dicta reflects the doctrine's roots in breach of confidence, and considered the continuing relevance of that emphasis under the *Campbell* reformulation.

In setting out the principles in *Campbell*, Lord Hoffmann stated that in striking a balance between freedom of expression and the protection of personal information, neither has 'automatic priority' or enjoys a presumption over the other.[79] This balancing approach might look like a move away from Lord Hoffmann's view that freedom of expression was a 'trump card' a decade earlier in *Central Independent Television*. However, *Campbell* is consistent with Lord Hoffmann's earlier view insofar as he always accepted that expression could be limited by exceptions recognised in statute or common law. What had changed was that, with the introduction of the HRA, privacy was now an exception established by statute.

Lord Hoffmann's judgment also indicated the limits of both Article 8 and Article 10 rights. For example, he noted that simply because a person has put parts of their life into the public domain does not mean they lose their claim to privacy.[80] This put an end to generic arguments that celebrities who live by publicity cannot complain when embarrassing private facts are revealed. Privacy claims also had limits. Simply being photographed in a public place without consent does not, according to Lord Hoffmann, amount to a breach of privacy.[81] However, to be photographed in a 'situation of humiliation or

---

[74] *Campbell* (n 15) [43].
[75] ibid [51].
[76] ibid [44].
[77] ibid [51].
[78] *Weller v Associated Newspapers Ltd* [2014] EWHC 1163 (QB).
[79] *Campbell* (n 15) [55].
[80] ibid [57].
[81] ibid [73].

severe embarrassment' in a public place could amount to such a breach.[82] That explains why publishing images of a person attempting suicide in a public place violates privacy rights,[83] while an image of a person simply going out to buy milk does not.[84] While this approach gives some definition to the scope of the rights in practice, it appears not to have constrained the subsequent development of the law. In both *Weller* and *Murray*,[85] the courts have accepted that privacy rights can be engaged even where photographs in a public place are not humiliating or embarrassing.[86]

Lord Hoffmann's judgment is also important as he dissented on the facts and would have allowed the newspaper to publish the photographs and refer to Campbell's treatment with Narcotics Anonymous. He argued that the decision to publish a photograph fell within the boundaries of editorial autonomy. Photographs provided a way for the press to tell their story:

> [J]udges are not newspaper editors. It may have been possible for the Mirror to satisfy the public interest in publication with a story which contained less detail and omitted the photographs. But the Mirror said that they wanted to show themselves sympathetic to Ms Campbell's efforts to overcome her dependency. For this purpose, some details about her frequency of attendance at NA meetings were needed.[87]

As with the judgment in *Jameel*, Lord Hoffmann stressed the realities and pressures faced in newsrooms. Accordingly, the 'practical exigencies of journalism demand that some latitude must be given'.[88] Newspapers could not be expected to 'always get it absolutely right' and such an expectation would have a chilling effect.[89] While that cannot be an excuse for poor standards, it warns against judges applying ideal standards to the press with the benefit of hindsight. He noted that: 'Editorial decisions have to be made quickly and with less information than is available to a court which afterwards reviews the matter at leisure.'[90] Underlying this approach is a respect for editorial autonomy, allowing journalists to decide what is likely to catch the audience's attention and how best to make their point.

When discussing *Jameel*, I noted that Lord Hoffmann's judgment came down unambiguously in favour of press freedom. By contrast, the assessment of *Campbell* appears more mixed. On the one hand, Lord Hoffmann

---

[82] ibid [75].

[83] ibid [122]–[123], discussing *Peck v UK* (2003) 36 EHRR 719.

[84] *Campbell* (n 15) [154]. See also Baroness Hale in *Campbell* and Eady J in *John v Associated Newspapers Ltd* [2006] EWHC 1611 (QB), [2006] EMLR 772.

[85] *Murray v Big Pictures (UK) Ltd* [2008] EWCA Civ 446, [2009] Ch 481.

[86] This broader approach to private information is supported in *Von Hannover v Germany* (2005) 40 EHRR 1.

[87] *Campbell* (n 15) [59].

[88] ibid [62].

[89] ibid [63].

[90] ibid [62].

helped to reformulate the law and set it off on a path that in practice has led to more privacy actions against newspapers and injunctions being awarded. On the other hand, he dissented, stressed the importance of editorial autonomy and pointed to some limits on the types of information that might be considered private. Yet the different starting points from which the court addressed the issues explain the contrast with *Jameel*. In *Jameel*, the court was concerned with a long established law of libel that had a well-known pro-claimant tilt. An expansion of a public interest defence improved the position of the press, but did not radically give the press carte blanche to publish what they want. Even with the liberalised *Reynolds* defence, the law still gave ample protection to reputation. By contrast, in *Campbell*, the courts were faced with a tradition in which the law recognised no right to privacy and where the tilt was in favour of press freedom. Any attempt to reformulate the law that put privacy interests on a firmer footing was therefore bound to be seen by some as an encroachment on the previous liberties of the press. Despite the apparent contrast between the pro-press outcome in *Jameel* and the mixed position in *Campbell*, in both decisions Lord Hoffmann took a similar stance that sought to strike a proper balance between press freedom and other competing rights and interests.

III. BROADCASTING LAW AND *PROLIFE ALLIANCE*

The third major decision relating to freedom of expression and media freedom to be considered here is *ProLife Alliance*, which concerned content controls on party election broadcasts. This time, the ruling proved to be particularly controversial and received much academic criticism. In the leading text, *Freedom of Speech*, Eric Barendt described the decision as 'most disappointing', in which the judges showed 'scant regard for freedom of expression'.[91] To Trevor Allan, the decision reflected an 'authoritarian conception of the legal order', in which 'the right to free speech is only a residue left by specific legislation, which may impose stringent limitations'.[92] Ivan Hare described the failure to 'address the questions of free speech principle' as 'very disappointing' and commented that parts of Lord Hoffmann's reasoning were 'surprising, if not actually dangerous'.[93] In his analysis of the case, Adam Tomkins says the court took 'a potentially enormous case concerned with a right that many legal constitutionalists consider to be the most important of all—the right to freedom of political expression' and turned it into 'a perfectly ordinary administrative law case about the proper

---

[91] E Barendt, *Freedom of Speech* (Oxford, Oxford University Press, 2005) 46–47.
[92] T Allan, *The Sovereignty of Law* (Oxford, Oxford University Press, 2013) 25–31.
[93] I Hare, 'Debating Abortion—The Right to Offend Gratuitously' (2003) 62 *CLJ* 525, 527.

construction and application of a particular set of statutory obligations'.[94]
The reaction to the decision stands in stark contrast to the general approval
of *Jameel*.

In *ProLife Alliance*, a small political party fielded a sufficient number
of candidates in the 2001 General Election to qualify for a party election
broadcast. The ProLife Alliance sought to broadcast a short film, which
included images of aborted foetuses. The broadcasters, however, refused
to carry the film on the grounds that such images did not comply with the
broadcasting standards on taste and decency provided for under the BBC
Charter and section 6 of the Broadcasting Act 1990. The ProLife Alliance
sought to argue that the broadcasters' refusal was a violation of the right to
freedom of expression under Article 10. While this argument was successful
in the Court of Appeal, the House of Lord reversed that decision and found
against the political party.

In rejecting ProLife's claim, Lord Hoffmann argued that primary Article 10 rights were not even engaged. He reasoned that there is no right
under Article 10 to have access to the broadcast media; instead, people can
only have access where provided by the broadcaster or the law. Along these
lines, if the law can determine whether to grant access or not, then it can
surely impose conditions on access too. Consequently, the Article 10 issue
for Lord Hoffmann was whether the conditions were arbitrary, discriminatory or unreasonable. ProLife Alliance argued that the taste and decency
requirements were discriminatory in preventing the party from getting its
core message across in the way it thought fit. Lord Hoffmann rejected this
argument, noting that the point of party election broadcasts is to encourage 'an informed choice at the ballot box'.[95] He then went on to say that it
is relevant to consider whether the taste and decency requirements had an
impact on the goal of informing the electorate. He found that as the ProLife
Alliance was contesting only a small number of constituencies and as abortion is not a 'party political issue', the party election broadcast 'had virtually nothing to do with the fact that a general election was taking place'.[96]
Consequently, the restriction of the ProLife Alliance's form of message did
not make the electorate any less informed in relation to the choice before
them, because ProLife's position was not a realistic choice.

Furthermore, Lord Hoffmann felt that enacting taste and decency requirements was an 'entirely proper decision for Parliament as representative of
the people to make' and that the separation of powers requires the court
not to disturb the outcome. The question was then whether the broadcasters

---

[94] A Tomkins, *Our Republican Constitution* (Oxford, Hart Publishing, 2005) 28. For criticism of this view, see Allan (n 92) 86, who argues that a proper application required consideration of free speech principles.
[95] *ProLife Alliance* (n 16) [66].
[96] ibid [68].

had erred in their application of the relevant standards. Lord Hoffmann found that the broadcasters had applied the right standards and, once this was accepted, it was not 'possible for a court to say that they were wrong'. Furthermore, he also showed respect for the expertise of the broadcasters, who had researched public opinion in relation to the contents standards. Just as he said in *Campbell* that judges are not newspaper editors, Lord Hoffmann stated in *ProLife Alliance* that the broadcast standards 'are not a matter of intuition on the part of elderly male judges'.[97]

There are a number of criticisms that have been made of this reasoning. First, Lord Hoffmann's conclusion that the party election broadcast about abortion had nothing to do with the choice facing voters takes a narrow view of electoral debate. Parties in an election should have the chance to make an issue relevant to the choice before the voters. That such a message has little chance of success does not mean that it has 'nothing to do' with the general election. However, Lord Hoffmann did not rely solely on that reasoning. He found that even if the ProLife Alliance's message was relevant to the election, it would not 'have been unreasonable to require it to comply with standards of taste and decency', as those 'standards are part of the country's cultural life and have created expectations on the part of the viewers as to what they will and will not be shown on the screens in their homes'.[98] Along these lines, he argued that political messages should not be exempt from those standards.[99]

A second line of criticism of the decision is that even if we accept that taste and decency requirements should apply to political broadcasts, Lord Hoffmann was too quick to approve the broadcasters' judgment in applying those standards. Allan argues that the majority let the broadcasters off the hook by reasoning as if they 'were only performing their statutory duty'.[100] That approach, Allan argues, takes a 'rigid' view of the separation of powers, which assumes that once Parliament has enacted a provision, the empowered agency only has the task of applying that statute in good faith. Of course, this is not the only path that was available and the court could have taken a closer look at the broadcasters' exercise of discretion. The taste and decency standards could have been narrowly construed, requiring a heightened threshold when applied to election broadcasts.[101] Along these lines, the taste and decency requirements could be used to filter out attempts to use extreme violence or pornography in an election broadcast.[102] However, a shocking or disturbing image connected to a party's core

---

[97] ibid [80].
[98] ibid [70].
[99] *Cf* Lord Scott's dissent, especially at ibid [95]–[100].
[100] Allan (n 92) 26.
[101] H Fenwick and G Phillipson, *Media Freedom under the Human Rights Act* (Oxford, Oxford University Press, 2006) 583, 587–88.
[102] See Barendt (n 91) 47.

message should not fall foul of the content standards under this narrower construction of the statute.

A more intensive judicial approach would, of course, make a greater inroad into the discretion of the broadcaster. To the critics of the decision, such an increase in judicial supervision is warranted as the broadcasters' decision touched on a fundamental right. By contrast, for Lord Hoffmann, such intervention would take the courts outside its sphere of responsibility and competence. That is consistent with the views expressed by Lord Hoffmann in other administrative law cases, which show respect for the expertise and the constitutional allocation of responsibilities. For example, in *Secretary of State for the Home Department v Rehman (AP)*, he commented that in assessing the threat from terrorism, the court should show respect for the decisions of the executive on account of its 'special information and expertise' and the legitimacy conferred by making executive members 'responsible to the community through the democratic process'.[103] In *R (on the application of Begum) v Headteacher and Governors of Denbigh High School*,[104] considering whether a school rule forbidding pupils from wearing a jilbab violated religious freedom, he stated that the school rather than the court 'was in the best position to weigh and consider' the effects of its uniform policy.[105] In *R (Alconbury Developments Ltd) v Secretary of State for the Environment, Transport and the Regions*, he stated that policy decisions about what lies in the public interest 'are a matter for democratically accountable institutions and not for the courts' and can be delegated by Parliament to an agency.[106] In such cases, he has stressed a particular vision of the separation of powers and the limits of the court's competence in relation to some issues.

Lord Hoffmann's respect for agency autonomy provides a connection between *ProLife Alliance* and the emphasis on editorial autonomy in *Jameel* and *Campbell*. One way to make that connection is to treat the media as quasi-constitutional actors—with important constitutional functions in checking government and disseminating valuable information. If such a view is taken, then maybe the respect for editorial autonomy is much like the respect shown to the judgment of other branches of government. To be clear, I do not suggest that Lord Hoffmann has argued for such a quasi-constitutional status for the press—that is a claim sometimes advanced by the press and is the subject of debate.[107] I raise this point merely to show

---

[103] *Secretary of State for the Home Department v Rehman (AP)* [2001] UKHL 47, [2003] 1 AC 153 [62].

[104] *R (on the application of Begum) v Headteacher and Governors of Denbigh High School* [2006] UKHL 15, [2007] 1 AC 100.

[105] ibid [65].

[106] *R (Alconbury Developments Ltd) v Secretary of State for the Environment, Transport and the Regions* [2001] UKHL 23, [2003] 2 AC 295 [76]. See also *R v Secretary of State for Work and Pensions, ex p Hooper* [2005] UKHL 29, [2005] 1 WLR 1681 [32].

[107] Eg, *Miranda v Secretary of State for the Home Department* [2014] EWHC 255 (Admin), [2014] 1 WLR 3140 [71] (Laws LJ, rejecting an argument that journalists have special constitutional status in relation to releasing information that could affect national security).

that if we recast *Jameel* and *Campbell* as public law cases, then a common theme runs through the three decisions.

However, the link between *Jameel*, *Campbell* and *ProLife Alliance* can be maintained without making a bold claim about the constitutional status of the press. If we move away from the administrative law framework in *ProLife Alliance* and recast this decision as one of media law (which it clearly was), the common theme also becomes apparent. In *ProLife Alliance*, the political party claimed a right to express its view in the form of its own choice, which is the most obvious free speech issue in the case. Yet the broadcasters, and not just the political party, also acted as speakers. If we approach the decision through the lens of administrative law—of which Tomkins complained—the broadcaster is viewed as a government functionary exercising statutory discretion. Through a media law lens, however, the broadcaster is itself a media organisation with its own claims to media freedom. Obviously, the fact that the broadcasters in this case were subject to statutory content controls meant that they did not have absolute autonomy. However, the broadcasters had discretion when applying those standards, which can be seen to be part of their own editorial judgment as to what content to carry.

When reframed in this way, the decision in *ProLife Alliance* is partly about balancing the speech claims of the political party with those of the broadcasters and determining which should have the final say as to what content can be communicated. Thinking about the case in this way highlights the complexity of a media organisation. There may be different components within media organisations that have slightly different speech interests. For example, the rights of the individual reporter and editor may come into conflict with one another. Along these lines, in *ProLife Alliance*, the right of the political party came into conflict with judgment of the broadcasters.

My account of the broadcasters acting as media speakers is open to challenge. For example, Fenwick and Phillipson describe the broadcasters in *ProLife Alliance* as 'regulators' carrying out a statutory function rather than as rights holders themselves.[108] In his own reasoning, Lord Hoffmann also tends to emphasise the role of the broadcasters in carrying out the instructions of Parliament. The characterisation of the broadcaster as a type of regulator is certainly accurate, but does not provide a complete picture. Acting in accordance with a statutory function does not exclude claims to editorial autonomy and press freedom. In a number of Ofcom adjudications relating to the duties on broadcasters, the regulator has stressed the need to

---

[108] Fenwick and Phillipson (n 101) 586.

respect editorial freedom in deciding how best to fulfil those duties.[109] While Ofcom makes the final call as to whether those duties have been fulfilled, it still gives weight to the broadcaster's judgment as an element of media freedom. So, in relation to party election broadcasts, while the political party decides the content of its message, the broadcaster also takes some responsibility for the content disseminated as part of its overall output. Accordingly, when applying the taste and decency requirements in *ProLife Alliance*, the broadcasters were also exercising their own editorial judgment.

Framing the issue in this way raises difficult issues. As I have written elsewhere, the rights of an editor should not always trump the rights of individual speakers seeking to access the media.[110] In some situations, media organisations can be subject to duties to respect the rights of others. This reframing still leaves much scope to criticise the decision in *ProLife Alliance*. One might argue that the House of Lords should not have given greater priority to the editorial discretion of the broadcasters over that of the political party. I do not seek to resolve these issues here. My point is merely to show that if we view *ProLife Alliance* as a media law case, then Lord Hoffmann's respect for the broadcasters' judgment seems to fit with his emphasis on editorial autonomy in *Jameel and Campbell*, and his view that it is not for the courts to interfere in this area. Despite the differing reactions to these cases, a common thread runs through each.

IV. CONCLUSION

Throughout his legal career, Lord Hoffmann has made a significant contribution to the law on freedom of expression and media freedom. Decisions such as *Jameel* are widely recognised as important milestones towards a legal environment that protects journalism on matters of public importance. Yet, on several occasions, his contributions have attracted controversy, such as the *ProLife Alliance* decision and his intervention in the libel reform debates. While his contributions have at various times prompted both approval and criticism from free speech campaigners, we should not mistake this for inconsistency. Whether he came down on the side of the

---

[109] See 'The Jeremy Kyle Show', *Ofcom Broadcast Bulletin* Issue 252 (14 April 2014) 6, 17: 'Broadcasters must have the editorial freedom to decide when and how it is most appropriate to provide information to mitigate offence in particular situations' (http://stakeholders.ofcom. org.uk/enforcement/broadcast-bulletins/obb252); 'Russia Today', *Ofcom Broadcast Bulletin* Issue 213 (10 September 2012) 19, 27: 'When considering whether or not a broadcaster has reported with "due accuracy", it is important to recognise the importance attached to freedom of expression and the broadcaster's right to be able to interpret news events as it sees fit' (http://stakeholders.ofcom.org.uk/binaries/enforcement/broadcast-bulletins/obb213/obb213.pdf).

[110] J Rowbottom, *Democracy Distorted* (Cambridge, Cambridge University Press, 2010) ch 7.

expression right or not depended on the nature and context of the case before him. On some occasions, the context of the case provided an opportunity to remind people of the importance of freedom of expression, while other cases may have highlighted the limits. While Lord Hoffmann recognised the importance of free speech, he was not a crusader who sought its absolute protection. He also saw the need to protect other competing rights and interests.

To conclude, I consider the future of two issues that were important to Lord Hoffmann's contribution. The first relates to the point at the start of this chapter, that when he described free speech as a 'trump card', he was really concerned with courts finding exceptions to speech on an ad hoc basis. He warned of the danger of judges being pulled in a direction due to their sympathy for a claimant. However, he was not opposing restrictions on expression established in the common law or by Parliament. It has already been noted that whatever he had in mind in 1994, expression can no longer be viewed as a trump card over privacy rights in domestic law and that the protection of private information is now an established exception. However, we might consider whether the legacy left by cases such as *Campbell* and *Jameel* fits with his earlier concerns about ad hoc decisions. The methodology in both decisions allows for the free speech considerations to be weighed up against reputation and privacy rights by looking at a range of considerations in the particular case. For example, in privacy cases, the courts look at the type of information, how the information was acquired, the identity and past behaviour of the claimant, the tone of the article, whether the article concerned a matter of public importance and so on.[111] As a result, many different factors come into the mix. While the law establishes the exception to expression rights in misuse of private information and libel, the extent of those exceptions are not 'clearly defined'. The methodology is open-textured, giving room for different judicial approaches when striking the balance between competing rights and interests on the facts of a particular case. Does this pose a danger of the ad hoc approach in which judges are too easily swayed by their sympathy for the claimant when striking the balance? The answer given by Lord Hoffmann in *Jameel* was that, over time, the precedents gradually build up a set of rules that define the scope of the exception. Such definition has still yet to come. Whether a sufficient number of cases will reach the appellate courts and whether the Convention jurisprudence allows for such stable rules to crystallise remains to be seen.

The second issue relates to Lord Hoffmann's emphasis on editorial autonomy in *Jameel*, *Campbell* and *ProLife Alliance*. In each case he warned against the courts intruding too closely on the prerogatives of an editor

---

[111] See *Axel Springer v Germany* [2012] ECHR 227.

or reporter. Such respect for editorial judgment is a key element of media freedom. This, of course, leaves open the question of why such editorial judgment is necessary and whether such leeway should be granted to amateur mass communications (such as blogs, social media and websites).[112] If the justification is based on respect for the professional judgment and expertise of journalists and editors, then that may suggest greater weight for editorial autonomy in the established and professional media. By contrast, if the leeway is granted to prevent courts imposing ideal standards with the benefit of hindsight, then that points to respect for editorial autonomy in amateur publications too. The question then is who is entitled to editorial autonomy and why. While this issue has yet to be addressed, it is likely to be only a matter of time before it comes to the courts.

---

[112] See J Rowbottom, 'In the Shadow of the Big Media: Freedom of Expression, Participation and the Production of Knowledge Online' [2014] *Public Law* 491, 507–09.

10

Lord Hoffmann and Purposive Interpretation in Intellectual Property Law

JUSTINE PILA*

I. INTRODUCTION

SINCE LORD HOFFMANN returned to Oxford in 2009 and decided that, of the many subjects on the Oxford Law curriculum, the one he wanted to teach was patent law, I have felt a bit like the cat that got the cream. But it is a natural choice, for intellectual property (IP) is not only a field in which Lord Hoffmann has expressed a special interest throughout his career, but also one in which he has made an enormous—and in this jurisdiction at least, an unrivalled—contribution. It is no exaggeration to say that most of the current law of patents and key aspects of the law of copyright are due to him, as well as significant aspects of the IP laws of other jurisdictions.

It would be impossible in one chapter to do justice to the breadth and depth of Lord Hoffmann's contribution to IP. So, rather than attempt to do so, I will focus instead on some of the criticisms that have been levelled at his opinions and will ask whether (to borrow an expression from patent law) they are 'fairly based'.[1] If these criticisms have a common theme, it is one of timidity—a word that some may be surprised to hear in connection with Lord Hoffmann. Nonetheless, it has been suggested that some of Lord Hoffmann's most important opinions in IP—for example, those concerning the patentability requirement of novelty and the substantial part test

* I am grateful to Chintan Chandrachud for his comments on an earlier draft of this chapter.

[1] See the discussion of *Biogen Inc v Medeva plc* [1996] UKHL 18, [1997] RPC 1 below (text to n 60 et seq).

of copyright infringement—have been timid in the face of three things: (a) European authority; (b) IP rights that trammel on public freedoms; and (c) legal uncertainty.[2]

In this chapter I consider these criticisms and reject them. In the argument I make, such ambivalence on these matters as can be read in Lord Hoffmann's opinions in IP is merely a reflection of his commitment to giving effect to the policy choices of the legislature. I also defend his particular, purposive, interpretive approach on substantive and methodological grounds, and support the ascendancy of proportionality as a methodological tool in IP—including as a test of fair dealing in copyright—as a means of perpetuating and extending its influence.

Before embarking on this argument, some context of relevance regarding the two IP regimes that I will be discussing is appropriate.

The first is the patent system. In England, a patent system has existed since the seventeenth century, when it was developed as a public interest exception to a general legal (and, some would say, constitutional)[3] prohibition against monopoly grants.[4] Despite its statutory basis, until the 1970s the substantive principles of patent law were developed largely by the courts with an eye to these origins. During the 1970s, however, English patent law underwent a dramatic change as a result of the introduction of the supranational European Patent Convention (EPC),[5] which introduced a new body of patent law and a new authority—the European Patent Office (EPO)[6]—to interpret it. Since then, a lot of domestic patent cases, including many of the cases decided by Lord Hoffmann during his time as a member of the Judicial Committee of the House of Lords, have focused on the impact of this new law on traditional English principles and policy. And that impact, it is fair to say, has been to extend the reach of patent protection and to entrench in England and Europe generally a conception of patent grants as rights of an inventor rather than limited privileges granted by a state in pursuit of certain public benefits, which has discomfited some members of the local patent community.

---

[2] See C Floyd, 'Novelty under the Patents Act 1977: The State of the Art after *Merrell Dow*' [1996] *European Intellectual Property Review* 480; and M Spence and T Endicott, 'Vagueness in the Scope of Copyright' (2005) 121 *LQR* 657, discussed below. Use of the word 'timidity' in connection with Lord Hoffmann's opinions is from Floyd, above at 480, discussing *Merrell Dow Pharmaceuticals Inc v HB Norton & Co Ltd* [1995] UKHL 14, [1996] RPC 76 as follows: 'One sees a stark contrast between the bold stand of the courts in controlling monopolies in the 17th century, and the timid approach to the decisions of the EPO adopted by our courts today.'

[3] See, eg, *Oakley Inc v Animal Ltd and others* [2005] EWHC 210 (Ch) [23]–[25] (Mr Prescott QC).

[4] See the authorities cited by Mr Prescott QC, ibid.

[5] Convention on the Grant of Patents (Munich, 5 October 1973) 13 ILM 268 (as amended).

[6] The European Patent Office is one of two arms of the European Patent Organisation established by the EPC, and includes Boards of Appeal and an Enlarged Board of Appeal that operate as European patent tribunals with primary responsibility for interpreting and applying the EPC. See EPC, arts 21 and 22.

The copyright system has also existed for hundreds of years[7] and has also undergone something of a transformation recently on account of European harmonisation. Of especial importance in that regard has been the European Union's (EU's) Information Society Directive,[8] which introduces a near-complete copyright code for the EU's 28 Member States by requiring that they recognise authors as having certain rights in respect of their works, subject to a closed list of mandatory and permissible exceptions and limitations.[9] While the domestic impact of this code and other sources of European copyright law has been ambivalent—in some ways extending and in other ways restricting the reach of copyright—it has nonetheless focused the attention of courts and commentators on aspects of traditional English copyright law and policy.

With this as background, let me explain some of the criticisms of Lord Hoffmann's opinions and how they have arisen.

II. PATENTS FOR EXISTING PRODUCTS AND COPYRIGHT PROTECTION FOR IDEAS: *MERRELL DOW* AND *DESIGNERS GUILD*

In English law, as under the EPC, an invention must be new in order to be patentable.[10] According to section 2 of the Patents Act 1977, implementing Article 54 of the EPC, an invention is new if and only if it does not form part of the state of the art in the sense of not having previously been made available to the public. In *Merrell Dow*, the House of Lords was called upon to consider the meaning of this requirement and what exactly being new entails. Giving the leading speech for the court, Lord Hoffmann described the answer as depending on the essentially epistemological question 'what does it mean to know something, so that it can be part of the state of the art?',[11] and that question as depending in turn on the purpose for which it is asked.[12] In his analysis, while an invention can be known under 'an infinite variety of descriptions'[13]—what it looks like, how it is made, what it does, etc—the purpose of the novelty requirement in patent law is to determine whether the public already had the information needed to work the invention. The basis for this understanding is clear, since if a patent were granted for an invention which the public already had the means to work, the public

---

[7] The original copyright legislation was the Statute of Anne 1710 (8 Ann 11 c 19).

[8] Directive 2001/29/EC of the European Parliament and of the Council of 22 May 2001 on the harmonisation of certain aspects of copyright and related rights in the information society [2001] OJ L167/10 (Information Society Directive).

[9] ibid arts 2–5.

[10] Patents Act 1977, s 1(1).

[11] *Merrell Dow* (n 2) [39].

[12] ibid [36] and [39].

[13] ibid [36].

would receive nothing of substance in exchange for the grant and would, on the contrary, be denied access to something which it had previously been free to use. It also explains Lord Hoffmann's conclusion in *Merrell Dow* that to know an invention for patent law purposes means to know it 'under a description sufficient to work [it]'.[14]

That is the law, but what does it mean in practice? According to Lord Hoffmann, following jurisprudence of the EPO, it means among other things that giving the public instructions for causing a chemical reaction in the human body by ingesting a drug is enough to make a metabolite produced by that ingestion known, even if the metabolite as such is not referred to or described in the instructions. By contrast, the actual ingestion of the drug by members of the public may not be enough, for making an invention known 'requires the communication of information',[15] and using a product will not necessarily communicate any information. In *Merrell Dow*, this meant that a patent for a metabolite created in the human liver following the ingestion of the previously patented product terfenadine was invalid, for the metabolite had been made available to the public by the instructions for ingesting terfenadine contained in the terfenadine patent. However, had the attack on the metabolite's novelty depended solely on the prior use of terfenadine, it would have failed, and the metabolite been new for patentability purposes. That, at least, is the implication of Lord Hoffmann's analysis.

Soon after the publication of that analysis, counsel for Merrell Dow—Mr Christopher Floyd QC (now Lord Justice Floyd of the Court of Appeal of England and Wales)—gave a lecture criticising its second limb (regarding the impact of the prior use of terfenadine).[16] In Mr Floyd QC's view, if a product is put into the public realm by any means, it is thereby made known to the public, and so becomes incapable of being patented. In addition, the reason for Lord Hoffmann's decision to the contrary, Mr Floyd QC suggested, was his concern not to contradict an earlier decision of the European Patent Office in G2/88 (*Mobil/Friction-reducing additive*)[17] that the prior public use of an invention will not necessarily deprive it of novelty. In *Mobil*, the Enlarged Board of the EPO had held that the use of an engine additive for the purpose of reducing friction was new and therefore patentable, notwithstanding the prior public use of the same additive in the same manner for the different purpose of inhibiting rust. The reason given by the Board was that the new purpose of the use (to reduce friction) revealed a new technical effect of the use (reducing friction) that, while inherent in the additive's prior use to inhibit rust, was not *made available to the public* by it. In Mr Floyd QC's view, *Mobil* was wrongly decided and by tiptoeing around it, Lord Hoffmann showed undue deference to the EPO and failed to

---

[14] ibid [41].
[15] ibid [28].
[16] The lecture was later published as Floyd (n 2).
[17] *Mobil/Friction-reducing additive* [1990] EPOR 73.

do as English courts have historically done by declaring 'odious monopolies' for existing inventions to be void.[18]

A similar criticism has been made of Lord Hoffmann's opinion in the copyright case of *Designers Guild Ltd v Russell Williams (Textiles) Ltd.*[19]

Designers Guild concerned the principle of copyright law that infringement of copyright requires the unauthorised use of a substantial part of a protected work[20] and the two consequent issues: what is a substantial part of a work; and what relevance does the so-called idea/expression distinction (according to which copyright protects expression but not ideas) have when determining copyright infringement? The premise of Lord Hoffmann's analysis, consistent with his analysis in *Merrell Dow* and made explicit the following year in his speech in *Newspaper Licensing Agency v Marks & Spencer plc,*[21] was that the answers to these questions depend on a further question—wherein lie the qualities or substance of a work?—which depends in turn on the purpose for which the question is asked. That purpose, as the Copyright, Designs and Patents Act 1988 (CDPA) makes clear, is to determine which aspects of a work may not be copied, etc without the permission of the copyright owner.[22] In addition, when considering the question wherein lie the qualities of a work, the connection with *Merrell Dow* continues. For just as there exist an infinite number of descriptions under which an invention might be known, so too there will be an infinite number of perspectives on the source of a work's substance—a commercial perspective, an aesthetic perspective, the author's perspective, a reasonable person's perspective, etc—raising the question of which perspective the law of copyright infringement prioritises. Implicit in Lord Hoffmann's analysis in *Designers Guild* and confirmed in his speech in *Marks & Spencer*[23] is that the answer is Parliament's perspective. Hence his decision that in order to determine the source of a work's substance or qualities, it is necessary to identify which aspects of the work are deemed by the CDPA to merit it protection. In the case of a literary work, they are its aspects of literary originality; in the case of an artistic work they are its aspects of artistic originality; and so on, according to the nature of the work and the statutory requirements for its protection by copyright.[24] The result underlines a fundamental principle of copyright law, which is that assessments of infringement differ according to the (statutory) category of protected work in issue. Consider, for example, an original set of instructions for weaving fabric. As an original

---

[18] See Floyd (n 2) 480 (excerpted at n 2) 487.
[19] *Designers Guild Ltd v Russell Williams (Textiles) Ltd* [2000] UKHL 58, [2000] 1 WLR 2416.
[20] See Copyright, Designs and Patents Act 1988, s 16(3).
[21] *Newspaper Licensing Agency v Marks & Spencer plc* [2001] UKHL 38, [2002] RPC 225 [19].
[22] For the acts reserved exclusively to the copyright owner, see CDPA, s 16(1).
[23] *Marks & Spencer* (n 21).
[24] See CDPA, s 1(1); *Designers Guild* (n 19) 2421–23.

literary work, such instructions will be protected by literary copyright.[25] Following Lord Hoffmann's decision in *Designers Guild*, that copyright will only be infringed by reproducing aspects of the instructions that, when considered cumulatively, reflect a substantial part of the instructions' literary originality, and *not* by reproducing aspects of the instructions that reflect a substantial part of the instructions' *artistic* originality, including by representing the visual form of the fabric that the instructions depict.[26] By contrast, if the instructions are, in addition to being an original literary work protected by literary copyright, also an original graphic work protected by artistic copyright—as the recent decision in *Abraham Moon & Sons Ltd v Thornber*[27] makes it clear that they may be—depicting the fabric visually in two or three dimensions, including by following the instructions to produce the fabric itself, *will* infringe their copyright, since the design of the fabric will be part of what constitutes the instructions as a work of visual significance, and thus part of what their artistic copyright protects.[28]

What implication does Lord Hoffmann's test of copyright infringement in *Designers Guild* have for the idea/expression distinction? Implicit in the reasoning of Lord Hoffmann is that it deprives the distinction of substantive relevance, for the ideas of a work—the plot of a novel, for example, or the brush technique of a painting—are part of what gives the work its literary or artistic originality, and thus are part of what constitutes it as a literary or artistic work protected by copyright. It follows that such ideas—the plot of a novel or the brush technique of a painting—are also part of what copyright in the work protects.[29] To conclude otherwise, Lord Hoffmann implied, would support the fallacy that a work's ideas can be distinguished from their expression, in addition to subverting the statutory law by reading things into it that are not there.[30]

---

[25] See CDPA, s 1(1)(a).

[26] See *Designers Guild* (n 19) 2423 (rejecting the possibility of infringement of literary copyright in a patent specification by reproducing the invention).

[27] *Abraham Moon & Sons Ltd v Thornber* [2012] EWPCC 37 (Birss J).

[28] See CDPA, s 17(3).

[29] See *Designers Guild* (n 19) 2422–23; *Marks & Spencer* (n 21) [19].

[30] See *IBCOS Computers Ltd v Barclays Mercantile Highland Finance* [1994] FSR 275 (Ch) (emphasising the need for courts in copyright cases to adhere strictly to the statutory tests of subsistence and infringement and thereby avoid being distracted by such extra-legislative policy aphorisms as 'what is worth copying is prima facie worth protecting' and 'there is no copyright in ideas'). In the UK, the idea/expression distinction is given statutory expression in the context of computer programs only, following art 1(2) of Directive 2009/24/EC of the European Parliament and of the Council of 23 April 2009 on the legal protection of computer programs [2009] OJ L111/16. While art 9(2) of the TRIPS Agreement 1994 also states that 'Copyright protection shall extend to expressions and not to ideas, procedures, methods of operation or mathematical concepts as such', when interpreted in the manner of equivalent 'as such' provisions of European and international IP instruments, this could be said to prevent only the recognition of copyright subsistence in ideas. Under the CDPA, such recognition is in any case precluded by the restriction of copyright subsistence to *works*, of which ideas are clearly not examples: see s 1(1). More generally, and as Lord Hoffmann said in *Designers Guild* (n 19) 2422, the distinction 'needs to be handled with care. What does it mean?

It is important to understand that with the possible exception of 'odious monopolies' for inventions previously in use by the public, there is no aspect of IP law that invokes more passion than the idea/expression distinction because of its association with freedom of expression rights and interests, and its effect in limiting the scope of copyright protection.[31] As a result, it is not surprising that Lord Hoffmann's speech in *Designers Guild* has been criticised. For example, soon after it was delivered, Michael Spence and Timothy Endicott published an article in the *Law Quarterly Review*[32] arguing that while the idea/expression distinction 'is not explicitly to be found in the Act ... it is undoubtedly a part of UK copyright law' and a 'crucial' part at that.[33] In their analysis, its treatment by Lord Hoffmann in *Designers Guild* was on the one hand 'confusing because copyright law only protects a substantial part of the expression of a work' and on the other hand symptomatic of his wider failure to have derived from the statute principles of sufficient precision and clarity to guide future decision-makers.[34]

From this and Mr Floyd QC's critique of *Merrell Dow*, three criticisms of Lord Hoffmann's opinions emerge. The first is that they are too quick to abandon traditional English IP law and policy; the second is that they are insufficiently concerned to protect third party freedoms; and the third is that they are unacceptably vague and imprecise. Are these criticisms fair?

It is impossible to read Lord Hoffmann's opinions in IP law without being struck by their eloquence and analytical rigour. Nonetheless, it is also impossible to ignore a certain ambivalence on each of the three matters above. On closer inspection, however, it becomes clear that that ambivalence is attributable less to any timidity on his part than to his unshakeable intellectual commitment to giving effect to the intentions of Parliament, objectively conceived, by interpreting IP statutes purposively.

III. LORD HOFFMANN'S AMBIVALENCE AS A FUNCTION OF HIS COMMITMENT TO PURPOSIVE INTERPRETATION AS A MEANS OF GIVING EFFECT TO PARLIAMENTARY INTENTION, OBJECTIVELY CONCEIVED

The central premise and insight of purposive interpretation is that meaning is conveyed by a speaker's choice of language and the context in which she speaks, including her purpose in speaking, whether subjectively or

---

As Lord Hailsham of St. Marylebone said in *LB (Plastics) Ltd v Swish Products Ltd* [1979] R.P.C. 551, 629, "It all depends on what you mean by 'ideas'."

[31] Note, however, that freedom of expression is also commonly cited as an argument in favour of copyright protection, since by promoting the creation and dissemination of expressive and informational works, copyright can be said to promote a public domain of ideas and information. See, eg, N Netanel, 'Copyright and a Democratic Civil Society' (1996) 106 *Yale Law Journal* 283.

[32] Spence and Endicott (n 2).

[33] ibid 659.

[34] ibid 658 and 670.

objectively conceived.[35] In IP, Lord Hoffmann has embraced an objective version of this theory, according to which the purpose of the relevant speaker must be gleaned from her choice of words and the context in which she speaks them rather than her subjective motivations in speaking them. He has done so most fully and expressly in the context of patent claims, notably in *Kirin-Amgen Inc v Hoescht Marion Roussel Ltd*, as a means of ensuring to patentees the full (but only the full) extent of the patent monopolies that they claim.[36] However, his commitment to purposive interpretation as a method for deriving meaning from all language-based communications, combined with his concern to decide cases in the manner required by legislation, has meant that it runs through all of his opinions in IP. Hence, in *Merrell Dow* and *Designers Guild*, when asked to interpret the statutory requirement of novelty and the substantial part test of copyright infringement, his focus was on identifying the essential questions raised by each—what does it mean to know an invention in patent law and what gives a copyright work its qualities or substance as such?—and answering them purposively, having regard to the reason for asking them as revealed by the relevant legislation.

Central to the method of purposive interpretation deployed by Lord Hoffmann in IP is the need to ensure that when interpreting and applying legal instruments, courts adhere closely to the language of the instrument itself and do not allow policy considerations to subvert its meaning, including by supporting a 'gloss' in the interests of legal certainty. As he said in *Kirin-Amgen*, for example, after rejecting a structured test of patent claim construction in favour of one based on purposive interpretation:

> No doubt there will be patent lawyers who are dismayed at [my decision]. They may feel cast adrift on a sea of interpretative uncertainty. But that is the fate of all who have to understand what people mean by using language.[37]

So too in other cases, Lord Hoffmann has made clear his view that the purposive interpretation of IP legislation will not always produce the best outcome from a policy perspective, underlining the restraint that it requires on the part of individual courts and judges. For example, in *Marks & Spencer*, concerning copyright in a newspaper as a typographical arrangement of a published edition under section 1(1)(c) of the CDPA, he held that while the original purpose of granting copyright in typographical arrangements was to protect publishers of new editions of works by such authors as Jane Austen and Beethoven against competition from pirate photo-lithographic copies, and not to protect publishers of newspapers:

> Nevertheless, copyright is a right to prevent copying and not merely to restrain unfair competition. It sometimes affords protection in unexpected situations ...

---

[35] On purposive interpretation in general, see A Barak, *Purposive Interpretation in Law* (Princeton, Princeton University Press, 2005).
[36] *Kirin-Amgen Inc v Hoescht Marion Roussel Ltd* [2004] UKHL 46, [2005] RPC 9.
[37] ibid [71].

If, as a matter of construction, the work is protected, then (subject to any special defences) the copyright owner is entitled to enforce it.[38]

So, he said, in a decision affirming his concern with *objective* rather than *subjective* parliamentary intent,[39] while 'the purpose of the copyright is something which can be taken into account in deciding [which aspects of a typographical arrangement] will attract protection', it cannot be allowed to subvert the legislative language itself.

Clearly, this is not without its difficulties, for even if we accept that meaning can both depend on and be subverted by context, how do we know which situation we are in and which aspects of context are relevant? And, as a related question, at what level of generality—and with reference to what supporting evidence—is the purpose of a statutory right or provision appropriately conceived? That these questions admit of no simple or abstract answers may be said to underline 'the sea of interpretive uncertainty' upon which purposive reasoning casts one adrift. But in my view, the extent of that uncertainty and the dangers of the waters in this area generally have a tendency to be overstated. Provided that one does take care to identify at the outset the relevant question which the law requires to be asked and provided that the purpose which the law reveals for asking that question is made the central reference point when answering it, the scope for uncertainty is substantially diminished, along with the risk of the case being decided according to individual judges' intuitive sense of justice, albeit that neither is capable of being removed entirely. In my view, this emerges clearly from Lord Hoffmann's explanation in *Designers Guild* of why the Court of Appeal had been wrong in that case to overturn the trial judge's decision that the aspects of the protected work which the defendant had copied were a substantial part of the work (in satisfaction of the test of copyright infringement) on the ground that an objective comparison of the protected and allegedly infringing works did not suggest substantial copying by the defendant. As he remarked:

> It is often difficult to give precise reasons for arriving at a conclusion one way or the other (apart from an enumeration of the relevant factors) and there are borderline cases over which reasonable minds may differ. But the first step in trying to answer any question (whether of impression or otherwise) is to be clear about what the question is. In the present case, it is whether the features which the judge found to have been copied from [the protected work] formed a substantial part of [it] as an artistic work. That is certainly a question of judgment or impression. But why, in answering that question, should it be relevant to consider whether [the claimant's work] did or did not look like [the defendant's work]?[40]

---

[38] *Marks & Spencer* (n 21) [30].
[39] See text following n 35.
[40] *Designers Guild* (n 19) 2420–21.

That the question in *Designers Guild* was as stated in this paragraph is clear from the statutory test of copyright infringement contained in section 16 of the CDPA, which defines infringement as the unauthorised exercise of an act reserved to the copyright owner in relation to a protected work in whole or substantial part. And so too it follows as a matter of logic from this test that, having established *in fact* that a reserved act has been done in relation to a work and which aspects of the work the act involved, the defendant's work will cease to be relevant and in particular will offer no assistance when deciding whether the relevant aspects of the work are a substantial part of it. It is difficult to explain the Court of Appeal's conclusion to the contrary other than as a product of its failure to have kept section 16 squarely in mind when deciding the case, and its persuasion to the policy view urged for the defendant that certain types of non-literal copying ought not to be regarded as infringing of copyright, whatever the CDPA provides.[41]

By Lord Hoffmann's own admission, his interpretation of the substantial part test of copyright infringement in *Designers Guild* entails a degree of uncertainty, since in each case it requires an assessment by the court of whether the parts of the protected work which have been copied sufficiently reflect those aspects of the work that merit it copyright. This may help to explain Spence and Endicott's criticism of his decision for having failed to translate the statutory test of substantial part into principles of sufficient precision and clarity to guide future decision-makers. But the question remains whether his approach could be improved upon. In the argument that Spence and Endicott make, it could be improved upon by being replaced with a test tailored to reflect (the authors' view of) the purpose of *granting* copyright, namely, to incentivise 'the creation, dissemination and efficient exploitation of protected works' and promote authors' 'expressive autonomy'.[42] Consistent with this, the particular test of substantial part infringement which they advocated involved an assessment by the court of the competing economic and expressive implications of permitting and prohibiting the relevant use of the protected work to decide what the justice of the case required.[43]

Far from revealing the deficiencies of Lord Hoffmann's approach in *Designers Guild*, this argument in my view underlines its strengths by drawing attention to its greater conceptual clarity and grounding in the statutory law. Why, it must be asked, should the scope of copyright protection be limited to unauthorised uses of a work that cause more commercial or expressive harm to the author than benefit to the unauthorised user when the

---

[41] See ibid 2420, quoting from the judgment of Morritt LJ (with whom Auld and Clarke LJJ agreed on this point) in the Court of Appeal.

[42] Spence and Endicott (n 2) 672–73.

[43] See ibid 673–74 (proposing that courts determine substantial part having regard to: '(i) the impact of the taking on the market for the original work; (ii) the effect of precluding the taking on the market for substitutes for the work; (iii) the importance of the part taken to the expressive effect of the original work; and (iv) the effect of precluding the taking on the normal conduct of expressive exchange').

legislation prohibits *any* unauthorised use of *any* substantial part of a protected work and makes separate provision for the protection of third party
interests and rights—including those of non-commercial use and freedom
of expression—in its fair dealing and other defences? Asking this question
underlines two things of importance regarding the Spence and Endicott test.
The first is its substantive legal effect, which is to reconceive copyright from
a (transferrable, exclusionary) *property* right to a right to prevent only such
uses of a work that would, in the view of the court, cause more harm to the
commercial and expressive interests of the copyright owner and author than
to the commercial and expressive interests of the public. And the second is
its methodological effect, which is to require that the question at the heart of
the substantial part test of copyright infringement—wherein lies the source
of a copyright work's qualities or substance?—be answered with reference
to a policy perspective supplied by the authors themselves rather than, as
in Lord Hoffmann's analysis, the express statutory conditions for copyright
subsistence. Hence my suggestion that the real focus of the authors' objection to *Designers Guild* is the statutory rules of copyright, and their failure
to protect the commercial and expressive interests of third parties in the
manner and to the extent that the authors would like. In the context of
EU copyright harmonisation in particular, driven largely by the EU's policy
commitment to ensuring a 'high level of protection for authors' in recognition of the nature of copyright as a property right[44] subject to a closed list of
exceptions and limitations,[45] this objection can perhaps be read as a lament
for a past in which English copyright law was thought to be more explicitly
concerned with the promotion of third party interests. Regardless, its effect
is to use both the substantial part test of copyright infringement and the
method of purposive interpretation itself as tools for subverting the policy
choices of the legislature with respect to the nature and scope of copyright
protection as expressed in the provisions of copyright legislation. In addition, in its claim to promote legal certainty, it is open to further challenge,
since it is unclear how an approach to copyright infringement based on the
reconciliation of competing commercial and expressive interests could be
applied with any degree of consistency in practice.

In criticising *Designers Guild*, Spence and Endicott do not take issue with
the purposive approach of Lord Hoffmann as such, but rather with his failure to define 'substantial part' with reference to (their view of) the purpose
of copyright overall. Nonetheless, purposive interpretation itself is often
regarded as a natural enemy of legal certainty, since even if there is general
agreement regarding the legislature's intention with respect to a particular
statutory right or provision (which often there is not), the implications of

---

[44] See, eg, Information Society Directive, recitals 4 and 9.
[45] See Information Society Directive, art 5.

that intention for the meaning of the right or provision in a specific case will frequently be unclear.

This can perhaps be seen in the context of patent claim construction, where Lord Hoffmann's deployment of purposive interpretation has proved controversial—albeit as much for its perceived literalism[46] as for its perceived uncertainty.[47] Consistent with the contradictory nature of these criticisms, this is in my view another example of an area of IP law the uncertainties of which have a tendency to be overstated, and the overstatement of which often masks an objection to the policy choices of Parliament. The key principle here, following Lord Hoffmann's opinion in *Kirin-Amgen*, is that patent claims are to be construed like any other language-based communication, including contracts and statutes, with due regard being paid to their statutory function in defining an invention (technical idea) and its associated monopoly. The task of the court is therefore to determine what the patent's notional addressee—the person skilled in the art to which the invention relates and armed with common general knowledge regarding that art (PSA)—reading the claims as a description and demarcation of an invention and monopoly would understand them to have been intended to mean, and in particular what subject matter the PSA would understand them to have been intended to cover.[48] It is only, he said, by adopting this approach that one can be assured of reading the claims in a way that ensures to the patentee the full extent, but not more than the full extent, of the protection which he has sought through his choice of language to claim.[49]

As noted above, a central aspect of the context in which patent claims are read is their statutory function to define an invention—ie, a technical idea—and an associated patent monopoly.[50] That function reflects the fundamental principle of patent law that it is inventors themselves who are charged with defining their monopoly rights through the definition of their patentable invention in the patent claims. That definition is then examined by the patent office, representing the public, for compliance with the requirements of legislation. If it is accepted and the patent application proceeds to grant, the definition functions as a formal notice to the public of the extent to which their freedoms are constrained by the patentee's monopoly. Hence the role of patent claims in defining both the rights of individual patentees and the corresponding obligations of third parties; a role premised on a view of patent grants as contracts between a patentee and the public that

---

[46] See, eg, RL Hoad, 'Non-literal Patent Infringement: More Honoured in the Breach than the Observance?' (2006) 17 *Australian Intellectual Property Journal* 121; H Laddie, '*Kirin Amgen*—The End of Equivalents in England?' (2009) 40 *International Review of Intellectual Property and Competition Law* 3.

[47] See n 70.

[48] See *Kirin-Amgen* (n 36) [34].

[49] ibid [47]–[48].

[50] See Patents Act 1977, ss 14(5) and 125.

are negotiated by the claimant and the patent office as the public's agent and enforced by the courts in the manner of other agreements. Among other things, this role underlines the importance of patent claims being interpreted with reference to their intended meaning *objectively* conceived by drawing attention to the need for patent claims to be sufficiently clear to inform the public of the impact of the grant on their freedoms.[51]

Once the function of patent claims to define and give public notice of an invention and an associated patent monopoly is acknowledged, the point at which contextual factors (including the claimant's purpose in drafting the claims) cease to support and begin to subvert the meaning of the claimant's language becomes easier to discern: depending always on the language itself, and the description and drawings which Article 69(1) requires to be used to interpret that language, it will generally be the point at which it supports a view of the claimant's invention and monopoly as covering more than the technical equivalent of that which a literal interpretation of the claims by the PSA would support.[52] This view of technical equivalence as representing the outer limits of legitimate (purposive) construction is supported by Lord Hoffmann's analysis in *Kirin-Amgen* of the earlier decision of Lord Diplock in *Catnic Components Ltd v Hill & Smith Ltd*[53] that the monopoly conferred by the patent in that case for a 'vertical lintel' also covered a lintel inclined at six degrees. The essence of this analysis was that the latter would be understood by the PSA as a technical approximation of the former and thus as substantively the same invention.[54] In those circumstances, to limit the patentee's monopoly to the lintel inclined at zero degrees would have had the perverse and arbitrary result of enabling a defendant to avoid infringement by manufacturing a lintel inclined at 0.0001 degrees. It would also have required

---

[51] The focus on the claimant's intention objectively conceived explains Lord Hoffmann's dismissal in *Kirin-Amgen* (n 36) [35] of the relevance of the patent office file recording the 'negotiations' between the claimant and patent office before the patent was granted as an aid to construing the patent claims. According to Lord Hoffmann, 'the meaning of the patent should not change according to whether or not the person skilled in the art has access to the file and in any case life is too short for the limited assistance which it can provide. It is however frequently impossible to know without access, not merely to the file but to the private thoughts of the patentee and his advisors as well, what the reason was for some apparently inexplicable limitation in the extent of the monopoly claimed.' In addition however, to use the patent office file as an aid to construing the subjective intentions of the claimant is to use it for an irrelevant purpose. And as a matter of policy, to concede that the meaning of a patent claim cannot be determined without regard to the patent office file would be to concede that patent claims are not capable of performing their statutory function of notifying the public of that which they are prevented by the patentee's monopoly from doing. This creates further difficulties for Arnold J's recent decision in *Actavis v Eli Lilly* [2014] EWHC 1511 (Pat) that resort *may* be had to the patent office file in certain circumstances when construing patent claims (see n 70).

[52] As Lord Hoffmann explained in *Kirin-Amgen* (n 36) [49], technical equivalence can 'be an important part of the background of facts known to the skilled man which would affect what he understood the claims to mean. That is no more than common sense. It is also expressly provided by the new art 2 added to the Protocol [on the Interpretation of Article 69]'.

[53] *Catnic Components Ltd v Hill & Smith Ltd* [1982] RPC 183 (HL).

[54] See, eg, *Kirin-Amgen* (n 36) [65].

one of two things on the part of the Court: either an assumption that in reading the claim, the PSA would understand the patentee to have used each word in its literal sense; or a policy commitment to hold the patentee to the literal meaning of its claim whatever the context and consequences. Both are problematic, however, since people do *not* use language in a literal sense—this being the central insight of the semantic theory that underpins purposive interpretation—and since to hold them to their literal meaning on policy grounds is expressly prohibited by patent legislation. According to the Patents Act 1977, importing the Protocol on the Interpretation of Article 69 of the EPC that was drafted in response to the perceived extremes of the interpretative approaches of English and German courts histori-cally,[55] patent claims must be construed with a view to achieving a balance between the interests of legal certainty and fair protection for patentees, and may therefore not be interpreted literally (as in England historically) or treated as a mere guideline in discovering the inventive contribution of the patentee (as in Germany historically). The clear implication of the Protocol, supported by purposive reasoning, is that to interpret patent claims literally would be to sacrifice the aim of protecting patentees on the altar of legal certainty, which would be inappropriate in an era in which patents are no longer conceived as exceptional grants requiring strict interpretation in the interests of protecting public freedoms.[56] Conversely, however, to construe patent claims as providing mere guidance in identifying the invention and monopoly which it is their express statutory purpose to define would be to ignore that purpose and the aim of claim interpretation in general to derive the meaning that the claimant through his language has sought to convey.[57]

This discussion implies a truth that has proved surprisingly elusive in IP law, which is simply the impossibility of deriving meaning from a com-municative act of any kind without construing it purposively. If one does accept this as truth, it follows that to deploy any other interpretive method is to make a policy decision that there is something more important in the particular context than discovering the communicator's apparently intended meaning per se, be it legal certainty or some other legal policy objective, such as securing greater protection for patentees.[58]

In sum, while purposive reasoning is not a science and will sometimes lead 'reasonable minds [to] differ' on the right result in an individual case,[59] that is not a valid criticism or conceptual shortcoming of the method itself. Indeed, the great virtue of its deployment by Lord Hoffmann in the cases

---

[55] See Patents Act 1977, s 125(3). On the background to the Protocol, see *Mobil* (n 17) [2.1] and [4.1].

[56] See n 4 and accompanying text.

[57] See text accompanying n 50.

[58] For a defence of this truth and Lord Hoffmann's interpretive approach generally, see A Kramer, 'Common Sense Principles of Contract Interpretation (and how we've been using them all along' (2003) 23 *OJLS* 173.

[59] See n 40.

considered herein has been the detailed explanation of IP law- and decision-making with reference to the relevant legal instrument which it has entailed.

In defending Lord Hoffmann's use of purposive interpretation in IP, I have drifted somewhat from my central aim in this chapter, which is to demonstrate that it is Lord Hoffmann's *commitment* to such interpretation that explains many aspects, and responds to many criticisms, of his decisions in this field. Thus, my suggestion is that when one reads his body of work with that commitment in mind, decisions that might at first seem difficult to understand or reconcile fall clearly into place as a product of his particular and distinctive analytical approach.

Let me mention another of Lord Hoffmann's decisions that reflects the policy ambivalence in the name of purposive interpretation that I have been referring to, which is his decision (from the bench of the Court of Appeal) in *H Lundbeck A/S v Generics (UK) Ltd*.[60] In that case Lord Hoffmann retreated from his earlier decision in *Biogen Inc v Medeva plc*[61] regarding the post-EPC requirement of section 14(5)(c) of the Patents Act 1977 that the claims of a patent (in which the invention is defined) be 'supported by the description' of the invention contained in the patent specification.[62] In *Biogen*, Lord Hoffmann had interpreted this requirement as accommodating the old English principle of fair basis to find that it was not enough for a patentee to disclose one way of performing the invention that it claimed; if it is 'possible to envisage other ways of achieving [its result] which make no use of the invention [as described]', the patent would be invalid for being 'wide or speculative', consistent with traditional English principles.[63] In doing so, he had again reasoned purposively from the Patents Act, emphasising both the social contract between the state and inventor that patents represent[64] and the need for 'care' to prevent patents from interfering unreasonably with 'further research and healthy competition'. In his conclusion, the monopoly which a patentee receives from a patent grant must correspond exactly in scope with the invention which the patentee discloses to the public via its patent description.[65] What he seems not to have contemplated at the time of *Biogen*, however, was that the old English principle of fair basis which his decision preserved conflicted with express provisions of modern UK statutory law guaranteeing the availability of patents for

---

[60] *H Lundbeck A/S v Generics (UK) Ltd* [2008] EWCA Civ 311, [2008] RPC 19, affirmed in [2009] UKHL 12, [2009] 2 All ER 955.

[61] *Biogen* (n 1).

[62] See also Patents Act 1977, s 14(3).

[63] *Biogen* (n 1) 22.

[64] See text accompanying n 51. In England the conception of patents as social contracts was cemented following *Liardet v Johnson* (1778) 481 NB 173 (KB). For a recent decision challenging this conception, see *Human Genome Sciences Inc v Eli Lilly* [2011] UKSC 51, [2012] RPC 6.

[65] *Biogen* (n 1) 52.

products as such.[66] The reason for the conflict is that, in the case of a product patent, there will always be a disjuncture between what a patentee receives from her monopoly and gives via her disclosure, since the scope of her patent protection will extend to all ways of making and using the product, and yet the teaching disclosed in her patent will necessarily be confined to a finite number of each. So it was that when this conflict emerged in *Lundbeck*, Lord Hoffmann felt compelled to distinguish *Biogen*.[67] However, on the policy implications of doing so, he was characteristically sanguine. 'It is … difficult', he said, 'not to sympathise with the judge's feeling that the distinction between [the inventors] in [the two cases] owes little to any difference in their original contributions to their respective arts',[68] but:

> Parliament has chosen to allow product claims and the jurisprudence of the EPO, which we have always regarded as carrying great weight, shows that such claims can be made in the latter case as well. It is too late to have regrets about the breadth of the monopoly which such claims confer.[69]

So, while the guarantee of product patents may upset the social contract on which patent law depends and thereby may restrict public freedoms beyond a point we might regard as desirable—just as the availability of copyright in typographical arrangements may give publishers rights they were not intended to have, the substantial part test of copyright infringement may enable copyright owners to prevent third parties from copying ideas, and patent claim construction may not give patent lawyers the legal certainty they would like—these are issues for Parliament and are not issues that it would be appropriate for the courts to seek to resolve.

On the whole, and despite the enduring authority of Lord Hoffmann's opinions in IP, this is a lesson that practitioners, academics and the general public have been reluctant to embrace. For example, there has been considerable resistance to the purposive construction of patent claims on the part of patent practitioners, who would seem to prefer the simplicity and security of a more certain test, be it interpretive literalism or the structured approach favoured by courts before Lord Hoffmann's decision in *Kirin-Amgen* (also, coincidentally, authored by Lord Hoffmann in his early years as a High

---

[66] See, eg, Patents Act 1977, s 60 (defining the rights conferred by a patent differently for product and process inventions). For a detailed discussion, see J Pila, 'Chemical Products and Proportionate Patents before and after *Generics v Lundbeck*' (2009) 20 *King's Law Journal* 489.

[67] In my view, and as I have elsewhere argued, even accepting the inconsistency between the *Biogen* (n 1) principle of insufficiency and the guarantee of product patents, it was not necessary for Lord Hoffmann to distinguish *Biogen* as he did in *Lundbeck*, since the inventions in the two cases were materially the same. See J Pila, 'Chemical Product Patents and *Biogen* Insufficiency before the House of Lords' (2009) 125 *LQR* 573. That, however, is a separate matter not germane to the current discussion.

[68] *Lundbeck* (n 60) [19].

[69] ibid [46].

Court judge).[70] Such resistance is related to a wider phenomenon in patent law whereby the courts themselves, concerned to satisfy the demands of practitioners and the public for legal certainty, formulate structured tests for resolving statutory questions only to discard those tests when they are revealed to produce results unsupported by the statutory law.[71] The dangers of this phenomenon will be obvious and are increased by the tendency of practitioners to continue to apply the structured tests even after the courts have abandoned them—a point made by Lord Justice Lewison in the context of the (judicially formulated) 'obvious to try' test of inventive step in *MedImmune Ltd v Novartis Pharmaceuticals UK Ltd*.[72]

IV. *MERRELL DOW* AND *DESIGNERS GUILD* REVISITED

Before moving too far from *Merrell Dow* and *Designers Guild*, I should return to those cases and their substantive outcomes. Was Lord Hoffmann right to decide each case as he did? I think the answer depends on one's view of his conception of the subject matter in each—the metabolite in *Merrell Dow* and the fabric design in *Designers Guild*—as a patentable invention and copyright work respectively. According to Lord Hoffmann, the metabolite properly conceived (qua invention) was a 'piece of information'[73] and therefore could not exist in the absence of information, and the fabric design properly conceived (qua artistic work) was a product of artistic originality, of which its underlying artistic ideas and techniques were an essential, constitutive part. These raise fascinating and complex questions regarding the subject matter of IP and their ontology, and in my respectful opinion Lord Hoffmann answered them correctly.[74] In the case of *Designers Guild*,

---

[70] See *Improver Co v Remington Consumer Product Ltd* [1990] FSR 181 (Pat). For a recent example of practitioner *and* judicial resistance to the purposive approach to patent claim construction adopted by Lord Hoffmann in *Kirin-Amgen* (n 36), see *Actavis v Eli Lilly* [2014] EWHC 1511 (Pat). In that case Arnold J lamented the 'falling out of fashion' of the structured *Improver* approach to claim construction, and relied on that approach in apparent defiance of *Kirin-Amgen* and more than 10 years of supporting appellate authority (eg, *Virgin Atlantic Airways Ltd v Premium Aircraft Interiors UK Ltd* [2009] EWCA Civ 1062, [2010] RPC 8) on the ground in part that the parties to the case supported its adoption.

[71] Lord Walker alluded to this phenomenon, encouraged perhaps by the scientific background of many patent lawyers, in *Synthon BV v SmithKline Beecham plc* [2005] UKHL 59, [2006] RPC 10—a case involving another watershed decision by Lord Hoffmann—[57].

[72] *MedImmune Ltd v Novartis Pharmaceuticals UK Ltd* [2012] EWCA Civ 1234, [2013] RPC 27 [179]–[181].

[73] *Merrell Dow* (n 2) [28].

[74] For some consideration of them, see, among other works, J Pila, *The Requirement for an Invention in Patent Law* (Oxford, Oxford University Press, 2010); J Pila, 'An Australian Copyright Revolution and its Relevance for UK Jurisprudence: *IceTV* in the Light of *Infopaq v Danske* (2010) 9 *Oxford University Commonwealth Law Journal* 77; and J Pila, 'The Future of the European Requirement for an Invention' (2010) 41 *International Review of Intellectual Property and Competition Law* 906.

the reason is that under section 1(1) of the CDPA, copyright subsists in and protects authorial (literary, dramatic, musical and artistic) and other works. To suggest that such works—be they novels, paintings, dance compositions, plays or more mundane subject matter such as product marketing material—do not include ideas or information is to engage in a legal fiction that can only be justified by clear parliamentary support. Outside the limited realm of computer programs, no such support exists in the UK.[75] This is why the authors sought to rely in their article on Article 9(2) of the Agreement on Trade-Related Aspects of Intellectual Property Rights and English case law.[76] But for constitutional reasons, and noting the CDPA's detailed regulation of all aspects of copyright, neither of these sources is sufficient to support their argument. For these reasons alone, Spence and Endicott's criticism of *Designers Guild* as having proceeded from a 'confusion' regarding what copyright protects must be rejected. So, in my view and for similar reasons, must Mr Floyd QC's criticism of *Merrell Dow* be dismissed.

V. EXTENDING LORD HOFFMANN'S INTERPRETIVE APPROACH TO FAIR DEALING VIA PROPORTIONALITY

Spence and Endicott are not the only ones to have baulked in the face of vague statutory concepts such as 'substantial part' and to have sought to pin them down with structured tests or bright line rules. Another example, also from copyright but this time involving a member of the public, is provided by the commentary entitled 'myths and ambiguities in copyright law' by the literary scholar Jonathan Bate that was published in the *Times Literary Supplement* in August 2010.[77] In a critique of the copyright law of fair dealing (according to which fair dealings with a work are permitted for and only for the specific statutory purposes of non-commercial research, private study, criticism or review of a work, quotation, reporting a current event, caricature, parody or pastiche, and illustration for instruction for a non-commercial purpose),[78] Bate lamented the absence of any statutory definition of 'fair', including the propensity for 'myths' regarding its meaning to arise. The law would be improved, he suggested, by a rule permitting the use of extracts of up to 400 words from a prose work, 40 words from a poem or more 'in certain circumstances'.[79] One sees in this proposal similarities to the proposal of Spence and Endicott above, including criticism of

---

[75] See n 30.
[76] ibid.
[77] J Bate, 'Fair Enough? Myths and Ambiguities in Copyright Law' *Times Literary Supplement* (London, 6 August 2010) 14.
[78] See CDPA, ss 29–32.
[79] n 77.

a key aspect of the copyright statute for its alleged vagueness.[80] As with the Spence and Endicott substantial part test, however, the Bate fairness test is both arbitrary (why 400/40 words?) and uncertain (how would the courts decide when fairness requires the 400/40 word rule to be set aside?).

The meaning of fair dealing in copyright law is one IP issue that Lord Hoffmann has not considered from the bench. Even here, however, the law can be said to reflect his analytical approach and can be predicted to do so increasingly in the future in England as it becomes increasingly aligned with the EU concept of proportionality.[81] Thus aligned, the fairness of a dealing with a work for one of the statutory purposes above depends on whether the dealing exceeds what is necessary to achieve that purpose. That this understanding of fairness is in the ascendancy seems clear from the increasing impact of EU law on UK copyright, and in particular from the harmonisation of permissible copyright exceptions and limitations via Article 5 of the Information Society Directive, and the requirement (following *Marleasing SA v La Comercial Internacional de Alimentacion SA*)[82] that UK courts interpret all of the fair dealing defences contained in the CDPA to be consistent with their Article 5 counterparts, most of which include a proportionality requirement.[83] For example, the provisions of Article 5(3)(a), (c), (d) and (f) permitting the use of works for the statutory purposes of illustration for teaching or research, reporting current topics, criticism or review, and information respectively only permit such use to the extent that it is justified by the (EU) statutory purpose itself. This is presumably why the recently introduced UK defence permitting fair dealings with a work for the purpose of quotation is similarly limited to proportionate quotations, ie, to individual quotations the extent of which 'is no more than is required by the specific purpose for which it is used'.[84]

Of related importance to the EU's harmonisation of copyright exceptions and limitations is the well-established conception of such exceptions and limitations in England and elsewhere as a site for reconciling competing fundamental rights and interests in respect of protected material,[85] and the also well-established role of proportionality as a tool for reconciling such rights and interests in individual cases, including those of authors to protection of their intellectual property and of third parties and society at large to freedom

---

[80] *Cf* Spence and Endicott (n 2) 662: 'It would be possible to create precise rules to determine the question of substantiality in some contexts, but such rules could give rise to more arbitrary decision-making than the application of a vaguer standard.'

[81] See Treaty on European Union, art 5(4).

[82] Case C-106/89 *Marleasing SA v La Comercial Internacional de Alimentacion SA* [1990] ECR I-4135.

[83] See also Case C-145/10 *Painer* [2011] ECR I-12533 [105]–[106].

[84] See CDPA, s 30(1ZA)(c).

[85] See, eg, Information Society Directive, recital 31; Case C-201/13 *Deckmyn* (3 September 2014); *Pro Sieben Media AG v Carlton UK Television Ltd* [1999] FSR 605 (CA) 612 (Robert Walker LJ) ('the wide variety of uses of copyright material permitted by the 49 sections comprised in Chapter III [of the CDPA] (acts permitted in relation to copyright works) are all directed to achieving a proper balance between protection of the rights of a creative author and the wider public interest').

of expression.[86] In addition, and as I have noted elsewhere, while the English courts have never themselves used proportionality expressly to determine the fairness of an unauthorised dealing with a work, deploying instead the so-called 'Laddie' factors (according to which fairness is determined in all cases having regard to the commercial or non-commercial motivation of the defendant, the extent of the work's unauthorised use, the impact of the use on the copyright owner's market and the extent of the work's prior public circulation),[87] they have on occasion expressed their conclusions in language suggestive of a proportionality analysis. Thus, in considering whether an unauthorised use of a work for a protected (statutory) purpose was fair, they have sometimes asked whether the use exceeded what was necessary to achieve that purpose.[88] The result is an interpretive approach that is remarkably similar to the interpretive approach deployed by Lord Hoffmann in *Designers Guild*. As seen above, in *Designers Guild*, Lord Hoffmann interpreted the question 'are these aspects of the work a substantial part of the work?' as depending on the reason for asking the question, which reason he sought from the statutory conditions for copyright subsistence. So too in the fair dealing context, a proportionality approach to fairness requires that the question 'is this use of the work fair?' be answered having regard to the reason for asking the question, which reason must similarly be sought from the statutory definition of each fair dealing defence, and the specific purposes for which it authorises use of the work. The fairness of a dealing under section 30(2) will then depend on whether a specific use goes beyond what is necessary to report the relevant current event, and in deciding this the courts will need to have regard to the fundamental (freedom of expression) rights and interests underpinning that section, including by considering the nature of the event in question, the importance of the public learning about it, and the ability of the defendant effectively to report it by means other than use of the protected work.[89] Following the decision of the Court of Justice of the European Union (CJEU) in *Deckmyn*,[90] they will also need to have regard to any other fundamental rights and interests engaged by the use to ensure that section 30(2) operates as a site for the reconciliation of *all* competing fundamental interests and

---

[86] See EU Charter, arts 11 (freedom of expression and information) and 17(2) (IP protection); Case C-467/08 *Padawan* [2010] ECR I-10055 and *Painer* (n 83); and in other areas of copyright Case C-275/06 *Productores de Música de Espana (Promusicae) v Telefónica de España SAU* [2008] EUECJ and *Golden Eye v Telefonica UK* [2012] EWHC 723 (Ch).

[87] See *Ashdown v Telegraph Group Ltd* [2001] EWCA Civ 1142, [2002] QB 546; *Newspaper Licensing Agency Ltd v Meltwater Holding BV* [2011] EWCA Civ 890, [2012] RPC 1.

[88] See, eg, *Ashdown* (n 87) [81]–[82]; *Hyde Park Residence Ltd v Yelland* [2001] Ch 143 (CA) [40].

[89] See *Painer* (n 83); *Ashdown* (n 87).

[90] In *Deckmyn*, the Court held that in deciding whether a parodic use of a copyright work is excluded from copyright infringement, domestic courts must identify *all* of the competing fundamental rights and interests which the use engages and resolve individual cases in a manner that reflects a fair balance of them, including the rights and interests of authors and copyright owners to prevent parodic and other uses of their works that have the effect of associating them with a discriminatory message in accordance with EU Charter, art 22.

rights, and not only those of IP protection and freedom of expression themselves. It could be said that this supports a version of proportionality that, while still closely linked to Lord Hoffmann's purposive approach, differs from that approach by requiring explicit judicial engagement with a wider range of rights and interests than those which it is the purpose of the relevant fair dealing defence to protect. Put differently, it replaces the necessity-focused test of proportionality with a more traditional, three-stage test to require, as a further condition of raising a defence, that the disadvantages of allowing the dealing not be disproportionate to the aims pursued. In so doing, it would likely be criticised by Lord Hoffmann for rejecting the judgement of the legislature as to the social importance of the object to be achieved by each defence and the burdens imposed by the means used to achieve it.[91]

But for the CJEU's controversial decision in the *Deckmyn* case, the shift in UK law towards a proportionality-based approach in which the fairness of a use depends on whether it exceeded what was necessary having regard to its legitimate (statutory) purpose is to be welcomed. In addition, just as Lord Hoffmann's use of purposive interpretation to support his approach in *Designers Guild* draws attention to the deficiencies of the Spence and Endicott test of copyright infringement above, so too in my view the use of purposive interpretation via a proportionality test of fairness draws attention to the shortcomings of the existing Laddie factors approach.[92] For one, the Laddie factors are capable of producing arbitrary results, since they treat the issue of fairness as unaffected by the legitimate (statutory) purpose of the use and thus deny that a person might need to use different amounts or parts of a protected work for different purposes. In this way they deny the context-specific nature of the fairness enquiry. For example, where a protected work is used without permission for the purpose of reporting a current event—defined in law to mean an event of real and current interest to the public[93]—the fact of the work's limited prior public circulation should *support* a finding of fair dealing, since in that case the public will have limited alternative means of learning about the event, increasing its dependence on the defendant's report of the event. Applying the Laddie factors, however, it will always support a finding of unfairness. In addition, why the commercial motivation of a defendant should always be relevant when deciding the fairness of any use of a protected work is unclear, since the value underpinning most of the fair dealing defences is that of freedom of expression, which is enjoyed and served as much by profit-making enterprises (such as the press) as by their non-profit counterparts.

---

[91] See in this regard L Hoffmann, 'The Influence of the European Principle of Proportionality upon UK Law' in E Ellis (ed), *The Principle of Proportionality in the Laws of Europe* (Oxford, Hart Publishing, 1999) 107, 109.

[92] For a fuller discussion, see J Pila, 'Patent Eligibility and Scope Revisited in the Light of *Schütz v Werit*, European Law and Copyright Jurisprudence' in RC Dreyfuss and JC Ginsburg (eds), *Intellectual Property at the Edge: The Contested Contours of IP* (New York, Cambridge University Press, 2014) 382.

[93] See, eg, *Pro Sieben* (n 85) 625; *Ashdown* (n 87) [64].

By requiring the courts to reason and justify their decisions having regard to the statutory exceptions themselves, a proportionality-based test of fairness also promotes legal coherence. While it is true that a structured test such as that based on the Laddie factors or a bright line rule such as that proposed by Bate provides the courts and others with a list of factors to check or definite criteria to apply, it is ultimately of limited assistance in deciding whether the use was *fair* and thus does little to promote the coherence of copyright. That is presumably why the Court of Appeal in the leading fair dealing case of *Ashdown* concluded its analysis of the implications of the Laddie factors for the issue of fairness by asking whether the defendant newspaper in that case needed to reproduce as much of the protected work as it did in order to inform the public of the event in respect of which (as the Court had held) the public had a real and current interest.[94] (The answer provided, in my view correctly given that the public was about to receive a copy of the work in its entirety by the copyright owner himself, was that it did not.) It is also presumably why Bate did not abandon the fairness requirement completely in his reform proposal.

VI. CONCLUDING REMARKS

In conclusion, my suggestion is that Lord Hoffmann has been less timid in the face of uncertain law, encroachments on public freedoms and attacks on traditional English legal values than committed intellectually to ensuring fidelity to IP legislation by means of a purposive interpretive approach in which policy plays an important but ultimately limited role. Indeed, even his frequent resort to comparative reasoning in patent law can be understood as having proceeded directly from his concern to give effect to the Patents Act, section 130(7) of which requires that its substantive provisions be interpreted to reflect the interpretation of corresponding European instruments. To give a further and memorable example of that concern, at a British Literary and Artistic Copyright Association (BLACA) event in January 2010 on the CJEU's contentious decision in *Infopaq International A/S v Danske Dagblades Forening*,[95] Lord Hoffmann remarked that if the European Court wanted the UK to rewrite its statutory laws of copyright to recognise the subsistence of copyright in all authorial works rather than merely in original literary, dramatic, musical and artistic works (as under the CDPA currently), it was going to have to say so more clearly than it had said in *Infopaq*. (Whether the courts will show Lord Hoffmann's restraint by waiting for the legislature to act rather than simply electing to rewrite the CDPA themselves remains to be seen, though is far from assured.)

---

[94] See *Ashdown* (n 87) [81]–[82].
[95] *Infopaq International A/S v Danske Dagblades Forening* [2009] EUECJ C-5/08.

A final example of Lord Hoffmann's view of the role of courts when interpreting statutory IP law may be seen in his scepticism regarding expansive judicial interpretation of human dignity-based exclusions from patentability, which he has described in his Oxford patent law seminars as representing the intrusion of religious values into patent law.[96] Underpinning this scepticism is the traditional view that since patents confer rights of exclusion rather than of use and protect artefactual (technical) ideas rather than naturally occurring phenomena, they are incapable of conferring rights of ownership in respect of the human body or otherwise offending the integrity of the person. In recent years, however, this view has been somewhat undermined by changes in the legal and socio-economic context in which patent rights exist and operate. For example, expanding conceptions of patentability combined with the increasing prominence of individual rights in EU law, advances in biotechnology and a growing EU agenda in the field of IP have brought patents into more direct and frequent conflict with third party freedoms and interests than historically, and increased the pressure on IP systems throughout Europe to recognise such conflicts as competitions between fundamental rights and interests—including property on the side of IP owners and one or more of human dignity, the integrity of the person, freedom of expression, education, privacy and freedom to conduct a business on the side of defendants. In effect, EU law has turned the private law of IP into an area of public law, confirming again that in the future we can expect the (public law) tool of proportionality to be of increasing importance for it.

I have described proportionality as consistent with a purposive interpretive approach. That consistency is apparent from the nature of the proportionality principle thus conceived and also (and relatedly) from Lord Hoffmann's discussion of that principle in *Campbell v Mirror Group Newspapers Ltd*,[97] a case of further interest for its reflection of his caution in the face of proliferating fundamental rights claims based on European instruments. In *Campbell*, Lord Hoffmann approved the recognition of a new tort of misuse of private information supported by the Human Rights Act 1998 (HRA) and the European Convention on Human Rights 1950 (ECHR) only a year after deciding in *Wainwright v Home Office*[98] that the HRA, by adding to the existing remedies protecting the value of privacy, had 'weakened' the argument for recognising 'a general tort of invasion of privacy' in English law.[99] 'There seems to me', he said in *Wainwright*, 'a great difference between identifying privacy as a value which underlies the existence of a rule of law (and may point the direction in which the law should develop)

---

[96] For support for this view see, eg, S Moyn, 'The Secret History of Constitutional Dignity' (2014) 17 *Yale Human Rights and Development Journal* 39.
[97] *Campbell v Mirror Group Newspapers Ltd* [2004] UKHL 22, [2004] 2 AC 457.
[98] *Wainwright v Home Office* [2003] UKHL 53, [2003] 3 WLR 1137.
[99] ibid [34].

and privacy as a principle of law in itself.'[100] Absent any clear statutory support for the recognition of a general privacy principle, he made clear, the courts would not be justified in recognising one.

The reason offered by Lord Hoffmann for his change of view in *Campbell* was his acceptance that the common law, supported by Article 8 of the ECHR, had moved on and 'adapt[ed] itself to the needs of contemporary life'.[101] Article 8 recognises the right of every person 'to respect for his family and private life, his home and his correspondence' and prohibits 'interference by a public authority with the exercise of this right' other than in exceptional circumstances, including 'for the protection of the rights and freedoms of others'. According to Lord Hoffmann in *Campbell*, such recognition supported two trends that it had become appropriate for the courts to validate. The first was the treatment of private information as something worth protecting, and the second was the expansion of the traditional English breach of confidence action to accommodate that treatment.[102] Having accepted these trends, he set about to identify the purpose of the new 'misuse of private information' tort with a view to interpreting and applying it. That purpose, he said, was not the same as the purpose of the old breach of confidence action, for the accommodation of privacy within the breach of confidence action represented 'a shift in [its] centre of gravity' from 'the duty of good faith applicable to confidential personal information and trade secrets alike' to 'the protection of information about one's private life and the right to the esteem and respect of other people'.[103] Having thus identified the aim of the tort as the protection of none other than human dignity, the requirements for its establishment were clear: the unauthorised use of private information would be tortious in any case in which it exceeded what was necessary to achieve a legitimate competing purpose, such as the protection of expression rights and interests.[104] Aside from demonstrating Lord Hoffmann's preparedness to adapt traditional principles of English law to take account of European human rights provisions in appropriate contexts, one sees in this decision his use of proportionality as a methodological tool for ensuring the purposive interpretation and application of rights in individual cases, much as was supported in the fair dealing context above.[105] This supports my suggestion that as IP rights do come into more frequent conflict with other fundamental rights and interests, and as IP conflicts in general are increasingly conceived as conflicts between such rights and interests, we can expect to see the courts use this tool increasingly, extending further the influence of the analytical approach which Lord Hoffmann has deployed so widely and shown such commitment to in the field of IP.

---

[100] ibid [31]–[32].
[101] *Campbell* (n 97) [46].
[102] ibid.
[103] ibid [51].
[104] ibid [55].
[105] For a fuller discussion, see J Pila, 'Pluralism, Principles and Proportionality in Intellectual Property' (2014) 34 *OJLS* 181.

11

Lord Hoffmann and the Law of Employment: The Notorious Episode of Johnson v Unisys Ltd

ALAN BOGG AND HUGH COLLINS

IN HIS LONG and distinguished judicial career, Lord Hoffmann rarely ventured into the field of labour law. Yet, among scholars of labour law, one of those rare forays has become one of the most notorious and controversial judgments of the twenty-first century. In *Johnson v Unisys Ltd*,[1] he led the Judicial Committee of the House of Lords to reject an employee's claim for substantial damages resulting from a summary dismissal. In reaching that conclusion, he took two contentious steps in the legal reasoning.

The first step involved a particular interpretation of the common law of the contract of employment. Lord Hoffmann held that, although it had been established in the English common law that the parties to a contract of employment were bound by an obligation to perform in good faith and not to destroy mutual trust and confidence, that obligation did not apply to the act of dismissal. This interpretation of the common law is controversial because it created an anomalous kind of contractual obligation, with unforeseeable ramifications with respect to other issues that arise in connection with employment. The contractual obligation is an incongruity because the employer's obligation to perform in good faith exists during performance of the contract, but suddenly disappears when the employer decides to dismiss an employee. This part of the reasoning in the case can be criticised for creating an anomaly in the common law that has unfortunately led to a succession of increasingly curious decisions by the Supreme Court.

The second controversial step in the reasoning in *Johnson v Unisys Ltd* involved an appeal to the intention of Parliament with respect to the legal questions posed by the case. Since the historical record disclosed no explicit statement by Parliament on the matter at all, this reference to parliamentary intention was clearly a matter of inference from circumstantial evidence

---

[1] *Johnson v Unisys Ltd* [2001] UKHL 13, [2003] 1 AC 518.

and the general history of parliamentary legislation in the field. Given these indeterminate materials, it is clearly possible to infer opposite conclusions, both for and against Lord Hoffmann's view of what Parliament must have intended. Moreover, there must also be a question whether it is appropriate for a court even to embark on such an attribution of parliamentary intention when the question before it is not about the meaning of legislation, but rather an interpretation of the common law.

This contribution takes the unusual form of a debate about the merits of the decision in *Johnson v Unisys Ltd* and its progeny. In section I, Hugh Collins sets out the main legal issues raised in the case and how Lord Hoffmann (joined by Lords Bingham and Millett) resolved them. In section II, Collins proceeds to criticise the reasoning with respect to the two contentious issues set out above. In section III, Alan Bogg sets out to defend the decision on its merits, though conceding that some of the subsequent cases have misunderstood the case. Bogg focuses primarily on the second contentious point about the interpretation of parliamentary intention.

I. THE DECISION AND REASONING IN *JOHNSON V UNISYS LTD*

Mr Johnson was employed in a senior position in a computer software company. With a gap of three years in the middle, he had been employed there from 1971 to 1994. In the 1980s, before the break of three years caused by dismissal for redundancy, he had taken time off for work-related stress and depression. Following three years of employment in the early 1990s, on 17 January 1994, he was asked to attend a meeting. No specific allegations were put to him. Yet later the same day, he was summarily dismissed and given a month's wages in lieu of notice. He lodged an internal appeal that was unsuccessful. He then made a successful claim for unfair dismissal, a statutory claim now contained in Part X of the Employment Rights Act 1996, receiving the maximum compensation at that time under the legislation of £11,691.88. Following his dismissal, Mr Johnson suffered a major psychiatric illness, involving admissions to hospital and a prolonged course of medical treatment. Despite making more than 100 applications for jobs, he remained unemployed. His lack of success was almost certainly due to his lengthy stays in hospital and the substantial period he was out of work in an industry that is constantly innovating. At the age of 52, it seemed unlikely that he would work again.

Mr Johnson then instituted proceedings in the county court for breach of contract and negligence under the common law. His principal claim was an alleged breach of the implied term in contracts of employment that his employer would not without reasonable and proper cause conduct itself in such a way so as to damage the relationship of trust and confidence between the parties. He further alleged that the manner of his dismissal caused his mental breakdown and his subsequent inability to work. He claimed a loss of earnings in excess of £400,000. The employer's application to strike out this claim was successful in the county court and on appeal to the Court of Appeal,[2] and to a unanimous House of Lords. Mr Johnson's claim for economic or financial loss resulting from breach of contract was dismissed.

A. The Contractual Argument

In itself, this statement that a claim for economic loss resulting from breach of contract was struck out looks puzzling. It could only make sense under the general principles of the common law of contract if it mischaracterises the situation. It may be that the claim was not regarded as one for economic loss, but rather for non-pecuniary loss such as injury to feelings. It may be that no term of the contract had been broken. It may be that the losses claimed were regarded as too remote to recover or not caused by the breach of contract. Unless one of those possibilities is satisfied, the decision must be incompatible with the general law of contract. The decision would therefore represent an anomalous limitation on liability that seems to be applied to contracts of employment alone and no other sorts of contracts. Each of those possible ways for justifying a striking out of the claim consistently with the general law of contract was considered extensively by the Judicial Committee.

i. Was the Claim One for Non-Pecuniary Loss Such as Injury to Feelings?

The stated claim was for loss of earnings during a period of unemployment following the dismissal, not injury to feelings. The harsh and unpleasant manner of a dismissal may certainly cause considerable distress, but ever since the decision in *Addis v Gramophone Co Ltd*,[3] the common law courts have rejected such claims in relation to breaches of the contract of employment. To avoid that undoubted limitation, the claim was instead framed as one regarding the economic loss resulting from an extensive period of unemployment. The suggestion in such a claim is that the manner of the dismissal damages the employability of the claimant because the stigma attached to the claimant resulting from the summary dismissal makes it far harder to obtain subsequent employment. The argument is that potential employers will not be willing to hire someone who has been dismissed under such circumstances; there is no smoke without fire. It is not clear whether such a claim for economic loss is possible under the common law. Unfortunately, the House of Lords in *Addis* did not explicitly address the

---

[2] [1999] ICR 809 (CA).
[3] *Addis v Gramophone Co Ltd* [1909] AC 488 (HL).

question properly, though by its decision in overturning the substantial award of damages given by the jury, it is possible that it intended to exclude such a claim as well as the claim for distress. In *Malik v Bank of Credit and Commerce International SA*,[4] Lord Steyn, for the Judicial Committee, stated that a claim for economic loss resulting from stigma caused by an employer's breach of contract (in the form of running a bank corruptly) was possible. Subsequently, however, the employees in that case were unable to prove their claims because they were unable to show that potential employers, who had rejected their applications for jobs, had done so because of the stigma they were suffering from as a result of the employer's corrupt practices in breach of contract.[5] It seems, therefore, that according to the principles of the common law, provided that the claim was for economic loss resulting from stigma caused by the employer's breach of contract, a claim for damages should have been permitted.[6]

ii. Was the Employer in Breach of Contract?

The employer had broken the term of the contract of employment requiring reasonable notice to be given prior to dismissal, but had paid a month's wages in lieu of that notice period. If any more compensation was due for breach of the duty to give notice, it would have been subsumed within the statutory claim for unfair dismissal. The issue in *Johnson v Unisys Ltd* was whether the employer was also liable for a different breach of contract, namely, a breach of the implied term of mutual trust and confidence. The House of Lords in *Malik v BCCI* had held that such an implied term should be included by law in every contract of employment. If that was correct, it seemed reasonably clear that the manner in which the employer had carried out the summary dismissal had involved a breach of that term, so the path towards a claim for stigma damages looked open. But on this point there was a disagreement in the House of Lords in *Johnson v Unisys Ltd*. Whilst Lord Steyn was prepared to follow the logic of that argument, the majority was not.

The first and perhaps principal reason given by Lord Hoffmann for rejecting a claim based upon the implied term of mutual trust and confidence was that the express terms of the contract precluded such a claim. The express terms of the contract between Mr Johnson and his employer stated:

> If you decide to leave UNISYS you are required to give the company four weeks' notice; equally, the company may terminate your employment on four weeks' notice ... In the event of gross misconduct, the company may terminate your employment without notice.[7]

---

[4] *Malik v Bank of Credit and Commerce International SA* [1997] ICR 606, [1998] AC 20 (HL).
[5] *Bank of Credit and Commerce International SA v Ali (No 3)* [1999] IRLR 508 (Ch D).
[6] In *Johnson*, Lord Hoffmann seems to agree with that conclusion: (n 1) [43]–[45].
[7] ibid [38].

Lord Hoffmann argued that this express provision was probably inconsistent with any possible implied term that required the employer only to terminate employment in good faith (or not in breach of the duty of mutual trust and confidence).[8] The express term makes no mention of any limits on the employer's right to terminate the contract, and it could be inferred that on its proper construction, the contract preserved the common law default rule that a master may dismiss his servant at any time, for any reason or no reason at all, without a hearing, on payment of damages for breach of the express or implied notice provision.[9]

Some would welcome a reversal of that common law tradition derived from the law of master and servant. Termination at will is the legal expression of the commodification of labour: it denies that employees should be treated like human beings, with dignity and respect. By applying the implied term of mutual trust and confidence to the manner of dismissal or perhaps some variant formulation of that implied term, such as a duty to exercise the power of dismissal fairly and in good faith, the common law would partly reverse the doctrine of termination at will by permitting claims for stigma damages resulting from the fact of the summary dismissal. Lord Steyn accepted that approach to the development of the common law, but Lord Hoffmann was of the opinion that although such a revision of the common law was 'jurisprudentially possible'[10] and 'finely balanced',[11] it would not be wise for the courts to make such a radical revision of the common law.

Why would such a development of the common law not be wise? Lord Hoffmann argued that the change in the common law of dismissal would not be 'incremental', but would be profound, and that such a major change is probably best left to the legislature. Whilst it is true that a requirement placed upon employers only to make dismissals in good faith would be a significant change in a default rule of the common law, it would not amount to a significant change in the legal standards applicable to the employment relation because the statutory law of unfair dismissal already requires an employer to act reasonably, which is possibly a higher standard. Moreover, as a default rule, an implied term requiring an employer not to act in bad faith could probably be excluded by a sufficiently clear express term in the contract. Lord Hoffmann expressed the opinion in this case that the express term was probably sufficiently precise to exclude the implied term, even assuming that the implied term existed and applied to dismissal, thereby demonstrating how straightforward it might be to exclude an implied term requiring good faith in dismissal.

---

[8] ibid [42].
[9] *Malloch v Aberdeen Corporation* [1971] 1 WLR 1578 (HL) 1581 (Lord Reid).
[10] *Johnson* (n 1) [47].
[11] ibid [50].

Lord Steyn insisted, however, that there is no contradiction or inconsistency between an express term permitting termination of the contract by giving notice and an implied term sounding in damages for a decision to terminate made in bad faith: 'the two can live together'.[12] Moreover, Lord Steyn hinted at a further argument that, as a term implied by law, the obligation of mutual trust and confidence, as an overarching legal principle, cannot be so easily displaced by express terms. He concluded that it would be consistent with the express term conferring the power to dismiss for any reason on giving notice to imply an obligation not to dismiss the employee in a harsh and humiliating manner.[13]

iii. Would the Damages Be Too Remote?

A claim for substantial damages for breach of a term of the contract of employment could also be struck out on the ground that it had no reasonable prospect of success on the facts of the case. It was on this ground that Lord Steyn joined the majority in striking out the claim. Mr Johnston needed to overcome two major hurdles: he would have to prove that it was the bad faith character of the dismissal and not simply the dismissal itself that had caused his nervous breakdown; and even if that contention could be established, in addition, it would have to be demonstrated that his psychiatric injury was not too remote because it had been foreseeable as likely by the employer. It was for these reasons that Lord Steyn joined the majority in striking out the claim as having no reasonable prospect of success. In particular, it would have been hard to establish that the employer was aware of the risk of psychiatric injury at the time of the dismissal, based solely on evidence of a period of stress and depression a decade earlier during Mr Johnson's previous employment with the company.[14]

Lord Hoffmann also discussed these points about proving causation and remoteness, but used them for a different purpose. Given the potential complexities involved in arguments about causation and remoteness, his argument was that it would probably be better to exclude liability altogether. In particular, he stressed how the liability might be 'open-ended' and disproportionate to the employer's degree of fault.[15] These are the crucial points—there is no cap on an employer's liability once the restriction drawn by the law of wrongful dismissal of limiting compensation to wages payable during the period of notice is removed. This reasoning marks a sharp

---

[12] ibid [24].
[13] ibid.
[14] Approving the remarks of Lord Woolf MR in the Court of Appeal: [1999] ICR 809, 817C–D. The principles governing foreseeability and remoteness were subsequently developed and specified in *Hatton v Sutherland* [2002] EWCA Civ 76, [2002] ICR 613 (CA) and *Barber v Somerset County Council* [2004] UKHL 13, [2004] ICR 457.
[15] *Johnson* (n 1) [49].

cleavage between an employer's liability in contract for dismissal and the indeterminate amount of liability that may arise for personal injuries suffered by employees. Lord Hoffmann wanted to protect employers against indeterminate and uncapped amounts of liability for dismissal. So, given the difficulties of introducing arbitrary caps on the amount of liability under the common law, the only option left to Lord Hoffmann appeared to be to deny liability altogether in every case, even those instances where issues of causation and remoteness do not present difficulties of proof.

This worry about the potential unlimited and disproportionate nature of liability needs to be unpacked. We need to recall first of all that a party who suffers loss caused by another's breach of contract rarely receives full compensation for every conceivable loss, because of the application of stringent tests of causation, a duty to mitigate loss and the exclusion of remote losses. Any claim for compensation for loss caused by breach of an implied term not to dismiss an employee in bad faith would be limited by these principles, especially the duty placed on the employee to mitigate loss by finding another job.[16] Moreover, it would surely be extremely unusual for any employee to be able to prove that the manner of a dismissal had actually caused an inability to obtain another job ever again. Such cases may sometimes happen, as where a high-profile dismissal destroys a professional reputation irretrievably, thereby preventing that person from working again in that trade or profession, for example, a consultant surgeon,[17] a music teacher in a school[18] or a director of social services for a local authority.[19] Even in those cases, however, the dismissed professional might be able to obtain some other kind of gainful employment, thereby reducing the loss caused by the breach of contract. Admittedly, in the *Johnson* case, there was the additional complexity of the allegation that the manner of the summary dismissal had caused a psychiatric injury, which in turn had allegedly incapacitated Mr Johnson from working again. If that argument could have been made out, it would have been hard to resist a claim for substantial damages reflecting the loss of an entire career. But this feature of the claim was unusual in comparison to the situation of most dismissed employees, who may be suffering from damage to their employability, but not from exclusion from the labour market altogether.

B. The Argument Based on Parliamentary Intention

The second reason given by Lord Hoffmann for not developing the common law of dismissal to require the employer to act in good faith when

---

[16] KD Ewing, 'Job Security and the Contract of Employment' (1989) 18 *Industrial Law Journal* 217.

[17] *Edwards v Chesterfield Royal Hospital* [2011] UKSC 58, [2012] ICR 201.

[18] *R(G) v Governors of X School* [2011] UKSC 30, [2011] ICR 1033.

[19] *R (Shoesmith) v Ofsted* [2011] EWCA Civ 642 [2011] ICR 1195.

making dismissals was that Parliament, by enacting the law of unfair dismissal in 1971, had intended to regulate the field and that it would not be a proper exercise of the judicial function to develop the common law in the same field. The legislation on unfair dismissal contains many rules based upon policy rather than principle, such as the exclusion of certain classes of employees and absolute upper limits on the amount of compensation. A development of the common law to apply an implied term of good faith in dismissals would circumvent such restrictions in some cases. The case vividly illustrated the problem: Mr Johnson's claim for unfair dismissal was limited to about £11,000, whereas his actual economic loss, assuming he could prove it, was in the order of £400,000. Lord Hoffmann concluded:

> For the judiciary to construct a general common law remedy for unfair circumstances attending dismissal would be to go contrary to the evident intention of Parliament that there should be such a remedy but that it should be limited in application and extent.[20]

In a brief judgment, Lord Nicholls made the same point:

> I am persuaded that a common law right embracing the manner in which an employee is dismissed cannot satisfactorily coexist with the statutory right not to be unfairly dismissed. A newly developed common law right of this nature, covering the same ground as the statutory right, would fly in the face of the limits Parliament has already prescribed on matters such as the classes of employees who have the benefit of the statutory right, the amount of compensation payable and the short time limits for making claims. It would also defeat the intention of Parliament that claims of this nature should be decided by specialist tribunals, not the ordinary courts of law.[21]

Since there was no evidence of any explicit parliamentary intention with regard to the consequences for the common law arising from the introduction of the law of unfair dismissal in 1971,[22] this appeal to the intention of Parliament is at best speculative.

Lord Steyn presented an alternative account of Parliament's intent.[23] He observed that the statutory law of unfair dismissal would continue to function without difficulty even if the common law were developed. He argued that, even if Parliament was fully aware of the common law of wrongful dismissal when it enacted the law of unfair dismissal, its new scheme was only ever capable of dealing effectively and justly with the less serious cases, and Parliament could not be assumed to have intended to prevent the development of the common law for other cases involving breach of contract where the remedy of the statutory claim for unfair dismissal would not fully address the issues.

---

[20] *Johnson* (n 1) [58].
[21] ibid [2].
[22] Industrial Relations Act 1971.
[23] *Johnson* (n 1) [23].

To these points of rebuttal to the majority view, I would add, first, the observation that when a similar issue arose in connection with workmen's compensation, the common law judges in England did not abolish the law of negligence for personal injuries incurred at work, but rather preserved the law precisely in order to fill the gaps in more serious cases.[24] And, second, the point about the upper limit on compensation under the law of unfair dismissal can be turned around completely—it could be said that this statutory remedial system is plainly adequate in the vast majority of cases, but where it does not provide an appropriate remedy, a claimant should be free to use other avenues offered by the common law, such as breach of contract or judicial review, to obtain appropriate redress. For example, this has been the approach adopted by the courts towards the use of judicial review by public sector officials.[25] Finally, it must be acknowledged that there are complex jurisprudential issues at stake in this debate about the interpretation of parliamentary intention, which not only involve the possibility and appropriateness of using statutes as a source of general principle (in this case that compensation for dismissal should always be capped to protect employers against excessive claims) and also views about whether private law, including contract law, essentially serves regulatory and instrumental purposes or whether its principles of corrective justice provide it with autonomous foundations that are quite distinct from parliamentary legislation.[26]

II. THE SUBSEQUENT INCOHERENCE OF THE COMMON LAW

Lord Hoffmann offered the following sound precept in *Johnson v Unisys Ltd*:

> [T]he common law decides cases according to principle and cannot impose arbitrary limitations on liability because of the circumstances of the particular case. Only statute can lay down limiting rules based on policy rather than principle.[27]

Admittedly, it may not always be straightforward to distinguish between principle and policy, but the common law can certainly strive to avoid arbitrary or ad hoc limitations on liability rather than employing rules that have a reasoned general application. Unless the common law sticks to principle, judicial decisions will become unpredictable and the law will become incoherent.

---

[24] PWJ Bartrip and SB Burman, *The Wounded Soldiers of Industry* (Oxford, Oxford University Press, 1983). Compare the position in the US: A Larson, 'The Nature and Origins of Workmen's Compensation' (1952) 37 *Cornell Law Quarterly* 206.
[25] *Ofsted* (n 19) [87] (Maurice Kay LJ).
[26] JA Pojanowski, 'Private Law in the Gaps' (2014) 82 *Fordham Law Review* 1689.
[27] *Johnson* (n 1) [49].

The question to be considered here is whether Lord Hoffmann, having made this wise observation, then promptly did the opposite. Did he lead a majority of the Judicial Committee in the same case to breach that precept by imposing an arbitrary limitation on liability either because of the circumstances of the particular case or for policy reasons? To answer this question, we need to consider the consequences of the decision for the coherence of the common law. It will be argued that subsequent decisions in the courts in the same field have revealed a resulting incoherence of the law, which is striking evidence that the precept was indeed abandoned.

We should briefly examine two subsequent developments in the common law, though these are not the only problems to have emerged. The first concerns constructive dismissal and the second relates to breach of the express terms of the contract.

A. Constructive Dismissal

The notion of constructive dismissal arises when an employer commits a fundamental or repudiatory breach of contract and the employee decides to accept the repudiation of the contract and bring further performance of the primary obligations under the contract (the wage/work bargain) to an end by quitting the job. This is a normal application of the general law of breach of contract to the contract of employment.[28] However, there is a reason for its added significance in employment law. In order to bring a statutory claim for unfair dismissal, an employee has to establish that he or she was dismissed.[29] Where the employee has resigned, it will be necessary under the statutory concept of dismissal to demonstrate that the employer was in fundamental breach of contract, thereby entitling the employee to terminate the contract for breach.[30] Usually an employee establishes that such a fundamental breach of contract has been committed by the employer by demonstrating a breach of the implied term of mutual trust and confidence.[31] If, as seemed to have been decided in *Johnson v Unisys Ltd*, the implied term of mutual trust and confidence did not apply in the context of dismissal, as opposed to during performance of the contract, the possibility of bringing a claim for constructive dismissal was largely blocked. In other words, the majority of the House of Lords had been so concerned to prevent the common law from being used to avoid the limitations placed by Parliament on

---

[28] *Geys v Société Génerale, London Branch* [2012] UKSC 63, [2013] 1 AC 523.
[29] Employment Rights Act 1996, s 95.
[30] *Western Excavating (ECC) Ltd v Sharp* [1978] ICR 221 (CA).
[31] *Lewis v Motorworld Garages Ltd* [1986] ICR 157 (CA); AL Bogg, 'Bournemouth University Higher Education Corporation v Buckland*: Re-establishing Orthodoxy at the Expense of Coherence?' (2010) 39 *Industrial Law Journal* 408.

the statutory right to claim unfair dismissal that they had inadvertently created a major gap in the protection afforded to employees under the statutory
claim for unfair dismissal. The near-elimination of the statutory concept of
constructive dismissal was a potential disaster for employees because this
concept determines the limits of harsh treatment that employers can mete
out to their employees before employees can say 'enough is enough' and go
off to a tribunal to claim unfair dismissal. By distorting the common law,
the House of Lords had inadvertently created a major gap in the protection
afforded by the statutory law of unfair dismissal.

The House of Lords took an early opportunity to plug this gap in *Eastwood v
Magnox Electric plc* and *McCabe v Cornwall County Council*.[32] The Judicial Committee drew a distinction between causes of action that concerned
conduct prior to a dismissal and other causes of action arising from the manner of dismissal. The test was whether the cause of action preceded and was
independent of the dismissal process, or whether it flowed directly from the
employer's failure to act fairly when taking steps leading to dismissal. If the
common law cause of action concerned the latter by forming part of a dismissal, it fell within the so-called 'Johnson exclusion zone' and would be
struck out. This distinction, of course, makes little sense in the context of
constructive dismissal. The point in these cases is that the employer's conduct
has provoked the constructive dismissal, so it is not possible to disentangle
breaches of contract prior to the dismissal from the dismissal itself. Fortunately, however, the House of Lords seems to have given a strong steer that the
implied term of mutual trust and confidence could be relied upon for the purposes of establishing constructive dismissal in order to bring a statutory claim.

Even so, the law was plainly incoherent and unsatisfactory. Lord Nicholls
pointed out some of the odd consequences of the boundary line or exclusion
zone established by *Johnson v Unisys Ltd*: 'An employer may be better off
dismissing an employee than suspending him ... an employee who is psy-
chologically vulnerable is owed no duty of care in respect of his dismissal
although, depending on the circumstances, he may be owed a duty of care in
respect of his suspension.'[33] In truth, it will be hard to distinguish claims for
breach of the implied term of mutual trust and confidence that have arisen
during the performance of the contract and those that have arisen in connection with the process of dismissal, whether constructive or by the act of
the employer. In conclusion, Lord Nicholls observed:

> It goes without saying that an interrelation between the common law and statute
> having these awkward and unfortunate consequences is not satisfactory ... This
> situation merits urgent attention by the Government and the legislature.[34]

---

[32] *Eastwood v Magnox Electric plc* and *McCabe v Cornwall County Council* [2004] UKHL
35, [2005] 1 AC 503.
[33] ibid [32].
[34] ibid [33].

B. Breach of the Express Terms of the Contract of Employment

Parliament did not heed this cry for help. Instead, the Supreme Court had the opportunity to sort out the mess, though arguably it proceeded to make things far worse in the decisions in *Edwards v Chesterfield Royal Hospital* and *Botham v Ministry of Defence.*[35] The claim in these cases was that the employer had broken an express term of the contract regarding a disciplinary procedure that had to be followed prior to dismissal. Assuming that such a breach had occurred, the employees claimed substantial damages on the basis that the stigma resulting from the dismissal had effectively destroyed their careers. In the case of *Edwards*, for instance, a consultant surgeon had been dismissed for gross professional and personal misconduct and he claimed in excess of £4.3 million for loss of income until retirement on the basis that he would not be able to work again in the NHS as a result of the stigma. In an unusual panel of seven justices in the Supreme Court, three justices (Lords Dyson, Mance and Walker) extended the *Johnson* exclusion zone to include the denial of a claim for damages for breach of the express contractual disciplinary procedure. Making up the majority, Lord Phillips, though expressing sympathy for that view, preferred to decide the case on the ground that *Addis* had decided that stigma damages were not recoverable and that, furthermore, this rule should be extended to a breach of an express contractual disciplinary procedure. In the minority, Lords Kerr and Wilson were also prepared to apply the *Johnson* exclusion zone to a breach of an express contractual procedure, but held that as the allegedly incorrect procedure had occurred the day before the dismissal, the breach of contract was separate from the dismissal and therefore the claim could proceed because it fell outside the *Johnson* exclusion zone. Lady Hale, having reminded everyone that she alone had once been an employee, declined to extend the *Johnson* exclusion zone beyond the implied term of mutual trust and confidence.

Why might this decision be regarded as incoherent? First, the view that breach of an express contractual term will not give rise to any claim for damages at common law is surely unique. Second, this odd result was compounded by the further view that Mr Edwards, if he had acted swiftly, could have obtained an injunction to prevent the use of the wrong procedure. This produces the curious result that the term of the contract is enforceable in equity, but not the common law. Third, the majority also suggested that the breach of the contractual disciplinary procedure would be actionable in damages, but only if the terms of the contract expressly stated that it should be so actionable. Where else in the common law is it required that the parties should expressly agree that they should be liable in damages for

---

[35] [2011] UKSC 58, [2012] ICR 201.

breach of contract? Fourth, the view that if the disciplinary procedure and the dismissal are separated by a day, the breach of procedure falls outside the *Johnson* exclusion zone (as suggested by the minority) almost seems perverse—why should legal rights to damages for breach of contract depend on which day the contract was broken? Fifth, the Supreme Court seems to have overlooked the point that a claim on very similar facts also for stigma damages that had damaged the career of a doctor as a result of breach of a contractual procedure had been accepted by the High Court in the 1950s. Although not binding on the Supreme Court, it is relevant to the speculation about what Parliament must have intended when it enacted the statutory law of unfair dismissal.[36] Sixth, the decision throws into doubt the legal enforce-ability of express terms of contracts that limit the substantive grounds for lawful dismissal, such as the clause that was enforced by the House of Lords in *McClelland v Northern Ireland General Health Services Board*,[37] which only permitted dismissal for 'gross misconduct', or for being 'inefficient and unfit to merit continued employment', or for 'failure to take the oath of alle-giance'. Lord Mance, in *Edwards*, doubted that such a reversal of substan-tive protections followed from his decision, but surely it must do so, because it provides a potential way of obtaining superior damages to those available under the statutory law of unfair dismissal. If that result does not follow, it simply creates yet a further anomaly by distinguishing between procedural and substantive terms of contracts of employment regarding dismissal.[38]

III. PARLIAMENTARY INTENTION

When Lord Hoffmann regarded the matter of Mr Johnson's common law claim in isolation from the statutory context, he suggested that the argu-ments for and against the development of the implied term of trust and con-fidence were 'finely balanced'.[39] This suggests a degree of diffidence about common law development that I would reject. As Hugh Collins' preceding arguments demonstrate, the development of the implied term of trust and confidence in the manner proposed by Mr Johnson would have been fully warranted from the perspective of common law principle. Lord Hoffmann made clear, however, that the principled coherence of the common law was not the only concern; it was also important to consider the development of the common law alongside the parallel statutory framework so as to ensure

---

[36] K Costello, '*Edwards v Chesterfield Royal Hospital*—Parliamentary Intention and Damages Caused by Maladministration of a Contractual Disciplinary Procedure' (2013) 76(1) *MLR* 134, 139, discussing *Barber v Manchester Regional Hospital Board* [1958] 1 WLR 181 (QB).
[37] *McClelland v Northern Ireland General Health Services Board* [1957] 1 WLR 594 (HL).
[38] Costello (n 36) 144.
[39] *Johnson* (n 1) [50].

a coherent composite body of common law and statutory norms in the regulation of dismissal. This reflects a particular view of the judicial role: 'their responsibility to do justice between the parties—to make a morally sound and justified resolution of the case—is always to be harmonized with the responsibility to make that resolution also fit—at least, not contradict—the community's existing law, *considered as a whole*'.[40] This envisages the maintenance of synchronic consistency between common law and statute,[41] reflecting a constitutionally appropriate division of responsibility between judges and legislators in the activity of law-making. In the English system of common law under a constitutional system of parliamentary democracy, this division would reflect the generally subordinate position of judges and the common law relative to legislators and statutes.

In *Johnson*, this constitutional conception of the judicial role was mediated through the concept of 'parliamentary intention'. It was expressed through the policies embodied in the unfair dismissal legislation:

> Employment law requires a balancing of the interests of employers and employees, with proper regard not only to the individual dignity and worth of the employees but also to the general economic interest ... The development of the common law by the judges plays a subsidiary role. Their traditional function is to adapt and modernise the common law. But such developments must be consistent with legislative policy as expressed in statutes. The courts may proceed in harmony with Parliament but there should be no discord.[42]

As we have already seen, Mr Johnson made a successful claim under the relevant legislation for unfair dismissal, a statutory claim now contained in the Employment Rights Act 1996, receiving the maximum compensation available at that time under the legislation of £11,691.88. It was this aspect of Mr Johnson's claim that troubled Lord Hoffmann the most, leading him to conclude that:

> [F]or the judiciary to construct a general common law remedy for unfair circumstances attending dismissal would be to go contrary to the evident intention of Parliament that there should be such a remedy but that it should be limited in application and extent.[43]

Professor Freedland has described this appeal to parliamentary intention as 'more than slightly artificial'.[44] This reflects a broader current of academic scepticism that views Lord Hoffmann's appeal to parliamentary intention as

---

[40] J Finnis, *Philosophy of Law Collected Essays: Volume IV* (Oxford, Oxford University Press, 2011) 128 (emphasis added).

[41] On the notion of 'synchronic' legal order, drawing upon the work of John Finnis, see J Horder, *Excusing Crime* (Oxford, Oxford University Press, 2004) 258–60.

[42] *Johnson* (n 1) [37].

[43] ibid [58].

[44] M Freedland, *The Personal Employment Contract* (Oxford, Oxford University Press, 2003) 304.

fictional and speculative, a cynical attempt to cloak a dodgy judicial decision in the robes of democratic legitimacy. Indeed, in *Eastwood*, Lord Steyn
observed that 'there is apparently no support for the analysis adopted in
Johnson', listing an impressive roll call of 'A-list' academic critics.[45] What
follows might be regarded as an attempt to break with the unanimous
chorus of criticism and disapproval that Lord Hoffmann's approach has
attracted, albeit from the 'B-list'.

In fact, and this has always been rather disconcerting given the considerable intellectual firepower that has been directed at *Johnson*, I have always
been left scratching my head to find an answer to the question posed by
Judge Ansell who considered Mr Johnson's claim at first instance:

> [T]here is not one hint in the authorities that the ... tens of thousands of people
> that appear before the tribunals can have, as it were, a possible second bite in
> common law and I ask myself, if this is the situation, why on earth do we have
> this special statutory framework? What is the point of it if it can be circumvented
> in this way?[46]

In this respect, at least, parliamentary intention is very clearly expressed in
the legislation: the compensatory award is limited through a statutory cap.
There is nothing speculative or artificial about that. Since the enactment of
the unfair dismissal legislation in 1971, Parliament has visited and re-visited
the appropriate remedial limits, reflecting shifting democratic decisions on
the meaning of corrective justice and its relationship with the general economic interest. Likewise, the length of continuity of service qualifications
for unfair dismissal protection has been modified from time to time. And,
most recently, the new status of 'employee-shareholder' creates a novel legal
structure whereby employees can effectively waive unfair dismissal protection in exchange for shares in the company.[47] And one might conceivably
imagine Judge Ansell scratching his head if an employee with one year's
continuous service (the qualifying period is now two years), an 'employee-
shareholder' (having contracted out of general unfair dismissal protection)
or a 'worker' (unfair dismissal is confined to 'employees' and is unavailable
to 'workers') were able to bypass the statutory restrictions and bring a common
law claim for wrongful dismissal on the basis of trust and confidence.

In this way, unfair dismissal legislation has not been frozen in time since 1971,
but it has evolved, and continues to evolve, dynamically through democratically enacted changes to the statutory framework. We might therefore regard
Lord Hoffmann's appeal to 'parliamentary intention' as an appeal to a living
concept. What Parliament intended in 1971 is neither here nor there for the
purposes of developing the common law in 2015. Neither is it relevant what the

---

[45] *Eastwood* (n 32) [43].
[46] *Johnson* (n 1) [57].
[47] Growth and Infrastructure Act 2013, s 31.

members of the Donovan Commission happened to think in 1968.[48] Still, it is one thing to suggest that parliamentary intention is clear and precise on the issue of whether the remedies for unfair dismissal ought to be limited. That much seems uncontroversial—the limitations are set out very precisely in the legislation. It is quite another thing to suggest that parliamentary intention is similarly clear on the issue of how the common law ought to be developed in the light of that legislative framework. That is a much more controversial and difficult matter, and we need to proceed cautiously in testing this proposition.

Before proceeding cautiously, however, we might identify a particular conception of the common law that seems to animate Lord Hoffmann's judgment. According to Lord Hoffmann, the common law is 'subsidiary' to democratically enacted legislation,[49] and common law developments must be 'consistent with legislative policy as expressed in statutes'.[50] This seems to convey something more than the rather obvious point that common law developments may be over-ridden by statute. It suggests that in a parliamentary democracy, the judicial antennae should be attuned acutely to the primacy of legislation as a source of interpretive principles for developing the common law. It suggests that in the judicial maintenance of a consistent legal order, the gravity of relevant legislation should exceed the gravity of common law doctrine, even in the development of common law principle. In its concern to respect the democratic superiority of legislation as a source of principle, Lord Hoffmann's minimalist judicial instincts echo a tradition of judicial non-intervention that was once widely regarded as appealing in the historical development of British labour law.[51]

Once we understand *Johnson* for what it *really* is, a constitutional law case that happens to be played out against the backdrop of an employment dismissal dispute, arguments about what Parliament intended in respect of common law development may be viewed in a different light. It is doubtful that Lord Hoffmann seriously entertained the view that Parliament had ever formulated actual intentions about the common law of wrongful dismissal and its future development. Here is an alternative way of thinking about the matter: perhaps Lord Hoffmann's concern with parliamentary intention is better understood as a counterfactual enquiry into what Parliament might think about the desirability of certain lines of common law development,

---

[48] *Cf* B Hepple, *Rights at Work: Global, European and British Perspectives* (London, Sweet & Maxwell, 2005) 49: 'There is no reason to believe that Woodcock and his fellow Commissioners thought that the common law they were preserving would stand still.' Here Hepple discusses the intellectual orientation of George Woodcock, a commissioner and then General Secretary of the TUC. The historical context is fascinating, though its relevance to the issue in *Johnson* is questionable.

[49] *Johnson* (n 1) [37].

[50] ibid.

[51] See, for example, the early discussion of judicial non-intervention in KW Wedderburn, *The Worker and the Law* (1st edn, Harmondsworth, Penguin, 1965) ch 1.

given its policies as expressed from time to time through legislation. This is necessarily a speculative enterprise. Different judges might well disagree about how to develop the common law in a manner that is faithful to legislative policy, deploying parliamentary intention in this counterfactual sense to structure that enquiry. There might also be disagreement about how much weight to attach to legislative policy in developing the common law, particularly in situations where legislative policy leads to the violation of citizens' fundamental human rights, leaving the common law as the only mechanism of legal redress for the citizen.

Yet this is something quite different from the idea that *judges should have no regard at all to legislative policy in developing the common law in a parliamentary democracy*, which is an altogether bolder and more controversial proposition. It would certainly be welcome if protagonists in the debates around *Johnson* clarified the nature of their disagreement with this aspect of the judgment: is it a disagreement over what Parliament (counterfactually) intended in respect of common law development and how much weight to attach to that, or is it a disagreement with the very idea that the common law should be sensitive at all to democratically enacted policies expressed in legislation? The second position seems to leave little space for the notion of the judicial role as maintaining a synchronic order between legislation and common law: it may be seen as an anti-democratic deriding of the dignity of legislation;[52] it reinforces a conception of the common law as a body of doctrine that is impervious to democratic influence; and in this respect it seems an unattractive position to hold. In a spirit of charity to the protagonists in the debate, it is better to assume that both the critics and the supporters of *Johnson* are engaged in a more modest disagreement about what the relevant legislative policy was, and how much weight to attach to it, in developing the common law of wrongful dismissal.

There is no knockdown argument to demonstrate the superiority of Lord Hoffmann's constitutional conception of the inter-relationship between common law and statute. Instead, I propose to consider four sets of concerns that have often been ventilated in discussions of Lord Hoffmann's approach in *Johnson*. In each case, I want to suggest that the concerns provide rather weak arguments against Lord Hoffmann's reasoning and, in some cases at least, actually count in favour of Lord Hoffmann's approach.

A. Oil and Water

Professor Hepple has engaged in a powerful critique of what had been described by Professor Beatson as an 'oil and water' approach to the

---

[52] See J Waldron, *The Dignity of Legislation* (Cambridge, Cambridge University Press, 1999).

inter-relationship between common law and statute.[53] The 'oil and water' approach is based on the idea that 'statutes in common law systems are not regarded as a *source of principle* upon which flesh is put by interstitial case law development', but that common law and statute are instead regarded 'as two bodies of law flowing next to but ... separately from each other in distinct streams'.[54] According to Hepple, *Johnson* is an exemplar of the 'oil and water' approach, and so much the worse for *Johnson*. It is preferable that courts use statutes analogically to develop the common law in a manner that treats inter-connected laws as elements of a coherent system of laws, even where this coherence is fairly localised (such as in respect of the legal event of dismissal).

Hepple argues that this 'oil and water' approach is descriptively false and normatively unappealing in the law of employment. It is descriptively false because it is at variance with the composite quality of modern employment legislation, which is often parasitic upon contractual concepts and doctrines. Examples include the contractual definition of constructive dismissal under the unfair dismissal legislation or the contractual implementation of the statutory right to equal pay. These examples attest to the fact that 'there could be no clearer evidence that Parliament intended the symbiotic relationship between common law and statute to continue than in the way in which statutory rights have been placed firmly within the framework of the contract of employment'.[55] The 'oil and water' approach is also normatively unappealing because protective employment statutes can be a valuable source of principle for shaping and refining the development of common law doctrine. For example, in the landmark decision of *Malik*, Lord Steyn observed that 'in the search for common law principle one is not compelled to ignore the analogical force of the statutory dispensation'.[56] In *Malik*, the approach to remedies under the unfair dismissal legislation supported the conclusion that economic loss caused by reputational injury ought to be recoverable where this was caused by a breach of the implied term of mutual trust and confidence during the life of the employment contract. By contrast, *Johnson* represented:

> [T]he failure of the judiciary to appreciate that the common law of employment and statutory rights are imbricated, like over-hanging roof-tiles, and keep each other in place. Their separation in *Johnson* and other cases means there is a leaky roof in the structure of employment law.[57]

---

[53] See Hepple (n 48) lecture 3. Hepple's Hamlyn Lecture has been extremely influential as a critique of *Johnson*.

[54] J Beatson, 'The Role of Statute in the Development of Common Law Doctrine' (2001) 117 *LQR* 247.

[55] Hepple (n 48) 51.

[56] *Malik v BCCI* (n 4) 52–53.

[57] Hepple (n 48) 53.

Certainly, there are good reasons to reject the 'oil and water' approach to the relationship between statute and common law, and Beatson puts the general case for its rejection very powerfully.[58] Yet the 'oil and water' characterisation of *Johnson* seems entirely misplaced. This was not a situation where (to use Lord Steyn's words from *Malik*) Lord Hoffmann ignored the 'analogical force of the statutory dispensation'. On the contrary, Lord Hoffmann referred approvingly to the tendency for the common law to adapt 'to the new attitudes' towards the employment relation as articulated in protective employment statutes, 'proceeding sometimes by analogy with statutory rights'.[59] Indeed, his reasoning justifying the freezing-out of trust and confidence in respect of dismissal was shaped powerfully by the analogical force of the statutory cap on the compensatory award. The effect of the statutory analogy was to impede a common law development that would otherwise have been very compelling in the absence of legislation. Since the substance of the wrongful dismissal right being asserted by Mr Johnson would effectively shadow that of the unfair dismissal right (albeit dispensing with the limitations stipulated by Parliament on the statutory remedy) it was necessary to block the natural evolution of the implied term of trust and confidence. In this way, the effects of the unfair dismissal legislation on common law development were very tangible indeed.

Whatever else might be problematic about Lord Hoffmann's reasoning, then, its 'oil and water' character is not one of them. It is of course possible to argue in favour of the opposite outcome in *Johnson* using analogies with different statutory principles that might be discerned in the dismissal legislation. One might point to the principle of corrective justice that underlies the unfair dismissal legislation and the ways in which the legislation fails to ensure corrective justice.[60] In this way, the implied term of trust and confidence might be seen as a legal technique for filling the gaps left by the legislation (albeit that those gaps have been inserted deliberately by Parliament rather than by mere oversight). Yet by now we have left the 'oil and water' objection far behind, for neither Lord Hoffmann nor Lord Steyn is guilty of it in *Johnson*. Instead, it is much more interesting to consider the underlying arguments that might help judges to decide when the analogical force of statutes should freeze, restrict or accelerate common law development in particular contexts.

In fact, Beatson's work on the role of statutes in developing the common law offers a highly nuanced perspective on that interaction, and he acknowledges

---

[58] Beatson (n 54) 251–52.

[59] *Johnson* (n 1) [35]. In this respect, Lord Hoffmann referred approvingly to the decision in *Goold (WA) (Pearmak) Ltd v McConnell* [1995] IRLR 516 (EAT), where Morison J. derived an implied term that an employer would afford an employee the opportunity to obtain the redress of a grievance, from the statutory provisions governing the issuing of written particulars of employment (now set out in s 1 of the Employment Rights Act 1996).

[60] See, eg, the speech of Lord Steyn: *Johnson* (n 1) [23].

that it is sometimes appropriate that legislation should freeze out common law development. For example, Beatson observes that 'the existence of a statute ... may mean that the legislature has taken over that area and removed it from further common law development'.[61] An example of this might be the freezing of the development of common law restraint of trade doctrine as a technique for tackling discriminatory practices, given that the field has now been occupied comprehensively by a detailed and intricate statutory regime of anti-discrimination law.[62] Which considerations might inform our assessment of when statutory analogies should freeze rather than propel common law development? I would suggest that there are four considerations relevant in *Johnson*.

First, Beatson argues that 'certain polycentric problems may not be susceptible to the incremental case-by-case method of the common law'.[63] This concern with polycentricity seems to underlie Lord Hoffmann's preference to avoid disrupting the delicate compromises contained in the legislative framework regulating dismissal, particularly the limitations on the compensatory award and the remedy of reinstatement, alongside the uncertain consequences of developing a parallel common law remedy in respect of the same legal event viz the dismissal. It is no answer to this to assert that wrongful dismissal and unfair dismissal are distinct causes of action. Certainly they are currently, but they would not have been so easily distinguished had Mr Johnson's claim succeeded, for the implied term of trust and confidence would have drawn its content from the statutory unfair dismissal regime (albeit without the remedial limitations imposed by Parliament on the statutory right).

Second, the existence of a comprehensive and detailed legislative regime tends to suggest that Parliament had intended statute to be the predominant form of regulation in a particular sphere of activity. Third, where legislation is concerned to *circumscribe* the extent of a defendant's liabilities, perhaps through statutory immunities or remedial limitations, this would seem to countervail against common law developments that have the effect of re-activating or escalating those liabilities. Finally, there are certain regulatory spheres where legislation has been the dominant form of law-making. Labour law is probably the most striking example of a statute-based legal discipline.[64] Indeed, much of that legislative activity has historically been directed at the exclusion of the common law, particularly in the area of collective labour relations. In these kinds of regulatory context, the centre of gravity should rest with legislation rather than pure common law principle, even in the development of common law doctrine.

---

[61] Beatson (n 54) 264.
[62] ibid 258.
[63] ibid 264.
[64] The classical treatment of labour law as a statutory discipline is PL Davies and MR Freedland, *Labour Legislation and Public Policy* (Oxford, Oxford University Press, 1993).

B. The 'Floor of Rights'

According to Hepple, there is another structural feature of English employment law that constitutes a fault line running beneath *Johnson*, and it is one that 'goes to the heart of the question why statutory rights were construed as a glass ceiling'.[65] This is the absence of a general legal principle of inderogability of labour rights.[66] At first sight, the link between the principle of inderogability and the *Johnson* problem is not obvious. Inderogability is usually concerned with regulating and limiting the erosion or waiver of labour rights, so-called downwards derogation.[67] In *Johnson*, of course, the problem was the opposite one of whether to permit derogation *upwards* from the statutory standard through the judicial development of common law standards.

In Hepple's schema, the principle of inderogability would seem to be asymmetric. On the one hand, downwards derogation from fundamental labour rights would not generally be permitted, since these rights should be treated as imperative norms. On the other hand, upwards derogation would generally be permitted simply because labour rights should always be regarded as a worker-protective floor. If more worker-protective norms emerge in other ways, perhaps through collective bargaining or individual negotiation or judicial development of the common law, rising standards of worker protection should always be facilitated by the legal system. Although Hepple does not put it this way, we might then see his particular rendering of the principle of inderogability as derived from an even more fundamental principle of 'favourability' prevalent in Continental labour law systems, whereby norms are always interpreted and developed in favour of the worker as the weaker party in the contractual relationship.[68]

There are two problems with this general 'floor of rights' argument. First, it depends upon the improbable assumption that different regulatory actors are subject to the same normative considerations in deciding whether to permit upwards derogation. The 'floor of rights' argument was developed most prominently in the 1970s as a rationalisation of the relationship between statutory rights and autonomous collective bargaining.[69] Statutory rights

---

[65] Hepple (n 48) 53.

[66] Hepple (ibid) acknowledges the important work of Lord Wedderburn, who introduced the concept of 'inderogability' to British labour lawyers, drawing upon his comparative expertise of European labour law systems. According to Hepple: 'Professor Lord Wedderburn has suggested, in the context of collective agreements, that we might use the concept of "inderogability". This he derives from concepts used in Italian labour law of *inderogabilita in pejus* (unalterable downwards) and *inderogabilita in melius* (unalterable upwards).' He cites Lord Wedderburn, 'Inderogability, Collective Agreements, and Community Law' (1992) 21 *Industrial Law Journal* 245.

[67] Hepple (n 48) 54.

[68] M Freedland and N Kountouris, *The Legal Construction of Personal Work Relations* (Oxford, Oxford University Press, 2011) 150–51.

[69] Lord Wedderburn, 'The Employment Protection Act 1975. Collective Aspects' (1976) 39 *MLR* 169.

were to be regarded as a floor that provided a minimum basis of decent work for all workers regardless of union membership or collective bargaining. Nevertheless, collective bargaining could build upon those minimum statutory standards in situations where workers were organised into trade unions. In this way, statutory rights provided a springboard for autonomous collective bargaining. Thus, Wedderburn observed of the individual statutory entitlements in the Employment Protection Act 1975 that 'bargaining begins from a materially raised floor of statutory entitlements'.[70]

In Wedderburn's hands, the 'floor of rights' analysis provided a sophisticated way of integrating the juridification of individual employment law within the wider concerns of collective laissez-faire. Where autonomous negotiation is concerned, this 'floor of rights' analysis remains compelling. There is no conceivable reason why private parties, whether trade unions or employees, should be prevented from agreeing terms and conditions of employment that improve upon those provided for by statute. Indeed, such restrictions would be both unjust and inefficient. It is for this reason that the judgment in *Edwards* is deeply flawed, contrary to principle and in no sense a logical consequence of the reasoning in *Johnson*. I shall return to *Edwards* in the next section. Yet even if it is still true that 'bargaining begins from a materially raised floor', it certainly does not follow that judges should be free to develop the common law in the same direction. Judges developing the common law stand in a different constitutional relationship to Parliament than trade unions, employees or employers engaged in the activity of self-interested bargaining.

This suggests a second problem with the general 'floor of rights' argument. Whether legislation should be viewed as a floor or a ceiling for the common law surely requires a particular consideration of the specific statute. The sheer variety of statutes in the sphere of employment would suggest that a general presumption in favour of derogation upwards by the common law on every occasion is inappropriate. Rather than seeking a generic answer, a careful consideration of the specific statutory context is likely to be more helpful in determining whether it is appropriate for judges developing the common law to regard this particular statute as a ceiling or a floor. For this reason, the fact that workmen's compensation legislation did not preclude the parallel development of common law negligence liability for workplace injuries is not necessarily an accurate guide as to whether the same should hold for the unfair dismissal context. That would depend upon whether the statutory contexts are similar in relevant respects.

It may even be that the 'floor of rights' calculus is more particularised still. So it may be the case that different dismissal scenarios would necessitate different common law responses, even under the umbrella of the same unfair dismissal legislation. As an example of how this might be so, Hepple

---

[70] ibid.

engages in a fascinating discussion of the development of implied terms following the enactment of the Human Rights Act 1998, suggesting that this is 'an example of statutory rights where derogation upwards must surely be allowed'.[71] The implied term of trust and confidence might be used by the courts to ensure that the employer respects the employee's Convention rights, providing stronger protection than would otherwise have been possible. This argument is compelling in the light of section 6 of the Human Rights Act, which requires public authorities (including courts) to refrain from acting in a way that is incompatible with a Convention right. Indeed, this seems to be envisaged by Lord Hoffmann himself in *Johnson*. Thus, Lord Hoffmann observes that:

> Employment law requires a balancing of the interests of employers and employees, with proper regard not only to the individual dignity and worth of the employees but also to the general economic interest. *Subject to observance of fundamental human rights*, the point at which this balance should be struck is a matter for democratic decision.[72]

That deference to employment legislation in developing the common law is 'subject to observance of fundamental human rights' might lend support to Hepple's thesis about the possibility of derogation upwards by the common law where fundamental human rights are engaged, *even in a dismissal situation*.

Consider the recent decision of the European Court of Human Rights in *Redfearn v UK*.[73] A member of the far-right British National Party was dismissed from his employment before the qualification period had elapsed for unfair dismissal protection. The dismissal was on the grounds of his party political membership, it having been conceded that Mr Redfearn had discharged his employment duties impeccably. His complaint that his freedom of association under Article 11 had been violated was upheld. The Government introduced specific legislative changes in response to the decision in *Redfearn*, but what if no legislative response had been forthcoming? This raises difficult constitutional questions, but it may be that in this scenario the courts could have developed the common law using trust and confidence to protect Mr Redfearn's Convention rights in a dismissal situation. The judicial responsibility to protect the claimant's fundamental human rights might over-ride the judicial responsibility to respect the unfair dismissal legislation as a ceiling. The delicate judgments required to resolve these difficult legal problems are unlikely to be well-served by crude general presumptions for or against the derogability of legislation through common law development.

---

[71] Hepple (n 48) 56.
[72] *Johnson* (n 1) [37] (emphasis added).
[73] *Redfearn v UK* [2012] ECHR 1878, [2013] IRLR 51.

C. The Incoherent Aftermath of *Johnson*

As Hugh Collins' critique of *Johnson* establishes with admirable lucidity, subsequent case law has given rise to some difficult distinctions and awkward consequences. In *Eastwood*, the House of Lords affirmed the existence of the *Johnson* exclusion zone while emphasising that contractual breaches prior to the dismissal itself remained actionable on the basis of ordinary contractual principles. In this way, disciplinary suspensions would remain subject to the implied term of trust and confidence, even if dismissals were not. This created numerous practical difficulties. It was forensically challenging to ascertain whether a particular loss was causally attributable to the dismissal itself or to any antecedent contractual breaches. It also led to the rather perverse situation that it might make economic sense for an employer to dismiss an employee without a procedure, thereby triggering the exclusion zone and the statutory cap on the compensatory award, rather than risk breaching the contract during the taking of the appropriate procedural steps.

Of course, having established an exclusion zone in *Johnson*, it was always going to be necessary for the courts to specify its boundary line. The House of Lords could have treated the exclusion zone as encompassing the entirety of the employer's disciplinary powers, including suspension and investigation, though that would have cut back the reach of trust and confidence quite significantly. *Eastwood* represented an attempt to position the boundary of the exclusion zone in a manner that was consistent with the reasoning in *Johnson*, whilst at the same time giving the implied term an important regulatory role in the exercise of disciplinary powers other than dismissal in the contract of employment. Following *Eastwood*, there was certainly much to be said for the intervention of Parliament to rationalise this area of employment law in order to finesse the wrinkles and inconsistencies at the interface between common law and legislation. That Parliament has not yet done so—whether its neglect is wilful or not is not clear—should serve as a cautionary tale to those who argue in favour of the free development of common law, with the onus on Parliament to intervene where it disapproves of a line of common law development.[74] This would seem to rest upon an optimistic view of the legislative process, which may be subject to the constraints of time, expediency and party political pressures.

The most recent wrongful dismissal decisions in *Edwards* and *Botham* represents another chapter in the *Johnson* saga, and it is a highly regrettable one. To recap, the claimants claimed damages at large for injury to reputation covering loss of future earnings, consequent upon dismissals following the employers' failure properly to follow a disciplinary procedure that was

---

[74] See, eg, A Burrows, 'The Relationship between Common Law and Statute in the Law of Obligations' (2012) 128 *LQR* 232.

an express term of the contract. As such, the focus was on the express terms of the contract rather than upon an implied term imposed upon the contract by the common law itself. A majority of the Justices held that this head of damages was not recoverable in contract, though some of them thought that an injunction could be sought to enforce the procedures prior to a dismissal taking effect; further, that it might be possible to claim contractual damages on the basis of ordinary contractual principles where there was a *further* express agreement that the procedure should be enforceable in this way. Following a hearing before no fewer than seven Justices, the decision resulted in separate speeches from five: Lord Dyson (with whom Lord Walker concurred), Lord Phillips, Lord Mance (who agreed with Lord Dyson), Lord Kerr (with whom Lord Wilson agreed) and Lady Hale. Whether there is even a ratio that can be gleaned from *Edwards* is a moot point, and the headnote to *Edwards* is likely to keep lawyers puzzling for years in much the same way as the mysterious headnote to *Addis*.[75]

I do not propose to parse the differences, sometimes subtle and often yawning, between the speeches in *Edwards*. Instead, I will consider the extent to which it was legitimate for the Supreme Court to rely upon parliamentary intention to justify the inclusion of the *Edwards* scenario within the scope of the *Johnson* principle. This argument from parliamentary intention was a strong element in Lord Dyson's and Lord Mance's reasoning.

The speech that places the heaviest reliance on parliamentary intention is that of Lord Dyson. It is also fair to say that Lord Hoffmann does not escape criticism, having offered some unhelpful obiter observations on the contractual incorporation of disciplinary procedures that regrettably proved influential in *Edwards*. According to Lord Hoffmann:

> My Lords, given this background to the disciplinary procedures, I find it impossible to believe that Parliament, when it provided in section 3(1) of the 1996 Act that the statement of particulars of employment was to contain a note of any applicable disciplinary rules, or the parties themselves, intended that the inclusion of those rules should give rise to a common law action in damages which would create the means of circumventing the restrictions and limits which Parliament had imposed on compensation for unfair dismissal. The whole of the reasoning which led me to the conclusion that the courts should not imply a term which has this result also in my opinion supports the view that the disciplinary procedures do not do so either.[76]

The logic of Lord Hoffmann is ingenious. It is also flawed, based as it is upon a misunderstanding of the legal effects of the issuing of written particulars under section 1 of the Employment Rights Act 1996. The first point

---

[75] For discussion, see E Barmes, 'Judicial Influence and *Edwards v Chesterfield Royal Hospitals NHS Foundation Trust* & *Botham v Ministry of Defence*' (2013) 42 *Industrial Law Journal* 192.

[76] *Johnson* (n 1) [66].

to note is that at the time that Mr Johnson's written particulars were issued, there was no statutory obligation to issue a written statement encompassing the employer's disciplinary procedures. Rather, the 'note' in section 3(1) referred to a specification of 'any disciplinary rules applicable to the employee' and required a description of 'a person to whom the employee can apply if he is dissatisfied with any disciplinary decision relating to him'. The statutory obligation to issue written particulars relating to a disciplinary procedure was only introduced into the Employment Rights Act 1996 in 2004. It is therefore difficult to attribute the written elaboration of a disciplinary procedure to the employer's statutory obligation to provide written particulars at the time that *Johnson* was decided.

Nor should the insertion of disciplinary procedures into the obligation to issue written particulars in 2004, following the enactment of the Employment Act 2002, be regarded as enhancing the legitimacy of the parliamentary intention argument in *Edwards*. According to Lord Dyson, the effect of this statutory provision 'is that Parliament has decided, at least in most cases, that contractual force should be given to applicable rules and procedures'.[77] It would have involved significant legal incoherence if Parliament had prescribed limits on the statutory remedy, while also providing for their circumvention through a contractual remedy that was generally available to those employees falling within the scope of the unfair dismissal legislation. Hence, the same considerations that applied in *Johnson* to implied terms were also applicable to the express terms at issue in *Edwards*. This is because the express terms were only notionally the product of an agreement, but were in effect statutorily mandated in most cases.

The history of the Employment Act 2002 means that Lord Dyson's claim is untenable. The Employment Act 2002 specified statutory minimum procedures governing disciplinary, dismissal and grievance procedures. It also contained a remarkable and radical provision. Section 30 provided that 'every contract of employment shall have effect to require the employer and employee to comply, in relation to any matter to which a statutory procedure applies, with the requirements of the procedure'. This attracted significant scholarly attention at the time of its enactment;[78] indeed, Lord Dyson himself makes passing reference to section 30 in the course of his judgment. At first glance, section 30 would seem to lend significant force to Lord Dyson's parliamentary intention argument based upon an analogy with the reasoning in *Johnson*. However, a closer examination of the history of section 30 leads to the opposite conclusion. For section 30 was deliberately never activated by the government of the day following a consultation process on the implementation of the Employment Act 2002. It was finally

---

[77] *Edwards* (n 17) [28].

[78] See, eg, B Hepple and GS Morris, 'The Employment Act 2002 and the Crisis of Individual Employment Rights' (2002) 31 *Industrial Law Journal* 245.

repealed in 2008, along with the general dismissal regime instituted by the 2002 Act.

The reasons for the Government's decision not to activate section 30 are illuminating and can be gleaned from debates in the House of Lords. In response to concerns expressed by Lord Wedderburn that section 30 would not be activated in accordance with the legislative scheme, the Government spokesman Lord Sainsbury of Turville observed that: 'If employers do not follow the procedures and the dispute subsequently escalates to employment tribunal proceedings, they will suffer the adverse consequences provided for in the 2002 Act. In dismissal cases they will face a finding of unfair dismissal.'[79] This suggests an intention to confine the legal consequences of non-compliance with the mandatory procedures imposed by the 2002 Act within the specific limits prescribed by the legislation. Baroness Miller of Hendon, for the Opposition, was perhaps more candid in welcoming the Government's decision not to proceed with section 30. She referred to a submission from the Confederation of British Industry (CBI), widely regarded as having been influential in the Government's change of position on section 30. Quoting the CBI submission, Baroness Miller stated the decision not to implement section 30:

> [E]nsures that businesses have flexibility to change elements of their procedures, for example to keep pace with changes in the business structure, without having to issue contracts of employment every time, a process which would be a huge bureaucratic burden ... and it prevents employees circumventing the one-year qualifying period for unfair dismissal claims by instead claiming 'breach of contract' for failure to follow one of these procedures.[80]

The fate of section 30 is devastating to Lord Dyson's argument from parliamentary intention. For Parliament in 2004 cannot have intended to avoid contractual incorporation by deciding not to activate section 30 whilst simultaneously intending to require contractual incorporation by including disciplinary procedures in the obligation to issue written particulars. That would make no sense.

In this way, and despite some unhelpful obiter suggestions by Lord Hoffmann in *Johnson* to the contrary, *Edwards* should not be regarded as the legitimate progeny of *Johnson*. Where express terms are at issue, the intention of Parliament is a red herring. What matters are the intentions of the contracting parties in determining what was agreed, objectively considered, against the backdrop of the statutory context. The statutory right in the unfair dismissal legislation should, following Wedderburn's conceptualisation of the 'floor of rights', simply be regarded as a 'materially raised floor of statutory entitlements'[81] from which bargaining takes place. If there is

---

[79] HL Deb 23 February 2004, vol 658, col 100.
[80] ibid col 93.
[81] Wedderburn (n 69).

an express term in the contract governing the disciplinary process, it should simply be treated as enforceable in the ordinary way, like any other term of a contract. None of this is to deny that some incoherence and odd consequences flow from the *Johnson* exclusion zone. The existence of the boundary line means that something of this nature is inescapable. It is to say that the mess of *Edwards* is a result of faulty reasoning and an over-extension of the *Johnson* exclusion zone beyond the legitimate constitutional rationale of *Johnson*.

D. The Ghost of *Rookes v Barnard*

The chapter began with the notoriety of Lord Hoffmann's speech in *Johnson*. When placed in historical perspective, however, the notoriety of *Johnson* is perhaps nothing next to the notoriety of *Rookes v Barnard*, a case familiar to all labour lawyers and tort lawyers and a cause célèbre of 1960s labour law.[82] Following a dispute between the trade union and Mr Rookes, Mr Rookes resigned his union membership. This resulted in the passing of a resolution at a union meeting, and a full-time union official and two fellow employees informed the employer that the workforce would engage in strike action unless Mr Rookes was given notice by the employer. Mr Rookes was duly given notice. The House of Lords decided that the actions of the conspirators amounted to a tort of intimidation, since the threat to strike was a threat to do something unlawful, viz to breach the employment contract, which contained a 'no strike clause'. The effect of this was to place the industrial action beyond the existing statutory immunities for tort liability in respect of strike activity, since the tort of intimidation had not been within the contemplation of Parliament when it drafted the statutory immunity which excluded liability in trade disputes for listed torts.

At the time, many labour lawyers regarded *Rookes* as a scandal because it represented a breach of the principle of judicial abstention and non-intervention in collective labour relations.[83] It was an example of judicial law-making which, in substance, was disruptive of a delicate balance that had been settled upon by Parliament in the law governing industrial disputes. The regressive tendencies of the common law had been unleashed again, despite the longstanding exclusion of the common law from collective labour relations through democratic legislation. The judicial defiance of Parliament's will as expressed through the statutory immunities meant that *Rookes* was, like *Johnson*, a constitutional law case of the first importance, played out against the backdrop of an employment dispute.

---

[82] *Rookes v Barnard* [1964] AC 1129 (HL).
[83] For a brilliant contemporary analysis of *Rookes v Barnard*, see the young Lord Wedderburn's note at (1965) 28 *MLR* 205.

What relevance does *Rookes* have in evaluating *Johnson*? Perhaps we should regard both cases as grist to the mill of the well-worn trope that you cannot trust English judges with anything as important as the law governing work relations. Their energies are better directed at things like bailment, charterparties and bills of lading. For Hepple, *Rookes* and *Johnson* both exemplify the 'oil and water' approach to legal reasoning of which he is justly critical.[84] Responding to the desire on the part of the House of Lords to rein in the economic torts in *OBG Ltd v Allan*,[85] with some of the judges justifying that common law restraint by reference to the legislation on industrial action,[86] Wedderburn observed that this was 'another brick in the wall' of *Johnson*.[87]

There is another perspective, however. It is dangerous to evaluate labour law cases on the basis of a score sheet between employers and workers; it is much better to evaluate them by the principles that they articulate. We may yet see *Johnson* as embodying a set of constitutional instincts that are fundamentally antithetical to those on display in *Rookes*. Had their Lordships in *Rookes* regarded the common law as Lord Hoffmann regarded it in *Johnson*, as subsidiary to democratically enacted legislation in the development of a composite body of employment law consisting of both legislation and common law, *Rookes* might well have been decided very differently.

It is tempting to reflect upon what might have been had that particular butterfly fluttered its wings in 1964. It is a matter of no small irony that the young Lord Hoffmann penned his spirited defence of *Rookes*, which was published in the *Law Quarterly Review* in 1965.[88] In this respect, we can see how many years spent serving on the bench with such distinction led to a maturation of his views on the constitutional proprieties of judging in a parliamentary democracy.

IV. CONCLUSION

To sum up, it seems plain that in the pursuit of a policy controversially attributed to Parliament, the courts have been determined to prevent dismissed employees from claiming awards of damages that would exceed the statutory maximum for a claim for unfair dismissal. To do so, taking their lead from *Johnson*, the courts have created a multitude of anomalies, with a particularly starring role to be given to the idea that in order to claim damages for a breach of contract, the contract must expressly provide that

---

[84] Hepple (n 48) 53.
[85] *OBG Ltd v Allan* [2007] UKHL 21, [2008] 1 AC 1.
[86] See particularly ibid [306] (Lady Hale).
[87] Lord Wedderburn, 'Labour Law 2008: 40 Years on' (2007) 36 *Industrial Law Journal* 397, 409.
[88] (1965) 81 *LQR* 116.

damages may be claimed for that breach. From the perspective of common law principle, the law may be regarded as an incoherent mess, the just deserts of an unwise departure from common law principle led by Lord Hoffmann. Against this, there must be set a wider group of concerns that might be described as constitutional in nature. These constitutional concerns would advocate a need for caution in developing the common law where, as is so often the case in employment law, those common law principles are embedded in a statutory context. These concerns, reflecting a particular conception of the judicial role in a parliamentary democracy, seem to underlie Lord Hoffmann's reluctance in *Johnson* to develop the common law in such a way as to facilitate a circumvention of the statutory cap by claimants in dismissal proceedings. Whatever the final resolution of this debate, Lord Hoffmann's notoriety amongst labour lawyers seems assured.

12

The Meaning of Commercial Contracts

PAUL S DAVIES*

T HE LEADING GUIDANCE about how written contracts should be interpreted was provided by Lord Hoffmann in *Investors Compensation Scheme Ltd v West Bromwich Building Society*:

(1) Interpretation is the ascertainment of the meaning which the document would convey to a reasonable person having all the background knowledge which would reasonably have been available to the parties in the situation in which they were at the time of the contract.

(2) The background was famously referred to by Lord Wilberforce as the 'matrix of fact', but this phrase is, if anything, an understated description of what the background may include. Subject to the requirement that it should have been reasonably available to the parties and to the exception to be mentioned next, it includes absolutely anything which would have affected the way in which the language of the document would have been understood by a reasonable man.

(3) The law excludes from the admissible background the previous negotiations of the parties and their declarations of subjective intent. They are admissible only in an action for rectification. The law makes this distinction for reasons of practical policy and, in this respect only, legal interpretation differs from the way we would interpret utterances in ordinary life. The boundaries of this exception are in some respects unclear. But this is not the occasion on which to explore them.

(4) The meaning which a document (or any other utterance) would convey to a reasonable man is not the same thing as the meaning of its words. The meaning of words is a matter of dictionaries and grammars; the meaning of the document is what the parties using those words against the relevant background would reasonably have been understood to mean.

* I am grateful to Jonathan Morgan for his comments on an earlier draft of this chapter.

The background may not merely enable the reasonable man to choose between the possible meanings of words which are ambiguous, but even (as occasionally happens in ordinary life) to conclude that the parties must, for whatever reason, have used the wrong words or syntax (see *Mannai Investment Co Ltd v Eagle Star Life Assurance Co Ltd* [1997] 3 All ER 352, [1997] 2 WLR 945).

(5) The 'rule' that words should be given their 'natural and ordinary meaning' reflects the common sense proposition that we do not easily accept that people have made linguistic mistakes, particularly in formal documents. On the other hand, if one would nevertheless conclude from the background that something must have gone wrong with the language, the law does not require judges to attribute to the parties an intention which they plainly could not have had. Lord Diplock made this point more vigorously when he said in *Antaios Cia Naviera SA v Salen Rederierna AB, The Antaios* [1984] 3 All ER 229 at 233, [1985] AC 191 at 201:

> 'if detailed semantic and syntactical analysis of words in a commercial contract is going to lead to a conclusion that flouts business commonsense, it must be made to yield to business commonsense'.[1]

These principles are set out with typical clarity and lucidity.[2] They have proved to be very influential. A leading treatise on the interpretation of contracts begins by citing this passage and then remarking that 'the lazy reader can stop here'.[3] Westlaw indicates that the decision in *Investors* has been cited 1,077 times.[4]

Nevertheless, problems concerning the correct approach to interpretation remain, and this issue continues to trouble the highest courts.[5] Lord Hoffmann fittingly returned to this topic in his final decision in the House

---

[1] *Investors Compensation Scheme Ltd v West Bromwich Building Society* [1998] 1 WLR 896 (hereinafter *ICS*), 912–13.

[2] Justice Dyson Heydon has praised 'Lord Hoffmann's brilliant expositions of the law, dripping with suave, glittering phrases' in both *ICS* (ibid) and *Chartbrook Ltd v Persimmon Homes Ltd* [2009] UKHL 38, [2009] 1 AC 1101: see JD Heydon, 'Implications of *Chartbrook Ltd v Persimmon Homes Ltd* for the Law of Trusts' (Trusts symposium, Adelaide, 18 February 2011) https://www.scribd.com/doc/249124509/Dyson-Heydon-Chartbrook.

[3] Sir K Lewison, *The Interpretation of Contracts* (5th edn, London, Sweet & Maxwell, 2011) para 1.01; the author also cites a short passage of Lord Bingham in *Bank of Credit and Commerce International v Ali* [2001] UKHL 8, [2002] 1 AC 251 (hereinafter *BCCI v Ali*) before making this comment.

[4] Search conducted on 3 June 2014.

[5] Post-*ICS*, see, eg, *BCCI v Ali* (n 3); *The Starsin* [2003] UKHL 12, [2004] 1 AC 715; *Chartbrook* (n 2); *Re Sigma Finance Corp (In Administration)* [2009] UKSC 2, [2010] 1 All ER 571 *(Re Sigma)*; *Multi-Link Leisure Developments Ltd v North Lanarkshire Council* [2010] UKSC 47, [2011] 1 All ER 175; *Rainy Sky SA v Kookmin Bank* [2011] UKSC 50, [2011] 1 WLR 2900; *Lloyds TSB Foundation for Scotland v Lloyds Banking Group plc* [2013] UKSC 3, [2013] 1 WLR 366. On 11 February 2014, the Supreme Court granted permission to appeal the decision in *Arnold v Britton* [2013] EWCA Civ 902, [2013] L & TR 24.

of Lords, *Chartbrook Ltd v Persimmon Homes Ltd.*[6] In that case, Lord Hoffmann said that:

> What is clear ... is that there is not, so to speak, a limit to the amount of red ink or verbal rearrangement or correction which the court is allowed. All that is required is that it should be clear that something has gone wrong with the language and that it should be clear what a reasonable person would have understood the parties to have meant.[7]

On this basis, a court may interpret a contract in a manner which does not accord with the words used in the written document. This approach is controversial and produces an overlap with the area traditionally occupied by rectification. This chapter will examine the impact of Lord Hoffmann's approach to interpretation in the commercial sphere and how the law might continue to evolve. Consideration of the role and elements of rectification will also be important; Lord Hoffmann's obiter comments on rectification in *Chartbrook*[8] have proved to be significant,[9] but their import is not yet fully clear.[10]

I. INTERPRETATION: NOTHING NEW UNDER THE SUN?[11]

Lord Hoffmann's re-statement of the principles of contract interpretation is sometimes seen as marking a shift away from a 'strict', almost 'literalist' approach to the meaning of a text towards a more 'contextual' approach which takes into account a wide array of background information and allows a court greater freedom to manoeuvre away from the language of the written contract itself.[12] However, it is not clear that the principles laid out in *ICS* were truly novel at all.[13] In *Chartbrook*, Lord Hoffmann himself commented that:

> [T]here was little in that statement of principle which could not be found in earlier authorities. The only points it decided that might have been thought in the least

---

[6] Lord Hoffmann also gave the influential judgment on implied terms in *Attorney-General of Belize v Belize Telecom Ltd* [2009] UKPC 10, [2009] 1 WLR 1988 in his final case in the Privy Council, but, for reasons of space, implication of terms is not considered further here.

[7] *Chartbrook* (n 2) [25].

[8] ibid [48]–[66].

[9] Eg, *Daventry DC v Daventry & District Housing Ltd* [2011] EWCA Civ 1153, [2012] 1 WLR 1333.

[10] In *Daventry*, Lord Neuberger thought that Lord Hoffmann's analysis 'may have to be reconsidered or at least refined': ibid [195].

[11] See Lord Bingham, 'A New Thing under the Sun: The Interpretation of Contract and the *ICS* Decision' (2008) 12 *Edinburgh Law Review* 374

[12] See, eg, C Staughton, 'How Do the Courts Interpret Commercial Contracts?' (1999) 58 *CLJ* 303; J Spigelman, 'From Text to Context: Contemporary Contractual Interpretation' (2007) 81 *Australian Law Journal* 322.

[13] Lewison (n 3) para 5.02: 'The five principles do not represent a new departure in the interpretation of contract. They are a restatement with differences of emphasis.' See also *Marley v Rawlings* [2014] UKSC 2, [2014] 2 WLR 213 [36] (Lord Neuberger): 'Most of the content of that passage is unexceptionable.'

controversial were, first, that it was not necessary to find an 'ambiguity' before one could have any regard to background and, secondly, that the meaning which the parties would reasonably be taken to have intended could be given effect despite the fact that it was not, according to conventional usage, an 'available' meaning of the words or syntax which they had actually used.[14]

In *Prenn v Simmonds*[15] and *Reardon Smith Lines Ltd v Hansen Tangen*,[16] Lord Wilberforce had already made clear that the 'surrounding circumstances' or 'matrix of facts' could be crucial in ascertaining the true meaning of a contract, insisting that: 'No contracts are made in a vacuum: there is always a setting in which they have to be placed.'[17] Even prior to *ICS*, Lord Hoffmann had supported this reasoning both in the Court of Appeal[18] and in the House of Lords.[19]

In many ways, the principles of *ICS* should have come as no surprise. They fit comfortably with the work done by philosophers of language.[20] Context is recognised to be crucial to the interpretation of a text.[21] Yet even if the logic and authority underpinning *ICS* were clear, the outcome of the case was undoubtedly controversial.[22] ICS concerned a large number of elderly investors who entered into 'home income plans' on the advice of a firm of independent financial advisers. This involved the investors re-mortgaging their homes and investing the proceeds in shares or bonds. The investments failed and the advisers were insolvent, so the investors claimed

---

[14] *Chartbrook* (n 2) [37].

[15] *Prenn v Simmonds* [1971] 1 WLR 1381 (HL).

[16] *Reardon Smith Lines Ltd v Hansen Tangan* [1976] 1 WLR 989 (HL).

[17] ibid 995–96.

[18] Eg, *Co-operative Wholesale Society Ltd v National Westminster Bank plc* [1995] 1 EGLR 97 (CA), citing too *Basingstoke and Deane Borough Council v Host Group Ltd* [1988] 1 WLR 348 (CA).

[19] For example, in *Charter Reinsurance Co Ltd v Fagan* [1997] AC 313 (QB, CA, HL), the phrase 'actually paid' was interpreted to cover sums not yet paid, and in *Mannai Investments v Eagle Star Assurance Co Ltd* [1997] AC 749, '13 January' was interpreted to mean '12 January'. Lord Hoffmann gave a reasoned speech in both cases, which clearly foreshadowed his judgment in *ICS*. See too, extra-judicially, L Hoffmann, 'The Intolerable Wrestle with Words and Meaning' (1998) *South African Law Journal* 656. Interestingly, in *Mannai*, Lord Hoffmann originally would have decided the case differently, but ultimately changed his mind; the case might have been decided differently had Lord Goff produced his—ultimately dissenting—judgment more quickly: A Paterson, *Final Judgment: The Last Law Lords and the Supreme Court* (Oxford, Hart Publishing, 2013) 129–30.

[20] For example, Lord Hoffmann was influenced by Oxford academics such as John Austin: see, eg, *Amoco (UK) Exploration Co v Teesside Gas Transportation Ltd* [2001] UKHL 18, [2001] 1 All ER (Comm) 865 [31]. See too M Chambers, 'Philosopher-Judge: Lord Hoffmann's Impact on the Law' (1997) 18 *Commercial Lawyer* 24.

[21] Eg, S Pinker, *The Language Instinct—The New Science of Language and Mind* (London, Penguin, 1995).

[22] 'The famous statement of principles of construction by Lord Hoffmann in that case should not obscure the radical nature of the decision on the facts': A Burrows, 'Construction and Rectification' in A Burrows and E Peel (eds), *Contract Terms* (Oxford, Oxford University Press, 2007) 93.

compensation and rescission of the mortgages from the building society which had provided the mortgages. This claim was actually brought by the Investors Compensation Scheme (ICS), which had agreed to compensate the investors from its own funds in return for an assignment of the investors' causes of action. A term in the contract of assignment between the investors and the ICS excluded:

> Any claim (whether sounding in rescission for undue influence or otherwise) that you [the investors] have or may have against the West Bromwich Building Society in which you claim an abatement of the sums which you would otherwise have to repay to the Society.

The 'natural meaning'[23] of the clause was that the ICS could not sue West Bromwich for the damages suffered by the investors: the clause allowed the investors to retain *any claim* for damages they had against West Bromwich. Nevertheless, the majority of the House of Lords felt able to *interpret* the clause to mean: 'Any claim sounding in rescission (whether for undue influence or otherwise).'[24] It is apparent that this interpretation does not correspond to the obvious meaning of the words used by the parties in the written contract. Lord Lloyd, dissenting in the House of Lords, said that:

> [S]uch a construction does violence to the language. I know of no principle of construction ... which would enable the court to take words from within the brackets, where they are clearly intended to underline the width of 'any claim,' and place them outside the brackets where they have the exact opposite effect. As Leggatt LJ said in the Court of Appeal, such a construction is simply not an available meaning of the words used; and it is, after all, from the words used that one must ascertain what the parties meant.[25]

ICS has been said to be a 'high water mark' of interpretation in departing from the face of a written document.[26] The fact that 'violence' may be wreaked upon the words chosen by the parties through interpretation at common law, rather than rectification in equity, continues to prove controversial. To some extent, differences in opinions are natural; in *Chartbrook*, Lord Hoffmann recognised that: 'It is, I am afraid, not unusual that an interpretation which does not strike one person as sufficiently irrational to justify a conclusion that there has been a linguistic mistake will seem commercially

---

[23] Solan has contended that the notion of language having a 'plain meaning' in a legal document is a concept fraught with difficulty, particularly if the wider context within which the language is used is not known: L Solan, *The Language of Judges* (Chicago, University of Chicago Press, 1993) especially ch 4. See too A Corbin, *Corbin on Contracts* (St Paul, MN, West Publishing, 1960) vol 3, especially §535 and §542. For further consideration of this point, see text to nn 109–22.

[24] *ICS* (n 1).

[25] ibid 904. See too the decision of the Court of Appeal: [1997] CLC 348, 368.

[26] R Calnan, *Principles of Contractual Interpretation* (Oxford, Oxford University Press, 2013) 119.

absurd to another.'[27] However, as McLauchlan has observed: 'Even so, the division that one finds in the cases is remarkable. Time and again judges will disagree on such elementary questions as whether particular words have a plain meaning and what is the "commonsense" or "commercially realistic" interpretation.'[28] This is troublesome in an area where certainty is highly prized by the commercial parties affected.

II. PRAGMATIC CONCERNS: COMMERCIAL CERTAINTY

Some commentators[29] and judges[30] have expressed unease with an approach which displays too ready a willingness to depart from the written document agreed by the parties.[31] Whereas Lord Hoffmann thought that it was important 'to assimilate the way in which [contractual] documents are interpreted by judges to the common sense principles by which any serious utterance would be interpreted in ordinary life',[32] others have argued that this is unhelpful.[33] Sir Kim Lewison has observed that:

> [I]n everyday life a listener may ask for clarification in cases of ambiguity; whereas it is precisely in those cases that the court is called upon to interpret a contract, with no possibility of seeking clarification. In addition, in everyday life a speaker whose words are interpreted in a way he did not intend may legitimately say that he has been misunderstood. It would be a churlish response to say that he has not, simply because his words conveyed a different meaning to a reasonable listener.[34]

---

[27] *Chartbrook* (n 2) [15]. See too the speech of Lord Hoffmann in *Kirin-Amgen Inc v Transkaryotic Therapies Inc (No 2)* [2004] UKHL 46, [2005] 1 All ER 667.

[28] D McLauchlan, 'Contract Interpretation: What is it About?' (2009) 31 *Sydney Law Review* 5, 6.

[29] Eg, Calnan (n 26); A Berg, 'Thrashing through the Undergrowth' (2006) 122 *LQR* 354.

[30] Eg, *National Bank of Sharjah v Dellborg* (CA, 9 July 1997); for discussion of more recent authorities, see below. See, too, extra-judicially, Staughton (n 12) 307 ('it is hard to imagine a ruling more calculated to perpetuate the vast cost of commercial litigation'); Spigelman (n 12).

[31] Even though in *ICS* Lord Hoffmann did say that 'we do not easily accept that people have made linguistic mistakes, particularly in formal documents': *ICS* (n 1) 913. See too Lord Hoffmann's comments in *Jumbo King Ltd v Faithful Properties Ltd* [1999] HKCFA 38, [1999] 3 HKLRD 757 [59]: 'Of course in serious utterances such as legal documents, in which people may be supposed to have chosen their words with care, one does not readily accept that they have used the wrong words. If the ordinary meaning of the words makes sense in relation to the rest of the document and the factual background, then the court will give effect to that language, even though the consequences may appear hard for one side or the other. The court is not privy to the negotiation of the agreement—evidence of such negotiations is inadmissible—and has no way of knowing whether a clause which appears to have an onerous effect was a quid pro quo for some other concession. Or one of the parties may simply have made a bad bargain. The only escape from the language is an action for rectification, in which the previous negotiations can be examined.'

[32] *ICS* (n 1) 912.

[33] See in particular J Carter, *The Construction of Commercial Contracts* (Oxford, Hart Publishing, 2013) [5-05]–[5-19].

[34] Lewison (n 3) para 1.03.

Lord Hoffmann has rightly highlighted that no words can be understood in a vacuum: some context is invariably necessary.[35] But it does not aid commercial certainty if a wide array of background material can be introduced even where the written contract is clear, and the court may interpret the bargain in a way which is not even 'available' from the language of the document. As Sir Richard Buxton has argued, 'the law of contract, which individuals and businessmen use to regulate their affairs in order to avoid litigation, should place a premium on certainty. Neither *ICS* nor *Chartbrook* achieve that end'.[36] Commercial contracts are intended to be read by businessmen and, often, lawyers; the particular context of commercial contracts should generally mean that recourse to background material and departure from clear contractual language should occur far less frequently than for everyday utterances.[37]

In *Chartbrook*, Lord Hoffmann expressed 'doubt whether the *ICS* case produced a dramatic increase in the amount of material produced by way of background for the purposes of contractual interpretation'.[38] Yet the experience of many judges suggests that the volume of bundles introduced in disputes surrounding interpretation has expanded.[39] This further increases the costs of commercial litigation.[40] Such effects may be particularly unfortunate, since in the vast majority of cases, the background material introduced will not be helpful.[41] It also makes it difficult to advise clients without

---

[35] *Kirin-Amgen* (n 27) [64] (Lord Hoffmann).

[36] R Buxton, '"Construction" and Rectification after *Chartbrook*' (2010) CLJ 253, 261.

[37] J Morgan, *Contract Law Minimalism: A Formalist Restatement of Commercial Contract Law* (Cambridge, Cambridge University Press, 2013) 228–36.

[38] *Chartbrook* (n 2) [38]. See similarly *Egan v Static Control Components (Europe) Ltd* [2004] EWCA Civ 392, [2004] 2 Lloyd's Rep 429 [39] (Arden LJ); Bingham (n 11) 387–88; G McMeel, *The Construction of Contracts: Interpretation, Implication and Rectification* (2nd edn, Oxford, Oxford University Press, 2011) [5.47]–[5.48].

[39] See, eg, *Scottish Power v Britoil* (1997) *The Times*, 2 December (CA) (Staughton LJ); *Dellborg* (n 30) (Saville LJ); *Wire TV Ltd v CableTel (UK) Ltd* [1997] EWCA Civ 2251, [1998] CLC 244, 257 (Lightman J); *Persimmon v Hall Aggregates* [2008] EWHC 2379 (TCC) [6] (Coulson J); *Standard Life Assurance Ltd v Oak Dedicated Ltd* [2008] EWHC 222 (Comm), [2008] 2 All ER (Comm) 916 [12]–[13] (Tomlinson J); *ICI Chemicals & Polymers Ltd v TTE Training Ltd* [2007] EWCA Civ 725 [13]–[14] (Moore-Bick LJ). Sir Kim Lewison has maintained that 'despite the confidence of some judges in robust case management, Lord Hoffmann's second principle continues to lead to excessive material being placed before the court': Lewison (n 3) para 1.04.

[40] 'There can be no doubt that the expanded scope has significantly increased the cost of legal dispute resolution': Spigelman (n 12) 323. Such an approach also makes it more difficult to be sure that clear drafting will necessarily be respected: P Clark, 'Business Common Sense' [2012] *Conveyance and Property Lawyer* 190.

[41] 'There appear to be very few cases in which the outcome was affected by reference to evidence of the surrounding circumstances or the wider context. In the vast majority of cases judges use the evidence of surrounding circumstances to confirm the decision they state they have already reached on the wording of the contract. To the extent that this evidence plays a confirmatory role it could be said that the cost of adducing it, in terms of the time of the court and the hourly rate of lawyers, outweighs the benefits which it produces': E McKendrick, 'The Interpretation of Contracts: Lord Hoffmann's Re-statement' in S Worthington (ed), *Commercial Law and Commercial Practice* (Oxford, Hart Publishing, 2003) 147.

expending much time and energy 'thrashing through the undergrowth' of external considerations which might have influenced the parties.[42] These considerations may detract from what is perceived to be a great virtue inherent in the objective approach to contract interpretation: 'absolute justice gives way to a practical method of enforcing people's bargains more quickly and with a greater degree of certainty than would otherwise be possible'.[43]

English law is often chosen by parties because of its pragmatic and predictable nature, and it is important that this is reflected in the interpretative process.[44] It may be that some of the principles highlighted by Lord Hoffmann in *ICS* will be, and perhaps are already being, a little tempered.[45] After all, as Munby J remarked when discussing this area in *Beazer Homes Ltd v Stroude*: 'Utterances, even of the demi-gods, are not to be approached as if they were speaking the language of statute.'[46] It is important now to consider some factors which courts might continue to develop as part of the interpretative exercise.

A. What Constitutes Background?

Lord Hoffmann said that there is 'no conceptual limit' to factors which can be considered to be part of the factual matrix.[47] Thus, in *Khan v Khan*, shared cultural traditions were admitted as part of the interpretative process,[48] and in both *Crema v Cenkos*[49] and *Pink Floyd Music Ltd v EMI Records Ltd*,[50] evidence of market practice was found to be part of the background information, even though the practice did not constitute

---

[42] Berg (n 29), using the language of Lightman J in *The Inntrepreneur Pub Co (GL) v East Crown Ltd* [2000] 2 Lloyd's Rep 611 [614]. See similarly R Calnan, 'Construction of Commercial Contracts: A Practitioner's Perspective' in A Burrows and E Peel (eds), *Contract Terms* (Oxford, Oxford Unviersity Press, 2007). *Cf* Thomas J in *Wholesale Distributors Ltd v Gibbons Holdings Ltd* [2007] NZSC 37 [111]–[122]; D McLauchlan, 'Contract Formation, Contract Interpretation and Subsequent Conduct' (2006) 25 *University of Queensland Law Journal* 77, 103–106.

[43] Calnan (n 26) 17. An interpretation which contradicts the parties' actual intentions is still unlikely to succeed: see, eg, *Blueco Ltd v BWAT Retail Nominee (1) Ltd* [2014] EWCA Civ 154 [55] (Etherton C).

[44] See, eg, M Bridge, 'The Future of English Private Transactional Law' [2002] *Current Legal Problems* 191, 213–14.

[45] Calnan has argued that Lord Hoffmann's approach 'underplays the importance of certainty as an element of fairness in contractual cases': Calnan (n 42) 20. See too the decisions of the Supreme Court of Ireland in *ICDL GCC Foundation FZ-LLC v European Computer Driving Licence Foundation Ltd* [2012] IESC 55 and *Marlan Holmes Ltd v Walsh* [2012] IESC 13.

[46] *Beazer Homes Ltd v Stroude* [2005] EWCA Civ 265 [28].

[47] *BCCI v Ali* (n 3) [39].

[48] *Khan v Khan* [2007] EWCA Civ 399, [2008] Bus LR D73

[49] *Crema v Cenkos* [2010] EWCA Civ 1444, [2011] 1 WLR 2066.

[50] *Pink Floyd Music Ltd v EMI Records Ltd* [2010] EWCA Civ 1429, [2011] 1 WLR 770.

trade custom. This is a broader approach than that previously adopted; in *Reardon*, for example, evidence of Japanese shipbuilding practices was rejected as inadmissible when seeking to interpret a contract between two foreign companies, even if those practices were known to both parties.

Lord Neuberger has recently commented that:

> Most of the content of that passage [in *ICS*] is unexceptionable, although, in one or two places, the language in which the propositions are expressed may be a little extravagant; thus, the words 'absolutely anything' in his second proposition required some qualification from Lord Hoffmann in *Bank of Credit and Commerce*.[51]

In *BCCI v Ali*, Lord Hoffmann emphasised that the background material adduced as evidence must be 'relevant' in order to play a role when interpreting a contract.[52] But 'relevance' is a malleable concept in the hands of counsel, and it is not clear that this greatly restricts the amount and nature of material upon which parties rely.

B. Business Common Sense

The *ICS* principles also draw upon a notion of 'business common sense'. This is somewhat nebulous and judges clearly differ as to how it should be applied. The warning of Neuberger LJ in *Skanska Rasleigh Weatherfoil Ltd v Somerfield Stores Ltd* should be heeded:

> [T]he court must be careful before departing from the natural meaning of the provision in the contract merely because it may conflict with its notions of commercial common sense of what the parties may must or should have thought or intended. Judges are not always the most commercially-minded, let alone the most commercially experienced, of people, and should, I think, avoid arrogating to themselves overconfidently the role of arbiter of commercial reasonableness or likelihood.[53]

Disputes regarding the 'commerciality' of a particular interpretation are common;[54] the weight that should be given to this notion, and its content, remain unclear.[55] As Arden LJ observed in *Re Golden Key*: 'The line

---

[51] *Marley* (n 13) [36].

[52] *BCCI v Ali* (n 3) [39].

[53] *Skanska Rasleigh Weatherfoil Ltd v Somerfield Stores Ltd* [2006] EWCA Civ 1732, [2007] CILL 2449 [22].

[54] Eg, *Re Golden Key* [2009] EWCA Civ 636; *Pink Floyd* (n 50); *ING Bank NV v Ros Roca SA* [2011] EWCA Civ 353, [2012] 1 WLR 472.

[55] In a different context, Lord Phillips has observed that there is no universal meaning of 'common sense': *Moore Stephens (A Firm) v Stone Rolls Limited (in Liquidation)* [2009] UKHL 39, [2009] 3 WLR 455 [5].

between giving weight to the commerciality of a provision and writing a provision into an agreement can become a fine one.'[56] Judges often disagree about whether or not a particular interpretation complies with 'business common sense',[57] and so do parties. In *Ardagh Group SA v Pillar Property Group Ltd*, Etherton C said: 'In the present case, as is now so often the case, each side says that its preferred interpretation is more commercial than the other side's and indeed that the other side's is absurd or some similar description.'[58] Underhill LJ agreed with the Chancellor and deprecated an 'illegitimate appeal to what is said to be the "commerciality" of a particular construction of a formally drafted agreement' where the language used is perfectly clear.[59] Similarly, in *BMA Special Opportunity Hub Fund Ltd v African Minerals Finance Ltd*, Aiken LJ endorsed:

> [T]he statements of Briggs J, in *Jackson v Dear*,[60] first, that 'commercial common sense' is not to be elevated to an overriding criterion of construction and, secondly, that the parties should not be subjected to '… the individual judge's own notions of what might have been the sensible solution to the parties' conundrum'. I would add, still less should the issue of construction be determined by what seems like 'commercial common sense' from the point of view of one of the parties to the contract.[61]

The distinction between holding that an agreement makes no commercial common sense and concluding that one of the parties simply made a bad bargain may be very fine indeed.[62] It might be better only to depart from the clear language of a written contract on the basis of 'business common sense' or 'commerciality' where the conventional meaning of the contract would lead to 'manifest absurdity'.[63] This is a high threshold.

---

[56] *Re Golden Key* (n 54) [29].

[57] Ward LJ has commented that 'the higher you go [in the judiciary], the less the essential oxygen of common sense is available to you': *Oceanbulk Shipping & Trading SA v TMT Asia Ltd* [2010] EWCA Civ 79, [2010] 1 WLR 1803 [41], but see subsequently [2010] UKSC 44, [2011] 1 AC 662.

[58] *Ardagh Group SA v Pillar Property Group Ltd* [2013] EWCA Civ 900, [2014] STC 26 [51].

[59] ibid [61].

[60] *Jackson v Dear* [2012] EWHC 2060 [40].

[61] *BMA Special Opportunity Hub Fund Ltd v African Minerals Finance Ltd* [2013] EWCA Civ 416 [24] (Aiken LJ).

[62] As Underhill LJ further remarked in *Ardagh* (n 58) [61], 'parties not uncommonly make contracts which work out expensively for them in particular situations for which they have failed to provide'. See similarly *ING Bank* (n 54) [80], where Rix LJ warned that there may have been 'errors of negotiation or commercial intuition, not errors of language in the expression of an agreement'.

[63] This was perhaps the 'traditional' approach to interpretation: *River Wear Commissioners v Adamson* (1877) 2 App Cas 743, 764–65 (Lord Blackburn): 'an absurdity or inconvenience so great as to convince the Court that the intention could not have been to use in their ordinary signification'. This may also underpin Underhill LJ's conclusion that *Ardagh* was 'a very long way from the sort of case considered in *Chartbrook*': *Ardagh* (n 58) [61]. See too *Bashir v Ali* [2011] EWCA Civ 707, [2011] 2 P&CR 12 [39]–[40] (Etherton LJ).

C. Pre-contractual Negotiations and Subsequent Conduct

The most significant restriction upon the factual matrix is that pre-contractual negotiations are inadmissible. Lord Hoffmann recognised this in *ICS* and observed that the 'boundaries of this exception are in some respects unclear'.[64] In *Prenn v Simmonds*, Lord Wilberforce had expressed the view that such material was 'unhelpful',[65] but others have emphasised that if the pre-contractual negotiations were objectively known to both sides, then they may help to cast light on the meaning of the contract later concluded.[66] It was thought by many commentators that the exclusion of pre-contractual negotiations could not survive the impetus given to the liberalisation of background material by *ICS*.[67] Yet in *Chartbrook*, Lord Hoffmann accepted the pragmatic basis for excluding prior communications: there may be an abundance of material which the court would have to consider, and the majority of statements presented would be 'drenched in subjectivity'.[68] Lord Hoffmann said that a system which ignores pre-contractual negotiations, even where helpful, might be 'justified in the more general interest of economy and predictability in obtaining advice and adjudicating disputes'.[69] His Lordship also noted other reasons in favour of the exclusionary rule, such as a possible adverse effect on third parties[70] and the danger of encouraging parties to lay a paper trail of self-serving documents.[71] These are powerful reasons for restricting the scope of background material. But such reasoning may apply equally to other material commonly introduced by the parties and is not limited to prior negotiations. It may be that a more limited approach to the range of admissible evidence should be adopted for commercial contracts more generally.

Some use continues to be made of pre-contractual negotiations in establishing 'the "genesis" and objectively the "aim" of the transaction'.[72] However, it is difficult to decide whether evidence of pre-contractual negotiations is being adduced to prove a fact which is objectively known to the parties or to establish what the contract means. Only the former is admissible as part of the relevant background used in the interpretative exercise.

---

[64] *ICS* (n 1) 912–13: see Principle 3 at text to n 1.

[65] *Prenn* (n 15) 1384.

[66] Eg, *Proforce Recruit Ltd v The Rugby Group Ltd* [2006] EWCA Civ 69 (Arden LJ) (though see, subsequently, [2007] EWHC 1621 (QB), [2008] 1 All ER (Comm) 569).

[67] Lord Nicholls, 'My Kingdom for a Horse: the Meaning of Words' (2005) 121 *LQR* 577; G McMeel, 'Prior Negotiations and Subsequent Conduct—The Next Step Forward for Contractual Interpretation?' (2003) 119 *LQR* 272; Burrows (n 22) 84.

[68] *Chartbrook* (n 2) [38]. Lord Hoffmann was also suspicious of arguments in favour of admissibility drawn from Continental legal systems (see [39]).

[69] ibid [41].

[70] ibid [40].

[71] ibid [38].

[72] *Prenn* (n 15) 1385 (Lord Wilberforce).

Flaux J has observed that the dividing line between admissibility and inadmissibility regarding pre-contractual negotiations is 'so fine it almost vanishes',[73] and in *Oceanbulk Shipping & Trading SA v TMT Asia Ltd*,[74] Lord Clarke acknowledged that it may not be easy to distinguish between the two. Given such practical difficulties, it may be preferable simply not to admit pre-contractual negotiations into the interpretative process at all.[75]

Even though pre-contractual negotiations remain excluded, the general drive to widen the scope of the 'factual matrix' may suggest that the parties' conduct *after* concluding the contract should be taken into account when ascertaining the objective meaning of the contract.[76] The New Zealand courts have recognised the utility of such evidence[77] and, in *ING Bank NV v Ros Roca SA*, Walker J was not prepared to reject this argument out of hand.[78] The traditional approach of English law is to exclude such evidence; as Lord Reid commented in *James Miller Partners Ltd v Whitworth Street Estates (Manchester) Ltd*, 'otherwise one might have the result that a contract meant one thing the day it was signed, but by reason of subsequent events meant something different a month or a year later'.[79] Demands for commercial certainty may support the maintenance of a rule excluding post-contractual conduct in the same manner as pre-contractual negotiations.

D. A More Restrictive Approach for Certain Types of Contracts? The Impact upon Third Parties

Calnan has proposed that, when interpreting commercial contracts, the matrix of fact should be limited to the identity of the parties, the nature and purpose of transaction,[80] and the market in which the transaction

---

[73] *Excelsior Group Productions Ltd v Yorkshire Television Ltd* [2009] EWHC 1751 (Comm) [25].

[74] *Oceanbulk* (n 57).

[75] See Lewison (n 3) para 3.09. Compare *Investec Bank (Channel Islands) Ltd v The Retail Group plc* [2009] EWHC 476 (Ch) [76] (Sales J).

[76] Bingham (n 11) 389–90; J Steyn, *Democracy through Law: Selected Speeches and Judgments* (Aldershot, Ashgate, 2004) 46; McLauchlan (n 42).

[77] *Wholesale Distributors Ltd v Gibbons Holdings Ltd* [2007] NZSC 37.

[78] *ING Bank NV v Ros Roca SA* [2010] EWHC 50 (Comm) [17]: 'Mr Stanley for ING added that under English law the conduct of the parties subsequent to a written agreement is not admissible as evidence to assist its interpretation: *James Miller & Partners Ltd v Whitworth Street Estates (Manchester) Ltd* [1970] AC 572 (HL) 603C–E (Lord Reid). Mr Colton for Ros Roca suggested that this rule, like the rule about negotiations, does not exclude the use of such evidence to establish that a fact which may be relevant as background was known to both parties. In principle I think Mr Colton's submission is likely to be correct. As I have not needed to examine the evidence about subsequent conduct in this regard I express no concluded view.' (This point was not discussed in the Court of Appeal: [2011] EWCA Civ 353, [2012] 1 WLR 472.)

[79] *James Miller Partners Ltd v Whitworth Street Estates (Manchester) Ltd* [1970] AC 583, 603.

[80] *Cf Lloyds TSB* (n 5).

took place.[81] Such contextual factors will invariably be well known to both the contracting parties and third party observers without the need for any extensive trawl through extrinsic material. This restrictive approach to background material represents a much more conservative approach to the surrounding circumstances than that suggested by Lord Hoffmann,[82] but it might increase parties' control over how their agreements will be interpreted[83] and make it easier to give advice on the meaning of a contract.

Lord Hoffmann himself recognised that in some circumstances, the scope of the factual matrix may be limited.[84] This idea has been developed in subsequent cases and may pose significant brakes upon any wholesale shift 'from text to context'.[85] In *Re Sigma*, a complicated commercial trust deed included a clause about how assets were to be distributed.[86] Lord Collins stated that:

> This is not the type of case where the background or matrix of fact is or ought to be relevant, except in the most generalised way. I do not consider, therefore, that there is much assistance to be derived from the principles of interpretation re-stated by Lord Hoffmann in *Investors Compensation Scheme* ... Where a security document secures a number of creditors who have advanced funds over a long period of time it would be quite wrong to take account of circumstances which are not known to all of them. In this type of case it is the wording of the instrument which is paramount. The instrument must be interpreted as a whole in the light of the commercial intention which may be inferred from the face of the instrument and from the nature of the debtor's business.[87]

Although Lord Collins agreed that the 'literal' interpretation of the courts below was not to be favoured,[88] he essentially limited the relevant 'background' to the document itself. This makes the task of interpretation more straightforward.

In *Re Sigma*, Lord Collins sought to ensure that third parties who might not be aware of 'surrounding circumstances' known to the signatories of the contract would not be unfairly prejudiced. A similar concern was evinced

---

[81] Calnan (n 26) 66.

[82] Lord Hoffmann's principles apply beyond commercial contracts, but also to patents (*Kirin-Amgen* (n 27)), trust instruments (*Re Sigma* (n 5)) and Lord Hoffmann has also held that it applies to jurisdiction and arbitration clauses: *Fiona Trust v Privalov* [2007] UKHL 40, [2007] 4 All ER 951.

[83] The parties have considerably less control over the context or purpose ascribed by a subsequent tribunal than they do over the text itself: Morgan (n 37) 229.

[84] *Mannai* (n 19) 779: 'There are documents in which the need for certainty is paramount and which admissible background is restricted to avoid the possibility that the same document may have different meanings for different people according to their knowledge of the background.' See too *Chartbrook* (n 2) [40].

[85] Spigelman (n 12).

[86] *Re Sigma* (n 5). The same *ICS* principles apply when interpreting the meaning of trust deeds. See the criticism of *Chartbrook* (n 2) in Heydon (n 2).

[87] *Re Sigma* (n 5) [37] (Lords Mance and Hope agreed).

[88] He thought such an approach was more appropriate to tax legislation which had undergone appropriate scrutiny: ibid [35].

by the majority of the Court of Appeal in *Cherry Tree Ltd v Landmain Ltd*.[89] In that case, Dancastle Associates Ltd had a registered charge over land owned by Landmain Ltd. The legal charge itself contained no indication that the statutory power of sale under section 101(3) of the Law of Property Act 1925[90] might have been varied, but Dancastle and Landmain also entered into a parallel 'facility agreement', executed on the same date as the registered charge in July 2010, which stated that the charge was immediately enforceable, even if there was no default in repayment. In December 2010, Dancastle exercised its extended power of sale and sold the property to Cherry Tree Ltd. Cherry Tree sought to become the registered proprietor of the property. However, Landmain was not in default and argued that, since there was nothing in the charge itself to extend the statutory power of sale, Dancastle was not authorised to enforce the legal charge. Cherry Tree therefore needed to be able to introduce the 'facility agreement' as part of the factual matrix in order to interpret the charge in a manner consistent with its becoming the registered proprietor of the property.

Only Arden LJ, dissenting, favoured this outcome. Her Ladyship took a broad approach to the *ICS* principles, which she preferred as 'more likely to achieve the meaning which the parties would themselves have intended'.[91] By contrast, the majority insisted that the task of the court is 'not … to ascertain "what the parties intended to agree" but what the instrument means'.[92] The former question should be better dealt with through the doctrine of rectification.[93] The majority emphasised that the Land Register is meant to be conclusive and complete;[94] only the charge was open to inspection on the register. Third parties who looked at the register would not be aware of the parallel facility agreement. As a result, the facility agreement should not form part of the admissible background.

The robust approach of the majority in *Cherry Tree* represents a significant inroad into the wide-ranging applicability of the *ICS* principles. Lewison LJ thought that a similarly restrictive approach to background material was required when considering 'negotiable and registrable contracts or public documents' generally, including planning permissions, companies' articles of association, injunctions and receivership orders.[95] As Lewison LJ explained, 'the justification for the restrictive approach is that third parties

---

[89] *Cherry Tree Ltd v Landmain Ltd* [2012] EWCA Civ 736, [2013] Ch 305.

[90] This provides that there is a power to sell the charged property which can be exercised when the mortgage money has become due.

[91] *Cherry Tree Ltd* (n 89) [37]. See too M Barber and R Thomas, 'Contractual Interpretation, Registered Documents and Third Party Effects' (2014) 77 *MLR* 597.

[92] ibid [99] (Lewison LJ).

[93] See section III below.

[94] See, eg, Land Registration Act 2002, ss 120(2), 58.

[95] *Cherry Tree Ltd* (n 89) [124]–[125].

might (not will) need to rely on the terms of the instrument under consideration without access to extraneous material'.[96]

The decision of the majority in *Cherry Tree* is sensible. But it does not sit entirely comfortably with the general tenor of the 'modern approach to interpretation'[97] encapsulated in *ICS*. After all, 'ordinary' commercial contracts may be assigned or charged, and their meaning should be equally clear to third parties.[98] This has troubled some judges, who, as a result, have adopted a conservative approach to contract interpretation.[99] Spigelman has remarked, extra-judicially, that 'the impact on, and the import to third parties is, in my opinion, significantly understated in this analysis' of Lord Hoffmann in *ICS*; that the background should, in Spigelman's view, be significantly restricted in a substantial range of commercial contracts, including derivatives, represents 'a significant defect in Lord Hoffmann's schema'.[100]

However, it would be wrong to suggest that Lord Hoffmann was unaware of the impact on third parties. In *Chartbrook*, he explicitly considered this issue. Having recognised that the impact upon third parties was a further pragmatic reason for excluding evidence of prior negotiations from the process of interpretation, his Lordship acknowledged that:

> The law has sometimes to compromise between protecting the interests of the contracting parties and those of third parties. But an extension of the admissible background will, at any rate in theory, increase the risk that a third party will find that the contract does not mean what he thought. How often this is likely to be a practical problem is hard to say.[101]

It has been suggested that the risk of prejudicing third parties may be sufficiently accommodated by the possibility of contractual estoppel if an assignee, for example, has acted to his detriment in reliance on the 'conventional' meaning of the written document which does not correspond to a more 'liberal' interpretation of the contract.[102] But it seems unsatisfactory for there to be a different meaning of a contract if the claimant is the original contracting party or an assignee.[103]

In *Chartbrook*, Lord Hoffmann said that 'an assignee must either inquire as to any relevant background or take his chance on how that might affect the meaning a court will give to the document'.[104] Yet this may place an excessive burden on the assignee. The robust, pragmatic approach of *Cherry*

---

[96] ibid [125].
[97] ibid [90] (Lewison LJ).
[98] Calnan (n 26) 63: 'Third parties frequently acquire rights under commercial contracts by assignment or charge. Similar arguments could be applied to these contracts, although these issues have yet to be tested in court.'
[99] Eg, *Dellborg* (n 30) (Saville LJ).
[100] Spigelman (n 12) 334.
[101] *Chartbrook* (n 2) [40].
[102] McLauchlan (n 28) 42–43; Carter (n 33) 7–42. See too Barber and Thomas (n 91).
[103] Cf *Mannai* (n 19) 779 (Lord Hoffmann).
[104] *Chartbrook* (n 2) [40].

Tree might be preferred. In *Cherry Tree*, the third party would not have been unfairly prejudiced by taking into account the background information. Nevertheless, the Court of Appeal held that the mere risk of prejudice and the requirement for there to be a single, consistent interpretation of the contract meant that the relevant background needed to be restricted.

Another significant restriction on a wide use of background material concerns standard form contracts.[105] There is a need for certainty and consistency in the interpretation of commercial standard forms.[106] As McMeel has written, 'it may often be more important that a particular clause or phrase has received an *authoritative* judicial interpretation, than that it has received the *best possible* judicial analysis'.[107] Given the widespread use of such terms, this again represents a significant limit on background material in the interpretative process.[108]

E. Ambiguous Language

In *Oceanbulk Shipping & Trading SA v TMT Asia Ltd*, Lord Clarke cited with approval a previous speech of Lord Steyn, in which he said of *Investors* that 'Lord Hoffmann made crystal clear than an ambiguity need not be established before the surrounding circumstances may be taken into account'.[109] Lord Hoffmann has expressed the view that to speak of a 'natural meaning' or 'plain meaning' of language can be misleading and unhelpful.[110] Language might invariably be somewhat ambiguous.[111]

Such an approach may be linguistically coherent, but the particular demands of the commercial environment may facilitate discussion of the 'plain meaning' of contractual terms.[112] As Farnsworth has observed:

> [T]he language of a contract is directed not at describing experience but at controlling human behaviour, ordinarily the behaviour of the contracting parties.

---

[105] Lewison (n 3) para 3.18; see generally McMeel (n 38) paras 1.52–1.53.

[106] See, eg, *The Nema* [1982] AC 724, 737 (Lord Diplock).

[107] McMeel (n 38) para 1.53.

[108] *Zurich Insurance (Singapore) Pte Ltd v B-Gold Design & Construction Pte Ltd* [2008] SGCA 27 [132]: 'In general, the court ought to be more reluctant to allow extrinsic evidence to affect standard form contracts and commercial documents.'

[109] *Oceanbulk Shipping & Trading SA v TMT Asia Ltd* [2010] UKSC 44, [2011] 1 AC 662 [36], approving *R (Westminster City Council) v National Asylum Support Service* [2002] UKHL 38, [2002] 1 WLR 2956 [5]. Compare the approach in Australia: *Codelfa Construction Pty Ltd v State Rail Authority of NSW* (1982) 149 CLR 337; *Western Export Services Inc v Jireh International Pty Ltd* [2011] HCA 45.

[110] *Charter Reinsurance* (n 19) 391. See too Solan (n 23) and Corbin (n 23).

[111] Although in *Melanesian Mission Trust Board v Australian Mutual Provident Society* (1997) 74 P&CR 297, 301, Lord Hope said that 'it is not the function of the court, when construing a document, to search for an ambiguity'.

[112] Eg, R Lord, *Williston on Contracts* (4th edn, Rochester, Lawyers Co-operative Publishing Company, 1999) §602. Solan (n 23) 98 has also noted that 'there are many cases in which these interpretive difficulties do not arise'.

The concern of the court is not with the trust of this language but with the expectations that it aroused in the parties. It is therefore to these expectations, rather than to the concern of the philosopher or semanticist, that we must turn in the search for the meaning of contract language.[113]

Judges appear to accept that a contract may have a 'plain meaning', even if that meaning is not given effect.[114] Lord Grabiner has argued:

Words are always used to convey meanings and, in the absence of contrary evidence, it is most likely that the parties intended their words to have the meaning they would convey to most people. The natural or ordinary meaning of words exists precisely because it is the way in which most people use and understand those words and the analysis should, therefore, begin with the most likely answer. Indeed, the existence of a power to correct a mistake as a matter of construction presupposes that the analysis starts with the conventional meaning of the words used in the contract. It makes no sense to correct a mistake without first identifying a conventional meaning that is said to have been unintended.[115]

The plain meaning of the contractual language agreed by the parties should be the starting point for the interpretative exercise.[116] But perhaps, at least where the language is clear and unambiguous, the issue of interpretation should not require further resort to other factors. It would appear that: 'Typical firms prefer courts to make interpretations on a narrow evidentiary base whose most significant component is the first written contract.'[117] Any context required might be very much restricted;[118] a threshold of ambiguity may be used as a gateway to a wider range of background material.

Some impetus for such an analysis has been provided by recent decisions of the Supreme Court. For instance, in *Rainy Sky SA*, Lord Clarke stated that: 'Where the parties have used unambiguous language, the court must apply it.'[119] Similarly, in *Multi-Link Leisure Developments Ltd v North*

---

[113] E Farnsworth, *Contracts* (4th edn, New York, Aspen Publishers, 2004) §7.7.

[114] Eg, *Charter Reinsurance* (n 19) 384; *Lloyds TSB* (n 5); *Lehman Brothers International (Europe) v Lehman Brothers Finance SA* [2013] EWCA Civ 188 [71] (Arden LJ). In *Pink Floyd* (n 50) [18], Lord Neuberger MR observed that 'it is clear that there will be circumstances where the words in question are attributed a meaning which they simply cannot have as a matter of ordinary linguistic analysis, because the notional reasonable person would be satisfied that something had gone wrong in the drafting'.

[115] Lord Grabiner, 'The Iterative Process of Contractual Interpretation' (2012) 128 *LQR* 41, 45.

[116] As Lord Hoffmann himself pointed out in *BCCI v Ali* (n 3) [39], 'the primary source for understanding what the parties meant is their language interpreted in accordance with conventional usage'. See too *Estafnous v London & Leeds Business Centres Ltd* [2011] EWCA Civ 1157 [26] (Warren J)

[117] A Schwartz and R Scott, 'Contract Theory and the Limits of Contract Law' (2003) 113 *Yale LJ* 541, 569. This was recognised by Lord Hoffmann in *Chartbrook* (n 2) [36]. See too Calnan (n 42); Bridge (n 44) 213–14.

[118] Calnan (n 26) 66.

[119] *Rainy Sky SA* (n 5) [23]. See too, eg, *Al Sanea v Saad Investments Co Ltd* [2012] EWCA Civ 313 [31] (Gross LJ); *Ardagh* (n 62) [50] (Etherton C).

Lanarkshire Council, concerning the interpretation of a lease, Lord Hope held that 'words ... should not be changed, taken out or moved ... until it has become clear that the language the parties actually used creates an ambiguity which cannot be solved otherwise'.[120] A requirement of ambiguity may be welcomed by the lower courts,[121] since it renders the task of a judge more straightforward where there is a clear, plain meaning of a contract and forces a claimant to seek rectification if that meaning is to be altered.[122]

F. Reducing Appeals: A Question of Fact?

The interpretation of a written contract is a question of law. This contrasts with the interpretation of an oral contract, which is a question of fact. Sir Christopher Staughton has commented that this situation is 'strange'.[123] In *Carmichael v National Power plc*, Lord Hoffmann said that: 'There could have been no precedent and no certainty in the construction of standard commercial documents if questions of construction had been left in each case to a jury which gave no reasons for its decision.'[124] But juries are no longer used in civil trials, and the correct interpretation of a particular contract has little value as a precedent since the matrix of fact is particular to each individual contract.[125]

This approach might conceivably be revisited. After all, judges speak of the *'factual* matrix' and Lord Hoffmann has said that interpretation should be a question of 'business common sense'.[126] The advantage of treating questions of interpretation as a matter of fact would be to reduce the number of appeals in this area. Parties should be able to achieve a final answer to disputes regarding interpretation quickly, and not be encouraged to pursue an endless spiral of appeals in the hope of eventually finding a court prepared to place more or less weight on, for example, the 'commerciality' of a provision.

---

[120] *Multi-Link* (n 5) [11]. For critical discussion, see D McLauchlan, 'A Construction Conundrum?' [2010] *Lloyd's Maritime and Commercial Law Quarterly* 428. See too *Thompson v Goblin Hill Hotels* [2011] UKPC 8, [2011] 1 BCLC 587.

[121] *William Hare Ltd v Shepherd Construction Ltd* [2010] EWCA Civ 283, [2010] BLR 358; *ING Bank* (n 54); *Swallowfalls Ltd v Monaco Yachting and Technologies SAM* [2014] EWCA Civ 186.

[122] B Davenport, 'Thanks to the House of Lords' (1999) 115 *LQR* 11. See section III below.

[123] Staughton (n 12) 303.

[124] *Carmichael v National Power plc* [1999] 1 WLR 2042, 2048–49; see further Lord Devlin, *Trial by Jury* (London, Stevens & Sons, 1956) 97–98. In *Thorner v Majors* [2009] UKHL 18, [2009] 1 WLR 776 [82], Lord Neuberger expressed support for the 'illuminating analysis' of Lord Hoffmann in *Carmichael*.

[125] In *Deeny v Gooda Walker Ltd* [1996] 1 WLR 426 (HL) 435, Lord Hoffmann said: 'No case on the construction of one document is authority on the construction of another, even if the words are very similar.' See too *BCCI v Ali* (n 3) [51]; *Schuler v Wickman* [1974] AC 235 256 (Lord Morris).

[126] *ICS* (n 1) 912–13: see Principle 5 at text to n 1.

However, it may be that treating the interpretation of written contracts as a question of fact rather than law is too blunt an approach; it would make it even more difficult to obtain an authoritative and reliable interpretation of an industry's standard terms.[127] But consideration of this issue might provide some impetus to limiting the scope of appeals.[128] As Lord Walker commented in *Re Sigma*:

> Although I was one of those who gave permission for a further appeal ... I find, on closer consideration, that the case involves no issue of general public importance. There is no doubt as to the principles of construction to be applied ... The only issue is as to the interpretation of the security trust deed in the light of those principles.[129]

The frequency of appeals in this area—and differences in approaches of the judges—perpetuates uncertainty and increases the costs of litigation yet further. First instance judges are best placed to adjudicate upon issues concerning the surrounding circumstances and context of an agreement; appeals should be rare. It is significant that such an approach is adopted in the context of rectification.

III. RECTIFICATION

The fourth and fifth principles of *ICS* overlap significantly with the equitable doctrine of rectification.[130] It has been said that Lord Hoffmann's principles in *ICS* seek to achieve rectification through interpretation[131] and that the continuing expansion of interpretation means that rectification may soon 'wither on the vine'.[132] However, it seems unlikely that rectification will soon disappear. Pre-contractual negotiations and evidence of the parties' subjective intentions are inadmissible for the purposes of interpretation, but

---

[127] Indeed, in Germany, the law now recognises that the interpretation of commercial contracts should properly be recognised as raising questions of law in order to be used as precedents when dealing with standard form contracts: see S Vogenauer. 'Interpretation of Contracts: Concluding Comparative Observations' in A Burrows and E Peel (eds) *Contract Terms* (Oxford, Oxford University Press, 2007) 130.

[128] CPR 52.3(6) states that: 'Permission to appeal may be given only where—(a) the court considers that the appeal would have a real prospect of success; or (b) there is some other compelling reason why the appeal should be heard.' This might be interpreted stringently.

[129] *Re Sigma* (n 5) [40].

[130] Eg, Buxton (n 36) 257–58.

[131] Sir A Mason, 'Opening Address' (2009) 25 *Journal of Contract Law* 1, 4: 'I doubt that the Hoffmann restatement promotes cost-efficient litigation. It may lead to attempts to achieve rectification through interpretation.' See too Bridge (n 44) 213: '[T]he House of Lords has signalled its support for an interpretative process that looks to the world like rectification under another name, but without the procedural safeguards relating for example to the evidential burden resting upon the party seeking rectification'. Calnan has thought correcting mistakes through interpretation is a form of 'rectification lite': see Calnan (n 26) 126.

[132] McMeel (n 38) para 17.01. See too Burrows (n 22).

may be crucial for rectification. More fundamentally, if a mistake has been made, 'would it not be better to correct it by a process which is designed for the job, rather than one which is not?'[133] Extra-judicially, a number of judges have sought to defend rectification and argue that correcting mistakes which are not patently obvious slips—such as 'typos'—should preferably be dealt with through rectification.[134] If the breadth of interpretation becomes more limited, this will allow greater scope for rectification.

It is important to decide whether mistakes should be corrected through interpretation or rectification. As Lord Neuberger recently said in *Marley v Rawlings*:

> At first sight, it might seem to be a rather dry question whether a particular approach is one of interpretation or rectification. However, it is by no means simply an academic issue of categorisation. If it is a question of interpretation, then the document in question has, and has always had, the meaning and effect as determined by the court, and that is the end of the matter. On the other hand, if it is a question of rectification, then the document, as rectified, has a different meaning from that which it appears to have on its face, and the court would have jurisdiction to refuse rectification or to grant it on terms (eg if there had been delay, change of position, or third party reliance).[135]

Moreover, whether or not a written document should be rectified is a question of fact, not law. The burden of proof on the party seeking rectification is not easy to discharge.[136] As a result, fewer appeals arise in the area of rectification than interpretation.[137]

Rectification remains important, but what exactly needs to be proved in order to obtain equitable relief is somewhat unclear after Lord Hoffmann's judgment in *Chartbrook*. The crucial area of debate now focuses upon

---

[133] Calnan (n 26) 100. See too *Campbell v Daejan Properties Ltd* [2012] EWCA Civ 1503, [2013] HLR 6 (Jackson LJ): 'In construing a written contract, the governing principle is that the parties mean what they say. The court must give effect to the express terms of the contract and must resist the temptation to re-draft or improve upon those terms. If by mischance the contract does not say what both parties intended, the normal remedy for the aggrieved party is an action for rectification.'

[134] Buxton (n 36); K LewisonSir, 'If it ain't Broke, Don't Fix it' in First Supplement (2010) to Lewison, *The Interpretation of Contracts* (4th edn, London, Sweet & Maxwell, 2009) 127; Lord Toulson, 'Does Rectification Require Rectifying?' (TECBAR Annual Lecture, 31 October 2013) https://www.supremecourt.uk/docs/speech-131031.pdf; N Patten, 'Does the Law Need to be Rectified? *Chartbrook* Revisited' (The Chancery Bar Association 2013 Annual Lecture, 29 April 2013) www.chba.org.uk/for-members/library/annual-lectures/does-the-law-need-to-be-rectified-chartbrook-revisited; P Morgan, 'Rectification: Is it Broken? Common Mistake after *Daventry*' [2013] *Restitution Law Review* 1. See too C Nugee, 'Rectification after *Chartbrook v Persimmon*: Where are We Now?' (2012) 26 *Trust Law International* 76.

[135] *Marley* (n 13) [40].

[136] *Countess of Shelburne v Earl of Inchiquin* (1784) 1 Bro CC 338, 341; *James Hay Pension Trustees Ltd v Kean Hird et al* [2005] EWHC (Ch) 1093 [81]. It is incumbent upon the claimant to prove that a mistake has been made, which may be more difficult than simply persuading the court that something 'must have gone wrong' with the language used.

[137] *Cf* Nugee (n 134).

whether intention is assessed 'objectively' or 'subjectively'. It is helpful to consider rectification for 'common mistake' and 'unilateral mistake' separately.

A. Common Mistake

In *Chartbrook*, counsel for the claimants thought that the written document was clear, but did not correspond to what both parties understood the bargain to be. He thought that the claimants would therefore lose on the point of interpretation and that the success of the claim depended on whether or not he could prove that the defendant actually knew that the written document did not correspond to the parties' actual agreement. He was wrong on both counts.[138] Briggs J at first instance found that the directors of Chartbrook honestly believed that there was no mistake in the written document;[139] on the traditional understanding that rectification would only be granted if there had been an actual mistake common to both parties,[140] the rectification claim failed at both first instance and the Court of Appeal. Yet in the House of Lords, Lord Hoffmann, obiter, expressed a contrary view.

Lord Hoffmann thought that a prior consensus was objectively established by an exchange of letters between the parties and that the written document was inconsistent with this. His Lordship concluded that both parties were mistaken in thinking that the written document reflected their prior accord, since there was no evidence of subsequent discussions or variation on this point after the initial consensus had been reached.[141] He insisted that 'rectification required a mistake about whether the written instrument correctly reflected the prior consensus, not whether it accorded with what the party in question believed that consensus to have been'.[142] Such an objective approach to rectification was foreshadowed by Lord Hoffmann himself in *Britoil plc v Hunt Overseas Oil Inc*[143] and in some academic commentary.[144]

---

[138] ibid 78, where Nugee self-deprecatingly wrote that *Chartbrook* proved that 'I don't know how to construe a contract after all' and 'it turns out that I didn't understand the requirements for rectification either'.

[139] On appeal, the view was expressed that this conclusion might be dubious: see, eg, [2008] EWCA Civ 183, [2008] 2 All ER (Comm) 387 [163]–[169] (Lawrence Collins LJ) and Lord Hoffmann in the House of Lords (n 2) [55].

[140] For unilateral mistake, see section III.B below.

[141] *Chartbrook* (n 2) [66].

[142] ibid [57].

[143] *Britoil plc v Hunt Overseas Oil Inc* [1994] CLC 561 (CA); Hoffmann LJ was in the minority in the Court of Appeal.

[144] Eg, M Smith, 'Rectification of Contracts for Common Mistake, *Joscelyne v Nissen*, and Subjective States of Mind' (2007) 123 *LQR* 116.

This approach makes rectification somewhat easier to establish, since there is no need to establish an *actual* mistake or what the parties' intentions *actually* were.[145] But this can lead to very hard results: in *Chartbrook*, the directors of the defendant company, in good faith, relied upon the language of a written agreement which the claimant (a significantly larger commercial entity) had drafted and checked. Both parties had numerous opportunities to inspect the written contract before signing it, yet the House of Lords was prepared to say that even though Chartbrook had not actually made a mistake and honestly relied upon the clear language chosen by Persimmon, it could not enforce that language and must be subject to a different bargain to which it did not actually agree. This seems very tough and particularly troublesome to classify the mistake as *common* to both parties.

Lord Hoffmann justified an objective approach by pointing out an apparent inconsistency if an objective approach were employed for interpretation, but not rectification.[146] This has garnered some support,[147] but has failed to convince others.[148] It may be that where the written document is simply meant to record a bargain which has already been agreed, but due to a mistake fails to do so, the parties' subjective intentions are not crucial because rectification in such circumstances is a form of specific performance of the concluded accord.[149] Much more common, though, is the situation such as that in *Chartbrook*, where the document *is* the bargain and all negotiations prior to signing the written document are understood to be 'subject to a written contract'. In such instances, rectification does not enforce any prior agreement. The preferable, and traditional, approach is for a judge only to interfere with the parties' bargain if it does not accord with what was actually intended by the parties.[150] The best objective evidence of the parties'

---

[145] Smith (ibid 130) expressed concerns about rectification not being readily available if such a stringent approach were to be adopted, but this does not seem obviously inappropriate: only rarely should a court rewrite a written contract which commercial parties have agreed.

[146] *Chartbrook* (n 2) [57]–[66].

[147] *Daventry* (n 9) [80], [104] (Etherton LJ); *PT Berlian Laju Tanker TBK v Nuse Shipping Ltd (The Aktor)* [2008] EWHC 1330 (Comm), [2008] 2 All ER (Comm) 784 (Christopher Clarke J); Calnan (n 26) para 9.51.

[148] *Daventry* (n 9) (Toulson LJ and Neuberger MR); D McLauchlan, 'Refining Rectification' (2014) 130 *LQR* 83; P Davies, 'Rectifying the Course of Rectification' (2012) 75 *MLR* 387. See too the references cited at n 134 and ICF Spry, *Equitable Remedies* (9th edn, London, Sweet & Maxwell, 2014) 630: 'Recent general assertions by Lord Hoffmann in the *Chartbrook* case have rendered the general law of rectification less certain.'

[149] This can explain the result in *George Cohen Sons & Co Ltd v Docks and Inland Waterways Executive* (1950) 84 Lloyd's Rep 97, which was relied upon by Lord Hoffmann in *Chartbrook* (n 2) [62]: see *Britoil* (n 143) 571 (Hobhouse LJ); J Ruddell, 'Common Intention and Rectification for Common Mistake' [2014] *Lloyd's Maritime and Commercial Law Quarterly* 48, 57–60.

[150] This is consistent with the equitable roots of rectification: L Bromley, 'Rectification in Equity' (1971) 87 *LQR* 532; J Cartwright, *Unequal Bargaining: A Study of Vitiating Factors in the Formation of Contracts* (Oxford, Oxford University Press, 1991) 57; Spry (n 148) 634–35.

intentions is to be found in the written document itself. Why should any prior objective consensus reached during the course of negotiations trump the later, written, formal document? This is particularly difficult to answer when it is borne in mind that commercial parties understand the importance of signed, written contracts and take such documents seriously. And if they do not, they should be encouraged to do so.[151]

The approach in *Chartbrook* represents a significant change in direction. It was approved by all members of the House of Lords, but was strictly obiter. Buxton has voiced disquiet about the fact that the decision was reached without the benefit of the opinions of the lower courts,[152] and in the Court of Appeal in *Daventry*, both Toulson LJ and Lord Neuberger MR expressed the view that *Chartbrook* may need to be reconsidered and refined on this point. *Daventry* was a very complicated case[153] that adopted the objective approach of *Chartbrook* since counsel assumed that it was correct and did not argue to the contrary. The result in *Daventry* was similar to *Chartbrook*: although the defendant signatories did not actually make a mistake about the meaning and effect of the written contract, rectification was granted on the basis of common mistake. This is an artificial conclusion, grounded on the basis that a reasonable observer would have thought the defendant was mistaken, even though it was found as a matter of fact at trial that the defendant was not mistaken. It is a shame that permission to appeal to the Supreme Court in *Daventry* was not granted. It leaves the law on rectification in an unfortunate state of uncertainty and has prompted a flurry of extra-judicial writing by chancery judges concerned with this issue.[154] The traditional concern of equity with the parties' actual intentions should not be lost.[155] Lord Toulson has suggested that, since the Court of Appeal in *Daventry* made it clear that it was not deciding that *Chartbrook* should be followed as regards rectification and that previous decisions of the Court of Appeal which favoured a subjective approach were not cited to the court in *Daventry*,[156] the rules of precedent may still require judges to follow earlier, binding decisions of the Court of Appeal, which require a subjective rather than objective test of common mistake.[157]

---

[151] *Aberdeen v Stewart Milne* [2011] UKSC 56, 2012 SLT 205 [21].
[152] Buxton (n 36) 261.
[153] McLauchlan (n 148) 96 called it 'one of the hardest contract cases I have read'. For fuller discussion, see too Davies (n 148).
[154] See the references provided at n 134.
[155] *Cf Ryledar Pty Ltd v Euphoric Pty Ltd* [2007] NSWCA 65, (2007) 69 NSWLR 603.
[156] In particular *Britoil* (n 143).
[157] Toulson (n 134).

B. Unilateral Mistake

In *Chartbrook*, Lord Hoffmann was prepared to allow rectification for common mistake even though only one of the parties was actually mistaken. This therefore cast doubt over the status of rectification for *unilateral* mistake. In *Daventry*, both Toulson LJ[158] and Lord Neuberger MR[159] would have preferred to decide the case on the basis of unilateral mistake. The fact that they felt constrained not to do so by *Chartbrook* is unfortunate and casts further doubt upon the merits of the objective approach to common mistake.

Etherton LJ thought that, in *Daventry*, any claim for rectification based upon the claimant's unilateral mistake should fail because the defendant did not act dishonestly.[160] Unilateral mistake rectification demands that the conscience of the non-mistaken party actually be affected in order to justify equitable relief.[161] Yet in *Daventry*, Toulson LJ expressed sympathy[162] with Professor McLauchlan's suggestion that unilateral mistake rectification should be awarded where the defendant *ought* to have been aware of the mistake and the claimant was led reasonably to believe that the defendant was agreeing to the claimant's interpretation of the bargain.[163] It is suggested that such an approach should not be adopted.[164] As Hodge has observed, the traditional, subjective approach ought to be maintained, since: 'Good reason must be demonstrated before holding a contracting party to terms which differ, not only from those which he subjectively intended, but also from those to which he objectively assented by his conduct in signing a

---

[158] Toulson LJ thought unilateral mistake to be a 'more satisfactory basis' for the decision: *Daventry* (n 9) [181].

[159] Lord Neuberger MR thought it 'counter-intuitive' to speak of a common mistake where only one party was actually mistaken: ibid [225].

[160] ibid [97]. Etherton LJ was prepared to accept, at [95], that the defendant's knowledge of the claimant's mistake must fall within one of the first three categories set out by Peter Gibson J in *Baden v Société Generale pour Favoriser le Developpement du Commerce et de l'Industrie en France SA (Note)* [1993] 1 WLR 509 (Ch): (1) actual knowledge; (2) wilfully shutting one's eyes to the obvious; and (3) wilfully and recklessly failing to make such inquiries as an honest and reasonable man would make. However, Toulson LJ was 'not sure that the legal principle is or should be so rigid': ibid [184].

[161] Eg, *A Roberts & Co Ltd v Leicestershire CC* [1961] Ch 555 (Ch D); *Thomas Bates v Wyndham's* [1980] EWCA Civ 3, [1981] 1 WLR 505; *Commission for New Towns v Cooper* [1995] Ch 259 (CA). As a result, rectification for unilateral mistake would not have been granted in *Chartbrook*, since the defendant did not act unconscionably in knowingly taking advantage of the claimant's mistake.

[162] *Daventry* (n 9) [173]–[178].

[163] D McLauchlan, 'The "Drastic" Remedy of Rectification for Unilateral Mistake' (2008) 124 *LQR* 608.

[164] D Hodge, *Rectification: The Modern Law and Practice Governing Claims for Rectification for Mistake* (London, Sweet & Maxwell, 2010) para 4–22.

document which records those terms.'[165] Under the approach favoured by
Toulson LJ, rectification would impose upon the non-mistaken party, who
had no idea that the claimant was labouring under a mistake, an agreement
to which he did not *actually* assent, simply because a reasonable person
might think the mistaken party was led to believe that he was contracting
on different terms. To impose such terms on a party who was not actually aware of them and signed no document which included them seems
very harsh. The later, objective agreement contained in the formal contract
should trump any earlier consensus which may have been formed, unless
the defendant actually knew of, or deliberately turned a blind eye to, the
claimant's mistake.

The weight of authority continues to support a subjective approach to
unilateral mistake rectification.[166] This has recently been supported by
Lord Hoffmann in *Kowloon Development Finance Ltd v Pendex Industries
Ltd*,[167] a decision of the Hong Kong Court of Final Appeal. His Lordship
emphasised that rectification for unilateral mistake is distinct from rectification for common mistake and insisted that the former 'is very much concerned with the subjective states of mind of the parties'.[168] This should be
made equally clear by the English courts.

IV. CONCLUSION

It is crucial that the principles employed to ascertain the content of commercial parties' bargains are clear. Lord Hoffmann has helped to frame the key
issues that need to be addressed when considering the language of a written
document. In the vast majority of cases, the document itself will be clear and
the question of interpretation will not pose much difficulty. But sometimes
the language chosen may be less precise. The broad approach promoted in
ICS offers the court great flexibility, but this leads to tension with the goals
of commercial certainty and predictability. Lord Hoffmann has legitimately
highlighted that no language can be understood in a vacuum, yet, as Calnan
has recently urged, 'the law does need to be clarified. Over the next few years
what is needed is a developing jurisprudence of precisely what is encom-
passed within the expression "background facts" and what is not—and the
extent to which it depends on the nature of the contract concerned'.[169] It
may be that there are already signs that the background should be limited,
at least where third parties might acquire an interest in the subject matter

---

[165] ibid.
[166] See eg nn 160–61.
[167] *Kowloon Development Finance Ltd v Pendex Industries Ltd* [2013] HKCFA 35.
[168] ibid [20].
[169] Calnan (n 26) 64.

of the contract, and that rectification rather than interpretation should be invoked if the meaning sought is simply not available from the language chosen by the parties.[170] Lord Hoffmann's final judgment in the House of Lords in *Chartbrook* emphasised a liberal approach to interpretation and also favoured an objective approach to rectification. This might make rectification much easier to obtain, but often it will not be necessary because interpretation can avail the claimant. This skews the balance away from the primacy of the written text. It would be preferable to insist that the courts can only accept an interpretation of a contract which is possible on the basis of the language chosen by the parties and that rectification operates as a 'safety valve' which can re-write the parties' bargain in instances where the parties are *actually* mistaken[171] or where the defendant unconscionably exploits the claimant's mistake. This issue continues to vex the appellate courts, and the applicable principles continue to be refined. The contribution of Lord Hoffmann to this process simply cannot be ignored.

---

[170] In *Charter Reinsurance* (n 19) 388, Lord Mustill argued, regarding interpretation: 'There comes a point at which the court should remind itself that the task is to discover what the parties meant from what they have said, and that to force upon the words a meaning which they cannot fairly bear is to substitute for the bargain actually made one which the court believes could better have been made. This is an illegitimate role for a court. Particularly in the field of commerce, where the parties need to know what they must do and what they can insist on not doing, it is essential for them to be confident that they can rely on the court to enforce their contract according to its terms.' See too *Eustis Mining Co v Beer, Sondheimer & Co* 239 F 976, 982 (SDNY 1917): 'there is a critical breaking point ... beyond which no language can be forced' (Judge Learned Hand).
[171] J Steyn, 'Interpretation: Legal Texts and their Landscape' in BS Markesinis (ed), *The Clifford Chance Millennium Lectures; The Coming Together of the Common Law and the Civil Law* (Oxford, Hart Publishing, 2000) ch 5, 80–81.

13

Tangling in the Undergrowth

FRANCIS REYNOLDS QC, FBA

T HE PURPOSE OF this chapter is to say a little about the decision of
the House of Lords in *The Starsin*,[1] in the second part of which Lord
Hoffmann contributed to a panoply of five different opinions, one
dissenting and the other four to the same effect but reaching the result by
different routes. It is a matter of dispute which should be regarded as the
leading judgment, and I have heard this discussed at conferences more than
once, so it may in fact not be that of Lord Hoffmann.

The decision has two separate parts: what may be called the demise clause
point and the Himalaya clause point. It is the second which justifies the title
of this chapter and which presents the theoretical problems.

I. THE DEMISE CLAUSE POINT

A bill of lading is in substance a contractual document. It might be expected
that contractual documents would identify the parties to the contract.
Unfortunately, people in commerce do not always act in the way that lawyers find convenient. So not only do bills of lading not necessarily identify
the party who has made a contract with a carrier to have the goods carried,
more importantly, they often do not even make clear who is the carrier, ie,
the party who has agreed to carry the goods.

One way of dealing with this has, since the Second World War, been to
insert on the back of the bill of lading something called the 'demise' or
'identity of carrier' clause. (I have no idea why it is called 'demise'—'identity
of carrier' is more self-explanatory, but lawyers stick to the terminology
they know.) This provides, to put it crudely, that whatever appearance the
front of the bill of lading may give as to who is the carrier, the carrier is the
owner of the ship, and other signatures are applied as agent for the owner
only. This curious device was invented to deal with problems of the Atlantic
convoys in that War, when the British Government was the charterer of

---

[1] *Homburg Houtimport BV v Agrosin Pte Ltd* [2003] UKHL 12, [2004] 1 AC 715 (hereinafter *The Starsin*).

most of the ships: I persuaded Lord Roskill, who claimed to have drafted the clause, to set out a short history in the *Law Quarterly Review*.[2] For some reason, this or something like it survives in many bills of lading. It has the advantage that it makes the owner the carrier, with the result that the ship concerned or a sister ship may fairly easily be arrested in connection with a claim on the contract of carriage. It has the disadvantage of being on the back of the bill of lading, often in small type, smudged and/or containing mistakes of transcription and easily overlooked by solicitors handling claims in haste (especially during August, when the partner is on holiday and a trainee may be doing some of the work).

The problem arising in *The Starsin* was this. Suppose that the front of the bill of lading makes absolutely clear (they do not all do so, but it can happen) who the carrier is: in this case, the wording accompanying the signature was: 'As agent for Continental Pacific Shipping (the Carrier).' Yet on the reverse was a demise clause (actually two, slightly differing and containing mistakes of copying), in which the key words were: 'If this vessel is not owned by … the company or line by whom this bill of lading is issued *as may be the case despite anything that appears to the contrary*' (emphasis added), then the contract is with the owner.

So, we have a clear statement on the front as to who is the carrier, Continental, who were actually charterers, but another fairly clear one (despite the mistakes) on the back indicating that the owner is the carrier. The goods arrived damaged. Who should be sued?

The case went first to a commercial judge, Colman J, who decided that the contract was with the person stated as carrier on the front.[3] It then went to a Court of Appeal consisting of two Chancery judges and one commercial judge, Rix LJ.[4] The two Chancery judges, accustomed no doubt to construing documents as a whole, said that the clauses on the back were clear enough to override the form of signature on the front. Rix LJ dissented and preferred to go by the front.

The House of Lords unanimously reversed the majority decision and held that the front of the bill of lading, being absolutely clear, prevailed. A main reason was that documents have to be handled quickly in business and that it is known that people do not always read the small print on the back; indeed, in the widely used Uniform Customs and Practices on Documentary Credits, it is specified that banks processing letters of credit need (in effect) read no further than the front.

This decision seems to me common sense. But it does raise problems, especially this: exactly how clear does the front have to be before it displaces

---

[2] See Lord Roskill, 'The Demise Clause' (1990) 106 *LQR* 403. It arises from the fact that at the time, charterers could not rely on overall tonnage limitation, which is no longer the case.
[3] [2000] 1 Lloyd's Rep 85.
[4] [2001] EWCA Civ 56, [2001] 1 Lloyd's Rep 437.

the back? And, in addition, what if the clause is printed on the *front* of the bill of lading, perhaps in rather clearer form—which shipowners certainly might start doing in response to the decision?

The only clear way out is to go for the cause of the difficulty, which is that bills of lading do not make clear who are parties to them. So the way out is adopt an international convention specifying requirements for what appears on bills of lading, requiring a clear statement of the name of the carrier and providing a default rule in some form for when the matter is not made clear—for example, that in case of doubt, it shall be presumed that the registered owner of the ship concerned is the carrier. The Hague Rules of 1924,[5] amended for some countries by the Visby Protocol,[6] say nothing about this; they merely provide that the bill of lading issued should contain particulars of the cargo.[7]

The proposed Rotterdam Rules, finalised in 2008 and opened for signature in 2009 and the result of some 10 years' work on the part of UNCITRAL, deal with this and other problems of the contents of the bill of lading in some detail.[8] They are conspicuously the result of American work and influence, but to date, despite having about 24 signatories, they have only been ratified by three countries, Spain, Congo and Togo. One assumes that the US Government has more on its mind than reform of private law, even if it is expected to give a lead and even if changes are needed—especially by the American maritime industry, which is still stuck with the Hague Rules as enacted in 1936, ie, without even the Visby Protocol[9] (and thus a package or unit limitation of $500).

II. THE HIMALAYA CLAUSE POINT

The Starsin involved a claim in respect of damaged timber. On the analysis accepted by the Court of Appeal, the shipowner was the carrier, its ship or a sister ship could be arrested if necessary, and the owner would be liable

---

[5] 1924 International Convention for the Unification of Certain Rules of Law relating to Bills of Lading and Protocol of Signature (Hague Rules) (adopted 25 August 1924, entered into force 2 June 1931) 120 LNTS 155. The Hague Rules were enacted in the UK in 1924 with the introduction of the Carriage of Goods by Sea Act 1924.

[6] Protocol to Amend the International Convention for the Unification of Certain Rules of Law Relating to Bills of Lading 1965 (Hague-Visby Rules) (adopted 23 February 1968, entered into force 23 June 1977) 1412 UNTS 127.

[7] Hague Rules (n 5) art III.3.

[8] See United Nations Convention on Contracts for the International Carriage of Goods Wholly or Partly by Sea (adopted 11 December 2008, opened for signature 23 September 2009) GA Res 63/122 (Rotterdam Rules) ch 8.

[9] The reason for non-adoption of the Protocol seems at least in part to misunderstandings on the part of some of those attending the relevant meetings: see A Mendelsohn, 'Why the US Did Not Ratify the Visby Amendments' (1992) 23 *Journal of Maritime Law and Commerce* 29; M Sturley and S Grover, '*Ad Valorem* Rates under Article 4(5) of the Hague Rules: A Response to Mendelsohn (and De Gurse)' (1992) 23 *Journal of Maritime Law and Commerce* 621.

in contract. The remaining problems would have been concerned with the condition of the goods on loading, any indications of this on the bills of lading, and the application of the package or unit limitation imposed by the Hague Rules.

However, as is often the case in litigation, a correct decision on one point opens up difficulties on another. If the carrier is, as was eventually decided, the party issuing the bills of lading (Continental Pacific), then, if it is desired to sue the shipowner, which actually performed the carriage and whose ship might be arrestable, the action must be in tort. In such cases, the shipowner is customarily referred to as the 'actual carrier', and the party signing the bill of lading, who is probably a charterer, may be called the 'contracting carrier'. We may get rid of one problem immediately: an action in tort would require title to sue, that is, a proprietary or possessory interest in the goods at the time they were damaged.[10] As they were damaged during loading, any claimant would require to have that interest at the time of loading unless one could say that as further deterioration occurred during transit, the tort was committed at some later time. This last was rejected, and in the result only one of a group of possible claimants could sue in tort.

But if the shipowner, the actual carrier, could be sued in tort, it would want to rely on the Himalaya clause in the contracting carrier's bill of lading either to exclude its liability altogether (which as I shall explain was the apparent effect of part of the clause) or at worst to take advantage the terms of the Rules under which the carrier was operating, especially the package or unit limitation. (This last was in fact the eventual upshot of the case.)

The Himalaya clause is a well-known device for extending the protections and exemptions of the contract of carriage to the carriers' servants or agents and, most importantly, sub-contractors, of which of course an actual carrier is one. It is so called because it originated to deal with a problem exposed by a case decided in 1955, when Lord Hoffmann and I were undergraduates, *Adler v Dickson*.[11] Mrs Adler sued the master and bosun of the P&O liner "Himalaya" in tort, in order to avoid extensive exemption clauses in her contract for passenger carriage (this being long before the Unfair Contract Terms Act 1977). She succeeded against them, and this caused alarm in commercial circles. So the issue was fought to the House of Lords in 1962 in a case called *Scruttons Ltd v Midland Silicones Ltd*,[12] in connection with commercial sub-contractors, independent stevedoring firms, who it was argued should be able to rely on the terms of the main contract, in that case the package or unit limitation of the Hague Rules. Lord Roskill

---

[10] See, eg, *Leigh and Sillavan Ltd v Aliakmon Shipping Co Ltd (The Aliakmon)* [1986] UKHL 10, [1986] AC 785.

[11] *Adler v Dickson* [1955] 1 QB 158 (QBD).

[12] *Scruttons Ltd v Midland Silicones Ltd* [1961] UKHL 4, [1962] AC 446.

once described to me appearing in that case[13] to support protection for the stevedores contrary to the principle of privity of contract as 'braving the wrath of Lord Simonds' for several days.[14]

The House of Lords upheld the principle, with the result that the stevedores were not protected by the carrier's terms. Attention was then given to drafting a clause which might confer such protection on them and, as with the demise clause, Lord Roskill claimed to have been its draftsman.[15] The clause was held to have the intended result in two Privy Council cases, *The Eurymedon* from New Zealand in 1974[16] and *The New York Star* from Australia in 1980.[17] It was held to do so by creating some sort of independent contract (I shall come back to this) between claimant and subcontractor; in both cases the sub-contractor was a stevedore.

The overall merits of the situation can be viewed in two ways. On one view, if the main contractor is by the terms of the contract not liable, it is simply evading the terms of the contract under which the goods (or, in *Adler v Dickson*, passenger) are carried if its servants, agents and sub-contractors can be sued. This may well be true of the master or bosun of a ship, but there was a respectable body of opinion that the normal commercial understanding as to carriage of goods was that subcontractors are not protected by the terms of the main contract; and there were decisions to that effect in Australia[18] and the US.[19] It can be said that where an independent contractor is involved such as a stevedore, it is an independent entity which ought not to act negligently and ought to make its own arrangements as to liability and insurance. As Murphy J had said in the High Court of Australia in *The New York Star*:

> The overseas carriage of goods and the stevedoring industry are enmeshed by restrictive practices. Australian importers have no real freedom in their arrangements; to regard these as being in the area of contract is a distortion … My conclusion is that a contract should not be conjured up out of the circumstances in

---

[13] As Mr EW Roskill QC.

[14] His argument was actually quite adventurous as seen in retrospect. Leading counsel on the other side, his elder brother Mr Ashton Roskill QC, began (as reported at 459): 'The respondents take their stand on orthodoxy.' At another point, the younger brother said in reply (at 464): 'Appeals to orthodoxy get one nowhere.'

[15] In his Presidential Address to the Holdsworth Society of the University of Birmingham in 1981, he said: 'Now, knowing the draftsman of the Himalaya clause as well as I do, it was inevitable that his drafting should not have been as good as perhaps it should have been.' The Rt Hon Lord Roskill, 'Half-a-Century of Commercial Law 1930–1980' (1982) 7 *Holdsworth Law Review* 1, 10.

[16] *New Zealand Shipping Co Ltd v AM Satterthwaite & Co Ltd* [1974] UKPC 1, [1975] AC 154 (hereinafter *The Eurymedon*).

[17] *Port Jackson Stevedoring Pty Ltd v Salmond & Spraggon (Aust) Pty Ltd* (1980) 144 CLR 300, [1981] 1 WLR 138 (PC) (hereinafter *The New York Star*).

[18] *Wilson v Darling Island Stevedoring and Lighterage Co Ltd* [1956] HCA 10, (1956) 95 CLR 43.

[19] *Robert C Herd Co Inc v Krawill Machinery Corp* 359 US 297 (1959).

order to extend the exemptions and immunities under the bill of lading to the stevedore.[20]

Murphy J was not one of most famous Australian jurists, but the point is one that can be made.

However, one curious feature of the Himalaya clause had so far escaped attention. It was that a standard version of it (of course there were and are other variants) was actually in two sections: the first purported to confer *complete exemption* from liability on the sub-contractor; and only the second purported to extend to the sub-contractor (in effect) the benefit of the Hague Rules. Since stevedores do not perform sea carriage functions, this meant that the main—perhaps only—thing they wanted was the package or unit limitation and the one-year time bar of the Rules. In the two stevedore cases I have just referred to, the claim was for the time bar; since that applied and made them not liable, they had not needed to seek to rely on the complete exemption contained in the first part of the clause.

But in *The Starsin*, the party sued was the shipowner carrying as sub-contractor to another, ie, as an actual carrier. This was a new sort of sub-contractor as regards assessment of the merits. Furthermore, in this case, the action was not time-barred, so in order to secure complete exemption from liability, the independent contractor had to rely on the mysterious first part of the clause, which had not hitherto been tested or indeed understood. I wish now that I had asked Lord Roskill why he drafted it this way; it would have added to the information I secured on the demise clause. In *The Starsin*, Lord Hoffmann suggested[21] that the first part of the clause was an example of the belt and braces principle; the second more limited protection was in case the complete exemption was invalid. The difficulty there is that the complete exemption may be appropriate to a stevedore, but not to a carrier.

It was therefore the first part of the clause which caused the trouble. The difficulty was that the shipowner, the actual carrier, was carrying in performance of a main contract entered into by the charterer which was governed by the Hague Rules. Under those Rules, a complete exemption from liability like this would certainly be invalid; what may be called the 'lock-in' clause (Article III.8) provides in substance that anything reducing the carrier's liability below what the Rules provide is void. So to allow the actual carrier to rely on the first part of the clause would be to enable it to carry on a basis quite different from that on which the contracting carrier was carrying and indeed from that under which very many bill of lading consignments were and still are carried worldwide. It might be acceptable

[20] *The New York Star* (n 17) [45].
[21] *The Starsin* (n 1) [112].

as regards stevedores, who do not perform any of the carriage functions, but it looks odder here.

It is this that caused the intellectual problems of the case. Lord Steyn, who dissented on this point, thought that the clause must be taken at its face value, that the actual carrier was not liable and that the purpose of the clause was to channel all claims through the main contractor (the contracting carrier). This is certainly what freight forwarders, who use a lot of sub-contractors, would like to achieve,[22] and provides a quite different backdrop from that of the application of principles of privity to stevedores. The actual carrier is simply free of responsibility. This of course means that the ship cannot be arrested—a point made by Lord Hoffmann[23]—and makes one wonder what the purpose of the second part of the clause, extending the protection of the Hague Rules, was. As Lord Hobhouse said, complete exemption might be appropriate for stevedores, but would be inappropriate for persons carrying goods under an international regime.

So if the objective is to keep the first part of the clause for stevedores, but to make it invalid for actual carriers, who should then rely on the second part of the clause which extends to them the benefit of the Hague Rules, the question is how is this to be done? For the cargo claimant sues in tort, not on the contract of carriage.

By far the most elaborate opinion is that of Lord Hobhouse. He plainly thought that the matter should have been solved by means of the bailment on terms doctrine, to which I shall briefly allude later. Counsel had not taken this route, so after explaining what he thought the right approach should have been, Lord Hobhouse turned to solving the case on the basis of what had been argued. The restriction of Article III.8 (terms reducing the carrier's liability below what the Rules provide are void) is based on the existence of a contract of carriage, to which alone the Rules apply. To secure the application of Article III.8, he rather surprisingly argued that the collateral contract between the claimant and the defendant, on which *The Eurymedon* and *The New York Star* based the efficacy of the Himalaya clause, was, once the carrier took possession of the goods, a contract of carriage (though not a contract *for* carriage). I said surprisingly, as this explanation of the Himalaya clause, as operating by way of collateral contract,[24] is the very matter which Lord Hobhouse as counsel had argued to be wrong in *The New York Star*. It was surprising (and courageous) that he had argued against it there before Lord Wilberforce, who had actually given

---

[22] They also seek to rely on the so-called 'circular indemnity', or '*Elbe Maru*', clause, whereby the 'merchant' promises not to sue the sub-contractor.

[23] *The Starsin* (n 1) [116].

[24] Which Lord Roskill in his Holdsworth Society lecture (n 15) claimed was 'soundly based on legal principle'.

the advice of the Privy Council in *The Eurymedon*. It was also surprising, however, to find him later adopting and using it himself.[25] But it is used with relish and is indeed a central part of the argument.

The central theoretical problem arises out of the fact that Lord Wilberforce said that the collateral contract between claimant and stevedore was a 'bargain initially unilateral but capable of becoming mutual'.[26] But what *is* a unilateral contract capable of becoming mutual? We all know the example of the man walking to York: he cannot claim until he reaches York, but until then the offeror may be unable to revoke the offer. It is, however, unusual to suggest that the walker can be sued, even after he has started, for not completing his walk. In *Treitel on Contract*,[27] it is suggested that once the performance (in the stevedore case, loading or unloading) commences, the contract may become mutual, ie, bilateral. This explains why the offeror cannot withdraw the offer, but I have more difficulty with the idea that once performance has started, the offeree promises to complete it. Lord Hobhouse skilfully weaves in the law of bailment to the effect that once the goods are on the ship and the owner is their bailee, he holds the goods under a contract of carriage which has become bilateral; presumably, therefore, he could be sued for abandoning the voyage. The coexistent bailment feature may make this more plausible, but the further step of saying that there is then a 'contract *of* carriage' (though not *for* carriage)—which is what is required for the Hague Rules to apply and make the term void—seems to me a bold step.

Lord Hoffmann's view is presented as in agreement with that of Lord Hobhouse, but it is slightly differently based on the proposition that the Himalaya clause operates by deeming sub-contractors parties to the contract for the purpose of taking the benefit of the exemptions, and the only part of these relevant to the present case was Article III.8, which renders void provisions, such as those of the first part of the clause, contrary to the Hague Rules regime. The reasoning of Lord Millett can be represented as somewhat similar, but Lord Bingham put the matter on a more general basis.[28]

A proper discussion of this intriguing clash of reasoning would require a half-day session and cannot be undertaken here. But if one sets aside the completely different policy reasoning of Lord Steyn, that one should not be

---

[25] He cited at some length the dissenting judgment of Barwick CJ in the High Court of Australia, in which Barwick CJ said (256 CLR 231 at 250): 'Their Lordships' decision in *The Eurymedon* was of great moment in the commercial world and, if I may say so, an outstanding example of the ability of the law to render effective the practical expectations of those engaged in the transportation of goods.' In his Holdsworth Society lecture (n 15), Lord Roskill described this judgment as 'magnificent'.

[26] See [1975] AC 154, 167–68.

[27] *Treitel on the Law of Contract* (13th edn, London, Sweet & Maxwell, 2011) para 2-051.

[28] Which Flaux J said in *The Marielle Bolten* [2009] EWHC 2552 (Comm), [2010] 1 Lloyd's Rep 648 put him in a 'minority of one' (at [42]).

able to sue sub-contractors at all (at any rate in the actual carrier context), one is left with the need to say that although one can sue sub-contractors, as regards actual carriers, partly because of the remedy of arresting the ship, they should by some means have the benefit of the terms of the main contract of carriage (the Hague or Hague-Visby Rules), but not, in the actual carrier situation, of complete exemption from liability. To secure this result, four lines of reasoning are deployed and it must partly be a matter of taste which is preferred.

But what is the purpose of all this? To get round the grip of the doctrine of privity of contract. In lecturing on the topic to civil law-trained lawyers, I am often struck by the fact that in this area of the common law, a lot of intellectual activity—often the most interesting intellectual activity—is devoted to circumventing this problem. The civil lawyers listen politely and one knows that they themselves have other difficulties within their own legal mechanisms in this area. But I personally think that all the devices for giving effect to the standard form of the Himalaya clause are of an unsatisfactory nature—to use Lord Bingham's words, they 'invest what is essentially a legal device with a wholly disproportionate legal significance'.[29]

It is therefore a great relief that the Contracts (Rights of Third Parties) Act 1999 takes a direct route to permitting a third party intended as a beneficiary to take the benefit of the main contract's exemptions and limitations.[30] This should solve most of the difficulties, though it is possible by ultra-careful thinking to envisage situations where the old collateral contract reasoning could be needed. And one has to remember that people will go on using these forms and clauses, and also that there are many, many common law countries where the gladsome light of the statute is not available and where the intricate skills required to deploy the reasoning of the English cases may not be easily available.

There is also one gap in the Act of 1999: it applies to exclusions and limitations of liability, but does not apply to arbitration or jurisdiction clauses in bills of lading, which any lawyer operating in the area will recognise as important in the context of privity of contract. For these, some new form of Himalaya clause may be needed; however, more likely at first blush is some newer reasoning, that of *The Pioneer Container*,[31] based not on the device of collateral contract, but on the more complex notion of bailment on terms, an explanation of which is outside the scope of this chapter. This may enable the actual carrier to rely on such clauses contained in *his own* contract for actual carriage, probably a charterparty. But a later case, *The Mahkutai*,[32] in which Lord Hoffmann also sat, warns of more problems.

---

[29] *The Starsin* (n 1) [34].
[30] Section 6(5).
[31] *KH Enterprise v Pioneer Container* [1994] UKPC 9, [1994] 2 AC 324.
[32] *The Mahkutai* [1996] AC 650 (HL).

First, Lord Goff of Chieveley set up reasoning which could enable the actual carrier to rely on clauses in the *main* contract, which would create the result of a Himalaya clause by different and perhaps more satisfactory means. But, second, he was unable to use it because there was also a Himalaya clause the wording of which was inconsistent with the result required. This shows that a draftsman of a Himalaya clause with a free hand must still be careful not to prevent the operation of other types of reasoning and thus, even if the intricacies of *The Starsin* may be ceasing to worry us, something else may appear in its place.

Again, a clean way out of the thicket is needed, and this could be found in the Rotterdam Rules, which contain (as did their predecessors the Hamburg Rules, which did not gain acceptance) provisions regulating the liability of actual carriers and making them jointly and severally liable with contracting carriers.[33] No doubt there will be more problems to wrestle with, but at least they will not be the same ones.

---

[33] Articles 19 and 20.

14

Lord Hoffmann and Remoteness in Contract

ANDREW BURROWS QC, FBA*

I. INTRODUCTION

WHEN I LECTURE to the Judicial College on contract, I refer to 'the great trilogy of cases that marked the end of Lord Hoffmann's time as a Law Lord': *The Achilleas*[1] on remoteness; *Attorney-General of Belize v Belize Telecom Ltd*[2] on implied terms; and *Chartbrook Ltd v Persimmon Homes Ltd*[3] on the exclusion of pre-contractual negotiations in interpreting a contract and on the objective common continuing intention needed for rectification. All three still provoke great interest and remain controversial. Of the three, *The Achilleas* is perhaps the most difficult. I am going to argue that the actual decision in *The Achilleas* was wrong and, with great respect to the great lawyer we are honouring, that some of the central reasoning of Lord Hoffmann may have been flawed.[4] Having said that, Lord Hoffmann's speech has had the welcome effect of making us all think again about remoteness and, above all, it has made clear that it is a false simplification to regard *Hadley v Baxendale*,[5] as clarified in subsequent cases, as providing the sole test of remoteness in contract.

---

* I would like to thank Lord Hoffmann for his comments on this chapter.

[1] *Transfield Shipping Inc v Mercator Shipping Inc* [2008] UKHL 48, [2009] 1 AC 61 (hereinafter *The Achilleas*).

[2] *Attorney-General of Belize v Belize Telecom Ltd* [2009] UKPC 10, [2009] 1 WLR 1988.

[3] *Chartbrook Ltd v Persimmon Homes Ltd* [2009] UKHL 38, [2009] 1 AC 1101.

[4] For similar criticisms of Lord Hoffmann's judgment, see, eg, the case note by E Peel, 'Remoteness Revisited' (2009) 125 *LQR* 6 and the articles by PCK Wee, 'Contractual Interpretation and Remoteness' [2010] *Lloyd's Maritime and Commercial Law Quarterly* 150 and M Stiggelbout, 'Contractual Remoteness, Scope of Duty and Intention' [2012] *Lloyd's Maritime and Commercial Law Quarterly* 97.

[5] *Hadley v Baxendale* (1854) 9 Exch 341.

II. THE LAW BEFORE *THE ACHILLEAS*

Prior to *The Achilleas*, one might say that the conventional or orthodox view on remoteness was that the single test for remoteness in contract, derived from *Hadley v Baxendale* and clarified and refined in subsequent cases such as *Victoria Laundry (Windsor) Ltd v Newman Industries Ltd*,[6] *Parsons (Livestock) Ltd v Uttley Ingham and Co Ltd*[7] and *The Heron II*,[8] was as follows. Loss is too remote in contract if the defendant could not reasonably have contemplated that type of loss as a serious possibility had it thought about the breach at the time the contract was made. This formulation unified the two rules of *Hadley v Baxendale* which respectively focused on ordinary and exceptional loss.

Very importantly, a more restrictive rule associated with *British Columbia and Vancouver's Island Spar, Lumbar and Saw-Mill Co v Nettleship*[9] and *Horne v Midland Railway Co*,[10] which appeared to require that exceptional loss could be recovered only if the defendant had not merely contemplated that loss, but had agreed to accept liability for it as a term of the contract, had been explicitly rejected in subsequent cases.

In the *Nettleship* case, a carrier failed to load a container of machinery, with the consequence that the erection of the claimant's saw-mill was delayed, with a consequent loss of profit. The loss of profit was held to be too remote. The carrier did not know what the machinery was to be used for or that it could not easily be replaced. But in any event, mere knowledge was thought to be insufficient. Willes J said:

> [T]he mere fact of knowledge cannot increase the liability. The knowledge must be brought home to the party sought to be charged under such circumstances that he must know that the person he contracts with reasonably believes that he accepts the contract with the special condition attached to it ... Knowledge on the part of the carrier is only important if it forms part of the contract.[11]

And earlier he said: 'I am disposed to take the narrow view that one of two contracting parties ought not to be allowed to obtain an advantage which he has not paid for.'[12] Bovill CJ said: 'It must be something which could have been foreseen and reasonably expected and to which he has assented expressly or impliedly by entering into the contract.'[13]

---

[6] *Victoria Laundry (Windsor) Ltd v Newman Industries Ltd* [1949] 2 KB 528 (CA).

[7] *Parsons (Livestock) Ltd v Uttley Ingham and Co Ltd* [1978] QB 791 (CA).

[8] *Koufos v C Czarnikow Ltd* [1969] 1 AC 350 (HL) (hereinafter *The Heron II*).

[9] *British Columbia and Vancouver's Island Spar, Lumbar and Saw-Mill Co v Nettleship* (1867–88) LR 3 CP 499 (CCP).

[10] *Horne v Midland Railway Co* (1872–83) LR 8 CP 131 (Exchequer Court).

[11] ibid 509.

[12] ibid 508.

[13] ibid 506.

Similarly, in the *Horne* case, a carrier failed to deliver shoes on time so that the claimants lost a lucrative contract with the French army. Notice had been given that the shoes had to be delivered by the fixed date, otherwise the claimants would be 'thrown on their hands'. It was held by a five-two majority that the loss of profits on the lucrative contracts was too remote. All of the judges reasoned that one needed notice plus acceptance of the liability and the minority merely differed from the majority on the application of that approach to the facts.[14] In Kelly CB's words, one needed an 'expressed or implied contract by the company to be liable to these damages'.[15] Martin B required 'something equivalent to a contract on his part to be liable to such damages'[16] and Blackburn J inclined to the view that 'in order that the notice may have any effect, it must be given under such circumstances as that an actual contract arises on the part of the defendant to bear the exceptional loss'.[17]

However, this narrower approach in *Nettleship* and *Horne* was subsequently rejected. Although not dealing with special loss, none of their Lordships in *The Heron II* thought it necessary to go beyond determining what degree of likelihood of the loss needed to be reasonably contemplated applying *Hadley v Baxendale*. The loss of profit from the fall in the market price of sugar at Basrah during the period of delay caused by the carriers' breach was therefore held to be recoverable and not too remote. Lord Upjohn expressly denied that there was a further test that needed to be applied over and above reasonable contemplation:

> In *British Columbia Saw Mill Co Ltd v Nettleship* it was decided on the second branch of the rule that there must not only be common knowledge of some special circumstances but liability for damages resulting therefrom must be made a term of the contract. This was followed in *Horne v Midland Railway Co*. I do not see why that should be so. If parties enter into the contract with knowledge of some special circumstances, and it is reasonable to infer a particular loss as a result of those circumstances that is something which both must contemplate as a result of a breach. It is quite unnecessary that it should be a term of the contract. I agree with the learned editor of the *Halsbury's Laws of England*, 3rd ed., Vol. II (1955), p 243, that those authorities ought not to be followed.[18]

The same view was taken by both Lord Denning MR and Lord Justice Bridge in *GKN Centrax Gears Ltd v Matbro Ltd*[19] in deciding that a manufacturer's

---

[14] Lush J dissenting (ibid 145) said: 'I agree … with the suggestion that the notice in such cases can have no effect except so far as it leads to the inference that a term has been imported into the contract making the defendant liable for the extraordinary damages' and he cited Willes J judgment in the *Nettleship* case. Pigott B dissenting (ibid 143) thought that the defendants had 'contracted on the special terms that they will be liable for those consequences'.

[15] *Horne* (n 10) 137.

[16] ibid 140.

[17] ibid.

[18] *The Heron II* (n 8) 422.

[19] *GKN Centrax Gears Ltd v Matbro Ltd* [1976] 2 Lloyd's Rep 555 (CA).

loss of repeat orders of fork-lift trucks, consequent on their suppliers' breach of contract in supplying defective axles for those trucks, was not too remote. Each expressly rejected the view that one needed to ask a further question, over and above reasonable contemplation, as to whether the defendant had expressly or impliedly undertaken to pay damages for such loss. Lord Denning expressly said that the narrower approach in the *Nettleship* case could not survive *The Heron II*, and Lord Justice Bridge said that the narrower approach in *Nettleship* and *Horne* had either been overruled in *The Heron II* or had been shown to add nothing.

However, it is perhaps significant that, while rejecting the need for there to be any express or implied term (of fact) to this effect, a watered-down version of acceptance of liability or assumption of risk continued to be supported in several texts even after *The Heron II* and before *The Achilleas* (see, for example, the books by Treitel,[20] McGregor,[21] and Harris, Campbell and Halson).[22] Admittedly though, it was far from clear what precisely, if anything, this watered-down version was seen as adding to the reasonable contemplation test.

Awkward hypothetical examples remained unresolved. The classic was the taxi-driver. This example is referred to in books and articles in various forms. Its essence is captured in the following formulation. A books a taxi for £50 with B, a taxi-driver. A explains to B when booking that it is essential for him to reach his specified destination on time as he is meeting a business client there to clinch a highly lucrative deal. In breach of contract, B takes the wrong route so that A arrives late at his destination. As a consequence, A loses the lucrative deal (worth an estimated £10 million net profit). The unresolved question was (and is) whether A is entitled to damages of £10 million from B and, if not, why not? We shall return to this later.

---

[20] E Peel, *Treitel on The Law of Contract* (12th edn, London, Sweet & Mawell, 2007) para 20-088 (and the same wording is in the current edition (13th edn, London, Sweet & Maxwell, 2011) para 20-108).

[21] H McGregor, *McGregor on Damages*, 17th edn (London, Sweet & Maxwell, 2003) paras 6-176–6-177: 'However a defendant will still only be liable for damages resulting from special circumstances when those special circumstances have been brought home to him in such a way as to show that he has accepted, or is taken to have accepted, the risk. Not only must the parties contemplate that the damage resulting from the special circumstances may occur. But they must further contemplate that the defendant is taking the risk of being liable for such consequences should they occur.'

[22] D Harris, D Campbell and R Halson, *Remedies in Contract and Tort* (2nd edn, Cambridge, Cambridge University Press, 2002) 97: 'The test is whether the reasonable man in D's position would have realised that, by making the promise in these special circumstances, he was *assuming responsibility* for the risk of causing this unusual type of loss.' See similarly Robert Goff J's words in *The Pegase* [1981] 1 Lloyd's Rep 175 (Comm) 184, where he asked whether it was 'within the reasonable contemplation of the defendant that he was assuming responsibility for the risk of such loss in the event of late delivery'.

III. *THE ACHILLEAS*

The Achilleas concerned loss consequent on a delay in returning a ship at the end of a time charter. Under the time charter, the defendant charterers should have redelivered the ship to the claimant owners by 2 May 2004. In breach of contract, they did not redeliver to the owners until 11 May. The owners had entered into a follow-on time charter under which they were bound to deliver the ship to the new charterers by 8 May. When they were unable to do so as a result of the defendants' breach, the owners renegotiated the follow-on charter and, because rates had fallen, they agreed to reduce the rate of hire on that follow-on charter from $39,500 to $31,500 a day, a loss of $8,000 a day. The defendants accepted that they were liable for damages of the difference between the market rate and the charter rate for the nine-day overrun period between 2 May and 11 May, which came to $158,301. However, the claimant owners sought damages for their full loss, namely, $8,000 a day for the whole period of the follow-on fixture, which came to $1,364,584. It was held by the House of Lords, unanimously, that the claimants were limited to $158,301. The rest of the loss was too remote.

In the House of Lords, two distinct lines of reasoning were taken by, on the one hand, Lord Rodger and Baroness Hale and, on the other hand, Lord Hoffmann and Lord Hope. What makes it difficult to determine the ratio is that Lord Walker agreed with both.

Lord Rodger and Baroness Hale applied the conventional 'reasonable contemplation' test. Surprisingly, they concluded that, applying that test, the loss on the follow-on charter was too remote. It is hard to see how that could be a correct application of the conventional test. That late delivery would lead to loss on a follow-on charter was surely reasonably contemplatable and the fact that the scale of that loss, consequent on volatile market movements during the days of the overrun period, was not contemplatable should have been irrelevant; that went to the quantum of the loss, not to its type. Lord Hoffmann in his article '*The Achilleas*: Custom and Practice or Foreseeability?'[23] has described applying *Hadley v Baxendale* to reach the result that the loss on the follow-on charter was too remote as involving 'an intellectual sleight of hand'.[24] I agree.

In contrast, Lord Hoffmann and Lord Hope—and Lord Hoffmann's judgment is the fuller of the two and the one we all focus on—reasoned that what was ultimately important in deciding on remoteness in contract was whether the defendant had assumed responsibility (or accepted liability) for the loss. Although the *Hadley v Baxendale* test normally provided the answer to whether there had been that assumption of responsibility,

---

[23] Lord Hoffmann, '*The Achilleas*: Custom and Practice or Foreseeability?' (2010) 14 *Edinburgh Law Review* 47.
[24] ibid 54.

satisfaction of the 'reasonable contemplation' test was not sufficient. Lord Hoffmann saw the assumption of responsibility as fitting logically with the theory underpinning contract, namely, that liability is agreement-based. In order to work out what has been the responsibility assumed, one construes the contract in the standard objective way, taking account of the context. Remoteness is therefore agreement-centred. It is not an externally-imposed rule of policy designed to achieve fairness between the parties where their agreement has run out. On these facts, the charterers had not assumed responsibility for the loss beyond the overrun period so that the loss on the follow-on charter was too remote.

Why in construing the contract in its context did Lord Hoffmann (and Lord Hope) think that the charterers had not assumed responsibility for the loss even though it was a loss that was reasonably contemplated as a serious possibility in the event of late delivery?

We can put disproportionate liability to one side. A traditional concern about the *Hadley v Baxendale* test is where the loss is disproportionate to the price. So an argument can be made that, where the loss is disproportionate to the price, notice to the defendant of extraordinary loss that is likely to be lost may not be enough; rather, one needs some price adjustment to reflect the added risk. It may be thought that this is the concern lying behind the classic taxi-driver example, and it may have been what was triggering the concern to impose a stricter test in the *Nettleship* and *Horne* cases. Certainly this has been a major concern in the US, as is reflected in section 351(3) of the *Second Restatement of Contracts*. This states that 'a court may limit damages for foreseeable loss … if it concludes that in the circumstances justice so requires in order to avoid disproportionate compensation', and by comment (f) 'disproportionate' means 'an extreme disproportion between the loss … and the price charged by the party whose liability for that loss is in question'. But neither Lord Hoffmann nor Lord Hope mentioned disproportion as being the problem in *The Achilleas*. This is understandable because, on the facts, the loss claimed was less than 25 per cent of the cost of the charter.

In contrast, two factors (or linked series of factors) were mentioned by their Lordships and appear to have been uppermost in their minds in deciding that the charterers had not assumed responsibility.

First, the loss was 'something over which they had no control'[25] and, at the time of contracting, was 'completely unquantifiable'[26] and 'completely

---

[25] *The Achilleas* (n 1) [34] (Lord Hope). Lord Hoffmann at [23] pointed out that the owners under a time charter have the contractual right to refuse instructions if the last voyage is bound to overrun, but it is hard to see why that should affect the position on remoteness (the charterers are still in breach by late redelivery), not least in a case where, as I understand it, there was no suggestion on the facts that there was an inevitability that the last voyage would overrun. (In the Court of Appeal [2007] 2 Lloyd's Rep 555 [13], Rix LJ stated that it would seem that the last voyage was 'a last minute spot charter, but we are told nothing otherwise about its date or rate'.)

[26] ibid [23] (Lord Hoffmann).

unpredictable'.[27] With respect, reliance on these linked factors is difficult to understand. Of course, one could not know at the time of contracting how the owner would deal with late delivery of the ship and nor could one quantify or predict market movements. But there was no suggestion that the owners' conduct was unreasonable so as to break the chain of causation or to constitute a failure in the owners' duty to mitigate, and such unpredictability or unquantifiability has often been present in past cases and has not led to the loss being too remote. So, for example, in *The Heron II*, the drop in prices in the sugar market in Basrah was unpredictable and unquantifiable at the time the contract was made and was out of the control of the carriers. Yet that loss was held by the House of Lords to be not too remote. Similarly, in *Brown v KMR Services Ltd*,[28] the magnitude of the underwriting loss was unpredictable, unquantifiable and out of the control of the underwriters. Yet the loss was held to be not too remote.

Second, reliance was placed on the view of the law in the industry being that, in this situation, the liability was limited to the difference between the (higher) market rate and the charter rate for the overrun period. In Lord Hoffmann's words, relying on the finding of the arbitrators, 'The general understanding in the shipping market was that liability was restricted to the difference between the market rate and the charter rate for the overrun period'[29] and later he said that one must consider 'what these parties, contracting against the background of market expectations found by the arbitrators, would reasonably have considered the extent of the liability they were undertaking'.[30] Yet there was no previous decision that laid down that the damages in this situation were limited to the overrun period. True it is that it was accepted in, for example, *Hyundai Merchant Marine Co Ltd v Gesuri Chartering Co Ltd, The Peonia*[31] that damages for the overrun period could be awarded for the charterers' breach, but no other decided case had had to deal with the sort of facts that arose in *The Achilleas*. It is therefore hard to see that the view of the law in the industry applied to these facts. Surely the industry had not taken a view on what the position was where the owners' loss was much higher than that represented by the difference in value during the overrun period. Indeed, one might make exactly the same argument about the decision in *The Heron II*, where there was the earlier long-established decision in *The Parana*[32] that a sea-carrier's liability for delay was limited to damages for the interest on the invoice value of the cargo during the period of delay. Yet the House of Lords in *The Heron II*

---

[27] ibid [34] (Lord Hope).
[28] *Brown v KMR Services Ltd* [1995] 4 All ER 598 (CA).
[29] *The Achilleas* (n 1) [6].
[30] ibid [23].
[31] *Hyundai Merchant Marine Co Ltd v Gesuri Chartering Co Ltd, The Peonia* [1991] 1 Lloyd's Rep 100 (CA) 108.
[32] *The Parana* (1877) 2 PD 118 (CA).

did not regard that understanding of the law as dictating that, on the facts of that case, the damages for the market fall were too remote. Even if there was a clear industry view about the facts in *The Achilleas*, it would seem odd for the House of Lords to have regarded what may have been a mistaken view of the law as overriding what might otherwise have been the correct solution. In this respect, it is noteworthy that the majority arbitrators themselves put to one side the legal understanding in the industry precisely because, in their view, it was mistaken as to the law.

It is submitted, therefore, that even accepting that there is an additional 'assumption of responsibility' test over and above the reasonable contemplation *Hadley v Baxendale* test, the charterers had assumed responsibility for the loss claimed by the owners. With respect, Lords Hoffmann and Hope therefore reached the wrong conclusion (as, for the different reasons mentioned above, did Lord Rodger and Baroness Hale). The majority arbitrators, the first instance judge (Christopher Clarke J) and the Court of Appeal (Ward, Tuckey and Rix LJJ) were correct that the loss claimed was not too remote.

Nevertheless, the reasoning of Lord Hoffmann has had an important beneficial effect. His clear recognition of the additional 'assumption of responsibility' test has marked an important step forward in the law of remoteness in contract. What is now essential is that we properly understand this additional test. It is to that task that the rest of this chapter is devoted.

IV. UNDERSTANDING 'ASSUMPTION OF RESPONSIBILITY'

A. Exclusionary and Inclusionary

Several cases subsequent to *The Achilleas* have had to grapple with what exactly the 'assumption of responsibility' test entails. A very useful summary was put forward by Hamblen J in *Sylvia Shipping Co Ltd v Progress Bulk Carriers Ltd*:[33]

> The orthodox [*Hadley v Baxendale*] approach remains the general test of remoteness applicable in the great majority of cases. However, there may be 'unusual' cases, such as *The Achilleas* itself, in which the context, surrounding circumstances or general understanding in the relevant market make it necessary specifically to consider whether there has been an assumption of responsibility. This is most likely to be in those relatively rare cases where the application of the general test leads or may lead to an unquantifiable, unpredictable, uncontrollable or disproportionate liability or where there is clear evidence that such a liability would be contrary to market understanding and expectations.

---

[33] *Sylvia Shipping Co Ltd v Progress Bulk Carriers Ltd* [2010] EWHC 542 (Comm), [2010] 2 Lloyd's Rep 81 [40].

It is noteworthy that Hamblen J here included reference to disproportionate liability, albeit that, as we have explained above, that traditional concern did not actually feature in the reasoning of Lords Hoffmann or Hope.

Hamblen J's summary was dealing with the situations in which the *Hadley v Baxendale* test might be cut back so as to hold a loss too remote that would otherwise be regarded, applying the conventional approach, as not too remote. That of course was the question in *The Achilleas* itself. It can usefully be referred to as the 'exclusionary effect' of the assumption of responsibility.

However, although not expressly mentioned by Lord Hoffmann, it is clear that applying the assumption of responsibility test might have the opposite effect to that in *The Achilleas* and render loss that would otherwise be too remote not too remote. This can usefully be referred to as the 'inclusionary effect' of the assumption of responsibility. This was what was in issue in the leading case since *The Achilleas* of *Supershield Ltd v Siemens Building Technologies FE Ltd*.[34] In the context of deciding that a settlement reached by the parties was reasonable, Toulson LJ (with whom Richards and Mummery LJJ agreed) said that, while *Hadley v Baxendale* remains the standard rule, it can be overridden if, on examining the contract and the commercial background, the loss in question was within or outside the scope of the contractual duty. In other words, the approach in *The Achilleas* might override the standard rule by making loss that would be recoverable under *Hadley v Baxendale* too remote (an 'exclusionary' effect)[35] or by making loss that would be non-recoverable under *Hadley v Baxendale* not too remote (an 'inclusionary' effect).[36] On the facts, it was unlikely that loss by flooding would occur as a consequence of the defendant's breach in failing properly to install a float valve in a fire-sprinkler water storage system because normally the drains would have taken away the overflow water, but here the drains were blocked. Applying *Hadley v Baxendale*, the loss would have been too remote. But the loss was held to be not too remote because the installer had assumed responsibility for that loss and it was within the scope of the installer's duty.

One can readily think of other analogous situations where the assumption of responsibility might have an inclusionary effect. So, for example, Lord Walker in *The Achilleas* gave the example of a lightning conductor:

> If a manufacturer of lightning conductors sells a defective conductor and the customer's house burns down as a result, the manufacturer will not escape liability by proving that only one in a hundred of his customers' buildings had actually been struck by lightning.[37]

---

[34] *Supershield Ltd v Siemens Building Technologies FE Ltd* [2010] EWCA Civ 7, [2010] 1 Lloyd's Rep 349.
[35] These were Toulson LJ's words: ibid [43].
[36] ibid.
[37] *The Achilleas* (n 1) [78]. Another example is that given by Lord Hoffmann ((n 23) 55) of the builder's liability for a roof collapsing on someone's head, however unlikely.

B. An Implied Term of Fact?

It has become clear, therefore, that *The Achilleas* requires us to accept that the reasonable contemplation test of *Hadley v Baxendale* is not the sole test of remoteness. There are exceptional situations where that test is overridden, whether in an exclusionary or inclusionary way. However, to explain the exceptions as ones where the defendant has or has not assumed responsibility for the loss is in itself extremely vague.

Moreover, to talk of the answer turning on the contract, as objectively and contextually interpreted, adds little, if any, light. Indeed, to think of the answer depending on construction would appear to send us on a search for a term implied in fact, now no doubt using Lord Hoffmann's approach to such terms in *Attorney-General of Belize v Belize Telecom Ltd*.[38] If so, this would take us right back to the approach in the *Nettleship* and *Horne* cases, which, as we have seen, was rejected in later cases.

Significantly, it was precisely the language of an implied term that the Court of Appeal used to explain *The Achilleas* in the recent case of *John Grimes Partnership Ltd v Gubbins*.[39] Here a consulting engineer's delay in breach of contract had led to lost profit for the developer because of a fall in property prices. That loss of profit was held to be not too remote and therefore recoverable. It was reasoned that *The Achilleas* did not here displace the standard application of *Hadley v Baxendale* and *The Heron II*. In that sense, the decision was unremarkable and clearly correct. The important point, however, is that Sir David Keene, with whom Tomlinson and Laws LJJ agreed, rationalised the law in terms of an implied term:

> I too agree with the summary of the law provided by Toulson LJ in *Supershield*, although I would put it in slightly different language. It seems to me to be right to bear in mind, as Lord Hoffmann emphasised in *The Achilleas*, that one is dealing with the law of contract, where the situation is governed by what has been agreed between the parties. If there is no express term dealing with what types of losses a party is accepting potential liability for if he breaks the contract, then the law in effect implies a term to determine the answer. Normally, there is an implied term accepting responsibility for the types of losses which can reasonably be foreseen at the time of contract to be not unlikely to result if the contract is broken. But if there is evidence in a particular case that the nature of the contract and the commercial background, or indeed other relevant special circumstances, render that implied assumption of responsibility inappropriate for a type of loss, then the contract-breaker escapes liability. Such was the case in *The Achilleas*.[40]

Have we therefore come full circle with *Nettleship* and *Horne* being good law and with Lord Hoffmann's 'assumption of responsibility' resting on an

---

[38] *Attorney-General of Belize v Belize Telecom Ltd* [2009] UKPC 10, [2009] 1 WLR 1988.
[39] *John Grimes Partnership Ltd v Gubbins* [2013] EWCA Civ 37.
[40] ibid [24].

implied term of fact? In my view, the answer to this is 'no', but to understand the position we have come to, we now need to clarify the theoretical underpinning of the remoteness doctrine and how it fits with the law of contract as a whole.

C. What is the Proper Explanation for the Qualifications to Reasonable Contemplation?

One major area of the law of contract comprises rules concerned with the terms of a contract: their incorporation, interpretation and implication. At a high level of generality, one can say that most of those rules turn on the objective intentions of the parties, albeit that some terms are implied by statute irrespective of the parties' intentions. Another major area of the law of contract comprises rules concerned with factors that render a contract defective. These include, for example, the rules on duress or undue influence or misrepresentation or illegality. These rules are plainly not based on the objective intention of the parties. At a high level of generality, they are imposed by law to further certain policies such as procedural fairness (as in the law of duress or undue influence) or avoiding inconsistency with the criminal law (as in the law of illegality).

The contrast between these two different sets of reasons for the rules of contract law can be expressed in various ways. One can talk of agreement-centred or intention-based rules on the one hand and externally imposed or policy-based rules on the other.

Indeed, comparative lawyers have distinguished between a term-based approach and a rule-based approach, and it has been stressed that English law has often traditionally favoured a term-based approach when civil law prefers rules.[41] Classic examples are the approaches to common mistake and frustration and a duty of good faith. English law has traditionally sought to manage without a doctrine of common mistake and to explain the cases as instead resting on an implied term (an implied condition precedent) in the contract. The juristic basis of frustration has traditionally been said to rest on an implied term of the contract and/or its construction. English law does not recognise a duty to perform in good faith, but instead relies on implied terms in particular situations to achieve similar results.

---

[41] B Nicholas, 'Rules and Terms, Civil Law and Common Law' (1974) 48 *Tulane Law Review* 946. At 948–49, Nicholas wrote: 'In the field of contract, a fundamental difference between French law and the traditional Common law is that the Common law habitually attempts to derive all the consequences of a contract from the will of those who made it (or at least ostensibly to do so, for the French lawyer would say that the will from which those consequences are derived is a very artificial or objective one), whereas the French law (and the Civil law generally) will often have recourse to rules.'

It can be strongly argued that the modern trend is for English law and doctrine to move closer to the civilian approach so that, for example, many would now accept that the doctrine of frustration is imposed for reasons of fairness in a situation where the parties' intentions have run out. Reference to the doctrine resting on an implied term is therefore to a term implied by law (and not by fact) which is linked to the parties' intentions only in the weak sense that the parties can exclude what would otherwise be the fair solution imposed by law.

At a theoretical level, one can say that the question raised by trying to understand the 'assumption of responsibility' in *The Achilleas* is whether the law on remoteness of damage in contract is best viewed as based on agreement or construction or an implied term of fact or, alternatively, as a fair solution imposed externally on the parties subject to their contrary intention.

I have always understood that the rules on contractual remedies are externally imposed. So if we ask 'where does the obligation to pay damages come from?', the answer is surely that this is imposed on the parties and is not dependent on an implied term of fact or on the interpretation of the contract.[42] It would then seem to follow automatically that the rules on the measure of damages and restricting damages cannot rest on an implied term of fact or interpretation. Remoteness, like the law on causation of loss, and the duty to mitigate, and the law on contributory negligence, and the rules generally denying damages for mental distress, are externally imposed rules and are based on the law seeking a fair solution in a situation not dealt with by the contract. Certainly, if remoteness is seen as based on an implied term of fact or construction of the contract, it is hard to see how one can take a different approach to other rules on damages. Adam Kramer in 'An Agreement-Centred Approach to Remoteness and Contract Damages',[43] which was cited by Lord Hoffmann and appears to have directly influenced his judgment, does not shy away from that startling conclusion. He precisely goes on to argue that these other rules are best rationalised in that way. Yet he does not see the starting point of the award of damages as resting on the parties' intentions. But if the award of damages is not so based, how can the further rules suddenly become so based?

The better view, therefore, is that the law on remoteness, like the law of damages generally, is externally imposed. The relevance to remoteness

---

[42] Although some may find it helpful to follow Lord Diplock's analysis in several cases (eg, *Photo Production Ltd v Securicor Transport Ltd* [1980] AC 827 (HL) 848–49) and to think of a 'secondary obligation' to pay damages, this seems a needlessly elaborate approach and, even if one uses the concept of a secondary obligation to explain damages, that obligation is best viewed as imposed by law. It would be fictional to rest it on the parties' intentions.

[43] A Kramer, 'An Agreement-Centred Approach to Remoteness and Contract Damages' in N Cohen and E McKendrick (eds), *Comparative Remedies for Breach of Contract* (Oxford, Hart Publishing, 2004) 249.

of the parties' intentions and the construction of the contract is limited to the standard law on remoteness being excludable by the parties, whether expressly or impliedly. So, for example, in many contracts there is an express clause excluding liability for consequential loss.

I therefore agree with the approach of Professor Andrew Robertson in his article 'The Basis of the Remoteness Rule in Contract'.[44] In his words:

> [T]he remoteness rule is not an agreement-based rule, which is concerned with identifying an implicit allocation of risk made by the contacting parties, but a gap-filling device, which is concerned with ensuring that a contract breaker is not subjected to an unreasonable burden.

Applying the external view of remoteness enables one to clarify why, exceptionally, one would wish to depart from the standard reasonable contemplation test. In this analysis, remoteness is seen as a rule of policy designed to ensure that the award of damages (to put the claimant into as good a position as if the contract had been performed) does not impose an unreasonable burden of liability on a defendant. In essence, where the parties' intentions run out, the law must decide who should bear the risk of the loss that has occurred. It must allocate the risk in a fair and reasonable way. Applying this approach, it is in general fair and reasonable to allocate the risk of loss to the contract-breaker if the defendant, at the time of the contract, could contemplate that type of loss as a serious possibility of the breach. That explains the force of the conventional *Hadley v Baxendale* approach. However, this general risk allocation must be qualified in two main situations.

The first is where the whole purpose of the duty broken is to guard against the risk of the type of loss that has occurred. In that situation, it is fair for the risk of that loss to be allocated to the defendant, however unlikely the loss. This is the proper explanation for the so-called inclusionary effect of *The Achilleas*. It explains the lightning conductor and water valve situations mentioned above.

The second is where the type of loss is so exceptional in relation to the standard purpose of the duty that the only reason why it was reasonably contemplated as a serious possibility by the defendant at the time of the contract is that the claimant informed the defendant of the special risk. This is the taxi-driver example.[45] Or, as another illustration, let us assume that in *Hadley v Baxendale*, the mill-owner *had* informed the carrier that the mill was stopped. The essential question here is whether mere knowledge of the special risk (and hence the opportunity to limit the liability) is sufficient for the law to allocate that risk to the defendant. I would suggest not and that

---

[44] A Robertson, 'The Basis of the Remoteness Rule in Contract' (2008) *Legal Studies* 172, 172. Note also that in *Supershield Ltd* (n 34) [40], Toulson LJ referred to the law on remoteness in contract as grounded on policy.

[45] See text immediately before section III.

further relevant factors should be taken into account in deciding on a fair and reasonable allocation of the risk. These may include whether there has been an adjustment to the price to take account of the risk, how disproportionate the loss is to the price and the extent to which the parties are insured against, or could be expected to insure against, that loss.[46] If we apply these factors to the taxi-driver example, we arrive at the conclusion that, because the loss is wholly disproportionate to the price and because one could not expect a taxi-driver to insure against this sort of liability, the loss will be too remote unless, for example, the price has been significantly adjusted to reflect that risk. It is submitted that it is this balancing of factors to reach a fair risk allocation that provides the true explanation for the so-called exclusionary effect of *The Achilleas*. But in *The Achilleas* itself, in contrast to the taxi-driver example, the type of loss was not so exceptional in relation to the standard purpose of the duty and, in any event, the loss was not disproportionate to the price. There was therefore no good reason for cutting back the normal allocation of risk laid down by the standard remoteness rule and according to which the loss should have been fairly borne by the charterers.[47] One *could* feed into the balance of factors the two articulated by Lords Hoffmann and Hope, but, for the reasons already given,[48] they do not seem of great relevance to the fair allocation of risk in that case. In particular, it is for the courts to decide what was a fair allocation of risk in a situation that had plainly neither been thought through by the parties themselves nor, it is submitted, by the market in which they operated.

It may be that Lord Hoffmann would accept much of what has been said above, but would argue that the relevant factors in what I have viewed as going to a fair and reasonable risk allocation are best seen as going to whether, objectively, the defendant agreed to accept responsibility for the loss. The objection to that is that it masks what is an externally imposed rule as if it were agreement-centred. It expands and fictionalises the role of the parties' intentions (albeit objectively construed) when it is cleaner and more transparent to list the policy factors.

---

[46] Andrew Robertson's articulation of factors similarly includes whether the defendant had a reasonable opportunity to limit his or her liability; the degree of disproportion between loss and benefit; and the insurance arrangements. But he also adds as potentially relevant the defendant's culpability which seems alien to the English approach in contract law.

[47] In the Court of Appeal [2007] 2 Lloyd's Rep 555 [96], Rix LJ also points out (and I would like to thank Professor Francis Reynolds for drawing my attention to this passage) that: '[I]n taking the risk of a delay on a last legitimate voyage, the charterers were of course seeking to squeeze the last drop of profit from what ... was a particularly strong market ... They may or may not have calculated that, if the delay which they had put in motion caused their owners to lose their next fixture, this would happen just at a time when there was a sudden crack in market rates. But if they had considered that possibility, they ought to have appreciated that, barring any unusual features of the subsequent fixture, the risk of that loss should fairly fall on themselves rather than the owners. Why should it fall on the owners?'

[48] See text to nn 25–30.

A useful parallel may be drawn with implied terms. Terms implied by fact rest on the parties' intentions objectively construed. In Lord Hoffmann's *Belize* world, there is a seamless web between the implication of terms by fact and the interpretation of the contract: both ask what the contract would reasonably be understood to mean. However, terms implied by law—and leaving aside terms implied by statute—have a different foundation. Terms are implied by law if, taking into account reasonableness and fairness, a term is required by the type of contract or relationship in question.[49] As Lord Steyn explained in *Mahmud v Bank of Credit and Commerce International SA*,[50] they are 'default rules' that, as Dyson LJ made clear in *Crossley v Faithful & Gould Holdings Ltd*,[51] rest on 'the balancing of competing policy considerations'. They are imposed by the law on the parties and the relevance of the parties' intentions is only that terms implied by law must be consistent with the express terms of the contract and, in particular, there can be an exclusion of such implied terms.

It is submitted that there is no question of treating remoteness as resting on an implied term of fact. It would be a fiction to treat a policy-based doctrine as essentially based on understanding what the contract meant. And, as has been pointed out above, this would take us back to the rejected *Nettleship* and *Horne* approach.[52] Again, it would be very odd to treat remoteness as resting on a term implied by law as if it were a default rule necessitated by the type of contract or relationship in question, not least because the law on remoteness applies to all contracts, not just to certain contracts or relationships.[53] Certainly, in the classic judicial discussions of terms implied by law, there has been no mention of remoteness of damage as exemplifying such a term. This is not to deny that, if the analysis I have been putting forward is correct, there is a close parallel between the remoteness rules and terms implied by law in the sense that both rest on external policy factors and may be excluded by the terms of the contract.

There is one final argument to consider. Much academic ink has been spilt in trying to understand the earlier decision of the House of Lords, led by Lord Hoffmann, in *South Australia Asset Management Corp v York Montague Ltd (SAAMCO)*.[54] In that case, it was held that valuers who had negligently overvalued property providing security for loans were liable for

---

[49] See, eg, *Liverpool CC v Irwin* [1977] AC 239 (HL).

[50] *Mahmud v Bank of Credit and Commerce International SA* [1998] AC 20 (HL), 45–46.

[51] *Crossley v Faithful & Gould Holdings Ltd* [2004] EWCA Civ 293, [2004] 4 All ER 447 [36].

[52] See text following n 38.

[53] At the end of his *Edinburgh Law Review* article (n 23), Lord Hoffmann suggests that his approach in *The Achilleas* rests on a term implied *by law*. With respect, this undermines his central argument (see especially at [9]–[12] of his speech in *The Achilleas*) that remoteness is agreement-centred rather than an external rule.

[54] *South Australia Asset Management Corp v York Montague Ltd (SAAMCO)* [1997] AC 191 (HL).

some, but not all, the losses suffered by lenders consequent on the collapse of the property market. The claims were brought in contract and tort, albeit that the case, at least in academia, is normally discussed more in the tort than the contract context. Lord Hoffmann said that, in deciding on the scope of the duty of care, one should not 'impose on the valuer a liability greater than he could reasonably have thought he was undertaking'[55] and 'a duty of care which imposed upon the informant responsibility for losses which would have occurred even if the information which he gave had been correct is not in my view fair and reasonable as between the parties'.[56] Writing before *The Achilleas*, I struggled to see exactly where the approach in *SAAMCO* fitted, not least because, if viewed as a case on remoteness, it appeared to conflict with the reasonable contemplation or foreseeability tests and was reminiscent of the rejected approach in *Nettleship* and *Horne*.[57] In *The Achilleas*, Lord Hoffmann relied on *SAAMCO*. In the light of that, it is now clear that *SAAMCO* is best viewed as a remoteness case and as an illustration of cutting back the usual test of remoteness in line with the valuer's 'assumption of responsibility'.[58] However, if we put on our tort glasses—and, as I have said, *SAAMCO* has been standardly discussed more in tort courses and books than in contract courses and books—we would surely not regard the scope of the duty of care in the tort of negligence as turning on an objective interpretation of the parties' intentions. In tort, we would more naturally say that this is an external policy-based rule designed, as Lord Hoffmann himself expressed it in *SAAMCO*, to impose what is fair and reasonable between the parties. What goes for tort also goes for contract. The most natural interpretation is that these decisions are external policy-based decisions and are not agreement-centred.

V. CONCLUSION

The exclusionary and inclusionary qualifications of the standard reasonable contemplation test of remoteness in contract are best understood as policy-based and not as agreement-centred. The law on remoteness in contract is concerned to impose a fair and reasonable allocation of risk where the parties have not themselves done so in the contract (whether expressly or impliedly). The reasonable contemplation test of *Hadley v Baxendale* in general determines the fair and reasonable allocation of risk. But it may

---

[55] ibid 212.

[56] ibid 214.

[57] A Burrows, *Remedies for Torts and Breach of Contract* (3rd edn, Oxford, Oxford University Press, 2004) 112.

[58] This is not to suggest that I agree with the decision. In my view, and in line with the criticisms set out ibid 109–22, the better view is that the valuers had 'assumed responsibility' for the losses claimed.

be qualified so as to extend recovery (the inclusionary effect) where the whole purpose of the duty is to guard against the risk of the type of loss that has occurred. And where the type of loss is so exceptional in relation to the standard purpose of the duty, it may be qualified to limit recovery (the exclusionary effect) because, even though the defendant has the requisite knowledge of the particular risk, the loss is, for example, wholly dispropor-tionate compared to the price or there has been no adjustment of the price to take account of the risk.

Although I have throughout used Lord Hoffmann's language of an 'assumption of responsibility', it follows from that conclusion that it may be better if that language were abandoned precisely because it gives the misleading impression that remoteness is agreement-centred. Without very careful handling, it is likely to mislead the courts if, instead of asking them to impose a fair and reasonable risk allocation taking into account specified factors and subject to contracting out, we ask them to determine whether there has been 'an assumption of responsibility'.[59]

Lord Hoffmann chose not to bow out in a quiet way and *The Achilleas* made the loudest noise of all. For those of us who have devoted many happy hours to interpreting and admiring Lord Hoffmann's rich prose and out-standing reasoning, there is a deep sense of loss with his 'retirement'. Quiet or loud, his judgments were never dull.

---

[59] For criticism of the language of a 'voluntary assumption of responsibility' in the context of pure economic loss in the tort of negligence, see K Barker, 'Unreliable Assumptions in the Modern Law of Negligence' (1993) 109 *LQR* 461.

15

Lord Hoffmann, Tax Law and Principles

JUDITH FREEDMAN

I. INTRODUCTION

IN THE REALM of tax law, as in other areas discussed in this book, Lord Hoffmann's strongest theme has been one of purposive construction. Lord Hoffmann helped to review and revise the judicial approach to tax avoidance at a time when it had moved away from purposive construction towards a judicial rule of doubtful propriety (the so-called 'Ramsay principle').[1] At one point, however, Lord Hoffmann's explanation of his approach to construction threatened to create another type of formula—a distinction between commercial and juristic concepts, which proved to be impractical. What might have worked if always in his expert hands would not necessarily work in the hands of others. An approach that cannot be applied at all levels of the legal system is unlikely to be a sensible way forward.

There is a tendency amongst lower courts, and those on the ground who have to implement legislation, to look for concrete rules and formulaic guidance. Purposive construction alone may appear to give rise to uncertainty, especially in an area where the purpose of the legislation can be elusive. In such circumstances, references to 'economic' or 'commercial' concepts do not provide the kind of guidance that is sought. This means that, despite the serious intellectual effort and judicial focus that have been brought to bear on the problem of construing tax legislation to give effect to the intention of

---

[1] The *Ramsay* principle emerged *in WT Ramsay Ltd v Inland Revenue Commissioners* [1982] AC 300 (HL) and was subsequently developed in a series of cases. For articles analysing the way in which the case law developed, see, eg, J Freedman, 'Defining Taxpayer Responsibility: In Support of a General Anti-avoidance Principle' [2004] *British Tax Review* 332; E Simpson, 'The Ramsay Principle: A Curious Incident of Judicial Reticence?' [2004] *British Tax Review* 358; J Tiley, 'Tax Avoidance Jurisprudence as Normal Law' [2004] *British Tax Review* 304; J Freedman, 'Interpreting Tax Statutes: Tax Avoidance and the Intention of Parliament' (2007) 123 *LQR* 53; M Gammie, 'Moral Taxation, Immoral Avoidance—What Role for the Law?' [2013] *British Tax Review* 577.

Parliament, the case law on tax avoidance remains unsatisfactory and resort is frequently taken to legislative 'solutions'.

Very often these legislative solutions take the form of specified tax avoidance provisions, but the apparent inability of the judiciary to solve the tax avoidance problem has led also to the introduction of a statutory general anti-abuse rule (GAAR). Lord Hoffmann participated in a study group advising on the development and adoption of a UK GAAR.[2] This suggests an acceptance that the judiciary cannot tackle the problem of tax avoidance resulting from abuse of tax legislation without assistance. The legislative approach in the GAAR is not, however, one that relieves judges of the need to look at the purpose of the legislation. In fact, it requires them to look very carefully at the purpose of the legislation, but provides a framework to guide them in this difficult endeavour and, in certain circumstances, allows them to go beyond the confines of pure purposive construction as it is usually applied in the UK. This solution neatly frames Lord Hoffmann's views of the role of the judiciary in such cases.

This chapter commences in Part II by examining the problem of finding principles in tax legislation. Part III examines Lord Hoffmann's views on statutory construction in a tax context. Against this background, Part IV discusses Lord Hoffmann's contribution to the case law on the judicial approach to tax avoidance. In the light of this discussion, Part V reviews the limits of purposive construction and the need for a GAAR. Part V concludes.

II. HUNTING FOR TAX PRINCIPLES

Tax law is sometimes seen as an area devoid of principle: those who are not involved in tax law (and, even more worryingly, many tax practitioners and some revenue officials and draftsmen) tend to think of it only as a mass of technical detail. It is an area where clear principles are badly needed, but are not always present. The underlying tax policy is often incoherent as well as very complex, so that the application of logic does not always offer a solution. The ultimate objective should always be to raise revenue, of course, but beyond that there may be many different and frequently conflicting objectives.[3] Redistribution of wealth may be a primary objective of taxation for some and less significant for others. Taxation may be seen as a legitimate device to subsidise taxpayers with certain needs, and most

---

[2] Lord Hoffmann was a member of the Aaronson Study Group which put forward a proposal for a statutory anti-abuse provision at the request of the UK Government. See G Aaronson, 'GAAR Study: A Study to Consider Whether a General Anti-avoidance Rule Should Be Introduced into the UK Tax System' (Report) (November 2011) http://webarchive.nationalarchives.gov.uk/20130605083650/http://www.hm-treasury.gov.uk/d/gaar_final_report_111111.pdf (hereinafter the Aaronson Report). The author was also a member of that study group. The proposed legislation was subsequently enacted in the Finance Act 2013.

[3] There is a vast literature on this topic, but for a convenient modern summary, see S Adam et al (eds), *Tax by Design: The Mirrlees Review* (Oxford, Oxford University Press, 2011).

twenty-first-century policy makers will consider that tax liability should reflect ability to pay. Tax is frequently used to encourage certain forms of behaviour, such as investment, saving, environmentally friendly energy use and even riding a bicycle to work. Some taxes aim to discourage certain behaviours, such as drinking alcohol, smoking or eating sugar. Tax law is also used to assist some efforts to manage the macro-economy as well as to allocate revenues between sovereign states.

Sometimes these objectives conflict: a tax which really did prevent smoking would reduce revenue substantially. Frequently, efficiency of taxation needs to be traded off against equity. This multiplicity of objectives creates complexity. Each objective needs to be balanced against an often expressed desire for simplicity in taxation. This process of trade-offs is described by economists as optimal tax theory.[4] In practice, this weighing-up process rarely takes place in a complete manner, if at all, and, when these issues are considered, the policy makers do not start with a clean sheet of paper. Often there are too many political pressures for any serious consideration of the fundamentals. So sometimes there are no clear objectives and, even where they are clear, they may clash with other objectives within the tax system as a whole. Further, objectives that are perfectly clear in a straightforward case may be difficult to implement or target. This confusion surrounds not only the creation of new taxes but also the addition of new reliefs.

Politicians treat tax law as a political football and compete with each other to introduce one relief after the other. The National Audit Office (NAO) has reported that there are more than 1,000 reliefs in the UK tax system.[5] This is not a particularly useful figure, given that it covers a range of reliefs of very different types. Some are essential to define the tax base, such as the ability to deduct losses, whilst others are specific incentives to encourage certain behaviour, such as the allowance for individual savings accounts (ISAs). The NAO report does, however, underline the range and extent of complexity introduced into the UK tax system (as in many others) by the variety of tax incentives and other reliefs available. The Public Accounts Committee (PAC) under Margaret Hodge's leadership has been particularly vociferous in criticising the proliferation of tax reliefs, having seen how many of the tax schemes that the PAC considers unacceptable have been based on such reliefs.[6] Even though a relief may appear to have a clear economic objective, as soon as the policy descends into practicalities, questions may arise which start to muddy the waters, and the reliefs start to be used for purposes not initially envisaged by the policy makers.

There is often pressure on civil servants and other policy advisers from ministers to find 'quick wins' and tax changes that will appeal to the electorate at the annual budget. This annual budget event generates a proliferation

---

[4] ibid 35, paras 2.2.1 et seq.
[5] National Audit Office, 'Tax Reliefs' HC (2013–14) 1256.
[6] Report from the Committee of Public Accounts, 'Tax Reliefs' HC (2014–15) C 282 (incorporating HC (2013–14) 1155).

of unnecessary and often unprincipled changes, as politicians feel the need to be seen to be acting and advisers are required to provide them with ideas for this purpose. The Office of Tax Simplification, which was set up to review the tax system with simplification in mind, also seems all too often to be under pressure to come up with ideas that can be implemented quickly and will therefore inevitably be piecemeal.[7]

Even tax incentives that seem to have a good policy rationale are often poorly targeted. So, for example, loss-making businesses that need financial help may not be able to utilise tax incentives for investment because they have no taxable profits, so they may enter into an arrangement with a bank whereby the bank takes the tax benefit and shares it with the taxpayer in some form. The finance leasing industry was built on the use of tax incentives for investment in plant and machinery (capital allowances) in this way, with the bank purchasing the asset and claiming the allowance. The asset is then leased on to the business. Some of the tax benefit is enjoyed by the bank, but this may mean that the bank will provide finance on better terms than it otherwise would do, which may said to be within the original policy. It is just one more step from this for a bank to take the benefit of the relief in other circumstances where it would not be available directly to the taxpayer because the taxpayer does not satisfy some other condition. At what point the sharing by the banks of the advantages of the incentive tips over from being within the 'intention' of the legislation to being outside it is a difficult question. Does it depend on how much of the benefit the bank keeps for itself and how much it shares with the business? Can the arrangement extend to a sale and leaseback? The question that may arise for the courts in a tax avoidance scheme will be at what point the 'normal and accepted trade of finance leasing'[8] becomes something outside the purpose of the tax incentive-giving legislation. Experience has shown that this is an extremely difficult

---

[7] For details of the Office of Tax Simplification (OTS), see www.gov.uk/government/organisations/office-of-tax-simplification. As an example to illustrate the point in the text, the terms of reference for the OTS employment status review issued on 11 July 2014 refer expressly to 'quick wins' for the 2015 Budget, despite acknowledging that the report could recommend more significant reforms that would need to be left until after the 2015 General Election (see https://www.gov.uk/government/uploads/system/uploads/attachment_data/file/336881/Letter_from_OTS_to_XST_re_employment_status_and_tax_penalties_TORs.pdf). This seems to be an area where piecemeal reforms have already caused a great deal of trouble and where a holistic view is needed, especially as it needs to consider the relationship between tax and employment law.

[8] See *Barclays Mercantile Business Finance Ltd v Mawson (Inspector of Taxes)* 76 TC 446 (HC, CA and HL); [2004] UKHL 51 (hereinafter *BMBF*), in particular per Carnwath LJ in the Court of Appeal: 'the tax advantage, which is said to have infected the whole scheme, is one which is a normal and accepted part of BMBF's finance leasing trade. As the Judge [in the High Court, Park J as he was then] recognised, in this trade: "the obtaining of capital allowances for the leasing company's expenditure on acquiring the machinery or plant is fundamental. The lease rates are set at levels which assume that the lessor (or companies grouped with it) will benefit from the allowances. If the allowances are not obtained after all, the transaction ceases to make financial and commercial sense"'. [52] Civ 1853 [2002] EWCA.

line to draw and not one where looking at the underlying principles and the purpose of the legislation gives every reasonable person the same answer.

The response to this difficulty in targeting incentives has been to add anti-avoidance provisions when introducing the legislation, with further provisions as and when an adviser finds a way around the original provisions. This creates the perfect conditions for 'creative compliance', as Doreen McBarnet has called it.[9] This phrase captures the way in which the legislation can be carefully followed, but used in a way that transactions can be argued to be 'legal' and effective, despite the fact that some, even most, observers would believe they undermine the purpose of that legislation. One of the best ways to create a good scheme for reducing tax is to take the carefully crafted and therefore watertight anti-avoidance legislation and stand it on its head by using it for a different purpose from that envisaged.[10] Nevertheless, policy makers continue to encrust new provisions with anti-avoidance provisions, based on the knowledge that new reliefs often result in new tax avoidance methods.

The creation of poorly targeted tax incentives can create honest confusion about the way in which incentives that have been deliberately granted can be used and the limits on that use. Further, anti-avoidance provisions may create problems for those engaged in complex transactions entered into for genuine commercial purposes. These transactions may become complicated, even convoluted, because the underlying tax law is not fit for purpose and fails to prevent double taxation or fails to provide for the circumstances that have arisen. At other times, a complex structure is needed for regulatory or other reasons. The interaction of the anti-avoidance provisions with other circumstances can create confusion.

The result of this process of legislating and then adding wide anti-avoidance provisions is that tax advisers complain of uncertainty and the traps for the unwary that arise when a system is complex. Recent years have seen an increase in consultation, which has been welcomed by many practitioners and can remove some difficulties, but consultation can also create further complexity, and ultimately greater uncertainty, despite the declared aim being the opposite effect.[11] The reaction of practitioners consulted on draft legislation is generally to suggest adding detail to cover this or that

---

[9] D McBarnet and C Whelan, 'The Elusive Sprit of the Law: Formalism and the Struggle for Legal Control' (1991) 54 *MLR* 848.

[10] See, eg, s 127 of the Taxation of the Chargeable Gains Act 1992 (TCGA), interpreted in *Harrison v Nairn Williamson Ltd* 51 TC 135, [1978] STC 67 (CA) as applying when there is an acquisition of an asset with no disposal. Although this was a win for the Revenue on the facts of that case, following this decision, the market value rule was frequently manipulated to the taxpayer's advantage. Section 17(2) TCGA was then introduced to restrict the operation of the market value rule (see HMRC, 'CG14550—Market Value Rule: Acquisition No Disposal: Disposal No Acquisition' (Capital Gains Tax Manual) TCGA92/S17 www.hmrc.gov.uk/manuals/cgmanual/cg14550.htm).

[11] HMRC, *The New Approach to Tax Policy Making* (December 2010) http://webarchive.nationalarchives.gov.uk/20130129110402/http:/www.hm-treasury.gov.uk/d/tax_policy_making_response.pdf.pdf.

point in the hope that this gives them precision. This runs counter to all experience—our tax legislation is close to being the longest in the world and we still need many pages of extra-statutory guidance of dubious status.[12] This hardly suggests that detail will solve the problem of lack of certainty, but the practitioners seem convinced that this is the correct way to proceed. Parliamentary draftsmen naturally respond to this message by adopting a detailed rather than a principles-based approach to drafting.[13] Thus, it is much easier to talk about having a tax system based on clear principles than to implement that idea.

III. LORD HOFFMANN'S VIEWS ON STATUTORY CONSTRUCTION, PRINCIPLES AND POLICY

The lack of principle and difficulty in targeting legislation described in the previous section of this chapter makes tax an unwieldy area for any judge, but in particular for one who, like Lord Hoffmann, believes in the primacy of construction and the search for principle in answering the question of how to interpret the legislation.[14] Whilst this approach clearly goes beyond pure literal interpretation, this does not mean that using this method opens the way for the judge to impose his own views on what the outcome should be; this remains a matter of statutory construction. In Lord Hoffmann's memorable phrase in the *Norglen* case:

> If [tax avoidance schemes] do not work, the reason, as my noble and learned friend Lord Steyn pointed out in *IRC v McGuckian*, [1997] 1 WLR 991, 1000, is simply that upon the true construction of the statute, the transaction which was designed to avoid the charge to tax actually comes within it. It is not that the statute has a penumbral spirit which strikes down devices or stratagems designed to avoid its terms or exploit its loopholes. There is no need for such spooky jurisprudence.[15]

According to Lord Hoffmann, he is searching for principle and not policy, in the sense in which Dworkin sets out that distinction in *Law's Empire*.[16] Lord Hoffmann has explained further his understanding of this distinction as follows: 'a principle which entitles a litigant to judgment should not be overridden by judges on grounds of utilitarian calculation'.[17]

---

[12] As to the status of extra-statutory guidance in tax law, see J Freedman and J Vella, 'HMRC's Management of the UK Tax System: The Boundaries of Legitimate Discretion' in J Freedman, C Evans and R Krever (eds), *The Delicate Balance: Revenue Authority Discretions and the Rule of Law* (Amsterdam, IBFD, 2011).

[13] J Freedman, 'Improving (Not Perfecting) Tax Legislation: Rules and Principles Revisited' [2010] *British Tax Review* 717.

[14] This approach is explained in Lord Hoffmann's review of S Lee, *Judging Judges* (London, Faber, 1989) in (1989) 105 *LQR* 140; see Lord Hoffmann in *Kleinwort Benson Ltd v Lincoln City Council* [1999] 2 AC 349 (HL) 401 (discussed by F Wilmot-Smith in ch 16 of this volume).

[15] *Norglen Ltd (in Liquidation) and Reeds Rains Prudential Ltd* [1999] 2 AC 1 (HL) 14.

[16] R Dworkin, *Law's Empire* (Oxford, Hart Publishing, 1998) chs 6 and 7.

[17] Hoffmann (1989) (n 14) 143; Dworkin (n 16) esp 244.

Dworkin's concept of principle rests on the idea of integrity. He comments that: 'The judge's decision—his post interpretive conclusions—must be drawn from the interpretation that both fits and justifies what has gone before, so far as this is possible.'[18] One critic, James Lee, writing on a different area, has suggested that: 'If integrity is a question of keeping the faith, then ... Lord Hoffmann has heretical tendencies.'[19] Lee argues that Lord Hoffmann's treatment of precedent (in the two cases that Lee discusses)[20] 'seems to view interpretation as a teleological process: reasoning backwards from the desired result (the justificatory principle) and making the cases fit the instant decision'.[21]

This description has resonances with the tax avoidance cases in which Lord Hoffmann has been involved. Lord Hoffmann has even stated, extrajudicially, that in developing and applying the *Ramsay*[22] line of cases on tax avoidance, the 'House had to rewrite history in a way which struck some people as a little disingenuous' and agreed that 'a sleight of hand covered this retreat to constitutional propriety'.[23]

Lord Hoffmann was not alone in this exercise, however. Indeed, the House of Lords in the leading case *of Barclays Mercantile Business Finance Ltd v Mawson (BMBF)*[24] was unanimous that the *Ramsay* line of cases had to be reviewed. The process undertaken has been described by Mummery LJ[25] as 'a significant judicial stocktaking of the "new approach" to the construction of revenue statutes first applied in *Ramsay*'. Mummery LJ recognised that the aim in the speech delivered by Lord Nicholls in *BMBF* was to 'achieve some clarity about basic principles', whilst recognising that it was:

> [T]oo much to expect that any exposition will remove all difficulties in the application of the principles because it is in the nature of questions of construction that there will be borderline cases about which people have different views.[26]

Lord Hoffmann would argue, no doubt, that in this process of 'judicial stocktaking', or reassessing the case law, he was seeking the original meaning

---

[18] Dworkin (n 6) 239.

[19] J Lee, 'Fidelity in Interpretation: Lord Hoffmann and the Adventure of the Empty House' (2008) 28 *Legal Studies* 1.

[20] The cases discussed by Lee (ibid) are *Barker v Corus* [2006] UKHL 20, [2006] 2 AC 572 (causation in tort) and *Barlow Clowes v Eurotrust International* [2005] UKPC 37, [2006] 1 All ER 333 (dishonest assistance).

[21] Lee (n 19) 5.

[22] *Ramsay* (n 1). This case is explained in more detail in Part IV below.

[23] L Hoffmann, 'Tax Avoidance' [2005] *British Tax Review* 197, 202–03.

[24] *BMBF* (n 8). Lord Steyn in *IRC v McGuckian* [1997] 1 WLR 991, [1997] STC 908 (HL) 916 had also been forceful in emphasising that the principle in *Ramsay* was based on 'an orthodox form of statutory interpretation' and that 'in asserting the power to examine the substance of a composite transaction the House of Lords was simply rejecting formalism in fiscal matters and choosing a more realistic legal analysis'. However, it was not until *Westmoreland* was decided in 2001 that the point really took hold.

[25] *Mayes v HMRC* [2011] EWCA Civ 407, [2011] 81 TC 247.

[26] *BMBF* (n 8) [27].

of the initial case in the chain, which had become distorted. He would say that he, and his judicial colleagues, were only returning to the origins of that case and that it was only the intervening cases that required a little judicial 're-writing' to make them fit the thesis.

This is plausible, though not in line with the commentaries on *Ramsay* at the time of that decision and those immediately following. Whilst their Lordships in *Ramsay* denied creating a new principle, they were intent on establishing a new approach, with Lord Wilberforce stating that 'While the techniques of tax avoidance progress and are technically improved, the courts are not obliged to stand still' and 'it would be an excess of judicial abstinence to withdraw from the field now before us'.[27]

The House of Lords in *Ramsay* had come up with the idea of looking at a composite transaction rather than applying the law step by step, and this was developed further in subsequent cases. To many, this looked very like a judicial principle and, if it was not, to what 'basic principles' was Lord Nicholls referring in *BMBF* when he described the wish to give them clarity? Were these really merely the principles of statutory construction?

Despite the fact that Lord Hoffmann and his judicial colleagues claimed they were doing no more than getting back to the 'normal' principles of statutory construction in *BMBF*, this has not been operationally straightforward in later cases and arguably has not proved successful, as explained below. Commentators have persisted in trying to find something more. The courts have also frequently appeared to search for some other prescription to enable them to reach the answer they seek intuitively. There are some members of the judiciary who are prepared to hunt for that something more—a general overriding 'principle'. Others do not think this is appropriate. We might characterise these two views as wide purposive interpretation and narrow purposive interpretation. The supporters of the narrow form look at the wording of the legislation and search for its meaning, whilst supporters of wide purposive interpretation may be prepared to support that search with a judicially created principle of a more general nature. In the tax avoidance context, this latter approach might, for example, involve analysing a transaction as a composite one and then, simply by virtue of the fact that this can be done, applying the legislation to the composite rather than to individual steps. The narrow approach permits this only where the wording and context of the legislation contain signals permitting that mode of application. The wide approach looks for a general principle, while the narrow approach looks for a specific principle arising from the legislation. Critics of the wide approach would argue that it goes beyond the limits of proper purposive construction and moves into judicial legislation.

The case law in this area highlights the difficulty of finding the narrow principle or statutory purpose when the statutes in question are so complex and the subject matter is so artificial in nature. The hunt for a principle of

---

[27] *Ramsay* (n 1) 326–27 (Lord Wilberforce).

this nature can seem hopeless. The temptation to skip directly to a more utilitarian calculation is then very great indeed and if there is a device such as an apparent general overriding principle that can help the judges to do this, then it is not surprising to find them resorting to that.

The UK GAAR may be seen as an attempt to provide an overriding principle, or set of principles, that can supplement purposive construction to give guidance in this difficult process. It has been argued by some that the judiciary could, and should, have found a way of achieving the same result purely by careful statutory analysis.[28] The GAAR recognises the need for statutory assistance in the crafting of a general principle and giving it legitimacy. Continuing experience suggests that the judicial process alone was never going to achieve a stable case law base. There would always be judicial willingness to be creative from some,[29] coupled with judicial resistance to anything that could be seen as going beyond the narrow purposive approach from others.[30] As Graham Aaronson QC put it:

> Judges inevitably are faced with the temptation to stretch the interpretation, so far as possible, to achieve a sensible result; and this is widely regarded as producing considerable uncertainty in predicting the outcome of such disputes. In practice this uncertainty spreads from the highly abusive cases into the centre ground of responsible tax planning. A GAAR specifically targeted at abusive schemes would help reduce the risk of stretched interpretation and the uncertainty which this entails.[31]

It is entirely consistent with Lord Hoffmann's view of the role of principles that it has been found necessary to introduce a statutory GAAR that legitimates the process of going beyond purposive construction in defined circumstances rather than relying on a judicial rule of uncertain constitutionality.

IV. 'REALITY', 'ECONOMIC EFFECT' AND 'COMMERCIAL MEANING'

A. The Tax Avoidance Chain of Cases

The judicial role in combating tax avoidance has a long history. The *Ramsay* case referred to above,[32] which some claimed to have established a new

---

[28] See, eg, Simpson (n 1).

[29] See, eg, *Tower MCashback LLP 1 v Revenue and Customs Commissioners* [2011] UKSC 19, [2011] AC 457 (hereinafter *Tower*) and *Flanagan, Moyles, Stennett v HMRC* [2014] UKFTT 175 (TC), where the decisions are supposedly based on purposive construction, but also take a great deal of note of the fact that there were pre-ordained transactions and view the facts 'realistically'.

[30] *Mayes* (n 25) above might be seen as the classic example of this resistance, as discussed further below. See also *Hancock v HMRC* [2014] UKFTT 695. Both cases cited Lord Hoffmann's statement (n 23) that 'sometimes there are holes in the net and the courts find that they cannot plug them by appealing to the economic event which, at a higher level of generality, it appears that Parliament wished to tax'.

[31] Aaronson Report (n 2) para 1.7(iii).

[32] *Ramsay* (n 1).

judicial approach to tax avoidance, was based on the self-contained legislation designed to tax capital gains.

A somewhat simplified version of the facts in *Ramsay* will help to highlight the issues under discussion here. The taxpayer acquired two loans, one of which (to a subsidiary company) was increased in value at the expense of the other (a loss that reflected in the value of shares in the subsidiary). The aim was that the profit on the sale of the first loan would not be a chargeable gain for tax purposes because it was not a 'debt on a security' within the capital gains tax legislation, but the loss on the shares would be allowable and therefore could be set off against a pre-existing chargeable gain of the taxpayer within the structure of the capital gains tax regime. The overall transaction produced no economic change, but there was, if the scheme worked, a tax advantage. The scheme was purchased 'off the shelf'; that is, it was not tailor-made, but was devised and marketed to many taxpayers.

The question was whether gains and losses which ultimately balanced each other out economically could be treated as cancelling each other out for tax purposes, despite the technical argument that the loss was allowable but the gain was not taxable under the legislation. The legislation itself did not refer to the overall economic outcome, but the House of Lords managed to apply the law on the basis that no overall loss had arisen within the meaning of the legislation.[33] Lord Wilberforce stated that:

> The Capital Gains Tax was created to operate in the real world, not that of make-belief ... To say that a loss (or gain) which appears to arise at one stage in an indivisible process, and which is intended to be and is cancelled out by a later stage, so that at the end of what was bought as, and planned as, a single continuous operation, is not such a loss (or gain) as the legislation is dealing with, is in my opinion well, and indeed essentially, within the judicial function.[34]

The idea that the capital gains tax is created to operate in the 'real world' (whatever that is)[35] requires something of a leap. In the UK, capital gains tax is created and governed by a self-contained code with its own definitions of what constitutes a loss and a gain.[36] In truth, the decision in *Ramsay* focuses far more on the fact that it is looking at the scheme as a whole than on a detailed analysis of the statute. The result of this was that most contemporary commentators thought that the case was about introducing a new doctrine to tax law which involved looking at a scheme as

---

[33] The technical arguments in the case were also held to fail, so that the wider approach was not strictly necessary, but the wider reasoning was clearly expressed as the ratio of the case.

[34] *Ramsay* (n 1) 326.

[35] Lord Hoffmann has expressed doubts about references to 'reality', as discussed below.

[36] TCGA 1992. If one were really looking at 'economic effect', then many economists would argue that capital gains should be treated in the same way as income gains, but that is not what UK policy makers have chosen to do. See J Freedman, 'Treatment of Capital Gains and Losses' in P Essers and A Rijkers (eds), *The Notion of Income from Capital* (Amsterdam, IBFD, 2005).

whole and disregarding steps. Over the course of the following 15 years, the courts proceeded on that basis, apparently hardening the 'new approach' in *Ramsay* into a judge-made rule of some complexity, sometimes known as the 'principle' in *Furniss v Dawson*.[37]

The judicial formulations of the *Furniss v Dawson* principle specified the need to find a pre-ordained, circular, self-cancelling transaction undertaken for no commercial purpose other than obtaining a tax advantage. Each of these factors became something that acquired a gloss and precedents. As the factors rigidified, the formulation became increasingly easy to plan around, as do all firm lines.

It was this outcome that Lord Hoffmann rejected very clearly in *Mac-Niven v Westmoreland Investments Ltd* in 2001, saying that it looked like an overriding legal principle without regard to the language or purpose of any particular provision.[38] Of course, he was right and it is not clear that Lord Wilberforce in *Ramsay* had intended quite such a formulaic development. But getting back to that position after the twists and turns that the courts had taken was not straightforward, hence the need for ingenuity and some rewriting of history. This could be seen as a lack of consistency, but is better explained as a reworking of the case law in a way that sacrificed complete consistency with every case along the chain in order to get back to the origins of the principle, and for the sake of overall coherence of the law and a return to constitutional propriety.[39]

B. Juristic versus Commercial: The 'Supposed Dichotomy'

Following the decision in *Westmoreland*, the problem became how to apply the purposive approach that had supplanted the so-called *Ramsay* principle. Was it purely normal statutory construction or was there a special element in the tax cases still, given the difficulties of finding purpose in tax legislation and the need to inhibit tax avoidance? At this point, the cases threatened to take a wrong turning, partly because Lord Hoffmann was applying an approach that worked for him, but that was not easily translatable into a

---

[37] *Furniss v Dawson* [1984] AC 474 (HL).

[38] *MacNiven (Inspector of Taxes) v Westmoreland Investments Ltd* [2001] UKHL 6 [2003] 1 AC 311 (HL). (hereinafter *Westmoreland*).

[39] Lee (n 19) 5, citing N MacCormick, *Rhetoric and the Rule of Law* (Oxford, Oxford University Press, 2006), is critical of Hoffmann's 'quasi-Dworkinian reasoning' in the cases he is considering, stating that it relies too much on an individual conception of coherence. However, in *Westmoreland* (ibid) and the subsequent case of *BMBF* (n 8), it was clear that the other members of the House of Lords panel shared Lord Hoffmann's concerns and were prepared to go along with his reasoning in order to return to a position that all members considered to have greater constitutional propriety than the one being claimed by proponents of the judge-made principle.

general rule of statutory construction based on the wording and context of the legislation. For a time, as explained further below, Lord Hoffmann was taken to have developed an alternative principle requiring a priori classification of concepts as 'juristic' or 'commercial'. This was said to come from the legislation itself, and so ostensibly fitted the narrow purposive approach rather than a wider one. But the link with the wording was not always easy to find, leading to a concern that this arose not so much from a hunt for a principle in the legislation as an application of intuition.

In *Westmoreland*, Lord Hoffmann expressed the view that:

> The innovation in the *Ramsay* case was to give the statutory concepts of 'disposal' and 'loss' a commercial meaning. The new principle of construction was a recognition that the statutory language was intended to refer to commercial concepts, so that in the case of a concept such as 'disposal', the court was required to take a view of the facts which transcended the juristic individuality of the various parts of a preplanned series of transactions.[40]

Some of those who felt that in *Westmoreland* they had lost the comfort of the *Ramsay* principle as it had developed in its rigid, possibly unconstitutional form, seized upon the dichotomy between the 'commercial' and the 'juristic' interpretation of words suggested in that case as a new 'overriding principle' to be applied. It can be said with reasonable assurance that this was not what Lord Hoffmann had meant at all.[41] He had seen his comments as an explanation of purposive construction, and guidance on how to determine whether the context permitted the court to look at the overall economic effect, but just like the explanation of how to approach these issues given by Lord Wilberforce in *Ramsay*, Lord Hoffmann's explanation too threatened to become formulaic. Unsurprisingly, it very soon became apparent that this was not a formula that could lead to any certainty, since the same word could lead to different conclusions in different contexts.[42] This is obvious when it is seen as part of the exercise of purposive construction, but was puzzling for those seeking a generally applicable rule.

---

[40] *Westmoreland* (n 38) [32].

[41] Indeed, in a talk to the International Fiscal Association in 2003, Lord Hoffmann reportedly said that 'his judgment in *MacNiven* had been much misinterpreted, to his dismay, as substituting one solve all magic formula (the "pure" *Ramsay* doctrine) for another (the juristic: commercial concept)': see P Way, 'The Ramsay Principle—Where are We Now?' *GITC Review*, Vol III No 2 (2004) www.taxbar.com/documents/ramsey_principle_pw_000.pdf.

[42] For example, see contemporaneous comment on the contrast between the meaning of 'paid' in *Westmoreland* (n 38) (juristic) and that of 'payment' (commercial) in *DTE Financial Services Ltd v Wilson (Inspector of Taxes)* [2001] EWCA Civ 455, (2001) 74 TC 14 A. A Roycroft, 'And "Payment" Means ...' *Taxation* (28 June 2001) www.taxation.co.uk/taxation/articles/2001/06/28/1137/and-payment-means.

Almost inevitably, therefore, this new formulation began to cause problems. One sparring partner of Lord Hoffmann's in this area, Lord Templeman, described the supposed commercial/juristic distinction as 'reflecting ingenuity but not principle'.[43] The formulation was criticised by the lower courts in *BMBF* and the criticisms reached Hong Kong, where Lord Millett,[44] a progenitor of the original *Ramsay* principle but by this time retired from the UK courts, was able to intervene from a distance. He took up the point in *Collector of Stamp Revenue v Arrowtown*,[45] where he commented:

> The supposed dichotomy between legal and commercial concepts has caused great difficulty. In *Barclays Mercantile* neither Peter Gibson LJ nor Carnwath LJ could understand it, and counsel were unable to explain it. Nor is its source discernible. It makes no previous appearance in the many authorities in which *Ramsay* has been applied.[46]

Lord Millet accepted that Lord Hoffmann might have been doing nothing more than supporting purposive interpretation, but he went on to remark that 'his speech has had most unfortunate consequences. It has led to arid debate in an endeavour to fit the statutory language into one or other conceptual category.'[47]

On the one hand, it could be said that it was unfair to blame Lord Hoffmann for the misunderstandings of the commentators. On the other hand, perhaps a judge should predict that advisers will seize on his every word and might misinterpret what he says, particularly in an area where there is a thirst for certainty and a near-impossibility of providing such comfort. If decided cases at the highest level do not give adequate guidance to lower courts, tribunals and the officials who have to operate the law on an everyday basis, then even a decision that is right on its facts and specific analysis has failed to perform a vital function. The commercial/juristic distinction was not a test with a predictive function. In any event, in *BMBF*, the House of Lords, with Lord Hoffmann participating, clarified the position and

---

[43] Lord Templeman, 'Tax and the Taxpayer' (2001) 117 *LQR* 575, 582.

[44] Lord Millett had appeared as the QC for the Inland Revenue in both *Ramsay* and *Furniss v Dawson* and has been responsible for introducing some of the more radical ideas into those cases, including references to the US cases on form and substance and the step doctrine: see P Millett, 'A New Approach to Tax Avoidance Schemes' (1982) 98 *LQR* 209; J Tiley, 'Judicial Anti-avoidance Doctrines: The US Alternatives' (Pts I and II) [1987] *British Tax Review* 180 and 220. Lord Hoffmann has expressed his view that whilst the House of Lords in *Ramsay* (n 1) did not accept these concepts ('Lord Wilberforce handled them gingerly'), after *Furniss v Dawson* 'it appeared that the full-blooded American doctrine had been imported into the UK': see Hoffmann (n 23) 200.

[45] *Collector of Stamp Revenue v Arrowtown Assets Ltd* [2003] HKCFA 46, (2004) 1 HKLRD 77.

[46] ibid [148].

[47] ibid [150].

removed the idea that this description of the analysis of words in a statute was intended to be an overriding principle of some kind:

> *MacNiven* shows the need to focus carefully upon the particular statutory provision and to identify its requirements before one can decide whether circular payments or elements inserted for the purpose of tax avoidance should disregarded or treated as irrelevant for the purposes of the statute. In the speech of Lord Hoffmann in *MacNiven* it was said that if a statute laid down requirements by reference to some commercial concept such as gain or loss, it would usually follow that elements inserted into a composite transaction without any commercial purpose could be disregarded, whereas if the requirements of the statute were purely by reference to its legal nature (in *MacNiven*, the discharge of a debt) then an act having that legal effect would suffice, whatever its commercial purpose may have been. This is not an unreasonable generalisation, indeed perhaps something of a truism, but we do not think that it was intended to provide a substitute for a close analysis of what the statute means. It certainly does not justify the assumption that an answer can be obtained by classifying all concepts a priori as either 'commercial' or 'legal'. That would be the very negation of purposive construction: see Ribeiro PJ in *Arrowtown* at paras 37 and 39.[48]

C. Commercial Meaning and 'Reality'

Despite the fact that the 'commercial'/'juristic' dichotomy failed as a useful tool for providing guidance in tax avoidance cases, it remains important in understanding Lord Hoffmann's approach to statutory interpretation in tax cases. Lord Hoffmann has complained frequently about the tendency of UK tax legislation to resort to a mass of detailed rules rather than putting faith in the courts to recognise economic effect. He has said extra-judicially:

> I am not one of those who heaps criticisms upon parliamentary draughtsmen. I think that they usually do an excellent job in trying to translate their instructions into legally-effective language. It is the instructions that concern me. To understand the general economic effect of transactions which one intends to tax is usually relatively easy. To understand the intricate and multifarious forms which some of them can take is often much more difficult. But the Revenue appear to have no faith in the ability or willingness of the courts to recognise the economic effect beneath the varied forms and often prefer to legislate by reference to form rather than substance. In those circumstances, it is essential that those instructing the draughtsman should have a complete understanding of the way that particular activity is conducted. Before anyone can sit down to draft such a statute, it is necessary to be clear about what the Revenue wish to achieve.[49]

Lord Hoffmann recognises that, where the legislation has been drafted by reference to form, it is pointless to look for 'economic principles' or a

---

[48] *BMBF* (n 8) [38].
[49] Hoffmann (n 23) 206.

'commercial concept' and that very often this is not the fault of the draftsman, but the result of a policy failure or confusion, as described at the beginning of this chapter. Tax law is not always based on economic outcome—it may be very artificial at its heart. The fact that Lord Hoffmann sometimes finds that he cannot apply a commercial meaning illustrates his recognition of this fact.

One question is how the concept of looking for the commercial meaning of a word (where appropriate in the context) differs from simply overlaying the legislation with an overriding principle requiring the courts to look at 'reality' or 'economic substance'. Lord Hoffmann was at pains to point out in *Westmoreland*[50] that he was not simply talking about 'reality', and he pointed out the dangers of references to 'reality'. Commenting on the speeches in *Ramsay* that refer to the 'real' nature of a transaction, he has said:

> These expressions are illuminating in their context, but you have to be careful about the sense in which they are being used. Otherwise you land in all kinds of unnecessary philosophical difficulties about the nature of reality and, in particular, about how a transaction can be said not to be a 'sham' and yet be 'disregarded' for the purpose of deciding what happened in 'the real world'. The point to hold onto is that something may be real for one purpose but not for another. When people speak of something being a 'real' something, they mean that it falls within some concept which they have in mind, by contrast with something else which might have been thought to do so, but does not ... Thus in saying that the transactions in *Ramsay* were not sham transactions, one is accepting the juristic categorisation of the transactions as individual and discrete and saying that each of them involved no pretence. They were intended to do precisely what they purported to do. They had a legal reality. But in saying that they did not constitute a 'real' disposal giving rise to a 'real' loss, one is rejecting the juristic categorisation as not being necessarily determinative for the purposes of the statutory concepts of 'disposal' and 'loss' as properly interpreted. The contrast here is with a commercial meaning of these concepts. And in saying that the income tax legislation was intended to operate 'in the real world', one is again referring to the commercial context which should influence the construction of the concepts used by Parliament.[51]

In other words, 'reality' as an abstract concept is not helpful; it assists only as part of a process of construction with the commercial context influencing the reading of the statute.[52] If the concepts used by Parliament do not permit a construction that applies the commercial context and accords with the judge's sense of 'reality', then he must abandon 'reality' as he understands it and rely on the construct before him, however artificial that might appear to be in commercial or economic terms.

---

[50] *Westmoreland* (n 38).
[51] ibid [40].
[52] ibid [40] and [41]. Lord Hoffmann does not eschew references to economic reality himself, but he uses them within the context of detailed statutory analysis, as in *Jerome v Kelley* [2004] UKHL 25, STC 887, where he examined the history of the TCGA 1992 in detail in reaching his decision about the meaning of some difficult wording on the question of who had made a disposal for capital gains tax purposes.

It might have been hoped that *BMBF* would have settled the position for good, but ironically we have seen yet another 'formula' emerging via the *BMBF* case, and one that refers to 'reality'. The phrase in question, which some have started to turn into a detailed prescription, was cited in *BMBF*, taken from the very *Arrowtown* case that criticised Lord Hoffmann's supposed formula.[53] It is the result, once again, not of the original judges wishing to impose a formula, but of the tax bar and other practitioners being eager to adopt one, and subsequent judges accepting this. This formulation came from Mr Justice Ribeiro, who almost certainly did not intend to lay down a prescription for the future, but was merely summarising the position as he understood it. Nevertheless, every subsequent tax avoidance case seems to contain this quote: 'The ultimate question is whether the relevant statutory provisions, construed purposively, were intended to apply to the transaction, viewed realistically.'[54]

This might sound unexceptional enough, and at least has an express reference to purposive construction, but some courts seem to have taken the invitation to review the transaction 'realistically' as taking them considerably further than normal purposive construction would go, despite the fact that they always make sure to refer to the need to analyse the statute.[55] Many of the cases are still heavily influenced by the existence of pre-ordained transactions and circularity, and tend towards disregarding transactions or elements of transactions that have no commercial purpose, in reliance on the supposed tests in *Furniss v Dawson*,[56] despite the rejection of these as tests or even principles of construction in *Westmoreland* and *BMBF*.[57] There is a tendency towards what Lord Hoffmann might call 'utilitarian calculation'.[58] The tension between the narrow and the wider view of purposive construction continues.

V. GOING FORWARD: THE NEED FOR GUIDANCE

A. The Limits of Purposive Construction

The rejection of 'spooky jurisprudence' in favour of primacy of construction and a search for principle amounts to a rejection of formulae and judge-made

---

[53] *Arrowtown* (n 45).

[54] ibid [35].

[55] See, eg, *Tower* (n 29). On the question of whether there was 'expenditure' within the meaning of the legislation arising in that case, the Special Commissioner (Howard Nowlan) and the Supreme Court decided against the taxpayer, viewing the facts 'realistically', but the judge in the High Court, Henderson J and the Court of Appeal judges would have found for the taxpayer, showing the extent of the differences in opinion amongst the judiciary in this area. It is notable that Howard Nowlan and Henderson J were both members of the Aaronson Study Group (see n 2) which recommended a GAAR (alongside Lord Hoffmann).

[56] *Furniss v Dawson* (n 37).

[57] *Westmoreland* (n 38) [49]; *BMBF* (n 8) [36]; and more recently *Hancock* (n 30).

[58] Hoffmann (1989) (n 14).

tests in tax avoidance cases. Unfortunately, the courts need rather more direction than Lord Hoffmann sometimes admits in his judgments in deciding how to approach the legislation they are applying. Attempts by the judges to provide such guidance have backfired or produced judge-made rules that have then had to be dismantled and denied. Replacement judicial guidance has caused confusion and uncertainty.

Pure purposive construction of tax legislation without any resort to a gloss or an overriding principle to fill gaps and produce sensible answers may result in some results which run counter to the intuition of the judiciary. The judicial dismay at having to come to such decisions is clear, especially at a time like the present when there is severe criticism of complex tax avoidance schemes. This is particularly apparent where there is a failure of those proposing and producing tax legislation to base the legislation on clear objectives and economic principles. There is sometimes little 'reality' in tax legislation, and what is meant by 'reality' can only ever be understood in a given context. If the objectives of the legislation are not properly articulated, the courts, viewing the facts 'realistically', may not ascertain the correct 'reality' for the legislation in question.

The major contribution of Lord Hoffmann's approach to construing tax legislation is not that it provides all the answers, but that it underlines the need for tax legislation to spell out the policy and principles on which it is based in order to give the courts the tools they need to work out the answers. The court cannot be expected to provide a formula to rescue poor legislation. If no underlying rationale based on economic substance can be found at all, then the hunt for economic substance in the legislation may require a stretching of the wording of the legislation, or a result which does not fit the scheme of the legislation. In some cases the result may be that the courts retreat behind literal interpretation. This was the outcome in *Mayes*,[59] where Mummery LJ was forced to admit that: 'This is legislation which does not seek to tax real or commercial gains. Thus it makes no sense to say that the legislation must be construed to apply to transactions by reference to their commercial substance.'[60] Toulson LJ concurred, but commented that it 'instinctively seems wrong, because it bears no relation to commercial reality and results in a windfall which Parliament cannot have foreseen or intended'.[61]

In this non-technical sense of Parliamentary intention,[62] effect could not be given to the intention of the legislature because of the poor quality of

---

[59] *Mayes* (n 25). In addition to *Mayes* and *Hancock* (n 30), see also *DB Group Services (UK) Ltd v HMRC* [2014] EWCA Civ 452, where the Court of Appeal overturned the Upper Tier Tax Tribunal on its application of the *Ramsay* principle and allowed the appeal in favour of the taxpayers.

[60] *Mayes* (n 25) [44].

[61] ibid [101].

[62] For further discussion of the jurisprudential meaning of parliamentary intention in a tax context, see Freedman (2007) (n 1).

the legislation. To criticise such legislation is not an argument for more detailed legislation to replace it, but rather a plea for tax legislation to give more direction as to underlying policy and to the principles to be applied.[63] Leaving the courts to look for the relevant 'effect' without any such direction leaves the courts with little choice. They must either apply legislation which has an outcome that permits tax avoidance or they have to create their own solution by stretching the legislation, which means leaving policy decisions to the unguided court, a solution that Lord Hoffmann has disavowed.

B. Statutory Intervention: The GAAR

It is consistent with his expressed philosophy that Lord Hoffmann has supported the introduction of a statutory anti-abuse rule, the GAAR. This has now been enacted in the Finance Act 2013[64] to provide the judiciary with properly based authority to go further than normal statutory construction would permit in specified cases and based on articulated principles. Critics argue that the GAAR principles are too vague, but as a member of the Aaronson Study Group, Lord Hoffmann appears to have been happy that they were adequate.[65] Having successfully operated similar provisions in Hong Kong, he seems to be content that the principles in the legislation are sufficient to be workable and justiciable.[66] The UK GAAR legislation gives express authority to look beyond the limits permitted by purposive construction and to apply an overriding principle, but it is an overriding principle within carefully defined statutory limits, so does not invite an unrestricted judicial gap-filling exercise based on intuition.[67]

---

[63] Freedman (n 13).

[64] Finance Act 2013, ss 206–15.

[65] The Aaronson Report (n 2) states at para 1.1: 'Subject to one reservation, the conclusions set out in this section, and developed in the rest of this Report, reflect the views of the Advisory Committee. The reservation is that the two members of the Advisory Committee who are serving judges in the United Kingdom (Sir Launcelot Henderson and Howard Nowlan) wish to maintain a position of strict public neutrality on the policy issues discussed in this Report, and therefore on the question whether or not a GAAR should be introduced. They do, however, agree with their colleagues on the Advisory Committee that, if a GAAR is to be introduced, a model of the type recommended in this Report appears to be the most suitable for adoption in the UK.'

[66] See, for example, Lord Hoffmann's judgment in *Commissioner of Inland Revenue v Tai Hing Cotton Mill (Development) Ltd* (FACV No 2/2007) [17], where he praised the Hong Kong GAAR in s 61A of the Hong Kong Inland Revenue Ordinance, Cap 112 as a 'powerful and flexible weapon'. See also [21], where Lord Hoffmann imposes what he sees to be sensible limits on the powers under this legislation.

[67] For more details on the UK GAAR and its operation, see J Freedman 'Designing a General Anti-abuse Rule: Striking a Balance' (2014) 20(3) *Asia-Pacific Tax Bulletin* 167 (International Bureau of Fiscal Documentation). The Aaronson Report (n 2) para 5.4 comments that the GAAR comes into action only if 'the arrangement would, on conventional purposive interpretation, succeed in achieving the advantageous tax result which it set out to obtain. The GAAR then provides an overriding statutory principle to which other tax legislation is subject'.

The operation of the UK GAAR is not going to be without difficulty because of the defects in the way in which the underlying tax law is conceived and formulated, as described by Lord Hoffmann above. Some have suggested that the statutory GAAR is intended to provide a formula to fill the gaps in shoddy legislation.[68] It is true that it provides some gap-filling tools and expressly allows shortcomings in legislation to be addressed, Yet the GAAR expressly refers the courts to the principles on which the legislative provisions are based and the policy objectives of those provisions. The GAAR requires the underlying legislation to have coherent underlying principles and policy if it is to be truly effective. In this sense, it should reinforce the need to produce better tax legislation rather than undermine this objective. As an overriding principle that gives the courts authority to go beyond normal principles of statutory construction, whilst still working within the framework of the substantive underlying legislation, this legislation takes on board Lord Hoffmann's objections to the formulaic version of the *Ramsay* principle produced in *Furniss v Dawson* and gives the courts the tools that they have been unsuccessfully trying to invent for themselves.

VI. CONCLUSION

Lord Hoffmann has been clear about the power of purposive construction in the context of tax law, as elsewhere, but also about its limitations. Whilst there is much that a judge can do, the legislature and policy makers must work with these judges to give them the tools they need to apply complex tax legislation in the circumstances described above. In the case of tax law, the objectives and underlying principles of the legislation can be severely lacking. One of Lord Hoffmann's most important contributions to tax law has been to rein back the creation of judge-made law that was attempting to deal with a problem that was beyond the ability of the courts to tackle effectively. The judicial developments risked going beyond constitutional propriety and causing confusion. The intervention by Lord Hoffmann, together with other members of the judiciary, made clear the need for legislation, and the draft produced by the Aaronson Study and the final legislation in the Finance Act 2013 reflects Lord Hoffmann's influence.[69] The legislative framework has been created, but the judiciary will continue to have a major role to play in developing this framework and ensuring that it operates effectively and consistently with both the case law and other legislation. Lord Hoffmann has left his mark not only on the tax case law but also on tax legislation.

---

[68] See, eg, Gammie (n 1).
[69] The UK legislation shares many features with those of the Hong Kong GAAR, not least the list of factors to be taken into account in deciding whether it applies.

16

Retrospective Mistakes of Law

FREDERICK WILMOT-SMITH[*]

I. INTRODUCTION

ALTHOUGH LORD HOFFMANN sat on relatively few cases concerning the law of unjust enrichment, his contribution to each was striking.[1] His speech in *Banque Financière de la Cité v Parc (Battersea) Ltd* is almost certainly the best known; it is also perhaps the most significant.[2] But this chapter is not about *BFC*. Instead, I want to examine Lord Hoffmann's contribution to the mistake of law cases and, in particular, his speech in *Kleinwort Benson v Lincoln County Council*.

This choice demands quite some justification. The decision in *Kleinwort Benson* has been examined on numerous occasions and one might well wonder if there is anything new that can be said about it. The case concerned a claim for restitution of money paid pursuant to an alleged mistake of law. The House of Lords allowed the claim, overruling nearly 200 years of law which stated that mistakes of law could not ground claims for restitution. Enormously valuable litigation has ensued—and continues to run.[3] In *Kleinwort Benson*, Lord Hoffmann was the third of a bare majority—and candidly admitted that he changed his mind about the crucial issue.[4] Practically, then, a great deal has turned upon the quality of Lord Hoffmann's

[*] I am particularly grateful to Professor Robert Stevens for his comments on an earlier draft of this chapter.
[1] The main contributions are *Banque Financière de la Cité v Parc (Battersea) Ltd* [1998] 1 AC 221 (HL) (hereinafter *BFC*); *Kleinwort Benson Ltd v Lincoln City Council* [1999] 2 AC 349 (HL); and *Deutsche Morgan Grenfell Group plc v Inland Revenue Commissioners* [2006] UKHL 49, [2006] 1 AC 558. Some would say that his speech in *Foskett v McKeown* [2001] 1 AC 102 (HL) is also a contribution to the law of unjust enrichment—but Lord Hoffmann would demur: see 115G.
[2] The speech is a lucid re-statement of the law of subrogation.
[3] See, eg, *DMG* (n 1); *Test Claimants in the FII Group Litigation v Revenue and Customs Commissioners* [2012] UKSC 19, [2013] 2 AC 337.
[4] *Kleinwort Benson* (n 1) 398E (Lord Hoffmann). Paterson says that Lord Hoffmann was 'open to persuasion on occasion', but that he 'did not often change his mind': A Paterson, *Final Judgment—The Last Law Lords and the Supreme Court* (Oxford, Hart Publishing, 2013) 150.

reasoning. But this alone would not justify revisiting the issue. Instead, we should return to the speech as it contains an argument which has not received sufficient attention. The key issue in *Kleinwort Benson* is one where 'different theoretical approaches [led] to different results, and by the narrowest of margins'.[5] Controversy continues in large part because of underlying theoretical disagreement. And Lord Hoffmann's argument, if successful, could justify the result without resort to contestable jurisprudential premises. It could therefore dispel some lingering doubts about the decision itself.[6]

The topic of mistake of law can be extremely complex. To delimit the inquiry, I will focus chiefly on the most difficult situation which the topic throws up.[7] Suppose that the highest court overrules one of its own precedents.[8] Let us call the first decision *P1* and the second decision *P2*. Suppose further that *P1* is decided at time *t*, the facts of *P2* arise at *t+1* and that *P2* is decided at *t+2*. *P1* decides that the law is X; *P2* decides that it is ¬X. Suppose now that C, at *t+1*, pays money to D because of a belief that X is the law. The problem is this: can C, given *P2*, say that she paid D the money by mistake?[9]

I will not consider a number of distinct issues. In particular, I am not going to examine whether *Hazell* changed the law or stated it as it always was;[10] nor whether there could be said to be a causative mistake in *DMG* given the mechanism of paying the tax in question.[11] Finally, I will not consider the inter-relation between mistake, doubt and 'risk-taking'.[12]

---

[5] RHS Tur, 'Time and the Law' (2002) 22 *OJLS* 463, 469.

[6] The decision receives a muted reception, for instance, in the leading practitioner work: C Mitchell, P Mitchell and S Watterson, *Goff and Jones: The Law of Unjust Enrichment* (8th edn, London, Sweet & Maxwell, 2011) para 9-79.

[7] See ibid paras 9-75–9-79. I will not consider the case of legislation being repealed as this seems to me to be a distinct case. See on this point *Commissioner of State Revenue (Vic) v Royal Insurance Australia Ltd* (1994) 182 CLR 51; and Law Commission, *Restitution: Mistakes of Law and Ultra Vires Public Authority Receipts and Payments* (Law Com No 227, 1994) para 5.3. For Lord Hoffmann's views on this point, see *Kleinwort Benson* (n 1) 400F–H.

[8] For a list of such cases, see J Harris, 'Towards Principles of Overruling—When Should a Final Court of Appeal Second Guess?' (1990) 10 *OJLS* 135, 143–46. C Sampford, *Retrospectivity and the Rule of Law* (Oxford, Oxford University Press, 2006) ch 5 has a helpful treatment of the range of possible cases.

[9] An example like this—said to be a 'paradigm case'—was employed by Nicholas Underhill QC in argument: see *Kleinwort Benson* (n 1) 390F (Lord Lloyd). Counsel for the banks conceded that there was no mistake in such a case: *Kleinwort Benson* (n 1) 391D–E (Lord Lloyd).

[10] See, generally, A Nair, 'Mistakes of Law and Legal Reasoning: Interpreting *Kleinwort Benson v Lincoln City Council*' in R Chambers, C Mitchell and J Penner (eds), *Philosophical Foundations of the Law of Unjust Enrichment* (Oxford, Oxford University Press, 2009) 391.

[11] R Stevens, 'Justified Enrichment' [2005] *Oxford University Commonwealth Law Journal* 141, 142–45.

[12] *Kleinwort Benson* (n 1) 401E–F (Lord Hoffmann); *DMG* (n 1) [26]–[27] (Lord Hoffmann). My own view on the last of these matters should be clear from F Wilmot-Smith, 'Replacing Risk-Taking Reasoning' (2011) 127 *LQR* 610.

II. BACKGROUND TO THE PROBLEM

A. The Law of Unjust Enrichment

While Lord Hoffmann was a Fellow of University College, Robert Goff (a Fellow of Lincoln College) and Gareth Jones published the first edition of *The Law of Restitution*, which said:

> The principle of unjust enrichment ... presupposes three things: first, that the defendant has been enriched by the receipt of a benefit; secondly, that he has been so enriched at the plaintiff's expense; and thirdly, that it would be unjust to allow him to retain the benefit.[13]

Thirty years later, Lord Hoffmann gave this formula his stamp of judicial approval.[14] This analytic framework can be traced to the *Restatement (First) Restitution*.[15] The first black letter reads: 'A person who has been unjustly enriched at the expense of another is required to make restitution to the other'.[16]

Although the framework is relatively new, the legal principles contained within it—that is, those propositions which the framework seeks to structure—are not. For instance, in 1760, Lord Mansfield's opinion in *Moses v Macferlan* proclaimed that an action lies:

> [T]o recover back money, which ought not in justice to be kept ... It lies only for money which, ex æquo et bono, the defendant ought to refund ... [I]t lies for money paid by mistake; or upon a consideration which happens to fail; or for money got through imposition, (express, or implied;) or extortion; or oppression.[17]

Even then, it had long been recognised that money paid by mistake could (in many cases) be recovered. For instance, in *Bonnel v Foulke* the claimant owed money to the City Chamberlain as rent.[18] In the belief that the money was owed instead to the Mayor, he paid the Mayor. This did not discharge the debt, so he had to pay the City Chamberlain. He was able to recover the money paid to the Mayor. The case is sometimes analysed as an early instance of money recoverable when paid by mistake.[19]

---

[13] R Goff and G Jones, *The Law of Restitution* (London, Sweet & Maxwell, 1966) 14. See further P Birks, *An Introduction to the Law of Restitution* (Oxford, Clarendon Press, 1985) 21.

[14] See *BFC* (n 1) 234 (Lord Hoffmann). His Lordship adds that a claim can be defeated if there are 'reasons of policy for denying a remedy'.

[15] There are similar phrases in earlier works, but these are less clearly statements of legal rules. For instance, Keener said that implied contracts are founded 'upon the doctrine that a man shall not be allowed to enrich himself unjustly at the expense of another'. See WA Keener, *A Treatise on the Law of Quasi-contracts* (New York, Baker, Voorhis & Co, 1893) 19.

[16] American Law Institute, *Restatement (First) of Restitution* (St Paul, MN, American Law Institute Publishers, 1937) §1.

[17] *Moses v Macferlan* (1760) 2 Burr 1005, 1012; 97 ER 676, 680 (KB).

[18] *Bonnel v Foulke* (1657) 2 Sid 4, 82 ER 1224.

[19] RM Jackson, *The History of Quasi-Contract in English Law* (Cambridge, Cambridge University Press, 1936) 58.

B. The Mistake of Law Bar

So it has long been held that an enrichment transferred to a defendant by mistake could be recovered. In the modern language, the mistake is a reason why the enrichment is regarded as unjust. Some have argued that the law once allowed recovery for mistakes of either fact or of law.[20] For instance, in *Farmer v Arundel*, De Grey CJ said that the action for money had and received would lie: 'When money is paid by one man to another on a mistake either of fact or of law'.[21] But in *Bilbie v Lumley*, Lord Ellenborough ruled instead that mistakes of law would not, in this respect, count.[22] His Lordship's reasoning, such as it was, was that: 'Every man must be taken to be cognizant of the law; otherwise there is no saying to what extent the excuse of ignorance might not be carried. It would be urged in almost every case'.[23]

The decision came under increasing criticism and was eventually overruled in *Kleinwort Benson*. Most people now accept that mistakes of law should *sometimes* count—as, for example, where a claimant is unaware of a statute.[24] The battle chiefly focuses upon two questions: first, *when* a claimant can be said to make a mistake; and, second, *which* mistakes should count. *Kleinwort Benson* will give us an opportunity to focus upon the first of these and to see Lord Hoffmann's answers to it.[25] But let me first clarify a few more background issues.

C. Three Key Issues

i. What is a Mistake?

This question can swiftly 'lead one into deep waters'.[26] At the general level—that is, before we get to the complications thrown up by the law—there are two important points to note.

---

[20] W Evans, *Essays: On the Action for Money Had and Received, on the Law of Insurances, and on the Law of Bills of Exchange and Promissory Notes* (Liverpool, Merritt & Wright, 1802) 21–22. See, further, the references collected in Mitchell, Mitchell and Watterson (n 6) para 9-71.

[21] *Farmer v Arundel* (1772) 2 Wm Bl 824, 825; 96 ER 485, 486 (KB).

[22] *Bilbie v Lumley* (1802) 2 East 469, 102 ER 448 (KB).

[23] ibid 449–50. The reasoning was regurgitated by even the more thoughtful treatise writers: CG Addison, *Treatise on the Law of Contracts and Rights and Liabilities Ex Contractu* (London, W Benning & Co, 1847) 231; JP Benjamin, *A Treatise on the Law of Sale of Personal Property* (London, H Sweet, 1868) 307. For a helpful historical overview, see E Keedy, 'Ignorance and Mistake in the Criminal Law' (1908) 22 *Harvard Law Review* 75, 77–81.

[24] P Birks, 'Mistakes of Law' (2000) 53 *Current Legal Problems* 205, 229; A Burrows, 'Common Law Retrospectivity' in A Burrows, D Johnston and R Zimmermann (eds), *Judge and Jurist: Essays in Memory of Lord Rodger of Earlsferry* (Oxford, Oxford University Press, 2013) 548.

[25] On the second, see (most recently) *Pitt v Holt* [2013] UKSC 26, [2013] 2 AC 108.

[26] *DMG* (n 1) [20] (Lord Hoffmann).

First, establishing a mistake involves a comparison between a belief and the world.[27] I will here assume that beliefs are propositional attitudes and that to ascertain whether an individual is mistaken involves asking whether the proposition in question is true or false. For instance, suppose that I pay you in the belief that I am obligated to do so. In this case, the proposition in question is that I am obligated to pay. In order for me to be mistaken, the proposition must be false. Its veracity depends upon something like this: whether, at the appropriate time, the proposition matches something in the world. If I believe that I owe you £10 and I do not owe you that money, I am mistaken in that belief.

The second key point is that, at least in law, the proposition can only be verified against the world as it stands at the time that the proposition itself is expressed. In our context, this time is set by the moment of the transfer which is caused by a belief in the proposition. In this respect, mistakes are to be distinguished from so-called 'mispredictions'.[28] As Lord Walker put it: 'A misprediction relates to some possible future event, whereas a legally significant mistake ... relates to some past or present matter of fact or law'.[29]

It is important to notice a complication to which this point gives rise. Although the proposition can only be tested against something in the world at the time of the transfer caused by the belief, it need not have been possible to *know* the state of the world at the time of the transfer (or even for knowledge to have been possible).[30] That is, we are not bound by the epistemic limits *of the time of payment*. The simple point is that one can be mistaken in a situation where it is impossible to know that one is mistaken.[31]

ii. The Retrospectivity of Common Law Adjudication

Retrospectivity is a topic of great interest and one to which relatively little attention has been paid.[32] There is a general consensus that retrospective

---

[27] L Smith, 'Restitution for Mistake of Law' [1999] *RLR* 148, 151; G Yaffe, 'Excusing Mistakes of Law' (2009) 9(2) *Philosopher's Imprint* 1, 3.

[28] There is an old debate in the philosophical literature over whether future contingent propositions are truth functional. See, eg, J Macfarlane, 'Future Contingents and Relative Truth' (2003) 53 *Philosophical Quarterly* 321. This debate might be relevant to those situations where a claimant pays money on the basis of an assumed legal state of affairs, but where there is no law on the question prior to a future court decision. Lord Hope appears to have regarded this as sufficient to constitute a mistake: *Kleinwort Benson* (n 1) 410 (Lord Hope).

[29] *Pitt v Holt* (n 25) [109]. On this distinction, see further: Birks (n 24) 223–24; Stevens (n 11) 148.

[30] Failure to make this distinction has led a number of commentators into error: see D Sheehan, 'What is a Mistake?' [2000] *Legal Studies* 538, 538, 545; Nair (n 10) 373.

[31] W Seah, 'Mispredictions, Mistakes and the Law of Unjust Enrichment' [2007] *Restitution Law Review* 93, 96. My thanks to V Niranjan and Tom Adams for pressing me on my expression here.

[32] See, however, Sampford (n 8) and B Juratowitch, *Retroactivity and the Common Law* (Oxford, Hart Publishing, 2008).

law making is problematic.[33] Given this, common law adjudication seems to be peculiarly problematic. As Justice Holmes put it: 'Judicial decisions have had retrospective operation for near a thousand years'.[34] To see what Holmes meant, recall our hypothetical case: *P2* decides that the law is ¬X. In so deciding, most people think that *P2* changes the law. In the normal run of things, the court will apply the newly declared law (ie, ¬X) to decide the dispute between the parties in the case.[35] The court does this even if the facts of *P2* arose (as I stipulated above) at *t+1*, ie, a time when the law was indisputably X. As the facts in question arose, by hypothesis, before the law was changed, the court's decision applies retrospectively.[36]

I do ultimately want to suggest that *this* is the most interesting issue that these cases throw up. The topic deserves much more attention than it has received. But for the purposes of this chapter, I will not examine the merits of this approach to adjudication. I will presuppose it: common law retrospectivity is a necessary part of the background to the problem.

iii. What is the Effect of Subsequent Overruling?

When people disagree over whether a particular claimant has made a mistake of law, their disagreement often concerns whether the law has been *changed* by a particular legal decision. To understand this point, it is helpful to consider a distinction made popular by John Searle.[37] Searle distinguishes between the 'direction of fit' of words-to-world.[38] For instance, suppose that a man goes shopping with a list of 'beans, butter, bacon and bread'. A detective follows him around, writing down everything the man buys. When the man leaves the shop, both the man's and the detective's

---

[33] For an interesting historical survey, replete with examples, see Sampford (n 8) ch 1.

[34] *Kuhn v Fairmont Coal Co* 215 US 349, 372 (1910) (Holmes J, dissenting opinion).

[35] *Pace* Lord Goff (see *Kleinwort Benson* (n 1) 377–78), there is no *inevitability* to this: K Diplock, 'The Courts as Legislators' in BW Harvey (ed), *The Lawyer and Justice* (London, Sweet & Maxwell, 1978) 281; Tur (n 5) 473–74. A court *could* apply X to the parties to the dispute and then declare the law to be ¬X for disputes in the future, but this is clearly not the normal run of things in common law adjudication.

[36] See Juratowitch (n 32) 119.

[37] Searle was in Oxford from 1952 to 1959 and was (and, indeed, still is) friends with Hoffmann. Searle's thinking has clearly influenced Hoffmann's—most obviously, in Hoffmann's approach to contractual interpretation.

[38] This terminology was first employed by JL Austin, *Philosophical Papers* (Oxford, Clarendon Press, 1962). However, the distinction appears to be first drawn—in different terms, but using the example I will shortly give—in a famous passage by GEM Anscombe, *Intention* (Oxford, Blackwell, 1957) 56. Strictly speaking, it is the propositional content of the words, not the words themselves, which we consider. But 'propositional content-to-world' is somewhat less catchy.

lists will be identical—but their purposes are quite different. As Searle puts it:

> In the case of the shopper's list, the purpose of the list is ... to get the world to match the words; the man is supposed to make his actions fit the list. In the case of the detective, the purpose of the list is to make the words match the world; the man is supposed to make the list fit the actions of the shopper.[39]

What is the direction of fit between a judge's words and the world?[40] It seems that there is no single direction of fit.[41] Suppose that a judge claims that the law is X. Sometimes, the judge might simply be reporting what the law already is; that is, her words might aim to fit the world. For instance, when a judge now claims that a prima facie right to restitution arises on payment of money caused by mistake, she simply reports what is already the case as a matter of law.[42] But almost everyone will accept that judges play a constitutive role in some cases. Here a judge might actually make it the case that the law is X simply by claiming that it is so. In Searle's terms, the world changes to fit the words.

Most people also accept that a judge does not have *tabula rasa*; the proper judicial role is to develop the law 'only interstitially'.[43] The precise limits of the legitimate use of this power and the appropriate way to exercise it are of course matters of quite some debate. For instance, in *Kleinwort Benson*, Lord Hoffmann said that the adoption of a rule 'founded purely upon policy' would be a 'legislative act'—and therefore an illegitimate use of the powers of the House of Lords, which should be 'to clarify and develop the common law by restating rules in accordance with principle'.[44] Given this incremental approach, it can be difficult to see whether, in a particular case, a judge has merely declared what the law is or has made new law.[45] Often, therefore, when there is a dispute over whether there was a mistake of law in a particular instance, the dispute essentially turns on how we should understand a judge's decision—as a declaration or as a constitution of the

---

[39] J Searle, 'A Classification of Illocutionary Acts' (1976) 5 *Language in Society* 1, 3.

[40] I here mean the propositional content of a judge's claim about the law when that judge is speaking in an official role (and in a majority etc). By 'the world', I mean 'the state of the law'.

[41] As Lord Hope says (*Kleinwort Benson* (n 1) 410): 'Experience has shown that the judges do from time to time change the law ... But it would be equally wrong to say that the judges never declare the law.'

[42] *Barclays Bank Ltd v W J Simms & Cooke (Southern) Ltd* [1980] QB 677 (QB) and *DMG* (n 1).

[43] *Southern Pacific Co v Jensen* 255 US 205, 221 (1917) (Holmes J).

[44] *Kleinwort Benson* (n 1) 401 (Lord Hoffmann). That distinction is generally attributed to Dworkin: R Dworkin, *Taking Rights Seriously* (Cambridge, MA, Harvard University Press, 1978) 22–28. See, further, *R v Governor of Brockhill Prison ex p Evans* [2001] 2 AC 19 (HL) 48E–F (Lord Hobhouse).

[45] R Zimmermann and S Meier, 'Judicial Development of the Law, Error Iuris, and the Law of Unjustified Enrichment' (1999) 115 *LQR* 556, 560.

law. For instance, as we shall see shortly, many of the debates surrounding *Kleinwort Benson* concern whether *Hazell* established what was always the law, made law where there was previously no law, or overruled what was previously the law.

We can forestall these debates—and so avoid intricate factual inquiries—if there is a mistake in a case where everyone accepts that the law has been changed since the time of payment.[46] Recall the problem posed above, where the highest court overrules one of its own precedents.[47] I called these decisions *P1* and *P2*. Everyone should accept that the law is changed by *P2*.[48] I stipulated that *P1* is decided at *t* and *P2* at *t+2*, but I also stipulated that the facts of *P2* arose at *t+1*. What does *P2* claim the law to have been at *t+1*? It seems to claim that the law somehow was ¬X; or, perhaps more accurately, that we should *treat it as being so*: the parties' rights are decided on that basis. More than this, though, ¬X is not simply the law inter partes: ¬X will be the applicable law in any future case (even with facts which arose at *t+1*). And this brings the problem of mistake of law into sharp relief. Recall: C, at *t+1*, pays money to D because of a belief that X is the law. Can C, given *P2*, say that she paid D the money by mistake?

III. THE *KLEINWORT BENSON* DECISION

A. The Case Itself

Kleinwort Benson entered into a swap transaction with Lincoln City Council, a deal that was widely (though not universally) thought to be valid. After the swap was fully executed, the House of Lords held in *Hazell* that such transactions were ultra vires the local authorities' powers.[49] The swap was, it followed, void. The ordinary limitation period for claims in unjust enrichment is six years from the accrual of the cause of action.[50] Of course, had Kleinwort Benson known of the contractual invalidity earlier, it could have sought restitution for a failure of consideration (as other banks were

---

[46] Those who deny that the law is changed by *P2* have an easier route to saying that there is a mistake: see n 64.

[47] On the use of *Practice Statement (HL: Judicial Precedent)* [1966] 1 WLR 1234 (HL), we should 'say "overrule" expressly. It is better to avoid euphemisms like "depart from"'. *Miliangos v George Frank (Textiles) Ltd* [1975] AC 443 (HL) 470 (Lord Simon).

[48] Tur (n 5) 472 (criticising Lord Goff's claims in *Kleinwort Benson* (n 1)). Dworkin might disagree with this in some situations, but only, I think, where *P1* is a total aberration: Dworkin (n 46) 208 et seq.

[49] *Hazell v Hammersmith & Fulham London Borough Council* [1992] 2 AC 1 (HL).

[50] In *Kleinwort Benson Ltd v Sandwell Borough Council* [1994] 4 All ER 890 (QB), Hobhouse J held that the limitation period applicable to claims in unjust enrichment is that found in s 5 of the Limitation Act 1980

able to).[51] But such claims were time-barred. So the bank sought to evade the limitation period by characterising its claim as one based upon a mistake of law. This allowed the bank to take advantage of section 32(1)(c) of the Limitation Act 1980, which provides for an extended limitation period where 'the action is for relief from the consequences of a mistake'.[52] In such cases, 'the period of limitation shall not begin to run until the plaintiff has discovered the ... mistake ... or could with reasonable diligence have discovered it'.[53]

The claimant faced two problems. Their first was *Bilbie*: the law barred restitution for a mistake of law. Its second problem was, as Lord Hoffmann put it, that 'the law requires that a mistake should have been as to some *existing* fact or ... the then *existing* state of the law'.[54] Given this, were the claimants mistaken? Or did they only *become* mistaken when *Hazell* was decided?

The first of these problems was surmounted relatively easily. All members of the House of Lords agreed that *Bilbie* was wrongly decided; it was overruled. But the second problem proved more controversial.[55] The House divided three to two on the question of whether there was, in the relevant sense, a mistake. While the majority (Lords Goff, Hoffmann and Hope) said that the bank was mistaken, the minority (Lords Browne-Wilkinson and Lloyd) thought that it was not. The claimant could not be mistaken at the time it made the relevant payments, the minority reasoned, as its view of the state of the law was not falsified until *Hazell*. This debate is about how best to understand *Hazell*. That makes it of relatively limited interest.[56] Nevertheless, the speeches of their Lordships in *Kleinwort Benson* give some indication of the way they would treat the case that I have posed. There are two relatively simple answers to that problem, each reflecting quite distinct jurisprudential premises: one says that C was mistaken; the other says that she was not. Let me explain those approaches before turning to Lord Hoffmann's analysis.

---

[51] *Guinness Mahon Co Ltd v Chelsea and Kensington Royal London Borough Council* [1999] QB 215 (CA).

[52] Limitation Act 1980, s 32(1)(c).

[53] ibid.

[54] *Kleinwort Benson* (n 1) 398G–H (Lord Hoffmann).

[55] Although the bank dedicated all its submissions to the first point—*Kleinwort Benson* (n 1) 354–55—counsel for the local authority simply conceded this point and argued for a more nuanced rule: *Kleinwort Benson* (n 1) 355C–D. The unfortunate consequence of the bank's approach was that they gave almost no argument on the crucial question, that is, whether there was a mistake *in this case*: see *Kleinwort Benson* (n 1) 355D (the local authorities), 356H–57B (the bank).

[56] For discussion of these issues, see Mitchell, Mitchell and Watterson (n 6) paras 9-80–9-83; Juratowitch (n 32) 139–40. For a consideration of whether there should be a 'settled understanding' defence, see D Sheehan, 'Mistaken Overpayments of Tax' in S Elliott, B Häcker, and C Mitchell (eds), *Restitution of Overpaid Tax* (Oxford, Hart Publishing, 2013) 62–68.

B. Two Simple Approaches

i. C was Mistaken

On one view of the law, judicial decisions—even those of the highest courts—do not *make* or *change* the law in the fullest sense of the word.[57] For instance, William Blackstone claimed that judges are 'not delegated to pronounce a new law, but to maintain and expound the old one'.[58] Subject to some interpretive complications (what does 'maintain and expound' mean?), this view claims that the courts discover what was always the case. Judicial decisions are said to be 'only conclusive as between the parties to them and their privies',[59] but do not make law in the fullest sense. Although this theory has been attacked many times, scholars continue to defend it.[60]

If the theory is correct, our problem is quite easy. We must assess the payor's mental state 'by measuring the party's *belief about* the transaction ... against the law applicable to the *transaction*'.[61] A declaratory theorist can say: when P2 declares the law to be ¬X, this shows that the law was ¬X at *t+1*; and, so, C was mistaken.[62] A number of academics have been attracted to these, or similar, views.[63] These people regard the subsequent legal decision as revealing what was always the case.[64] For instance, Burrows says that: 'With the benefit of hindsight, we now know that the view of the law taken by the banks was mistaken'.[65]

In *Kleinwort Benson*, this manner of reasoning was adopted by Lord Goff and, perhaps, by Lord Hope. Although Lord Goff joined the bandwagon of

---

[57] A distinct, but similar, approach to the one of this section is this. One might think that courts have the power to change what the law *was* in the past. So, when P2 is decided, on this view, it *makes it the case* that the law was ¬X at *t+1*. I find this approach too implausible to justify dealing with it in the main text; but it is worth highlighting as something of a bridge between the Blackstonian approach and that of Lord Hoffmann (which accepts that the law *was not* ¬X, but says that if we are to treat it as having been so in one case, we must do so in all others).

[58] W Blackstone, *Commentaries on the Laws of England, 1765* (Chicago, University of Chicago Press, 1979) 69–70. See, further, M Hale, *Hale's Common Law of England* (6th edn, London, Butterworths, 1820) 90.

[59] *Evans* (n 44) 45E–F (Lord Hobhouse).

[60] For a rebuttal, but not a full-blooded defence, see A Beever, 'The Declaratory Theory of Law' (2013) 33 *OJLS* 1.

[61] J Finnis, 'The Fairy Tale's Moral' (1999) 115 *LQR* 170, 171. Compare *Kleinwort Benson* (n 1) 362E–F, where Lord Browne-Wilkinson fails to note the second limb of Finnis' proposition.

[62] Both natural lawyers and Dworkinians can make similar claims. These theories have conceptual space to say there is a mistake because they do not regard social facts (eg, the fact of a court's decision) as definitive of the legal position. See, eg, R Dworkin, 'The Law of the Slave-Catchers: A Review of Robert M Cover's *Justice Accused: Antislavery and the Judicial Process*', *Times Literary Supplement* (London, 5 December 1975) 1437; J Finnis, *Natural Law, Natural Rights* (2nd edn, Oxford, Oxford University Press, 2011) 289–91.

[63] Sheehan (n 31); Finnis (n 61); Burrows (n 24).

[64] For our problem, this assumes that the law stated in P2 is, unlike that in P1, correct.

[65] Burrows (n 24) 549.

critics of this 'fairytale' analysis of the law,[66] his Lordship's speech is hard
to distinguish from such a view.[67] While accepting that judges change the
law, his Lordship said it was 'inevitable' that a judicial statement of the law
must 'have a retrospective effect'.[68] His Lordship did not perceive a distinction between the case at hand and one where there is 'a judicial development of the law ... of a more radical nature, constituting a departure, even
a major departure, from what has previously been considered to be established principle'.[69] He would not be troubled by the case I have proposed.
He would say that:

> The payor believed, when he paid the money, that he was bound in law to pay
> it. He is now told that, on the law as held to be applicable at the date of the pay-
> ment, he was not bound to pay it. Plainly, therefore, he paid the money under a
> mistake of law.[70]

Lord Hope would appear to be similarly untroubled. However, his Lordship
was more circumspect about the jurisprudential basis of his decision. He says
that it is 'preferable to avoid being drawn into a discussion as to whether a
particular decision changed the law or whether it was merely declaratory'.[71]
The 'critical question' is 'whether the payor would have made the payment
if he had known what he is now being told was the law'.[72] In *P2*, the law is
said to be ¬X; C would not (by hypothesis) have paid if she had known that
¬X, and so she can recover for mistake of law.

ii. C was Not Mistaken

The minority in *Kleinwort Benson* propose an equally clear, entirely contrary, analysis of the Problem. They reasoned in this way. When *P2* overrules
P1, it changes the law from X to ¬X. It follows that the law *was* X in the
period between *P1* and *P2*; to say otherwise is to 'falsify history'.[73] Therefore, as Lord Browne-Wilkinson puts it, 'at the time of payment, the payor
was not labouring under any mistake'.[74] Similarly, Lord Lloyd claimed that:
'The payor was not mistaken. The subsequent change in the law could not

---

[66] See, for instance, *Kleinwort Benson* (n 1) 377.
[67] *Cf Evans* (n 46) 48B (Lord Hobhouse).
[68] *Kleinwort Benson* (n 1) 378–79.
[69] ibid 378E.
[70] ibid 379G–H (Lord Goff).
[71] ibid 411B (Lord Hope).
[72] ibid 411C–D (Lord Hope). Compare, however, the less guarded suggestion that what
matters is whether the payment would have been made if the payor 'had known the true state
of the law ... at the time of the payment': *Evans* (n 46) 37E (Lord Hope).
[73] *Kleinwort Benson* (n 1) 358B (Lord Browne Wilkinson).
[74] ibid 357H. Lord Browne-Wilkinson's claims are about a settled understanding of the law;
my hypothetical is a fortiori. His Lordship's analysis in *Kleinwort Benson* is not easy to square
with that in *Evans* (n 46) 27E.

create a cause of action which, ex hypothesi, did not exist at the relevant time.'[75] There are numerous academic supporters of this analysis.[76]

These people rely upon a different theoretical premise about the nature of common law adjudication. They emphasise the creative role that judges have—and, they would say, *had* in *Hazell*—in developing and changing the law. But they need not deny that common law adjudication operates retrospectively in the ordinary case. They will simply claim that Lords Goff and Hope did not answer the key question we face in a mistake of law case, which is:

> [W]hether the fact that the later overruling decision operates retrospectively so far as the substantive law is concerned also requires it to be assumed (contrary to the facts) that *at the date of each payment* the plaintiff made a mistake as to what the law then was.[77]

Lord Hoffmann's speech accepts the challenge. If his argument succeeds, we need not endorse the controversial jurisprudential positions of either the majority or the minority; instead, we need only accept that common law adjudication functions retrospectively.

C. Lord Hoffmann's Approach

i. An Underlying Anxiety

Lord Hoffmann's speech begins with a confession: 'on this point I have changed my mind'.[78] The anxiety underlying this change of mind comes from a more sensitive appreciation of the precise problem in a case like *Kleinwort Benson*—and in the one that I have posed—such that his Lordship was troubled by both majority and minority views. On the one hand, the majority's approach (and in particular that of Lord Goff) seems unduly simplistic in two respects. First, the problem cannot in every case be reduced to an epistemological one. In other words, we cannot say that the law was *always* ¬X and that we simply did not *know* it was ¬X until a court pronounces on the issue.[79] Any theory of adjudication which accepts that courts play even *some* constitutive role must accept this. So, as Lord Hoffmann rightly points out in *DMG*, in some cases at the time of payment, the claimant 'could not have discovered the truth because the truth did not yet exist'.[80] Unlike Lords Goff

---

[75] *Kleinwort Benson* (n 1) 397B–C (Lord Lloyd).
[76] Zimmermann and Meier (n 47); C Mitchell, 'Retrospective Mistakes of Law' [1999] *King's College Law Journal* 121; Birks (n 24); Nair (n 10).
[77] *Kleinwort Benson* (n 1) 359B (Lord Browne-Wilkinson).
[78] ibid 398E.
[79] To repeat, this *may* have been the case in *Hazell* and *Kleinwort*, but that does not answer our problem.
[80] *DMG* (n 1) [31]. See, further, *Kleinwort Benson* (n 1) 399E–F. The 'truth' might not yet exist either because the law on the matter was vague before the decision in question or, as in my hypothetical, because a subsequent decision changes what the law was.

and Hope, therefore, Lord Hoffmann appreciated that the mistake in these cases (if there is a mistake) is 'of a very special kind'.[81] Second, the key problem that the majority's approach has to face is that posed so clearly by Lord Browne-Wilkinson. As Lord Hoffmann characterises it, the key question is whether we should 'carry' the retrospectivity of legal decisions 'through into the question of whether the payor made a mistake'.[82] Some have supposed that the one entails the other;[83] but, absent a commitment to a particular theory of law,[84] that seems too strong. We need an argument to justify carrying the retrospectively through in this way.

However, the minority's dismissal of the relevance of the retrospectivity of common law adjudication to the problem was also too swift.[85] As we have seen, P2 might change the law, but it also applies the law to fact situations in the past. P2 therefore claims that the relevant law *was* ¬X at some time in the past. It is for this reason that there is justified unease about the minority's analysis. So Lord Hoffmann's anxiety arose because both answers—that the claimant was mistaken and that it was not—seem flawed. And this prompted a novel analysis of the problem.

ii. The Non-Contradiction Argument

Lord Hoffmann begins by saying that mistakes of law demand a particularly *legal* answer. He points out that:

> The common sense notion of a mistake as to an existing state of affairs is that one has got it wrong when, if one had been better informed, one could have got it right. But common sense does not easily accommodate the concept of retrospectivity. This is a legal notion.[86]

In ordinary common law adjudication, as we have seen, judicial decisions operate retrospectively. This means that, to recall my example, the House of Lords can in P2 treat the law as being ¬X at t+1 (or even before).[87] For C to be mistaken, the proposition—which is that X—must be false at t+1. If we were to examine this question at t+1, we would have to say that there is no mistake. But the House of Lords has now, in P2, adjudicated a dispute on the basis that the law at t+1 is ¬X. Does this make a difference? Does it, in Lord Hoffmann's terms, mean that we should 'carry through' the claim of P2 into the past when considering whether C has made a mistake?

---

[81] *DMG* (n 1) [23] (Lord Hoffmann).

[82] *Kleinwort Benson* (n 1) 399G. See further *DMG* (n 1) [23] (Lord Hoffmann): whether the claimant should 'be treated as having made a mistake'.

[83] Juratowitch (n 32) 141; Burrows (n 24) 549.

[84] See n 64 et seq.

[85] See *Kleinwort Benson* (n 1) 363 (Lord Browne-Wilkinson) and 391, 393–94 (Lord Lloyd).

[86] *Kleinwort Benson* (n 1) 399A–B (Lord Hoffmann). See, further, his Lordship's response to Beatson: *DMG* (n 1) [23] (Lord Hoffmann).

[87] For instance, *Anderton v Ryan* [1985] AC 560 (HL) was handed down on 9 May 1985; the key facts of *R v Shivpuri (Pyare)* [1986] AC 1 (HL) arose on 30 November 1982.

I believe that Lord Hoffmann's central argument for why we should carry through the claim of *P2*, that is, why the appropriate law is ¬X, can be deduced from his thought experiment.[88] He asks us to imagine a client in a position like that of C—ie, who has paid in the belief that X (and, on Lord Hoffmann's hypothetical case, in the belief that X requires her to pay). The House of Lords declares that the obligation is void (ie, that ¬X). The client asks his lawyer whether he can recover the money for mistake. If the applicable law is X, the lawyer must tell the client that he cannot recover 'because if you had consulted me at the time, I would have told you that you were certainly right to pay. Therefore you made no mistake'.[89] The key passage in Lord Hoffmann's speech is the following:

> The client asks: 'Does that mean that the obligation was actually valid? If so, what has made it invalid?' The lawyer has to answer 'No, the House of Lords has told us that it was always void. Nevertheless, you made no mistake.'[90]

This thought experiment is intended to demonstrate the absurdity of accepting the retrospectively of common law adjudication and simultaneously saying that there is no mistake. On that analysis, the law would contradict itself, saying that an obligation is both valid and invalid (ie, that both X and ¬X).

To illustrate his point, let us return to our hypothetical case. The test of whether C was mistaken is whether the proposition (X) is true at *t+1*. This requires the court to compare this proposition against the legal world, that is, against what the law was at *t+1*.[91] To say that C was *not* mistaken, we must say that the law at *t+1* was X. But *P2* adjudicated the litigants' rights at *t+1* on the basis that the law was ¬X. Given these two points, if the law says that C was *not* mistaken, it is committed to a contradiction: in *P2*, the law is said to be ¬X at *t+1*; in *C v D*, the law is (on this hypothesis) said to be X at *t+1*. To avoid this contradiction, we can either say that *P2* is incorrect, or we can say that the law at *t+1* was as it has been declared to be by *P2*.[92] If we take the latter course, we must also say that C is mistaken.[93]

---

[88] The full thought experiment is found at *Kleinwort Benson* (n 1) 399G–400E.

[89] *Kleinwort Benson* (n 1) 399–400 (Lord Hoffmann).

[90] ibid 400A–B (Lord Hoffmann).

[91] The distinctively legal aspect of this test is emphasised by Finnis (n 63) 174.

[92] A querulous objector might ask what is so bad about contradiction. Why can the law not join Whitman in saying 'Do I contradict myself? Very well then I contradict myself': W Whitman, *Whitman: Complete Poetry and Collected Prose* (New York, Library of America, 1982) 87, 246. Contradictions are rightly avoided in systems of thought as it is possible to derive *any* proposition from a contradiction. This can easily be proved:

1. P
2. P ∨ Q
3. P ∧¬P ∨Q
4. ∴Q.

This demonstrates that permitting contradictions shows we are not committed to *anything*—and thereby rejects the project of law making.

[93] The same analysis can be applied to *Evans* (n 46). For a thoughtful comment, see P Cane, 'The Temporal Element in Law' (2001) 117 *LQR* 5.

This interpretation of Lord Hoffmann's analysis explains why his Lordship uses the language of deeming in both *Kleinwort Benson* and *DMG*. In *Kleinwort Benson*, he says that 'it has turned out that the state of affairs at the time was not (or was deemed not to have been) what the payor thought'.[94] In *DMG*, his Lordship wondered if 'it would make objectors feel better if one said that because the law was now deemed to have been different at the relevant date, [the claimant] was *deemed* to have made a mistake'.[95]

This language has been deprecated as a '[slide] into fiction'.[96] But this is too swift. Now, there is clearly fiction in saying that the claimant was mistaken; there is a real sense in which she was not mistaken at the time of the transfer. But the retrospectivity of common law adjudication means that it is not a *mere* fiction to deem her to have been mistaken. In particular, it would be too crude to say that the impairment of the claimant's intention is precisely the same as if she had mispredicted the future. Or so I will argue.

IV. TWO OBJECTIONS

A. Can Retrospective Mistakes Justify Restitution?

i. The Objection

Birks once argued that restitution is justified in mistake cases because the claimant's intention to make the transfer in question is vitiated.[97] He contrasted mistakes with mispredictions. Mispredictions, he said, do not justify restitution. Here is the key explanation:

> [R]estitution for mistake rests on the fact that the plaintiff's judgement was vitiated in the matter of the transfer of wealth to the defendant. A mistake as to the future, a misprediction, does not show that the plaintiff's judgement was vitiated, only that as things turned out it was incorrectly exercised.[98]

With this in mind, consider Peter Cane's claim that 'it seems a more natural interpretation of what happened that the payors made not a mistake about the law, but rather a mistaken prediction about what the law would be held to be'[99] and Charles Mitchell's objection that 'the rewriting of history entailed by *Lincoln* ... makes it very hard to see "retrospective mistakes"

---

[94] *Kleinwort Benson* (n 1) 399F–G.
[95] *DMG* (n 1) [23].
[96] Birks (n 24) 225.
[97] Birks (n 13) 146–73.
[98] ibid 147.
[99] Cane (n 93) 8.

as having much to do with mistake as a factor vitiating the claimant's intent'.[100]

The objection is that a retrospective mistake of law does not justify restitution. But there are two strands to the objection: first, that the nature of the payor's impairment in *Kleinwort Benson* is just the same as that of a mispredictor; and, second, that—regardless of whether we should assimilate mistakes of law and misprediction—there is no genuine impairment of the payor's intention such as to justify restitution.

ii. Distinguishing Retrospective Mistakes and Mispredictions

There are two important distinctions between retrospective mistakes and mispredictions. The first distinction concerns the truth of the proposition at the time of the payment. At the time the payment is made, a misprediction is neither true nor false.[101] In our problem, by way of contrast, the proposition is actually true at the time of payment.[102]

The second distinction is both subtler and more important. With a misprediction, the proposition's truth—if that is the correct word—depends upon some event in the future. Even if one is tempted by the suggestion that a future contingent proposition can be true or false, its truth or falsehood can only be established with reference to facts about the future, ie, after the proposition itself is put forward. Retrospective mistakes of law are superficially similar in their dependence on a future event: the court's judgment. But in a deeper sense, the two cases come apart. In the case of a mistake of law, the proposition must still be tested against the world *at the time of the payment*. However, the common law's retrospective approach to adjudication means that the world must be understood in the light of later decisions. While it might be right to say that the claimant mispredicts, there is a sense in which she fails to predict what the law *actually is*. This sentence sounds confused, but the confusion arises from the nature of common law adjudication, not the mistake of law test.[103] Accepting (for now) this retrospective

---

[100] C Mitchell, 'Mistaken Tax Payments' [2007] *RLR* 123, 127. See, further, R Chambers, '*Deutsche Morgan Grenfell Group PLC v IRC* [2006] UKHL' [2006] *Oxford University Commonwealth Law Journal* 227, 232.

[101] Of course, this assumes an indeterministic world at least in respect of the prediction.

[102] I here presume that the family of theories considered under the umbrella heading of declaratory theories are incorrect. If they are correct, however, the same point remains—but the proposition would be false, not true.

[103] Bernard Lewis describes: 'a meeting of historians in Rome where we were discussing whether historians should or should not attempt to predict the future. That was when the Soviet Union was still alive and well. A Soviet colleague among us remained silent through the discussion and then we turned to him to ask him what his view was. He said, "In the Soviet Union, the most difficult task of the historian is to predict the past"'. B Lewis and BE Churchill, *Notes on a Century: Reflections of a Middle East Historian* (London, Weidenfeld & Nicolson, 2012) 157.

power of the common law, retrospective mistakes of law are importantly distinct (conceptually) from mispredictions.

iii. Justifying Restitution

All this shows that the simple elision of mistakes of law and mispredictions is too swift. But it does not answer the deeper objection that a retrospective mistake of law does not justify the response of restitution.[104] Lord Hoffmann himself does examine the justification of restitution in both *Kleinwort Benson* and *DMG*. Unfortunately, his argument appears to depend upon the view that the money in question was never *actually* owing. For instance, his Lordship claims that 'it is prima facie unjust for the recipient to retain the money when, if the payor had known the true state of affairs, he would not have paid'.[105] On the facts of *Kleinwort Benson*, of course, this is a perfectly plausible analysis: the case concerned a settled understanding of the law and perhaps *Hazell* did not change the law. But this does not answer the objection in a case where the law in question is changed by the subsequent decision. The objectors deserve an answer on this point.

Any response is inevitably contentious, requiring as it does an explanation of why restitution should be awarded in a normal case. For our purposes, the key question is why the claimant might be thought to have an interest in restitution.[106] Birks' explanation, as we have seen, turned on the claimant's vitiated intention to make the transfer. But at a more fundamental level, the concern is with the reasons the claimant assumed that she had. In a normal mistaken payment case, the claimant takes various facts to give her a reason to make her payment. If those facts do not hold, the 'but for' test means that—by her own lights[107]—she did not have sufficient reason to make the payment. The award of restitution seems to be an attempt to ensure that the claimant acts only for the reasons she takes herself to have.

This justification has a natural limit. When there is no rational failure on the claimant's part, no similar story can be told. This goes some way to explaining the law's antipathy to mispredictions. In such cases there is no

---

[104] I will not here examine whether there is sufficient normative justification for the claims to be brought under s 32(1)(c) of the Limitation Act 1980.

[105] *Kleinwort Benson* (n 1) 399D (Lord Hoffmann). See, similarly, 400E ('it subsequently turns out that he was not') and 401A ('would not have received if the payor had known the law to be what it has since been declared to have been'). In *DMG* (n 1) [23], the same point is made in the language of fairness. This notion might have some work to do in this context: if the claimant is said not to be mistaken, she can call her treatment unfair in that the law treats her differently from others in respect of its claims about the law in the past.

[106] This means that we can leave to one side the more difficult question of why the defendant should be the one to provide it.

[107] One way to understand some debates surrounding the 'but for' mistake test is whether it is enough that the claimant *took herself* to have such a reason or whether the facts in question would *actually* have given her a reason.

'false data' in the claimant's head at the time she makes the payment.[108] Therefore, the explanation of rational failure which I gave in mistake cases cannot hold in these cases.

Consider now a mistake of law case. Here, the claimant acts because she takes the legal position—in our case, the position that X—to give her a reason to pay. When the law declares that ¬X, it is inevitably tempting to assimilate her position with that of a mispredictor. But it is important to keep in mind that the claimant's position depends ultimately not upon the *fact* of the law, but upon the *reasons* she took the law to give. If the law can make it *as if* the position was ¬X at the time the payment was made, the claimant's rational non-conformity can be the same as if it had been ¬X all along. The law certainly aims to make it as if the position was always ¬X: its manner of adjudication is retrospective. And whenever it manages to treat the claimant in this manner, she is like (though not the same as) the orthodox mistaken payor, and a similar justificatory story applies.

A concrete example might help illustrate the point. In *Kleinwort Benson*, the claimants paid in part due to the belief that the swaps were valid. *Hazell* said that they were invalid. Had Lincoln County Council 'lost' the swap, it would have been entitled to claim restitution of the excess due to the principles of *Auckland Harbour Board*.[109] So retrospective common law adjudication combined with *Hazell* meant that the swap became, for Kleinwort Benson, a case of 'heads I win; tails you lose'. This demonstrates that the common law's retrospectivity can undermine the claimant's course of action in just the same way as if she got the facts wrong to begin with. It explains why restitution is a justifiable response to a retrospective mistake of law— and why its justification is closely related to that of a mistake of fact.

B. A *Condictio Indebitii*?

In his *Introduction to the Law of Restitution*, Peter Birks argued that English law required the identification of a 'factor' which rendered enrichments unjust.[110] As regards the law of 'subtractive unjust enrichment', Birks identified a set of such factors, including mistake, ignorance, duress and failure of consideration. He placed these factors within abstract categories of 'vitiation' and 'qualification'.[111] However, in his last book he argued that: 'In the swaps cases English law changed direction.'[112] Being firmly of the view that 'There was no mistake' in *Kleinwort Benson*,[113] Birks thought

---

[108] Sheehan (n 31) 551; Seah (n 32) 100.
[109] *Auckland Harbour Board v The King* [1924] AC 318 (PC).
[110] Birks (n 13) 62.
[111] ibid 105.
[112] P Birks, *Unjust Enrichment* (2nd edn, Oxford, Oxford University Press, 2005) 127.
[113] Birks (n 24) 233.

that the only possible explanation of liability in the case was that English law had embraced the civilian approach, whereby liability turns on whether there is a valid legal ground for the receipt of the enrichment. Similarly, Zimmermann and Meier claim that the effect of *Kleinwort Benson* is 'the (re)introduction of the *condictio indebiti* through the back door of mistake of law'.[114] To be clear, the objection is not to a legal system employing an absence of basis system. Instead, the objection is that the argument is an elaborate hoax. It hides the fact that the absence of a legal basis for the transfer is what is really doing the work in justifying restitution.

Lord Hoffmann himself appears sympathetic to these concerns. In *DMG*, his Lordship admits that his argument might be thought to extend 'the concept of a mistake to compensate for the absence of a more general condictio indebiti'.[115] He adds that some further remarks of his:

> [M]ay be said to support the view of Professor Birks that English law should be less concerned with whether the person who paid the money made a mistake (involving an inquiry into his subjective state of mind) than with whether there was a valid causa for the payment, such as a debt, compromise or gift.[116]

Whether this is really the case turns largely upon the plausibility of the explanation given in the previous pages. I will not recapitulate. Instead, I want to make three points on the absence of basis explanation of mistake of law cases. The first is a rather dull doctrinal point. As Stevens has pointed out:

> One significant problem with Birks's account of the law is that, if correct, it leads to the result that *Kleinwort Benson* itself was wrongly decided. If restitution follows because there was no basis for the payment made, this absence of basis was not caused by a mistake, but rather by the local authority's lack of capacity to enter into the transaction. The extended limitation period applicable to claims for the 'relief from the consequences of a mistake' would not therefore apply.[117]

Following the Supreme Court decision in *FII*, this point is unanswerable. That case decided that section 32(1)(c) of the Limitation Act 1980 only applies to claims where mistake is an essential element of the cause of action.[118] And if restitution is justified by an absence of basis, mistake is not an essential element of the cause of action.

The second point is less footling. It concerns how the claim should be understood in absence of basis terms. If the claimant had to show that there was *never* an absence of basis, the account would stumble upon the same problems that we have faced in this chapter: there *was* a basis initially, but it was subsequently removed. So the absence of basis account, to avoid

---

[114] Zimmermann and Meier (n 47) 565.
[115] *DMG* (n 1) [23].
[116] ibid [28].
[117] Stevens (n 11) 149. See, for a further problem with *DMG*, Chambers (n 102) 233.
[118] *FII* (SC) (n 3).

the problems, could say that what matters is that there is no basis *now*. Whenever limitation is an issue, this leads to the following problem: when does the cause of action arise? Presumably it arises when the basis is avoided. But this means that the approach has to take a stand on when a particular decision changes the law or merely declares it—and in a case like *Hazell*, that can be highly contentious.

Finally, consider Birks' claim:

> There was no mistake, in the sense that there was no impairment by wrong data. But there was, retrospectively, a *solutio indebiti*, a payment of a sum not due ... One can create an absence of legal ground retrospectively, one cannot create an impairment retrospectively.[119]

Birks denies that a fact about the world (the impairment) can be changed retrospectively. It is certainly true that empirical facts cannot be changed in this way. But I have claimed that the law's retrospective amendment does matter to the payor in the same way that an impairment matters. What is most striking about the passage, though, is Birks' unreasoned acceptance that *the law* can change things retrospectively. This gets to the heart of the matter. In the cases I have considered, the problem arises because of the common law's approach to adjudication, and the key question is what the normative consequences of that commitment are. This is an important question. But our concentration on the question should not blind us to the more difficult and more important theoretical question: the justification of the law's commitment to retrospectivity.

V. CONCLUSION

Peter Birks said that that mistake of law cases require us to have a fully fledged understanding of jurisprudence.[120] In this chapter I have argued that Lord Hoffmann's approach can justify restitution without a need to commit ourselves to any contestable jurisprudential positions regarding a theory of law. All we must presuppose is common law retrospectivity and non-contradiction. But the first presupposition must not go unexamined. Finnis rightly characterises the issue of this chapter as one of comparatively minimal importance.[121] Retrospective common law adjudication is the camel; retrospective mistakes of law are mere gnats in comparison. Perhaps we should not swallow retrospective adjudication. Or perhaps we should swallow it, but note its bitter taste. Either way, our attention should focus firmly on *that* issue.

---

[119] Birks (n 24) 233.
[120] ibid 205.
[121] Finnis (n 63) 174.

17

The Jurisprudence of Lord Hoffmann in Property Law

ROGER SMITH

I. INTRODUCTION

IN CONSIDERING THE legacy of Lord Hoffmann, this chapter concentrates upon just one of his judgments in the House of Lords. This is *Bruton v London and Quadrant Housing Trust*,[1] in which it was held that a licensee is capable of creating a lease with exclusive possession. Accordingly, this chapter makes no attempt to survey his judgments across a wide array of diverse topics within the property context, though I did re-read his judgments in that context. In reading this material, a couple of general points stood out, though neither is really surprising. The first is the frequency with which Lord Hoffmann relied on his sense of what a reasonable conclusion should be. Thus, there are references to arguments that should be rejected as involving 'remarkably silly consequences'[2] or being 'quite irrational'.[3] Similarly, agreements should not be construed so as to lead to 'highly unreal' consequences.[4]

A danger of this type of approach, of course, is that different lawyers will disagree as to whether such descriptions are justified or—perhaps more likely—whether the oddity justifies departing from what would otherwise be the outcome. Indeed, in several of the cases I read, the Court of Appeal had expressed itself in similar terms prior to being reversed by Lord Hoffmann and his fellow judges in the House of Lords.[5] However, Lord Hoffmann's

---

[1] *Bruton v London and Quadrant Housing Trust* [1999] UKHL 26, [2000] 1 AC 406.
[2] *Scottish and Newcastle plc v Raguz* [2008] UKHL 65, [2008] 1 WLR 2494 [10].
[3] *Walker v Birmingham City Council* [2007] UKHL 22, [2007] 2 AC 262 [10].
[4] *West Bromwich Building Society v Wilkinson* [2005] UKHL 44, [2005] 1 WLR 2303 [20].
[5] An interesting example is *Bruton* (n 1), which will be investigated in more detail below. In the Court of Appeal, Sir Brian Neill had dissented, but had made clear his unease with the conclusion he reached: *Bruton v London and Quadrant Housing Trust* [1997] EWCA Civ 2255, [1998] QB 834, 837. Kennedy LJ observed (at 846) that 'common sense rebels' against that minority view. Yet Sir Brian Neill's conclusion was upheld by Lord Hoffmann and a unanimous House of Lords.

judgments are much more than a call for a reasonable conclusion (perhaps in contrast with the later judgments of Lord Denning)—they are all marked by a full and generally compelling analysis of the case law. That is my second general point: persuasive legal analysis is employed to justify the conclusions Lord Hoffmann felt appropriate to reach. Of course, not everybody will have been persuaded by the analysis, but that is inevitable whenever there is complex and controversial legal analysis.

A. A Case on Options

Before turning to *Bruton*, mention will be made of one case decided by Lord Hoffmann at first instance. This is largely because it illustrates the style adopted by Lord Hoffmann, but also because it was the first of his cases in the property context which really made an impression on me in the early 1990s. That case is *Spiro v Glencrown Ltd.*[6] In many respects, it was a quite straightforward case on options. Like, I suspect, many others, I had rather unthinkingly accepted the analysis of the option that it operates as an irrevocable offer by the owner to sell—the exercise of the option operating as an acceptance of that offer.[7] The problem in *Spiro* was that, under that analysis, the contract to sell the land arises when the option is exercised. Section 2 of the Law of Property (Miscellaneous Provisions) Act 1989 would then require writing signed by both parties at that stage.[8] As is obvious, the exercise of the option is a unilateral act on the part of the purchaser: it would be quite exceptional for it also to be signed by the seller.

It may be suspected that virtually every judge would strive to hold that it is the option agreement that has to satisfy the 1989 Act rather than the exercise of the option or, perhaps more accurately, the contract resulting from the exercise. That Hoffmann J so held is, accordingly, not surprising. What is more interesting is the reasoning employed. He stressed that other cases have treated options as a form of conditional contract. Counsel argued that Hoffmann J had to decide between these rival ideas and that the irrevocable offer analysis was supported by most of the cases. Section 2 itself would pose a problem only if the irrevocable offer theory was adopted.

Hoffmann J recognised that there was authority supporting both the irrevocable offer and conditional contract theories. However, he wisely declined the invitation to determine which of them is correct. To quote from his

---

[6] *Spiro v Glencrown Ltd* [1991] Ch 537 (ChD).

[7] The authorities supporting this analysis are fully discussed in *Spiro* (ibid). A recent example was *J Sainsbury plc v O'Connor* [1990] STC 516, 531 (Millett J), though the analysis goes back at least as far as Lord Herschell LC and Lord Watson in *Helby v Matthews* [1895] AC 471 (HL). The text discusses an option to buy: there can of course also be an option to sell.

[8] A signed offer followed by a signed acceptance does not suffice, as was subsequently confirmed by the Court of Appeal in *Commission for the New Towns v Cooper (Great Britain) Ltd* [1995] Ch 259 (CA).

judgment: the earlier judges 'were not using "offer" in its primary sense but, as often happens in legal reasoning, by way of metaphor or analogy. Such metaphors can be vivid and illuminating but prove a trap for the unwary if pressed beyond their original context' and later:

> The purchaser's argument requires me to say that 'irrevocable offer' and 'conditional contract' are mutually inconsistent concepts and that I must range myself under one or other banner and declare the other to be heretical. I hope that I have demonstrated this to be a misconception about the nature of legal reasoning. An option is not strictly speaking either an offer or a conditional contract. It does not have *all* the incidents of the standard form of either of these concepts. To that extent it is a relationship sui generis. But there are ways in which it resembles each of them. Each analogy is in the proper context a valid way of characterising the situation created by an option.

Looked at in this way, it was easy to conclude that the irrevocable offer theory does not mean that section 2 requires the exercise of the option to be signed by both parties.

This tells us much about legal reasoning. It is all too easy to explain areas such as options by way of metaphor or analogy: it helps us to see what is happening and how a legal rule can be justified. However, we must not fall into the trap of equating the metaphor or analogy with the underlying legal principle. That may sometimes be appropriate, but on other occasions there may, as Hoffmann J observes, be a *sui generis* situation.

B. The *Bruton* Controversy

The remainder of this chapter concentrates upon the controversial decision in *Bruton*. This case is especially interesting because it received a decidedly hostile response from commentators. Nearly all the numerous notes and articles discussing it have been sharply critical. Nor has the response been limited to the years immediately following the decision in 1999; articles continue to be written on *Bruton*. The original hostile response has become more nuanced in more recent writing and I should say at once that my own views are very close to those of Dr Nicholas Roberts writing in 2012.[9] Whether this necessarily means that the views of commentators have changed may not be entirely obvious; an alternative explanation might be the need for authors to find fresh perspectives on a controversial topic!

It is relatively easy to summarise the problem in *Bruton*. Landlords have statutory duties relating to the state of the premises[10] and Mr Bruton claimed

---

[9] N Roberts, 'The Bruton Tenancy: A Matter of Relativity' [2012] *Conveyancer and Property Lawyer* 87.
[10] Landlord and Tenant Act 1985, s 11.

that there was a breach of those duties. The problem was that his landlord (the Housing Trust) was in fact a licensee from Lambeth Borough Council: could a mere licensee confer a lease on Mr Bruton? The background was that the premises were scheduled for demolition. In the intervening period, the Council licensed the premises to the Housing Trust for occupation by homeless individuals. The Housing Trust purported to grant a licence to Mr Bruton. It might be observed that Mr Bruton would clearly have had a lease if either the Council had entered into the agreement with him or, alternatively, if the Housing Trust had itself a lease of the premises. This would have been the result of the well-known decision in *Street v Mountford*,[11] which reasserts exclusive possession as the touchstone in deciding whether there is a lease or a licence.

II. THE MERITS OF THE CLAIM FOR DISREPAIR

If we step back from the technical issues in the case, the merits are not entirely clear. If there were to be relatively onerous repairing obligations, this would inhibit the use of such short life premises for housing those most in need. On the other hand, it seems difficult to justify the provision of substandard housing, especially when it would clearly have been unlawful had the agreement been between the Council and Mr Bruton. Should public sector landlords be permitted to avoid obligations which would clearly attach to private sector tenancies? In *Bruton* itself, Sir Brian Neill in the Court of Appeal[12] clearly thought it unfortunate if public sector landlords were unable to lease such property to the homeless—this was a telling comment, as he dissented in holding that there was a lease and the repairing obligations did apply. The House of Lords agreed with the conclusion of Sir Brian Neill; similar reservations were expressed by Lords Slynn and Jauncey. However, these reservations related more to the applicability of the legislation to public sector landlords than the finding of a lease in *Bruton*. Those doubts as to the practical outcome of *Bruton* have been strongly echoed by some commentators.[13] On the other hand, Susan Bright[14] has regarded the issues as being more complex than was recognised by the Court of Appeal, observing that Mr Bruton had lived there for 10 years; meanwhile, Michael Bridge has

---

[11] *Street v Mountford* [1985] UKHL 4, [1985] AC 809.

[12] *Bruton* (CA) (n 5) 837; see also 846 (Millett LJ).

[13] W Barr, 'The Big Society and Social Housing: Never the Twain Shall Meet?' in N Hopkins (ed), *Modern Studies in Property Law*, vol 1 (Oxford, Hart Publishing, 2012) ch 14; D Rook, 'Whether a Licence Agreement is a Lease: The Irrelevance of the Grantor's Lack of Title' [1999] *Conveyancer and Property Lawyer* 517.

[14] S Bright, 'Case Comment—Exclusive Possession, True Agreement and Tenancy by Estoppel' (1998) 114 *LQR* 345.

described the application of repairing obligations as 'perfectly acceptable'.[15] I must confess to having sympathy with the decision in favour of the tenant, but it is clearly not a straightforward matter.

III. THE ISSUES AND DECISION

The principal issues facing the courts in *Bruton* were: (1) whether a licensee (the Housing Trust) could grant a lease to Mr Bruton; and (2) if not, whether there could be a lease by estoppel. In the Court of Appeal, the leading majority judgment was delivered by Millett LJ. He responded to the first issue in the following manner:

> A tenancy is a legal estate. The essence of a legal estate is that it binds the whole world, not just the parties to the grant and their successors. The hallmark of a tenancy is the grant of exclusive possession. In this context, therefore, exclusive possession means possession to the exclusion of the whole world, not merely of the grantor and those claiming through him. If the grantor has no power to exclude the true owner from possession, he has no power to grant a legal right to exclusive possession and his grant cannot take effect as a tenancy.

This reasoning, it may be observed, has been adopted by many commentators.

Turning to the tenancy by estoppel issue, Millett LJ concluded that there was no scope for a lease by estoppel where the transaction stated on its face that there was a licence. But could the *Street v Mountford* analysis (that exclusive possession for a term is conclusive of a lease) operate within the tenancy by estoppel context? Millett LJ held not: 'the two doctrines cannot be combined in the way contended for. They are, when analysed, mutually exclusive'.[16] How far this reasoning is insurmountable may be questioned: in advance of the appeal to the House of Lords, doubts had been expressed by Susan Bright.[17]

In the House of Lords, the principal analysis turned on the first issue: can a licensee grant a lease? Lord Hoffmann[18] was emphatic that lack of title did not preclude the grant of a tenancy. His analysis is best seen in the following quotation, which has been the source of much debate over the past 15 years:

> [T]he term 'lease' or 'tenancy' describes a relationship between two parties who are designated landlord and tenant. It is not concerned with the question of whether the agreement creates an estate or other proprietary interest which may be binding

---

[15] M Bridge, 'Leases—Contract, Property and Status' in L Tee (ed), *Land Law: Issues, Debates, Policy* (Cullompton, Willan, 2002) 119.

[16] *Bruton* (CA) (n 5) 845.

[17] Bright (n 14); see also P Routley, 'Tenancies and Estoppel—After *Bruton v London and Quadrant Housing Trust*' (2000) 63 *MLR* 424, 426.

[18] Lords Slynn, Jauncey and Hobhouse delivered short concurring judgments; Lord Hope agreed with Lord Hoffmann.

upon third parties. A lease may, and usually does, create a proprietary interest called a leasehold estate or, technically, a 'term of years absolute'. This will depend upon whether the landlord had an interest out of which he could grant it. Nemo dat quod non habet. But it is the fact that the agreement is a lease which creates the proprietary interest. It is putting the cart before the horse to say that whether the agreement is a lease depends upon whether it creates a proprietary interest.[19]

On the basis that exclusive possession had been given to Mr Bruton, there was a lease. It might be added that there are dicta in *Street* that it is fatal to a lease if the grantor has 'no power to grant a tenancy'.[20] However, Lord Hoffmann limits those dicta to the context in which it would be ultra vires for a lease to be granted—this does not include lack of title.

Why are these dicta controversial? There are, perhaps, two interlocking points. The first is the nemo dat principle: how can a person who has no estate in the land (or exclusive possession) create a lease? The second revolves around the argument that there can be a lease which does not create an estate. It is objected that the essence of a lease is its status as an estate: a purely contractual tenancy (as the *Bruton* lease is frequently characterised) is a contradiction in terms. Indeed, commentators have suggested that Lord Hoffmann has created a completely new legal category. Before we investigate these arguments, we should look at what later cases have said.

IV. *BRUTON* IN SUBSEQUENT CASES

In most of the cases in which *Bruton* has been mentioned, this has been simply to record its analysis; certainly, no case has sought to question it.[21] There are two cases which tell us something interesting about *Bruton*. In *Islington Borough Council v Green*,[22] the question was whether the freeholder (licensor) could determine the *Bruton* lease. Blackburne J stressed that the *Bruton* principle operates regardless of whether the lease creates an estate binding third parties. Although Lord Hoffmann in *Bruton* had left open the effect of the lease on the freeholder,[23] Blackburne J had no hesitation in holding the freeholder unaffected. This fits principle well: it would be a significant breach of the nemo dat principle if the licensee could create rights affecting the licensor that were greater than those enjoyed by the licensee.[24]

---

[19] *Bruton* (n 1) 415.

[20] *Street v Mountford* (n 11) 821.

[21] Some dicta in *London Development Agency v Nidai* [2009] EWHC 1730 (Ch) might be read as inconsistent. However, this was in the context of a claim by the freeholder, who (as will be seen below) has been held to be unaffected by the lease.

[22] *Islington Borough Council v Green* [2005] EWCA Civ 56, [2005] HLR 591.

[23] *Bruton* (n 1) 416. As Blackburne J stressed, in the Court of Appeal Sir Brian Neill was emphatic that the licensor would not be bound: *Bruton* (CA) (n 5) 842.

[24] An argument that the licensor could be bound on an agency analysis was rejected as inconsistent with the facts.

Rather more interesting is *Kay v Lambeth London Borough Council*. Though the Court of Appeal decision was before *Green*, the House of Lords decision came just over a year later. The Court of Appeal[25] was clear that the freeholder's title was superior to that of the tenant and this appears not to have been challenged in the House of Lords.[26] Two interesting points arise from Lord Scott's analysis in the House of Lords. First, he appears to accept the idea that the *Bruton* lease does not create an estate—referring to it as a 'non-estate' tenancy. This, of course, is entirely in accordance with what Lord Hoffmann had said; the 'non-estate' terminology will be adopted in this chapter (alongside its description as a contractual tenancy). The second point concerns the main argument on this aspect of the appeal: that surrender of the licence had the effect of making the tenant's rights binding on the freeholder. This was based upon the principle in *Mellor v Watkins*.[27] This principle relates to the status of a sublease when the head lease terminates. Normally, the sublease terminates together with the head lease, for example, when the head lease is forfeited following breach. However, surrender of the head lease has the effect that the sublease survives and becomes binding on the freeholder: the head tenant cannot by a voluntary act terminate the sublease. Contrast with this the case where the head lease provides for termination (or is a periodic tenancy): here notice to terminate given by the head tenant falls outside the *Mellor v Watkins* principle.[28]

Lord Scott had no difficulty in dismissing this argument. The principle does not allow a licensee to create a situation in which a lease binds the freeholder. As was stressed, we may allow an estate carved out of the head lease to bind the freeholder, but the *Bruton* lease cannot be seen as being carved out of the licence. That reasoning seems to be eminently justified. However, is there any reason why *Mellor v Watkins* should not be extended to a *sub-licence* carved out of the original licence? This would, of course, mean that the occupier could have no more than a licence against the freeholder, but that might be sufficient to justify continued occupation. Lacking the protection of a secure tenancy, however, it would provide no protection if either the original licence or the sub-licence provides for termination. It may appear odd for the occupier to have a lease as against the licensee (the *Bruton* lease) and a licence as against the freeholder, but this does no more than recognise the ideas of relativity underpinning titles in English law.

---

[25] *Kay v Lambeth London Borough Council* [2004] EWCA Civ 926, [2005] QB 352 [58]–[73]; the tenant's argument was largely based on the statutory provisions relating to secure tenancies.

[26] *Kay and others v London Borough of Lambeth; Leeds City Council v Price and others* [2006] UKHL 10, [2006] 2 AC 465, [137]. Much of the interest of the case lies in the human rights context, on which it was not followed in *Manchester City Council v Pinnock* [2010] UKSC 8, [2011] 2 AC 104.

[27] *Mellor v Watkins* (1874) LR 9 QB 400.

[28] *Pennell v Payne* [1995] QB 192 (CA); *Barrett v Morgan* [2000] UKHL 1, [2000] 2 AC 264.

V. CRITICISM OF *BRUTON*: THE NEMO DAT PRINCIPLE
AND RELATIVITY

We can now turn to the consternation expressed by commentators. It has already been observed that *Bruton* has been widely criticised, particularly in the numerous notes and comments in the years immediately after the decision.[29] Around that time, Lord Hoffmann visited Oxford for an informal seminar to discuss *Bruton*. My recollection is that he mounted a stout defence of the decision, though in the face of considerable scepticism expressed by my colleagues who were present.

We have seen that one major concern relates to the nemo dat argument: how can a person who does not have an estate create a lease? A variation on this theme is whether a person who does not enjoy exclusive possession (the Housing Trust, as licensee) can give the exclusive possession to the tenant— all would agree that exclusive possession is essential for a lease to exist. At first impression, these look to be strong arguments. However, it will be argued that they are misguided.

The core of the answer to these concerns lies in the acceptance by English law of relativity of titles. This point was developed in some detail by Dr Nicholas Roberts a few years ago,[30] though there had been earlier support for it in the literature.[31] It enjoys the influential support of Lord Neuberger MR: 'The *Bruton* case was about relativity of title which is the traditional bedrock of English land law.'[32]

It has long been recognised that there can be more than one fee simple: the adverse possessor holds a fee simple well before the period of adverse possession is completed. This goes back to Coke[33] and is illustrated by the right of adverse possessors to reclaim the land from anybody who dispossessors them: a right best illustrated by *Asher v Whitlock*.[34] Perhaps most

---

[29] Rook (n 13); S Bright, 'Leases, Exclusive Possession and Estates' (2000) 116 *LQR* 7; M Dixon, 'The Non-proprietary Lease: The Rise of the Feudal Phoenix' [2000] *CLJ* 25; Routley (n 17); M Harwood, 'Leases: Are They Still Not Really Real?' (2000) 20 *Legal Studies* 503; M Pawlowski and J Brown, '*Bruton*: A New Species of Tenancy?' (2000) 4 *Landlord and Tenant Law Review* 119 (views repeated and developed in M Pawlowski, 'Occupational Rights in Leasehold Law: Time for Rationalisation?' [2002] *Conveyancer and Property Lawyer* 550; M Pawlowski, 'Feeding Forfeitures by Estoppel' [2004] *Conveyancer and Property Lawyer* 337; M Pawlowski, 'Contractual Intention and the Nature of Leases' (2004) 127 *LQR* 222; M Pawlowski, 'The Bruton Tenancy—Clarity or More Confusion?' [2005] *Conveyancer and Property Lawyer* 262; M Pawlowski, 'Personal and Proprietary Tenancies' (2009) 234 *Property Law Journal* 19).

[30] Roberts (n 9).

[31] It was mentioned by Harwood (n 29) 512, though the point is more strongly made by K Lewison [2009] *Conveyancer and Property Lawyer* 433; see also J-P Hinojosa, 'On Property, Leases, Licences, Horses and Carts: Revisiting *Bruton v London and Quadrant Housing Trust*' (2005) 69 *Conveyancer and Property Lawyer* 114; Bright (n 29) discusses exclusive possession as a relative concept.

[32] *Berrisford v Mexfield Housing Co-operative Ltd* [2011] UKSC 52, [2012] 1 AC 955 [65].

[33] Co Litt 2a, 297a; *Rosenberg v Cook* [1881] 8 QB 162, 165 (Jessel MR).

[34] *Asher v Whitlock* [1865] 1 QB 1.

interesting for us is that a person who adversely possesses as against a tenant obtains a fee simple. This formed part of the basis for the *Tichborne v Weir*[35] rejection of the argument that the adverse possessor obtains the tenant's lease. The Law Commission recognises that this survives in the modern land registration system, though since the Land Registration Act 2002,[36] the registration of the adverse possessor will convert the fee simple into a lease. If adverse possession against a tenant gives rise to a fee simple, this sits uneasily with the supposed principle that a lease cannot be granted by a licensee.

To develop this reasoning, suppose an adverse possessor, prior to the completion of adverse possession,[37] grants a lease. Clearly, the true owner has a superior title to both the adverse possessor and the tenant. Suppose we were to construe exclusive possession in an absolute sense, such that it has to give possession as against everybody. In that case, there would be no exclusive possession and no lease. This is plainly an unacceptable and erroneous result. Such a lease is good relative to the adverse possessor and those deriving title from the adverse possessor. If the true owner has effectively abandoned the land, then the risks to the adverse possessor are small.[38]

Relativity of title is generally encountered in the context of adverse possession, as in the discussion above.[39] *Bruton* is not such a case. However, there is no reason why relativity should not apply where a licensee purports to grant a lease. Indeed, the law pre-*Bruton* appeared content to do this where there was a tenancy by estoppel.[40] We shall see that Lord Hoffmann states that the estoppel is the result of there being a lease rather than the basis of there being a lease. However, even the latter view (which many would have adopted before *Bruton*) accepts that there can be a lease when the landlord has no title. Indeed, it was held that such tenancies would fall within the statutory protection of tenants.[41] At this point, we are not concerned with the question whether a tenancy by estoppel could be justified on the facts of *Bruton*; rather, the point is that the tenancy by estoppel is

---

[35] *Tichborne v Weir* [1892] 67 LT 735 (CA). *Tichborne* itself does not analyse the title of the adverse possessor, but Sedley J in *Central London Commercial Estates Ltd v Kato Kagaku Co Ltd* [1998] 4 All ER 948, 951 spells it out as a fee simple.

[36] Schedule 7, para 9(1) (read together with paras 1(1), 4, 6(1) and 7); Law Commission, 'Land Registration for the Twenty-First Century: A Conveyancing Revolution' (Law Com No 271, 2001) [14.71]. This is discussed further below.

[37] Since the Land Registration Act 2002 (LRA), completion of adverse possession requires compliance with sched 6: see s 96.

[38] As in *Perry v Clissold* [1907] AC 73 (PC) (claim for compulsory acquisition of adverse possessor's title).

[39] Similar analyses apply to the law relating to finding of chattels, as the famous case of *Armory v Delamirie* [1722] EWHC KB J94, (1722) 1 Strange 505, 93 ER 664 shows.

[40] The classic analysis is by AM Prichard, 'Tenancy by Estoppel' (1964) 80 *LQR* 370.

[41] *Bell v General Accident Fire and Life Assurance Corporation Ltd* [1998] L&TR 1 (Landlord and Tenant Act 1954).

designed for cases where the landlord has no title—it was never suggested that the law precluded a tenancy in such cases.

Seen in this way, the nemo dat argument falls away. When we deal with nemo dat, we are dealing with the question whether one person can affect others who already have interests in the property. To take an example from personal property, nemo dat means that a person who has merely contracted to buy property is unable to confer ownership on a sub-purchaser. As is well known, section 25 of the Sale of Goods Act 1979 enables the purchaser to pass good title if in possession—an exception to the nemo dat rule. All this is relative to the title of the seller. In the *Bruton* context, of course, nobody argues that the freeholder is affected by the *Bruton* lease—we have seen that this is confirmed by *Green* and *Kay*.

So far, the state of the pre-*Bruton* authorities has not been given much consideration. Unsurprisingly, the problem of the landlord without title arises in relatively few situations. Insofar as there are relevant dicta in the earlier cases, they are generally not directed towards the problem arising in *Bruton*. In most cases, it is enough to establish that there cannot be a lease affecting the freeholder; that is uncontroversial, whether before or after *Bruton*. Furthermore, most such cases would fall within the scope of the traditional tenancy by estoppel. The situation where the parties purport to create a licence (as in *Bruton*) has given rise to problems only since *Street v Mountford* placed so much stress on exclusive possession. It is true that *Street* may be said to restore the law to how it was perceived to operate prior to the mid-twentieth century (clearly the view of Lord Templeman), but before that time, it would have been most unusual to attempt to create a licence in circumstances where exclusive possession is intended to be conferred.

However, one case that causes real difficulty is the Court of Appeal decision in *Milmo v Carreras*.[42] The case involved a purported sublease that would last longer than the head lease held by the sub-lessor. The Court of Appeal held that the sublease took effect as an assignment. Lord Greene MR observed that the relationship of landlord and tenant:

> [M]ust depend on privity of estate. I myself find it impossible to conceive of a relationship of landlord and tenant which has not got that essential element of tenure in it, and that implies that the tenant holds of his landlord, and he can only do that if the landlord has a reversion. You cannot have a purely contractual tenure.[43]

If we accept a relativity analysis, should this not have applied in the *Milmo* context? The claim in the case was by the sub-lessor seeking to claim possession under the terms of the sublease. If a mere licensee can create a tenancy (as in *Bruton*), should not the same be true of a person with an

---

[42] *Milmo v Carreras* [1946] KB 306 (CA), not cited in *Bruton* (n 1). Bright ((n 29) 9) drew attention to its significance and it has been relied upon by several commentators, with an extended analysis by Roberts ((n 9) 99–101).

[43] *Milmo v Carreras* (ibid) 311.

inadequate title to support the duration of the tenancy (as in *Milmo*)? The last sentence of the quoted passage need not trouble the relativity analysis, as that analysis does not treat the relationship as purely contractual. However, the insistence on the landlord holding a reversion is more problematic.[44] Perhaps the complexity of the situation may provide a justification for the decision. The rule that a sublease cannot be for a term longer than the head lease does not operate only as between sub-lessor and sub-lessee. Thus, the ruling that it takes effect as an assignment has an obvious effect as between the freeholder and the sub-lessee: the sub-lessee becomes a tenant of the freeholder. It would be unduly complex to say that the sub-lessee is a tenant of both the freeholder and (by a relativity analysis) the sub-lessor—to whom should rent be paid? We might say (and there is much in Lord Greene MR's analysis that supports this) that the sub-lessor did have a title, but this has been removed from him. It might conceivably be treated as a form of deemed surrender to the freeholder.

More generally, the rule in *Milmo v Carreras* does appear to have been accepted: it was based upon prior authority. However, it has consequences that cause considerable unease. The terms of a sublease may well be very different from those in the head lease as regards both rent and other obligations. An assignment opens the assignee to obligations in the head lease, which may be both an unpleasant surprise and may also make a nonsense of the structure of the sublease. Though the rule has the benefit of simplifying the leasehold structure, this may be at a considerable cost to the intentions of the parties. In other words, if *Bruton* really is inconsistent with *Milmo*, then it might be no bad thing to reconsider *Milmo*![45]

VI. THE NON-ESTATE TENANCY

The idea of relativity in the *Bruton* scenario is one that can be made to fit with property principles. More difficult is the proposition that a lease may operate merely as a contract between the parties. It has been observed that Lord Hoffmann thought that a lease does not necessarily 'create a proprietary interest called a leasehold estate'.[46] If that argument is correct, it is then unnecessary to rely on relativity analyses.

---

[44] It might be queried whether a tenancy by estoppel might have been relied upon in *Milmo*. However, the tenancy by estoppel does not operate where the landlord has a legal title, but one insufficient to support the lease: see C Harpum, S Bridge and M Dixon, *Megarry and Wade: The Law of Real Property* (8th edn, London, Sweet & Maxwell, 2012) para 17-129 and the authorities cited therein (including *Cuthbertson v Irving* [1859] 4 H&N 742, 754; 157 ER 1034, 1039 (Martin B), in which the principles applying to the estoppel are explained).

[45] Note the criticism of *Milmo* in A Hill-Smith, 'The Principle in *Milmo v Carreras*: When the Term of a Sub-lease Equals or Exceeds that of the Head Lease' [2002] *Conveyancer and Property Lawyer* 509.

[46] Text accompanying n 19.

One point should be mentioned at the outset. In at least some contexts, the idea that a tenancy does not involve an estate is completely orthodox. Thus, we have the tenancy at will and (somewhat more problematical) the tenancy at sufferance. These are long-established forms of tenancies, though they do not involve estates. The underlying point is that estates (whether freehold or leasehold) are all about duration, whereas these forms of tenancies have no duration; instead, they describe the relationship between the parties. As expressed by Megarry and Wade: 'Although an estate cannot exist without tenure, there seems no reason why tenure should not exist without any estate.'[47]

In the *Bruton* context, of course, the lease does have a duration: nobody suggests that there was a tenancy at will. All that these forms of lease show is that a simple 'no estate, therefore no tenancy' analysis is erroneous.[48] Lord Hoffmann refers to the possibility of there being a lease without any estate or other proprietary interest—without, therefore, any leasehold estate. This is what was described by Lord Scott in *Kay* as a 'non-estate tenancy'; it has also been described by commentators as a 'contractual tenancy'. They have objected that this is a new form of tenancy, not based upon any previous form of tenancy. Furthermore, it is inconsistent with dicta in a number of cases, including *Milmo*, discussed above.

As has been observed, some more recent commentators have been more supportive of *Bruton*. We have seen that Roberts supports a relativity approach. He concludes that this is not consistent with what Lord Hoffmann said and proceeds to reject the broader non-estate analysis propounded by Lord Hoffmann.[49] Other authors[50] try to consider *Bruton* as an example of the notion of property being given a wider scope, though it may be doubted whether this is what Lord Hoffmann intended; this last analysis will be put on one side.

The idea of a purely contractual tenancy is genuinely difficult. Once we recognise that a tenancy can exist without an estate, perhaps the idea is, at a very fundamental level, compatible with principle. On the other hand, it would be a form of tenancy quite different from anything else recognised: it is not a term of years, a periodic tenancy, a tenancy at will or any other of the categories presently recognised. The closest one can get to rationalising it is as a tenancy coupled with a purely contractual right as regards duration; a mixture of tenancy at will and contractual licence perhaps. Yet the

---

[47] Harpum, Bridge and Dixon (n 44) para 17-106.

[48] Pawlowski, 'Occupational Rights in Leashold Law' (n 29) discusses the links between *Bruton* (n 1) and tenancies at will as both constituting hybrid tenancies. He argues for a restructuring of the categories in this area in order to better distinguish between personal and proprietary claims.

[49] Roberts (n 9) 102 and fn 5.

[50] Probably the best example is Hinojosa (n 31), who also stresses relativity in a useful fashion.

law denies the parties' ability to vary the rule that a tenancy at will is terminable by either party at any time.[51] However, in *Berrisford v Mexfield Housing Co-operative Ltd*,[52] it was contemplated that a periodic tenancy might be subject to contractual constraints on termination. This flexibility might extend to a tenancy at will. However, this is to take us too far into the realms of speculation; it is difficult to justify a contractual tenancy of this type on the present state of the authorities. When reading the criticisms of the contractual tenancy, one is struck by the range of dicta which at least assume that no such entity is recognised. *Bruton* could be a game changer in this respect, but is that necessary when a relativity analysis would work just as well?

All this prompts the following question: what did Lord Hoffmann really intend in his dicta in *Bruton*? Did he intend that there would be no estate *as between the Housing Trust and Mr Bruton*? We might start with two observations. Lord Hoffmann explains his analysis as being driven by the nemo dat principle. Yet it has been seen that it is consistent with that principle for a relativity analysis to apply. The second is that the thrust of counsel's argument appears to have been based upon relativity.[53]

We may all agree that the *Bruton* tenancy is not an estate binding the world; it is quite clear (and would have been tolerably obvious even at the time of *Bruton*) that it does not bind the freeholder. But did Lord Hoffmann intend to deny that there was an estate as between the Housing Trust and Mr Bruton? It may be that this would not matter most of the time—though these are issues which will be investigated towards the end of this chapter. The crucial aspect of an estate is that it is capable of binding successors in title. Suppose the Housing Trust had decided to assign its licence to another Housing Trust working in the same geographical area, with the permission of the freeholder (the council). Could the assignee renounce the lease on the basis that there was no privity of contract between it and Mr Bruton? Or suppose that a private sector licensee creates a *Bruton* lease and then dies, leaving his property to X.[54] Could X evict the tenant? These situations may be unlikely to arise, but it is submitted that they hold the key to our understanding of the *Bruton* lease. There is a strong argument that the successor should be bound. This is consistent only with the relativity analysis; it does not work with a purely contractual lease. But it is difficult to discern what Lord Hoffmann intended; certainly, the relativity analysis is not supported

---

[51] *Errington v Errington* [1951] EWCA Civ 2, [1952] 1 KB 290 (Denning LJ); *Binions v Evans* [1972] EWCA Civ 6, [1972] Ch 359 (Lord Denning MR and Megaw LJ); *Colchester BC v Smith* [1991] Ch 448, 483.

[52] *Berrisford* (n 32) [69] (Lord Neuberger MR); see also Lord Mance [104].

[53] *Bruton* (n 1) 408. Counsel was Kim Lewison, who has subsequently asserted that *Bruton* (n 1) is to be explained on relativity of title (see n 31).

[54] Two factors make this situation unlikely. Where there is exclusive possession, it will be very difficult to persuade the courts that there is a licence rather than a lease. In addition, any licence may well be terminable on the licensee's death.

on a natural reading of what he said (though he was not, of course, considering the position of purchasers). As already observed, Dr Roberts believes that Lord Hoffmann really did intend a purely contractual tenancy (without using those words, of course). There is certainly support for this when Lord Hoffmann asserts[55] that the tenancy relationship 'is not concerned with the question of whether the agreement creates an estate or other proprietary interest which may be binding upon third parties'. I would like to regard the construction of the dicta as rather more open, but I must confess that this would require considerable qualification of Lord Hoffmann's words.

VII. POSTSCRIPT

The question as to what Lord Hoffmann intended in *Bruton* was discussed following the oral presentation of this chapter. It is most interesting that Lord Hoffmann was quite clear that the relativity analysis was the basis of his approach; he did not intend to suggest that there could be a purely contractual principle. As we have seen, this is far more readily reconciled with traditional property analyses as to how estates work.

Two aspects of this are worthy of attention. The first is that it is not authority: it is what was actually written in the judgment in *Bruton* which provides the ratio decidendi of the case. Nevertheless, it lends support to the argument that the words used can (contrary to the analysis of Roberts) be treated as being based upon the relativity analysis.

The second aspect is a far more general one: it is dangerous to interpret a judgment (even of a judge like Lord Hoffmann, who is renowned for using language in a precise and accurate manner) as if it were an Act of Parliament. Especially as one moves away from the very precise point upon which a case is decided, not every dictum should be taken literally. This is even more true where it is inconsistent with principles in the area and not necessary for the resolution of the case.

VIII. TENANCY BY ESTOPPEL

It has been seen that the Court of Appeal treated the question whether there was a tenancy by estoppel as being the central issue in *Bruton*. One might have expected that the question whether *Street v Mountford* could operate in conjunction with the tenancy by estoppel would constitute the major issue in the House of Lords. However, Lord Hoffmann was able to side-step this by employing the analysis discussed above. He did consider the tenancy by estoppel, but dismissed it with the imperious observation that 'as the

---

[55] *Bruton* (n 1) 415.

authorities show, it is not the estoppel which creates the tenancy, but the tenancy which creates the estoppel'.[56]

What is the estoppel that Lord Hoffmann refers to? There is a well-known rule that the tenant cannot deny the landlord's title (so that rent has to be paid even though the landlord has no title) and the landlord cannot rely on his own lack of title (to deny a repairing covenant, for example). In these types of case, there is indeed authority[57] supporting the idea that there is a lease and that the estoppel operates within the lease rather than creating it—this fits Lord Hoffmann's analysis. Yet it may be that the earlier cases also recognised a somewhat broader form of estoppel, operating where there would not otherwise be a tenancy.[58] The relationship between these categories appears somewhat elusive. It is also said that some estoppels are based upon representation and others upon a common law rule.[59] Perhaps Lord Hoffmann's analysis fails to do justice to the range of ideas previously operating, but it may well be thought that it introduces welcome simplicity and clarity.

It may be added that Lord Hoffmann saw[60] no inconsistency between 'what the trust [ie, the Housing Trust] purported to do and its denial of the existence of a tenancy'. Despite the words used, 'the trust did plainly purport to create a tenancy'. Just as landlords cannot contract out of the Rent Acts by applying the label of licence, nor can they avoid the effect of estoppel. This reasoning (a brief paragraph at the end of his speech) indicates that a lease would have been found on the tenancy by estoppel analysis if the case had proceeded on the basis employed by the Court of Appeal. This, of course, vindicates doubts that had been expressed by commentators about the treatment of the tenancy by estoppel argument by the Court of Appeal.

Two observations may be added. The first is that a tenancy by estoppel renders the entire controversy regarding contractual leases unnecessary: the appeal could have been allowed on a basis which, despite splitting the Court of Appeal, would not have raised the broad issues that have troubled commentators. Perhaps Lord Hoffmann's response would be that to rely upon a tenancy by estoppel would have been inconsistent with both: (1) the true operation of tenancies by estoppel; and (2) a proper understanding as to how tenancies operate.

The second observation is directed towards commentators. If the decision could have been analysed on tenancy by estoppel grounds, why do the actual grounds for the decision cause so much controversy? If we were to employ a tenancy by estoppel analysis, the practical result is that a licensee

---

[56] *Bruton* (n 1) 416.

[57] Lord Hoffmann relied upon Kelly CB in *Morton v Woods* (1869) LR 4 QB 293, 304.

[58] This is reflected in the earlier editions of Megarry and Wade (n 44); see, eg, R Megarry and HWR Wade, *The Law of Real Property* (4th edn, London, Sweet & Maxwell, 1975) 646.

[59] Explained by Millett LJ in *First National Bank plc v Thompson* [1996] Ch 231 (CA); Harpum, Bridge and Dixon (n 44) para 17-125. See also Prichard (n 40) 394–96.

[60] *Bruton* (n 1) 416.

has created a lease which attracts the statutory repairing obligations. Virtually all the consequential issues raised by commentators (discussed in the following section) would seem to be equally applicable to the tenancy by estoppel. We may still be puzzled by the concept of a contractual tenancy, but would it really be any more difficult to apply in practice?

One specific, but quite important, point may be worth investigation. It is clear that the tenancy by estoppel operates to bind successors in title.[61] If the *Bruton* analysis really is of a purely contractual tenancy, can the *Bruton* tenancy be combined with a tenancy by estoppel so that a successor in title can be bound? Though it was suggested above that a contractual tenancy itself would not bind purchasers, there appears to be no reason why that result should not be achieved by the estoppel analysis. After all, Lord Hoffmann is clear that the estoppel flows from the existence of the tenancy. This takes away much of the significance of the difference between the relativity analysis and the contractual tenancy analysis. This goes to emphasise the point that the significance of *Bruton* may have been vastly over-rated.

IX. HOW DO RELATIVE TITLES AND NON-ESTATE TENANCIES WORK?

We will split this analysis into two parts: issues relating to the impact on third parties and other issues. With each of them, we will need to ask whether the relativity analysis and the non-estate tenancy analysis lead to different results.

A. The Impact on Third Parties

Some aspects of this have already been investigated. The nature of the relativity analysis is that the *Bruton* lease will bind successors in title from the landlord. Although one would not expect the non-estate tenancy to have that effect, it was seen in the previous section that there might be a tenancy by estoppel which could bind successors.

We will start with an investigation of registration rules. It is commonly observed that the relativity central to unregistered conveyancing (and rights to chattels) has no role in registered conveyancing. The very language of absolute titles encompasses ideas that are far closer to civilian concepts of *dominium*. Of course, the fact that the legislation both states the effect of and guarantees absolute titles goes a long way towards supporting this view. Thus, first registration with an absolute title will defeat any unprotected

---

[61] See Harpum, Bridge and Dixon (n 44) para 17-127 and the authorities cited therein; Prichard (n 40) 386. The assertion by Routley ((n 17) 428) that a tenancy by estoppel 'is not a tenancy: not a proprietary interest' must be regarded as misguided.

rival claims to the land.[62] If two persons are both registered as proprietor, this is generally regarded as a calamity which the system struggles to cope with.[63] On this basis, it may be thought difficult for the system to recognise a lease which binds some people (the licensee/landlord) but not others (the registered proprietor of the freehold/licensor).

Yet this may underestimate the flexibility of the system. What happens if there is adverse possession—the most obvious application of relativity? The original owner will have the registered fee simple, but what right can be claimed by the adverse possessor? Under the 1925 Act, the law imposed a trust when the period of adverse possession was completed. However, the Law Commission viewed this trust as both giving rise to problems and (more relevant to us) unnecessary.[64] It was perfectly happy to see the squatter as having a legal fee simple—overtly applying the relativity that is central to unregistered conveyancing. Even more interesting is a proposal that was never implemented: that a person who adversely possesses as against a tenant should be registered as proprietor of a qualified fee simple—alongside the absolute fee simple registered in the freeholder/landlord.[65] The final solution[66] that the adverse possessor should be registered as proprietor of the lease is far more satisfactory. However, what is of interest to us is that the original proposal regarded it as fully consistent with the operation of land registration to have two registered fee simple titles to the same plot. Doubtless it would be unacceptable to have two absolute titles, but where one is qualified, the system can operate satisfactorily.

What does this mean for the *Bruton* lease? There are three possibilities: the lease as a registered estate, as an overriding interest and as an interest protected by notice. Registration of leases is generally relevant only for those exceeding seven years—in practice unlikely for *Bruton* leases.[67] However, there appears to be no reason why the lease should not be registered with qualified title—analogous to the qualified title contemplated by the Law Commission for the adverse possessor.[68] This would most obviously be relevant under the relativity analysis for non-estate tenancies, though it should also be relevant for a lease by estoppel.

---

[62] LRA, s 11.

[63] A recent example is provided by *Parshall v Bryans* [2013] EWCA Civ 240, [2013] Ch 568 (mistake by land registry).

[64] See Law Commission, 'Land Registration for the Twenty-First Century: A Consultative Document' (Law Com No 254, 1998) [10.27] et seq. The trust is removed from the legislation by the 2002 Act: Law Com No 271 (n 36) [14.70].

[65] Law Com No 254 (n 64) [10.71]. C Jessel, 'Concurrent Fees Simple and the Land Registration Act 2002' (2014) 130 *LQR* 587 argues against a proliferation of registrable fees simple, though primarily in the context of a mesne seignory.

[66] Law Com No 271 (n 36) [14.69] and [14.71].

[67] Though such leases may become more common as a consequence of the lease for life analysis adopted by the Supreme Court in *Berrisford* (n 32) (leases of uncertain duration).

[68] Good leasehold title may also be possible (LRA, ss 10 and 12(6)). Possessory leasehold title is probably limited to the adverse possession context.

Turning to overriding interest status, this seems unlikely to be relevant to the enforcement of the lease. As regards the freeholder, we have seen that the *Bruton* lease provides no protection to the tenant—the freeholder is not a purchaser and overriding interest status is accordingly irrelevant. The same is necessarily true as regards successors in title from the freeholder. It should be remembered that being an overriding interest does not guarantee that the interest is enforceable—all it achieves is that the registration of a successor in title does not by itself defeat the interest.[69] Nor can overriding status be relevant as regards successors in title from the landlord (the licensee). Overriding interests give protection against registered disponees from registered proprietors. The landlord plainly cannot be a registered proprietor. Registration is generally limited to the fee simple and lease,[70] whereas the landlord has only a licence which is not even a proprietary interest. Accordingly, successors in title from the landlord will be bound according to the unregistered land priority principles.

A small digression may give rise to slightly greater difficulty. What happens if the landlord subsequently acquires a legal estate in the land? Under the principle of feeding the estoppel, a tenancy by estoppel immediately becomes a full estate. Is this relevant to the *Bruton* lease? We have seen that Lord Hoffmann thought that there was no reason why estoppel should not apply, though this was not the basis for his decision in favour of Mr Bruton. The effect of feeding the estoppel is that the tenant will thereafter have a full legal lease. In this context, the landlord's title will often be registered,[71] in which case there could well be a subsequent registered disposition by the landlord. Once the estoppel has been fed, the tenant should have no difficulty in asserting an overriding interest under Schedule 3 paragraph 1 to the LRA. But what if the tenancy by estoppel is not adopted? It seems then that a non-estate tenancy would not be an overriding interest because it is not an interest in land (capable of binding purchasers) at all.[72] This provides a good reason for recognising estoppel overlapping with the *Bruton* lease. Turning to the relativity analysis, this would treat the interest as proprietary as regards successors in title from the landlord and accordingly it should have overriding status—presuming that it otherwise fits into paragraph 1 (not exceeding seven years) or paragraph 3 (actual occupation).

That leaves protection by notice. This seems inappropriate. Leaving aside the prohibition of such protection for leases not exceeding three years,[73] it simply does not affect a registered estate.[74] The sole relevant registered

---

[69] *City of London BS v Flegg* [1987] UKHL 6, [1988] AC 54; *Paddington BS v Mendelsohn* [1985] EWCA Civ 17, (1985) 50 P&CR 244.

[70] Section 2 LRA provides for registration of other interests, but these are of no concern to us.

[71] But not if the landlord acquires a lease not exceeding seven years.

[72] Cf *National Provincial Bank Ltd v Ainsworth* [1965] UKHL 1, [1965] AC 1175.

[73] LRA, s 33(b).

[74] ibid, s 34(1). It might be otherwise if the landlord/licensee later acquires and registers a legal estate: a notice could be entered on that title.

estate is that of the freeholder and that estate is not affected by the *Bruton* lease. We have seen that a registered disponee from the freeholder is not affected by the *Bruton* lease, so protecting it by notice would in any event be futile.[75] Given that the landlord's title is unregistered, might the land charges scheme operate? However, legal leases are not registrable; further, the only possible category would be estate contracts and these require a contract by the holder of a legal estate.[76] Even allowing for the role of the tenancy by estoppel, this seems to be an insurmountable stumbling block.

Other issues impacting upon third parties relate to assignability and the running of covenants. Most *Bruton* leases are likely to be short and expressed not to be assignable. Given that there is likely to be a full rent, a tenant who wishes to leave is far more likely to surrender the lease or wait until the lease can be terminated; assignment is improbable. However, the nature of both the relativity analysis and the tenancy by estoppel[77] is that they result in estates that can be assigned just like any other lease. How this relates to the non-estate tenancy is less clear. It may depend upon whether assignment is viewed as being of the estate or of the tenancy.[78]

Does the Landlord and Tenant (Covenants) Act 1995 apply so that the benefit and burden of covenants run to assignees?[79] The Act applies to tenancies, which are defined to mean 'any lease or other tenancy'.[80] One would expect this to be interpreted so as to include a *Bruton* tenancy—the actual decision shows how statutory provisions can apply. This remains the case even if we adopt the non-estate tenancy analysis. This would be especially important if there were an assignment of the landlord's title (licence)—any question whether the tenancy is assignable does not then arise.

B. Other Issues

Is the *Bruton* lease a legal estate, applying the principles established by the Law of Property Act 1925? The relativity analysis and the tenancy by estoppel both appear to be consistent with there being a legal estate. It is true that the estate has to be absolute (see section 1(1)), but absolute is used in the

---

[75] *Kitney v MEPC Ltd* [1977] 1 WLR 981 (CA) confirms that protection by notice does not guarantee the status of the interest—it simply prevents an interest being defeated by a later registration.

[76] Land Charges Act 1972, ss 2(4)(iv) and 17 (applying the Law of Property Act 1925, s 205(1)(v)).

[77] There is authority supporting this assertion as regards the tenancy by estoppel: Harpum, Bridge and Dixon (n 44) para 17-127.

[78] The rule that a tenancy at will cannot be assigned (*Pinhorn v Souster* (1853) 8 Exch 763, 772) might well not apply to the very different non-estate tenancy, which does have a duration.

[79] It does not apply to pre-1996 leases, but it would be very rare for a *Bruton* (n 1) lease today to have been created so long ago.

[80] Landlord and Tenant (Covenants) Act 1995, ss 1 and 28(1).

sense of not being qualified—in other words, not conditional, determinable or subject to an executory limitation over. The fact that it is not valid against the world is of no relevance. This is very similar to the position where an adverse possessor has a fee simple.[81] What of a non-estate tenancy? This seems to be outside section 1, as that refers to 'estates' and by definition there is no estate in a non-estate tenancy. The better view, based on the analogous tenancy at will,[82] may be that the tenancy can be legal. Given that this tenancy would not affect third parties (unless linked with a tenancy by estoppel), its legal status would have very limited consequences.

An element of all property interests (in contrast with, for example, licences) is that they attract formality requirements. These apply both to the creation or disposition of interests (sections 52 and 53 of the Law of Property Act 1925) and contracts for their creation or disposition (section 2 of the Law of Property Act (Miscellaneous Provisions) Act 1989). These provisions would naturally apply to leases operating under the relativity analysis and also to leases by estoppel.[83] Whether a non-estate tenancy requires formalities seems less clear. It is not a 'legal estate' so as to fall within section 52 and it is probably not an 'interest in land' so as to fall within section 54. In any event, most *Bruton* leases are likely to fall within the exemption for leases not exceeding three years.[84]

Every lawyer is aware that there are numerous statutes controlling the operation of leases. Whether the *Bruton* lease satisfies these statutes is primarily a matter of construction, though it should be expected that they will apply if the relativity analysis is employed. *Bruton* itself held that the repairing obligations imposed by section 11 of the Landlord and Tenant Act 1985 applied. This provision refers to 'a lease of a dwelling-house ... for a term of less than seven years'. Plainly, there was no perceived problem in saying that a *Bruton* lease involves a 'term', even if it is not an estate. There may be reasons why a specific provision would not apply to (in particular) a non-estate tenancy, but one would expect that to be quite rare.[85] Some further

---

[81] As explained by the Law Commission: Law Com No 254 (n 64) [10.23]; see also *Turner v Chief Land Registrar* [2013] EWHC 1382, [2013] 2 P&CR 223, esp [15].

[82] R Megarry and HWR Wade, *The Law of Real Property* (5th edn, London, Sweet & Maxwell, 1984) 655 (a fuller analysis than in the 8th edn, para 17-106). It might be more difficult to avoid the impact of s 1(2),(3) that the only interests in land that are recognised as legal are those listed.

[83] This is most clear if Lord Hoffmann is correct in asserting that the estoppel rises from the relationship of landlord and tenant. Although estoppel can be used to avoid the consequences of failure to comply with formality requirements, that is not the role of the tenancy by estoppel (however analysed).

[84] Law of Property Act 1925, s 54(2), provided that the requirements of taking effect in possession and best rent are satisfied.

[85] An analogous question concerns the position of the tenancy at will. In *Wheeler v Mercer* [1956] UKHL 5, [1957] AC 416, this was held to fall outside the Landlord and Tenant Act 1954. Though the tenancy at will might have been thought to fall within the definition section, the operation of the Act as a whole showed that it was not intended to extend to tenancies at will.

guidance may be obtained from the decision in *Bell v General Accident Fire and Life Assurance Corporation Ltd*[86] that the Landlord and Tenant Act 1954 applies to tenancies by estoppel and the dicta in *Stratford v Syrett*[87] that they fall within the Rent Acts. These authorities should apply a fortiori under the relativity analysis. In the light of the *Bruton* decision on repairing obligations, there must be moderate confidence that the same applies to non-estate tenancies.

X. CONCLUSIONS

The outcome of the discussion above is that most of our leasehold principles apply to the *Bruton* lease, however it is analysed. This doubtless requires some careful explanation, especially in the registration context, but it would be wrong to think of the *Bruton* lease as such a strange beast that a wholly different and novel set of rules apply to it. If, as was argued earlier, a relativity analysis is employed to explain the *Bruton* lease, it can be treated as very naturally attracting virtually all the normal rules. As has been observed, there will be few examples of successors from the landlord/licensee and therefore little practical role for registration rules. The conclusion—here as with *Bruton* more generally—may be that the outrage expressed by so many commentators has been substantially and unnecessarily exaggerated.

---

[86] *Bell v General Accident Fire and Life Assurance Corporation Ltd* [1998] L&TR 1.
[87] *Stratford v Syrett* [1958] 1 QB 107 (CA) 112 (Evershed MR) and 115 (Romer LJ).

18

Proprietary Estoppel: The Importance of Looking Back

BEN McFARLANE*

I. INTRODUCTION

G IVEN THE NATURE of this book, it is appropriate that this chapter
is about the importance of looking back. It also seeks to demonstrate
that, in assessing the impact of a particular judge's jurisprudence, we
cannot focus solely on the decisions that are currently the best known and
most discussed. It is impossible to be sure as to which judgments will prove
most influential. As Lord Hoffmann reminded us in one of his final speeches
in the House of Lords: 'The owl of Minerva spreads its wings only with the
falling of the dusk.'[1] It will be argued here that this metaphor is not only an
apt reminder of the dangers of prediction, but is also a very helpful means of
understanding the nature of the most important form of proprietary estoppel. This argument will be made by considering the judgment of Hoffmann
LJ in *Walton v Walton*,[2] which eloquently set out the 'backwards-looking'
nature of particular proprietary estoppel claims. Unfortunately, as will be
seen, that judgment has only recently gained the prominence it deserves, and
much confusion has been caused by the fact that, in looking back over the
relevant precedents, the courts, until recently, overlooked that potentially
seminal contribution.

Lord Hoffmann's borrowing of Hegel's crepuscular metaphor came in
Thorner v Major, a decision that demonstrates the significance of the strand
of proprietary estoppel that may apply where B has acted in reasonable
reliance on a belief as to A's future action.[3] Indeed, *Thorner* is one of the

* I am grateful to the Leverhulme Trust for the support provided by a Philip Leverhulme
Prize and to John Williams for his research assistance.

[1] *Thorner v Major* [2009] UKHL 18, [2009] 1 WLR 776 [8].
[2] *Walton v Walton* (CA, 14 April 1994).
[3] As has been argued by J Mee, 'Proprietary Estoppel, Promises and Mistaken Belief' in S Bright
(ed), *Modern Studies in Property Law: Volume VI* (Oxford, Hart Publishing, 2011) 175, 181–83,
two further distinct forms of proprietary estoppel can also be identified. The acquiescence-based

three cases presented to visitors to the Supreme Court as evidence of the relevance of the UK's top court 'to everyday life'.[4] Peter Thorner, a taciturn farmer from Somerset, had indicated to David, son of a cousin of Peter, that David would inherit Peter's farm. As a result, David had continued to work on that farm, for very low pay, for a further 15 years. When Peter died without having made a valid will, the statutory intestacy rules imposed a duty on Peter's administrators to hold the farm for the benefit not of David, but of other relatives of Peter, closer to him in blood if not in life. The House of Lords confirmed, however, that equitable estoppel operated to impose a duty on Peter (and now on his administrators) to transfer to David the farm and associated assets. The decision meant not only that David was around £2.1 million better off than he would have been had no estoppel claim been possible,[5] but also that, in the words of the Supreme Court's exhibition's display, 'if a verbal promise is made to someone who subsequently relies on that promise to their own detriment, that promise can be enforced under the principles of fairness and equity'.

As will be seen, and as one would expect, the principle applied in *Thorner* is not quite as simple as that formulation would suggest. Even the casual visitor to the Supreme Court's exhibition might wonder if, in the absence of a contractually binding agreement, 'fairness and equity' provide a sufficient basis for holding a party to a promise. Going further, and taking a perhaps unduly optimistic view of the attention paid by our hypothetical visitor, a linked question concerns the role of formalities: given that a contract to dispose of an interest in land must be concluded in writing signed by both parties, why did the House of Lords permit the enforcement of an oral promise?

In this chapter, these questions will be answered in the following way. First, the specific principle operating in *Thorner* recognises that one party (A) can come under a non-contractual liability to another (B) where A makes a promise to B which B reasonably believed to have been seriously

---

strand, considered in, eg, *Fisher v Brooker* [2009] UKHL 41, [2009] 1 WLR 1764, applies where B adopts a particular course of conduct in reliance on a mistaken belief as to B's current rights and A, knowing of both B's belief and of the existence of A's own, inconsistent right, fails to assert that right against B: see further K Low, 'Nonfeasance in Equity' (2012) 128 *LQR* 63. The representation-based strand, applied for example by Lord Evershed MR in *Hopgood v Brown* [1955] 1 WLR 213 (CA) simply consists of the application of the general, preclusive doctrine of estoppel by representation. See further B McFarlane, *The Law of Proprietary Estoppel* (Oxford, Oxford University Press, 2014) 1.01–1.35.

[4] This exhibition is housed in the basement of the former Middlesex Guildhall on Parliament Square.
   [5] This estimate included the development potential of the land. Indeed, in February 2013, the local council, by a seven to five vote, approved an application for the construction on the farm site of a Sainsbury's superstore. There is an argument that, whilst the development value of the land is not subject to agricultural property relief from inheritance tax, David's acquisition of the land through proprietary estoppel, rather than under Peter's will, means that no inheritance tax is payable: see further McFarlane (n 3) 10.11–10.17.

intended by A as a promise on which B could rely. If B then adopts a course of conduct in reliance on that promise and, as a result, would suffer a detriment if A were wholly free to renege on the promise, A is under a prima facie liability to ensure that B suffers no such detriment. This liability cannot exceed, will often be less than, but may consist of A's doing what is necessary to ensure that B is placed in the position that B would have been in had A's promise been performed. Second, this principle is distinct from, and can exist alongside, contract law as it does not seek to identify situations in which A is under an immediate duty to honour an agreement with, or (in the case of a unilateral contract) a promise made to, B. As a consequence, there is no reason to think that its operation should be confined by formality provisions regulating the recognition of a contract.

A crucial source of support for these arguments is the relatively unheralded, and certainly unreported, judgment of Hoffmann LJ in *Walton v Walton*.[6] Dating from 1994, it remained relatively obscure until 2009, when it was highlighted, in *Thorner v Major*, by both Lord Walker[7] and Lord Neuberger.[8] Lord Hoffmann, in his own short speech, did not refer to his earlier judgment. Nonetheless, it will be argued here that, whilst it was in fact adopted by him in a slightly different context,[9] Lord Hoffmann's Minervan metaphor brilliantly illuminates not only the key point decided in *Walton* and confirmed in *Thorner*, but also the very nature of the promise-based form of proprietary estoppel.

II. *WALTON v WALTON* (1994)

Whilst it may be true that every unhappy family is unhappy in its own way, this is not immediately evident in the proprietary estoppel case law. In *Walton*, as in *Thorner*, the claimant had worked for low pay, long hours and many years on a family farm, albeit in this case one owned by his mother.[10] Following the death of her husband in 1962, Mrs Walton ran the farm with the assistance of the claimant (Alfie) and a hired worker. Her determination was remarked on in a local newspaper article of 1964, headlined 'An Amazing Widow Down on the Farm'. In 1963, the son married and moved

---

[6] *Walton* (n 2).

[7] *Thorner* (n 1) [52]–[57].

[8] ibid [101].

[9] See section IV below.

[10] It is also true that, unlike Peter Thorner, Mrs Walton later 'developed a fantasy life' and claimed that her son had shot at her ('On two occasions she called the local policeman to complain that he had fired shots at her. Once she showed him holes in the kitchen door which she said had been made by shotgun pellets. The policeman said that they were plainly woodworm. On another occasion she called him and said the plaintiff had shot at her with a rifle. She showed him a dent in the refrigerator which the policeman said had been made with an axe which still lay nearby').

into a bungalow, built by himself and his wife, next to the farmhouse. By the time of Mrs Walton's death, in 1989, family relations had deteriorated. Mrs Walton had attempted to sell the farm during her life, and the terms of her will required that the farm be sold to pay substantial pecuniary legacies, chiefly to her niece, with residue to Alfie's children and nothing to Alfie himself. Alfie had frequently complained about his low wages and Mrs Walton had consistently met those complaints by assuring him that his reward lay in the future: her stock phrase was that: 'You can't have more money and a farm one day.' In 1977, at Alfie's prompting, she had effectively retired from the partnership with Alfie, reducing her share to 10 per cent. From this point, Alfie obtained the benefit of being able to draw whatever the farming profits would allow, but, as noted by Hoffmann LJ, this did not change 'the fact that from ages 23 to 32, as a young man with two small children, his family did not have the money which he could have earned as a farm worker, let alone in some other occupation'. Moreover, the continued efforts put in by Alfie after 1977, and the money spent by him on maintenance and improvements to the farm, was expended 'on the assumption that the land would one day be his'.

Walton thus seems to display the now-familiar elements of proprietary estoppel. As noted by Hoffmann LJ, Alfie, crucially, was not resting his case merely on the making of the promise:

> [A]s if there had been nothing more than the promise, [Mrs Walton] would have been free to change her mind. It would have been a matter for her conscience and not the law. But the position is different if the person who has been promised some interest in property has, in reliance upon it, incurred expense or made sacrifices which he would not otherwise have made. In such a case the law will provide a remedy.

The first instance judge, however, had found against Alfie on the basis that, whilst Mrs Walton had made promises to him: 'They were never in my judgment words that were intended to create a legal obligation, nor were they treated as such.' Hoffmann LJ accepted, of course, that 'an intention to bring into existence an immediately binding contract' is a requirement of a contractual claim. On the facts of *Walton*, no such intention could be found: as 'Mrs Walton did not know what the future might hold', her promises were likely to have been subject to 'unspoken and ill-defined qualifications' and so it could not be reasonable for Alfie to have believed that his mother had intended to enter into a contract which 'subject to the narrow doctrine of frustration, must be performed come what may'. Crucially, however, this did not prevent a claim based on estoppel, as, in contrast to contract law, the relevant principle:

> does not look forward into the future and guess what might happen. It looks backwards from the moment when the promise falls due to be performed and asks whether, in the circumstances which have actually happened, it would be unconscionable for the promise not to be kept.

This distinction between the nature and operation of proprietary estoppel on the one hand, and contract law on the other, is vital to a proper understanding of the former doctrine and has important implications, to be discussed below. However, the absence of a requirement of intention to enter into an immediately binding agreement does not mean that *any* promise may suffice for a proprietary estoppel claim. The question, identified by Hoffmann LJ, is 'whether a person in the position of the plaintiff would reasonably have regarded the promises which the judge found to have been made as serious statements upon which he could rely'. The mere fact of a promise's having been made in a family context does not render such a belief unreasonable. The key point in *Walton*, it seems, was that the promises were often made in response to Alfie's complaints as to his wages. As the promise of inheritance was therefore made with the aim of influencing Alfie's behaviour, the prima facie position, it is submitted, is that it was reasonable for him to understand the promises as seriously intended. And, in analysing the evidence, Hoffmann LJ found no reason to reject that prima facie position; indeed, even in the newspaper interview from 1964, Mrs Walton had emphasised that the farm would remain in the family and would go to her son on her death.

Having decided, in contrast to the first instance judge, that the required promise had been made, Hoffmann LJ went on to consider the questions of reliance and detriment. The latter was easily established as a result of the time spent by Alfie working for low pay. It is worth noting, however, the formula used by Hoffmann LJ in summarising Alfie's case:

> He cannot have his life over again. If he does not get the farm, he will have to start again at the age of nearly 50, whereas if Mrs Walton had never promised him the farm, he might by now have established himself in some other way. So it would be unjust, or, in the language of equity, 'unconscionable' for the plaintiff now to be turned off the land.

The point here, often obscured by an unthinking use of the phrase 'detrimental reliance', is that action taken by B in reliance need not be immediately, or intrinsically, detrimental.

As for reliance, Hoffmann LJ found that it was clear that Alfie's decision to continue working for low wages and to make improvements to the land was of such a nature that reliance on the promises could be inferred; there was 'no evidence that his conduct was attributable to any other reason'. It is again significant that the promises were made in response to complaints by Alfie. It therefore seems that a simple 'but for' causation test was, on the facts, satisfied: the prospect of detriment arose from conduct that, but for the promises, Alfie would not have undertaken. Hoffmann LJ nonetheless called on the then-recent decision in *Wayling v Jones*,[11] in which he and Leggatt LJ had agreed with Balcombe LJ's leading judgment, to show that

[11] *Wayling v Jones* (1993) 69 P&CR 170 (CA).

'when a promise has been made, one does not test reliance by asking what the plaintiff would have done if it had never been made. One asks what he would have done if, the promise having been made, he had been told that it would not be kept'. Alfie's task was further eased by reference to Balcombe LJ's statement that:

> Once it has been established that promises were made, and that there has been conduct by the plaintiff of such a nature that inducement may be inferred, then the burden shifts to the defendants to establish that he did not rely on the promises.

It will be submitted below that these claimant-friendly departures from the standard causation tests are very difficult to justify.

As Alfie's claim was successful, Hoffmann LJ had to assess the extent of Mrs Walton's liability at her death; in other words, it was necessary to determine how best to satisfy the equity arising through proprietary estoppel. The crucial point here again consists in a contrast with contract law. As noted by Hoffmann LJ: 'The choice of remedy is flexible'; whilst it is possible that, as occurred in *Walton* itself, a court will order A's promise to be kept, this is neither a necessary nor, it seems, a presumptive outcome. The logic of this position, which has recently been challenged by the appellate courts in both England and Australia, will be defended below.

III. LATER DEVELOPMENTS

The purpose of this section is to consider developments in the promise-based strand of proprietary estoppel in the light of Hoffmann LJ's analysis of the doctrine in *Walton*. In that case, his Lordship divided his examination of Alfie's claim into four parts: promise; reliance; detriment; and satisfying the equity. The same scheme will be adopted here to consider developments in the case law after *Walton*. The question of formality requirements will also be considered; although it was not raised in the case itself, the application of Hoffmann LJ's analysis can aid in removing the courts' current confusion.

A. Promise

i. No Requirement that B Must Have Reasonably Believed A to Have Been Under an Immediate Duty to B

It is unfortunate that, until recently, *Walton v Walton* was not widely known. As a result of the failure to look back to this case, time and money has been wasted re-fighting some of its battles. An example is provided by *Sutcliffe v Lloyd*.[12] In an unsuccessful appeal against a judgment in favour

---

[12] *Sutcliffe v Lloyd* [2007] EWCA Civ 153, [2007] 2 EGLR 13.

of B (a builder and property developer), A (an entrepreneur) argued that B's proprietary estoppel claim should have failed as A had never suggested that his promise to B was legally binding. Wilson LJ rejected this contention as 'misconceived in law': as proprietary estoppel does not in any case operate so as to make A's promise immediately binding, there was no need for A to 'mis-state the law in this regard'.[13] *Walton* was not referred to, but Hoffmann LJ's analysis is unmistakably echoed by that of Wilson LJ:

> Equity intervenes to make the promise unable to be revoked (and able to be enforced) not at the time when it is made but only at a significantly later stage, namely in the events both that the promisee should have acted to his detriment in reliance upon it and that the promisor should have sought unconscionably to withdraw from it.[14]

The decision in *Sutcliffe* usefully demonstrates that Hoffmann LJ's analysis in *Walton*, resting as it does on the nature of proprietary estoppel, cannot be confined to the domestic context. The factual context will of course be relevant in determining if A has made a promise that B reasonably believed to have been seriously intended by A as capable of being relied upon, but the underlying conceptual question is the same. It is unfortunate, therefore, that neither *Walton* nor *Sutcliffe* was referred to by the House of Lords in *Cobbe v Yeoman's Row Management Ltd*,[15] where the analyses of Lord Scott and Lord Walker demonstrate that easy cases often make bad dicta. The result in the case, it is submitted, is consistent with the approach in *Walton*: whilst A had made a promise that, if planning permission was granted, A would sell land to B at a particular price, the context of pre-contractual negotiations, and the fact that no sufficiently detailed agreement in principle had been made,[16] meant that it could not be said that B had reasonably believed A to have made a promise seriously intended as capable of being relied upon by B.

In *Cobbe*, however, both Lord Walker and Lord Scott went further and suggested that an additional hurdle had to be surmounted in a proprietary estoppel claim. Lord Walker stated that, where such claims had succeeded in the past, B had acted in reliance not merely on A's promise, but also on a belief that 'the assurance on which he or she relied was binding and irrevocable'.[17] This requirement is inconsistent not only with *Walton* and *Sutcliffe v Lloyd*, but also with the judgments of Robert Walker LJ himself in *Gillett v Holt*[18] and *Jennings v Rice*.[19] In each of these cases, B had relied

---

[13] ibid [38].

[14] ibid.

[15] *Cobbe v Yeoman's Row Management Ltd* [2008] UKHL 55, [2008] 1 WLR 1752.

[16] Perhaps putting it at its highest, Lord Neuberger described *Cobbe* as a case in which 'there was total uncertainty as to the nature or terms of any benefit (property interest, contractual right, or money) and, if a property interest, as to the nature of that interest (freehold, leasehold, or charge) to be accorded to Mr Cobbe': *Thorner* (n 1) [93].

[17] *Cobbe* (n 15) [66].

[18] *Gillett v Holt* [2001] Ch 210 (CA).

[19] *Jennings v Rice* [2002] EWCA Civ 159, [2003] 1 P&CR 8. See too Mee (n 3) 179–181.

on promises that land would be left to him and there was nothing to suggest that B had believed those testamentary promises to be immediately binding on A. In *Cobbe*, Lord Walker did suggest that 'some of the domestic cases might have been decided differently if the nature of [B's] belief had been an issue vigorously investigated in cross-examination',[20] but in *Gillett*, for example, B had expressly conceded that he did not believe A's promise to have been immediately binding on A: a different result could have resulted only from different judging, not different cross-examination.

In *Cobbe*, Lord Scott took a different route to the same conclusion that a successful proprietary estoppel claim depends on B's having relied on a mistaken belief as to his or her current rights. His approach depended on taking proprietary estoppel literally; that is, considering it simply as a means by which A may be precluded from denying a matter of fact, or mixed fact and law.[21] On this view, a promise by A as to A's future action, such as a promise to transfer land to B in the future, cannot support a proprietary estoppel, whereas a representation that A is *already* under a legal duty to B may assist B by leading to A's being stopped from denying the truth of that representation. This view of proprietary estoppel is inconsistent not only with *Walton*, but also with the many other decisions that have employed proprietary estoppel as a means to ensure that B does not suffer a detriment as a result of B's reliance on a promise as to A's future action.[22] However, Lord Scott's analysis serves a useful role in emphasising that, despite its name, proprietary estoppel cannot be properly understood as simply[23] an application, to the proprietary context, of the general, preclusive doctrine of estoppel by representation. In *Walton*, for example, Hoffmann LJ noted that whilst the term equitable estoppel 'sounds very technical', the principle invoked in that case is 'really quite simple' and consists of the provision of a remedy where B has acted in reliance on a promise. There is much to be gained, and little to be lost, by clearly differentiating the promise-based principle applied in, for example, *Walton* from doctrines that simply control the assertions that a party is allowed to make in litigation.

It is true that Lord Hoffmann was a member of the panel in *Cobbe* and simply stated his agreement with the speech of Lord Scott. It is worth emphasising, therefore, that even if the approach advocated in *Walton* had been applied on the facts of *Cobbe*, no proprietary estoppel claim would have arisen. In contrast, the facts of *Thorner* quickly provided a genuine test of the limited approach adopted by Lord Scott in *Cobbe*. If proprietary

---

[20] *Cobbe* (n 15) [67].

[21] ibid [14].

[22] As discussed by B McFarlane and A Robertson, 'The Death of Proprietary Estoppel' [2009] *Lloyd's Maritime and Commercial Law Quarterly* 449.

[23] In some cases, resting on the representation-based strand of proprietary estoppel, the doctrine is indeed no more than an application of the preclusive doctrine of estoppel by representation: see, eg, the analysis of Lord Evershed MR in *Hopgood v Brown* [1955] 1 WLR 213 (CA).

estoppel has no more than a preclusive effect, then even if Peter Thorner had made a seriously intended promise, the doctrine would have been of no assistance to David. Yet the House of Lords allowed David's appeal, and the limited approach to proprietary estoppel was adopted by only one member of the panel: Lord Scott. The decision in *Thorner* thus approved both of the reasoning and the result in *Walton*.

ii. A Promise is Required Where B Relies on a Belief as to A's Future Conduct

Its emphasis on the need for A to have made a promise to B is one of the notable features of Hoffmann LJ's analysis in *Walton*. There is an important inconsistency, which is yet to be expressly recognised or addressed by the courts, in the language used when describing the requirements of proprietary estoppel. In many cases, the term 'promise' is avoided, and the conduct of A on which B's claim is based is described instead as 'encouragement'.[24] A clear example is provided by the influential scheme adopted by Kenneth Handley and applied in both his judicial[25] and extra-judicial analyses.[26] On this scheme, two separate strands of proprietary estoppel are identified: one based on A's acquiescence in a mistaken belief of B and another on A's encouragement of B's belief. Formulations focusing on encouragement all derive, directly or indirectly, from that of Lord Kingsdown in his brief dissenting speech in *Ramsden v Dyson*.[27]

However, it is far from clear that, in a case where B has formed and relied on a belief as to A's future conduct, A's non-promissory encouragement of that belief provides sufficient basis to place A under a liability to ensure that, if B's belief is falsified, B suffers no detriment as a result of that reliance. In the absence of an express or implied promise by A committing A to a particular course of conduct, A can reasonably object to having to bear the costs of B's reliance. This point seems to be borne out by both *Cobbe* and *Thorner*. In the former case, Etherton J found as 'proven facts' that A 'encouraged [B] to believe that, if [B] succeeded in obtaining planning permission in accordance with [the parties' agreement in principle] that

---

[24] See, eg, *Taylors Fashions Ltd v Liverpool Victoria Trustees Co Ltd* [1982] QB 133 (Ch) 151–52; *Scottish & Newcastle plc v Lancashire Mortgage Corporation Ltd* [2007] EWCA Civ 684 [45] (Mummery LJ).

[25] See, eg, *DHJPM Pty Ltd v Blackthorn Ltd* [2011] NSWCA 348, (2011) 285 ALR 311 [93].

[26] See, eg, K Handley, *Estoppel by Conduct and Election* (London, Sweet & Maxwell, 2006) 11–003.

[27] *Ramsden v Dyson* (1866) LR 1 HL 129, 170: 'If [B], under a verbal agreement with [A] for a certain interest in land, or, what amounts to the same thing, under an expectation, created or encouraged by [A], that [B] shall have a certain interest, takes possession of such land with the consent of [A] and upon the faith of such promise or expectation, with the knowledge of [A] and without objection by him, lays out money on the land, a Court of equity will compel [A] to give effect to such a promise or expectation.'

agreement would be honoured, even though it was not legally binding'.[28] A's conduct clearly amounted to 'inducement and encouragement'[29] as, even after forming the intention to withdraw from the agreement in principle, A had hidden that intention and had continued to encourage B's work. The House of Lords' denial of B's proprietary estoppel claim can be explained on the basis that, whilst A had encouraged B, A had made no express or implied promise that the land in question would be transferred to B. Equally, in *Thorner*, with both Lord Walker and Lord Neuberger expressly relying on *Walton*,[30] the success of B's claim depended on the finding of a 'promise or assurance' by A.[31]

The requirement of a promise is important for both practical and conceptual reasons. First, it provides a means for A to have some control over when liability may arise. This is important not only in commercial cases such as *Cobbe*, but also in the domestic or testamentary sphere, where B may well have developed and relied on entirely rational beliefs as to A's future conduct even in the absence of an express or implied promise by A.[32] Second, an emphasis on the need for a promise permits this particular strand of proprietary estoppel, which can apply where B's belief is simply as to A's future conduct, to be distinguished from other forms of the doctrine, such as that applying where A is precluded from denying the truth of a representation, or the acquiescence-based strand that can apply where A fails to disabuse B of a mistake, known to A, as to B's current rights. Any formula which seeks to include all three of those different strands has to employ a broad term such as 'encouragement' to capture the forms of A's conduct that may give rise to the estoppel, but this simply disguises the very clear difference between, for example, the 'classic example of proprietary estoppel, standing by whilst one's neighbour builds on one's land believing it to be his property'[33] and cases such as *Cobbe* and *Thorner*, where a promise is required.[34]

---

[28] *Cobbe v Yeomans Row Management Ltd and others* [2005] EWHC 266 (Ch) [123].

[29] ibid [89].

[30] *Thorner* (n 1) [60] (Lord Walker) and [77] (Lord Neuberger).

[31] ibid [5] (Lord Hoffmann). Indeed, the need for a promise or assurance was also emphasised in the first instance and Court of Appeal decisions: see *Thorner v Curtis and others* [2007] EWHC 2422 (Ch) [136] (John Randall QC); *Thorner v Curtis and others* [2008] EWCA Civ 732, [54] (Lloyd LJ).

[32] See J Mee, 'The Limits of Proprietary Estoppel: *Thorner v Major*' (2009) 21 *Child and Family Law Quarterly* 367 and eg, *Lissimore v Downing* [2003] 2 FLR 308 (Ch) and *Cook v Thomas* [2010] EWCA Civ 227. The former case arose between former cohabitants and HHJ Norris (in what Lord Walker extra-judicially described as an 'exemplary' judgment: 'Which Side "Ought" to Win?' [2008] *Singapore Journal of Legal Studies* 229, 236) found that the causal statements of A did not amount to a promise to give B a beneficial share of the property.

[33] Lord Neuberger in *Fisher v Brooker* [2009] UKHL 41, [2009] 1 WLR 1764 [62].

[34] Note that in *Thorner* (n 1), Lord Walker at [29] put forward a general test for proprietary estoppel, which included the requirement of a 'representation or assurance' by A, but was then forced (at [55]) into the fiction that, in a pure acquiescence case, A's 'standing by in silence serves as the element of assurance'.

B. Reliance

As noted above, in *Walton*, B's task in establishing reliance was simplified in two ways. First, the '*Wayling* test' of causation was applied:[35] the facts that had occurred were compared not with what would have happened in the absence of A's promise, but rather with what would have happened if A, having made the promise to B, had then informed B that it would not in fact be kept. On this test, reliance can be established even if, in the absence of any promise by A, B would have acted in exactly the same way. Second, the so-called 'presumption of reliance' was referred to: at least as applied by Lord Denning MR in *Greasley v Cooke*,[36] this presumption departs from the general rule that it is for B to establish the elements of his or her case.

On the facts of *Walton*, it seems clear that B's claim would have succeeded without the benefit of these indulgences: A's promises were made in order to induce B to act in a particular way that was immediately detrimental to B. As in certain other proprietary estoppel cases, it could be said that B had 'based his whole life' around A's promises.[37] It therefore seems that A's promises were a clear 'but for' cause of B's course of conduct in continuing to work on the farm for low wages and to make improvements to the farm. Indeed, it will be argued here that each of the two indulgences to B is impossible to justify.

First, consider the *Wayling* test. The reliance element of proprietary estoppel raises an issue of causation: as in other areas of law, causation must be proved in order to attribute to A responsibility for B's position. In the context of proprietary estoppel, this depends in turn on establishing a relevant link between A and the prospective detriment B may suffer. This is done by showing that the particular action or inaction of B that has exposed B to the prospect of such detriment was caused by A's conduct. If B would have adopted the same course of conduct in the absence of A's promise, then, it is submitted, the causal link is not established. When B seeks to establish a cause of action, the purpose of a causation test is to compare what has actually occurred with what would have happened in the absence of the events constituting the cause of action. Where a proprietary estoppel claim is based on A's promise, A's promise is an element of the cause of action; A's failure to inform B of an intention not to perform the promise is not. Indeed, as demonstrated by the facts of cases such as *Wayling* and *Thorner*, where A's failure to leave promised property to B is a result of A's inadvertence,[38] B's claim can arise even if A never formed the intention not to perform the promise.

---

[35] *Wayling* (n 11).
[36] *Greasley v Cooke* [1980] 1 WLR 1306 (CA).
[37] See, eg, *Gillett* (n 18) 235; *Suggitt v Suggitt* [2012] EWCA Civ 1140, [2012] WTLR 1607 [36] and [40].
[38] In *Wayling* (n 11), A made a will leaving his former hotel to B and, after selling that hotel and buying another, failed to update the will so as to leave the new hotel to B. In *Thorner* (n 1), A made a will leaving his farm to B, but then destroyed that will after falling out with one of the intended pecuniary legatees and failed to make a replacement will.

It is therefore submitted that the *Wayling* test cannot be supported.[39] Indeed, on the facts of *Wayling* itself, its adoption was not necessary.[40] It is also significant that, when carefully examining the reliance element in *Campbell v Griffin*,[41] Robert Walker LJ, whilst adopting much of Balcombe LJ's analysis in *Wayling*, made no reference to the idea that reliance can be established by considering how B would have behaved had A's promise been expressly withdrawn.

It was argued above that the separation of the acquiescence-based and promise-based forms of proprietary estoppel is crucial when considering if mere encouragement of B's belief as to A's future conduct may give rise to a claim. Similarly, it may be that confusion between these two forms of the doctrine lie behind the *Wayling* test. In an acquiescence case, A's *failure* to assert a right against B is one of the ingredients of B's cause of action. It is therefore appropriate to compare the events that have occurred with those that would have resulted from A's asserting his or her right, and thus informing B that B's belief was mistaken. In contrast, in a promise-based case, it is the fact of A's promise, not A's failure to tell B that A will not perform it, on which B's claim depends. Indeed, the underlying point has been made by Lord Hoffmann.[42] Causation is one of the elements used in order to attribute to A responsibility for B's position: as B's claim differs, so does its possible impact on A, and so may the applicable causation rules.[43]

The so-called 'presumption of reliance' also seems to be based on a false analogy. It derives chiefly from the decision of the Court of Appeal in *Greasley v Cooke*.[44] Lord Denning MR there relied on two decisions concerning the effect of a *fraudulent* misrepresentation.[45] It would be dangerous to assume that the approach taken in such cases must necessarily extend to cases where no fraud is present; for example, when considering whether a loss suffered by B is too remote a consequence of A's wrong, the courts have adopted a special rule in cases of deceit.[46]

---

[39] For further criticism of the test, see, eg, E Cooke, 'Reliance and Estoppel' (1995) 111 *LQR* 389; J Mee, *The Property Rights of Cohabitees* (Oxford, Hart Publishing, 1999) 108; McFarlane (n 3) 3.114–3.132.

[40] B had accepted in cross-examination that he would have 'stayed with' A even if no promise had been made. It was argued by B on appeal that this simply meant that the parties' relationship would have continued and did not mean that B would have continued to work for A without receiving a reasonable wage. It seems that Balcombe LJ was minded to accept that submission, as he stated that: 'I am by no means clear that [B] was thereby saying that he would have worked for pocket money even if there had been no promises': *Wayling* (n 11) 175.

[41] *Campbell v Griffin* [2001] EWCA Civ 990.

[42] See, eg, L Hoffmann, 'Causation' (2005) 121 LQR 592, 594–96, contrasting the causation tests applied in cases of negligence and of strict liability.

[43] See too Lord Mance in *Durham v BAI (Run Off) Ltd* [2012] UKSC 14, [2012] 1 WLR 867 [66].

[44] *Greasley* (n 36).

[45] *Reynell v Sprye* (1852) 1 De GM & G 600, 42 ER 710 and *Smith v Chadwick* (1884) 9 App Cas 187 (HL).

[46] See, eg, *Doyle v Olby Ironmongers Ltd* [1969] 2 QB 158 (CA).

It is important to note that the trend in the authorities is to minimise the significance of the reasoning in *Greasley*. First, it seems clear that, on Lord Denning MR's reasoning, B did not need to establish detriment, but could again rely on a presumption. However, this position has been rejected; in *Gillett v Holt*,[47] for example, it was held that B must prove that he or she would suffer detriment were A free to renege on A's promise to B.[48] Second, in a thorough analysis in *Steria Ltd v Hutchison*, Neuberger LJ cast doubt on the presumption of reliance and refused to extend it beyond proprietary estoppel.[49] Third, even in the context of proprietary estoppel, the presumption has been decisively rejected by the High Court of Australia.[50] The point is that, in particular factual circumstances, it may be reasonable to infer that A's promise was in fact a sufficient cause of B's conduct:[51] this will be the case if, as in *Walton*, B's conduct is immediately and objectively detrimental. The possibility of such a factual inference,[52] however, does not amount to a shift in the burden of proof, and the commonly employed notion of a presumption of reliance is therefore apt to mislead.

C. Detriment

On the facts of *Walton*, the course of conduct adopted by B in reliance on A's promises was immediately and objectively detrimental; as Hoffmann LJ put it, B 'made sacrifices in working for low wages' and also incurred expenditure 'by making improvements [to the farm] with his own labour

---

[47] *Gillett* (n 18).

[48] See too *Coombes v Smith* [1986] 1 WLR 808 (Ch) and *Steria Ltd v Hutchison* [2006] EWCA Civ 1551, [2007] ICR 445: each case rejects the notion of any presumption of detriment.

[49] *Steria* (n 48) [128]–[129]. See too *Nationwide Building Society v Lewis* [1998] Ch 482 (CA), where, in the context of a claim that A had held himself out to be a partner, Peter Gibson LJ (at 491) made the powerful point that: 'Given that reliance is a necessary requirement, it is not obvious that there should be a presumption in favour of the person who claims reliance and is in a better position to know whether he did rely on the holding-out and who should thereby be able to prove it.'

[50] *Sidhu v van Dyke* [2014] HCA 19. See, eg, per French CJ, Kiefel, Bell and Keane JJ at [58]: 'Reliance is a fact to be found; it is not to be imputed on the basis of evidence which falls short of proof of the fact' and at [61]: 'The approach suggested by Lord Denning should not be applied in Australia. The legal burden of proof borne by a plantiff did not shift. To speak of a shifting onus of proof is both wrong in principle and contrary to authority.'

[51] In *Sidhu* (ibid), the High Court of Australia, adopting the view of Neuberger LJ in *Steria* (n 48) [117], stated that it is sufficient for B to show that A's 'representation was a significant factor which [B] took into account when deciding whether to [act as he did]'. The difficulties with such a 'sufficient' or 'contributing' cause test of causation are examined in McFarlane (n 3) 3.135–3.173. It is argued there (at 3.174–3.212) that the standard 'but for' test of causation should instead be applied when determining if B relied on A's promise.

[52] See W Swadling, 'Explaining Resulting Trusts' (2008) 124 *LQR* 72, 74–77 for a very useful discussion of the nature and operation of presumptions, and the distinction between a presumption of law and a factual inference.

and money'. Whilst it was thus a simple task for B to establish the detriment element of his claim, the analysis in *Walton* nonetheless contains three important points on detriment, each of which has been developed in later decisions.

First, and linked to the backwards-looking nature of B's claim, is the fact that the detriment with which proprietary estoppel is concerned is that which *would* be caused to B from A's being free to act entirely as A wishes. This point was eloquently made by Dixon J in his seminal judgment in *Grundt v Great Boulder Pty Gold Mines Ltd*[53] and, in *Gillett v Holt*, Robert Walker LJ made explicit the point implied by Hoffmann LJ's summary: 'The issue of detriment must be judged at the moment when the person who has given the assurance seeks to go back on it.'[54] An example is provided by *Crabb v Arun District Council*.[55] B's reliance on an expectation of an easement over A's neighbouring land consisted of selling off part of his land without reserving a right of access from the public road to B's retained land. This action was not immediately detrimental and, in fact, presumably conferred a benefit on B by avoiding any reduction in the purchase price obtained. However, the prospect of detriment arose from the fact that, owing to this irrevocable action, B would clearly suffer a detriment if A then failed to grant B the expected easement over A's land.

The second point can be seen in Hoffmann LJ's observation in *Walton* that Alfie's acts in reliance on his mother's promises were:

> irrevocable. He cannot have his life over again. If he does not get the farm, he will have to start again at the age of nearly 50, whereas if Mrs Walton had never promised him the farm, he might by now have established himself in some other way.

On this analysis, it is clear that detriment is not simply a financial matter. At first instance in *Gillett v Holt*, no reference was made to *Walton*, and this point was unfortunately overlooked. When allowing B's appeal in *Gillett*, Robert Walker LJ stated that the first instance judge[56] 'must have taken too narrowly financial a view of the requirement of detriment'.[57] Instead, when considering detriment, a judge should 'stand back and look at the matter in the round'.[58] As a result, in cases where it can be said that B has 'based his whole life' on A's promises and has not received sufficient compensating benefits, detriment can be established.[59]

---

[53] *Grundt v Great Boulder Pty Gold Mines Ltd* (1937) 59 CLR 641 (High Court of Australia).
[54] *Gillett* (n 18) 232.
[55] *Crabb v Arun District Council* [1976] Ch 179 (CA).
[56] Carnwath J: see *Gillett v Holt* [1998] 3 All ER 917.
[57] *Gillett* (n 18) 235.
[58] ibid 233. As noted by Floyd LJ in *Davies v Davies* [2014] EWCA Civ 568, the proper assessment of detriment is not 'an exercise in forensic accounting' (at [51]), but is rather a 'classic evaluative exercise' (at [56]).
[59] See, eg, *Suggitt v Suggitt* (n 37).

This reference to compensating benefits leads to the third point implicit in *Walton*. As a result of the backwards-looking nature of B's claim, B's potential detriment is not necessarily assessed immediately after B's reliance. This means, for example, that countervailing benefits acquired by B after that initial reliance must be taken into account when evaluating B's detriment.[60] In *Walton* itself, for example, Hoffmann LJ carefully considered whether B's acquisition of 90 per cent of the partnership that ran the farm could constitute such a benefit. This important point was confirmed by the Court of Appeal in *Jennings v Rice*.[61] Nonetheless, the need to consider such benefits has, in some later cases, been overlooked. In *Henry v Henry*,[62] for example, the Court of Appeal of the Eastern Caribbean Supreme Court assumed that, as the prospect of detriment had been established, A's promise should be enforced. The Privy Council—correctly it is submitted—allowed A's appeal as B had received substantial countervailing benefits that had reduced the extent of B's potential detriment and therefore had to be taken into account when determining the appropriate relief.

D. Remedy

In *Walton*, Hoffmann LJ emphasised that when a promise-based proprietary estoppel claim arises: 'The choice of remedy is flexible.' For example, whilst a court might require A's promise to be kept, it might instead 'order [A] to pay compensation for the expense which has been incurred'. On this view, the variety in the relief available is not simply a product of the different forms that A's promise might take or of the fact that in some cases, there may be practical difficulties in specifically enforcing that promise. The point is rather the conceptual one that the doctrine does not operate to impose a duty on A to put B in the position that B would have been in had A's promise been performed.

It is, again, unfortunate that the decision in *Walton* was not reported. In *Jennings v Rice*,[63] for example, B's proprietary estoppel claim succeeded and A's administrators were ordered to pay B £200,000 from A's estate. B appealed, arguing that he had been promised (at least) A's house and furniture, valued at £435,000, and that 'the basic rule was that the established equity should be satisfied by making good the expectation'.[64] This appeal was unsuccessful; as Aldous LJ pointed out, B's argument, if correct, meant that the court should award B the same sum even if B 'had been left £5 or

---

[60] See, eg, *Watts v Story* (1983) 134 NLJ 631 (CA).
[61] *Jennings v Rice* (n 19). See too *Davies v Davies* (n 58) [54]–[55].
[62] *Henry v Henry* [2010] UKPC 3, [2010] 1 All ER 988.
[63] *Jennings v Rice* (n 19).
[64] ibid [16].

£50,000 or £200,000 in [A's] will, or [A] had died one month, one year or twenty years after making the representation relied on'.[65] The first instance judge had therefore been correct to emphasise the importance of proportionality in assessing the duty that should be imposed on A's administrators. Similarly, in *Henry v Henry*,[66] Sir Jonathan Parker, giving the advice of the Privy Council, rejected the view, taken by the Court of Appeal of the Eastern Caribbean Supreme Court, that 'there is no power in the court to say that the promise (and the resulting benefit) is disproportionate to the detriment'. This statement was said to betray a 'fundamental misconception as to the nature and purpose of the doctrine of proprietary estoppel ... Proportionality lies at the heart of the doctrine of proprietary estoppel and permeates its every application'.[67]

Whilst *Walton* was not cited in either *Jennings* or *Henry*, those later cases provide support for Hoffmann LJ's analysis. The conclusion of a contract can be seen as imposing an immediate duty on A to comply with A's promise to B; this is reflected in the fact that, if that duty is breached, A will be ordered to ensure that B is in the same position that B would have been in if the promise had been performed. In contrast, when the facts necessary for a promise-based proprietary estoppel claim have occurred, A instead comes under a liability to ensure that B suffers no detriment as a result of B's reasonable reliance on A's promise. The prospect of B's suffering a detriment is a crucial part of B's cause of action and, if A can remove that detriment, then, it seems, A cannot be said to have acted unconscionably, even if B has not been placed in the position B would have occupied had the promise been performed.[68]

The analysis in *Walton* also demonstrates that a promise-based proprietary estoppel claim differs not only from a contractual action, but also from the general, preclusive doctrine of estoppel by representation. True estoppels, as noted, for example, by Lord Scott in *Cobbe*,[69] have the effect of preventing A's asserting a particular fact, or matter of mixed fact and law. In that way, they necessarily protect B's 'expectation' and are not subject to any remedial flexibility. In themselves, however, such estoppels do not constitute a cause of action; they simply provide B with a means of establishing a fact, or matter of mixed fact and law, that may be essential to an independent cause of action. As was made clear by Hoffmann LJ's analysis in

---

[65] ibid [37].
[66] *Henry v Henry* (n 62).
[67] ibid [65].
[68] See, eg, *Powell v Benney* [2007] EWCA Civ 1283 and note the argument made by A Robertson, 'The Reliance Basis of Proprietary Estoppel Remedies' [2008] *Conveyancer and Property Lawyer* 295, 302.
[69] *Cobbe* (n 15) [14].

Walton, promise-based proprietary estoppel operates in a different way. The problem is that, partly as a result of the continued use of the term 'estoppel', the courts have often failed to separate the promise-based doctrine from its preclusive cousin. A good example is provided by the judgment of Deane J in *Waltons Stores (Interstate) Ltd v Maher*,[70] where it is stated that 'once regard is paid to substance, the principles of estoppel by conduct can be applied as effectively to a representation or induced assumption of future conduct as they can to one of existing fact'. This overlooks the key point, made by Gaudron J in the same case,[71] that, as made clear by *Jorden v Money*,[72] the preclusive logic of estoppel by representation simply cannot apply to a promise of A's future conduct: even if A can be prevented from denying that a promise was made, B's ability to establish that fact does not provide a cause of action. As can be seen in Deane J's influential judgment, the equation of the two quite different forms of estoppel leads to the mistaken assumption that, where a promise-based proprietary estoppel is established, the prima facie result must be that A is bound not to depart from A's promise. There are clear logical difficulties with this position,[73] yet it seems to represent the law in Australia[74] and has also recently been adopted by the Court of Appeal.[75] However, an emphasis on the backwards-looking nature of promise-based proprietary estoppel makes clear that the doctrine differs not only from contract law but also from estoppel by representation, and can thus ensure that the liability imposed on A does not go beyond its rationale of ensuring that A does not leave B to suffer a detriment as a result of B's reasonable reliance on A's promise.

---

[70] *Waltons Stores (Interstate) Ltd v Maher* (1988) 164 CLR 387 (High Court of Australia) 450.

[71] ibid 459: 'Because common law or evidentiary estoppel operates by precluding the assertion of facts inconsistent with an assumed fact, the assumption must necessarily be as to an existing fact and not as to a future event.' See further B McFarlane, 'The Limits to Estoppels' (2013) 7 *Journal of Equity* 251, 257–61.

[72] *Jorden v Money* (1854) 5 HL Cas 185, 10 ER 868.

[73] As pointed out by J Mee, 'Expectation and Proprietary Estoppel Remedies' in M Dixon (ed), *Modern Studies in Property Law: Volume V* (Oxford, Hart Publishing, 2009) 389, 403–04. To adopt (and slightly adapt) Mee's example: consider *Jennings v Rice* (n 19). It was held that it would be disproportionate for B to receive £435,000 and B was instead awarded £200,000. What if A's house and furniture had been worth not £435,000, but only £250,000? On an approach (such as that adopted by Arden LJ in *Suggitt v Suggitt* (n 37) [44]) that enforces B's expectation unless that is 'out of all proportion to the detriment which [B] suffered', B might well then receive £250,000. Yet, as Mee observes, it makes no sense that this reduction in the value of the promised property leads to an increase in A's liability.

[74] See, eg, *Sidhu* (n 50) [85]: 'While it is true to say that "the court, as a court of conscience, goes no further than is necessary to prevent unconscionable conduct", where the unconscionable conduct consists of resiling from a promise or assurance which has induced conduct to the other party's detriment, the relief which is necessary in this sense is usually that which reflects the value of the promise.' See too *Delaforce v Simpson-Cook* [2010] NSWCA 84, (2010) 78 NSWLR 483 [57]–[69] and *Harrison v Harrison* [2013] VSCA 170 [138].

[75] *Suggitt v Suggitt* (n 37).

E. Formal Requirements

As was later confirmed in *Thorner*, it is clear from *Walton* that a proprietary estoppel claim can be based on a purely oral promise, even if the effect of such a claim is to lead to a transfer of a right in a context where formalities are usually required. No point was taken on formalities in *Walton*,[76] and this is consistent with a, perhaps surprising, feature of the case law: formal requirements are raised only in those cases where B comes closest to meeting them. In *Crabb v Arun District Council*, for example, it was clear that no contract had been concluded between the parties,[77] and there was no objection from A that permitting B's claim would subvert the formal requirements applying to contracts for the sale or other disposition of an interest in land. In *Kinane v Mackie-Conteh*,[78] by contrast, A's promise was made in writing signed by A, and a contractual claim was barred only by B's failure to ensure that the written record was signed by *both* A and B. A did then object that, were A's promise enforced by means of proprietary estoppel, the policy of section 2 of the Law of Property (Miscellaneous Provisions) Act 1989 would be undermined. As in *Yaxley v Gotts*[79] and, later, in *Herbert v Doyle*,[80] the Court of Appeal met that objection by holding that B's claim gave rise to a constructive trust and so was excepted from the formal requirements by section 2(5) of the 1989 Act.

There are, however, insurmountable difficulties in the resort to constructive trusts as a general means to permit promise-based proprietary estoppel claims.[81] The first point is that, even on the facts of cases such as *Kinane*, *Yaxley* and *Herbert*, it is very difficult to find a genuine trust. In *Kinane*, A was ordered to comply with his promise to grant B a charge over A's home. In *Yaxley*, A was ordered to grant B a lease or to pay B the value of such a lease. In *Herbert*, A was again ordered to grant B a lease. There was no point in time, in any of those three cases, where A held a right on trust for B. The second point is that a proprietary estoppel claim has been allowed even in a case where the Court of Appeal expressly rejected the possibility of a trust.[82] Third, in *Stack v Dowden*,[83] Lord Walker admitted that, whilst he had, in his judgment in *Yaxley*, 'given some encouragement' to an assimilation of proprietary estoppel and '"common interest" constructive trusts', he was 'now rather less enthusiastic'. This change of heart was based on the fact that, whilst finding a common intention constructive trust of land

---

[76] *Crabb v Arun District Council* (n 55).
[77] See P Millett, '*Crabb v Arun District Council*: A Riposte' (1976) 92 *LQR* 342.
[78] *Kinane v Mackie-Conteh* [2005] EWCA Civ 45, [2005] WTLR 345.
[79] *Yaxley v Gotts* [2000] Ch 162 (CA).
[80] *Herbert v Doyle* [2010] EWCA Civ 1095.
[81] See further McFarlane (n 3) 6.74–6.88.
[82] *McGuane v Welch* [2008] EWCA Civ 785, [2008] 2 P & CR 24.
[83] *Stack v Dowden* [2007] 2 AC 432 (HL) [37].

concerns the identification of the 'true beneficial owner or owners, and the size of their beneficial interests', proprietary estoppel depends on:

> asserting an equitable claim against the conscience of the 'true' owner. The claim is a 'mere equity'. It is to be satisfied by the minimum award necessary to do justice[84] which may sometimes lead to no more than a monetary award.[85]

Lord Walker's analysis of a proprietary estoppel claim is consistent with that proffered by Hoffmann LJ in *Walton* and it provides the explanation for why, even in the absence of a constructive trust, such a claim does not undermine section 2 of the 1989 Act. The simple point is that the formality rule regulates *contracts* for the sale or other disposition of an interest in land and a proprietary estoppel claim, even if based on a promise, is not a contractual claim.[86] Similarly, in the case of a promise to leave property on A's death, the Wills Act 1837 is not in issue as B's claim is not based on a testamentary disposition by A; it is instead based on A's inter vivos promise. Where B's claim is not caught by the basic scope of a formality rule, there is, of course, no need for B to rely on an exception to that rule. It is unfortunate, however, that this straightforward point, which is clear from the analysis in *Walton*, has yet to be expressly recognised by the courts.[87]

Indeed, in *Cobbe v Yeoman's Row Management Ltd*,[88] Lord Scott adopted the contrary position, stating, in an expressly obiter passage, that section 2 does present a significant obstacle as:

> [P]roprietary estoppel cannot be prayed in aid to render enforceable an agreement that statute has declared to be void. The proposition that an owner of land can be estopped from asserting that an agreement is void for want of compliance with the requirements of section 2 is, in my opinion, unacceptable.

The first difficulty with this analysis is that it mis-states the effect of section 2: it may prevent an agreement from having a contractual effect, but it does not render an *agreement* void. Indeed, Lord Scott, along with the rest of the panel of the House of Lords, permitted B's restitutionary claim in *Cobbe*, based on B's performance of services under his agreement with A, so it cannot be the case that the policy of section 2 is to deny all legal effect to an agreement that does not meet the formal requirements of contractual validity. The second difficulty is caused by the failure to separate promise-based proprietary estoppel from the general, preclusive model of estoppel. As was made clear in *Walton*, B, when making the former type of claim, is

---

[84] Lord Walker here cited *Crabb v Arun District Council* (n 55).

[85] *Stack v Dowden* (n 83) [37].

[86] See, eg, B McFarlane, 'Proprietary Estoppel and Failed Contractual Negotiations' [2005] *Conveyancer and Property Lawyer* 501.

[87] Although it has been accepted, extra-judicially, by Lord Neuberger: see 'The Stuffing of Minerva's Owl? Taxonomy and Taxidermy in Equity' [2009] *CLJ* 537, 546.

[88] *Cobbe* (n 15) [29].

not seeking to make a contractual claim by preventing A from relying on section 2;[89] rather, B takes advantage of the fact that promise-based proprietary estoppel is itself a cause of action. As noted extra-judicially by Lord Neuberger, 'the fact that, if there was a contract, it would be void is irrelevant: indeed, the very reason for mounting the proprietary estoppel claim is that there is no enforceable contract'.[90]

This also explains why the reasoning of the House of Lords in *Actionstrength Ltd v International Glass Engineering SpA*[91] does not apply to a promise-based proprietary estoppel claim. In that case, B argued that A was estopped from relying on section 4 of the Statute of Frauds 1677 to show that a contract of guarantee was unenforceable. This attempt to rely on a preclusive estoppel was doomed to failure as A had made no representation that the contract was enforceable despite the lack of signed writing, or that A would not rely on the statute. As Lord Hoffmann made clear in his speech, B's claim was therefore based on no more than the unenforceable guarantee. Indeed, his Lordship distinguished between contracts of guarantee and contracts for the sale of land. In the former context: 'It will always be the case that the creditor will have acted to his prejudice on the faith of the guarantor's promise. To admit an estoppel on these grounds would be to repeal the statute.'[92] In contrast, agreements for the sale of land 'almost always start by being executory on both sides'.[93] As a result, permitting a promise-based proprietary estoppel claim where B has gone on to rely on such an informal agreement does not render the formality rule in section 2 redundant.

F. Later Developments: Conclusion

The basic argument made above is that, had subsequent courts paid consistent attention to the analysis of Hoffmann LJ in *Walton*, much appellate time and effort would have been saved, and the courts' current approach to promise-based proprietary estoppel claims would be far more coherent. The question of reliance provides the chief exception: in *Walton* itself, there was no doubt that B could prove reliance and, presumably as a result, Hoffmann LJ was content to follow the conventional wisdom on that issue.

---

[89] Compare *Waltons Stores* (n 70): whereas Deane and Gaudron JJ regarded B's claim, on the facts, as depending on A's being estopped from denying the existence of a contract (see 436–41 and 461–63), Mason CJ and Wilson J (at 398) as well as Brennan J (at 430–31) saw B's claim as resting on A's promise to take a lease of B's land.

[90] Neuberger (n 87) 546.

[91] *Actionstrength Ltd v International Glass Engineering SpA* [2003] UKHL 17, [2003] 2 AC 541.

[92] ibid [26].

[93] ibid [24].

As discussed above, that wisdom has since been challenged and, indeed, those challenges can be supported by using the key insight in *Walton*. That insight is that a promise-based proprietary estoppel claim differs from each of a contractual claim and a preclusive estoppel by representation. Unlike the latter, it is a cause of action and can impose a liability on A. Unlike the former, it does not impose an immediate duty to perform a promise, but instead allows a court to consider what A must do to ensure that A does not commit the specific form of unconscionable conduct that consists in leaving B to suffer a detriment as a result of B's reasonable reliance on A's unperformed promise. It is submitted that the imposition of such a liability on A can only be justified if B proves, inter alia, that the course of conduct giving rise to B's prospective detriment would not, in the absence of A's promise, have been entered into by B. If B would have acted in the same way, and so faced the same detriment, even in the absence of A's promise, it cannot be said that leaving B to bear that detriment without recourse against A would 'shock the conscience of the court'.[94]

It is appropriate that one of Lord Hoffmann's final cases in the House of Lords, *Thorner*, can be seen as a vindication of the specific point decided, almost 15 years earlier, in *Walton*: a promise-based proprietary estoppel claim can succeed without B's needing to show that B acted in reliance on a reasonable belief that A's promise was immediately, legally binding on A. More importantly, the reasoning of Hoffmann LJ in the earlier case can address some of the concerns that led Lord Scott in *Thorner* to maintain his scepticism as to the very existence of the promise-based strand of proprietary estoppel. One of the concerns expressed by his Lordship was that any promise as to A's future conduct, such as a promise to leave a farm to B must be 'in a sense, conditional', as it would not be intended to provide an absolute bar on A's ability to sell the farm if, for example, A had to do so in order to fund the costs of necessary medical treatment and care.[95] For this reason, Lord Scott preferred to exclude such promises from the scope of proprietary estoppel, leaving B's protection, if any, to come from the possible availability of a remedial constructive trust.[96] Lord Scott is correct in his diagnosis of the problem, but mistaken in the remedy he prescribes. For Hoffmann LJ's analysis in *Walton* shows that, as a result of its backwards-looking nature, the promise-based strand of proprietary estoppel does not impose an immediately binding duty on A and so can accommodate Lord Scott's concern. A relevant change of circumstances can be taken into account in considering whether, at any particular time, it would have been unconscionable for A to act in a particular way.

---

[94] In *Cobbe* (n 15) [92], Lord Walker suggested that even if the ingredients of a proprietary estoppel claim appear to be present, if the 'result does not shock the conscience of the court, the analysis needs to be looked at again'.

[95] *Thorner* (n 1) [19].

[96] ibid [14] and [20].

The point here is not that B can succeed in a proprietary estoppel claim simply by showing that A's actual or threatened behaviour is unconscionable in a general sense.[97] Rather, promise-based proprietary estoppel deals with a specific form of unconscionability: leaving B to suffer detriment as a result of B's reasonable reliance on A's unperformed promise, where B reasonably understood that promise as seriously intended by A as capable of being relied on by B. Nor is the point that a court can exploit the vagueness of unconscionability in order arbitrarily to reject B's claim even in a case where B has established the core elements of a promise, reliance and the prospect of detriment. It is rather that the notion can provide a means by which a court can develop specific rules to address two key issues: first, when is a change of circumstances significant enough to have an effect;[98] and, second, how should the effect of such circumstances be determined?

As for the first question, for example, it was suggested in *Germanotta v Germanotta* that subsequent events can be taken into account where their result is that A would have to perform his or her promise 'in radically different circumstances than were ever envisaged'.[99] The basic point here is that, as A's liability depends on A's having made a voluntary promise, A should not be made to bear a burden radically more onerous than that initially contemplated. Any event that would have led to the frustration of a contract should suffice, but, given the lower hurdles imposed for a prima facie liability to arise in proprietary estoppel,[100] it seems that, as implied by Hoffmann LJ in *Walton*, a change of circumstances may be relevant even if it would not have led to the frustration of a contract.[101] This contrast with contract law can carry over to the second question: even if a change of circumstances is sufficiently serious to have an impact, it should not necessarily entail the complete rejection of B's claim. If, as hypothesised by Lord Scott,

---

[97] As rightly noted by Lord Scott in *Cobbe* (n 15) [16]: 'unconscionability of conduct may well lead to a remedy but, in my opinion, proprietary estoppel cannot be the route to it unless the ingredients for a proprietary estoppel are present'.

[98] In *PW & Co v Milton Gate Investments Ltd* [2003] EWHC 1994 (Ch), [2004] Ch 142, for example, Neuberger J at [201] invoked the notion of unconscionability in explaining why events occurring after B's reliance may be taken into account in determining whether an estoppel by convention has been established: 'Estoppel is a doctrine designed to do justice, and, at least normally, it seems scarcely consistent with doing justice to ignore facts, which have occurred since the date upon which an action was taken in reliance upon the estoppel, and which may well impinge significantly, or even determinatively, on the issue of unconscionability.'

[99] *Germanotta v Germanotta* [2012] QSC 116 [151].

[100] A similar point is made by EA Farnsworth, *Changing Your Mind: The Law of Regretted Decisions* (New Haven, Yale University Press, 1998) 85–88.

[101] In *Delaforce v Simpson-Cook* [2010] NSWCA 8, (2010) 78 NSWLR 483, Handley AJA, in an obiter discussion, referred to *Walton*, but took the view (at [85]–[89]) that a change of circumstances may be relevant only if it affects 'the reasonableness of [B's] reliance, and the significance of [B's] changes of position' or if the contractual test for frustration is met. This view, it is submitted, is too narrow, and accords insufficient weight to the important differences between contract law on the one hand and a promise-based proprietary estoppel claim on the other.

a serious illness caused A to sell part of a farm promised to B, a duty to leave the remaining land to B would not impose a radically different burden on A. A useful analogy can be made with a point discussed by Lord Neuberger in *Thorner*, which equally depends on a distinction with contract law. His Lordship there noted that if A's promise is capable of bearing more than one meaning, that ambiguity 'should not deprive a person who reasonably relied on the assurance of all relief: it may well be right, however, that he should be accorded relief on the basis of the interpretation least beneficial to him'.[102]

Over time, specific rules can be developed to deal with these, and other,[103] questions. The point is that, in developing these rules, the courts can keep in mind the backwards-looking nature of B's claim and the crucial question of whether it would be unconscionable for A to leave B to suffer some detriment. In this way, unconscionability, rather than being a fifth wheel on the bus, can operate like stabilisers on a child's bicycle: at an early stage, helpful in avoiding accidents; if retained for too long, a source of embarrassment.

IV. THE OWL OF MINERVA

'The owl of Minerva spreads its wings only with the falling of the dusk.' The metaphor provides a nicely epigrammatic link between *Walton* and *Thorner*: quoted by Lord Hoffmann in the latter case, it is a memorable reminder of the backwards-looking nature of proprietary estoppel, as set out in *Walton*. Yet some care is needed. Indeed, as noted by Hoffmann J in *Spiro v Glencrown*: 'Such metaphors can be vivid and illuminating but prove a trap for the unwary if pressed beyond their original context.'[104] Indeed, the metaphor was used to support a different, narrower point in *Thorner*. There it concerned the question of whether Peter Thorner could be said to have made a promise, reasonably understood by David Thorner as seriously intended by Peter as capable of being relied on, to leave his farm to David. It was in that context that Lord Hoffmann noted that: 'Past events provide context and background for the interpretation of subsequent events and subsequent events throw retrospective light upon the meaning of past events.'[105]

---

[102] *Thorner* (n 1) [86]. Compare eg, *Raffles v Wichelhaus* (1864) 2 Hurl & C 906, 159 ER 375: the same ambiguity would be inconsistent with the finding of a contract.

[103] There is, for example, the question of the effect of possible vitiating factors (such as misrepresentation or duress) on B's claim. In *McGuane v Welch* [2008] EWCA Civ 785, [2008] 2 P & CR 24, for example, it was found that, before agreeing to sell his land at an undervalue to an erstwhile stranger, A had not had any independent legal advice, and that B had provided misinformation to A's solicitors and other parties. These 'unsettling features of the transaction' (at [46]) were taken into account in the Court of Appeal's conclusion that it would not be unconscionable for A to refuse to honour that agreement (at [46], [51] and [57]).

[104] *Spiro v Glencrown* [1991] Ch 537, 543. See too *In re K (Enduring Powers of Attorney)* [1988] Ch 310, 314.

[105] *Thorner* (n 1) [8].

It is certainly true that in other proprietary estoppel cases, the courts have taken into account the parties' subsequent conduct in determining if the required promise was made by A.[106] Nonetheless, even in such cases, care must be taken when evaluating such later conduct. For example, different weight has been attached to A's refusal, after the time of an alleged promise to B, to formalise A and B's arrangement. In some cases, that refusal has confirmed the court in its view that no promise had been made;[107] in other cases, even in commercial contexts, the later conduct of A has not interfered with the finding of an earlier promise.[108] Moreover, it may be important that Lord Hoffmann's statement refers to the interpretation of past events; certainly, the prevailing rule, in England and Australia at least,[109] is that subsequent conduct should not be taken into account when interpreting the provisions of a contract.[110] It has been suggested that this rule can be justified by the fact that 'a contract has an objectively ascertainable meaning when it is entered into, and that to take account of subsequent conduct would result in the possibility of the contract meaning different things at different times'.[111] Again, a contrast can be drawn with the backwards-looking nature of proprietary estoppel: as A is not under an immediate duty to honour A's promise, there is no inconsistency in the extent of A's liability changing over time as, for example, there are changes to the degree of prospective detriment that B may suffer. It therefore seems that, in understanding the limits of the Minervan metaphor as an aid to interpretation, it is necessary to advert to the nature of the particular claim made by B and, in particular, to the difference between a contractual claim and a promise-based proprietary estoppel claim. And it is at that more abstract level that, as shown by the analysis in *Walton*, the metaphor in *Thorner* is most useful.

As suggested at the start of this chapter, there is a still further level on which the metaphor succeeds: the one which Hegel had in mind. It reminds

---

[106] See too *Creasey v Sole* [2013] EWHC 1410 (Ch), [2013] WTLR 931 [105]. In *Campbell v Griffin* [2001] EWCA Civ 990, [2001] WTLR 981, in finding a promise to leave property to B on the death of the survivor of A1 and A2, it was noted that A1 had made a later codicil to his will in favour of B and that A1's solicitor, when corresponding with the Benefits Agency, had confirmed that A1 planned for B to inherit the home and that B's removal would 'distress [A1] enormously'. In *Jiggins v Brisley* [2003] EWHC 841 (Ch), [2003] WTLR 1141 [46], A's having referred to a property as 'B's flat' supported the court's finding of an earlier promise.

[107] See, eg, *Lissimore v Downing* [2003] 2 FLR 308 (Ch) [52]; *Cook v Thomas* [2010] EWCA Civ 227 [79].

[108] See, eg, *Gillett* (n 18) 228 and, in the commercial context, *Lloyd v Dugdale* [2001] EWCA Civ 1754, [2002] 2 P & CR 13 and *Chaudhary v Yavuz* [2011] EWCA Civ 1314, [2013] Ch 249.

[109] For the position in New Zealand, see *Gibbons Holdings v Wholesale Distributors* [2008] 1 NZLR 277 (Supreme Court of New Zealand).

[110] See, eg, *James Miller v Whitworth Street Estates* [1970] AC 583 (HL); *Schuler v Wickman Machine Tool Sales* [1974] AC 235 (HL); *Agricultural and Rural Finance v Gardiner* (2008) 238 CLR 570 (High Court of Australia) [35].

[111] R Calnan, *Principles of Contractual Interpretation* (Oxford, Oxford University Press, 2013) 4.101.

us of the difficulty of predicting the future, of reading the runes before the dust has settled. In that sense, it can apply to the evaluation of a judge's jurisprudence—even though, whilst dusk falls in the west, eminent judicial careers often end in the east. However, a proper evaluation of such careers must depend on the judge's influence and, as the common law never stops developing, the extent and nature of that influence can never be definitively established. It may be the case, for example, that as well as shaping the future of proprietary estoppel, the backwards-looking model of *Walton* can usefully be extended to other types of claim, such as those arising in unjust enrichment.[112] Certainly, the model can demonstrate that private law claims do not depend solely on the vindication of claim-rights and the enforcement of correlative duties, but may also ask a court to give effect to liabilities.[113] In any case, whilst we cannot make confident predictions, we can express fervent hopes, and one such is that the brief but masterly analysis of Hoffmann LJ in *Walton*, having been brought to prominence in *Thorner*, will continue to inform the development of the promise-based strand of proprietary estoppel.

---

[112] Note in particular the liability-based analysis of unjust enrichment proposed by S Smith: see, eg, 'Unjust Enrichment: Nearer to Tort than Contract' in R Chambers et al (eds), *Philosophical Foundations of the Law of Unjust Enrichment* (Oxford, Oxford University Press, 2009) 181 and 'The Restatement of Liabilities in Restitution' in C Mitchell and W Swadling (eds), *The Restatement Third: Restitution and Unjust Enrichment* (Oxford, Hart Publishing, 2013) 227. It is also worth noting that in *Australian Financial Services and Leasing Pty Ltd v Hills Industries Ltd* [2014] HCA 14, the High Court of Australia, in analysing the change of position defence, drew analogies with the assessment of detriment in proprietary estoppel and thus favoured a backwards-looking approach which asks 'whether it would be unconscionable for a recipient who has changed its position on the faith of the receipt to be required to repay' (at [88], per Hayne, Crennan, Kiefel, Bell and Keane JJ).

[113] See S Smith, 'Duties, Liabilities and Damages' (2012) 125 *Harvard Law Review* 1727.

19

Corporate Attribution and the Lessons of Meridian

JENNIFER PAYNE

I. INTRODUCTION

LORD HOFFMANN HAS delivered many important judgments in company law. The one considered in this chapter is that in *Meridian Global Funds Management Asia Ltd v Securities Commission*, a decision of the Privy Council.[1]

It is well established in company law that where a sole trader incorporates a company, even if he is the only shareholder and controller of that company and he is carrying on the same business after incorporation as before, the process of incorporation creates a separate and distinct legal person, possessing rights and subject to duties in just the same way as a natural person. That 'one man' behind the company, after incorporation, cannot in law be identified with the company.[2]

While the company is a separate legal person, however, it is not a natural person and consequently it cannot *itself* act. In order to determine whether a company has acted, for example to determine whether it has committed a tort or a crime, it will be necessary to attribute the acts of others to the company. As Lord Hoffmann stated in *Meridian*:

> A company exists because there is a rule (usually in a statute) which says that a persona ficta shall be deemed to exist and to have certain of the powers, rights and duties of a natural person. But there would be little sense in deeming such a persona ficta to exist unless there were also rules to tell one what acts were to count as acts of the company. It is therefore a necessary part of corporate personality that there should be rules by which acts are attributed to the company.[3]

---

[1] *Meridian Global Funds Management Asia Ltd v Securities Commission* [1995] UKPC 5, [1995] 2 AC 500.
[2] *Salomon v A Salomon & Co Ltd* [1897] AC 22 (HL).
[3] *Meridian* (n 1) 506.

Lord Hoffmann's judgment in *Meridian* explores the parameters of corporate attribution, setting out clear and coherent principles for tackling this complex topic. It is undoubtedly the leading case on the topic of attribution in English company law. The issue of corporate attribution and the decision in *Meridian* are discussed in section II. These principles have had an enormous impact on the way in which subsequent cases have tackled the issue of corporate attribution. However, the principles set out in *Meridian* have not been consistently followed by subsequent courts. Section III discusses the issue of corporate attribution after *Meridian*. Broadly, two uses are made of corporate attribution: in order to impose liability on a company; and in order to construct a defence against a claim brought by the company. It will be seen that in both cases the lessons of *Meridian* have not been wholly learned, but that the problems appear more pronounced in the second category, where attribution is used to provide a defence against a claim by a company. Section IV concludes. It is suggested that a return to the principles set out in *Meridian* can provide clarity in what has otherwise become a rather confused area of the law.

II. CORPORATE ATTRIBUTION AND THE DECISION IN *MERIDIAN*

There are various bases on which acts and states of mind can be attributed to a company. The first is that a specific statutory provision has been put in place to deal with the issue. So, for example, in the context of corporate manslaughter, a specific Act, introduced in 2007, provides that a company will be guilty of an offence only if the way in which its activities are managed or organised by its 'senior management' is a substantial element of the breach.[4] 'Senior management' for these purposes means the persons who play significant roles in: (i) the making of decisions about how the whole or a substantial part of the firm's activities are to be managed or organised; or (ii) the actual managing or organising of the whole or a substantial part of those activities.[5] Prior to this Act, it had been necessary to demonstrate that a single individual in the company had committed the crime and that this individual was the 'controlling mind' of the company.[6] As a result, successful prosecutions tended to only occur in relation to small, one-man companies.[7] Following the Act, however, no single individual has to be identified whose acts constitute the offence of manslaughter and who can then be identified with the company. Instead, it becomes an offence for companies to cause a

---

[4] Corporate Manslaughter and Corporate Homicide Act 2007.
[5] ibid s 1(4)(c).
[6] *Attorney-General's Reference (No 2 of 1999)* [2000] EWCA Crim 91, [2002] Cr App R 207.
[7] See, eg, *R v Kite and OLL Ltd* (Winchester Crown Court, 9 December 1994).

person's death as a result of the way in which its activities are organised, where that organisation amounts to a gross breach of a duty owed by the company to the deceased. This creates the possibility of larger companies being liable for corporate manslaughter.

The next basis is that there may be rules regarding attribution in the company's constitution. For instance, the articles of association of a company may specify that for a particular purpose, such as appointing members of the board, the decision of a certain person or group will be regarded as a decision of the company, so, for example, a majority vote of the shareholders will be regarded as a decision of the company for this purpose.[8] Some of these rules of attribution are not found in the company's constitution per se, but are implied from company law; for example, it is clear from *Multinational Gas and Petrochemical Co v Multinational Gas and Petrochemical Services Ltd*[9] that a unanimous decision of all the shareholders in a solvent company about anything which the company has power to do will be a decision of the company.

Third, the application of ordinary legal principles, particularly vicarious liability and agency principles, can be used to determine when the acts of an individual can be treated as the acts of the company. So, to determine whether a company, A Ltd, will be bound by a contract with B entered into on A Ltd's behalf by C, the answer is found, predominantly, in the rules of agency.[10] The starting point is to ask whether C acted with actual or apparent authority. Where the agent does have authority and the company is found to be bound to the contract, in general the agent then drops out of the picture and the company alone is liable to the third party. By contrast, where vicarious liability is used to impose liability on the company, the company's liability is in addition to that of the individual. For instance, where the individual is driving the company's van and negligently causes injury to another road user, then, in addition to the driver being liable, the company can be liable to the third party if there is a sufficiently close connection between the wrongful acts of the agents or employees and the activities which those persons were employed to undertake.[11]

---

[8] This point was recognised by Hoffmann LJ (as he then was) in *El Ajou v Dollar Land Holdings Ltd* [1993] EWCA Civ 4, [1994] 2 All ER 685, 705, a case which can be regarded as a precursor to *Meridian*.

[9] *Multinational Gas and Petrochemical Co v Multinational Gas and Petrochemical Services Ltd* [1983] Ch 258 (CA).

[10] Some additional third party protection is to be found in s 40 of the Companies Act 2006 and in *Royal British Bank v Turquand* (1856) 6 El & Bl 327. For discussion, see PL Davies and S Worthington (eds), *Gower & Davies: Principles of Modern Company Law* (9th edn, London, Sweet & Maxwell, 2012) 178–88.

[11] For a discussion of this test, see, eg, *Dubai Aluminium Company Ltd v Salaam* [2003] 1 BCLC 32 (QBD).

In general these three bases of attribution will be enough to determine whether the acts of a natural person can be attributed to the company, and indeed the existence and application of these three bases of corporate attribution is relatively uncontroversial. As Lord Hoffmann acknowledged in *Meridian*, however: 'In exceptional cases ... they will not provide an answer.'[12] These exceptional cases tend to arise where the provision in question requires some act or state of mind on the part of a person herself rather than via that person's servants or agents. It is in the exceptional cases that the difficulties regarding corporate attribution tend to lurk. This was the subject matter of the decision in *Meridian*.

In this case the question was whether the company, Meridian, was in breach of a requirement under New Zealand securities law to disclose its shareholding in another company. The provision was only breached if Meridian itself 'knew' that it was a 'substantial security holder' in the second company. On the facts, the purchase of the shares had been carried out by two investment managers on Meridian's behalf. They therefore knew all of the relevant facts, but the issue was whether their knowledge could be attributed to the company such that Meridian could be held to be in breach of the statutory provision.

The issue of attribution of a state of mind to a company in such circumstances was an area in need of some sensible judicial scrutiny. Thankfully, Lord Hoffmann provided that scrutiny. This issue had been dealt with prior to *Meridian* via the identification principle, ie, the notion that in some instances the acts of the individual are the acts of the company. Early in the twentieth century, the courts developed the 'directing mind and will' test. This test bases identification on the concept of the person 'who is really the directing mind and will of the corporation, the very ego and centre of the personality of the corporation'.[13] On the basis of this test, therefore, there could only be attribution to the company of the acts and state of mind of those who can properly be said to be the 'directing mind and will' of the corporation.

There were two interlinked difficulties with this test that Lord Hoffmann in *Meridian* sought to resolve. The first is that the 'directing mind and will' test, if rigidly interpreted, will tend to mean that attribution will only be possible where the board of directors or some senior officer is in charge of the activity in question. This is not always appropriate, however, and there may well be occasions on which the behaviour and state of mind of less senior members of the company should be attributed to the company.[14]

---

[12] *Meridian* (n 1) 507.
[13] *Lennard's Carrying Co Ltd v Asiatic Petroleum Ltd* [1915] AC 705 (HL) 713. See also *Tesco Supermarkets Ltd v Nattrass* [1971] UKHL 1, [1972] AC 153.
[14] See, eg, *Tesco Supermarkets* (n 13).

The second is that it is easy to slide from the identification principle to the idea that the company is an entity with a mind of its own able to engage in behaviour *itself*. So, for example, in *Lennard's Carrying Co Ltd v Asiatic Petroleum Co Ltd*, in which the directing mind and will test was first developed, Viscount Haldane stated:

> For if Mr Lennard was the directing mind and will of the company, then his action must, unless a corporation is not to be liable at all, have been an action which was the action of the company itself within the meaning of [the relevant statutory provision].[15]

Viscount Haldane's speech was 'open to the interpretation that he was expounding a general metaphysic of companies'.[16] Indeed, subsequent judges then developed an unfortunate anthropomorphic approach to this issue; for example, Denning LJ (as he then was) in *HL Bolton (Engineering) Co Ltd v TJ Graham & Sons Ltd*[17] likened a company to a human body: 'It has a brain and nerve centre which controls what it does. It also has hands which hold the tools and act in accordance with directions from the centre.'

This is to misunderstand company law and corporate attribution, however. When it is determined that a company is personally liable for an act, this does not mean that the company has actually done something or thought something *itself*. Companies cannot act immaculately, but only through human intermediaries. Even in cases of direct liability, the company is only a deemed wrongdoer because of the actions of its agents.[18]

In *Meridian*, Lord Hoffmann warned against the danger of anthropomorphism:

> Any statement about what a company has or has not done, or can or cannot do, is necessarily a reference to the rules of attribution (primary and general) as they apply to that company. Judges sometimes say that a company 'as such' cannot do anything; it must act by servants or agents. This may seem an unexceptionable, even banal remark and of course the meaning is usually perfectly clear. But a reference to a company 'as such' might suggest that there is something out there called the company of which one can meaningfully say that it can or cannot do something. There is in fact no such thing as the company as such, no 'ding an sich', only the applicable rules. To say that a company cannot do something means only that there is no one whose doing of that act would, under the applicable rules of attribution, count as an act of the company.[19]

---

[15] *Lennard's Carrying Co Ltd* (n 13) 713.
[16] *Meridian* (n 1) 509 (Lord Hoffmann).
[17] *HL Bolton (Engineering) Co Ltd v TJ Graham & Sons Ltd* [1957] 1 QB 159 (CA) 172.
[18] See, eg, P Watts, 'The Company's Alter Ego—An Imposter in Private Law' (2000) 116 LQR 525; P Watts, 'Corrupt Company Controllers, their Companies, and their Companies' Creditors—Dealing with Pleas of *Ex Turpi Causa*' [2014] *Journal of Business Law* 161.
[19] *Meridian* (n 1) 506–07.

So, there are two dangers with the identification test, but they are closely linked and Lord Hoffmann was able to deal with both dangers together. The anthropomorphism lurking in the test 'distracts attention'[20] from the purpose for which the test is created, namely the question of: 'Whose act (or knowledge, or state of mind) was *for this purpose* intended to count as the act etc of the company?'[21] The context is all-important. The issue is therefore 'one of construction rather than metaphysics'.[22] It is necessary to look at the particular statutory provision in question to determine whose act or knowledge can be attributed to the company for the particular purpose in question. So, in *Lennard's Carrying Co Ltd*, the provision provided a shipowner with a defence to a claim for the loss of cargo put on board his ship if he could show that the accident occurred 'without his actual fault or privity'.[23] The relevant person for this purpose was therefore the person within the company responsible for monitoring the condition of the ship, authorising repairs and so on. On the facts, this was Mr Lennard and it was therefore his fault that could be attributed to the company.[24]

In *Meridian*, the Privy Council held that the knowledge of the employees of the company who acquired shares for the company could be counted as the company's knowledge for the purpose of determining the application of a disclosure obligation under New Zealand securities law. The employees in *Meridian* were two senior investment managers who were not even members of the company's board. They could not be regarded as the 'directing mind and will' of the company as that term was understood prior to *Meridian*. Lord Hoffmann stated that the purpose of the statute in question was rapid disclosure of shareholdings and it was therefore appropriate to treat those in charge of the company's dealings in the market on its behalf as its controllers for this purpose. A focus on 'construction rather than metaphysics' therefore also solves the first problem identified in relation to the directing mind and will test.

Lord Hoffmann's innovation in *Meridian* was to recognise specifically that special rules of attribution exist over and above the primary rules (eg, those found in the company's constitutional documents) and the general rules (eg, those derived from agency and vicarious liability). *Meridian* did not spell the end to the 'directing mind and will' test: Lord Hoffmann recognised that, on occasion, it will still be relevant to attribute liability to a company on this basis.[25] Instead, Lord Hoffmann advocated an end to the view that where an act or state of mind is required on the part of the company

---

[20] ibid 509.
[21] ibid 507.
[22] ibid 511.
[23] Merchant Shipping Act 1894, s 502.
[24] *Lennard's Carrying Co Ltd* (n 13).
[25] *Meridian* (n 1) 511.

itself, this can *only* arise by attributing the acts or state of mind of someone who may be described as the 'directing mind and will' of the company.[26]

Lord Hoffmann's judgment also, helpfully, moved away from the anthropomorphic 'metaphysical' approach to company attribution towards a more context-driven approach.[27] This latter point is particularly important. There are downsides to the test: it is not possible to provide a precise answer to the general question of whose acts and knowledge will be attributed to the company since the analysis depends on the particular rule and context in question. Nevertheless, this approach is a significant improvement on the prior identification approach.[28] Companies cannot act or think immaculately and therefore it is preferable to understand that attribution does not involve the company itself committing the act. A better way to understand the role of the company in these circumstances is perhaps to borrow an analogy provided by Lord Hoffmann in *Standard Chartered Bank v Pakistan Shipping Corp*,[29] in which he described a company as being like an owner who lives in the south of France.[30] The acts of an employee in England are not the acts of the owner, but may be attributed to the owner in certain circumstances. Likewise, for a company, attribution is simply the process of determining that, for a particular purpose, the acts of an individual can be deemed to be those of the company such that the company can be held responsible for them.

Unfortunately, the clarity of this view of attribution has not always been maintained, as will be discussed in the next section. It has been noted that 'a kind of anthropomorphism [is] very hard to eradicate from this branch of the law'[31] and, indeed, this has proved to be the case.

III. CORPORATE ATTRIBUTION AFTER *MERIDIAN*

Corporate attribution can be relevant in two broad ways. First, it can be used to impose contractual, criminal, tortious or statutory liability on a company. So, for example, it can be used to determine whether a company

---

[26] Lord Hoffmann explained those cases where the 'directing mind and will' test has been stretched to include relatively junior employees as examples of the application of special rules of attribution (see, eg, LS Sealy, 'The Corporate Ego and Agency Untwined' [1995] *Cambridge Law Journal* 507 on this point).

[27] For discussion, see E Ferran, 'Corporate Attribution and the Directing Mind and Will' (2011) 127 *LQR* 239.

[28] It is notable that despite the uncertainty inherent in the *Meridian* approach, the Law Commission has commended this approach to the courts in all cases where the statute does not deal specifically with the issue of corporate liability: Law Commission, 'Criminal Liability in Regulatory Contexts' (Law Com Consultation Paper No 195, 2010) [5.103]–[5.110].

[29] *Standard Chartered Bank v Pakistan Shipping Corp* [2002] UKHL 43, [2003] 1 AC 959 [23].

[30] See also Staughton LJ in *PCW Syndicates v PCW Reinsurers* [1996] 1 WLR 1136 (CA) 1143, who analogised a company to an owner who spends his days on the grouse moors.

[31] RB Cooke, 'A Real Thing: *Salomon v A Salomon & Co Ltd*' in RB Cooke, *Turning Points of the Common Law* (London, Sweet & Maxwell, 1997) 26–27.

should be held responsible for the theft by its employee of a customer's coat,[32] or will be bound by a contract entered into by an individual purporting to contract on the company's behalf. *Meridian* is an example of this kind of corporate attribution, involving as it did the question whether the knowledge of the investment managers should be deemed to be that of the company such that the company could be held liable under the relevant provisions of New Zealand securities law. This first use of corporate attribution is perhaps the best known, and of course it was this form of attribution that was being addressed directly in *Meridian*. Some of the lessons of *Meridian* appear to have been learned in this context, particularly in civil law cases, but the 'directing mind and will' test continues to cast a long shadow.

A second use of corporate attribution is its use to help defend against a claim being brought by the company. A number of cases have sought to utilise the principle of *ex turpi causa non oritur actio* in this context. This is a defence based on the idea that 'no court will lend its aid to a man who founds his cause of action upon an immoral or an illegal act'.[33] So, for example, where a director of a company is engaged in fraud, the question may arise whether that fraud can be attributed to the company such that if the company seeks to bring an action in relation to that fraud against the director or against a third party, it can be claimed that the company is seeking to rely on its own wrongdoing, and the *ex turpi causa* maxim can be used to bar the company's claim. This second use of attribution has arisen in a rash of recent cases, starting with the House of Lords' decision in *Stone & Rolls Ltd v Moore Stephens*.[34] Here, in some cases at least, the lessons of *Meridian* need to be reiterated and reapplied in order to introduce some clarity into this area.

A. The Use of Corporate Attribution to Impose Liability on a Company

Meridian was a criminal law case, but it has been widely cited and applied in civil law cases. In general, the lessons of *Meridian* have been taken to heart in this context, and the courts have moved away from the identification principle and the view that a state of mind or acts of the company itself can only be attributed to the company via the acts or knowledge of a person who is a directing mind and will of the company. Instead, the courts in civil cases have been prepared to develop special attribution rules in construing both statutory provisions and common law rules.[35] The courts in civil cases

---

[32] *Morris v CW Martin & Sons Ltd* [1966] 1 QB 716 (CA).
[33] *Holman v Johnson* (1775) 1 Cowp 341, 343; 98 ER 1120, 1121 (Lord Mansfield CJ).
[34] *Stone & Rolls Ltd v Moore Stephens* [2009] UKHL 39, [2009] 1 AC 1391.
[35] For a discussion of recent cases in this context, see E Ferran, 'Corporate Attribution and the Directing Mind and Will' (2011) 127 *LQR* 239, 249–50.

do still make use of the 'directing mind and will' concept in order to attribute liability to the company in some instances, but, following *Meridian*, they are not wedded to this concept and are prepared to attribute liability on the basis of the acts or knowledge of those who cannot be so described.[36]

By contrast, the judges in criminal law cases involving mens rea have tended to prefer to attribute liability on the basis of the state of the mind of senior management.[37] The view has persisted that 'it is impossible to find a company guilty unless its alter ego is identified'.[38] Some criminal law cases have regarded *Meridian* as a re-statement and not an abandonment of the identification principle,[39] on the basis that a narrow formulation of the rule of attribution is necessary to avoid corporations being convicted of mens rea crimes when 'in truth they have no guilty mind'.[40] The recent decision of *R v Regis Paper Co Ltd*[41] is an example of the difficulties that can arise for courts attempting to apply the principles of *Meridian* to criminal law cases.

In this case the question arose whether a company could be held criminally liable for intentionally making a false entry in a record required for environmental pollution control. The acts and the state of mind were located in Mr Steer, the company's technical manager, who was convicted of deliberately falsifying the records under the relevant legislation. The focus of the enquiry for the Court of Appeal was whether Mr Steer could be regarded as the 'directing mind and will' of the company. Ultimately their Lordships determined that he could not be so regarded, and therefore his state of mind could not be attributed to the company. The Court of Appeal in *Regis* did take on board the context-specific approach advocated by Lord Hoffmann in *Meridian*. Their Lordships analysed the statutory provision in question,[42] but concluded that there was no basis within the regulations for departing from the 'directing mind and will' test. This is an odd reading of the relevant provisions. Of course, one of the potential disadvantages of the context-specific approach advocated by Lord Hoffmann is that courts may on occasion find it difficult to determine the policy and purpose behind a substantive rule in order to apply the special rules of attribution, or, in applying rules where the policy is obscure, may come to a conclusion different from that which other courts or commentators might have reached. The purpose of the regulation in this instance seems clear, however, namely to ensure that environmental

---

[36] See, eg, *Odyssey Re (London) Ltd v OIC Run-Off Ltd* [2000] EWCA Civ 71, [2001] Lloyd's Rep I R 1; *cf* Buxton LJ (dissenting).

[37] *Attorney-General's Reference (No 2 of 1999)* (n 6). Note, however, that in this case, it was suggested that *Meridian* reaffirmed rather than departed from the identification doctrine (at 816). For a discussion, see Law Commission, 'Criminal Liability in Regulatory Contexts' (Law Com Consultation Paper No 195, 2010) [1.64]–[1.67] and ch 5.

[38] *Attorney-General's Reference (No 2 of 1999)* (n 6) 216 (Rose LJ).

[39] ibid.

[40] *Odyssey Re (London) Ltd v OIC Run-Off Ltd* (n 36) [107] (Buxton LJ).

[41] *R v Regis Paper Co Ltd* [2011] EWCA Crim 2527.

[42] Pollution Prevention and Control (England and Wales) Regulations 2000, reg 32(1)(g).

pollution records are accurate. Mr Steer was the person within the company in control of the operations at the company in relation to the submission of these records. If the analysis in *Meridian* is followed, it would appear that Mr Steer was in a similar position to the investment managers in that case. Looking at the purpose and function of the provision, it would seem to be appropriate to attribute Mr Steer's state of mind in relation to this matter to the company, despite the fact that he was some way below board level.

As discussed by Professor Ferran, the application of the 'directing mind and will' test to attribute criminal liability to a company need not per se be regarded as a reason to doubt the value or benefit of the *Meridian* decision.[43] Lord Hoffmann in *Meridian* clearly recognised that attribution on that basis may be correct in some circumstances. The attribution rule must be tailored to the terms and, crucially, to the policies of the substantive rule, and it may be appropriate for the judges to determine that a serious criminal offence be attributed to the company only via the acts or state of mind of a senior manager. It is problematic if judges are placing undue weight on this test, however, such that they are insufficiently willing to take account of the relevant context in order to allow the state of mind of someone other than the 'directing mind and will' of the company (such as Mr Steer in *Regis*) to be attributed to the company. It may be that the enduring language of the 'directing mind and will' of the company is problematic in this context. As Lord Walker stated recently: '[to] refer instead to "the relevant responsible director or employee", or some such expression, would be less arresting but a good deal more accurate'.[44]

B. The Use of Corporate Attribution to Defend Against a Claim Brought by a Company

A second possible use of corporate attribution, which has come to the fore in recent cases, is its use to found a defence based on the *ex turpi causa* maxim where a claim is being brought by a company against a third party. Problems have arisen in this context as a result of the decision of the House of Lords in *Stone & Rolls Ltd v Moore Stephens*.[45]

In *Stone & Rolls*, the House of Lords considered a claim by a company in liquidation against its former auditor. The company was essentially a one-man company (it had one shareholder and effectively a single controller) and the one man behind the company, Mr Stojevic, had used the company to perpetrate a fraud against banks. The fraud involved the presentation

---

[43] E Ferran, 'Corporate Attribution and the Directing Mind and Will' (2011) 127 *LQR* 239.
[44] *Moulin Global Eyecare Trading Ltd (in Liquidation) v The Commissioner of Inland Revenue* [2014] HKCFA 22, [2014] 3 HKC 323 [67].
[45] *Stone & Rolls Ltd* (n 34).

by the company of false documents to banks, the receipt of funds by the company, and the payment of those funds to other parties involved in the fraud. This case involved the liquidator seeking to claim that the auditor had failed to act with due care and skill and had increased the company's losses by failing to detect the fraud. The question was whether the auditor could make use of the maxim of *ex turpi causa* to strike out the company's claim, on the basis that the fraud of the 'one man' could be attributed to the company, and therefore the company could be seen as seeking to rely on its own wrongdoing in bringing this claim against the auditor. It was accepted that for this defence to operate, the fraud had to be attributed to the company as its own conduct, and not as conduct for which it was vicariously liable, or liable under normal agency principles.

There is an exception to the *ex turpi causa* principle: the so-called *Hampshire Land* principle may be invoked to preclude the attribution of liability in circumstances where the company as a distinct legal entity is deemed a victim of the very illegal or immoral act that would otherwise have triggered the application of the maxim *ex turpi causa*.[46] So, for example, the principle may be invoked to enable a company to enforce a compensatory action where the company is considered a victim of an illegal act perpetrated by an agent of the company.[47] However, the majority of the House of Lords in *Stone & Rolls* held that the *Hampshire Land* principle could not be applied to a one-man company where the company was suing to recover on behalf of all those that it itself had defrauded. Their Lordships were of the view that it would be impossible in such circumstances to describe the company as a victim.

The House of Lords in *Stone & Rolls* by a 3:2 majority held that the fraud of Mr Stojevic was the company's fraud such that the auditor could rely on the *ex turpi causa* maxim. The company was consequently barred from recovering compensation for the consequences of its own illegal conduct. There are a number of problems with the analysis and reasoning of the majority in *Stone & Rolls*. Crucially, it ignores the lessons of *Meridian*. There is an undue fixation by the majority in *Stone & Rolls* with the idea that the 'one man' behind the company was the 'directing mind and will' of the company and that the fraud of the directing mind and will of the company should be attributed to the company: 'In the present case Mr Stojevic and [the company] were in effect one and the same person.'[48] In addition, Lord Brown quoted with approval the statement in *Tesco Supermarkets v Nattrass* that the 'one man' behind the company 'is an embodiment of the

---

[46] See *Re Hampshire Land Co* [1896] 2 Ch 743.
[47] See *Belmont Finance Corp Ltd v Williams Furniture* [1979] Ch 250 (CA).
[48] *Stone & Rolls* (n 34) [199] (Lord Brown).

company ... his mind is the mind of the company. If it is a guilty mind then that guilt is the guilt of the company'.[49]

This analysis falls into the trap identified by Lord Hoffmann in *Meridian*. The fraudster and the company are not the same person. Neither is the company itself actually fraudulent. It cannot itself carry out the acts or have the state of mind necessary to be fraudulent; rather, the company is *deemed* to be fraudulent if the fraud of the natural person (Mr Stojevic) is attributed to the company.

The correct question then, as set out in *Meridian*, is to determine whether the acts of the natural person should be deemed to be the acts of the company *for this purpose*. Context was important in *Meridian* in determining *whose* acts can be attributed to a company in a given scenario, but it is just as important in a situation like *Stone & Rolls* where the question is *whether* to attribute wrongdoing of an individual, even someone who is the 'directing mind and will', to the company. As Lord Mance, in the minority in *Stone & Rolls*, said, when and how far a company will be attributed with the wrongdoing of individuals that have acted for it 'depends on the circumstances and context'.[50] By contrast, the majority decision of the House of Lords in *Stone & Rolls* appears to suggest that wrongdoing on the part of the 'directing mind and will' of the company will automatically be attributed to the company unless there is an exception, such as the rule in *Hampshire Land*. However, it does not, and should not, follow that just because wrongdoing has been committed by an individual who is the 'directing mind and will' of a company, even if that individual is the one man in a one-man company, that the wrongdoing should be attributed to the company for any and all purposes.

To see this more clearly, it is instructive to analyse the decisions of two subsequent Court of Appeal decisions in which the court had to determine whether the *ex turpi causa* maxim can be utilised to bar a claim by the company against the wrongdoers themselves, namely *Safeway Stores Ltd v Twigger*[51] and *Bilta (UK) Ltd v Nazir*.[52]

Both of these cases effectively involved the same scenario. Wrongdoers within the company in each case had their acts or state of mind attributed to the company such that the company was found to be in breach of a particular statutory provision. The company subsequently sought to bring actions against those wrongdoers for breach of their duties to the company in relation to the wrongdoing that had led to the company being found in breach of those provisions. In each case, the wrongdoers sought to utilise

---

[49] *Tesco Supermarkets* (n 13) 170 (Lord Reid).
[50] *Stone & Rolls* (n 34) [220].
[51] *Safeway Stores Ltd v Twigger* [2010] EWCA Civ 1472.
[52] *Bilta (UK) Ltd v Nazir* [2013] EWCA Civ 968 (also known as *Jetivia SA v Bilta (UK) Ltd*).

the *ex turpi causa* maxim to bar the company's claim. On the face of it, it seems extraordinary that the wrongdoers should be able to use their own wrongdoing, then attributed to the company, to bar the company's claim against them for that very wrongdoing.[53] Nevertheless, in *Safeway Stores Ltd v Twigger*, that is what the Court of Appeal allowed.

In *Safeway Stores*, a number of employees and directors of the claimant company sought to strike out an action brought against them. The company claimed that the defendants had caused it to become liable for penalties imposed under the Competition Act 1998 as a result of the defendants allegedly engaging in (illegal) price fixing with their counterparts in other supermarkets. The defendants claimed, inter alia, that the company's claim was barred by *ex turpi causa* and the Court of Appeal accepted this argument.

In this case, the relevant provision of the 1998 Act makes illegal 'agreements between undertakings, decisions by associations of undertakings or concerted parties' that adversely affect competition, ie, the prohibition is placed on 'undertakings'. The company had admitted that it was party to such an agreement. Longmore LJ, giving the principal judgment, held that because the Act made undertakings directly, not vicariously, liable, the claimant company was 'personally' liable and therefore caught by the *ex turpi causa* defence. Oddly, the judge seemed to consider that the liability of the company had not arisen because of the acts of its agents since 'to talk of liability for the acts of one's agents is to talk of vicarious liability and the company's liability was not vicarious';[54] rather, the view seems to have been that the company had made the agreement *itself*. This is the same error as that made by the majority in *Stone & Rolls*: the company cannot think or act for itself. The company in *Safeway Stores* is not in breach of these provisions because it entered into this agreement itself. It is only liable because the acts of its employees are attributed to it for that purpose and as such it is deemed to be liable. In addition, the fact that the company is in breach of a statutory provision as a result of the attribution of the wrongdoing of those acting for it does not necessarily mean that the company cannot then bring a claim against those wrongdoers if they have breached their duty to the company. The fact that the wrongdoing is attributed to the company for one purpose (the company's liability under the Competition Act) does not necessarily mean that it should be attributed to the company for a different purpose (the company's claim against the wrongdoing employees and directors). This is not an exception to the rules of attribution; rather, it is a situation in which the rules of attribution have no relevance, and therefore the *ex turpi causa* maxim has no relevance.[55]

---

[53] Indeed, there are plenty of examples of the courts recognising the injustice and absurdity of allowing such a defence; see, eg, *Gluckstein v Barnes* [1900] AC 240 (HL).

[54] *Safeway Stores Ltd* (n 51) [27] (Longmore LJ).

[55] For discussion, see P Watts (ed), *Bowstead & Reynolds on Agency* (19th edn, London, Sweet & Maxwell, 2013) para 8-213.

A far more satisfactory approach to these issues was adopted by the Court of Appeal in *Bilta (UK) Ltd v Nazir*[56] and, indeed, Lord Walker, giving judgment in the Court of Final Appeal in Hong Kong in 2014, has stated that this decision 'has achieved a welcome clarification of the law in this area'.[57] *Bilta* involved a company with two directors and only one shareholder. The company had traded in the purchase and sale of European emissions trading scheme allowances on the Danish emissions trading registry, and was said to have been part of a VAT fraud. The purchases were from traders carrying on business outside the UK and were therefore zero-rated for VAT purposes. The sales were to VAT-registered persons in the UK and were standard-rated. The company was unable to pay the VAT due on its supplies. Revenue and Customs raised VAT assessments of £38 million which the company could not pay and it subsequently went into liquidation. The Court of Appeal considered a strike-out application against claims brought by the company's liquidators against the directors of the company in respect of various breaches of directors' duties, including alleged fraudulent trading under section 213 of the Insolvency Act 1986 and breach of section 172 of the Companies Act 2006. The basis of the application was that the company was party to illegal tax evasion and was disabled from suing any parties that had assisted in that illegality by reason of the principle of *ex turpi causa*. The Court of Appeal rejected this application.

Patten LJ explained that attribution of the wrongs to the company will not necessarily be available to found a defence should the company sue its directors for the wrongdoing. Following the reasoning in *Meridian*, context is all-important.[58] It is necessary to look at the purpose behind the application of the attribution rules and to consider the policy circumstances in order to determine whether attribution can be used as a defence. In relation to a claim by a company against its directors, the question is whether there has been a breach of duty by the directors. In *Bilta*, it was held that such a breach had occurred and therefore the company (in a claim by the liquidator since the company was insolvent) could sue those directors for their breach of duty. The question of whether the company was a victim or a villain here was irrelevant. It is clear that the maxim of *ex turpi causa* should be irrelevant to a case where the issue is whether a director has breached his duties to the company.

---

[56] *Bilta* (n 52); and see Watts, 'Corrupt Company Controllers' (n 18). See also the decision of the Court of Appeal in *Brumder v Motornet Service and Repairs Ltd* [2013] EWCA Civ 195, which involved a different issue, namely whether the director had a claim for compensation from the company, but nevertheless recognised that despite attribution of a director's acts and state of mind to a company leading to the company being in breach of the Provision and Use of Work Equipment Regulations 1998, the director still owed a duty to the company in relation to that wrongdoing which had been breached.

[57] *Moulin Global* (n 44) [106]. In this decision, Lord Walker, who was part of the majority in *Stone & Rolls* (n 34), recognised some of the difficulties with that judgment (see [100]).

[58] *Bilta* (n 52) [34]–[35].

The decision in *Bilta* is clearly correct and, indeed, similar reasoning should have been applied in *Safeway Stores* in order to allow the company to bring a claim against its agents in that scenario. It was irrelevant that in *Bilta* the company was effectively a one-man company (both directors and the sole shareholder were involved in the fraud). Once the context is understood, ie, the question to be answered is whether the company can sue its directors for a breach of duty to the company, it becomes clear that the wrongdoing of the directors should not be attributed to the company *for this purpose* and therefore the question of the application of the *ex turpi causa* maxim becomes irrelevant.[59]

In *Bilta*, the company was insolvent, but of course this did not mean that the directors' duties had come to an end. It is well understood in company law that the directors' duty to act in the interests of the company comprises, broadly, the interests of the shareholders as a whole when the company is solvent,[60] but requires the directors to take account of the interests of the creditors as a whole when the company is insolvent or on the verge of insolvency.[61] Similarly, it is well understood that while the shareholders can ratify breaches of duty by directors to the company while the company remains solvent,[62] they cannot do so once the company is near to insolvency, since to do so would override the interests of the creditors in the company's assets. Once insolvent, then, in general the company can no longer be equated with the shareholders. There was therefore no difficulty with the liquidator asserting this breach of duty claim even though the company was insolvent; the directors' duties to the company are understood to incorporate the creditors' interests at this point in time.

This decision stands in sharp contrast to the decision in *Stone & Rolls*, where on similar facts the breach of duty claim brought by the liquidator was struck out as a result of the application of the *ex turpi causa* maxim. Of course, *Bilta* is factually distinct from *Stone & Rolls* in that *Stone & Rolls* involved not a claim by the company against the fraudster, but a claim against a third party, the auditors, who then sought to utilise the *ex turpi causa* maxim by attributing the wrongdoing of the fraudster to the company. The question arises whether this distinction is meaningful in terms of this analysis.

Patten LJ in *Bilta* thought so, but he was in a difficult position in that case. After all, the majority of the House of Lords in *Stone & Rolls* had held that where a company is under the sole ownership and control of a wrongdoer,

---

[59] Similar reasoning was employed in the Singapore Court of Appeal in *Ho Kang Peng v Scintromix Corp Ltd* [2014] SGCA 22.

[60] Section 172(1) of the Companies Act 2006, although note the list of factors which the directors must take into account, such as the interests of the company's employees, in determining what is in the long-term interests of the shareholders.

[61] *West Mercia Safetywear Ltd v Dodd* [1988] BCLC 250; see also Companies Act 2006, s 172(3).

[62] See now Companies Act 2006, s 239.

the principle of *ex turpi causa* will inevitably be applied. In *Bilta*, the sole shareholders and both directors were involved in the fraud and so, on its face, the *ex turpi causa* maxim should have been applied. The Court of Appeal in *Bilta* was potentially in some difficulty if it wished to hold that the *ex turpi causa* maxim was irrelevant. Understandably, therefore, Patten LJ distinguished *Stone & Rolls* on the basis that that case did not concern the company's litigation against the 'one man' behind the company, but rather was concerned with litigation against the company's auditor, ie, a third party. With respect, however, his reasoning in *Bilta* can and should be applied equally to the situation in *Stone & Rolls* where the *ex turpi causa* defence is being raised by a third party in response to a claim by the company. This case has been appealed to the Supreme Court. Judgment of that court is awaited, and it is to be hoped that the opportunity will be taken to clarify these issues.

The starting point in *Stone & Rolls* should not have been the question of whether Mr Stojevic was the directing mind and will of the company, followed by an automatic attribution of his fraud to the company for all purposes. Instead, the question should have been whether his wrongdoing should have been attributed to the company *for this purpose*. Where the company brings a claim against a third party, such as an auditor, the starting point should be whether that third party has breached its duty to the company. Undoubtedly, auditors do owe a duty to the company, the scope of which is determined by the contract between the auditor and the company and statutory provisions governing auditing standards. Generally, however, an auditor's duty to the company has been understood to comprise an undertaking to protect the shareholders of the company.[63] If the company had been solvent in *Stone & Rolls* and there had been an innocent constituency present, ie, minority shareholders not implicated in the fraud, it seems clear that the *ex turpi causa* maxim would not operate.[64] In such circumstances, the minority shareholders would retain their ability to claim against the wrongdoers.[65] The minority shareholders in such a scenario are an innocent group who should not be barred from compensation because the majority have been involved in a fraud which the company's auditor, in breach of duty to the company, has failed to detect.[66]

---

[63] *Caparo Industries plc v Dickman* [1990] UKHL 2, [1990] 2 AC 605.

[64] If the company is solvent and all of the shareholders are party to the fraud, then, for this purpose, the shareholders can be regarded as embodying the company, because their unanimous decision is regarded in company law as a decision of the company: *Multinational Gas and Petrochemical Co* (n 9); *Re Duomatic Ltd* [1969] 2 Ch 365.

[65] *Belmont Finance* (n 47).

[66] A number of the judges in *Stone & Rolls* (n 34) suggested that a claim against the company's auditor would have been possible if the company had been solvent and innocent shareholders had been present: *Stone & Rolls* (n 34) [192] (Lord Walker), [203] (Lord Brown) and [241] (Lord Mance); *cf* [63] (Lord Phillips).

In *Stone & Rolls*, however, the company was insolvent. Therefore, the question should be whether the auditor's duty to the company extended to an undertaking to protect the creditors' interests, and therefore whether the creditors can be regarded as an innocent constituency akin to innocent minority shareholders in a solvent company. There is no clear line of authority on whether, in general terms, an auditor's duty encompasses the creditors' interests.[67] Further, the specific point that arose in *Stone & Rolls*, namely whether loss arising from a failure by the auditor to spot a fraud by someone such as Mr Stojevic fell within the scope of the duty owed by an auditor to a client company, had not been previously addressed by the courts.

If an auditor is to be regarded as undertaking to protect only the shareholders' interests, even where the company subsequently becomes insolvent, then the outcome in *Stone & Rolls* would be correct, albeit that the reasoning would not. If an auditor's duty to the company is interpreted as encompassing the interests of the creditors once the company is insolvent, however, then the reasoning of the minority judges should be followed, the *ex turpi causa* defence would have no application and the company could have continued with its claim against its auditor.

A compelling argument in favour of regarding the auditor's duty as extending to creditors in this situation was put forward by Lord Mance (dissenting) in *Stone & Rolls*, namely that the duties of auditors, by analogy with those of directors, must take account of creditors' interests rather than shareholders' interests once the company is insolvent.[68] As discussed, it is well established that, in relation to directors' duties, the interests of the creditors override the interests of the shareholders when the company approaches insolvency, and the creditors' interests will clearly be affected by the auditors' breach of duty just as the shareholders' interests would be affected were the company to remain solvent. In the same way that innocent shareholders in a solvent company can be regarded as an 'innocent constituency' and therefore, potentially, able to preserve a claim against the auditors, so too can creditors in an insolvent company be regarded in this way. In *Bilta*, there was therefore no difficulty with the liquidator asserting the company's claim against the wrongdoing directors even where the one-man company was insolvent and all of the shareholders were involved in

---

[67] See *Re Gerrard (Thomas) & Sons* [1968] Ch 45 (in which auditors were held liable to pay compensation to companies in liquidation in relation to unlawful dividends); however, *cf Galoo Ltd v Bright Grahame Murray* [1993] EWCA Civ 3, [1995] 1 WLR 1360.

[68] *Cf* Lord Walker and Lord Brown in *Stone & Rolls* (n 34), who seem to say that the duty owed by an auditor to a client company is owed only for the benefit of the interests of the shareholders and not of the creditors. Support for this view can be found in P Watts, 'Audit Contracts and Turpitude' (2010) 126 *LQR* 14, in which Professor Watts argues that the audit contract is not intended by the parties to give legal (as opposed to incidental) protection to creditors.

the fraud. A similar argument can be applied to auditors and, on that analysis, it would be odd if the auditor's undertaking to the company did not encompass the creditors' interests. The insolvency of the company should not exonerate the auditor for breach of duty to the company.

The main policy argument against the extension of an auditor's duty in this way is the view that making auditors liable to creditors for huge losses suffered by the company may have the effect of reducing or weakening audit services in the long term. There has been a growing appreciation in recent years of the potentially important role that auditors can perform in detecting corporate fraud.[69] They lend their professional reputation to issuers regarding the accuracy and credibility of an issuer's financial statements. Given that auditors are 'repeat certifiers' and need to maintain that reputation, rational auditors should not collude in their clients' wrongdoing. Auditors can therefore be regarded as 'gatekeepers', with a role in protecting investors in the financial markets.[70] Since the Enron and Worldcom scandals at the turn of the century, there has been increasing regulation of auditors to enhance their gatekeeping function. While private enforcement can have a potential role in enhancing that function, alongside public oversight and enforcement, excessive civil liability could have a negative effect on the audit market.[71]

In the event, these issues were not fully argued in *Stone & Rolls*. The case involved a strike-out application and, as discussed, the majority judges got sidetracked by the 'directing mind and will' issue, thereby putting 'the cart (the status of the fraudster as the company's directing mind and will) ... before the horse (the scope of the duty owed by the auditor)'.[72] In addition, the facts of *Stone & Rolls* were somewhat extreme, involving as they did a one-man company in which that one man set out to use the company to deliberately defraud others. The issue of the scope of an auditor's duty to the company, and specifically whether that duty encompasses an undertaking to the creditors in some circumstances, therefore remains to be decided another day.

What can and should be taken from *Stone & Rolls*, however, is an appreciation of where the majority in that case went wrong. In particular, the error seems to rest on an undue regard for identifying Mr Stojevic as the 'directing mind and will' of the company, and it then being regarded as

---

[69] See JC Coffee Jr, *Gatekeepers: The Professions and Corporate Governance* (New York, Oxford University Press, 2006) esp ch 6.

[70] See J Payne 'The Role of Gatekeepers' in N Moloney, E Ferran and J Payne (eds), *The Oxford Handbook of Financial Regulation* (New York, Oxford University Press, 2015).

[71] JC Coffee, 'Gatekeeper Failure and Reform: The Challenges of Fashioning Relevant Reforms' in G Ferrarini, KJ Hopt, J Winter and E Wymeersch (eds), *Reforming Company and Takeover Law in Europe* (Oxford, Oxford University Press, 2004).

[72] E Ferran, 'Corporate Attribution and the Directing Mind and Will' (2011) 127 *LQR* 239, 251–52.

inevitable that his fraud should be attributed to the company such that the auditor could make use of the *ex turpi causa* maxim to block the company's claim against them. This approach seems to forget the lessons of *Meridian*, namely, first, that the company and the natural person acting for it, even if that is the one man in a one-man company, are not one and the same and, second, that when determining whether to attribute an act or state of mind to the company, context is key. It is not automatic that just because wrong-doers have acted for the company that their wrongdoing will be attributed to the company. As *Meridian* makes clear, it is necessary to examine the context to determine whether the wrongdoers' state of mind or acts should be attributed to the company for this purpose; the answer will differ according to the nature of the provision and the factual matrix, including the nature of the company, the position occupied by the wrongdoer in the company and so on. Furthermore, even if the act or state of mind is attributed to the company such that the company becomes liable (eg, for breach of a particular statutory provision), this does not mean that the company is somehow imprinted with that wrongdoing such that the *ex turpi causa* maxim can be brought into effect to prevent the company suing either the wrongdoers or a third party, such as the auditor in *Stone & Rolls*. Whether the company can bring a claim should, again, require a consideration of the context of the claim. In general, the primary enquiry will be the existence and scope of the duty owed by the wrongdoer or third party to the company. Where there is a breach of duty to the company, such as the breach of directors' duties in *Jetivia*, the *ex turpi causa* maxim has no relevance.

IV. CONCLUSION

Lord Hoffmann's judgment in *Meridian* laid down some key principles in relation to corporate attribution. Not only did he clarify the existing bases for corporate attribution, he also recognised the special rules of attribution that will be needed to determine when a company itself can be deemed to have acted in a particular way or to have had a particular state of mind in order to be liable under a statute. Two particularly important lessons need to be drawn from his judgment: these special rules do not mean that a company itself has done something or had a particular state of mind; and the issue of attribution depends on the context. It is always necessary to ask whether an act or state of mind of a particular individual should be attributed to the company for *this particular purpose*.

The cases of corporate attribution since *Meridian* demonstrate that these lessons have not always been taken to heart. The issue seems less acute in relation to those cases where attribution is being used to impose liability on a company. Here the need for a contextual approach seems to have been accepted, although the need to identify a wrongdoer who is the 'directing mind and will' before liability can be imposed seems to have cast a long shadow in this context, particularly in criminal law cases. More problematic, however, is the use of attribution to deny a claim to a company via the use of the *ex turpi causa* maxim. Decisions such as that of the majority of the House of Lords in *Stone & Rolls* and that of the Court of Appeal in *Safeway Stores* suggest that the courts do not always sufficiently recognise that the company and the wrongdoer are distinct entities, or that the context of the attribution needs to be carefully borne in mind. These decisions conflate the attribution of liability to the company for one purpose (to make the company liable for a statutory provision) with attribution to the company for another purpose (application of the *ex turpi causa* maxim). It is suggested that a return to the lessons of *Meridian* can help to clarify these issues and therefore, hopefully, lead to more satisfactory outcomes in similar cases in the future.

Index